My iPod touch®

SECOND EDITION

Brad Miser

800 East 96th Street,
Indianapolis, Indiana 46240 USA

My iPod touch®, Second Edition

ISBN-13: 978-0-7897 4715 0
ISBN-10: 0-7897-4715-4

Library of Congress Cataloging-in-Publication Data

Miser, Brad.
My iPod touch / Brad Miser. — 2nd ed.
p. cm.
Includes index.
ISBN 978-0-7897-4715-0
1. iPod touch (Digital music player) I. Title.
ML74.4.I48M56 2011
006.5—dc22
2010040179

Printed in the United States on America

First Printing: November 2010

Trademarks

All terms mentioned in this book that are known to be trademarks or service marks have been appropriately capitalized. Que Publishing cannot attest to the accuracy of this information. Use of a term in this book should not be regarded as affecting the validity of any trademark or service mark.

iPod touch is a registered trademark of Apple Inc.

Warning and Disclaimer

Every effort has been made to make this book as complete and as accurate as possible, but no warranty or fitness is implied. The information provided is on an "as is" basis. The author and the publisher shall have neither liability nor responsibility to any person or entity with respect to any loss or damages arising from the information contained in this book.

Bulk Sales

Que Publishing offers excellent discounts on this book when ordered in quantity for bulk purchases or special sales. For more information, please contact

U.S. Corporate and Government Sales
1-800-382-3419
corpsales@pearsontechgroup.com

For sales outside of the U.S., please contact

International Sales
international@pearsoned.com

Associate Publisher
Greg Wiegand

Acquisitions Editor
Laura Norman

Managing Editor
Kristy Hart

Development Editor
The Wordsmithery LLC

Senior Project Editor
Lori Lyons

Copy Editor
Apostrophe Editing Services

Indexer
Erika Millen

Proofreader
Apostrophe Editing Services

Technical Editor
Kate Binder

Publishing Coordinator
Cindy J. Teeters

Book Design
Anne Jones

Composition
Nonie Ratcliff

Table of Contents

About the Author

Brad Miser has written extensively about technology, with his favorite topics being the amazing "i" gadgets, iPod touch and iPhone, that make it possible to take our lives with us while we are on the move. In addition to *My iPod touch*, Second Edition, Brad has written many other books, including *My iPhone*, Fourth Edition; *Easy iLife '09*; *Absolute Beginner's Guide to iPod and iTunes*; *Special Edition Using Mac OS X Leopard*; *Absolute Beginner's Guide to Homeschooling*; *Teach Yourself Visually MacBook Air*; and *MacBook Pro Portable Genius*. He has also been an author, development editor, or technical editor on more than 50 other titles.

Brad is or has been a sales support specialist, the director of product and customer services, and the manager of education and support services for several software development companies. Previously, he was the lead proposal specialist for an aircraft engine manufacturer, a development editor for a computer book publisher, and a civilian aviation test officer/engineer for the U.S. Army. Brad holds a Bachelor of Science degree in mechanical engineering from California Polytechnic State University at San Luis Obispo and has received advanced education in maintainability engineering, business, and other topics.

In addition to his passion for silicon-based technology, Brad likes to ride his steel-based technology, aka, a motorcycle, whenever and wherever possible.

Originally from California, Brad now lives in Brownsburg, Indiana, with his wife Amy; their three daughters, Jill, Emily, and Grace; a rabbit; and a sometimes inside cat.

Brad would love to hear about your experiences with this book (the good, the bad, and the ugly). You can write to him at bradmiser@me.com.

Dedication

To those who have given the last full measure of devotion so that the rest of us can be free.

Acknowledgments

To the following people on the *My iPod touch* project team, my sincere appreciation for your hard work on this book:

Laura Norman, my acquisitions editor, who envisioned the original concept for *My iPhone* and applied it to the equally amazing iPod touch. Laura and I have worked on many books together, and I appreciate her professional and effective approach to these projects. Thanks for letting me work on this one!

Kate Binder, my technical editor, who did a great job to ensure that the information in this book is both accurate and useful.

San Dee Phillips, my copy editor, who corrected my many misspellings, poor grammar, and other problems.

Lori Lyons, my project editor, who skillfully managed the hundreds of files and the production process that it took to make this book.

Anne Jones, for the interior design and cover of the book.

Nonie Ratcliff, for laying out the book.

Que's production and sales team for printing the book and getting it into your hands.

We Want to Hear from You!

As the reader of this book, *you* are our most important critic and commentator. We value your opinion and want to know what we're doing right, what we could do better, what areas you'd like to see us publish in, and any other words of wisdom you're willing to pass our way.

As an associate publisher for Que Publishing, I welcome your comments. You can email or write me directly to let me know what you did or didn't like about this book—as well as what we can do to make our books better.

Please note that I cannot help you with technical problems related to the topic of this book. We do have a User Services group, however, where I will forward specific technical questions related to the book.

When you write, please be sure to include this book's title and author as well as your name, email address, and phone number. I will carefully review your comments and share them with the author and editors who worked on the book.

Email: feedback@quepublishing.com

Mail: Greg Wiegand
Associate Publisher
Que Publishing
800 East 96th Street
Indianapolis, IN 46240 USA

Reader Services

Visit our website and register this book at www.quepublishing.com/register for convenient access to any updates, downloads, or errata that might be available for this book.

Soon you'll wonder how you ever got along without one

In this chapter, you learn how to get going with your iPod touch. The topics include the following:

→ Touring your iPod touch
→ Preparing iTunes
→ Preparing MobileMe
→ Using this book

Getting Started with Your iPod touch

The good news is that getting started with an iPod touch is a simple, painless process. In this chapter, you get a tour of the iPod touch so that you can use its controls and work with its interface quickly and easily. You also learn about installing iPod touch's required partner, iTunes, which you use to move content onto iPod touch and keep it in sync. An optional, but valuable, partner for your iPod touch is Apple's MobileMe service, which is great for keeping your iPod touch connected to your email, calendars, and other valuable information wherever you are. Last, you learn a bit about how you can get the most out of this book.

Touring Your iPod touch

Your iPod touch is one of the most amazing handheld devices ever because of how well it is designed. It has only a few external features you need to understand. For most of the things you do, you just use your fingers on your iPod touch's screen (which just seems natural), and the touch's consistent interface enables you to accomplish most tasks with similar steps.

Getting to Know the iPod touch's External Features

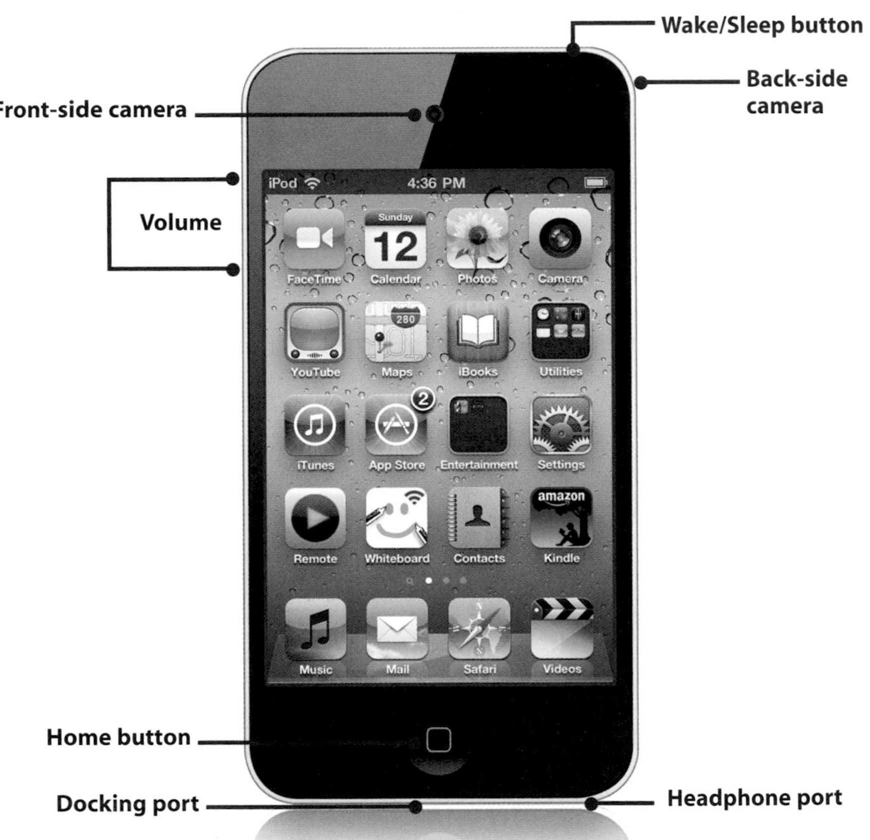

Take a quick look at the iPod touch's physical features:

- **Wake/Sleep button**: Press this to lock the iPod touch's controls and put it to sleep. Press it again to wake up the iPod; slide the on-screen slider to unlock and start using the iPod. Note that if you use the iPod to listen to audio when you press this button, that audio keeps playing while the touch is locked. If you hold this button down for a few seconds while the iPod touch is awake, you're prompted to shut it down. If the iPod touch is turned off and you press and hold this button for a second or two, it starts up; you can tell an iPod touch is starting up when you see the Apple logo on its screen.

- **Headphone port**: Plug the iPod touch's earbuds or external speakers into this port.
- **Docking port**: Use this port to connect the iPod touch to a computer using the included USB cable. You can also plug an iPod into a dock to connect it to other devices, and some devices connect directly to this port.
- **Home button**: If the iPod is asleep, press this button once to wake it up (which does the same thing as the Wake/Sleep button). If the iPod is awake and unlocked, press this button once to move to the all-important Home screens, or press it twice to open the App toolbar.
- **Volume**: Press the upper button to increase volume; press the lower button to decrease it. The volume you change is contextual; for example, when you use the Music app, you change the music's volume level, but if you don't have audio playing, the buttons change the volume of the iPod's ringer and alerts.
- **Cameras:** The iPod has a camera on the front side (facing you) and one on the backside. You can use these cameras to take photos and video and to use the very cool FaceTime app to videoconference with someone.

Knowing Why It's Called a Multi-Touch Interface

Apple designed the iPod touch to be touched. (That might have something to do with its name, I suspect.) The previous section describes the only physical features an iPod touch has; as you saw, there aren't many. Most of the time, you control your iPod touch by using your fingers on its screen to tap buttons, select items on lists, scroll, zoom, type text, and so on. After you use it a while, you might want everything to work this way because it's so easy and intuitive.

Going Home

Most iPod touch activities start at the Home screen (or Home screens, to be more accurate because the Home screen has multiple pages), which you get to by pressing the Home button. Along the bottom of the Home screen, you see the Home Screen toolbar; this toolbar is visible when you view most of the Home screen's pages so that you have easy access to the buttons it contains (more on the Home screen shortly); up to four buttons can be installed on this toolbar. Above the toolbar, you see applications that do all sorts of cool things. You can also create bookmarks for websites and store them as buttons on the Home screen. As you add applications and bookmarks, the number of pages of the Home screen increases. You can organize the buttons on the pages of the Home screen in any way you like. You can also place buttons into folders so that you can make accessing the buttons you use most frequently convenient.

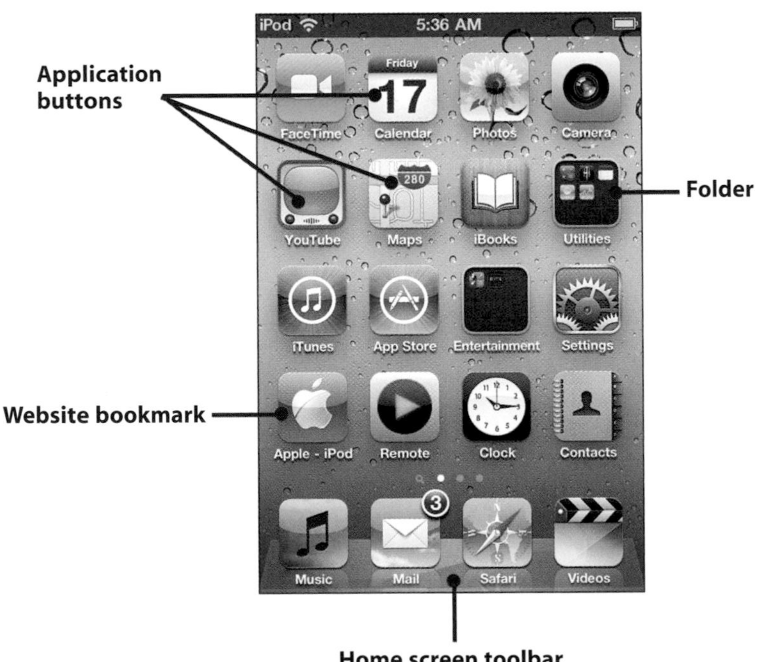

Touching the touch's Screen

The following figures highlight the major ways you control an iPod touch. A tap is just what it sounds like; you briefly press a finger to the iPod touch's screen over the item you want to control and then lift your finger again. Sometimes, you double-tap, which is also exactly what it sounds like; you simply tap twice. To drag, you place your finger on the screen and move it across the screen without lifting it up; the faster you move your finger, the faster the resulting action happens. (You don't need to apply pressure, just make contact.) To pinch or unpinch, place two fingers on the screen and drag them together or move them apart; the faster and more you pinch or unpinch, the "more" the action happens (such as a zoom in).

Tap a link to move to it

Drag your finger up, down, left, and right to scroll

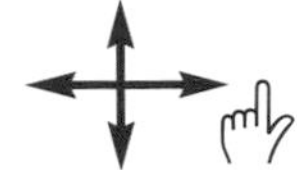

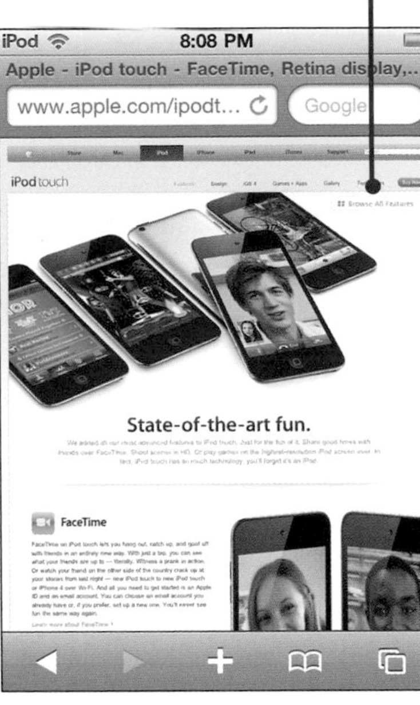

Unpinch your fingers or tap twice to zoom in

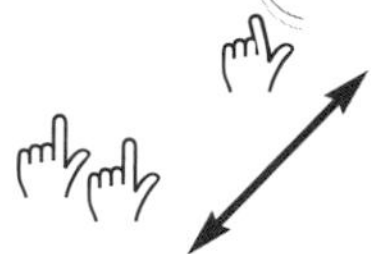

Pinch your fingers or tap twice to zoom out

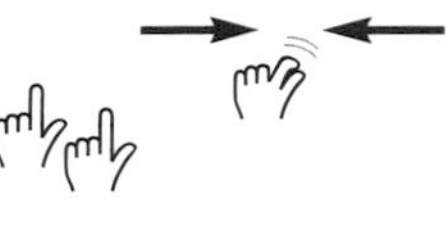

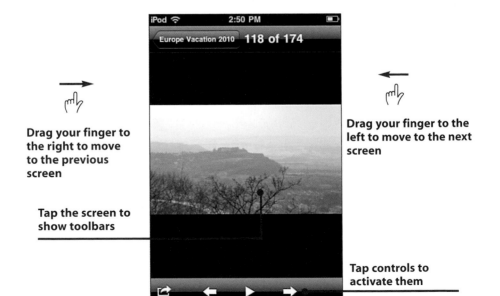

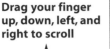

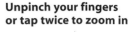

Drag your finger to the right to move to the previous screen

Drag your finger to the left to move to the next screen

Tap the screen to show toolbars

Tap controls to activate them

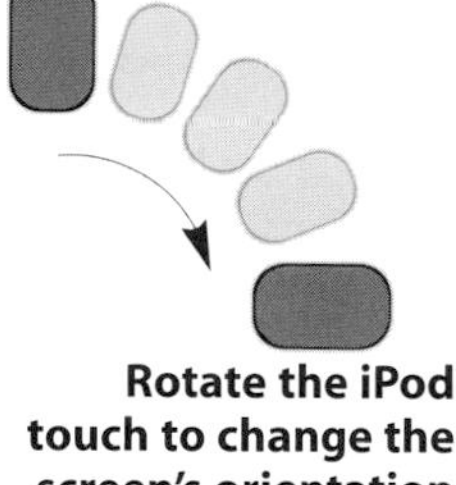

Rotate the iPod touch to change the screen's orientation

Working with iPod touch Applications

One of the best things about an iPod touch is that it can run all sorts of applications. It includes a number of apps by default, such as Mail, Safari, and so on, but you can download and use thousands of other apps through the App Store. You learn about many of these applications as you read through this book. And as you learned earlier, to launch an app, you simply tap its icon. The app launches, and it fills the iPod's screen.

When you launch an app, it fills the screen

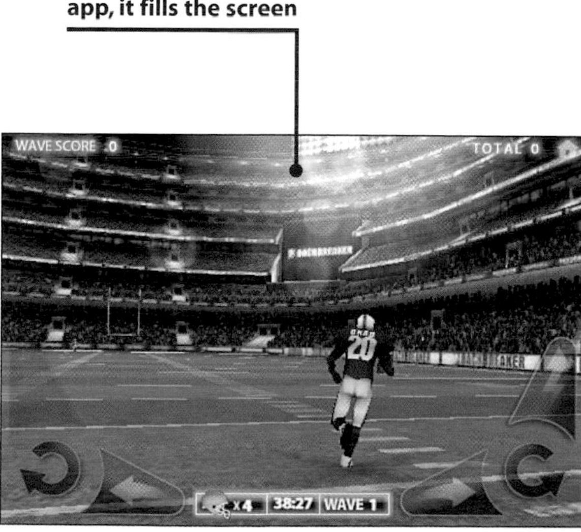

As you learn in Chapter 14, "Customizing an iPod touch," you can organize apps in folders. To access an app that is in a folder, tap the folder. The folder opens, and you see the apps it contains.

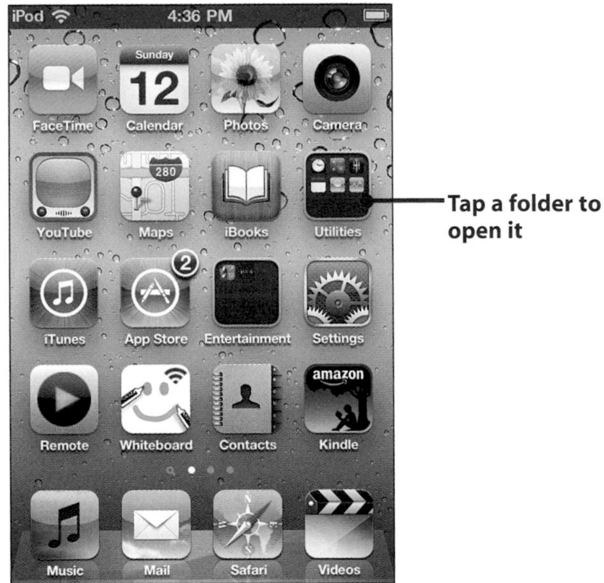

To launch an app within a folder, tap its button.

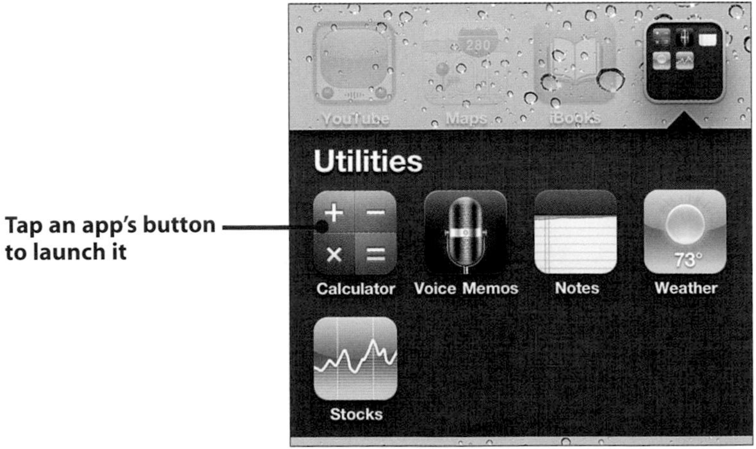

To stop using an application, you can use its exit or quit commands (some apps have these, some don't) or simply press the Home button. You return to the Home screen you were most recently using.

However, because the iPod touch multitasks, when you move out of an app by pressing the Home button, the app moves into the background, but it doesn't stop. So if the app has a task to complete, such as uploading photos or playing audio, it continues to work behind-the-scenes. In some cases, notably games, the app becomes suspended at the point you leave it. In addition to the benefit of completing tasks when you move into another app, the iPod's capability to multitask means that you can run multiple applications at the same time. For example, you can run an Internet-radio application to listen to music while you switch over to Mail to work on your email.

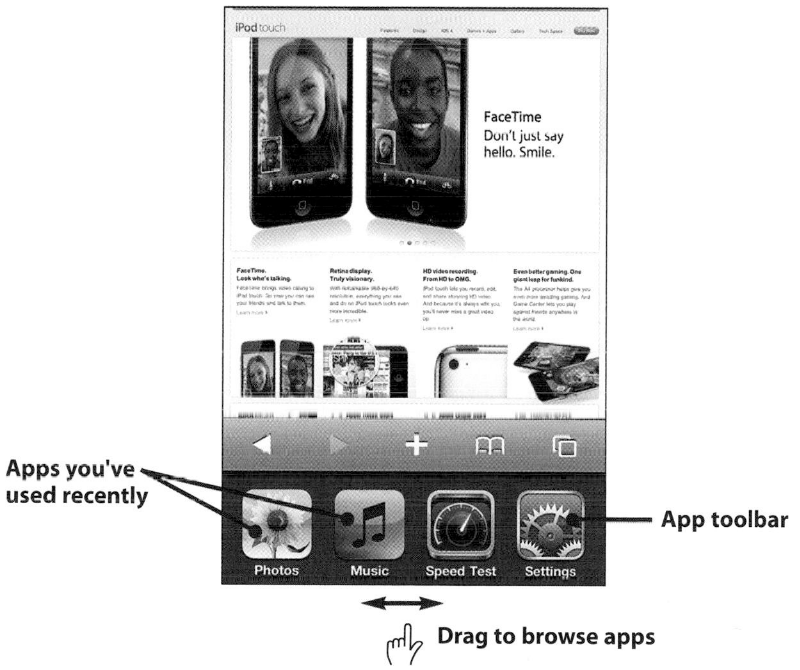

You can control apps by using the App toolbar. To see this, press the Home button twice. The front-most app slides to the top of the screen, and the App toolbar appears. On this toolbar, you see the apps that you've used recently. To see all the apps you've used recently, drag on the toolbar to the left or right. When you drag all the way to the right, you see playback controls for audio and video along with a button that locks the iPod touch's screen in its current orientation.

Tap an app to move into it

To jump quickly into a different app, tap its button. That app takes over the screen, and you can work with it. It also picks up right where you left off.

To close the toolbar without moving into a different app, press the Home button once.

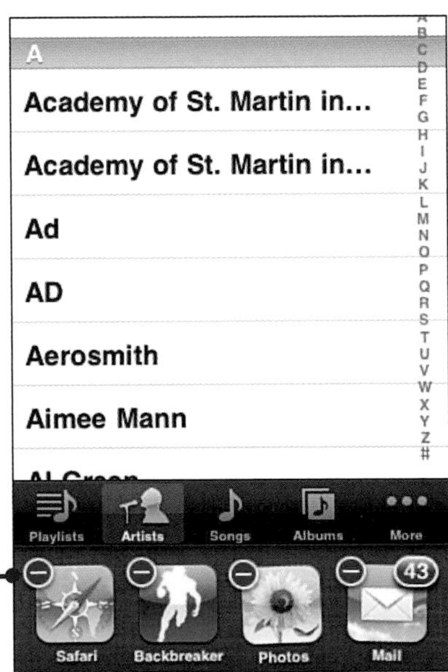

Tap to force an app to quit

Third Generation or Newer iPod touch Required

If you have the first or second generation of iPod touch, it can't multitask; it doesn't have enough processing power to manage multiple applications at the same time. So with one of these older iPods, you can only have one application running at a time. And there is no App toolbar either. You were looking for a reason to upgrade anyway, right?

In some cases (such as when it doesn't work correctly), you might want to force an app to quit. To do this, press and hold its button on the toolbar. When the icons start jiggling and the "-" appears, tap it. The app is forced to quit. You should be careful about this, though, because if the app has unsaved data, you will likely lose it when you force the app to quit. You can then move to other apps and make sure you save all open data that you want to keep. (In some cases, you should exit the app by using its commands to save its data.) After you are sure you've saved all the data you want, you should also restart your iPod touch.

Working with Text on an iPod touch

You can do lots of things with an iPod touch that require you to type, and iPod touch's keyboard is quite amazing. Whenever you need it, whether it's for emailing, entering a website URL, performing a search, and so on, it pops up automatically.

Use the iPod touch's virtual keyboard to type

To type, just tap the keys. As you tap each key, the character you tap pops up in a small window so that you can see what you entered, which is useful feedback for you. You also hear audio feedback if you haven't disabled it. The keyboard includes all the standard keys you expect. To change from letters to numbers and special characters, just tap the .?123 key. Tap the #+= key to see more special characters. Tap the 123 key to move back to the numbers and special characters or the ABC key to return to letters. The keyboard also has contextual keys that appear when you need them. For example, when you enter a website address, the .com key appears so that you can enter these four characters with a single tap.

What's Your Typing Orientation?

Like many other tasks, you can rotate the iPod to change the screen's orientation while you type. When the iPod is in the landscape orientation, the keyboard is wider, making it easier to tap individual keys. When the iPod is in portrait orientation, the keyboard is narrower, but you can see more of the typing area. So try both to see which mode is most effective for you.

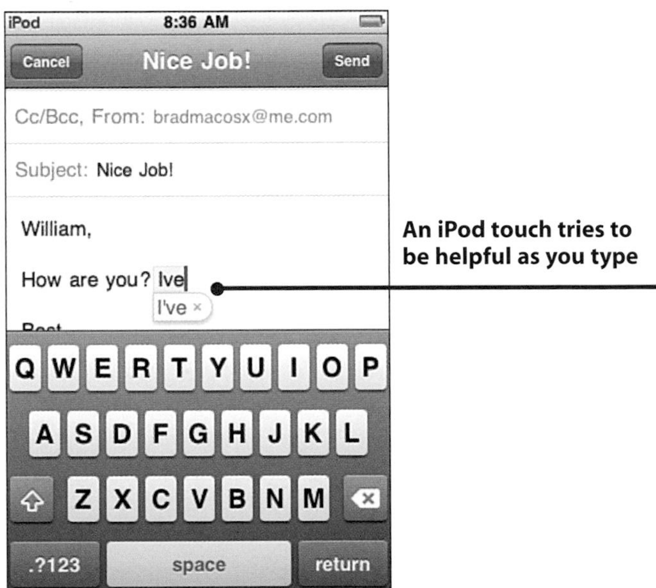

An iPod touch tries to be helpful as you type

If you type a word that the iPod touch doesn't recognize, it makes a suggestion about what it thinks is the correct word in a pop-up box. To accept the suggestion, tap the Space key. To reject the suggestion, tap the pop-up box to close it and keep what you typed. You can also use this feature for shorthand typing. For example, to type "I'll" you can simply type "Ill," and iPod touch will suggest "I'll," which you can accept by tapping the Space key.

Typing Tricks

Many keys, especially symbols and punctuation, have optional characters. To see a character's options, tap it and hold down. If it has options, a menu pops up after a second or so. To enter one of the optional characters, drag over the menu until the one you want to enter is highlighted and then lift your finger off the screen. The optional character you selected is entered.

The iPod also attempts to correct the capitalization of what you type. It also automatically selects the Caps key when you start a new sentence, start a new paragraph, or in other places where its best guess is that you need a capital letter. If you don't want to enter a capital character, simply tap the caps key.

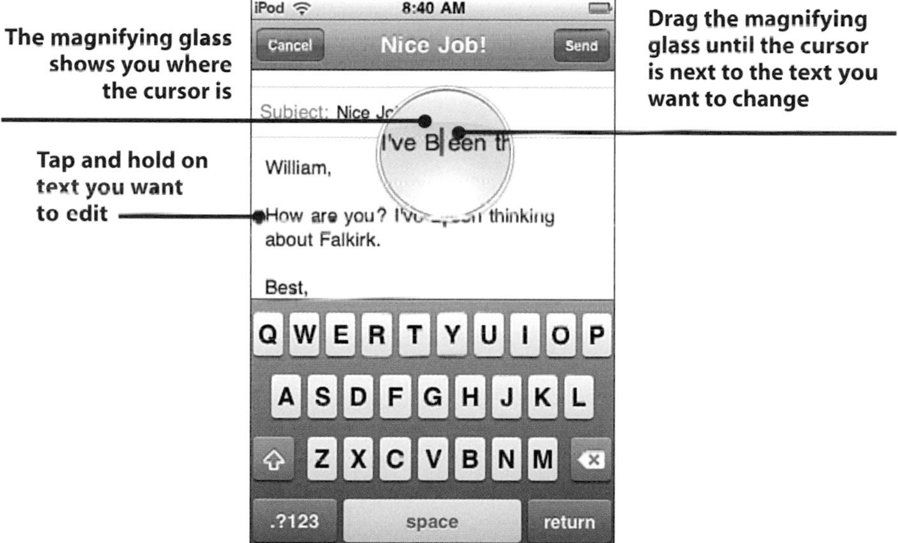

To edit text you've typed, tap and hold on the text you want to edit. A magnifying glass icon appears on the screen, and within it you see a magnified view of the location of the cursor. Drag the magnifying glass to where you want to make changes and then lift your finger from the screen; the cursor remains in that location, and you can use the keyboard to make changes to the text or to add text at that location.

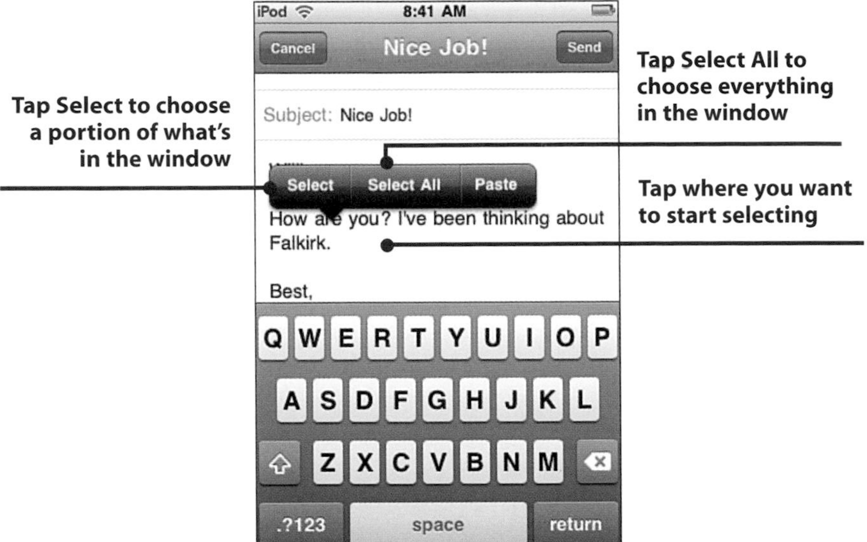

You can also select text or images to copy and paste the selected content into a new location. Tap and hold down briefly where you want to start the selection until the magnifying glass icon appears; then lift your finger off the screen. The Select menu appears. Tap Select to select part of the content on the screen, or tap Select All to select everything in the current window.

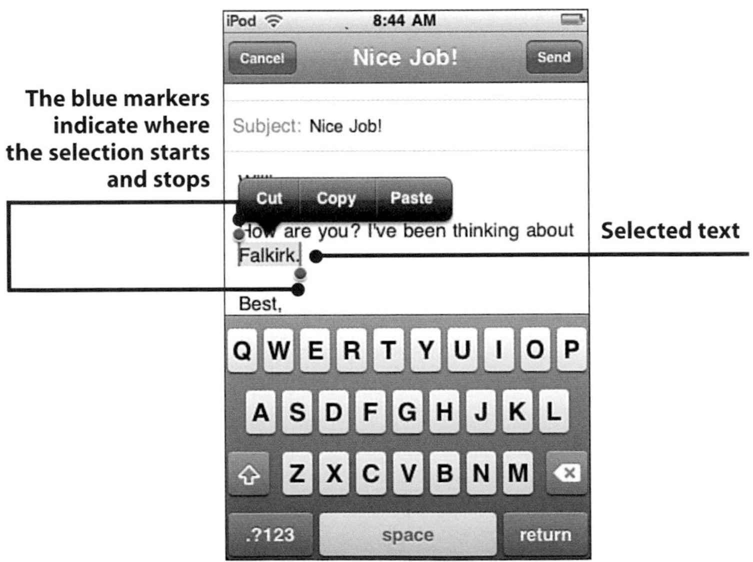

You see markers indicating where the selection starts and stops. (The iPod attempts to select something logical, such as the word or sentence.)

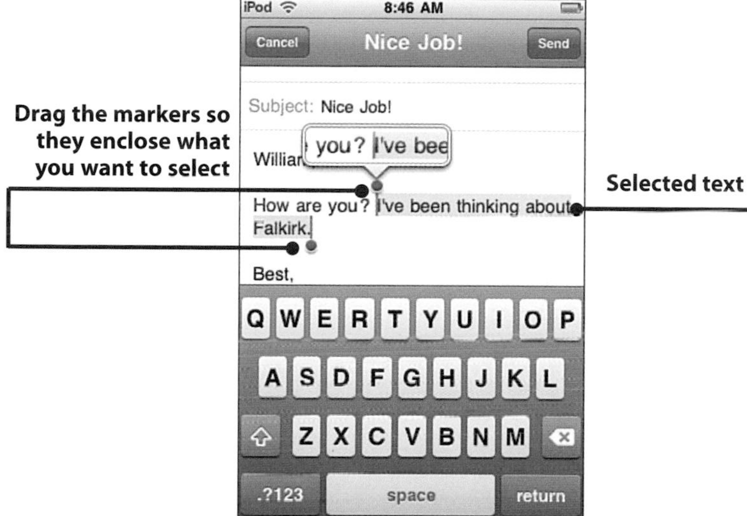

Drag the two markers so that the content you want to select is between them; the selected portion is highlighted in blue. As you drag, you see a magnified view of where the selection marker is, which helps you place it more accurately. When the selection markers are located correctly, lift your finger from the screen. (If you tapped the Select All command, you don't need to do this because the content you want is already selected.)

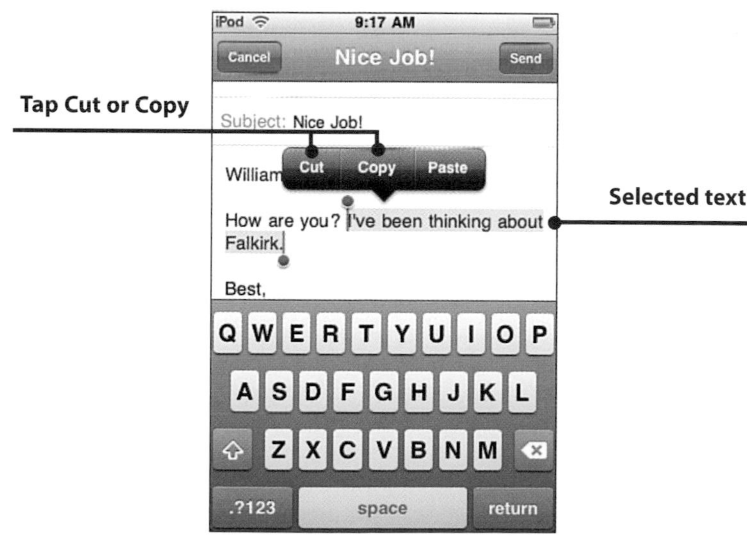

Tap Cut to remove the content from the current window, or tap Copy to just copy it.

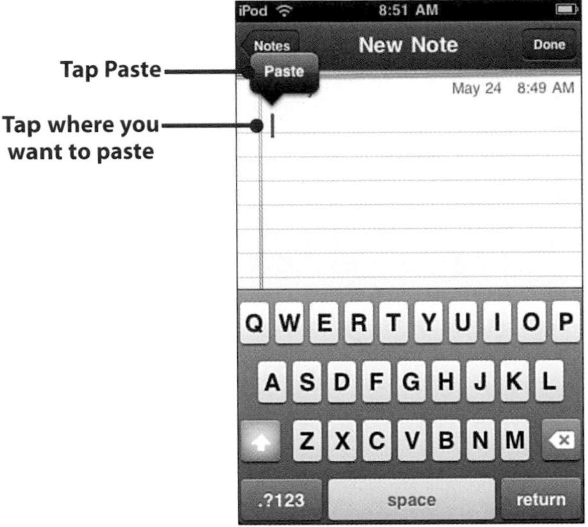

Move to where you want to paste the content you selected. Tap where you want the content to be pasted; for a more precise location, tap and hold and then use the magnifying glass icon to move to a specific location. Tap Paste.

The content you copied or cut appears where you placed the cursor.

The iPod also has a spell-checking feature that comes into play after you have entered text (as opposed to the auto-correct feature that changes text as you type it). When you've entered text that the iPod doesn't recognize, it is underlined in red.

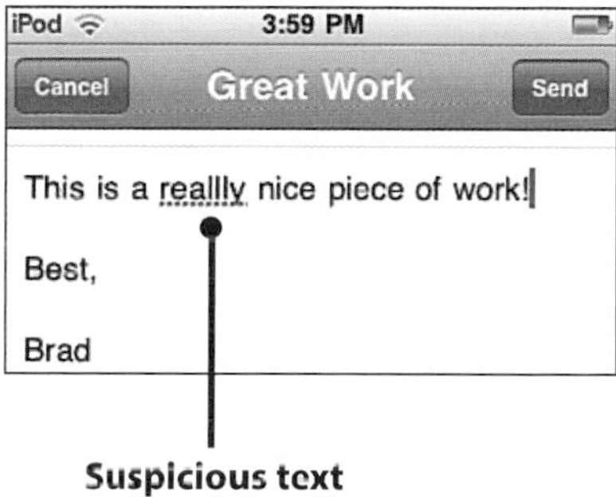

Suspicious text

Tap the underlined word; it is shaded in red to show you what is being checked, and a menu appears with one or more replacements that might be the correct spelling; if one of the options is the one you want, tap it. The incorrect word is replaced with the one you tapped.

Tap to accept the corrected word

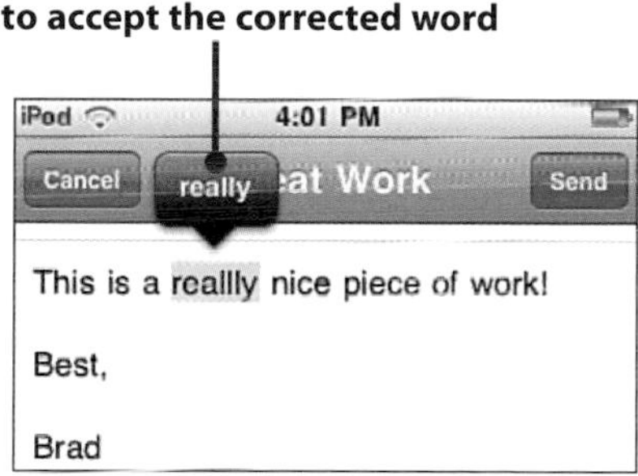

Other Text Options

In some apps, tapping a word causes a menu with other kinds of actions to appear; you can tap an action to make it happen. For example, in the iBooks app, when you tap a word, the resulting menu enables you to look up the word in a dictionary. Other apps support different kind of actions, so it's a good idea to try tapping on words in apps that involve text to see what is available.

Using the Home Screens

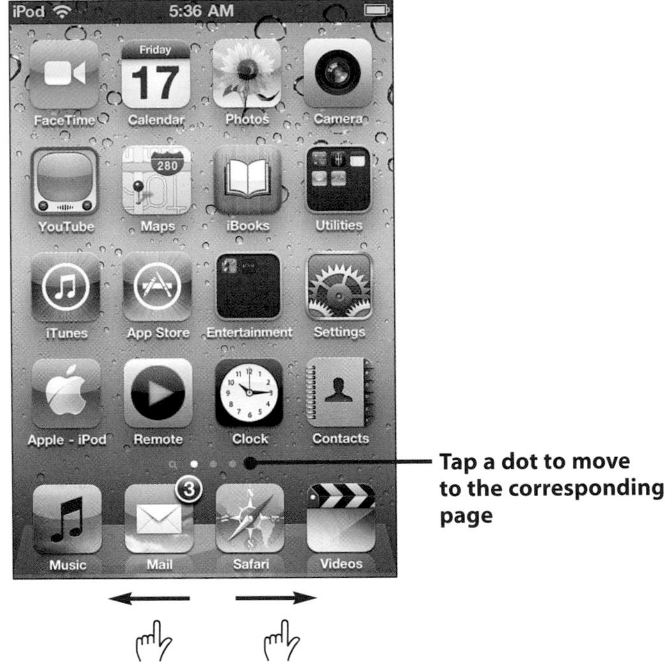

Tap a dot to move to the corresponding page

Drag to the left or right to move between Home screen pages

Earlier you read that the Home screen is the jumping-off point for many of the things you do with your iPod touch because that is where you access the buttons you tap to launch applications, move to website bookmarks you've saved there, and configure your iPod touch's settings.

The Home screen actually has multiple pages. To move to a page, drag to the left to move to later pages or to the right to move to earlier pages. Or tap the dot corresponding to the page you want to move to.

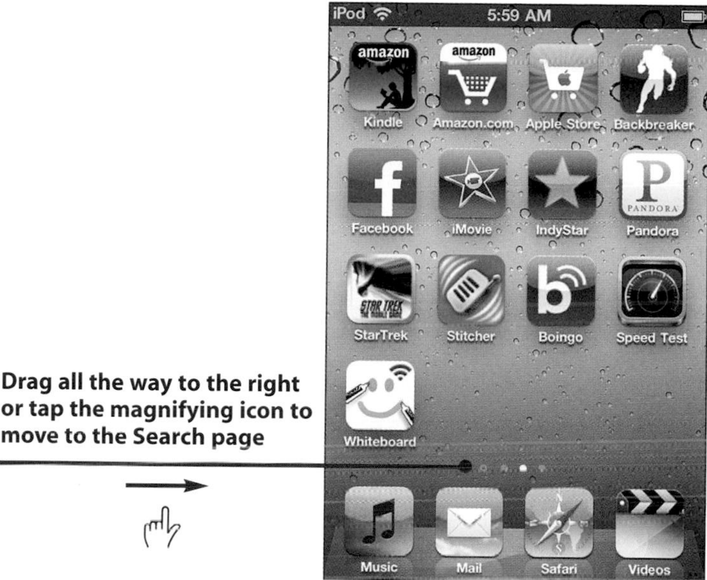

If you move all the way to the "left," you see the Search page. Using this tool, you can search your iPod touch. The objects you search, such as email, music, and such are determined by settings you can configure. (This is covered in Chapter 14, "Customizing an iPod touch.")

To perform a search, tap in the Search bar and type. As you type, items that meet your search are shown on the list below the Search bar. When you finish typing the search term, tap Search.

The results are organized into sections, which are indicated by icons along the left edge of the screen, such as email, contacts, and so on. To see the detail of an item, tap it. The results remain so that you can always move back to the results screen to work with other items you found.

Monitoring the iPod touch's Condition

At the top of the screen, you see various icons that provide you with information, such as if you are connected to a Wi-Fi network, the time, the state of the battery, and so on. Keep an eye on this area as you use your iPod.

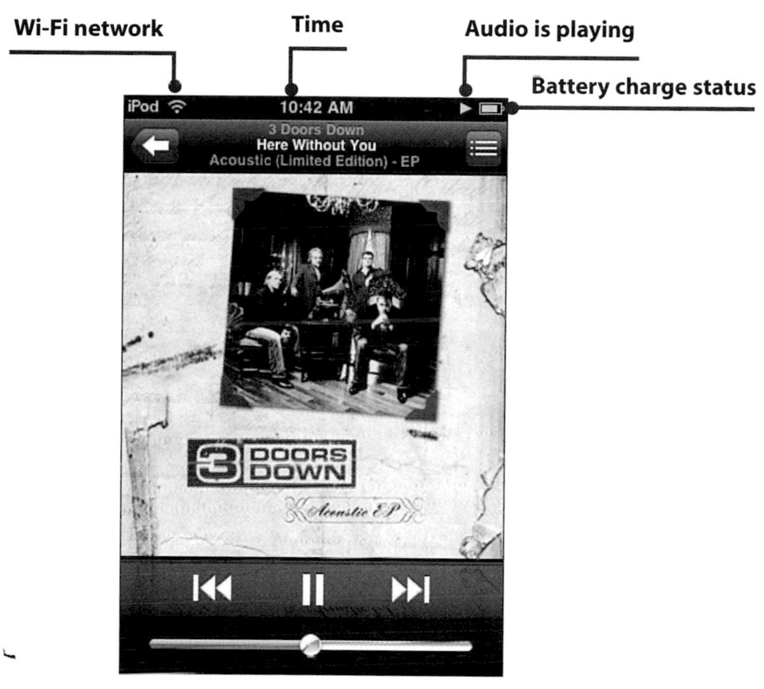

Sleeping/Locking and Waking/Unlocking

When an iPod touch is asleep and you press the Wake/Sleep button or the Home button, the iPod wakes up, and its screen activates; you see the Unlock slider. Drag the slider to the right to unlock the iPod so that you can work with it. You move to the last screen you were using. (In Chapter 14, you learn how to secure your iPod with a passcode so that it can't be unlocked until the correct passcode is entered.)

The Time Is Always Handy

If you use your iPod touch as a watch the way I do, just press the Home button or the Wake/Sleep button. The current time and date appear; if you don't unlock it, iPod touch goes back to sleep after a few seconds.

In most cases, you should just put iPod touch to sleep when you aren't using it instead of shutting it off. It doesn't use much power when it sleeps, and it wakes up immediately when you want to start using it again. (You seldom need to turn an iPod touch off.)

Changing Volume

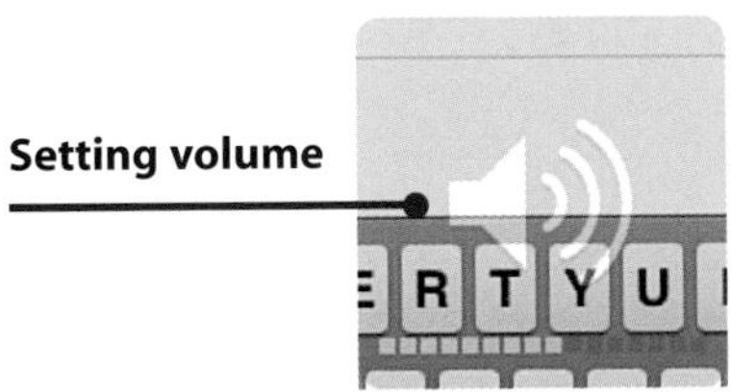

To change the touch's volume, press the up or down Volume button. If you aren't on a screen that shows the Volume slider, an icon pops up to show you the relative volume you are setting. When the volume is right, release the volume button.

Shutting an iPod touch Down

If you want to turn your iPod touch off, press and hold the Wake/Sleep button until the red slider appears at the top of the screen. Drag the slider to the right to shut the iPod down.

To restart your iPod touch, press and hold the Wake/Sleep button until the Apple logo appears on the screen, and then let go of the button. After it starts up, you see the Home screen, and it's ready for you to use.

Preparing iTunes

iTunes is the application you use to move content (music, podcasts, movies, books, and so on) and information (such as email account configurations) onto your iPod touch. You need to download and install iTunes on your computer or make sure that you use the most current version if it's already installed. To start, jump into any of the following sections that apply to your particular situation.

---

iPod touch and iTunes

This isn't a book about iTunes, so I cover only the details you need to know to use your iPod touch. iTunes is a powerful application that you can use to manage all your digital entertainment and, of course, to move content onto an iPod, CD, DVD, iPhones, and so on.

You might find yourself in one of two situations on the iTunes front. If you are a Windows user and have never installed iTunes, you have to download and install it, which is covered in the next section. (If iTunes is already installed, skip over that section.) If you're a Windows or Mac user and already have iTunes installed on your computer, update it to make sure that you use the latest version; the section titled "Updating iTunes" covers how to do so.

After iTunes is installed and updated, you should get an account at the iTunes Store, which enables you to purchase content or rent movies. As you might guess, there's a section called "Obtaining an iTunes Store Account" if you don't already have an account there.

Downloading and Installing iTunes on a Windows PC

If your PC doesn't have iTunes installed, perform the following steps.

1. Open a web browser.
2. Move to www.apple.com/itunes/download/.
3. Check or uncheck the two check boxes to suit your preferences.
4. Click Download Now. The installer application starts.

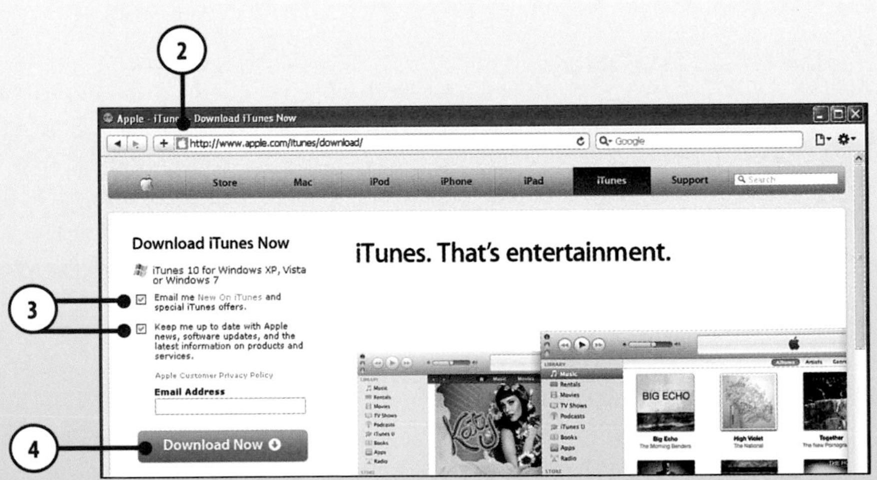

5. Follow the onscreen instructions to open and run the installer to install iTunes.

Mac Installation Section Missing?

If you happen to be wondering why there isn't a section on installing iTunes on a Mac, it's because Macs come with iTunes pre-installed. If you weren't wondering, never mind.

Updating iTunes

You should check to make sure you use the most current version of iTunes.

1. Open iTunes.
2. On a Windows PC, choose Help, Check for Updates. On a Mac, choose iTunes, Check for Updates. The application checks your version of iTunes against the current version.

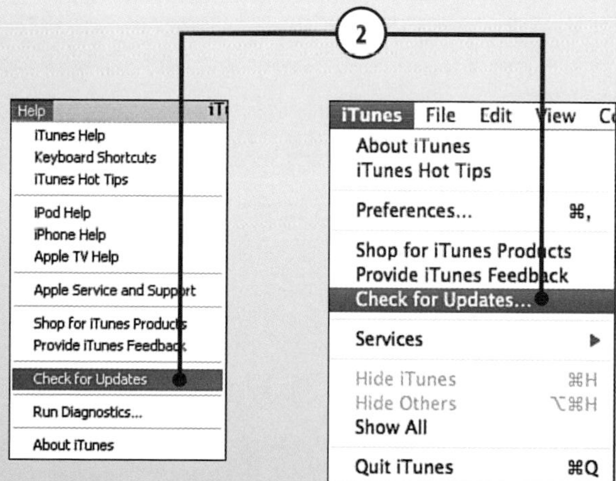

3. If you are using the current version, click OK to clear the dialog telling you so. If you aren't using the current version, you're prompted to download and install it. Follow the onscreen instructions to download and install the newer version.

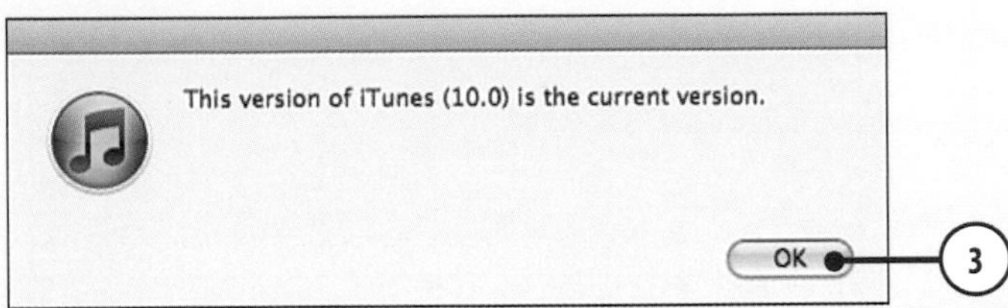

Obtaining and Signing In to an iTunes Store Account

An account on the iTunes Store enables you to purchase or rent audio and video content that is then downloaded to your iTunes Library from where you can move it onto your iPod touch. And you can purchase and download content directly onto your iPod touch as well. Even if you don't intend to purchase content or rent movies, you need an account to download and install applications for your iPod touch. To obtain and sign into an account, perform the following steps.

1. Open iTunes.
2. Click iTunes Store. You connect to the Internet and move into the iTunes Store.
3. Click Sign In. The Sign In dialog appears. If you see your Apple ID instead of the Sign In button, iTunes is already logged into an iTunes Store account. If the account is yours, skip the rest of these steps. If the account isn't yours, click the account shown and click Sign Out so that you can create your account.

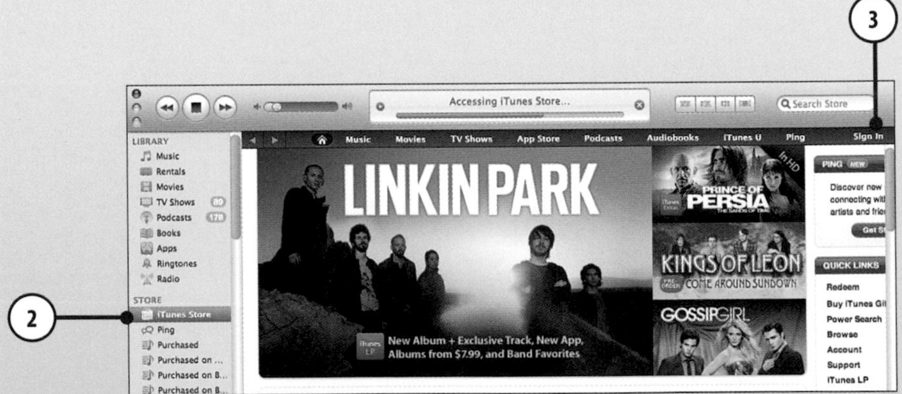

Got iTunes Store Account?

You can log in to an existing iTunes Store account by entering your Apple ID or AOL screen name and password and then clicking Sign In. Skip the rest of these steps.

4. Click Create New Account. You move to the first screen in the account creation process.

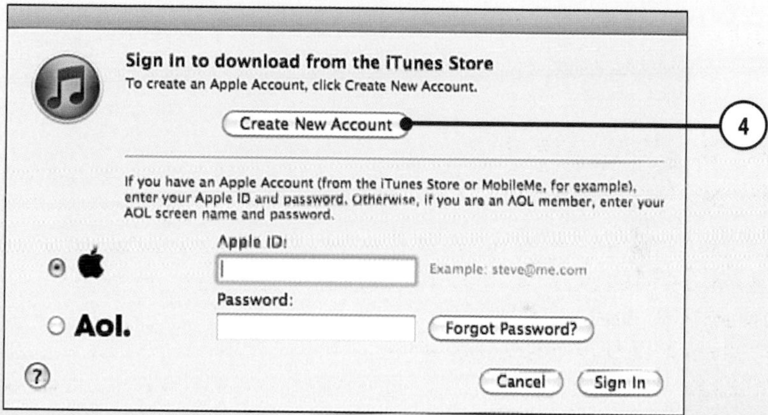
Sign In to download from the iTunes Store
To create an Apple Account, click Create New Account.
Create New Account
4
If you have an Apple Account (from the iTunes Store or MobileMe, for example), enter your Apple ID and password. Otherwise, if you are an AOL member, enter your AOL screen name and password.
Apple ID:
Example: steve@me.com
Password:
Aol.
Forgot Password?
Cancel
Sign In

5. Read the information and follow the onscreen instructions to create an Apple ID. After you complete the steps, you receive your Apple ID and password.

Welcome to the iTunes Store
Preview, buy, and download the latest music, movies, TV shows, apps, and more.
Start shopping on iTunes as soon as you've created your Apple ID. Click Continue to begin.
5
Cancel
Continue

6. Click the Sign In button.

7. Enter your Apple ID and password.
8. Click Sign In. You are logged into your iTunes Store account.

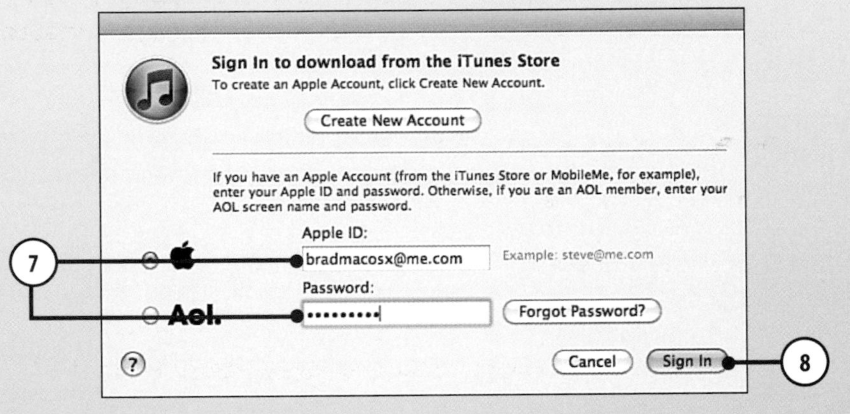

Preparing MobileMe

Apple's MobileMe service provides you with a number of features including online disk space, an email account, an online photo gallery, and more. When it comes to your iPod touch, MobileMe offers one primary benefit, and it is a good one. With MobileMe, you can keep your contacts, calendar, web favorites, and MobileMe email in sync between computers and your iPod touch wirelessly. Instead of connecting your iPod touch to a computer to move information over a USB cable, information (such as your email) is moved directly from the Internet onto iPod touch via its Wi-Fi Internet connection. Not only is this easier, but also your information remains more current on all your devices.

MobileMe works by moving information from a computer or an iPod touch to the MobileMe "cloud" on the Internet. The information is downloaded from the cloud to each device so that all devices have the same information on them.

MobileMe isn't free. Currently, an individual MobileMe account is $99 per year, whereas the cost of a family account is about $149 per year. However, you can sign up for a free trial account available for 60 days. At the end of that period, you can choose to cancel the account if you don't find it valuable.

Three general steps are required to use MobileMe with your iPod touch. The first is to obtain a MobileMe account. The second is to configure MobileMe on your computers; this task is slightly different on Windows PCs or Macs, so you can find a section for each kind of computer. The third step is to configure your iPod touch to access the information provided by MobileMe; this step is described in the relevant chapters (such as Chapter 9, "Emailing") but are primarily discussed in Chapter 4, "Configuring and Synchronizing Information on an iPod touch."

Obtaining a MobileMe Account

To begin your free trial MobileMe account, follow these steps:

1. Use a web browser to move to www.apple.com/mobileme/.
2. Click Free Trial.

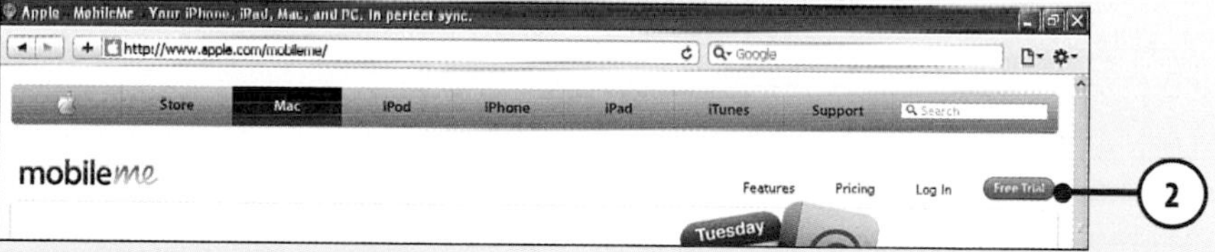

Your Member Name Is Important

Be careful about what you choose as your member name; in addition to using this to log in to MobileMe, it becomes part of your primary email address. You can't change your member name after you create your account.

3. Follow the onscreen instructions to obtain your MobileMe account. This involves creating your member name and password and providing contact information and a credit card (which isn't charged until the end of your free trial period). At the end of the process, you'll have a MobileMe member name and password. You use this information to access MobileMe services on all your devices.

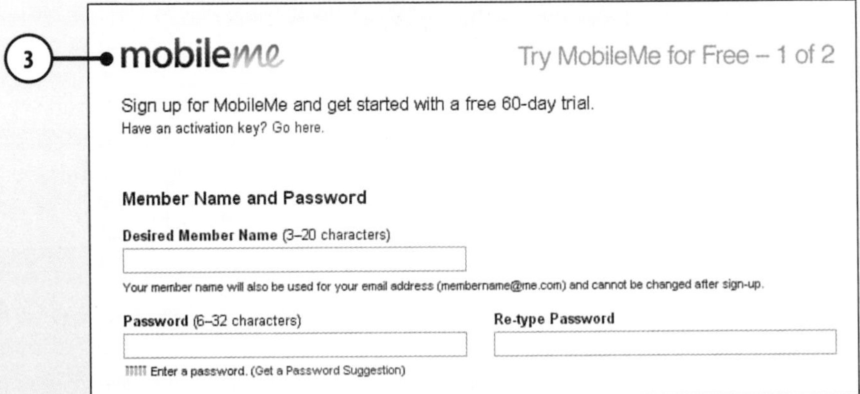

Configuring MobileMe on a Windows PC

Use the MobileMe Control Panel to configure MobileMe syncing on a Windows PC.

1. Open the MobileMe Preferences Control Panel. (If you don't have this Control Panel, you aren't using the current version of iTunes. Go back to the section called "Updating iTunes" and update your version.)

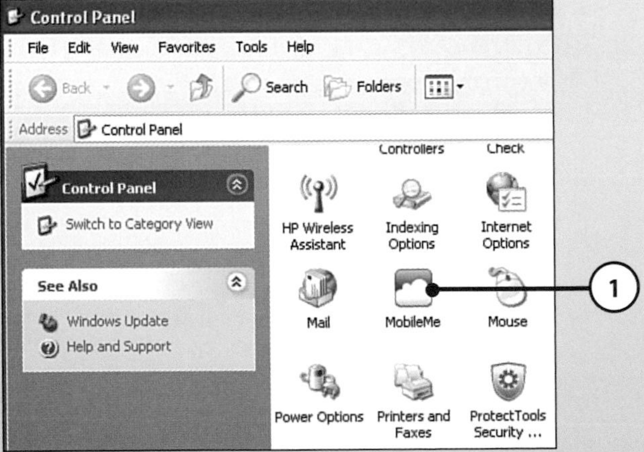

2. Enter your MobileMe member name and password.
3. Click Sign In. Your computer connects to your MobileMe account. In the Account Status section, you see information about your account, such as the amount of disk space you have, when the account expires, and so on.

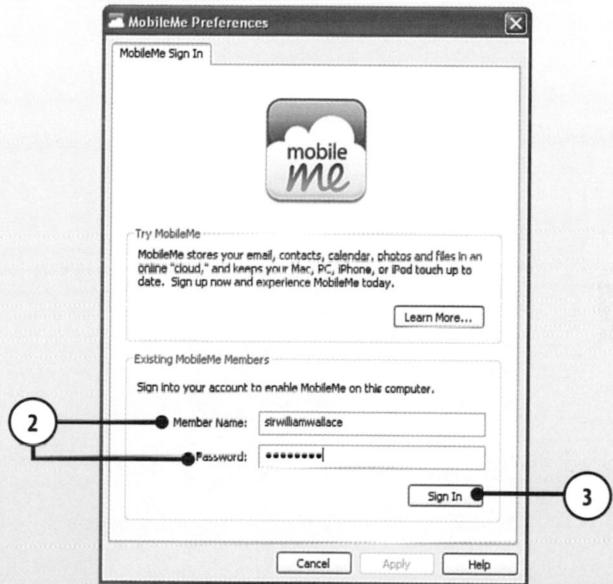

Exchange Handled Separately

If you have an Exchange account, you don't use MobileMe to sync your calendar or contact information. Instead you configure the Exchange account on your iPod touch and choose which information to sync with it. (This is explained in Chapter 9.)

4. Click the Sync tab.
5. Check the Sync with MobileMe check box.
6. On the top drop-down menu, choose how frequently the sync happens. Choose from Hourly, Automatically, and Manually. If you select Manually, you must click the Sync Now button to sync your MobileMe information between your computer and your MobileMe account.

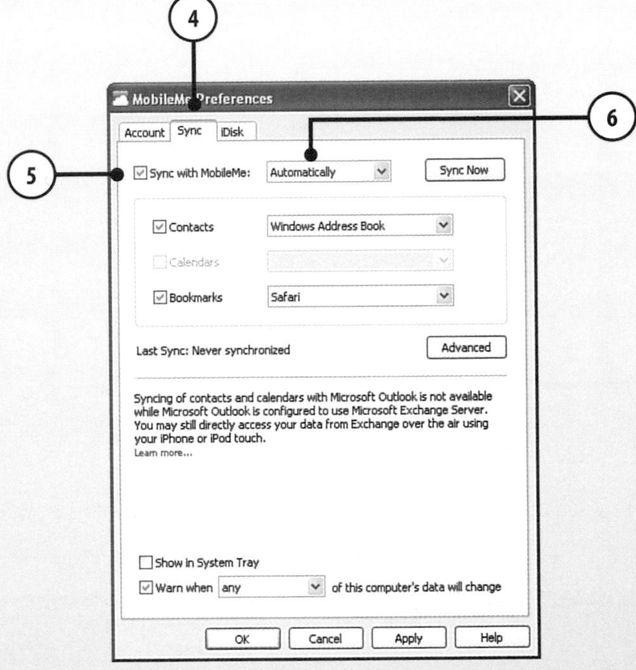

7. If you want your MobileMe contact information to be included in the sync, check the Contacts check box and choose where you want the contact information stored, such as Windows Address Book.
8. To include MobileMe calendar information in the sync, check the Calendars check box and choose the location of the calendars to be synced from the drop-down list.
9. To have your bookmarks moved into the MobileMe cloud, check the Bookmarks check box and choose the web browser where the bookmarks you want to sync are maintained (Internet Explorer or Safari).
10. Click OK. If you selected any option but Manually in step 6, the information you selected is copied from the computer to the MobileMe cloud where you can access it on iPod touch, and the process is repeated according to the schedule you set. If you selected Manually, click the Sync Now button to move the information.
11. Skip to the section titled "Managing MobileMe Syncs."

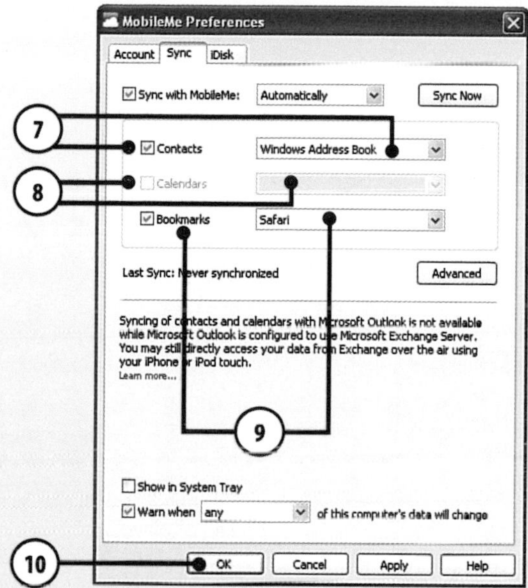

Configuring MobileMe on a Mac

Use the MobileMe pane of the System Preferences application to configure MobileMe syncing on a Mac.

1. Open the System Preferences application and click the MobileMe icon.

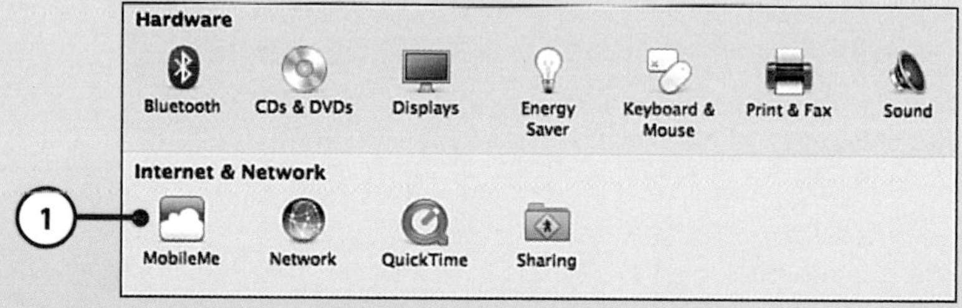

2. Enter your member name and password.

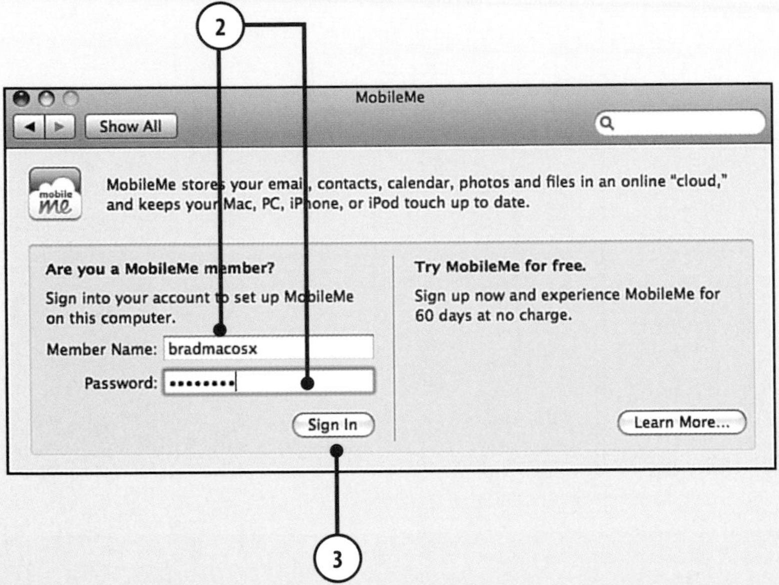

3. Click Sign In. Your account information is configured, and the MobileMe pane updates to show that you have configured MobileMe.
4. Click the Sync tab.
5. Check the Synchronize with MobileMe check box.
6. On the pop-up menu, select how you want synchronizations to occur. You can choose Manually to sync manually; choose a time period, such as Every Hour, to sync at those times; or choose Automatically to have syncs performed whenever included data changes.
7. Check the check box next to each item you want to include in the syncs.
8. Click Sync Now. The information you selected is copied onto the MobileMe cloud where you can access it from iPod touch. Future syncs happen according to the schedule you set, or if you selected Manually, you have to click the Sync Now button whenever you want to sync your information.

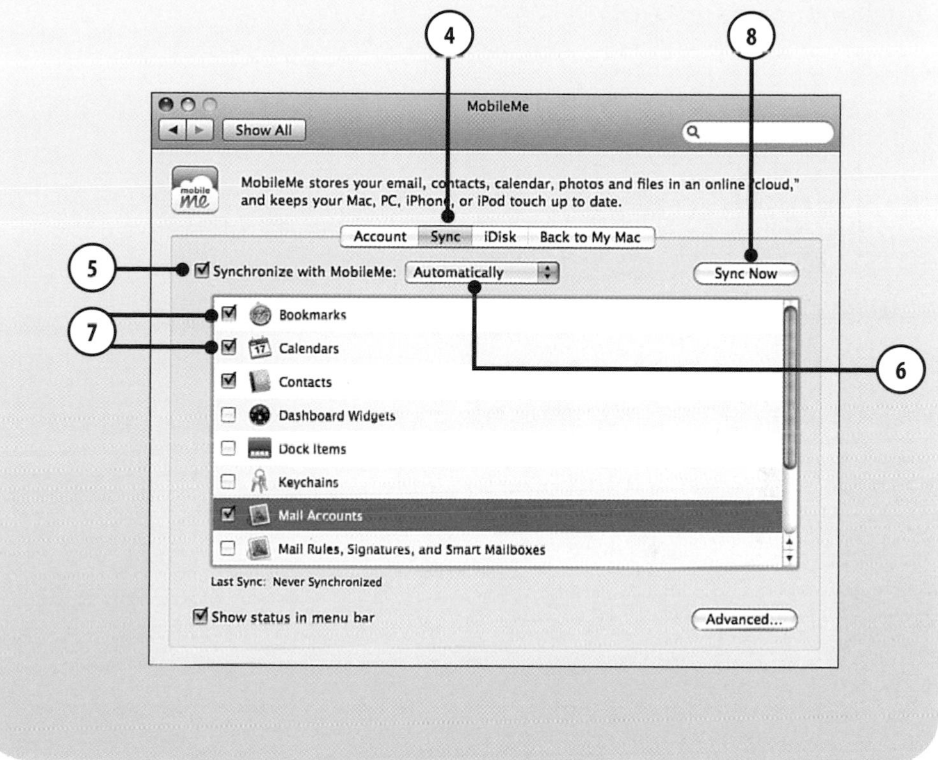

Managing MobileMe Syncs

As information changes on your iPod touch or on a computer, that information is synced via the MobileMe cloud. When this happens, the differences between the data on each device must be managed. You decide what happens the first time you sync, and you manage the process each time thereafter.

Syncing for the First Time

The first time you sync information via MobileMe (or if you reset your sync options), you decide how you want information to be moved. You are prompted via the MobileMe Sync Alert dialog.

1. At the prompt, choose how you want information to be moved. Choose Merge Data if you want the data on MobileMe to be merged with the information on your computer. Choose Replace Data on Computer to replace the information on your computer with information stored on the MobileMe cloud. Choose Replace Data on MobileMe to have the information on your computer replace the data on the MobileMe cloud. Choose Ignore for now if you don't want any action taken.

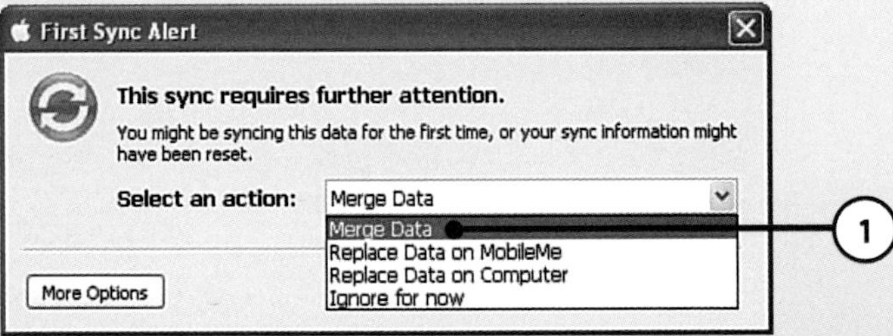

2. Click Allow. The sync proceeds.

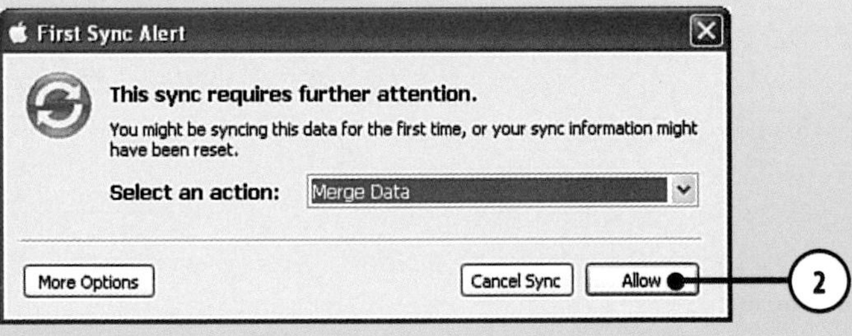

Managing Sync Alerts

During syncs, you are prompted when the amount of data changes beyond the limits you set on the MobileMe Preferences Control Panel or the MobileMe pane of the System Preferences application. For example, you might choose to be notified when more than 5% of the computer's data changes. When this happens, you see a dialog that enables you to make selections about how data is moved. You can use the controls in this dialog to review the changes and accept or prevent them as you see fit. When you decide, you click the appropriate Sync button to allow the sync to proceed. If these prompts get too annoying, move back to the MobileMe preferences and increase the percentage of data change that triggers a notification or disable the notifications entirely.

This Isn't a Book on MobileMe Either

If you get a MobileMe account, make sure you explore all it has to offer, including the great web applications for email, contacts, and calendars. And you may find that its iDisk online disk space is worth the cost of an account on its own.

Using This Book

This book has been designed to help you transform an iPod touch into *your* iPod touch by helping you learn to use it easily and quickly. As you can tell, the book relies heavily on pictures to show you how an iPod touch works. It is also task-focused so that you can quickly learn the specific steps to follow to do all the cool things you can do with your iPod touch.

Using an iPod touch involves lots of touching its screen with your fingers. When you need to tap part of the screen, such as a button or keyboard, you see a callout with the step number pointing to where you need to tap. When you need to drag or slide your finger along the screen, such as to browse lists, you see the following icon:

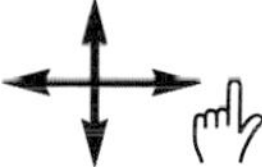

The directions you can drag are indicated with arrows.

To zoom in or zoom out on screens, you unpinch or pinch, respectively, your fingers on the screen. These motions are indicated by the following icons:

When you can drag quickly across the iPod touch's screen to flip through pages, you see this icon:

When you need to tap twice, such as to zoom out or in, you see the following icon:

When you need to rotate iPod touch, you see this icon:

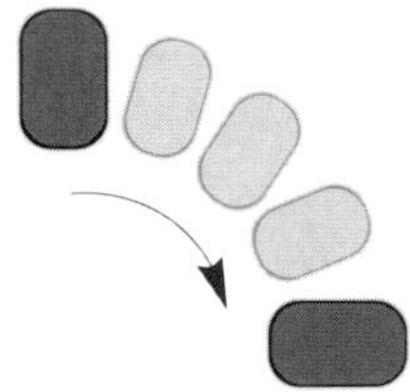

Sometimes you shake the iPod touch to activate a control. When you do, you see this icon:

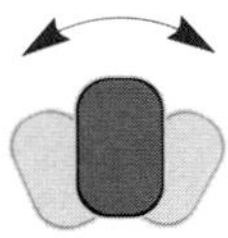

Because iTunes and the iPod touch work with both Windows computers and Macs, this book is designed for both platforms. When significant differences exist, such as with applications you use to store photos, you see task sections devoted to each type of computer. You can safely skip over sections focused on a type of computer you don't use.

Go here to connect an iPod touch to the Internet and to connect to other devices using Bluetooth

Use peer-to-peer applications to play games or share information with other touches, iPhones, or iPads

In this chapter, you explore how to connect your iPod touch to the Internet and to other touches, iPhones, or iPads. Topics include the following:

- → Connecting to the Internet
- → Connecting to other devices using Bluetooth
- → Connecting to other iPod touches, iPhones, or iPads

Connecting to the Internet, Bluetooth Devices, and iPods/iPhones/iPads

Many of the iPod touch's default applications rely on an Internet connection, with the most obvious being Mail, Safari, the App Store, and so on. Many third-party applications must also have an Internet connection to function. Fortunately, you can connect your iPod touch to the Internet by connecting it to a Wi-Fi network that provides Internet access.

Using Bluetooth, you can wirelessly connect your iPod touch to other devices, such as Bluetooth headphones or a wireless keyboard.

With peer-to-peer applications, you can also connect your iPod touch to other iPod touches, iPhones, or iPads to create a local network to exchange information, play games, and so on.

Connecting an iPod touch to the Internet

To connect your iPod touch to the Internet, you need to connect it to a Wi-Fi network that provides Internet access. You can use a variety of Wi-Fi networks, including those available in your home or business or in public places, such as airports, restaurants, hotels, and schools.

After you configure your iPod touch to join a network, it remembers that network by default and joins it automatically when you move the touch within the network's range. So, connecting to a network is a one-time task; after you connect the first time, your touch connects to the network automatically when it is the best choice (if multiple networks are available). You can tell your touch to ignore networks that you don't want to join automatically.

Automatic Prompting to Join

By default, when you access one of your iPod touch's Internet applications, such as Safari, and your iPod touch isn't connected to the Internet, it automatically searches for networks to join. A dialog appears showing all the networks available to you. You can select and join one of these networks similar to how you join one via Settings, as you learn how to do in the following steps. If you don't want your iPod touch to do this, use the Settings application to move to the Wi-Fi Networks screen and turn off Ask to Join Networks. When this function is disabled, you need to manually connect to networks you've never used before, as described in the following steps.

Connecting to an Open Network

Many Wi-Fi networks broadcast their identification—their names and whether they are secure—so that you can easily see them on your iPod touch; these are called open networks because anyone who is in range can attempt to join the network because it appears on Wi-Fi devices automatically. These are the easiest to join.

Not All Access Is Free

Be aware that some open networks charge access fees for Internet access, especially in public places such as airports and hotels; in these situations, you need a username and password to access the Internet over a network you connect to.

Without a username and password, you can connect to the network, but you can access only the provider's login page that you can use to log in or obtain an account that you use to connect to the Internet. Some of these networks provide some information or functions you can access free without connecting to the Internet, such as a news page. This is common for Wi-Fi networks in airports; you can often freely connect to the network and can access some content, such as streaming video or the airport's home page. If you want to connect to the Internet, you need an account, which might require that you pay a fee of some type. Fortunately, many airports and other public areas provide free Internet access, in which case all you must do to connect is to agree to that network's terms and conditions and sometimes provide an email address.

---

1. On the Home screen, tap Settings. Next to Wi-Fi, you see the status of your Wi-Fi connection, which is Not Connected if you aren't currently connected to Wi-Fi.
2. Tap Wi-Fi.
3. If Wi-Fi is turned off, tap the OFF button to turn it on (if the ON button appears, skip this step). The Wi-Fi status becomes ON, and your iPod touch immediately starts searching for available networks.
4. Review the networks that your iPod touch finds; these are shown in the Choose a Network box. For each network, you see its name, whether it is secure, and its signal strength. (I've found that the signal strength icon on this screen isn't very reliable; you won't actually know how strong a signal is until you connect to the network.)

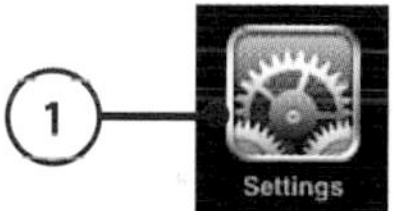

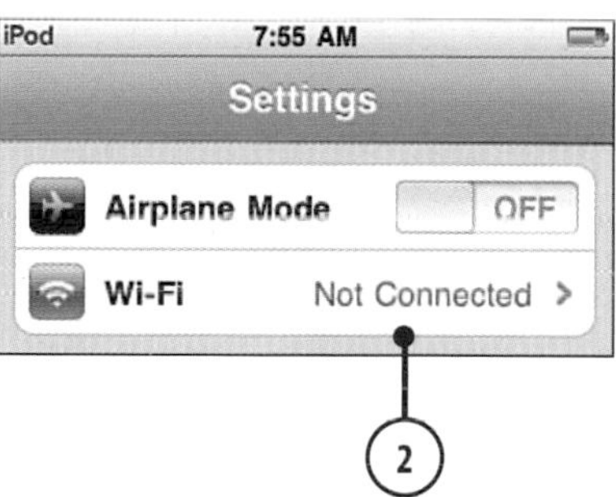

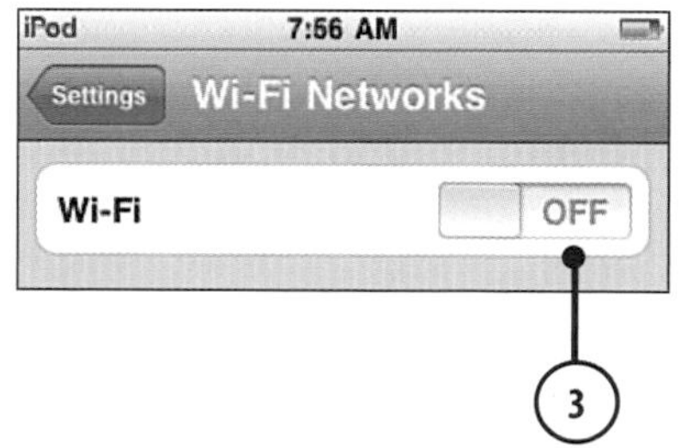

5. Tap the network you want to join. Before you tap, however, consider the security of the network; if you see the padlock icon next to the network's name, you need a password to join it—the Enter Password screen appears when you tap a secure network. If a network is not marked with the padlock icon, it is not secure, and you skip to step 8 after you tap that network to join it.

6. Enter the password for the network.

7. Tap Join. If you provided the correct password, your iPod touch connects to the network and gets the information it needs, such as an IP address. If not, you're prompted to enter the password again. After you successfully connect to the network, you return to the Wi-Fi screen.

Secure network (requires a password)

iPod 8:03 AM
Settings Wi-Fi Networks
Wi-Fi ON
Choose a Network...
Foxtrot
The iMac Network
Other...
Ask to Join Networks ON
Known networks will be joined automatically. If no known networks are available, you will be asked before joining a new network.

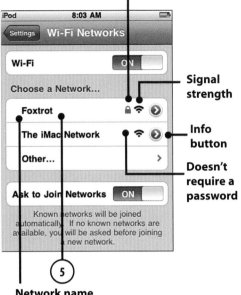

Signal strength

Info button

Doesn't require a password

5

Network name

Typing Passwords

As you type a password, the last character you typed remains on the screen for a period of time and then is hidden by a dot in the Password field. This is helpful because you see the most recent character you entered, which can prevent you from getting all the way to the end of a sometimes long password only to discover you've made a mistake along the way and have to start all over again.

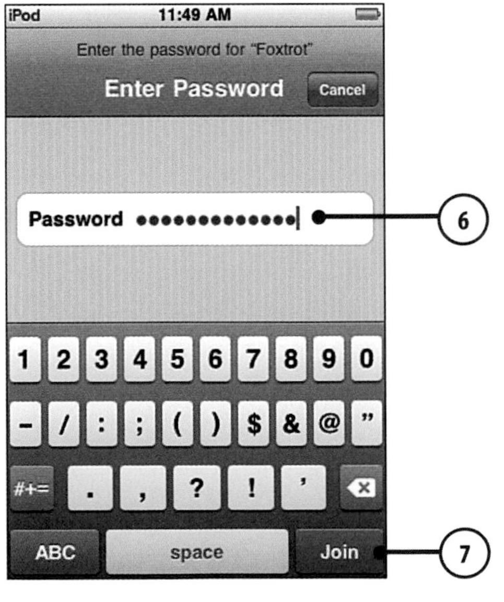

8. Review the status of the network to which you connected. The name of the connected network is in blue and is marked with a check mark. You see the signal strength for that network. (This indication is typically more accurate than the one you see before you are connected.)
9. Tap the Info button for the network to which you are connected. You see the Info screen, which is labeled with the name of the network.
10. Scroll the screen to review the network's information. The most important item is the IP Address. If there is no number here or the number starts with 169, the network is not providing an IP address, and you must find another network. You can safely ignore the rest of the information on the screen in most situations. If you want to access some of the more advanced settings, such as HTTP proxy, you need information from the network administrator to access the network, so you need help to get your iPod touch connected.
11. Tap Wi-Fi Networks to return to the Wi-Fi Networks screen.
12. Move to the Home screen. You should see the Wi-Fi connection icon next to iPod; this indicates that you are connected to a Wi-Fi network and shows the strength of the signal.

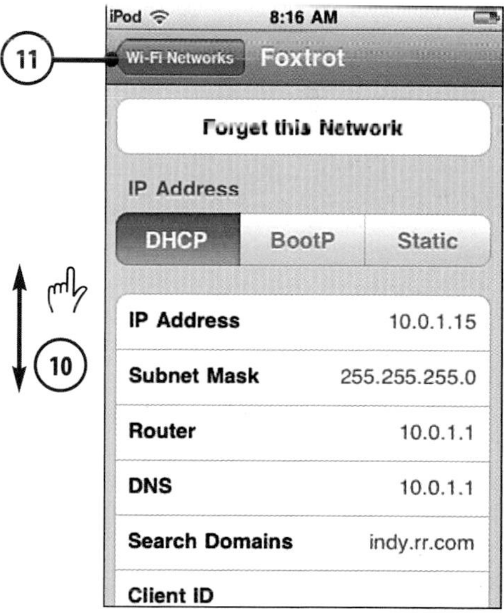

Was Connected but Now I'm Not

If you've been using a network successfully, and at some point your iPod touch cannot access the Internet but remains connected to the network, move to the network's Info screen and tap Renew Lease. Confirm this action at the prompt. This refreshes your iPod touch's IP address, sometimes enabling you to access the Internet again.

13. Tap Safari.
14. Try to move to a web page, such as www.apple.com/ipodtouch/. (See Chapter 7, "Surfing the Web," for details.) If you move to a web page that is not from a Wi-Fi provider, you're good to go. If you are taken to a web page for a Wi-Fi provider, you need an account to access the Internet. If you have a username and password for that network, enter them on the login form. If you don't have an account, you must obtain one; use the web page to sign up. After you have an account with that provider, you can get to the Internet. If you see an error message that the iPod touch is not connected to the Internet, make sure you are connected to a Wi-Fi network; if you are, there is a problem with the network's connection to the Internet, which needs to be resolved before you can access the Internet. In most cases, your best alternative is to find a different network to use. (Sometimes using the Renew Lease function described in the previous sidebar helps.)

Security Key Index

Some private networks require a key index in addition to a password. Unfortunately, there's no way to enter a specific key on your iPod touch. If a network requires this key, you can't connect your iPod touch to it. You might join the network, but you probably won't get an IP address from it—and you must have one to get to the Internet. If you cannot join a Wi-Fi network that you know is available, check with the administrator to make sure that you have the right configuration information and don't need a key index.

Connecting to a Commercial Network

Many networks in public places, such as hotels or airports, require that you pay a fee or provide other information to access that network and the Internet. In many cases, you can connect for free but must provide an email address and agree to the network's terms and conditions. When you connect to one of these networks, you're prompted to log in. Check out these steps:

1. Tap the network you want to join. The iPod touch connects to the network, and you see the Log In screen for that network.

2. Provide the information required to join the network. If you need a username and password, provide it. If the network requires a fee, you need to provide a credit or debit card to create an account. These accounts typically have various durations, such as by the hour, day, month, and so on. The fee depends on the duration you select. In most cases, you also have to indicate that you accept the terms and conditions for the network, which you typically do by checking a check box.

3. After you provide the required information or payment, tap the button to join the network. This button can have different labels depending on the type of access, such as Free Access, Login, and so on. After your account has been verified, you see a confirmation screen and can move onto the Internet.

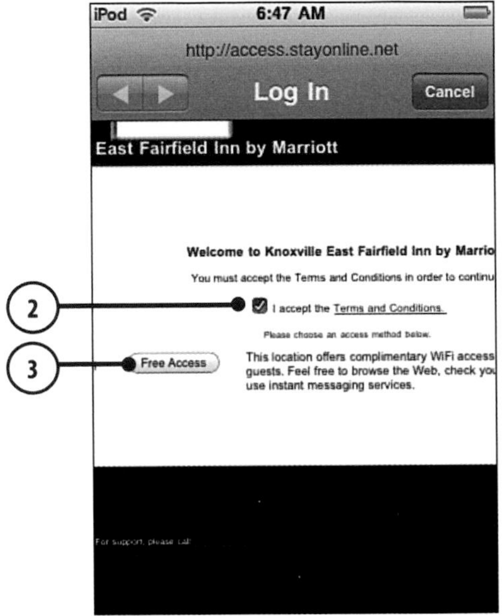

Not Always

Not all commercial networks prompt you to log in as these steps explain. Sometimes, you use the network's homepage to log in instead. You join the network as described in the previous section, and when you try to move to a web page as explained in step 14 in that section, you're prompted to log into or create an account with the network's provider.

>>> Go Further

BOINGO BOINGO

Boingo is a network/Internet provider available in many locations, such as airports, either directly or through sharing arrangements with other providers. In addition to being widely available, this service has an app that you can download from the App Store. This app does a couple of cool things. One is that you can purchase access time on an hourly basis for $1.99/hour (less if you buy 10 hours at once); you purchase these as credits via the iTunes Store using the same process you use to buy music, movies, or other apps. The other is that when you launch the app, it automatically finds and logs into Boingo or compatible networks, which gets you onto the Internet quickly and easily. The app also shows you how much time remains in the current session so that you can decide whether you need more time. When your current hour expires, you're prompted to use another session. When you run low on credits (hours of access), you can easily purchase more through the Boingo app. Your hours never expire, and you don't have to make a monthly commitment; the price per hour is quite low compared to many other options, making this is an excellent option when free access isn't available.

Connecting to a Closed Network

Some networks don't broadcast their names or availability; these are called closed networks because they are hidden to Wi-Fi devices; you must know they exist. To connect to one of these networks, you must know the network's name because it won't show up on the iPod touch's list of available networks. You also need to know the type of security the network uses and its password. You have to get this information from the network's provider.

1. Follow steps 1 through 3 in the previous section to turn Wi-Fi on and to move to the Wi-Fi Networks screen.
2. Tap Other.

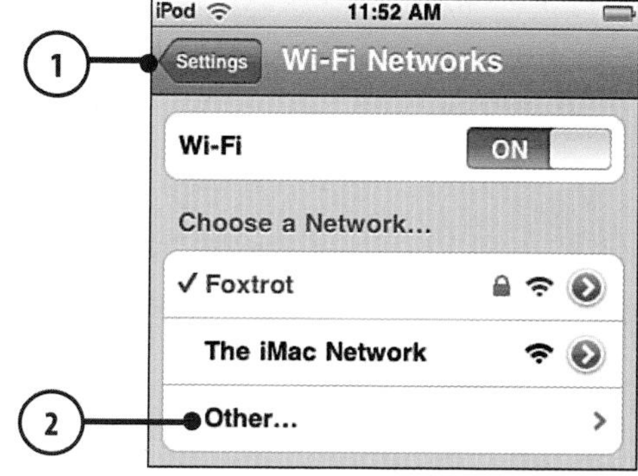

3. Enter the name of the network.
4. Tap Security.
5. Tap the type of security the network uses. The options are None, WEP, WPA, WPA2, WPA Enterprise, or WPA2 Enterprise. You don't need to worry about what each of these options means; you just need to pick the right one for the network. You need to get the type of security from the person who manages the network. (The None option is for unsecured networks, but it's very unlikely that a hidden network doesn't require a password.) When you select an option, it is marked with a check mark.
6. Tap Other Network. In the Security field, you see the type of security you selected. The Password field appears.
7. Enter the password.
8. Tap Join. If the information you entered matches what the network requires, you join the network and can begin to access its resources. If not, you see an error message and have to try it again until you can join. When you successfully join the network, you move back to the Wi-Fi Networks screen and see that you are connected to the closed network, which now appears on the Choose a Network list.

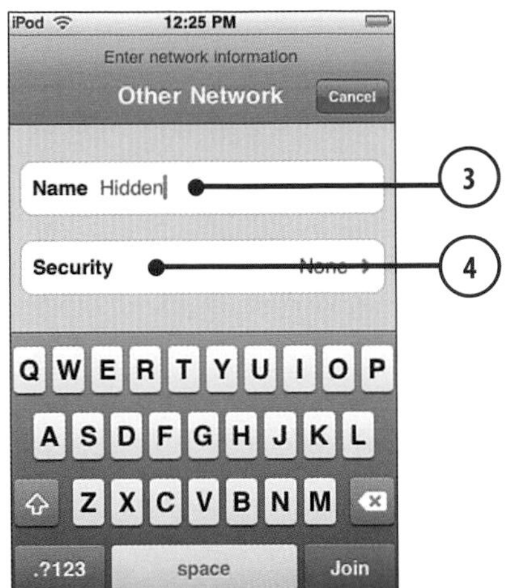

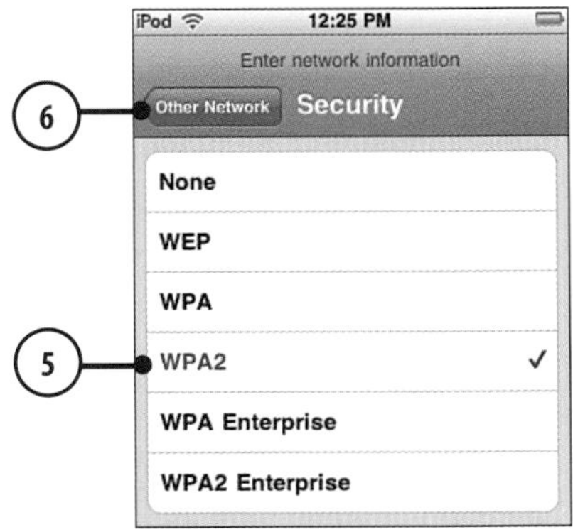

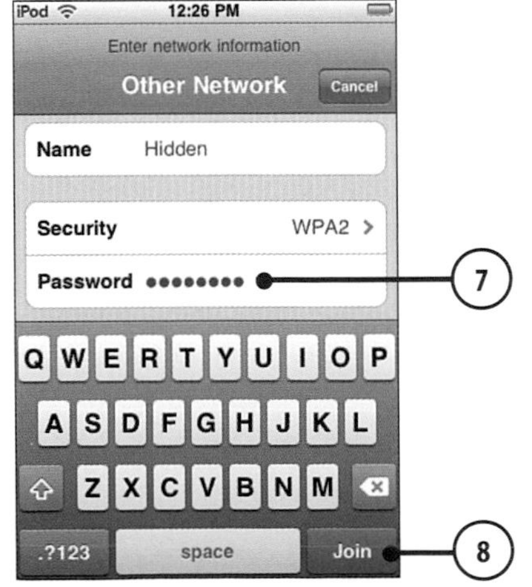

>>> Go Further

NETWORK SNIFFERS

Sniffers are devices and software that can detect wireless networks, both open and closed. These can help you know that a closed network is available, but because most (dare I say all?) closed networks are secure, you need to know a password to connect to that network. So just knowing it exists isn't actually of much value, but a sniffer can help you know when a network exists so that you can try to find out the password by contacting the administrator.

Changing Networks

You can change the network that your iPod touch uses at any time. For example, if you lose Internet connectivity on the current network, you can move your iPod touch onto a different one.

1. Move to the Settings screen. The network to which your iPod touch is currently connected is shown.
2. Tap Wi-Fi. Your iPod touch scans for available networks and presents them to you in the Choose a Network section.
3. Tap the network that you want to join. Your iPod touch attempts to join the network. If you haven't joined that network previously and it requires a password, enter it when prompted to do so. After your iPod touch connects, you see the new network's name highlighted in blue and marked with a check mark. Your touch then starts using that network, such as to connect to the Internet.

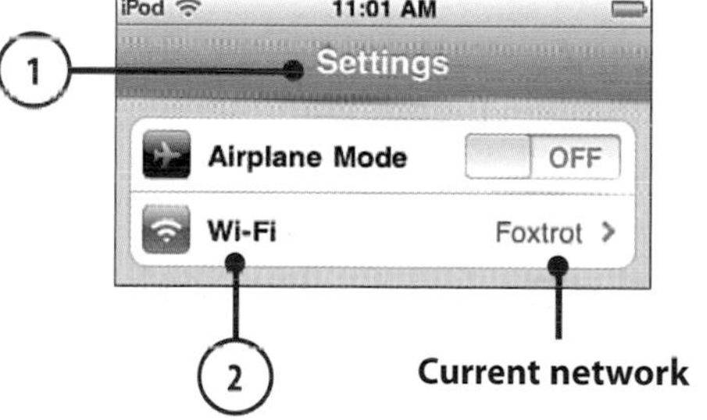

Be Known

After your iPod touch connects to a Wi-Fi network (open or closed) successfully, it becomes a known network. Your iPod touch automatically connects to known networks when it needs to access the Internet. So unless you tell your iPod touch to forget about a network, you need to log in to it only the first time you connect to it.

Forgetting Networks

As you previously learned, your iPod touch remembers networks you have joined and connects to them automatically as needed. Although this is mostly a good thing, occasionally you won't want to use a particular network any more. For example, when moving through an airport, you might connect to a network for which you have to pay for Internet access, but then you decide you don't want to use that network after all. Each time you move through that airport, your iPod touch connects to that network automatically, which can be annoying. So you might want your iPod touch to forget about that network so that it doesn't automatically connect to it in the future.

1. Move to the Wi-Fi Networks screen.
2. Tap the Info button for the network that you want your iPod touch to forget.
3. Tap Forget this Network.

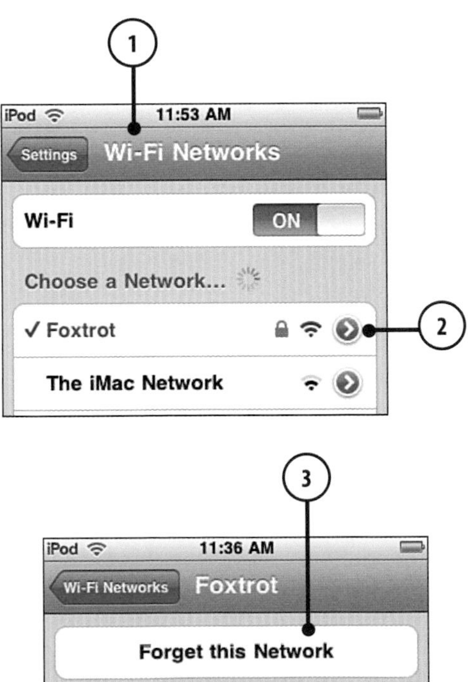

4. Tap Forget Network in the resulting prompt. Your iPod touch forgets the network, and you return to the Info screen. If your iPod touch had been getting an IP address from the network, that address is cleared, and your iPod touch attempts to connect to a different network automatically.

5. Tap Wi-Fi Networks. You return to the Wi-Fi Networks screen. If a network you've forgotten is still available to your iPod touch, it continues to appear in the Choose a Network list, but your iPod touch will no longer automatically connect to it. You can rejoin the forgotten network at any time just as you did the first time you connected to it.

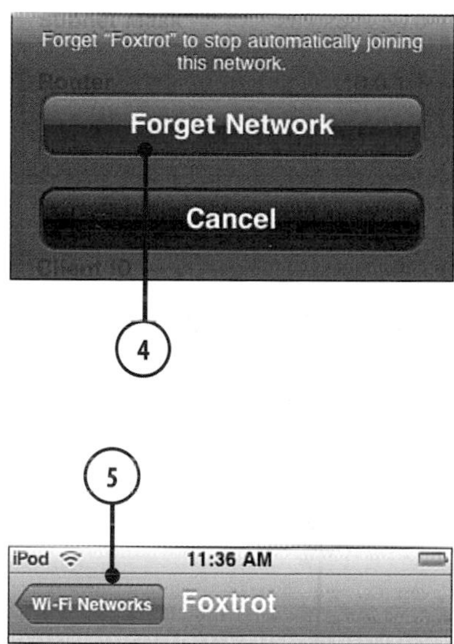

Connecting to Other Devices Using Bluetooth

An iPod touch includes built-in Bluetooth support so that you can use this wireless technology to connect to other Bluetooth-capable devices. There are many kinds of devices that support Bluetooth and to which you can connect your iPod touch; these include, wireless keyboards, headphones, iPhones, iPads, and other iPod touches. To connect Bluetooth devices together, you pair them.

In Bluetooth, *pairing* is the lingo for two Bluetooth devices connecting. The requirement is that the devices can communicate with each other via Bluetooth. There is also a "sometimes" requirement, which is a pairing code, passkey, or PIN. All those terms refer to the same thing, which is a series of numbers entered in one or all devices being paired. Sometimes you enter this code on both devices, whereas for other devices you enter the first device's code on the second device. Some devices don't require a PIN, in which case you don't even have to think about it.

When you need to pair devices, you're prompted to do so, and you need to complete the actions required by the prompt to communicate via Bluetooth.

To enable Bluetooth on your iPod touch and connect to another device, do the following.

1. Move to the Settings screen.
2. Tap General.
3. Tap Bluetooth.
4. Tap OFF. Bluetooth starts up, and the status becomes ON. The iPod touch immediately begins searching for Bluetooth devices. You also see the status Now Discoverable, which means that other Bluetooth devices recognize the iPod touch.
5. Put the other device in Discoverable mode. (See the instructions provided with the device.) The two devices find each other. On iPod touch, the other device is listed but shown as not paired. You might be prompted to enter a passkey on one device or both.
6. Tap the device to which you want to connect. If a passkey is required, you see a prompt to enter it on the device with which you are pairing.

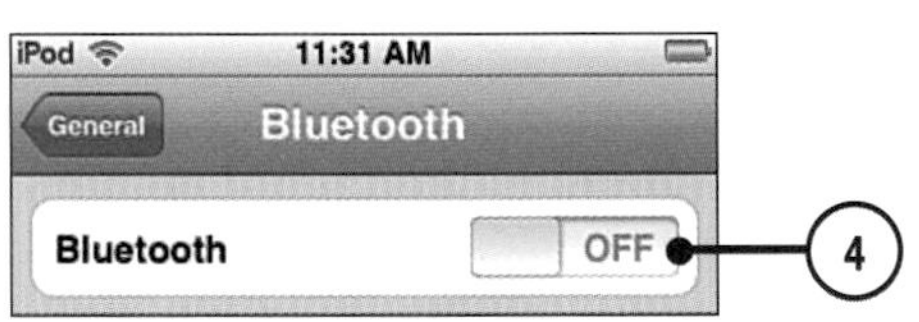

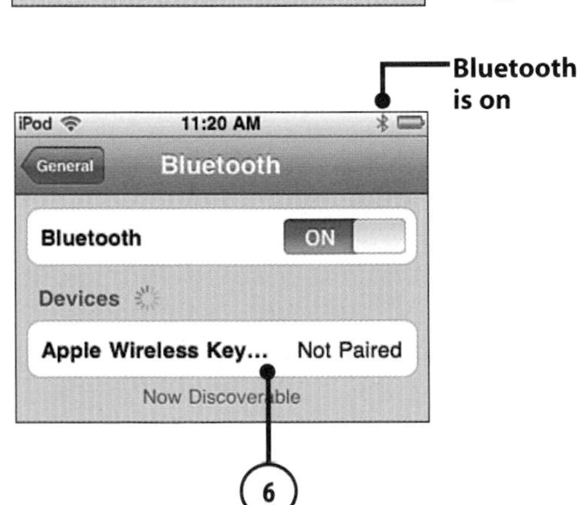

Bluetooth On

When Bluetooth is active (whether the iPod touch is connected to other devices or not), you see the Bluetooth icon at the top of the screen.

7. Input the required passkey, such as typing the passkey on a keyboard if you are pairing with a Bluetooth keyboard.

8. If required, tap Connect; some devices connect as soon as you enter the passkey and you won't need to do this. You see the device to which the iPod touch is connected in the Devices section of the Bluetooth screen. If the device works without any further configuration, you can use it. In some cases, you need to configure the device to work with the iPod touch.

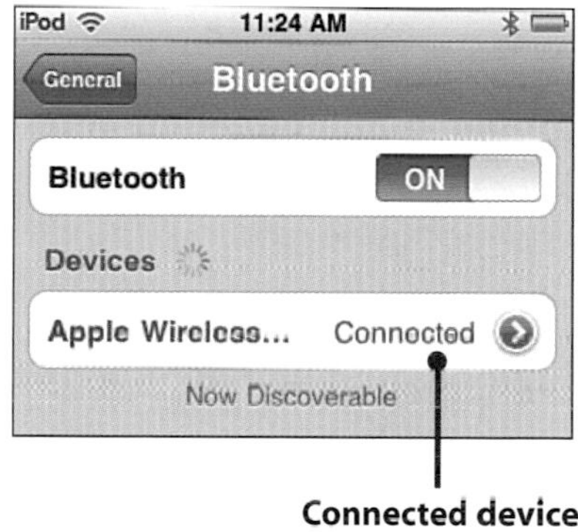

Ah, Forget About It

Like other connections you make, your touch remembers Bluetooth devices to which you've connected before and reconnects to them, which is convenient—most of the time anyway. If you don't want the touch to keep connecting to a device, move to the Bluetooth screen and tap the device's Info button. Tap the Forget this Device button and then tap Forget Device. The pairing is removed. Of course, you can always pair the devices again at any time.

Connecting to Other touches, iPhones, and iPads

The iOS 4 operating system includes peer-to-peer connectivity, which is an overly complicated way of saying that devices running this operating system (iPod touches, iPhones, and iPads) can communicate with one another directly. Developers can take advantage of this in their applications to enable great functionality, especially multiplayer gaming, information sharing, and other collaborative activities.

Unlike Internet or Bluetooth connections, you don't configure the peer-to-peer connection directly. Instead, you use applications that have this capability built into them.

There are two ways that iPhone OS devices can communicate with each other: via a Wi-Fi network or via Bluetooth. The method you use in any specific situation depends on the application that you use.

There are two basic ways applications employ peer-to-peer communication. Some applications are designed to mostly work in this mode, and the connection configuration is more obvious. Other applications, especially games, offer peer-to-peer communication as an option.

If the application you want to use communicates over a Wi-Fi network, such as a network you use to access the Internet, all the devices with which you want to communicate must be on that network (which was previously covered in this chapter). If the application uses Bluetooth, you must enable Bluetooth on each device and configure them so they can communicate with one another. (See the previous section for the details of configuring Bluetooth.)

Also each device that will be communicating via the application must have the application installed on it. (See Chapter 13, "Installing and Maintaining iPod touch Applications," for help finding and installing applications.)

Following are general steps showing examples of each type of application. The detailed steps you use depend on the specific applications you use, but the general process is similar.

Using an Application with Peer-to-Peer Networking by Default

Some applications are designed to primarily function via communication with other iPod touches and iPhones. These applications typically prompt you to connect to other devices as soon as you launch them.

1. Launch the application on your iPod touch.
2. Have the other people launch the application on their devices.
3. At the prompt, tap the device to which you want to connect. The other user is prompted to allow your connection request. If he does so, you see a notification on your device.
4. Tap Continue.

5. Use the application. (This example is an application called Whiteboard that enables each user to write or scrawl on a shared whiteboard. Of course, the writing might not be legible, but that isn't the iPod touch's fault.)

Configuring an Application to Use Peer-to-Peer Networking

Some applications need to be configured to communicate with other devices. This is typical of games that offer both single player and multi-player options. Before you can play, you need to configure the application to communicate on each device.

1. Launch the application.
2. Open the application's configuration menu.

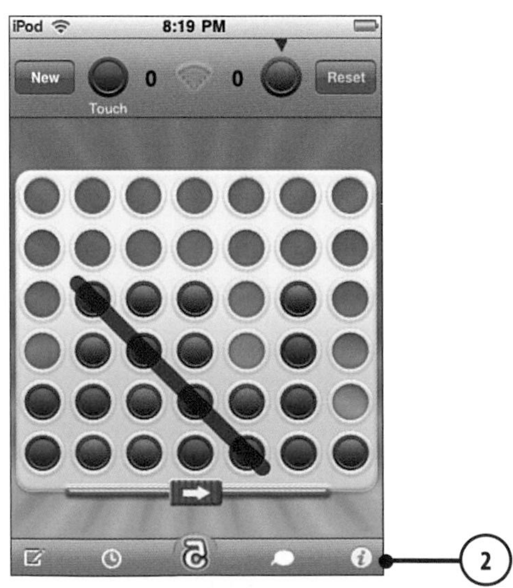

3. Tap the communication option you want to use.
4. Select the player you want to be for the game. (Some games prompt you for a name as soon as you choose a communication option.)
5. Tap Done.
6. Have the other players perform steps 1 through 5 on their devices.
7. Start the game. You see the results of what other people do on their iPod touches while they see the results of what you do on yours in real time.

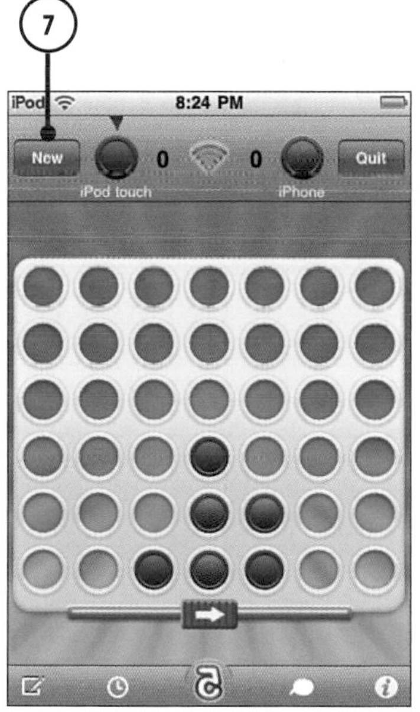

View and work with photos added from your computer

Carry a library of books with you and read whatever you want, whenever you want

Download content from the iTunes Store onto your iPod touch

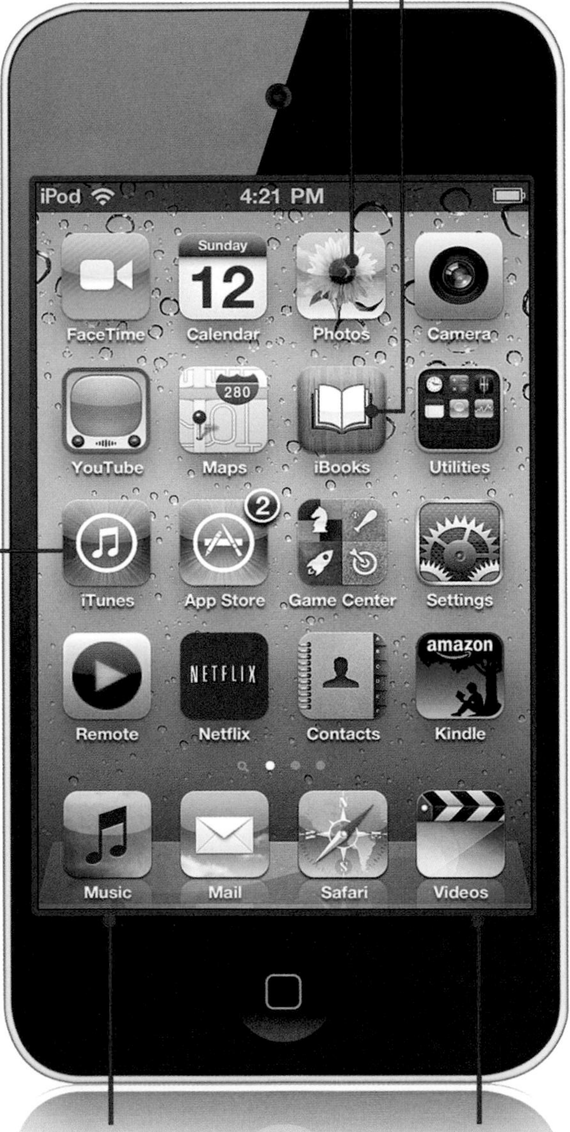

Enjoy great audio and video from your iTunes Library on your iPod touch

In this chapter, you learn how to stock your iPod touch with audio, video, books, and photos. The topics include the following:

- → Moving audio and video content from your iTunes Library onto the iPod touch
- → Adding books to your iPod touch
- → Using iTunes to move photos onto your iPod touch
- → Using the iPod touch iTunes application to download content directly from the iTunes Store
- → Using the iBooks application to download books directly from the iTunes Store

3

Moving Audio, Video, Books, and Photos onto Your iPod touch

One of the best things about an iPod touch is that you can use it to listen to audio content of various types (see Chapter 5, "Listening to Music, Podcasts, and Other Audio"). You can also watch video on the iPod touch's high-resolution screen (see Chapter 6, "Watching Movies, TV Shows, and Other Video"). And with the iBooks app, you can have a library of books in the palm of your hand (see Chapter 12, "Using Cool iPod touch Applications"). You can view and work with photos stored on it, too (see Chapter 11, "Storing, Viewing, and Sharing Photos").

However, before you can do all these things, you must move content with which you'll work onto your iPod touch. There are two basic ways to do this. One is to move content from your iTunes Library onto the touch; you can also use iTunes to move photos from a photo application to your iPod touch. The second method is to move content directly from the iTunes Store onto your iPod touch.

Using iTunes to Add Audio and Video Content to the iPod touch

iTunes is a great application that you can use to store, organize, and enjoy all sorts of audio and video. It's also the primary way to move audio and video content onto your iPod touch. You first add the content to your iTunes Library and then move that content onto the iPod touch through the sync process.

The most common ways to add content to the iTunes Library are by importing audio CDs or purchasing content from, renting movies from, and subscribing to podcasts in the iTunes Store.

After you stock your iTunes Library, you can create playlists to organize that content to move it onto your iPod touch.

When your content is ready, sync the iPod touch with the iTunes Library so that the content you want to be available is moved from your Library onto the iPod touch.

Importing Audio CDs to the iTunes Library

Importing audio CDs is one of the most useful ways to get music and other audio content into your iTunes Library.

1. Launch iTunes by double-clicking its application icon, choosing it on the Windows Start menu, or clicking it on the Mac's Dock.

Only the First Time

You need to perform steps 2 through 10 only before the first time you import CDs or when you want to change settings.

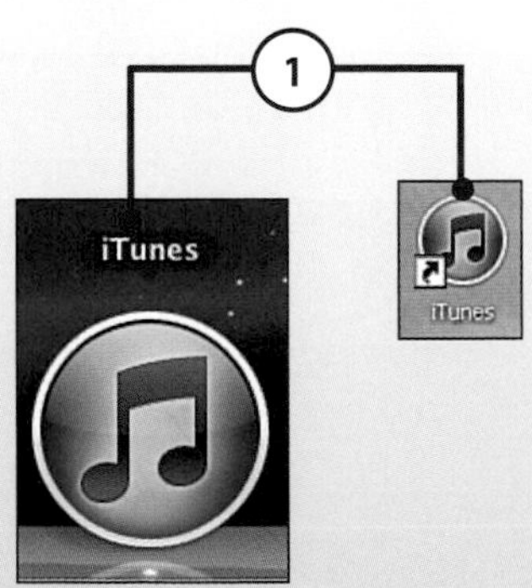

2. Choose Edit, Preferences (Windows) or iTunes, Preferences (Mac). The Preferences dialog appears.
3. Click the General tab.

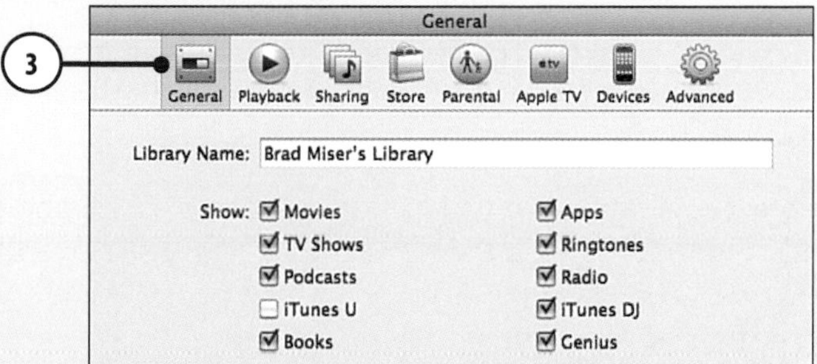

4. On the When you insert a CD menu, choose Import CD and Eject.
5. Click Import Settings.

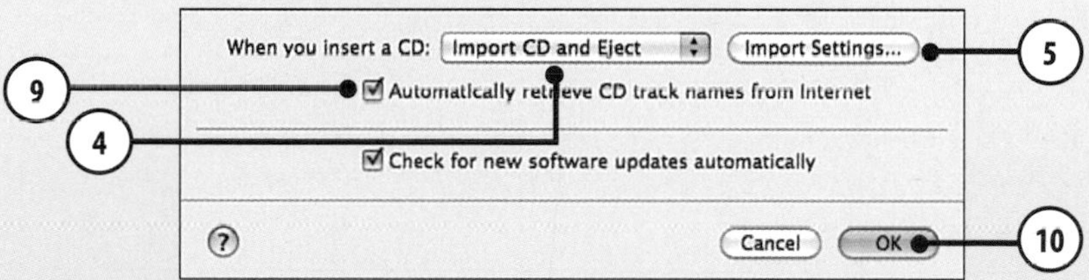

6. On the Import Using drop-down menu, choose AAC Encoder.
7. On the Setting drop-down menu, choose iTunes Plus.
8. Click OK.

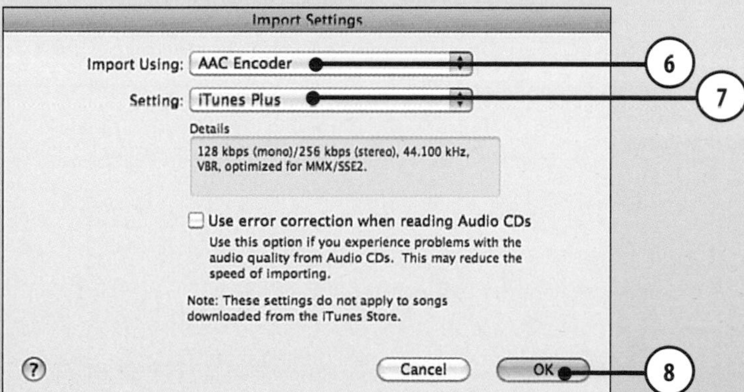

9. Check Automatically retrieve CD track names from Internet.
10. Click OK.

11. Insert a CD into the computer. iTunes connects to the Internet and identifies the CD. When that's done, the import process starts. You don't have to do anything else because iTunes manages the import process for you. When the process finishes, iTunes plays an alert sound and ejects the disc.

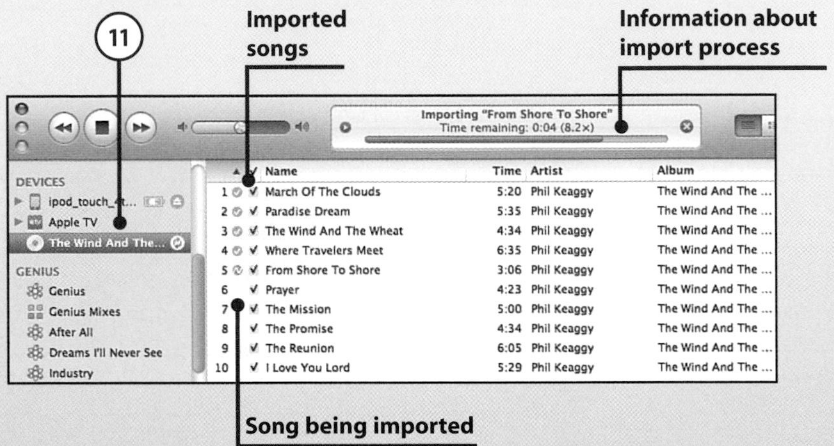

12. Insert the next CD you want to import. After it has been ejected, insert the next CD and so on until you've added all the CDs that you want to listen to on your iPod touch to your iTunes Library.

>>> Go Further

TAGGING YOUR MUSIC

To browse and find music in your iTunes Library, you must tag (label) the tracks you import so that iTunes can identify and organize that content. When iTunes finds a CD's information on the Internet, it takes care of this for you, including the album artwork associated with that CD (as long as the music is available in the iTunes Store).

If iTunes doesn't find information for CD content you import, you should add tags manually. Do this by selecting a track and choosing File, Get Info. Use the Info dialog to update the track's tags, including name, album, artist, and even artwork. If you select multiple tracks before you open the Info dialog, you can update the tags on the selected tracks at the same time.

No Duplicates Please

After you import a CD, you won't likely ever need to use it again on your computer. So after you import all your CDs, change the iTunes On CD Insert setting to Ask to Import CD so that you don't accidentally import multiple copies of the same CD in the rare case when you do insert the CD into your computer again.

Purchasing Content from the iTunes Store

The iTunes Store has a large selection of music, movies, TV shows, and other content that you can preview, purchase or rent (movies), and download to your iTunes Library. To do this, you must have an Apple Store account, also known as an Apple ID. (You can preview content without an Apple ID.) If you have an AIM/AOL screen name, you can also use that to sign into the store. (You have to provide credit card information to use an AIM/AOL account to make purchases.) For the steps to obtain an Apple ID and log into the iTunes Store, see Chapter 1, "Getting Started with Your iPod touch."

Sign Me In!

If you see the Sign In button instead of your Apple ID in the upper-right corner of the iTunes window, click that button and sign in to your account.

1. Click iTunes Store on the Source list. iTunes connects to the iTunes Store, and you see the Home page.
2. Click the Power Search link in the Quick Links section located along the right side of the Home page.

The Store in Full Screen

By default, when you browse the iTunes Store, you do so in the right pane of the iTunes window. However, the Store is best when you have plenty of screen space in which to view it. You can have the Store fill the entire width of the iTunes window (the Source pane is hidden) by opening Preferences, clicking the Store tab, checking the Use full window for iTunes Store check box, and clicking OK. When you finish with the Store, click the Close button (x) in the upper-left corner of the Store window to return to the standard iTunes view. The rest of the figures in this chapter show this configuration.

3. To limit your search to a specific kind of content, choose it on the pop-up menu. For example, choose Music to search for music. The Search tool updates to include fields appropriate for the kind of content for which you are searching.
4. Enter the information for which you want to search, such as Artist, Song, Genre, and such.
5. Click Search. Items that meet your search criteria display in the lower parts of the window. The results are organized into logical collections based on the type of content for which you searched. For example, when you search for music, you see albums, songs, and music videos. You see different kinds of information for each category of content. When you search for music, you see the Songs category that lists name, album, artist, and so on for each song.

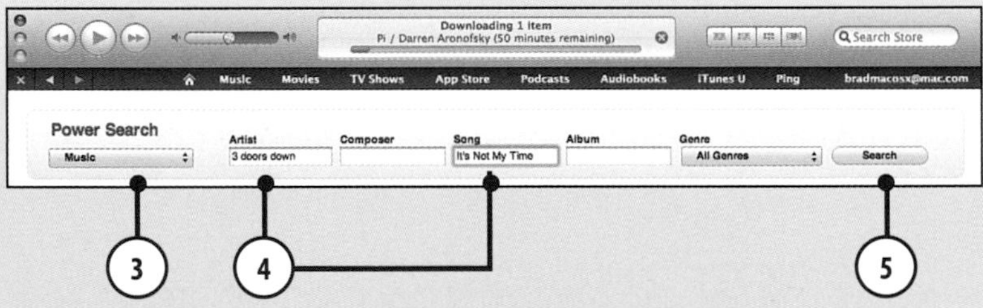

This Store Is Made for Browsing

The iTunes Store is designed to be browsed. Just about every graphic and almost all the text you see is linked to either categories of content or to specific content. You can browse the store just by clicking around. For example, you can click the Music link to browse music, or you can click any of the other links you see on the Home page to browse some other type of content. There are numerous ways to browse, but all of them involve just clicking around. If you don't have something specific in mind, browsing is a great way to discover, preview, and purchase content.

6. To preview content, move the pointer over it and click the Play button that appears; where it appears depends on what you hover over. When you hover over a song, the Play button replaces the track number; when you hover over video, the Play button appears in the lower-right corner of the thumbnail. After you click the button, a 30-second preview plays. To move the item's detail screen, click its text or graphic.

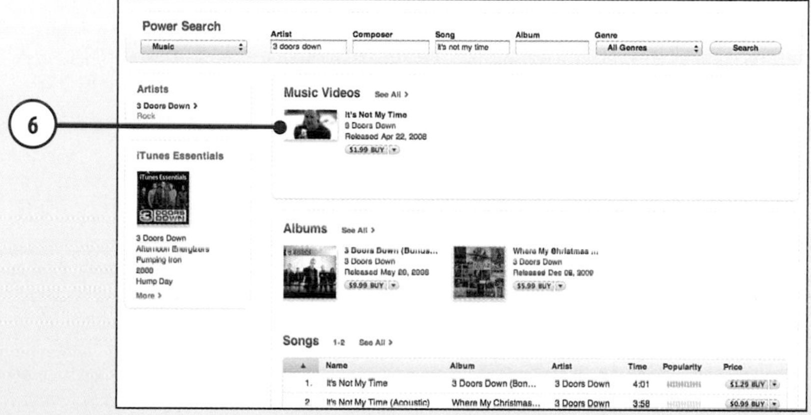

7. If you select video, watch the video in the preview window that appears. Click the close button (x) in the upper-left corner of the preview window to close it.

8. Continue previewing content.

9. When you want to purchase and download content, click the BUY button. This button can include different information depending on the screen it appears on. It always shows the price of the content. It can also describe what you are buying. For example, when you browse a TV show, one Buy button enables you to purchase the entire season while you can use the Buy buttons next to each episode to purchase one episode at a time.

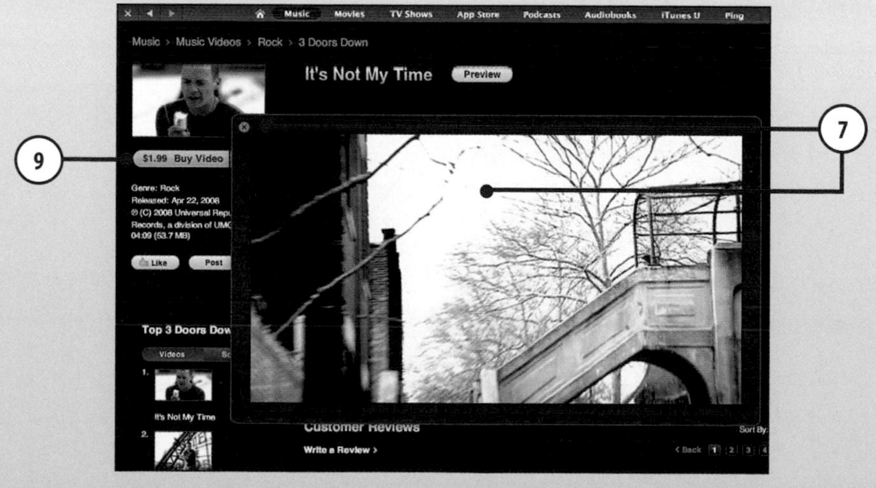

HD Movies and TV

Some movie and TV content is available in the HD format. Your iPod touch can't play this content. However, when you purchase HD content, you actually get two versions. Along with the HD version that you can play on a computer or a home entertainment system, you get an iPod touch-compatible version that you can move onto and watch on your iPod touch.

10. If prompted, enter your account's password and click Buy. (If you enable iTunes to remember your iTunes Store account information for purchasing, you can skip this step.) The content you purchase is downloaded to your computer and added to your iTunes Library.

Sign In to download from the iTunes Store
To create an Apple Account, click Create New Account.
Create New Account
If you have an Apple Account (from the iTunes Store or MobileMe, for example), enter your Apple ID and password. Otherwise, if you are an AOL member, enter your AOL screen name and password.
Apple ID:
bradmacosx@me.com
Example: steve@me.com
Password:
Aol.
Remember password
Cancel
Buy
10

11. Click the Purchased playlist on the iTunes Source list to see content you've downloaded from the iTunes Store.

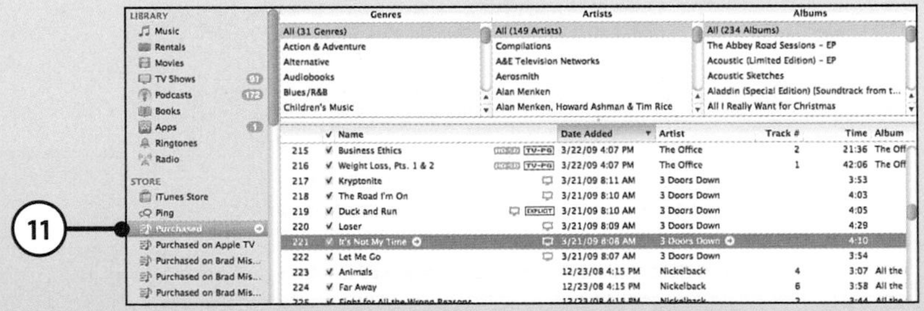
11

More Than Buy

If you click the downward-facing arrow to the right of the Buy buttons, you see a menu with various commands, such as gift, which enables you to give the content to someone else, share via Facebook, and so on. One useful option enables you to add content to your wish list, which is much like a shopping cart where you can store content you might be interested in purchasing at a later time; after you add content to your wish list, you can move back to it by clicking the My Wish List item on the Quick Links section of the iTunes Store home page. From your wish list, you can preview or purchase content.

Renting Content from the iTunes Store

You can also rent movies, TV shows, and other content from the iTunes Store. When you rent content, you can watch it as many times as you'd like within a 24-hour period (starting when you play the rented content) within a 30-day window (starting when the content is downloaded into iTunes). After either the 24-hour viewing or 30-day rental period expires (whichever comes first), the rented content is removed from iTunes (or from your iPod touch) automatically. To rent a movie, follow these steps (renting episodes of a TV series is similar—just move to the TV Shows area instead).

1. Move into the iTunes Store and click the Movies button.
2. Browse or search for movies in which you might be interested; for example, click the See All link next to the New to Rent or Own section title to see new releases.

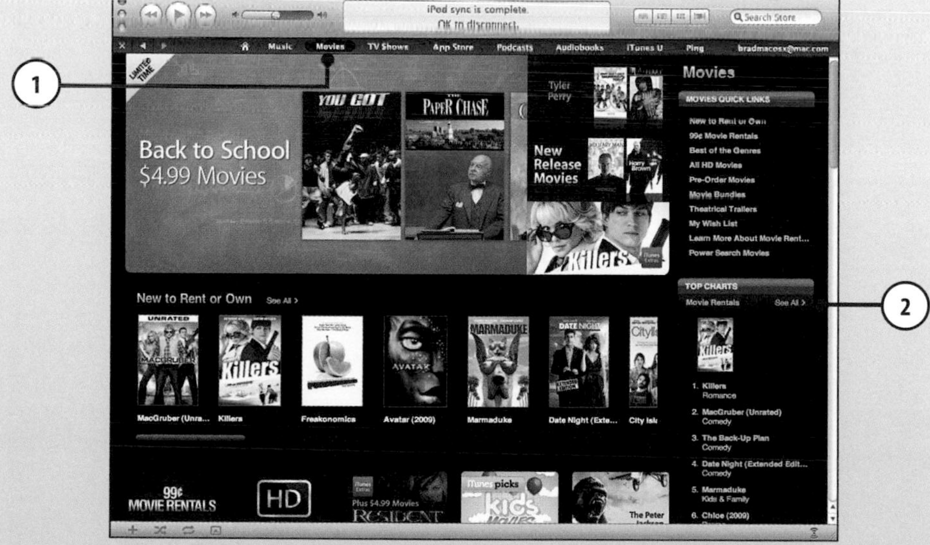

3. Click a movie's thumbnail or links to see detailed information about it, including the cost to rent it.

4. To watch the movie's trailer, click the View Trailer button.

5. To rent the movie, click the Rent Movie button. If you've allowed iTunes to remember your Apple ID information for purchasing, the movie downloads immediately. If iTunes doesn't remember your Apple ID, provide your information and click the Rent button.

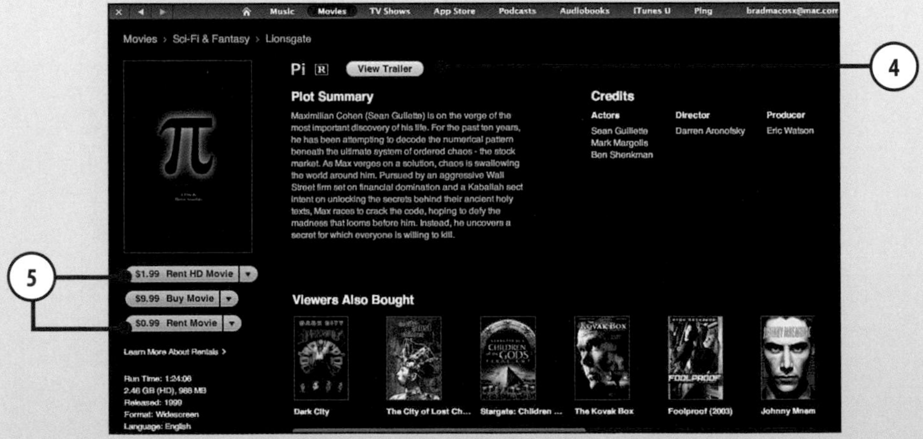

One Place Only

Unlike other content you get from the iTunes Store, rented content can be on only one device at a time. So when you move rented content from the iTunes Library onto an iPod, it disappears from the iTunes Library. You can move rented content between devices as many times as you'd like.

6. To access content you've rented, click the Rentals source. (Be sure not to play a rented movie until you're sure you will can watch all of it within 24 hours because the viewing period starts as soon as you play it.)

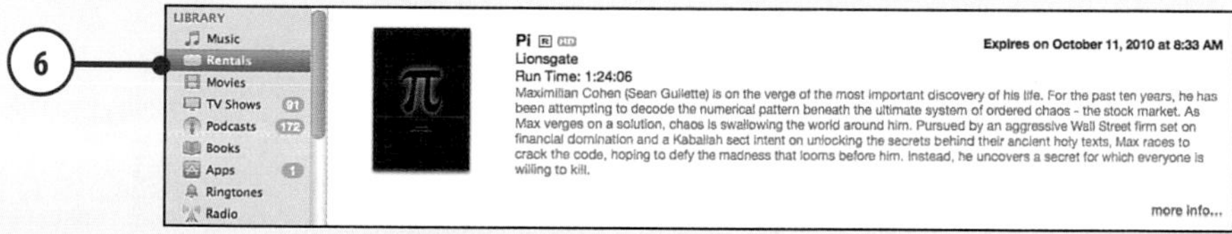

Subscribing to Podcasts in the iTunes Store

Podcasts are radio-like audio or video episodes that you can subscribe to and listen to or watch. Even better, most podcasts are free.

1. Move into the iTunes Store.
2. Click the arrow on the Podcasts button.
3. Click a category you are interested in, such as Business.

Searching

You can search for podcasts using the Power Search tool on the Home page and choosing Podcasts on the Power Search menu. You can also type the podcast name in the Search iTunes Store bar in the upper-right corner of the screen; when you do this, you search across all content so you might see music, movies, and so on, in addition to podcasts.

4. Browse the results.
5. Click a podcast to get more information about it.

Settings

With the Podcasts source selected, click the Settings button at the bottom of the iTunes window to configure how your podcasts are managed by iTunes, such as when it checks for new episodes, if new episodes are downloaded automatically, and so on.

6. Read about the podcast.
7. Hover over an episode and click the Play button to preview it.
8. To subscribe to the podcast so it is automatically downloaded, click Subscribe; like other action buttons, the Subscribe button shows the cost of the podcast. In most cases, they are free, so the button is Subscribe Free.

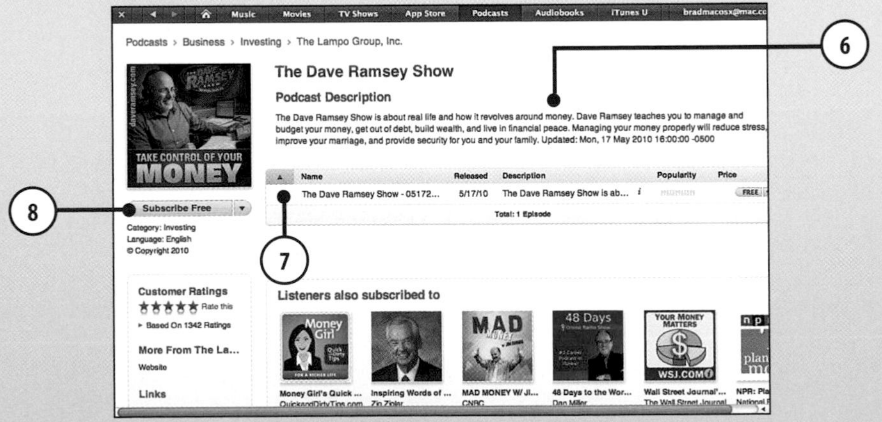

9. Click Subscribe at the prompt. The most recent episodes are downloaded to your iTunes Library; future episodes will be downloaded automatically.

10. Click the Podcasts source in the Source list. (The number you see indicates how many episodes of all the podcasts to which you've subscribed have been downloaded but not yet listened to.) You see all the podcasts to which you've subscribed. Under each podcast, you see the episodes that have been downloaded; click a podcast's triangle to show or hide its episode list. The blue dot next to episodes indicates you haven't listened to them yet.

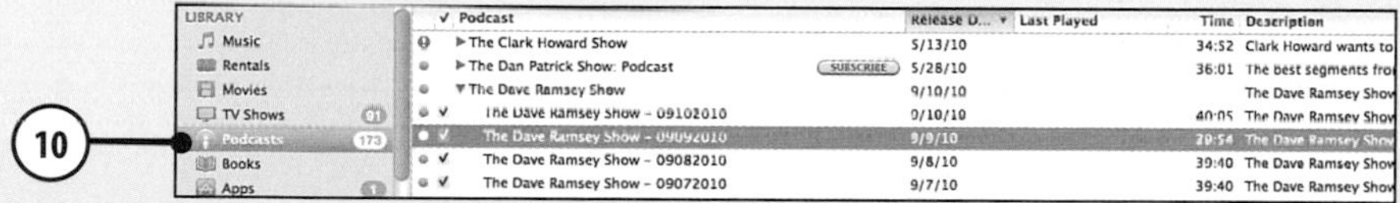

Building Music Playlists

One of the best ways to collect content that you want to place on your iPod touch is to create a playlist and manually place content onto it.

1. Click the New Playlist button. A new playlist is created with its default name selected for you to change.

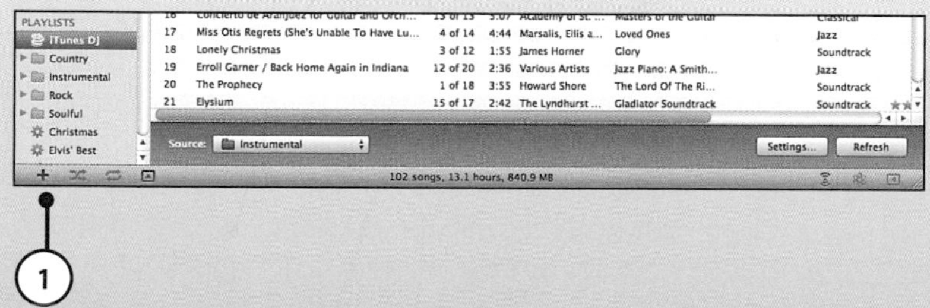

2. Rename the new playlist and press Enter (Windows) or Return (Mac).

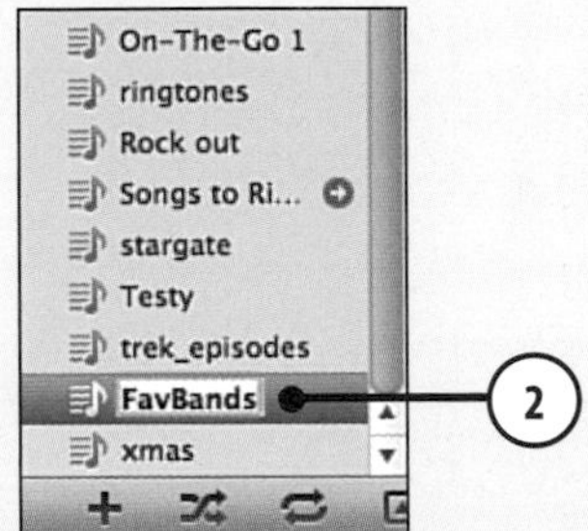

3. Select Music on the iTunes Source list.

4. Browse or search for songs you want to add to the playlist.

Playlists for All

These steps explain how to create playlists for music, but they work just as well for any content in your Library, including audiobooks, movies, episodes of TV shows, and so on. Just find the content you want to add and drag it onto the playlist's icon. You can mix types together, such as songs and movies, in the same playlist, too.

5. Drag songs from the Content pane onto the playlist you created.

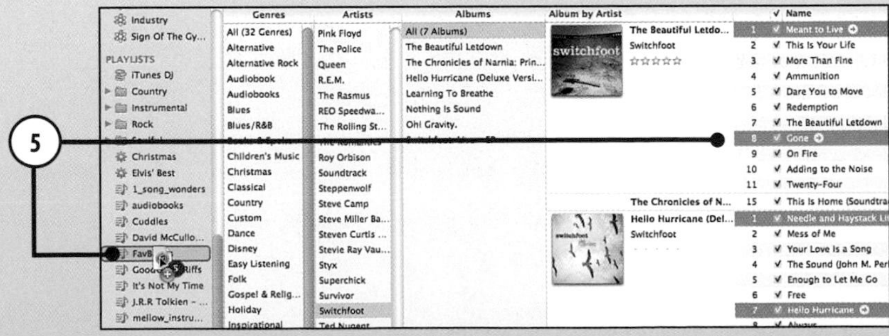

6. Repeat steps 3–5 until you place in the playlist all the songs that you want it to contain. You can place any combination of songs in a single playlist.

7. Select the playlist. Its contents appear in the Content pane.

8. Drag songs up and down the playlist until they are in the order in which you want them to play.

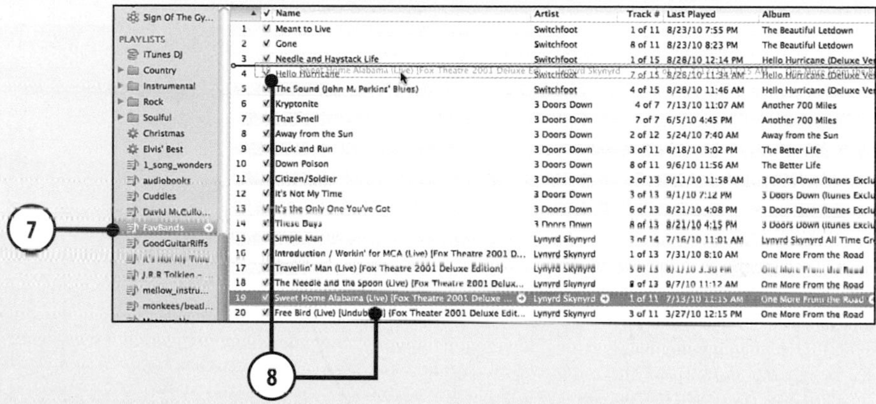

iTunes Folders

Over time, you are likely to create a lot of playlists to keep your iTunes content organized. You can use folders to store playlists on the Source list to make them easier to work with. To create a folder, choose File, New Playlist Folder. Name the folder and then drag playlists into it to store them there. You can expand or collapse a folder by clicking the triangle next to its name. You can place folders within other folders, too.

Building Smart Playlists

A smart playlist does the same basic thing as a playlist, which is to collect content that you want to listen to or watch and to move onto your iPod touch. Instead of placing content in a playlist manually, a smart playlist adds content automatically based on criteria you define.

1. Select File, New Smart Playlist. The Smart Playlist dialog box appears.

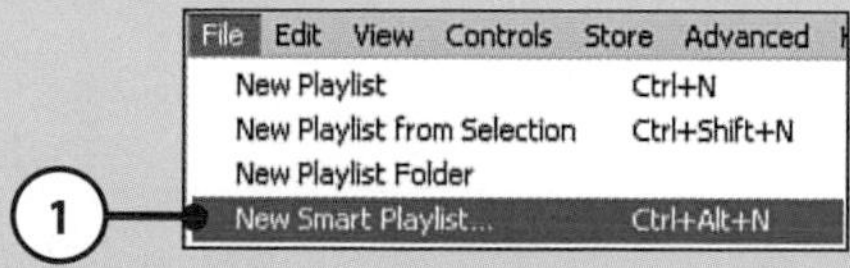

2. Select the first tag on which you want the smart playlist to be based on the Tag menu. For example, you can select Artist, Genre, My Rating, or Year tag, among many others.
3. Select the operand you want to use on the Operand menu. For example, if you want to match data exactly, select is. If you want the condition to be looser, select contains.
4. Type the condition you want to match in the Condition box. The more you type, the more specific the condition is.
5. To add another condition to the smart playlist, click the Add Condition button. A new, empty condition appears. At the top of the dialog box, the All or Any menu appears.

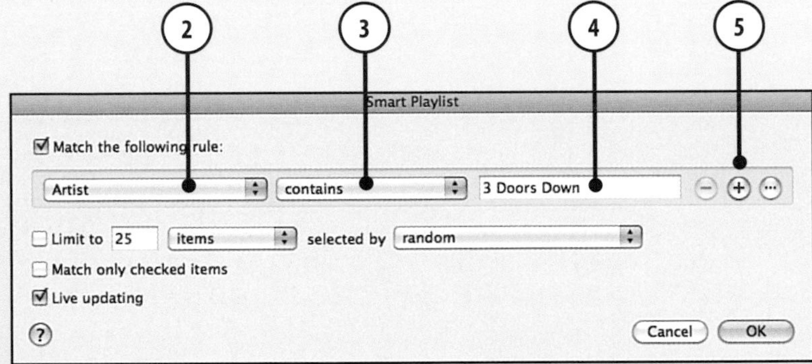

6. Select the second tag on which you want the smart playlist to be based in the second condition's Tag menu.
7. Select the operand you want to use in the Operand menu.

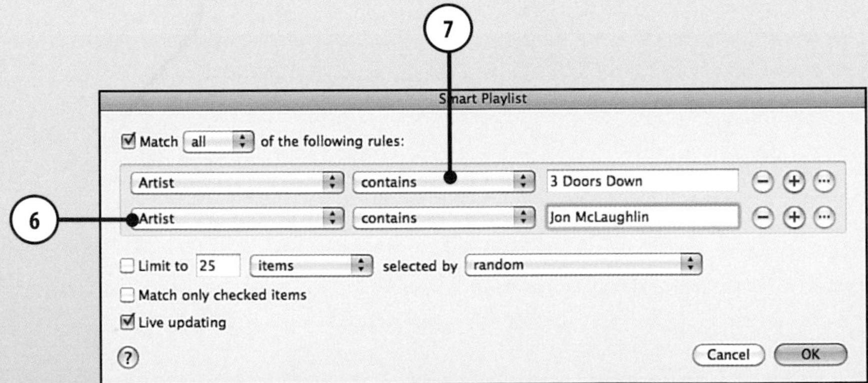

8. Type the condition you want to match from the Condition box.
9. Repeat steps 5–8 to add more conditions to the playlist until you have all the conditions you want to include.
10. Choose all on the menu at the top of the dialog if all the conditions must be met for a track to be included in the smart playlist or choose any if only one of them must be met.

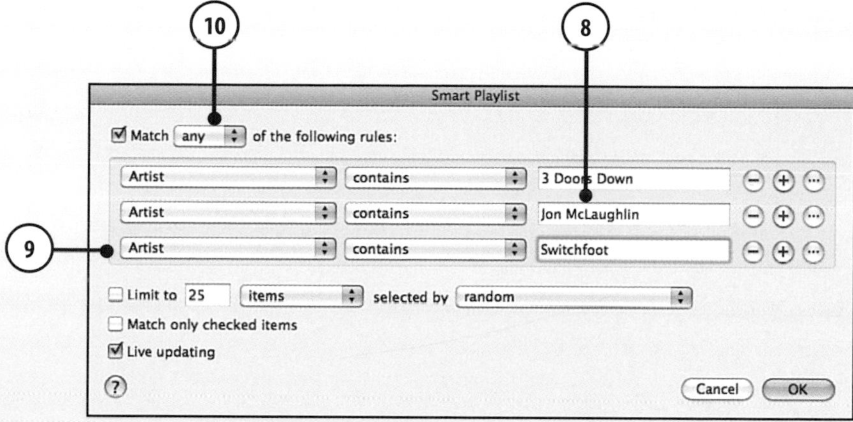

11. If you want to limit the playlist, check the Limit to check box.
12. Select the parameter by which you want to limit the playlist in the first menu; this menu defaults to Items. Your choices include the number of items, the time the playlist will play (in minutes or hours), or the size of the files the playlist contains (in MB or GB).
13. Type the data appropriate for the limit you selected in the Limit to box. For example, if you selected minutes in the menu, type the maximum length of the playlist in minutes in the box.

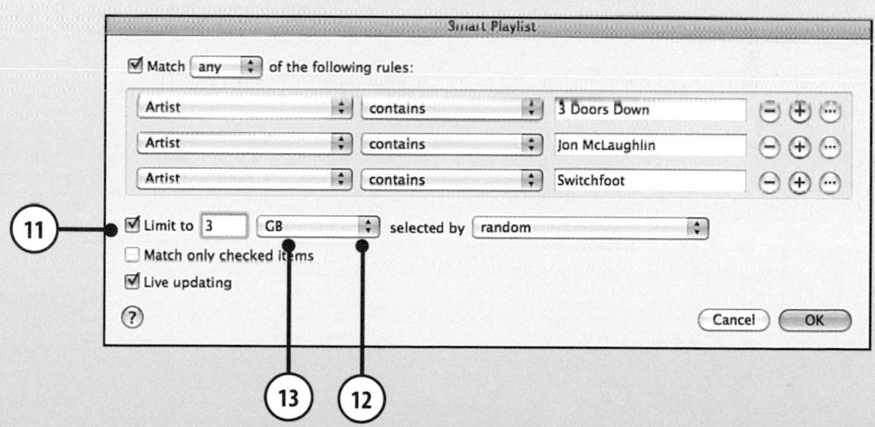

iTunes Is Helpful

As you make selections on the Tag menu and type conditions in the Condition box, iTunes attempts to automatically match what you type to tags in your Library. For example, if your Library includes Elvis music and you use Artist as a tag, iTunes enters Elvis Presley (or Elvis Costello if your Library contains any of his music) in the Condition box for you when you start typing Elvis.

14. Select how you want iTunes to choose the songs it includes based on the limit you selected by using the selected by menu. For example, to have iTunes include tracks you've added to the Library most recently, select Most Recently Added.

15. If you want the playlist to include only songs whose check boxes in the Content pane are checked, check the Match only checked items check box.

16. If you want the playlist to be dynamic, meaning that iTunes updates its contents over time, check the Live updating check box. If you uncheck this check box, the playlist includes only those songs that meet the playlist's conditions when you create it.

17. Click OK. You move to the Source list; the smart playlist is added and selected, and its name is ready for you to edit. Also the songs in your Library that match the criteria in the playlist are added to it, and the current contents of the playlist are shown.

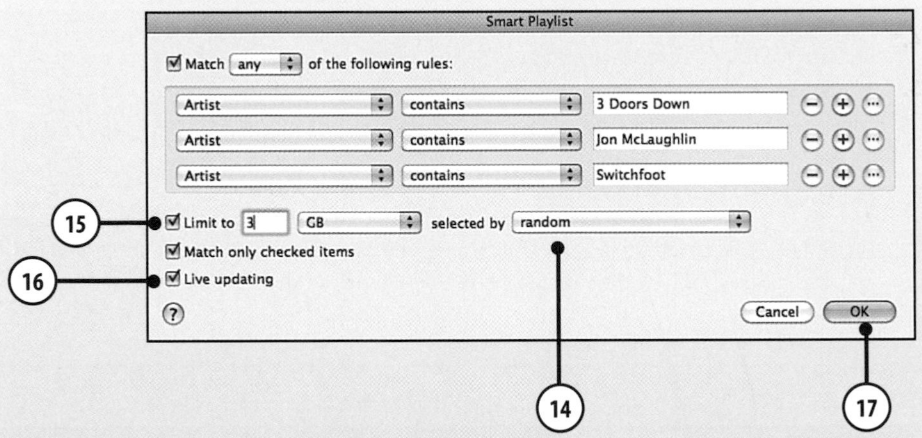

18. Type the playlist's name and press Enter (Windows) or Return (Mac).

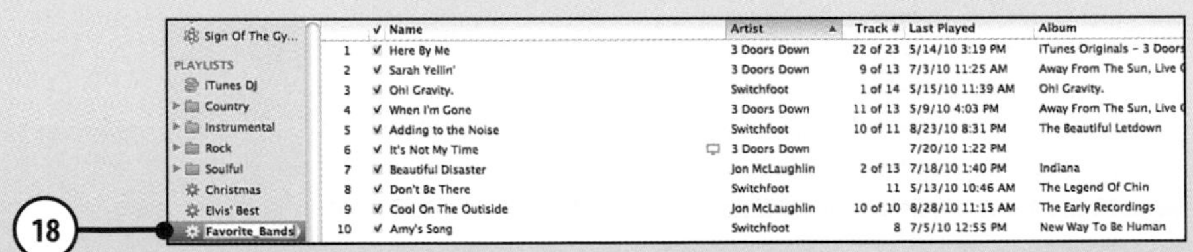

Check Please!

Each item in iTunes has a check box. You use this to tell iTunes if you want it to include the item (such as a song or podcast) in whatever you happen to be doing. If you uncheck this box, iTunes ignores the item when the related option is selected, such as the Match only checked items check box when you create a smart playlist. Or if a song's check box is unchecked, it will be skipped when you play a source containing that song.

Moving Audio and Video from the iTunes Library onto an iPod touch

To move audio and video content onto an iPod touch, you need to choose the content you want to move there and then synchronize the iPod touch with your iTunes Library.

1. Connect the iPod touch to your computer using its USB cable. The iPod touch is mounted on your computer and appears in the iTunes Source list.
2. Click the iPod touch icon. The iPod touch synchronization screen appears. It has a Summary button for general configuration and a button for each type of content you can move onto the iPod touch.
3. Click the Music button.
4. Check the Sync Music check box.
5. If you have enough room on the iPod to store all the music content in your Library on the iPod, check the Entire music library radio button. Unless you have a small amount of music and other content in your Library, you'll probably need to check the Selected playlists, artists, and genres radio button instead; this enables you to select specific music to move onto the iPod. The rest of these steps assume this option is selected. When you select it, the Playlists, Artists, and Genres selection tools appear.

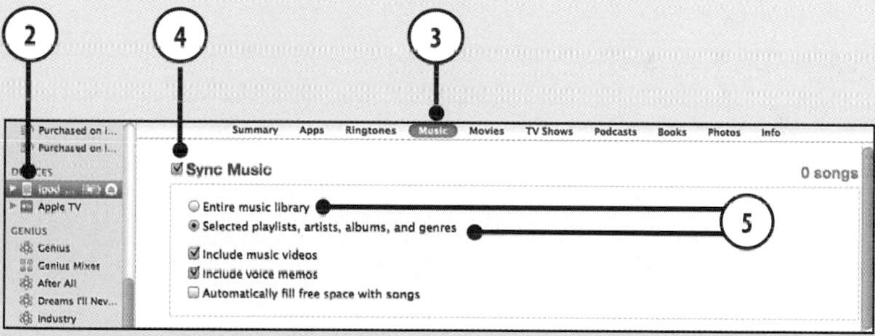

How Much Room Do I Need?

To see how large the music collection in your Library is, click Music on the Source list and ensure that All is selected in each column of the browser. In the center of the bottom border of the iTunes window, you see the number of songs in your library along with the number of days (or hours) those songs will play if you play all of them and the total amount of space required to store them. If the last number is larger than your iPod's memory, you must select the music you want to move onto the iPod. Of course, you'll also want to store videos, applications, books, and such on the iPod, which also requires memory. If you try to sync too much content, you see a warning dialog during the process and have to reduce the amount of content included in the sync.

6. Check Include music videos if you want music videos in your collection to be moved onto the iPod touch.

7. Check Include voice memos if you use the Voice Memos application to record audio notes and want those memos to be moved from the iPod touch into your iTunes Library. (You have to use an external microphone to record audio on your touch.)

8. If you want any free space on the iPod to be filled with music that iTunes selects, check the Automatically fill free space with songs check box.

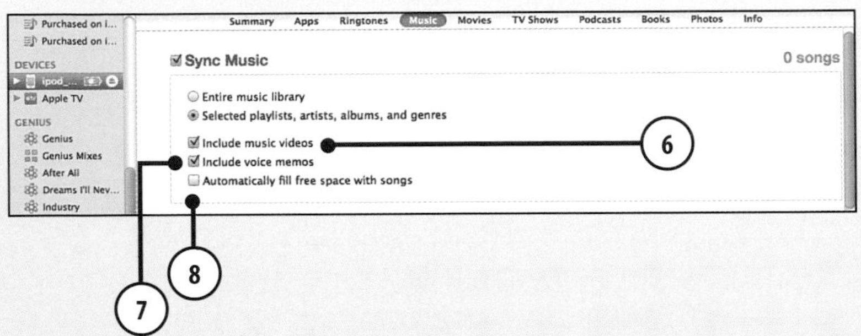

Scrolling, Scrolling, Scrolling

Each section on the Music button has its own scroll bar that you can use to browse the content in that section. You can also use the iTunes scroll bar to move up and down the pane, which you might need to do to see all its contents.

9. To expand or collapse a folder to see or hide the playlists it contains, click its triangle.

10. To move all the items within a folder of playlists onto the iPod touch, check the folder's check box.

11. To include a playlist in the sync so that all the items that playlist contains are moved onto the touch, check the check box next to it on the Playlists list.

12. To move all the songs by specific artists' onto the iPod, check the artist's name on the Artists list.

13. Click the check box next to each genre whose contents you want to move onto the iPod. For example, to move all the music in the Blues genre, check that check box.

14. To move the contents of an album onto the iPod, check its check box.

15. As you add content, check the Capacity bar at the bottom of the window. This bar shows you how the space on the iPod will be used. The color coding shows the amount of each type of content you are syncing, and the empty part of the bar shows how much free space you have. In order to complete the sync, you need you ensure that the content of all types you include in the sync is equal to or less than the space available on your iPod.

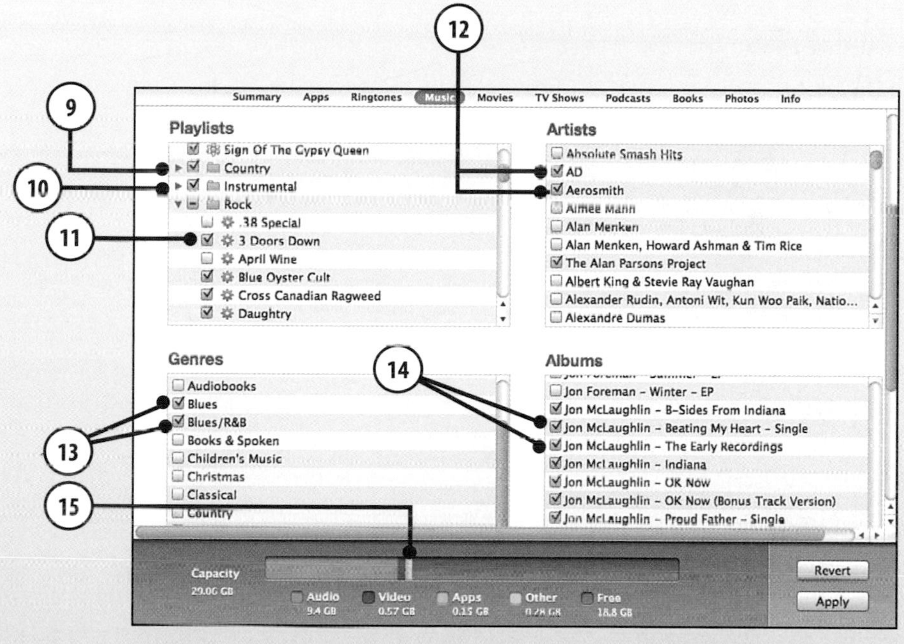

Searching for Artists

If you type in the Search box to the right of the Artists section title, iTunes limits the artists shown to those whose names include what you type. You're likely to end up with many different artists in your Library, and this is a quick way to find specific artists to include in the sync.

16. Click the Movies button. In the Rented Movies section, you see the movies you are currently renting. (If you don't have any rented movies in your Library, you don't see this section.) The rented movies currently stored in your Library are shown in the box on the left, and the rented movies on the iPod are shown in the box on the right.
17. Click a rented movie's right-facing Move button to move it from the iTunes Library onto the iPod touch. The movie's icon moves to the right pane of the window, which indicates it will be moved onto the iPod touch during the next sync.
18. Check the Sync Movies check box.

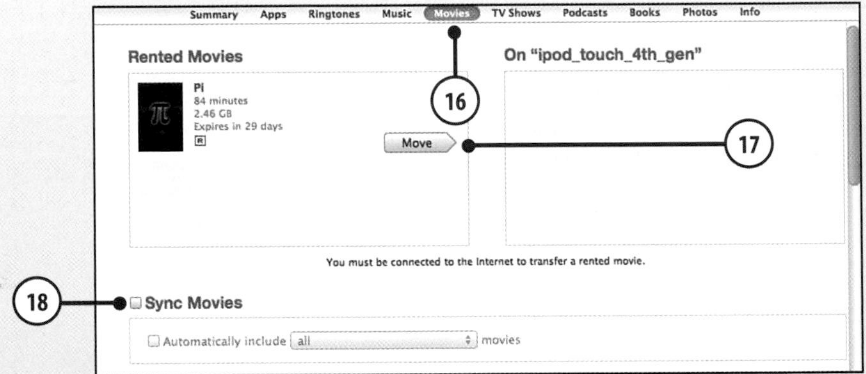

19. To automatically copy movies onto the touch, check the Automatically include check box and choose which movies you want to copy on the pop-up menu. For example, to automatically include the five movies you most recently added to your Library, but haven't watched yet, choose the 5 most recent unwatched option.

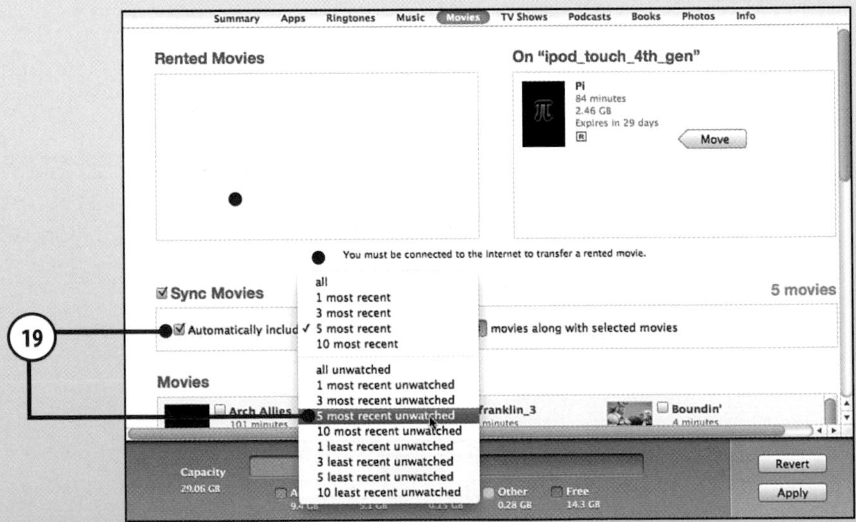

Returning a Rental

To move a rented movie from the iPod touch back into the iTunes Library, click the left-facing Move button next to the movie you want to move. During the next sync, it is removed from the iPod touch and placed back into the iTunes Library.

20. To move specific movies onto the iPod touch, uncheck the Automatically include check box.
21. Check the check box next to each movie you want to copy onto the iPod touch.
22. To remove a movie from the iPod touch, uncheck its check box.

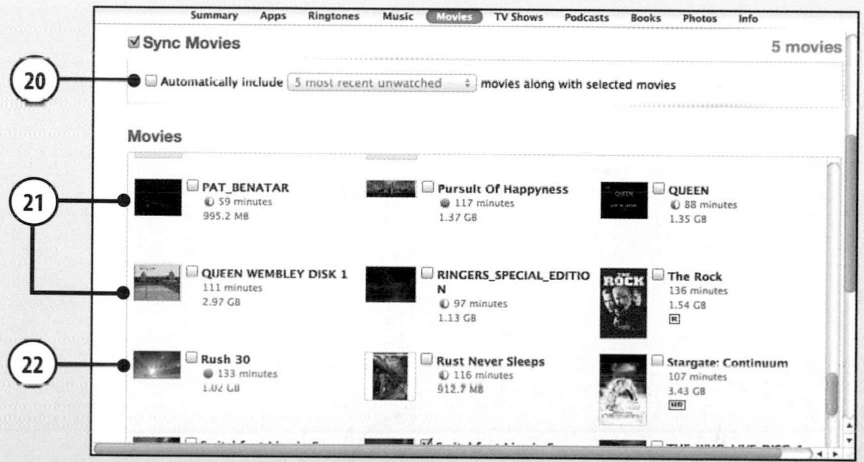

Formats Matter

Movies can be in many different formats; some can be played on your iPod while others can't. Unfortunately, you can't tell if a movie is in the correct format on the Movies button. Any movies you obtain from the iTunes Store are in the correct format, but if you add movies from other sources, they might not be. If you try to include a movie not in the iPod's format, you see an error dialog during the sync process that shows you which movies aren't formatted for the iPod. You can create an iPod-formatted version by selecting the movie in your Library and choosing the Create iPod or iPhone Version on the Advanced menu. This creates a copy of the movie in the correct format; you should name this copy so that you know which is which. Then, select the iPod version on the Movies button to include it in the sync.

23. Scroll down to see the Include Movies from Playlist section.

24. Use the playlist check boxes and folder triangles to choose playlists whose movies you want to move onto the iPod; these work just like the music playlist section tools.

25. As you add content to the sync, monitor the Capacity bar. If you select more content than your iPod can store, you see a warning icon and the Over Capacity text; you also see the amount of over capacity you've selected. To be able to complete the sync, you need to remove at least the amount shown as the over capacity amount so that the warning goes away. In other words, the total space required by all the content you select must be equal to or less than the storage capacity of your iPod.

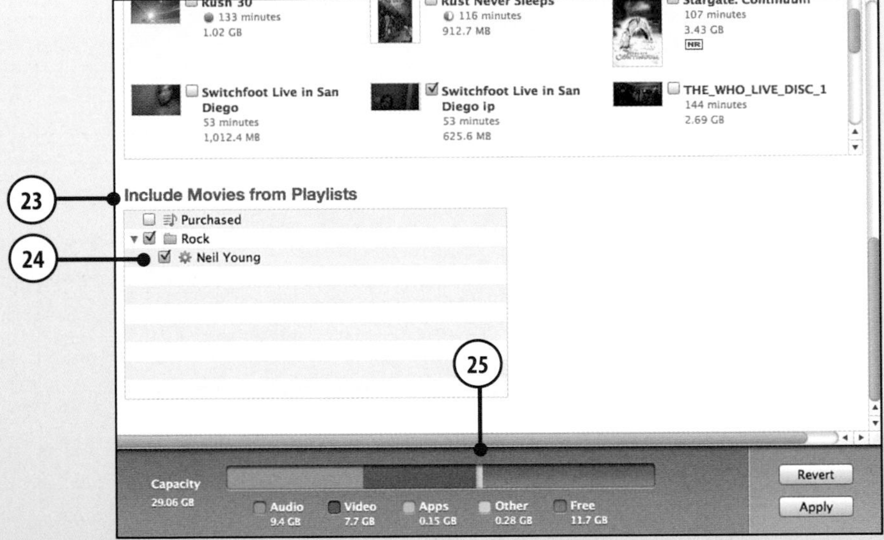

26. Click the TV Shows button.

27. To move rented TV shows onto the iPod, click the right-facing Move button next to the shows you want to include in the sync.

28. Check the Sync TV Shows check box.

29. To have iTunes automatically select shows to copy, check the Automatically include check box.

30. On the first pop-up menu, choose how you want iTunes to select the shows to move. For example, to choose the three shows you most recently added to your Library, but haven't watched yet, choose the 3 newest unwatched option.

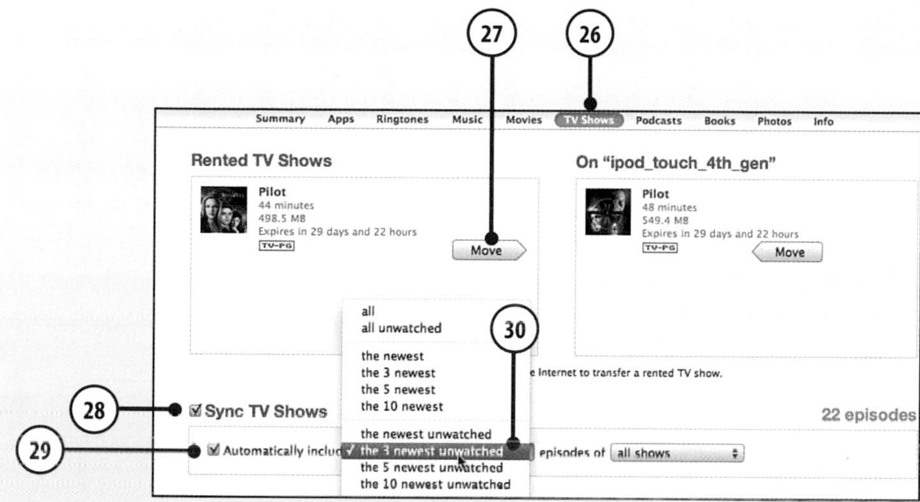

31. On the second pop-up menu, choose all shows to include all your shows in the sync or selected shows to include only certain shows in the sync.

32. If you use the selected shows option, check the check box next to each series whose shows you want to include in the sync automatically.

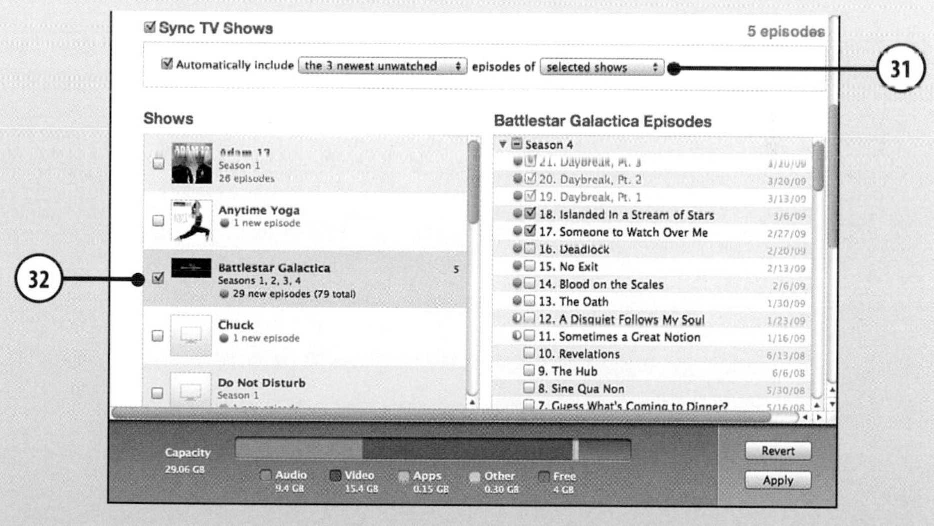

33. To manually select the shows to move, uncheck the Automatically include check box.

34. Select the series containing episodes you want to move onto the touch manually. In the right pane, you see the episodes of that series in your Library, organized by season.

35. To expand a season to see all the episodes it contains, click its triangle; to collapse it, click the triangle so it points to the right.

36. To include an entire season, check the season's check box.

37. To include specific episodes, check their check boxes.

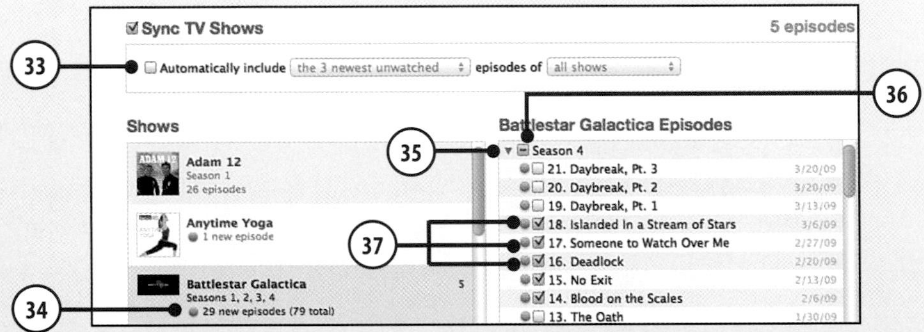

38. If you have playlists containing TV shows, use the controls in the Include Episodes from Playlists area to include those in the sync; these work just like the other playlist selection tools.

39. Keep an eye on the Capacity bar to make sure you aren't trying to add too much content.

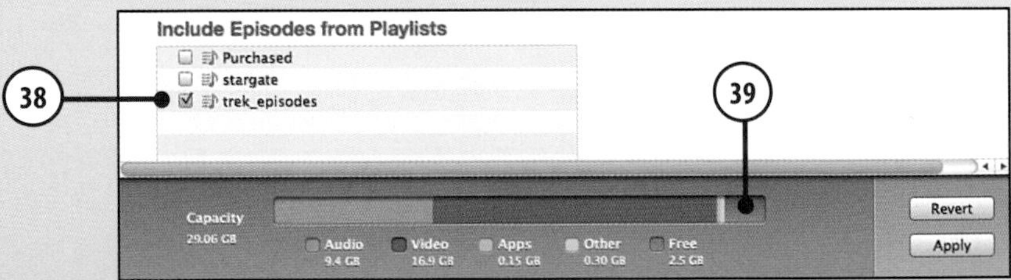

Seen It?

Movies or TV shows that you haven't watched are marked with a blue circles. If you've watched part of a movie or show, its circle is partially filled. If you've watched all of a movie or TV show, it doesn't have a circle.

40. Click the Podcasts button.
41. Check the Sync Podcasts check box.
42. To have iTunes automatically sync podcasts, check the Automatically include check box; if you want to manually select podcasts to sync, uncheck this check box and skip to step 46.
43. On the first pop-up menu, choose the number and type of episodes you want to include in the sync, such as the 5 most recent unplayed.

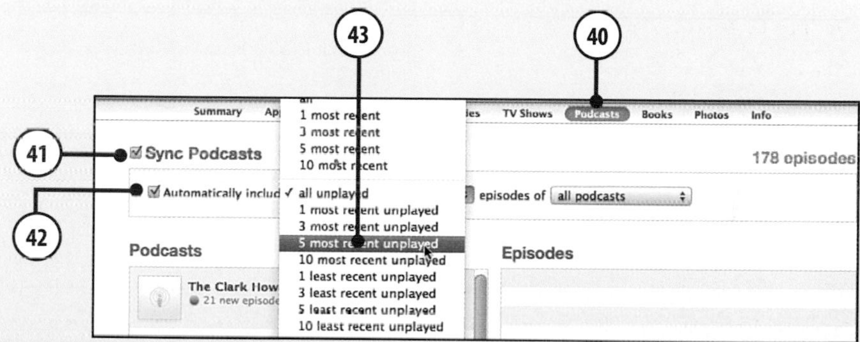

44. On the second pop-up menu, choose all podcasts to include all your podcasts in the sync or selected podcasts to choose specific podcasts.
45. If you selected specific podcasts, check the check box next to each podcast you want to include the sync and skip to step 49.

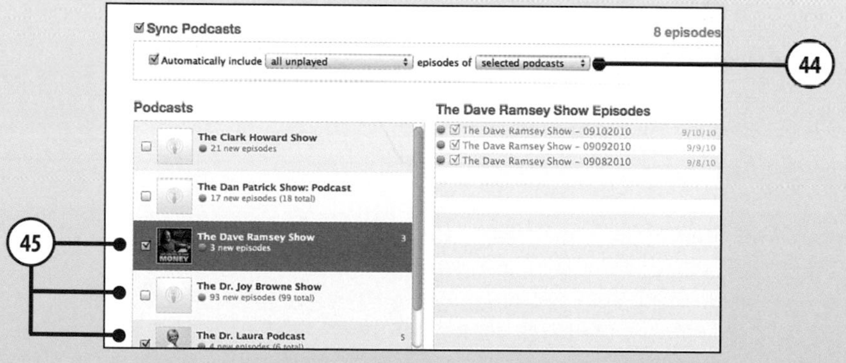

46. Select the podcast containing episodes you want to move onto the touch.

47. Check the check box next to each episode you want to sync.

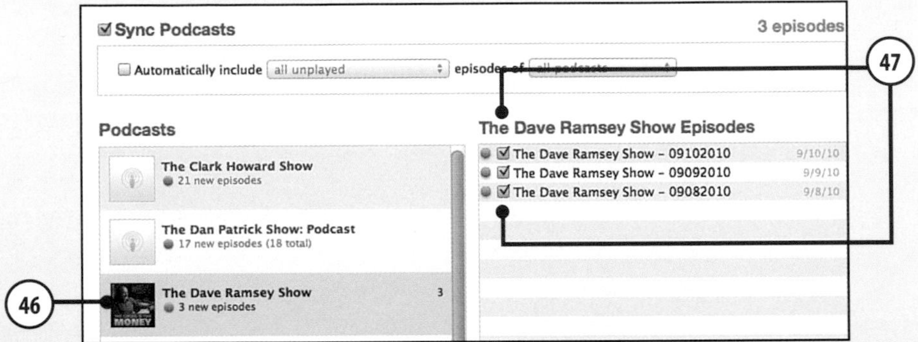

48. Repeat steps 46 and 47 until you've included all the episodes you want to have available on the iPod.

49. Check that the iPod is able to store the content you've selected. If so, continue. If not, use the previous steps to remove content until it does fit.

50. Click Apply. iTunes starts the sync process and moves the selected content from the iTunes Library to the iPod touch. You see the progress of the sync in the Information area at the top of the iTunes window. If there are no problems with the sync, it completes without further action from you.

Check First, then Unplug

Wait until the iPod touch sync is complete message appears in the Information area located at the top of the iTunes window before disconnecting the iPod touch from the computer. If you remove it during the sync process, some of the content might not be moved onto the iPod touch correctly. While the sync is in process, you also see the Sync in progress message on the iPod touch's screen. Wait until this disappears before disconnecting.

51. If there are any problems with the sync, such as content being in the wrong format, view information about the problem in the dialog.

52. Click the Expansion triangle to get more detail.

53. Click OK to close the dialog. The sync completes best it can given the issues noted. To be able to complete the sync without any problems, use the sync and other tools to solve the specific problems you encountered.

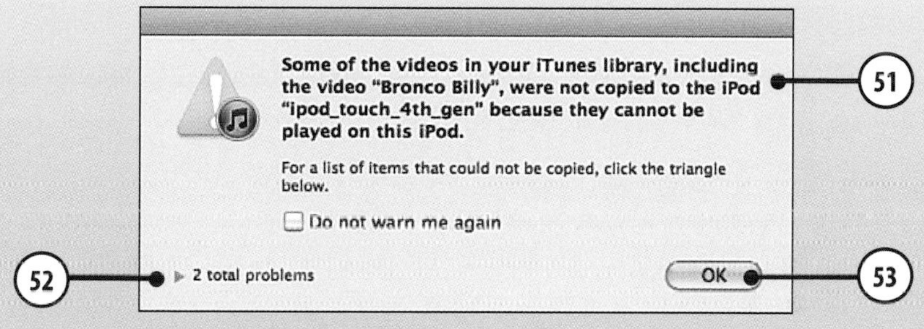

>>> Go Further

OPTIONS, OPTIONS

The Summary button has an Options section that contains several general synchronization settings. Checked by default, the Open iTunes when this iPod is connected option does just what it says; when you connect your iPod, iTunes opens if it isn't open already. If you don't want content whose check box isn't checked to be moved onto the iPod, check the Sync only checked songs and video check box. To cause iTunes to convert songs that have been encoded so they are high quality (larger file sizes) to files that have smaller sizes (so more content fits onto the iPod), check the Convert higher bit rate songs to 128 kbps AAC check box. (You aren't likely to hear the difference when playing this content with your iPod.) If you check the Manually manage music and videos check box, you can place content on the iPod touch by dragging songs, movies, and other content onto the iPod touch icon on the Source list. To protect the backup of your iPod touch's data (used to restore your iPod touch) with encryption, check Encrypt iPod backup, create and verify a password, and click Set Password; this password will be required to restore the backed up information onto the iPod touch. On third-generation or later iPod touches, the Configure Universal Access button takes you to a dialog where you can enable features designed for hearing- or seeing-impaired people.

Using iTunes to Add Books to Your iPod touch

The iBooks app enables you to read books on your iPod. Of course, to read books on your touch, you have to store books on it. You can use iTunes to store your books and then move them onto the iPod through syncing, just like audio and video content. You can download books in the ePub format from many different websites and add them to your iTunes Library. After books are in iTunes, you move them onto the iPod.

Adding Books to Your iTunes Library

The iBooks application can be used to read any electronic book in the ePub format. The good news is that this format is becoming the standard for electronic publishing; the other good news is that there are a lot of sources of ebooks in this format that you can download, so there isn't really a limit to how many books you can read with your iPod.

1. Move to the website from which you want to download books, such as epubbooks.com.
2. Browse or search for a book you want to read on your touch.
3. Download the book.

4. In iTunes, choose File, Add to Library (Mac) or Add File to Library (Windows).
5. Choose the folder where the books you've downloaded are stored.
6. Select the books you want to add to iTunes.
7. Click Choose (Mac) or Open (Windows). The books you selected are added to your Library and are ready to move onto the iPod.

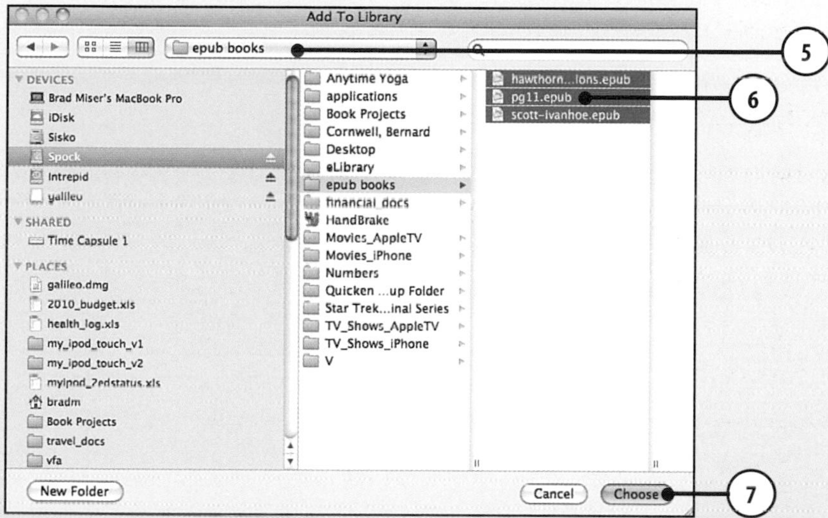

Where Can I Download Books?

There are many sources of ebooks on the Internet. Some of these are commercial sites, whereas others are nonprofit sites, such as www.gutenberg.org. To find sources of ebooks, perform a web search for "ePub books" and you'll find many sources from which you can obtain books. The commercial sites typically enable you to download a sample of a book for free so that you can try it. If you like it, you can go back and purchase the full book. Many sites offer books you can download for free.

Book Formats

Although ePub is the modern standard for ebooks, a lot of ebooks are in other formats. Some require specific applications to read, such as books from Amazon.com. (You can use the Kindle app to read those.) Like Amazon.com's Kindle application for the iPod touch, the application you need to read books in these other formats is free, so the biggest downside is that you need to have and use more than one book-reading application on your touch to read books from sources that don't offer books in the ePub format.

Moving Books onto an iPod touch

You can move books onto your iPod like you move other content there.

1. Select the iPod touch on the Source list.
2. Click the Books button.
3. Check the Sync Books check box.
4. To move all your ebooks onto the touch, click All books and skip to step 6; to choose specific books to move, click Selected books.
5. Check the check box for the books you want to move onto the touch.
6. Click Apply. The books included in the sync are copied onto the touch and will be available on the iBooks bookshelf.

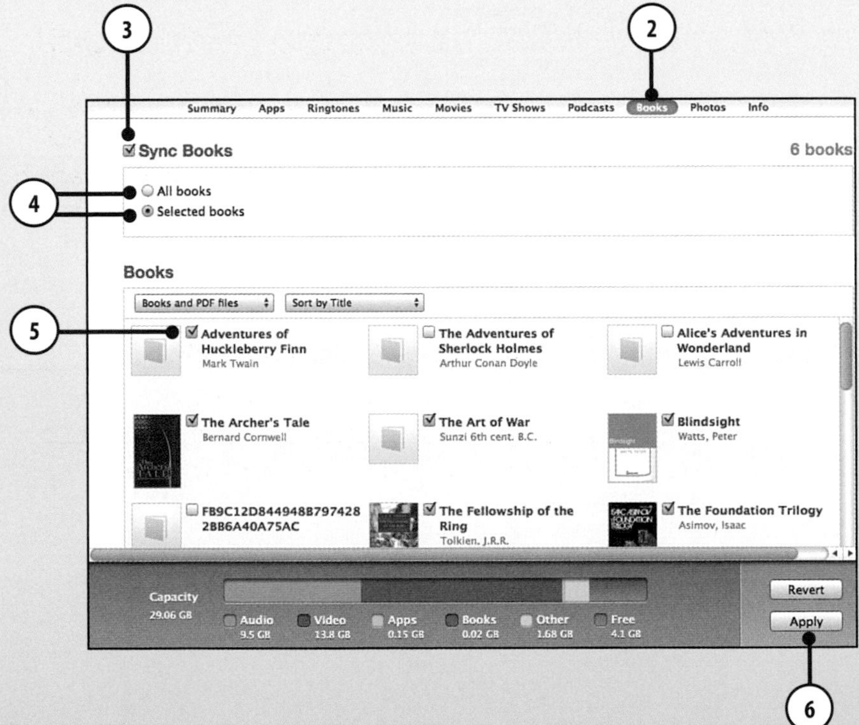

Sorting, Searching, and Browsing

You can sort the books on the Books button by author by choosing Sort by Author on the pop-up menu or by title by choosing Sort by Title. You can also search for books by typing in the Search bar located on the right side of the window. You can browse the books displayed using the scroll bar for the Books section.

Audiobooks

You can also use iTunes to store audiobooks (available from the iTunes Store and many other sources) and then sync them on the iPod using the audiobook sync tools located at the bottom of the Books button. These work similarly to podcasts and other kinds of audio.

PDFs

You can also use the iBooks app to read documents in PDF format. If you add PDFs to your iTunes Library, you can select them for syncing onto the iPod just like ebooks. You can use the pop-up menu just under the Books heading to choose if you see Only Books, Only PDFs files, or Books and PDF files.

Using iTunes to Add Photos to Your iPod touch

As you learn in Chapter 11 your iPod touch is a great way to view your photos while you are on the go. You can move photos from a computer onto iPod touch so that you can view them individually and as slideshows. The steps to move photos from a computer to iPod touch are slightly different between Windows PCs and Macs. See the section that applies to your computer.

Moving Photos from a Windows PC onto an iPod touch

You can use iTunes to move photos you're storing on your PC using Adobe Photoshop Album 2.0 or later or Adobe Photoshop Elements 3.0 or later. You can also move photos from your My pictures folder onto the iPod. The following steps show how this works; moving photos from one of the Adobe applications works similarly.

1. Connect the iPod touch to your computer and open iTunes (if it doesn't open automatically).
2. Click the Photos button.
3. Check the Sync Photos from check box.
4. On the pop-up menu, choose My Pictures to sync photos in your My Pictures folder, choose folder to select a different folder containing photos you want to move, or choose the application containing the photos you want to move onto your iPod touch, such as Photoshop Elements.
5. If you want all the photos in the selected source to be moved onto your iPod touch, click the All option and skip to step 8.

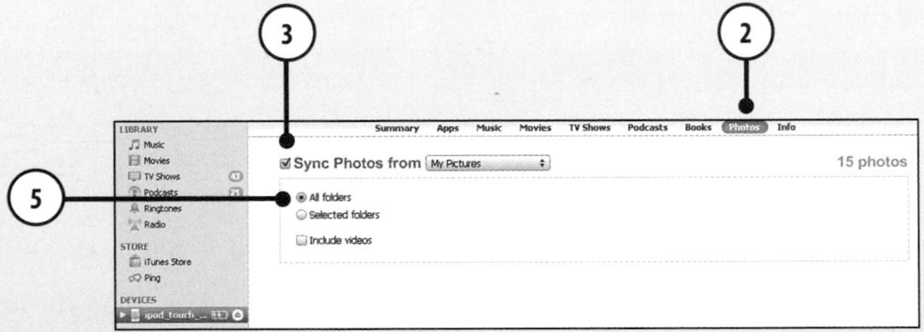

6. If you want only selected albums to be moved onto the iPod touch, click the Selected options.
7. Check the check box next to each folder or photo album that you want to sync with the iPod.
8. If you want videos in the selected source to be moved onto the iPod, check the Include videos check box.

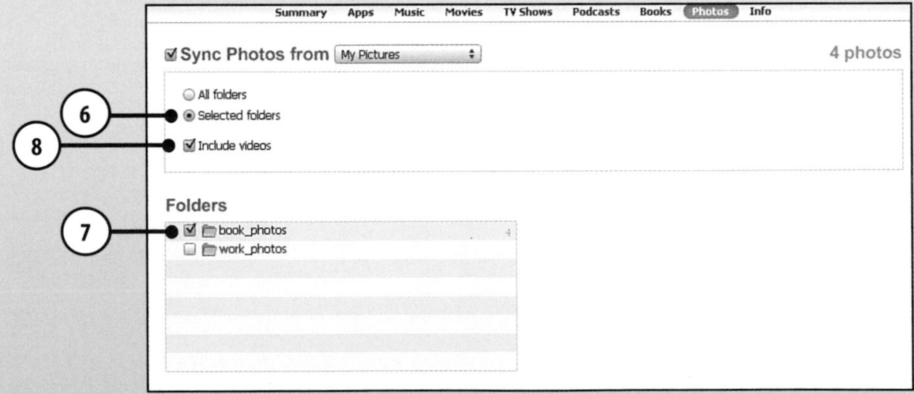

9. Click Apply. The photos you selected move onto your iPod. If you make changes to the photo albums or folders, or to the photos you selected, the updates move onto the iPod touch the next time you sync it.

Moving Photos from a Mac to an iPod touch

iTunes is designed to work seamlessly with iPhoto. You can move all your photos or selected photo albums from iPhoto to your iPod touch by using iTunes' syncing. You can also move photos you've stored in a folder on your Mac almost as easily.

1. Connect the iPod touch to your computer and select it on the iTunes Source list.
2. Click the Photos button.
3. Check the Sync Photos from check box.
4. On the pop-up menu, choose iPhoto.
5. If you want all the photos in iPhoto to be moved onto your iPod touch, click the All photos, albums, events and faces radio button and skip to step 9.

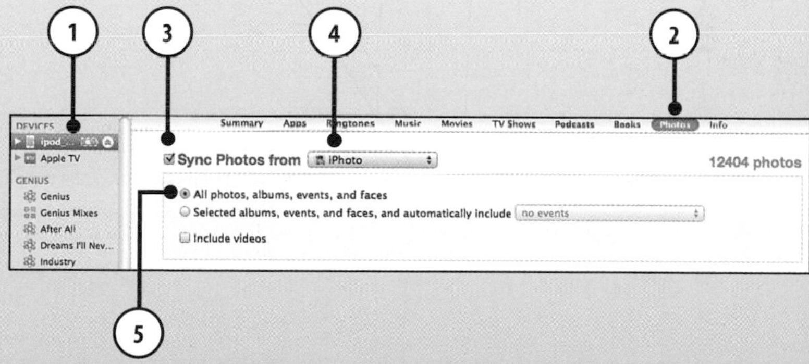

6. To choose specific photos to move onto the iPod touch, click the Selected albums, events, faces, and automatically include radio button.
7. On the pop-up menu, choose which events you want to be moved onto the iPod automatically, if any.

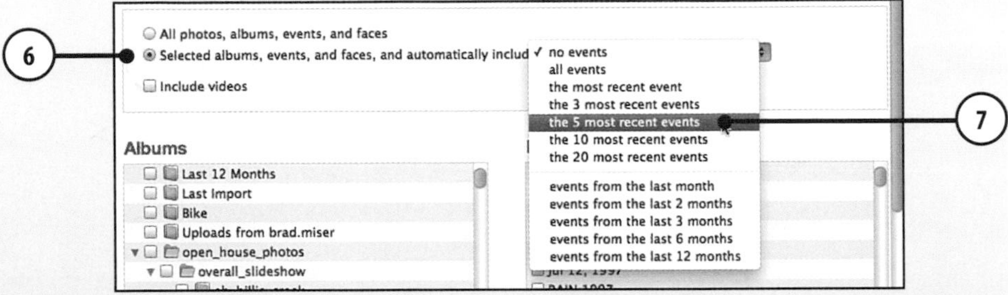

8. Choose the albums you want to move onto the touch by checking their check boxes. Like other content, you can expand folders, browse albums, and so on.
9. Choose the events whose photos you want to include by checking their check boxes. (You can search for events by typing date information in the Search bar.)
10. Choose the people who have been identified with the Faces feature whose photos you want to have available on the iPod by checking the check boxes next to their names.

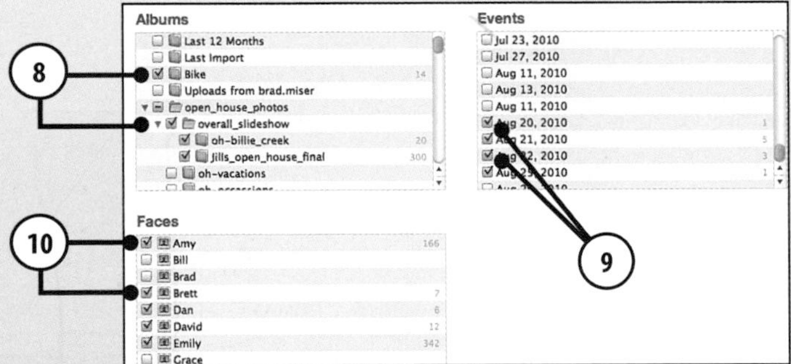

Number of Photos

Each time you select a source of photos to sync, you see the number of photos that will be moved onto the iPod from that source. This is shown at the right edge of the Albums, Events, and Faces panes.

11. If you want videos stored in iPhoto to be moved onto the touch, check the Include videos check box.
12. Click Apply. The photos you selected move onto your iPod touch. If there's not enough memory to store the photos you selected, you're warned; you'll need to remove some of the photos from the sync or remove other kinds of content to make more room.

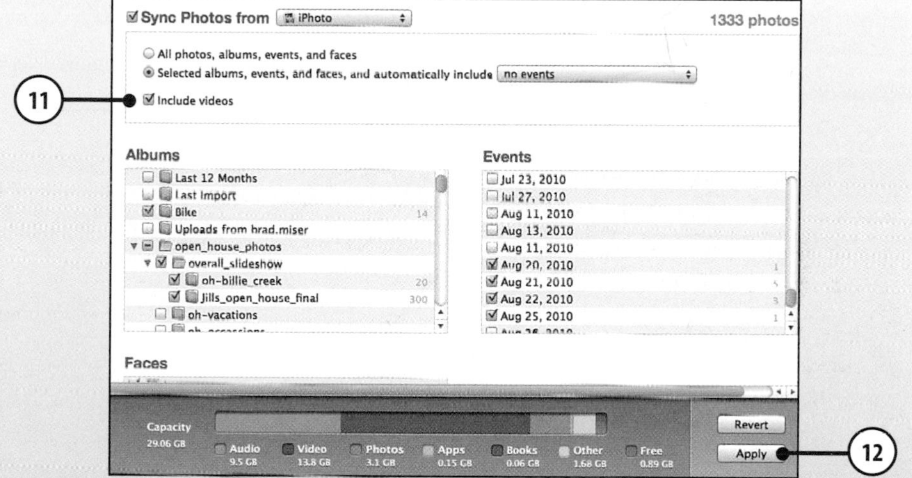

Other Sync Options

If you choose Pictures on the Sync photos from pop-up menu, you can move photos stored in your Pictures folder onto the iPod touch. If you select Choose Folder, you are prompted to select a folder of photos that you want to move. Depending on the option you choose, you might or might not be able to select specific collections of photos to move into the iPod touch. For example, if you select a folder that contains other folders, you can select the contents of each folder individually (which is similar to selecting a photo album to sync).

Using the iTunes iPod touch Application to Add Audio and Video to an iPod touch

You can use the touch's iTunes application to download audio and video content from the iTunes Store directly onto your iPod touch, where you can play it just like content you've moved onto the iPod touch using iTunes on your computer.

In the iTunes application on your iPod touch, you can use the following options that appear at the bottom of the app's screen:

- Music enables you to browse for music.
- Videos provides tools you can use to find and download movies, TV shows, and music videos.
- Podcasts enables you to find and download episodes of audio and video podcasts.
- Search makes it possible for you to search the iTunes Store for any type of content.
- More presents other tools to you: Audiobooks provides tools you use to find audiobook content, iTunes U takes you to content provided by universities and other organizatins, such as courses, special exhibits, and so on, and Downloads moves you to the Downloads screen where you see the progress of your downloads.

The next time you sync the iPod touch after downloading content using the iTunes application, the content you downloaded is moved into your iTunes Library so that you can enjoy it on a computer, too. (This also backs up your purchased content on your computer.)

1. On the iPod touch's Home screen, tap iTunes. You move to the iTunes Store application. At the bottom of the screen, you choose how you want to look for content by tapping one of the buttons. The rest of these steps explain how to use the Search tool; however, using the other options is similar.

2. Tap Search.
3. Tap in the Search box.

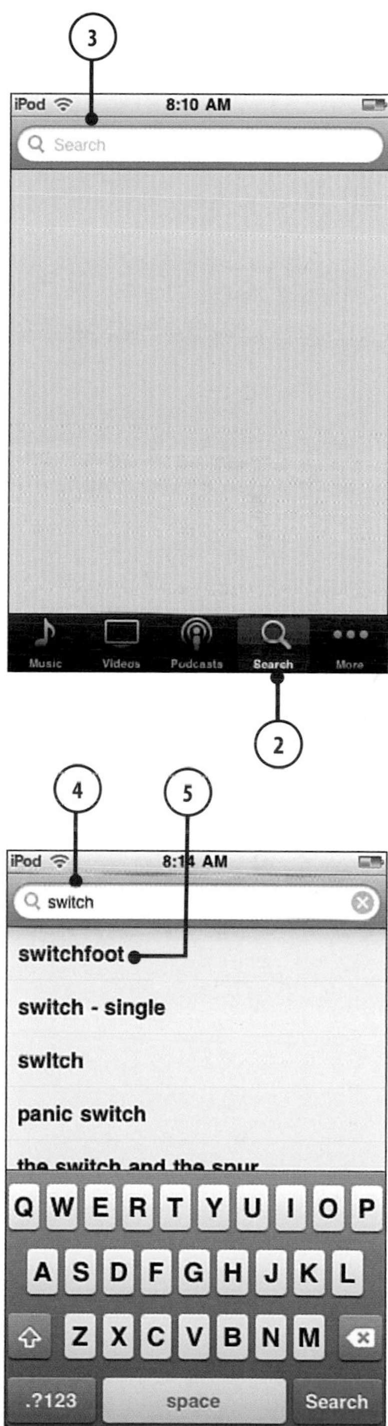

Reconfiguring the iTunes App Toolbar

To change the buttons shown at the bottom of the iTunes app's screen, tap More and then tap Edit. Then drag the buttons you want to see from the Configure screen down to the location on the toolbar where you want to place them, and then tap Done. The only button you can't replace on the toolbar is the More button, which is what you tap to see the buttons that currently aren't on the toolbar.

4. Type search criteria, such as an artist's name or movie title. As you type, content that matches your search appears under the Search bar.
5. When you see something of interest on the results list, tap it. For example, tap an artist's name. You see a list of content related to your search, organized by albums or songs. You see different results and options when you select movies or other types of content, but the general process you use to preview and purchase content is the same.

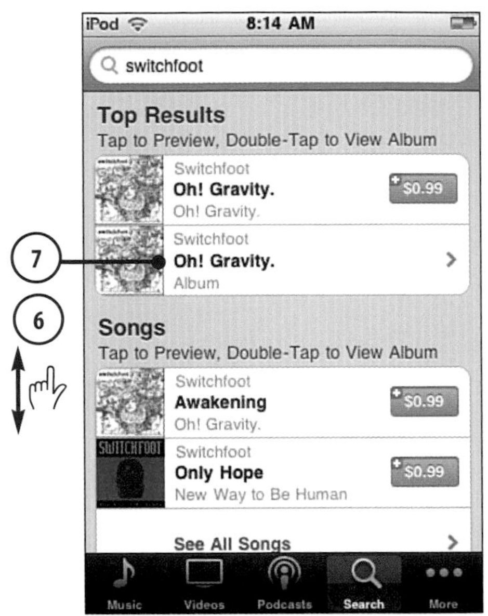

6. Drag your finger up or down the screen to browse the search results, which are organized into categories, such as Top Results, Songs, Albums, Music Videos, and so on.
7. To explore the contents of an album or category, tap it. When you tap an album, at the top of the screen you see the album's general information, such as when it was released and how many songs it contains. In the lower part of the window, you see the tracks on that album. If you tap a different kind of content, such as a music video, you see options appropriate for that type. The rest of these steps focus on an album, but you can download other types of content using similar steps.
8. If you tapped an album, drag your finger up or down the screen to browse the entire list of tracks.
9. To preview a track, tap it. A 30-second preview plays. While it's playing, the track's number is replaced by the Stop button, which you can tap to stop the preview, and the Volume slider appears at the bottom of the screen.
10. To buy an album, tap its BUY button, which also shows the price of the album. The button becomes the BUY ALBUM button.
11. To buy a song, tap its Buy button, which shows the price of the song. The button becomes the BUY NOW button.

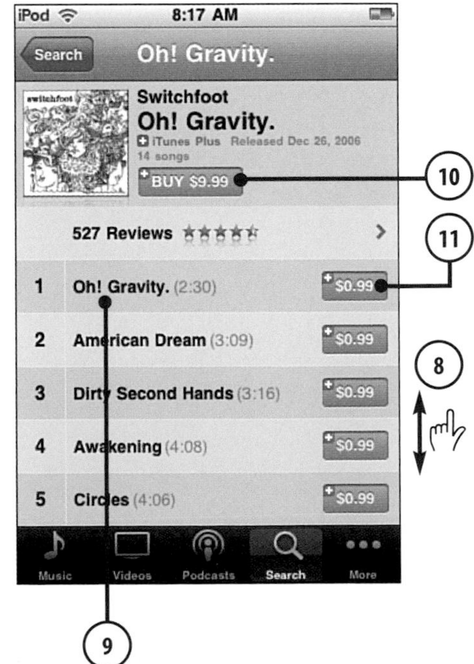

Previewing and Buying Songs

You can preview and buy songs directly from the results screen, too.

12. Tap the BUY ALBUM or BUY NOW button. You see the iTunes Password prompt.

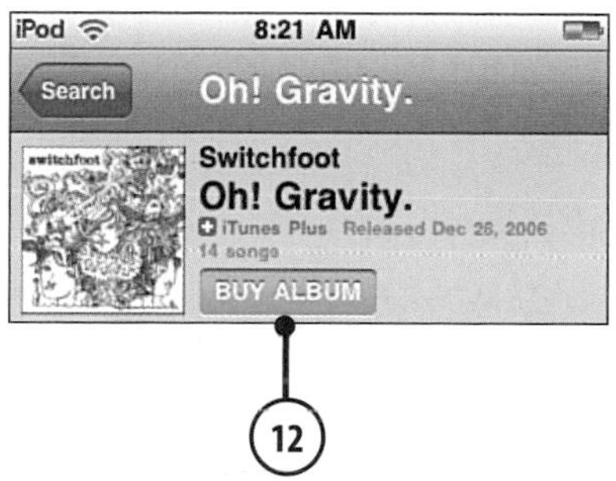

13. Enter the password for your iTunes Store account and tap OK. A flashing red indicator appears over the More button to show you how many tracks are being downloaded to the iPod touch.

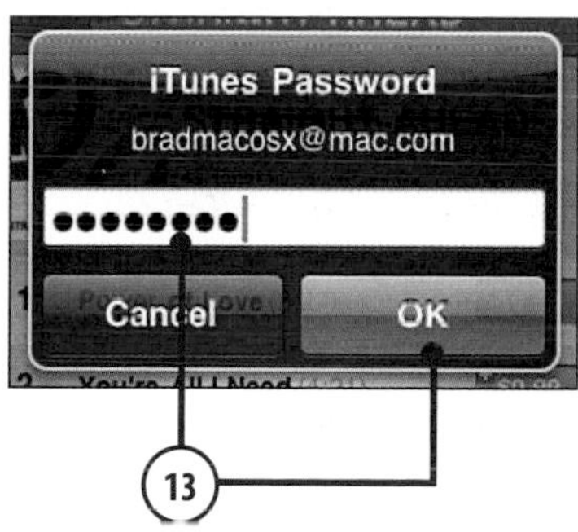

Move from Song to Album

When you browse a list of songs, tap a song twice to move to the album that the song comes from.

14. Tap More. (If you've moved the Downloads button onto the toolbar, you can skip this step.)

15. Tap Downloads. You move to the Downloads screen where you see the details about the tracks you are purchasing, including the amount of time the download process will take to finish for the item currently being downloaded.

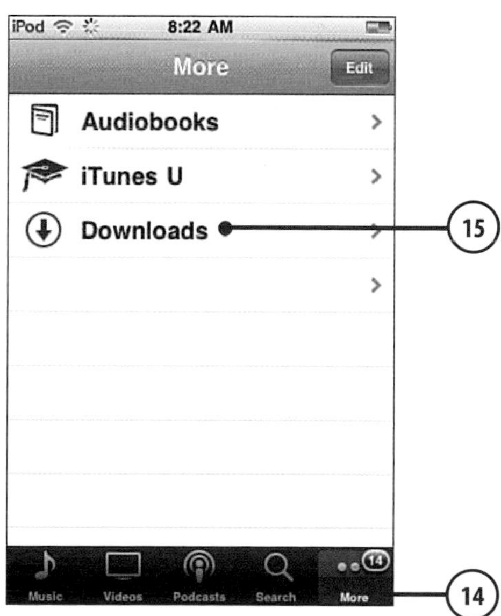

When the process is complete, the Downloads screen becomes empty. This indicates that the content you purchased has been added to the iPod touch and is ready for you to listen or watch.

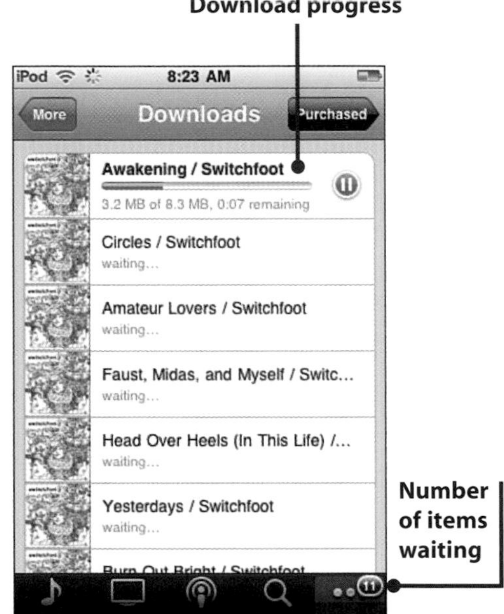

The Next Time You Sync

The next time you sync after purchasing content from the iTunes Store on the iPod touch, that content is moved into your iTunes Library. It is stored in a playlist called Purchased on *iPod touchname* where *iPod touchname* is the name of your iPod touch. If you've created any smart playlists with live updating enabled and the new content matches that playlist's criteria, the new content becomes part of those playlists automatically. It's a good idea to sync your touch as soon as possible after purchasing new content so that you back up your purchases; that way, if something happens to that content on the touch, you can always recover it using iTunes. If you don't sync and something happens to the purchased content on your touch, you'll have to pay for it again.

Using the iBooks Application to Add Books to an iPod touch

You can add books to your iPod touch by accessing the iBooks Store through the iBooks application. When you move into the store, you see tools you can use to browse or search for books in many ways:

- At the top of the screen, you can tap Categories to browse books by their category. When you tap Categories, a list of categories appears; tap a category to browse the books it contains. This works in context of the other options. For example, when you tap Browse and then tap Categories, you can select a category to browse. When you tap Featured and then tap Categories, you select a category in which to show featured books.
- Tap Featured to browse the featured books.
- Tap Charts and then tap Top Charts to browse books by various top lists or tap New York Times to see *The New York Times* bestseller list.
- Tap Browse to browse books by author; tap Top Paid or Top Free to see books you have to buy or those you can download for free. You can browse the list or tap the index to jump to a specific author. If you tap Categories, you can browse books by category instead of by author.
- Tap Search to search for books by author, title, and so on by typing text in the Search bar.
- Like in the iTunes Store, you can tap just about any graphic, button, or text to move to the object to which that link is connected.

After you've downloaded books, you can tap the Purchased button to see the books you've downloaded.

If you aren't sure you want to purchase a book, you can download a sample to read for free and then buy and download the entire book later when you are sure.

Got iBooks?

If iBooks isn't installed on your touch, use either iTunes or the App Store application to add it. See Chapter 13, "Installing and Maintaining iPod touch Applications," for the details on finding and installing applications.

---

1. On the Home screen, tap iBooks.
2. Tap Store. Use the options (described in the intro to this section) you see to find books of interest to you. The rest of these steps demonstrate browsing for a book by category; the other search and browsing tools work in a similar fashion.
3. Tap Browse.
4. Tap Categories.

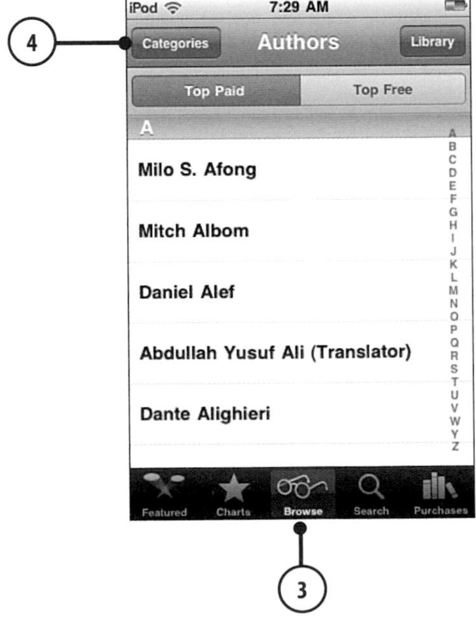

5. Drag the list to browse the categories.
6. Tap a category you want to browse. A list showing authors with books in that category appear.
7. Tap Top Paid to browse books you have to pay for or Top Free to browse free books.
8. Browse the list of books or tap the index to jump to a specific section of the list.
9. Tap an author. What you see depends on the number of books the author has. For example, if you tap an author containing only one book in the category, you see a screen showing the book with a link to see other books by the same author. If you tap an author with multiple books in the category, you see a list of books by that author.
10. Browse the list of books.
11. Tap a book in which you are interested. The detail screen for that book appears. Here you see a description of the book, its user rating, and other information.

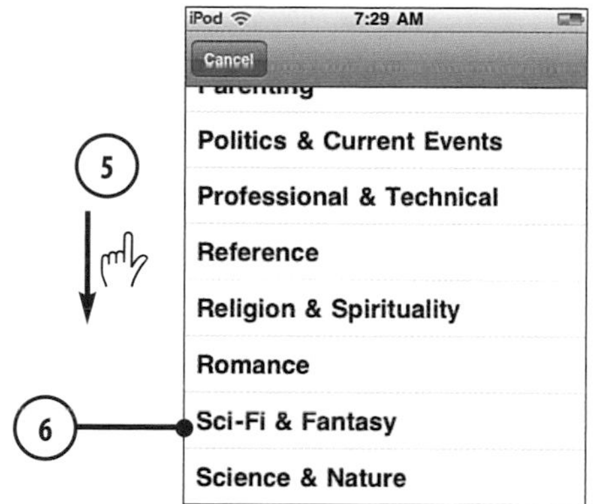

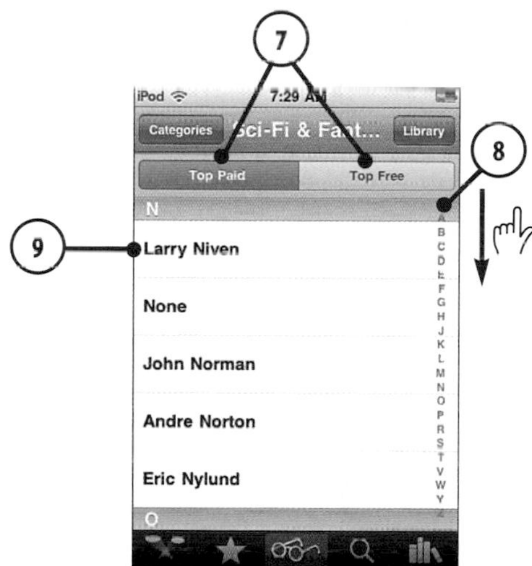

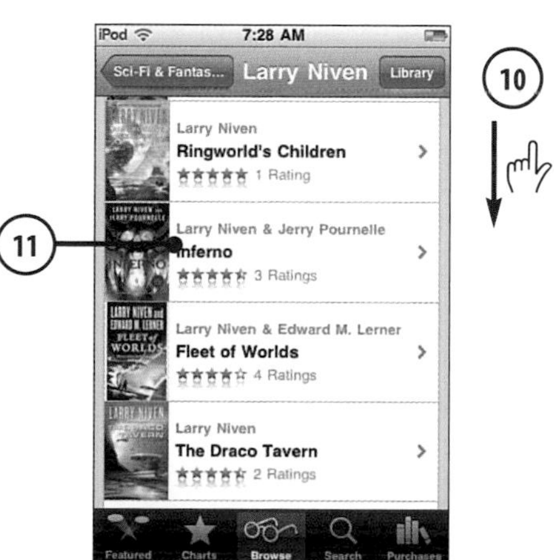

12. Browse the book's information, including its publication details, summary, and so on.
13. To read customer reviews tap the review section.
14. To download a sample of a book to try for free, tap GET SAMPLE; you move back to your Library and see the cover of the book whose sample you downloaded. (Samples have the word "Sample" on their covers in a red banner.) You're ready to use iBooks to read the sample and can skip the following steps.
15. To purchase and download a book, tap its Price button.

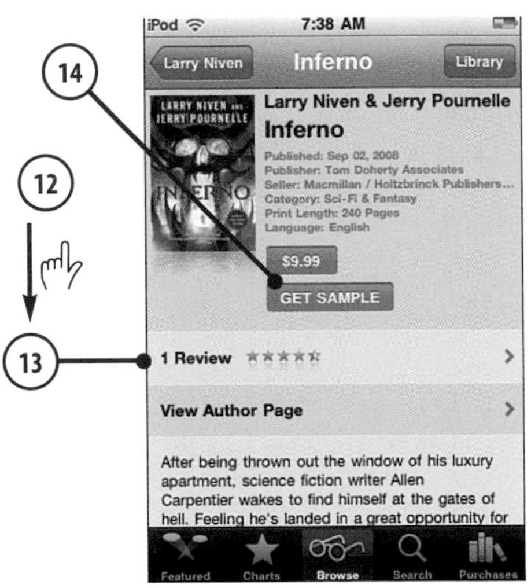

Happy with a Sample?

After you read a sample and decide you want the whole book, you can tap the BUY that appears in iBooks when you read a sample. This takes you to a screen showing the price of the full book. Tap the Price button to start the purchase process.

Buy a Free Book!

There are quite a few free books available; these are marked with the FREE button. When you tap this button, the process is the same as when you buy a book, meaning that you have to sign into your iTunes account. Of course, it is different in that you aren't charged for the free book!

16. Tap the BUY BOOK button.

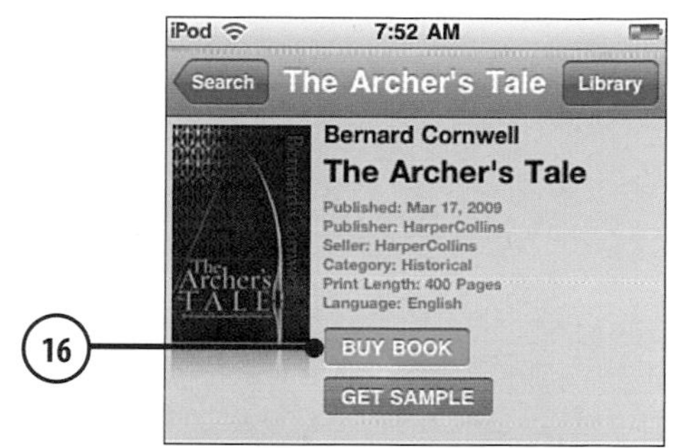

Books Everywhere

If you have more than one device that can run iBooks, you can allow the app to sync your books across all your devices. Information you add to books, such as notes and bookmarks, appear in your books on each device.

17. Enter your iTunes password and tap OK. You move back to your Library, and the book is downloaded to your iPod. New books are marked with the text New in a blue banner. The book you just purchased is ready for you to read.

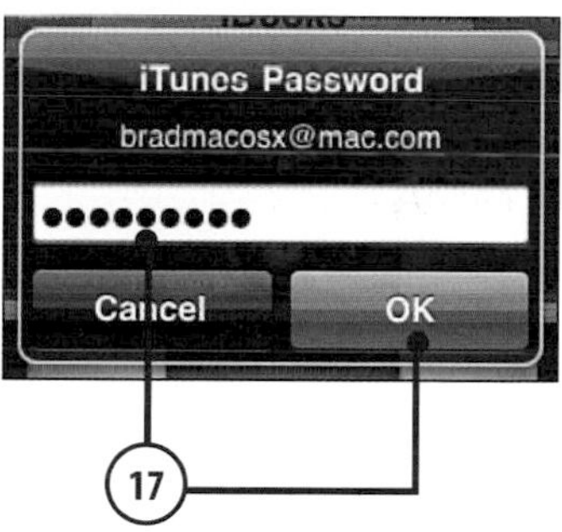

Save My Books!

Unlike music and video content you purchase from the iTunes Store, you can re-download books at any time on any device. So, your books are backed up because should something happen to them on your iPod, you can simply download them again. To download a book you've already purchased, open the iBooks Store within the iBooks app and tap Purchases. Tap Redownload next to the book you want to download.

Tap to set up MobileMe or Exchange accounts for syncing

Tap to use information that's been synced

In this chapter, you learn how to get information onto an iPod touch and keep it in sync with computers and other devices. The topics include the following:

- → Syncing with iTunes on a computer
- → Syncing with MobileMe
- → Syncing with Exchange

Configuring and Synchronizing Information on an iPod touch

In later chapters, you learn how you can use your iPod touch for email, contacts, calendars, and web browsing. All these tasks are easier and better when you sync information that you have on a computer with your iPod touch. That's because when synced, you don't have to manually configure information on the iPod touch. More important, you always have the same information available to you on your computers and your iPod touch.

There are three ways you can sync an iPod touch with your computer. You can sync with iTunes, MobileMe, or Exchange, and you can use one, two, or all three of these techniques simultaneously.

Syncing Information with iTunes

In Chapter 3, "Moving Audio, Video, Books, and Photos onto Your iPod touch," you learned how to move audio and video content from your iTunes Library onto an iPod touch. Using a similar process, you can move email accounts, calendars, contacts, and bookmarks from your computer onto your touch. This information also gets synced each time you connect your iPod to the computer, so any changes you make on the iPod touch move back to the computer and vice versa.

The only downside to syncing with iTunes is that you have to physically connect the iPod touch to a computer, but that isn't a big deal. The primary benefit is that you don't need any additional accounts to sync this information.

As with some other tasks, the details to use iTunes to sync are slightly different on a Mac than they are on a Windows PC, so read the section that applies to the kind of computer you use.

Go Wireless

Using MobileMe or an Exchange account are the better ways to sync information because you don't have to connect an iPod touch to a computer. Your syncs can happen automatically whenever you connect to a Wi-Fi network.

Using iTunes to Sync Information on Macs

To set up information syncing on a Mac, perform the following steps.

1. Connect the iPod touch to your Mac.
2. Select the iPod touch on the Source list.
3. Click the Info button.
4. To sync your Address Book contacts, check Sync Address Book Contacts; if you don't want to sync this information (such as if you use MobileMe to sync), skip to step 11 instead.
5. To sync all your contact information, click All contacts and skip to step 8.

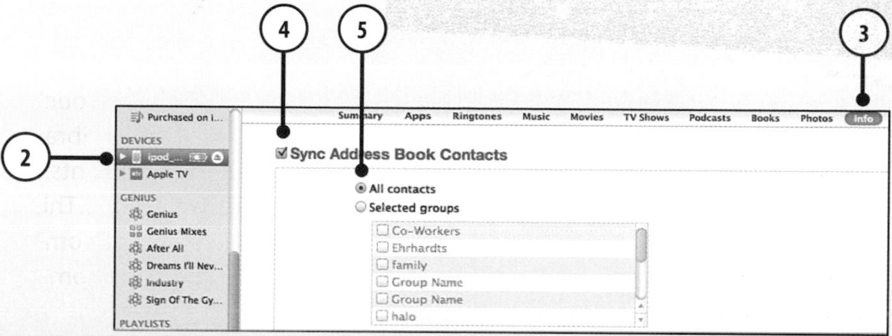

6. If you organize your contact information in groups and want to move only specific ones onto the iPod touch, click Selected groups.
7. Check the check box next to each group you want to move to the iPod touch. If you leave a group's check box unchecked, the contacts it contains are ignored during the sync process.
8. If you want contacts you create on the iPod touch to be stored in a specific Address Book group when you sync, check the Add contacts created outside of groups on this iPod to check box and select the group on the pop-up menu. If you don't want them placed into a specific group, leave the check box unchecked.
9. To sync with your contacts stored on Yahoo!, check Sync Yahoo! Address Book contacts, click Agree, and follow the onscreen prompts to log into your Yahoo! Address Book.
10. To sync with your contacts stored in your Google account, check Sync Google Address Book contacts, click Agree, and follow the onscreen prompts to log into your Google account.

No Duplicates Please

You don't need to set up the same information to sync in more than one way. For example, if you have a MobileMe account, use that to sync your email account, contacts, and calendars rather than iTunes because with MobileMe, your information is synced wirelessly. If you sync this information using MobileMe and iTunes, you end up with duplicate information on your touch.

Do You Use Entourage?

iCal for calendars, Mail for email, or Address Book for contact information are the only Mac applications that you can directly sync with the iPod touch via the iTunes sync process. If you use Entourage, see the next tip.

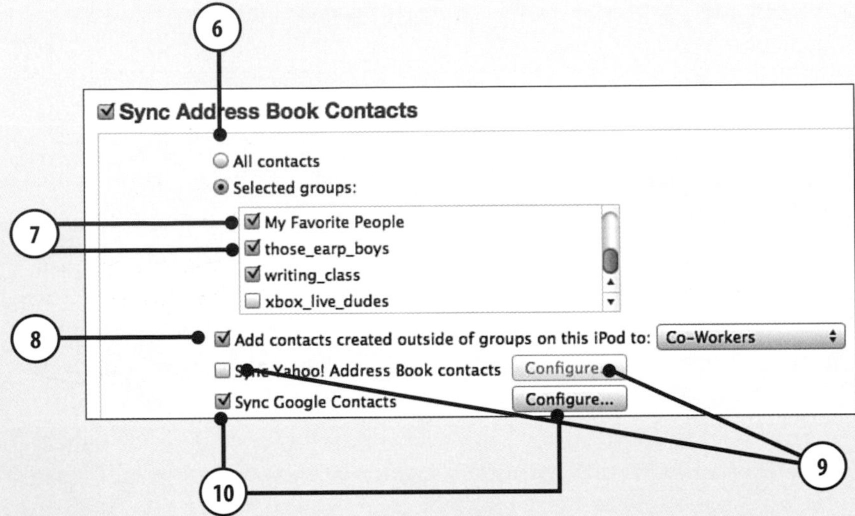

11. Scroll down until you see the Calendars section.

12. Check Sync iCal Calendars to move your iCal calendars onto the touch; if you don't want to sync calendar information (such as if you use MobileMe), skip to step 17.

13. If you want all the calendars you access in iCal to be synced on the iPod touch, click the All calendars radio button and skip to step 16.

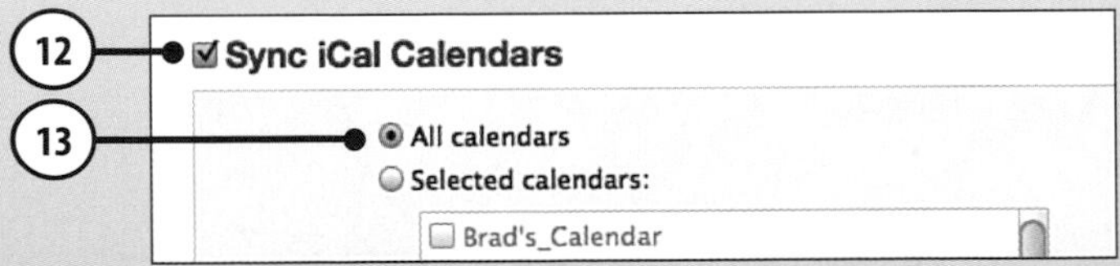

Syncing Entourage

If you use Entourage, you can sync its information with your iPod touch indirectly by syncing its information with Address Book and iCal, which in turn are synced with your iPod touch via iTunes. Open Entourage's Preferences and configure the Sync Services preferences to synchronize contacts with Address Book and events with iCal. Then configure Address Book and iCal syncing in iTunes as described in these steps. To sync your Entourage email, simply manually configure your email account on the iPod touch, as described in Chapter 9, "Emailing."

14. If you want only selected calendars to move onto an iPod touch, click the Selected calendars radio button.
15. Check the check box next to each calendar that you want to sync on the touch.
16. If you want to prevent older events from syncing, check the Do not sync events older than check box and enter the number of days after which events should be excluded from the sync in the box.

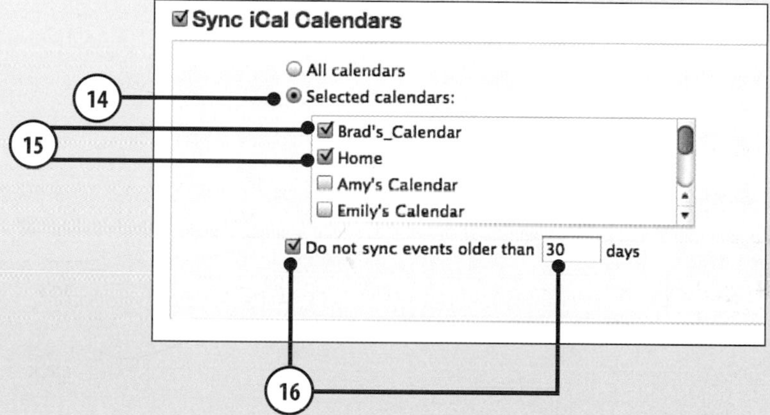

17. Scroll down until you see the Mail Accounts section.
18. Check Sync Mail Accounts if you want to add email accounts configured in Mail to the iPod touch; skip to step 20 if you don't want any of your email accounts synced. (For example, configure MobileMe email or Exchange accounts directly on the iPod).
19. Check the check box for each account you want to move onto iPod touch.
20. Check the Sync Safari bookmarks check box if you want to sync your Safari bookmarks, so you can use them with the iPod touch's web browser; if you don't want this, skip this step.
21. If you want any notes you create in Mail to be moved onto the touch and notes you create on the touch to be moved into Mail, check the Sync notes check box; if not, skip this step.

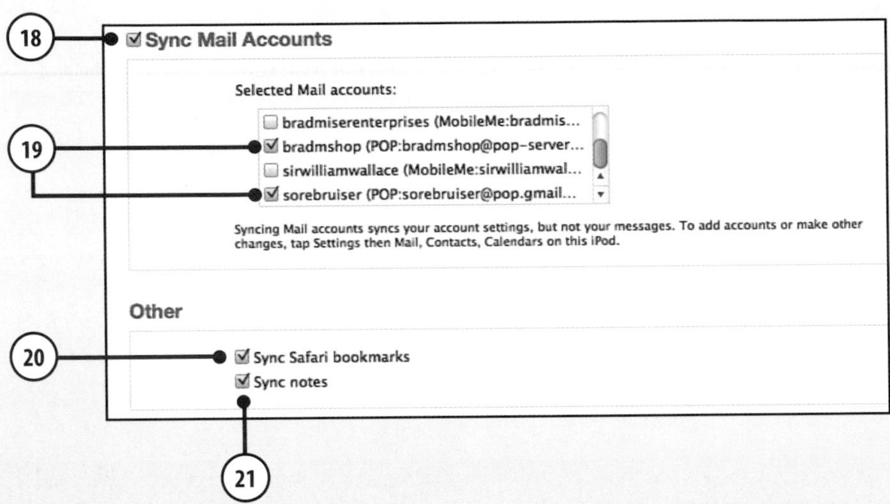

22. Scroll down to the Advanced section.
23. Check the check boxes next to any information that you want to be replaced on the iPod touch with information from the computer. If you don't check a check box, its information will be merged with that information on the iPod touch instead.
24. Click Apply. A sync is performed, and the information you selected is moved onto the iPod touch.

    Each time you sync the iPod touch (this happens automatically when you connect the iPod touch to your Mac), any updated information included in the sync settings on the computer is moved to the iPod touch, and updated information on the iPod touch is moved onto the computer.

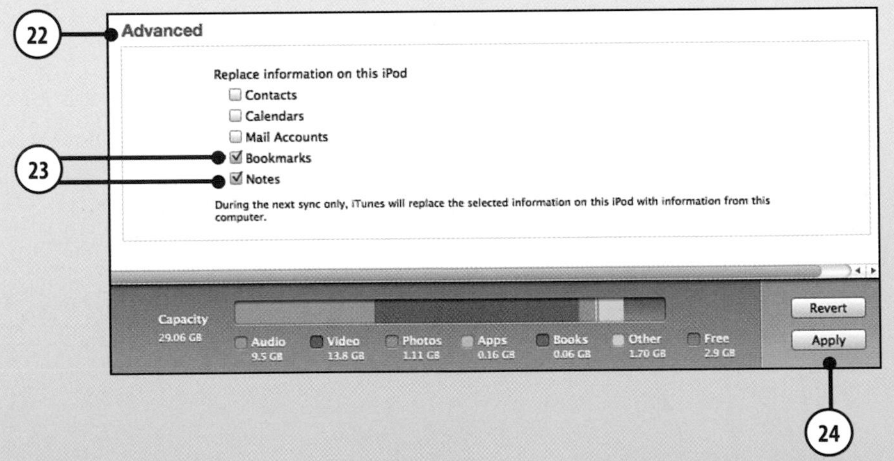

It's Not All Good

If you prefer Firefox as your web browser, you can't sync your bookmarks via iTunes. That's too bad and is quite annoying for those of us who use Firefox regularly. There's currently just no simple way to move bookmarks to or from an iPod touch from or to Firefox. (There are ways to do this, but they are clunky and require more room to explain than I have here.) Hopefully, Apple will remove this web browser discrimination in an update to its software soon.

Locating Synced Notes?

When you sync notes, they are stored in the Mail application under the Notes subsection of the Reminders section shown in the mailbox pane on the left side of the window. If you don't see your notes, expand the Notes item and select On My Mac. You should see your notes in the List pane at the top of the Mail window. Select a note on the list to read it in the Reading pane at the bottom of the window.

Sync Versus Apply

Whenever you make changes to the sync settings for the iPod touch, the Apply button replaces the Sync button and the Cancel button appears. When you click Apply, the new settings are saved and used for subsequent syncs, a sync is performed, and the button becomes Sync; click Cancel to keep the current sync settings. When the sync settings haven't changed since the last sync, click Sync to perform a sync using the current settings.

Syncing with More Than One Source

If you configured iPod touch to sync with more than one source of contact information, perhaps Outlook on a Windows PC and Address Book on a Mac, when you sync, you're prompted to replace or merge the information. If you select Replace Info, the existing information on whatever you are syncing with replaces all the contact information on iPod touch. If you choose Merge Info, the information you are syncing moves onto iPod touch and merges with the existing contact information.

Using iTunes to Sync Information on Windows PCs

You can sync information on a Windows PC with an iPod touch by performing the following steps.

1. Connect the iPod touch to your computer.
2. Select the iPod touch on the Source list.
3. Click the Info button.
4. To sync your contacts, check Sync Contacts with and choose the source of contact information with which you want to sync on the drop-down list. The options are Outlook, Google Contacts, Windows Address Book, or Yahoo! Address Book. If you choose Yahoo! or Google, log into your account at the prompt. If you don't want to sync contact information stored on your computer (such as if you use MobileMe), skip to step 8.
5. To sync all contact information, click All contacts and skip to step 8.

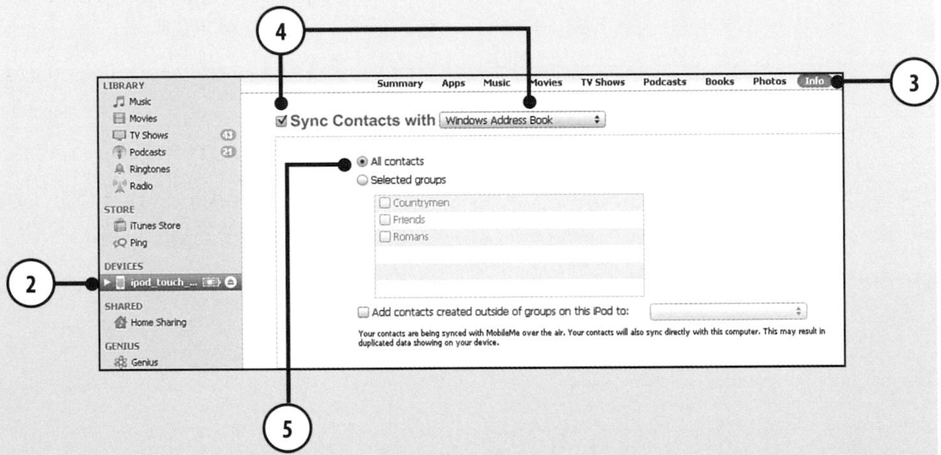

6. If you organize your contact information in groups and want to move only specific ones onto the iPod touch, click Selected groups.
7. Check the check box next to each group you want to move into the iPod touch. If you leave a group's check box unchecked, it will be ignored during the sync process.
8. If you want contacts you create on the iPod touch to be moved into a specific contact group when you sync, check the Add contacts created outside of groups on this iPod to check box and select the group on the pop-up menu. If you don't want them placed into a specific group, leave the check box unchecked.

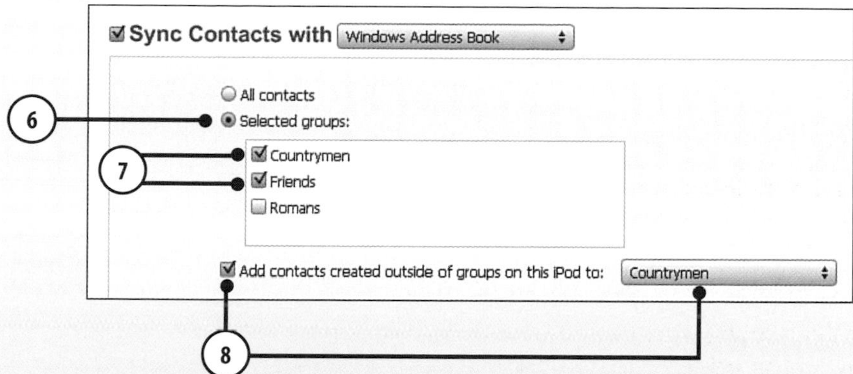

9. Scroll down until you see the Calendars section.
10. Check Sync Calendars with and choose the calendar application that contains the calendars you want to sync; if you don't want to sync calendar information (such as if you use MobileMe), skip to step 15.
11. If you want all the calendars you access in the application you selected to be synced on the iPod touch, click the All calendars radio button and skip to step 14.
12. If you want only selected calendars to move onto an iPod touch, click the Selected calendars radio button.
13. Check the check box next to each calendar that you want to sync on the iPod touch.
14. If you want to prevent older events from syncing, check the Do not sync events older than check box and enter the number of days after which events should not be included in the sync in the box.
15. Scroll down until you see the Mail Accounts section.

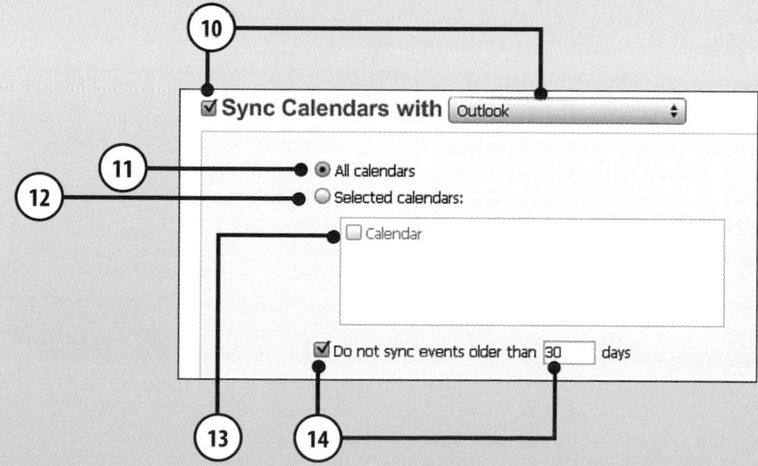

16. Check Sync Mail Accounts from if you want to configure email accounts configured on your computer on the iPod touch; skip to step 19 if you don't want them configured (such as if you use MobileMe or Exchange email accounts).
17. Select the email application containing the accounts you want to sync on the drop-down list.
18. Check the check box for each account you want to move onto iPod touch.
19. Check the Sync bookmarks with check box if you want to move your bookmarks so you can use them with the iPod touch's web browser; if you don't want this, skip to step 21.
20. Select Safari or Internet Explorer on the drop-down list to choose the browser containing the bookmarks you want to sync.
21. If you want any notes you create with the iPod touch's Notes application to be moved onto the computer and notes you create on the computer to be moved onto the touch, check the Sync notes with check box and select the application where the synced notes should be stored on the drop-down list; if you don't want to move your notes onto the computer, skip this step.
22. Scroll down to the Advanced section.

Synced Notes?

In the current version of iTunes, Outlook is the only Windows application that supports notes syncing. When you sync notes, they are stored in the Notes area, which you can access by clicking the Notes icon.

It's Not All Good

If you prefer Firefox as your web browser, you can't sync your bookmarks via iTunes. That's too bad and is quite annoying for those of us who use Firefox regularly. There's currently just no simple way to move bookmarks to or from and iPod touch from or to Firefox. (There are ways to do this, but they are clunky and require more room to explain than I have here.) Hopefully, Apple will remove this web browser discrimination in an update to its software soon.

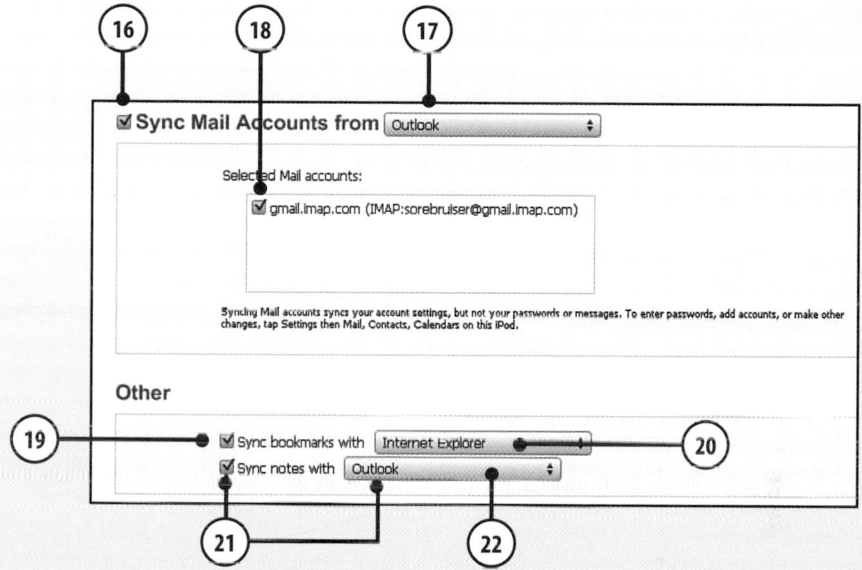

23. Check the check boxes next to any information that you want to replace on the iPod touch with information from the computer. If you don't check a check box, that information will be merged with the information on the iPod touch instead.

24. Click Apply. A sync is performed, and the information you selected is moved onto the iPod touch.

    Each time you sync the iPod touch (automatically when you connect the iPod touch to your computer), any updated information included in the sync settings on the computer is moved to the iPod touch, and updated information on the iPod touch is moved onto the computer.

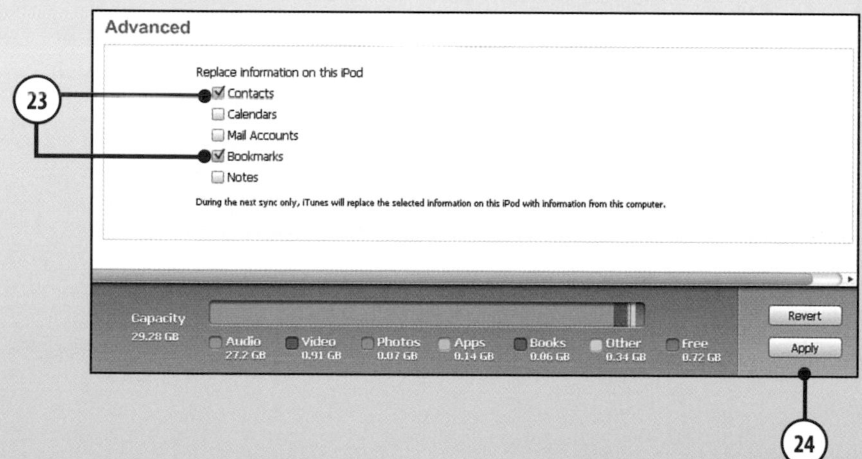

Sync Versus Apply

Whenever you make changes to the sync settings for the iPod touch, the Apply button replaces the Sync button and the Cancel button appears. When you click Apply, the new settings are saved and used for subsequent syncs, a sync is performed, and the button becomes Sync; click Cancel to keep the current sync settings. When the sync settings haven't changed since the last sync, click Sync to perform a sync using the current settings.

Syncing with More Than One Source

If you configured iPod touch to sync with more than one source of contact information, perhaps Outlook on a Windows PC and Address Book on a Mac, when you sync, you're prompted to replace or merge the information. If you select Replace Info, the existing information in whatever you sync with replaces all the contact information on iPod touch. If you choose Merge Info, the information you sync moves onto iPod touch and merges with the existing contact information.

Syncing Information with MobileMe

One of the great things about a MobileMe account is that you can sync email, contacts, calendars, and bookmarks wirelessly. Whenever your iPod touch can access the Internet, no matter where you are, the sync process can occur.

Of course, to sync information with MobileMe, you must have a MobileMe account. See Chapter 1, "Getting Started with Your iPod touch," for information about obtaining a MobileMe account.

If you have a MobileMe account, it is simple to access your MobileMe information on your iPod touch by configuring your account on the iPod touch and configuring its sync options. Here's how:

1. On the Home screen, tap Settings.

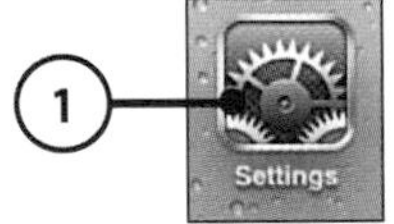

2. Tap Mail, Contacts, Calendars. (You might need to scroll down the screen to see this command.)
3. Tap Add Account.
4. Tap mobileme.
5. Enter your name.
6. Enter your MobileMe email address.
7. Enter your MobileMe account password.
8. Change the default description, which is your email address, if you want to. This description appears on various lists of accounts.
9. Tap Next. Your account information is verified. When that process is complete, you see the MobileMe screen that you use to choose which elements of your MobileMe account are going to be synchronized on iPod touch.

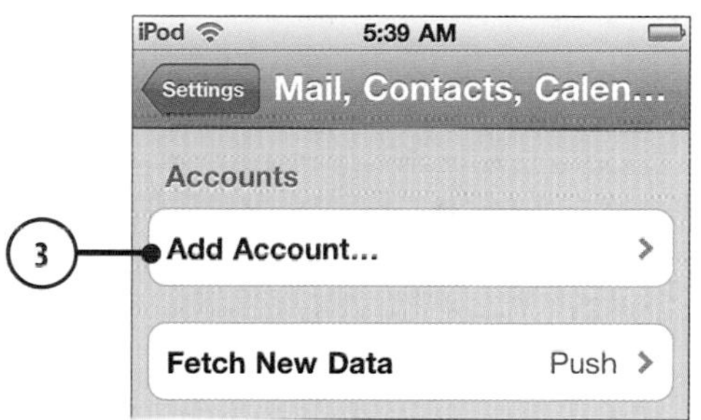

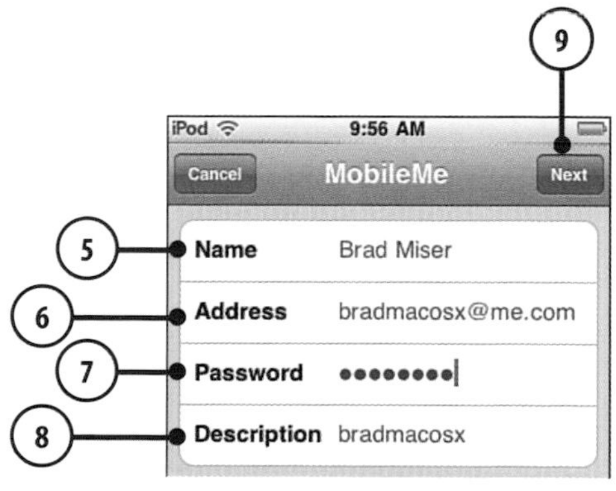

10. Tap OFF next to each kind of information you want to sync on the iPod touch; its status becomes ON to show you that information will be synced. If you leave a type's status set to OFF, that information is ignored.

To Merge or Not to Merge

If you previously synced information with a computer, such as calendar information, when you enable syncing for that information, you are prompted to Merge with MobileMe or Do not Merge. If you tap Merge with MobileMe, the information you previously synced combines with the information on MobileMe. If you choose Do not Merge, you are prompted to Keep on My iPod touch or Delete. If you tap Keep on My iPod touch, the information you previously synced is kept on the touch. If you tap Delete and then tap Delete again at the warning prompt, the information you previously synced is deleted from the iPod touch. (The source with which you synced is not affected.)

11. Tap OFF next to Find My iPod touch to activate this feature, which enables you to access your touch remotely (when it is connected to the Internet); if you don't want to turn this on, skip to step 13.

12. Tap Allow.

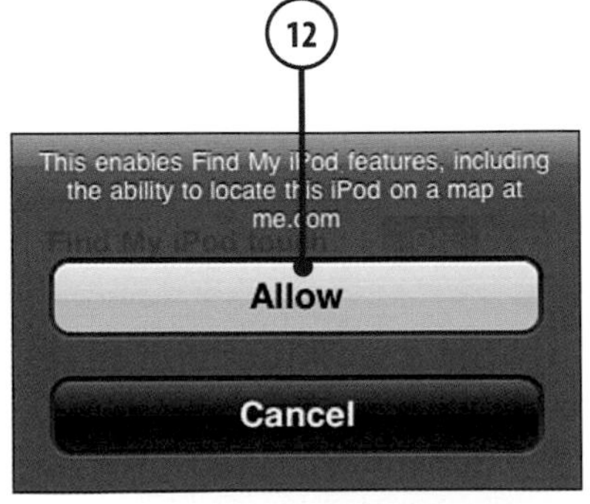

13. Tap Save. The account is synced to the iPod touch. You return to the Mail, Contacts, Calendar screen where you see your MobileMe account on the Accounts list. The account is ready to use as is; however, you should also configure how and when information is synced.

14. Tap Fetch New Data.

15. To enable information to be synced with your iPod touch whenever there are updates and the iPod touch is connected to the Internet, ensure the Push status is ON (if it isn't, tap OFF to turn it on); or to disable push to extend battery life, tap ON so the status becomes OFF. This setting impacts all your wirelessly synced accounts.

16. Tap the amount of time when you want an iPod touch to sync information when Push is OFF or when an account doesn't support Push; tap Manually if you want to sync manually only. This setting also impacts all your wirelessly synced accounts.

17. Scroll down the screen.

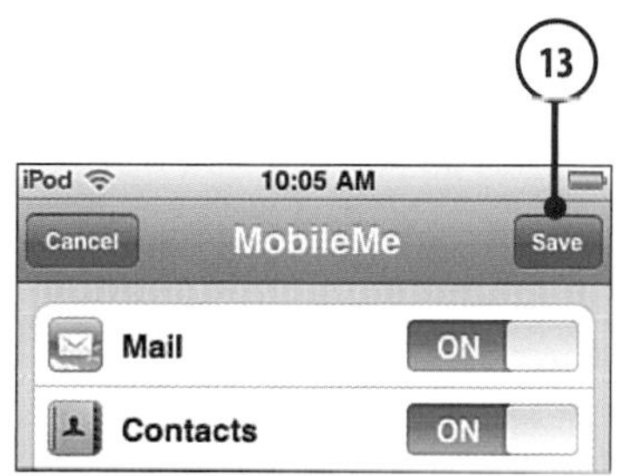

18. Tap Advanced. You see a list of all your active accounts. Next to each account, you see if it is configured to use Push, Fetch, or Manual. You also see the kinds of information included in the sync settings for each account, such as Mail, Contacts, Calendars, and so on.

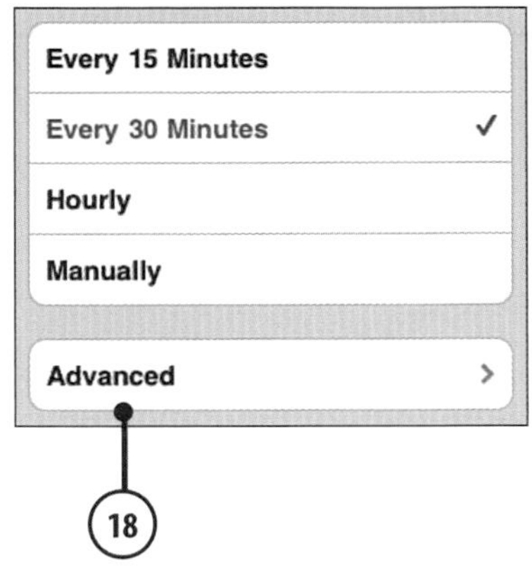

19. Tap the account you want to configure.

20. Tap the option you want to use for syncing; the options can include Push, Fetch, or Manual. If you choose Push, syncing occurs when the iPod touch is connected to the Internet and new information is on the iPod touch or in the MobileMe cloud; this keeps information on the touch the most current but also causes the largest energy use and shortest working time until you need to recharge the iPod. If you choose Fetch, information is automatically retrieved according to the time you selected in step 17; this enables automatic syncing but uses less battery power than Push. If you choose Manual, information is synced only when you manually start the process; while requiring you to take action to update your information, it does provide the longest battery life.

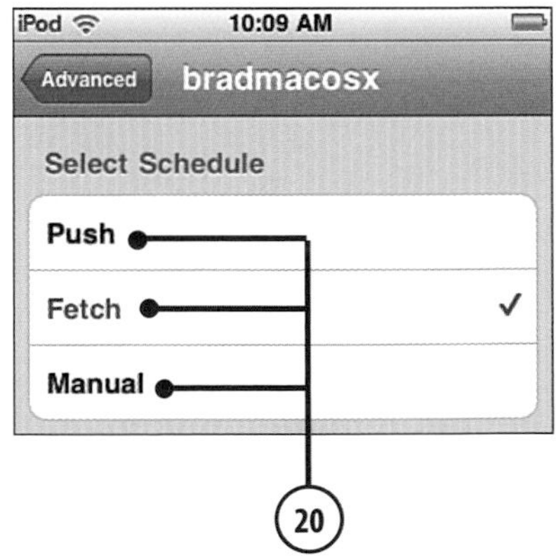

The MobileMe account is ready to use and its information syncs wirelessly according to your configuration settings.

Syncing Information with Exchange

If you have a Microsoft Exchange account, you can sync its email, contact, and calendar information on your iPod touch; this works similarly to synchronizing with MobileMe. Configuring an Exchange account on an iPod touch is explained in Chapter 9. After you set up an Exchange account on your iPod touch, you can configure its sync options similarly to doing so for a MobileMe account, the details of which are provided in the previous section.

Duplicate MobileMe and Exchange Syncs

Make sure you enable calendar and contacts syncing from the same source only once or you end up with the same information on your iPod touch multiple times, which can be confusing. For example, If you use Outlook on a PC and have an Exchange account, you don't want to sync your calendar information both via MobileMe and Exchange because you'll get the same calendar information twice. Disable Calendar syncing using the MobileMe control panel, and only the information you get via Exchange moves onto your iPod touch.

Tap here to configure an iPod touch for audio

Tap here to enjoy audio bliss

In this chapter, you explore all the audio functionality the iPod touch offers. The topics include the following:

- → Finding and listening to music
- → Controlling audio content quickly
- → Finding and listening to podcasts
- → Customizing iPod touch for music

Listening to Music, Podcasts, and Other Audio

The primary reason iPods have become such a phenomenon is that they are amazingly powerful devices for listening to all kinds of audio, including music, podcasts (which came into existence because of iPods), audiobooks, and others. After you move audio content onto your iPod touch (learn how to stock your touch with great audio in Chapter 3, "Moving Audio, Video, Books, and Photos onto Your iPod touch"), you can use the iPod touch's fantastic and fun tools to enjoy that content.

Finding and Listening to Music

There are two fundamental steps to listening to music and other audio content. First, find the content you want to listen to by using one of the many browsing and searching features your iPod touch offers. Second, after you find and select what you want to hear, use the iPod touch's playback controls to listen to your heart's content.

Turn It Up! (Or Down!)

No matter which technique you use to find and play music, you can control the volume using the Volume keys on the left side of iPod touch. Press the upper part of the rocker switch to increase volume or the lower part to decrease it. While you are pressing the switch, a volume indicator appears on the screen to show you the relative volume level as you press the keys. When you are on the Now Playing screen or viewing the iPod control bar, you can use the Volume slider to set the sound level. And if you listen with the headphones included with your touch, you can use the buttons on the right earbud wire to crank it up (or down).

Using the Cover Flow Browser to Find and Play Music

The Cover Flow Browser simulates what it's like to flip through a stack of CDs; you can quickly peruse your entire music collection to get to the right music for your current mood.

1. On the Home screen, tap the Music button.
2. Rotate your iPod touch 90 degrees in either direction, and the Cover Flow Browser appears. Each cover represents an album from which you have at least one song stored on your iPod touch.

Jump to an Album

Tap any album cover you see on the screen to quickly bring that album into focus.

3. To browse your tunes, drag a finger to the right to move ahead in the albums or to the left to move back; the faster you drag, the faster you "flip" through the albums. The album cover directly facing you, front and center on the screen is the album in focus, meaning that it's the one you can explore.

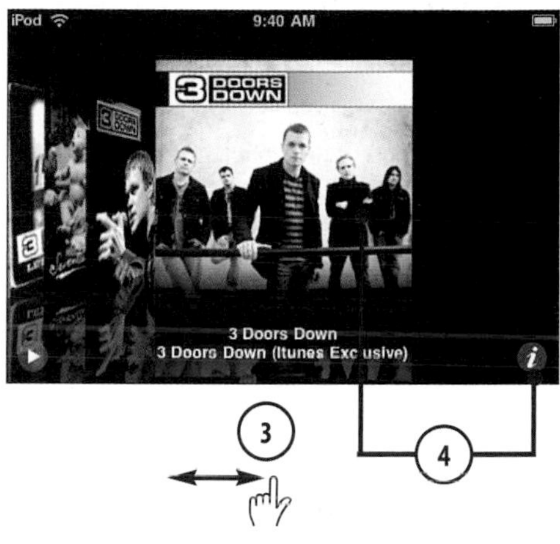

4. To see the songs on an album, move it into focus and tap its cover or tap the Info button. The Contents screen appears, showing you a list of all the songs on that album.
5. To browse the list of songs, drag your finger up or down the screen.
6. To play a song, tap it. The song plays and is marked with a blue Play button arrow on the list of songs.

7. To pause a song, tap the Pause button. The music pauses, and the Play button replaces the Pause button.
8. To play a different song, tap it.
9. To return to the album's cover, tap its title information, tap the Info button, or just tap outside of the album cover.
10. While you're listening, you can continue browsing to find more music you want to listen to. (When the iPod touch starts playing the next song in the album you are currently playing, the cover for that album jumps back into focus.)

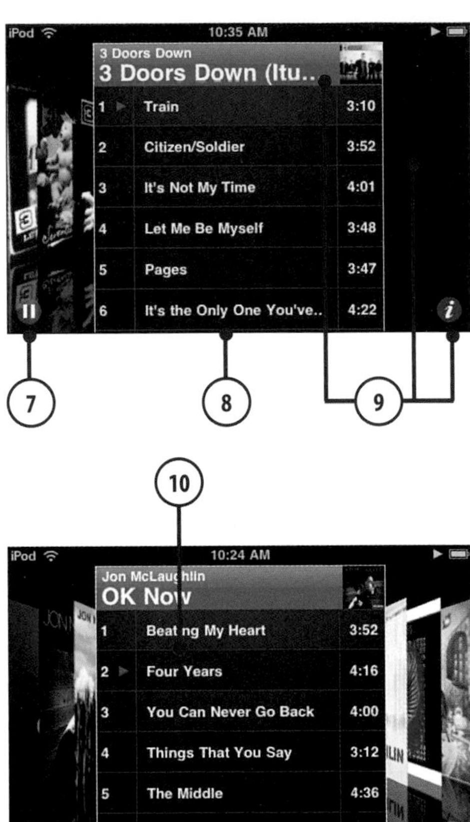

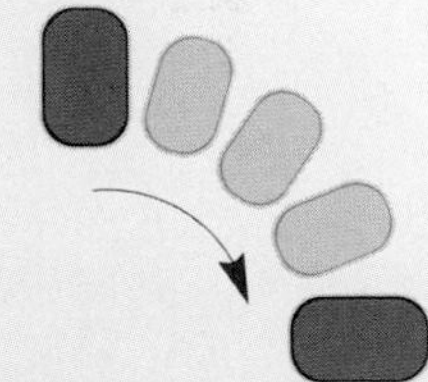

11. Rotate the iPod touch 90 degrees to see the Now Playing screen.
12. Use the Now Playing screen to control the music (covered in detail in the "Playing Music" task later in this section).

Missing Album Artwork

When an iPod touch doesn't have artwork for an album, you see a generic musical note icon as the album cover in the Cover Flow Browser. You can use iTunes to associate artwork with albums that don't currently have it. The next time you sync your iPod touch, the new album artwork appears in the Browser.

Using Playlists to Find Music

Finding and listening to music in your iTunes playlists that you moved onto your iPod touch is simple.

1. On the Home screen, tap the Music button.
2. Tap the Playlists button. The list of all playlists on your iPod touch appears. These playlists are organized just as they are on the Source list in iTunes; if you use folders to organize your playlists, you see those folders on the Playlists screen.
3. Slide your finger up and down the list to browse your playlists.
4. Tap a playlist or folder that you'd like to explore. The list of songs in that playlist or the list of playlists within the folder appears with the title of the playlist or folder at the top of the screen.

5. If you move into a folder, tap the playlist you want to see.
6. Drag your finger up and down to browse the songs the playlist contains. (You can also search a playlist by browsing up until you see the Search bar; learn how in the section "Searching for Music" later in this chapter.)
7. When you find a song you want to listen to, tap it. The song begins to play, and the Now Playing screen appears.

Back to the Browser

No matter how you end up there, you can always move between the Now Playing screen and the Cover Flow Browser by rotating the iPod touch from vertical to horizontal. Whenever the iPod touch is oriented horizontally, the Browser appears.

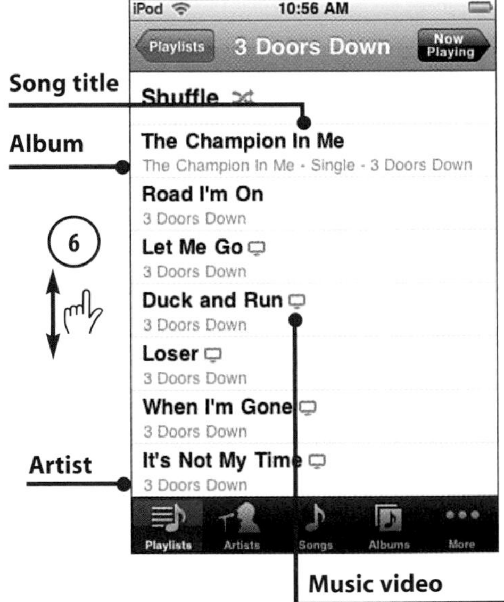

8. Use the Now Playing screen to control the music (covered in detail in the "Playing Music" section later in this chapter).
9. Tap the Return button to move back to the playlist's screen. (When you view a playlist's screen, the song currently playing is marked with the speaker icon.)

Using Artists to Find Music

You can find music by browsing artists whose music is stored on the touch.

1. On the Home screen, tap the Music button.

See All, Know All

The various All commands you see, such as All Albums just under the Search tool at the top of the Artists screen, enable you to browse all the content, organized as indicated. For example, when you tap All Albums on the Artists screen, you see all the music on your touch, organized by the albums in which it is contained.

2. Tap Artists. The list of all artists whose content is on iPod touch appears. Artists are grouped by the first letter of their first name or by the first letter of the group's name (not counting "The" as the first word in a name).

3. Drag your finger up and down the list to browse all available artists. (At the top of the screen, you see the Search tool by which you can search for specific artists. See "Searching for Music" later in this chapter for more information.)

4. To jump to a specific artist, tap the letter along the right side of the screen for the artist's or group's first name; to jump to an artist or group whose name starts with a number, tap # at the bottom of the screen.

5. Tap an artist whose music you'd like to explore. A list of songs by that artist appears. If you have more that one album by that artist, the songs are organized by album; otherwise, you simply see a list of the songs.

6. Drag your finger up and down the screen to browse the artist's albums.

7. To see the contents of an album, tap it, and the list of contents screen appears with the album's title, album art, and information (such as playing time) at the top of the screen. Or to view all the songs by the artist, skip to step 13.

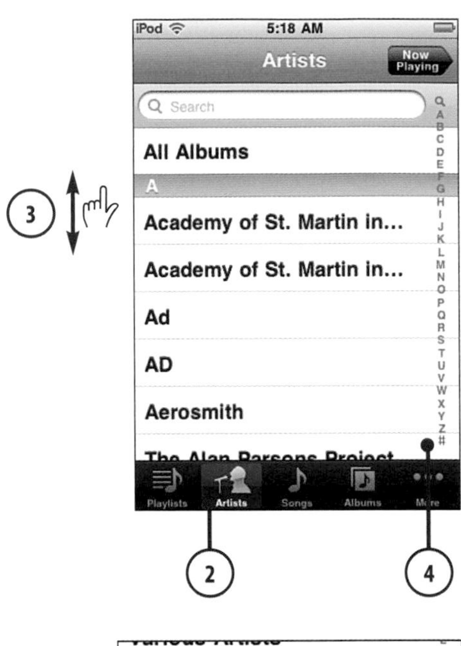

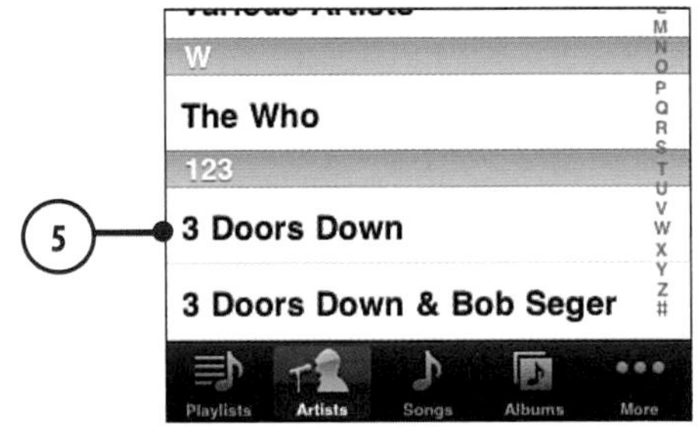

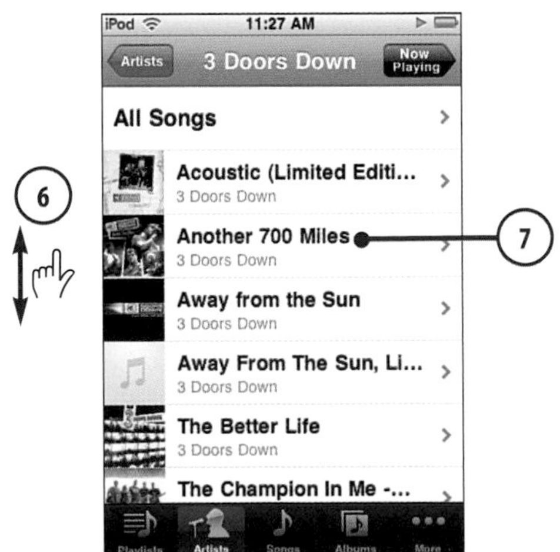

8. Drag your finger up and down the screen to browse all the songs on the selected album.
9. When you find the song you want to listen to, tap it. The song begins to play, and the Now Playing screen appears.
10. Use the Now Playing screen to control the music (covered in detail in the "Playing Music" task later in this section).
11. To move back to the album's screen, tap Return.
12. To move back to the artist's screen, tap Return (which is labeled with the artist's name).

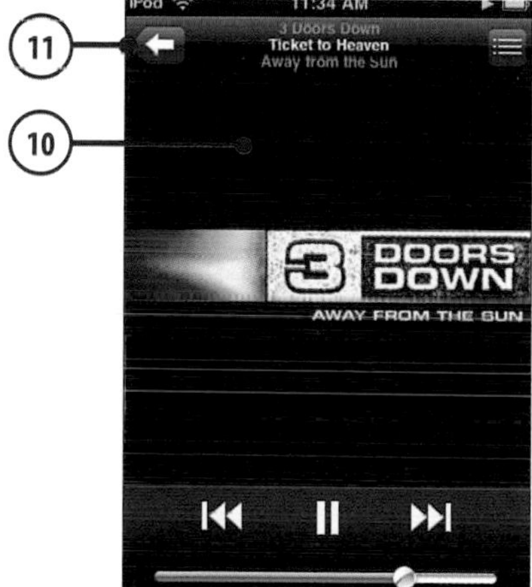

13. To see all the songs by the artist, tap All Songs. You see the list of all songs by the artist, organized alphabetically.
14. Browse the list or tap a letter to move to a song you want to hear.
15. Tap the song you want to hear. The song begins to play, and the Now Playing screen appears.

To Now Playing and Back

Whenever music is playing or paused, the Now Playing screen is active even when it isn't visible. You can move to the Now Playing screen by tapping the Now Playing button located in the upper-right corner of the screen. You can return from the Now Playing screen back to where you were by tapping the Return button located in the upper-left corner of the Now Playing screen.

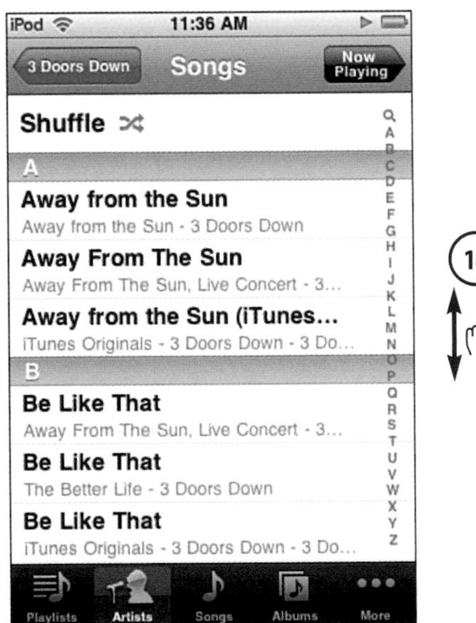

16. Use the Now Playing screen to control playback of the music (covered in detail in the "Playing Music" task later in this section).
17. Tap Return to move back to any of the previous screens to find and play more music.

Using the More Menu to Find Music

The More menu shows you all the content categories on your iPod touch. You can use this menu to access content when it can't be found by one of the category buttons at the bottom of the screen.

1. On the Home screen, tap the Music button.
2. Tap More. The More screen appears, showing you the content categories on your iPod touch that aren't shown on the toolbar at the bottom of the screen.
3. Tap the category in which you are interested, such as Genres. That category's screen appears.

4. Browse the category and drill down into its detail to get to songs you want to hear. Browsing categories is similar to browsing playlists, artists, songs, and albums. (If you browse to the top of the screen, you see the Search tool with which you can search in most categories. See "Searching for Music" later in this chapter.)

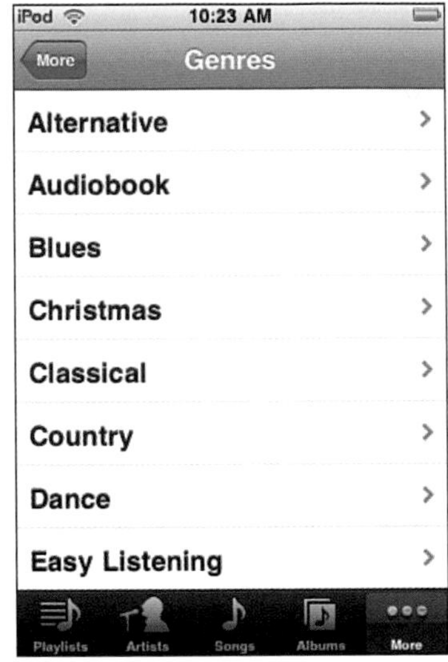

Songs and Albums

The Songs browser enables you to browse and search your music by individual song while the Albums browser does the same for albums. These tools work similar to the Artists tool. Tap the tool to use it. You can then browse the music and tap something to drill down into what it contains until you get to a list of songs, in which case, when you tap a song it plays. All these screens have a Search tool at the top to enable you to find specific content.

Your Favs

As you learn a little later in this chapter, you can configure the Music toolbar to have buttons for the categories you use most frequently.

Searching for Music

Browsing is a useful way to find music, but it can be faster to search for specific music in which you are interested. You can search most of the screens that you browse, and when a category has a lot of options, such as Songs, searching can get you where you want to go more quickly than browsing. Here's how:

1. Move to a screen you can browse; this example uses the Songs screen, but you can search most screens similarly.
2. Browse to the top of the screen until you see the Search tool or tap the magnifying glass icon at the top of the screen's index.
3. Tap in the Search tool.
4. Type the text or numbers for which you want to search. As you type, the items that meet your search criterion are shown; the more you type, the more specific your search becomes. Below the Search tool, you see the results organized into categories, such as Album and Song.
5. When you think you've typed enough to find what you're looking for, tap Search. The keyboard disappears.

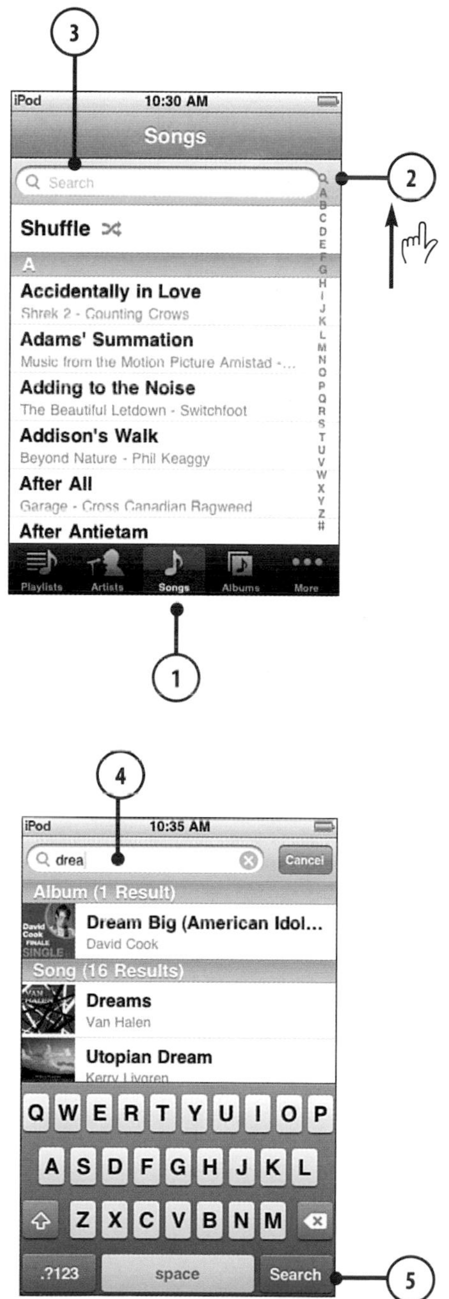

6. Browse the results.
7. Tap songs or albums to get to the music you want to play.

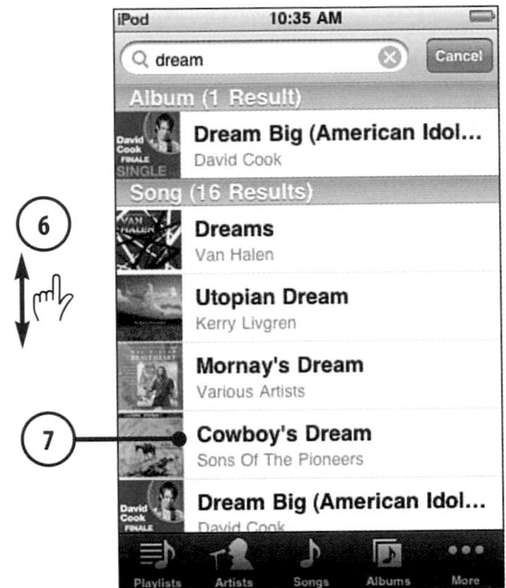

Clearing or Editing a Search

You can clear a search by tapping the "x" that appears on the right end of the Search tool when you have entered text or numbers. You can edit the search text just like you edit any other text (see Chapter 1, "Getting Started with your iPod Touch" to learn about entering and editing text).

Using Genius to Find Music

The Genius feature finds music and builds a playlist based on songs that "go with" a specific song. How the Genius selects songs that "sound good" with other songs is a bit of a secret, but it works amazingly well. You can have the Genius build a playlist for you in a couple of ways and then listen to or update it.

Creating a Genius Playlist Based on the Current Song

1. Find and play a song using any of the techniques you learned earlier in this chapter.
2. On the Now Playing screen, tap the screen so the Timeline and controls appear.
3. Tap the Genius button. While the music plays, the Genius playlist is created, and you move to the Genius screen where you see the songs that the Genius selected; the song that is currently playing is at the top of the list and is marked with the Genius and speaker icons.
4. Tap any song on the playlist to start playing it.
5. Tap the New button to start a new Genius playlist. (See the "Creating a Genius Playlist by Selecting a Song" section in this chapter.)
6. To have the Genius change the playlist, tap Refresh. Songs may be added, and the order in which they are listed may be changed.
7. To save the playlist, tap Save. The name of the playlist changes from Genius to be the name of the song on which the playlist was based. The New button disappears, and the Delete button appears.

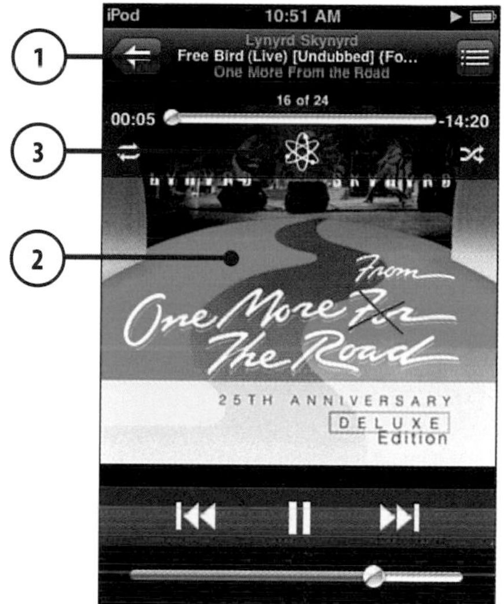

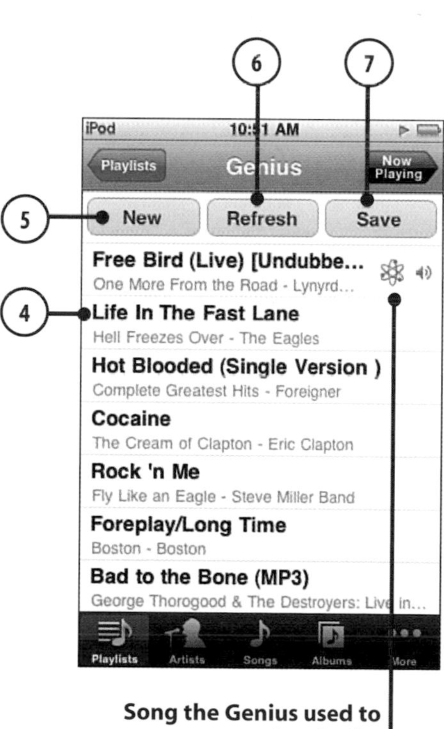

Song the Genius used to create the playlist

They Really Are Genius

Genius playlists appear on the Playlists screen like other playlists you have created, except they are marked with the Genius icon. Genius playlists appear at the top of the Playlists screen (instead of being listed alphabetically). You can play Genius playlists just like others on the Playlists screen, and you can edit them (covered in the "Refreshing a Genius Playlist" section). Genius playlists are also moved into your iTunes Library on your computer the next time you sync your iPod touch.

Creating a Genius Playlist by Selecting a Song

1. Move to the Playlists screen.
2. Tap Genius Playlist. You see the Genius screen showing the most recent Genius playlist.
3. Tap New.

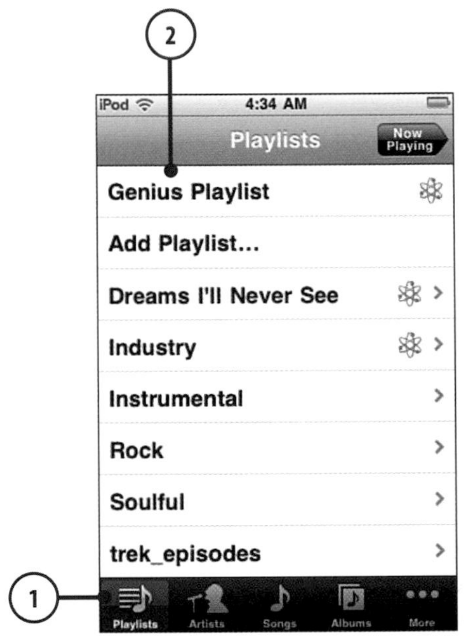

4. Browse or search for the song on which you want the new playlist to be based.
5. Tap the song on which you want the new playlist to be based. The Genius creates the playlist; it appears on the Genius screen and starts to play automatically.
6. Use steps 4 through 7 in the previous task to work with the playlist.

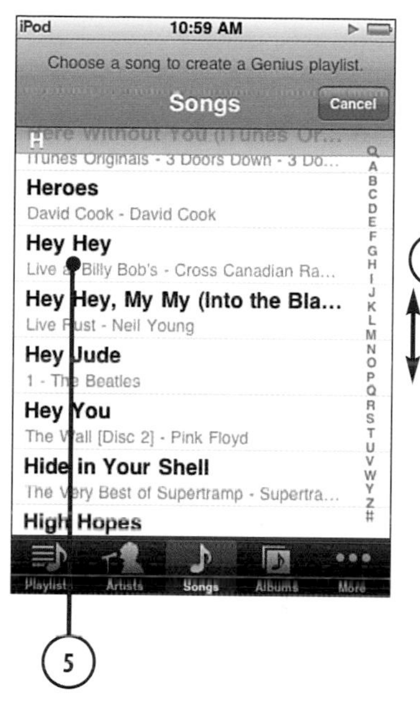

Refreshing a Genius Playlist

1. Move to the Playlists screen.
2. Tap the Genius playlist you want to manage; Genius playlists are named with the name of the song on which they are based, and they have the Genius icon. The Genius playlist's screen appears.

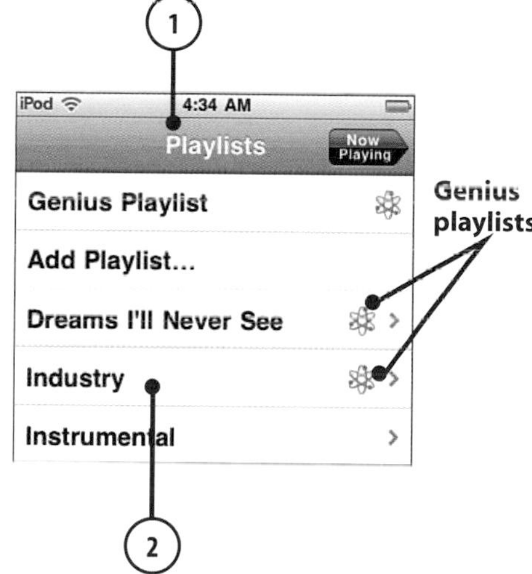

Deleting a Genius Playlist

To delete a genius playlist, move to its screen and tap the Delete button. The playlist is deleted. (Of course, the songs on your iPod touch are not affected.) If you have synced your iPod touch since you saved the playlist, you won't see the Delete button because the playlist has been saved to your iTunes Library. To delete a playlist after you've synced your iPod touch, delete it from your iTunes Library.

3. Tap Refresh. The Genius builds a new playlist based on the same song. The resulting playlist might have the same or different songs, and they might be in a different order. The refreshed playlist replaces the previous version.

Roll Your Own Playlist

You can be your own genius by manually creating a playlist. Tap Add Playlist on the Playlists screen. Name and save the playlist at the prompt. The Songs screen appears. Tap a song's Add button (+) to add it to the new playlist; the song is grayed out to show you it has been added. Add as many songs as you want in the same way. Tap Done. You move to the playlist's screen. Tap Edit. Change the order of songs in the playlist by dragging the Order button on the right edge of the screen up or down. Swipe over a song to delete it. Tap the Add button to add more songs. The next time you sync, the new playlist is added to iTunes so you can listen to it on the computer, too.

Finding Music by Shuffling

This section is a bit of a contrivance because when you shuffle music, you don't really find it, but rather you rely on your iPod touch to select music "randomly." There are two ways to shuffle music: You can use the Shuffle option, or your can shake your iPod touch.

Shuffling with the Shuffle Option

1. Move to a source of songs using one of the techniques you learned earlier, such as selecting a playlist, browsing an artist, and so on.
2. Browse to the top of the screen if you aren't there already.
3. Tap Shuffle. Your iPod touch selects a song from the group you were browsing and plays it; you move to the Now Playing screen. After that song plays; the iPod touch selects another one and plays it. This continues until all the songs in the source have played.

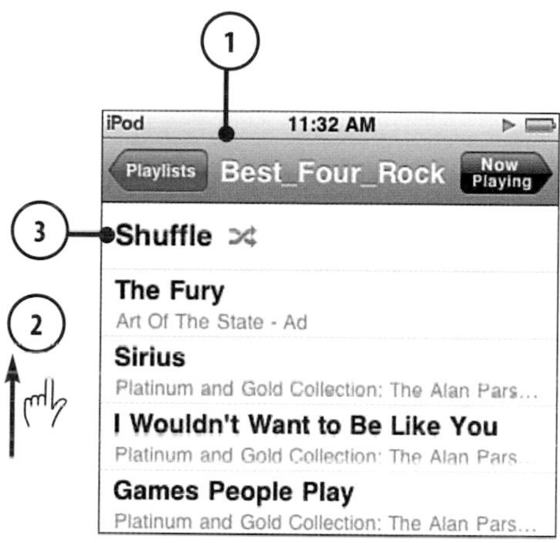

Shuffling by Shaking

1. Move to a source of songs that you want to shuffle through. There are many ways to do this, such as selecting a playlist, browsing an artist, and so on.
2. Tap a song. It starts to play, and you move to the Now Playing screen.
3. Gently shake your iPod touch in a back and forth motion. A song is selected at random and begins to play. You can shake your touch at any time to move to the next randomly selected song.

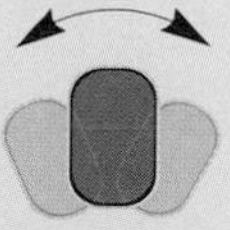

Playing Music

As you have seen, the Now Playing screen appears whenever you play music. This screen provides many controls and options for playing music.

1. Find and play a song or album. The Now Playing screen appears, and you can use its controls.
2. Tap the Track List view button. The Album Cover view is replaced by the Track List view. Here you see the list of all tracks on the album from which the current song comes, even if you aren't listening to the album itself (such as when you are listening to a playlist). You see the order of tracks on the album along with their names and playing times.

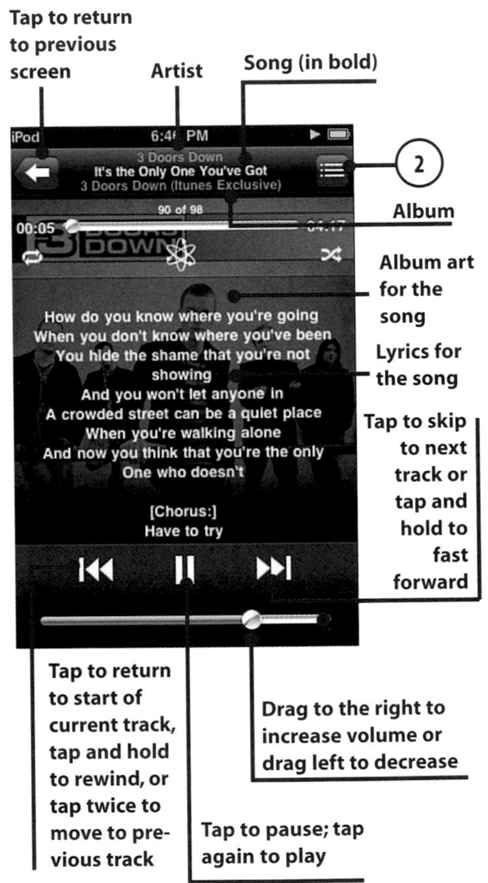
Tap to return to previous screen
Artist
Song (in bold)
2
Album
Album art for the song
Lyrics for the song
Tap to skip to next track or tap and hold to fast forward
Tap to return to start of current track, tap and hold to rewind, or tap twice to move to previous track
Drag to the right to increase volume or drag left to decrease
Tap to pause; tap again to play
iPod
3 Doors Down
It's the Only One You've Got
3 Doors Down (Itunes Exclusive)
90 of 98
00:05
How do you know where you're going
When you don't know where you've been
You hide the shame that you're not showing
And you won't let anyone in
A crowded street can be a quiet place
When you're walking alone
And now you think that you're the only
One who doesn't
[Chorus:]
Have to try

Lyrics and the Timeline Bar

You can add lyrics to songs in iTunes. Tap the screen once to show the lyrics in the center of the screen; these appear along with the Timeline bar and controls at the top of the screen. (If you see the Timeline but not lyrics, the song doesn't have lyrics saved for it in iTunes.) Tap the screen again to hide them. Lyrics and the Timeline bar are in the state they last were each time you were on the Now Playing screen. If you display lyrics and the Timeline bar and move away from the Now Playing screen, they will display the next time you move back. Likewise, if they are hidden when you move away, they remain hidden when you return.

3. Drag your finger up and down to browse through the tracks in the album.
4. Tap a song to play it.
5. Rate the song currently playing by tapping one of the dots. Stars fill up to the dot you tapped to give the song a star rating between one and five stars.
6. Tap the Album Cover button. You return to the Album Cover view.
7. If you don't see the Timeline bar, tap the album cover once. The Timeline bar appears. (If a song has lyrics, they appear along with the Timeline bar.)
8. To repeat the current album until you stop playing it, tap the Repeat button. When the album is set to repeat indefinitely, the Repeat button turns blue. To repeat the album one time, tap the Repeat button again. When the album is set to repeat once, the button turns blue and contains a small "1." To turn off repeat, tap the button again so it is white.
9. To move ahead or back in the song, drag the Playhead to the right or left.
10. To play the songs on the album randomly, tap the Shuffle button.
11. If the song has lyrics, browse up and down the screen to read all the lyrics.
12. Tap the album cover again. The Timeline bar and lyrics (if there are any) disappear.

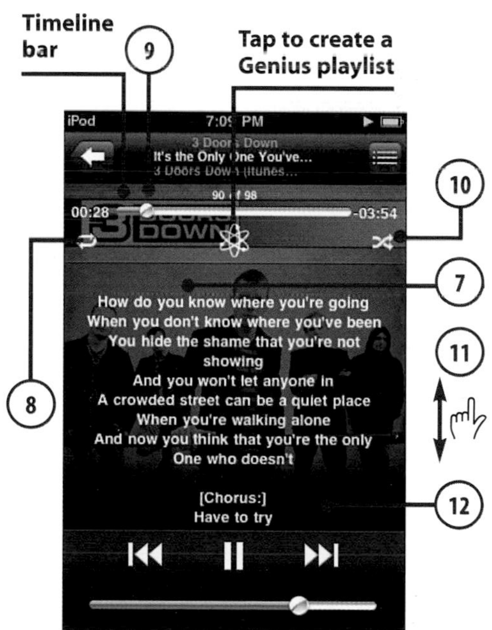

13. Tap the Return button. You move back to the screen from which you selected music to play.

14. Tap the Now Playing button. You return to the Now Playing screen.

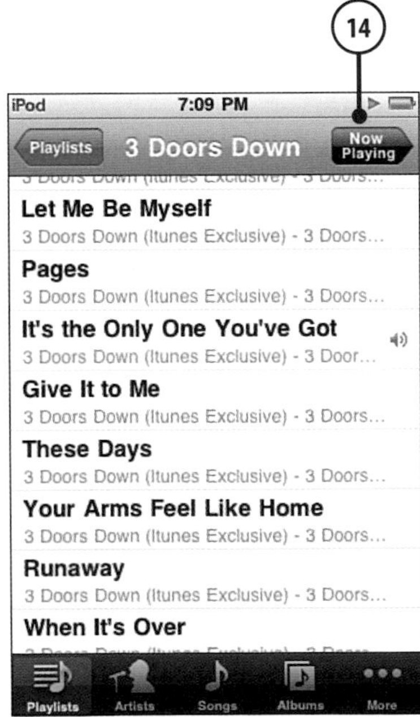

Viewing Albums

As soon as you play a song from the Track List view screen, you jump to Album mode. From that point on, you work only with the album from which the current song came. For example, if you play a playlist, switch to Track List view and play a different song on the same album, you change the content to only that album, so the next song that plays is the next one on the album, not the next one in the playlist. When you tap the Return button, you move to the album's screen instead of the playlist's screen. If you view only the song's information or give it a rating in Track List view, when you move back to the Cover view, you still work with the original source, such as a playlist.

Controlling Audio Content Quickly

While the touch is perfect for listening to audio content, you obviously will use it for a lot more than just that function. Of course, you can always get back to the Music app by moving to the Home screen and tapping the Music button. However, this requires more steps than necessary. There are faster ways to control your music; which you use depends on if your iPod is Locked/Asleep or you are doing something with it.

Controlling Audio When the iPod Is Locked

When audio is playing and your iPod locks, it would be a hassle to move back to the Music app to control that audio; you'd have to tap the Home button or Sleep/Wake button to wake the iPod up, slide the Unlock slider, and then move to the Music app (which can require several steps depending on what you were last doing). There is a faster way.

1. Wake the iPod by pressing the Sleep/Wake or Home button.
2. When the Locked screen appears, press the Home button twice. Album art for the currently playing audio appears along with basic playback tools. (You can also jump directly to the playback controls by pressing the Home button twice when the iPod is asleep/locked.)
3. Use the playback tools to control the tunes. These work just like they do on the Now Playing screen.

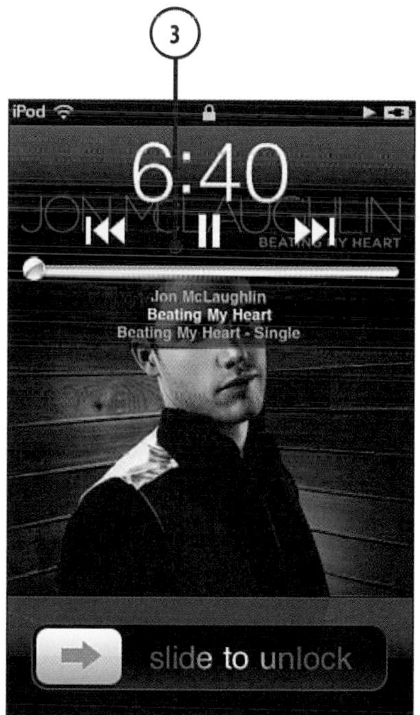

More Control

After a period of time passes without you using them, the playback tools are hidden and you see only the album art. To restore the tools, press the Home button twice. You can also hide the tools by pressing the Home button twice. For example, if you keep the iPod in your pocket, you might want to hide the tools before you put it back in there to prevent the tool's buttons from activating accidentally.

Controlling Audio When You Do Something Else

Audio plays in the background when you switch to a different app, which is a good thing. You can control the audio by going back to the Music app. One way to do this is to press the Home button once to move back to the Home screen and then tap the Music button, but if you don't have the Music app placed at the bottom of the Home screen, you might have to move to a different Home screen to tap it. This works fine, but you can use the App toolbar to jump directly to the Music app, regardless of where its icon is stored. Press the Home button twice; the App toolbar appears. Tap the Music button to move into the Music app; you return to the screen you were on the last time you used that application. You may need to drag to the left or right on the App toolbar to see the Music app icon.

You can also browse all the way to the left on the App toolbar to expose playback controls instead of moving into the Music app.

On Music and Locked iPods

When you wake up an iPod and audio is not playing, you see its wallpaper image. If audio is playing, you see the album art for that audio instead. In either case, if you press the Home button twice the playback tools appear. If no audio is currently playing, you can start the most recently selected content again; to change the source of content, you need to go back into the Music app.

Finding and Listening to Podcasts

An iPod touch is a great way to listen to your podcasts. Like all other audio functions, you first find the podcast you want to listen to and then use iPod touch's audio playback controls to hear it.

1. On the Home screen, tap the Music button.

More Episodes

If you tap Get More Episodes, you move into the iTunes application where you can find and download more episodes of the podcast or add different podcasts to your iPod touch. This is covered in Chapter 3.

2. Tap the More button.
3. Tap Podcasts. The Podcasts screen appears, showing you the podcasts available to you.
4. Browse or search for a podcast to which you want to listen.
5. Select a podcast by tapping it. The list of episodes for that podcast is shown; the name of the list screen is the name of the podcast. Podcasts to which you haven't listened are marked with a blue dot.

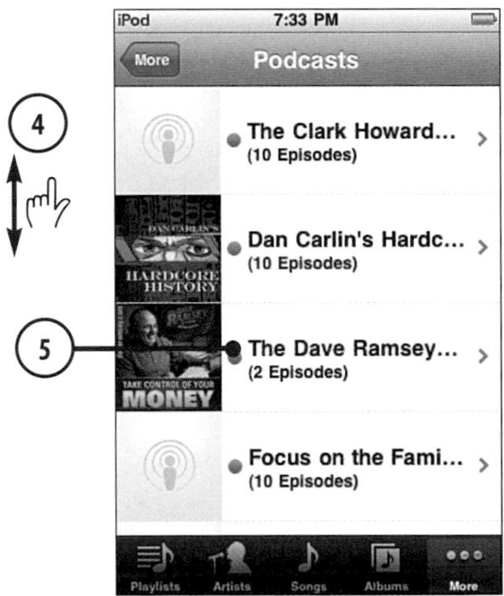

Video Podcasts

When a podcast is a video podcast, the video plays on the Now Playing screen. You can also play video podcasts using the iPod touch's video playback tools, which you learn about in the next chapter.

Audiobooks

Another excellent iPod function is the capability to listen to audiobooks. You can get these from the iTunes Store, Audible.com, and many other locations. After you add audiobooks to your iTunes Library, you determine whether they are moved to iPod touch by using the book-syncing tools. The tools and techniques for listening to audiobooks are similar to listening to podcasts.

Podcast Info

If an episode of a podcast includes a text description, that description appears along with the Timeline bar just like lyrics to music.

6. Tap the episode you want to hear. The podcast begins to play, and the Now Playing screen appears.
7. If the Timeline bar isn't showing, tap the screen. The Timeline bar appears. Some of the controls are the same as for music while some are unique to podcasts.
8. To repeat the last 30 seconds, tap the Repeat button.
9. To change the speed at which the podcast plays, tap the 1x button; the podcast plays at twice the normal speed, and the button shows 2x. Tap it again to play the podcast at one-half speed, and the button shows 1/2x. Tap the button again to return to normal speed.
10. Tap the Envelope button to share the episode you are listening to with someone else. When you tap this, a new email message is created. This message contains a link to the podcast that the recipient can click to access it. You address and complete the message and then send it. (See Chapter 9, "Emailing," for the steps to send email.) The recipient clicks the link to move to the iTunes Store to try out the podcast. (This function is enabled only for those podcasts to which you can subscribe in the iTunes Store.)
11. Use the other controls on the Now Playing screen, which work just as they do when you are playing music.

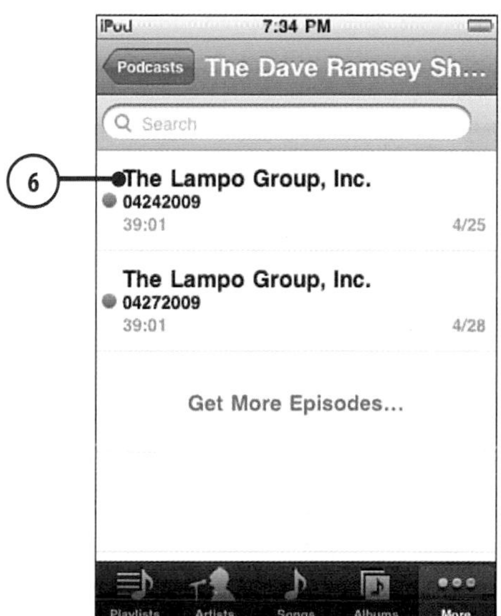

Customizing Your iPod touch for Music

You can use iPod touch as an iPod just fine without performing any of the steps in this section. However, because this book is named *My iPod touch*, you should explore these options to make iPod touch your own.

Configuring the Music Toolbar

The five buttons at the bottom of the Music screen enable you to get to specific content quickly. You can choose four of the buttons that appear on the screen to make accessing content by the categories that are most useful to you even easier and faster.

1. Move to the More screen.
2. Tap Edit. The Configure screen appears.

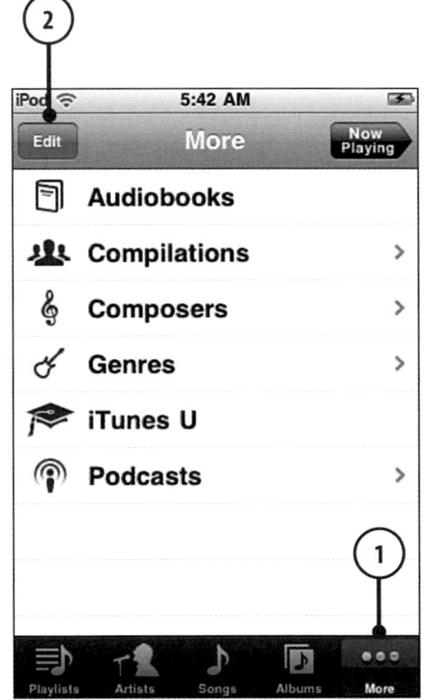

3. Drag a button you want to add to the toolbar to the location of one of the buttons currently there. As you hover over the current button, it lights up to show you that it will be the one replaced when you lift your finger. The button you dragged replaces the button over which you placed it. The original button is moved onto the Configure screen.
4. Repeat step 3 until the four buttons you want to be on the toolbar are there. (The fifth button is always the More button.)
5. Drag the buttons on the toolbar around until they are in the order you want them to be.
6. Tap the Done button.

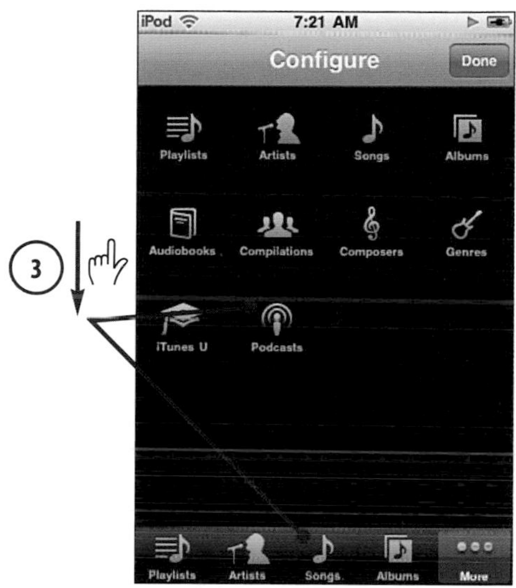

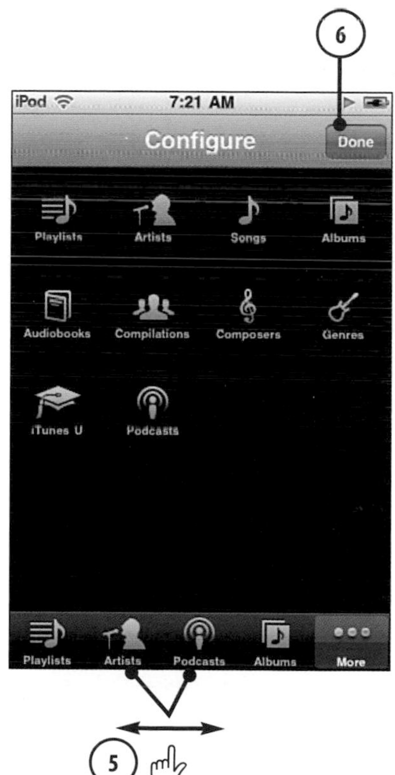

Configuring iPod touch's Music Settings

You can use the Music settings to configure various aspects of iPod touch's audio functionality.

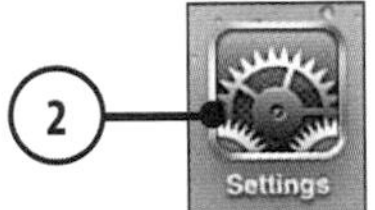

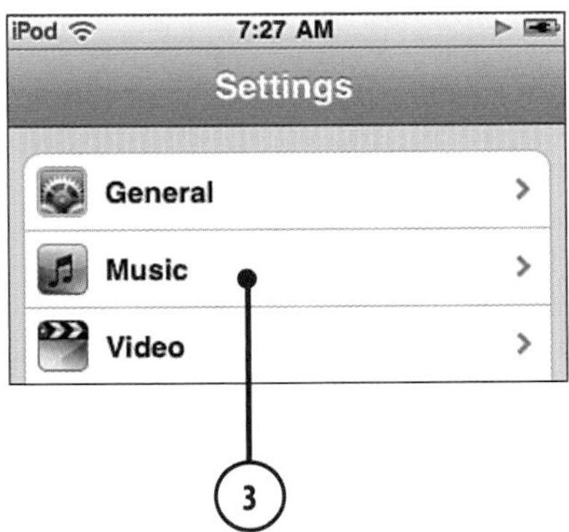

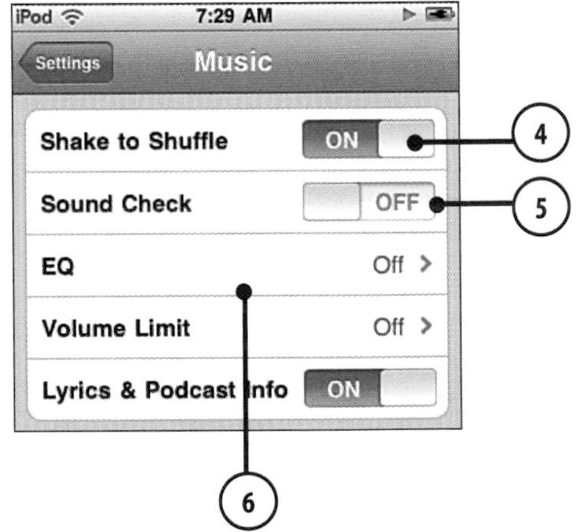

1. Press the Home button to move back to iPod touch's Home.
2. Tap Settings.
3. Tap Music.
4. Tap ON next to Shake to Shuffle if you don't want your iPod touch to shuffle to the next song when you shake it. The status becomes OFF, which means if you shake your iPod touch, songs play in the order they are listed in the source you are playing. Press OFF to enable shuffling by shaking again.
5. Tap Sound Check OFF if you want the touch to attempt to even the volume of the music you play so that all the songs play at about the same relative volume level. Sound Check's status is indicated by OFF or ON. When you tap its current status, Sound Check's status toggles from one to the other.
6. To set an equalizer, tap the EQ bar. The EQ screen appears.

7. Scroll the screen to see all the equalizers available to you.
8. Tap the equalizer you want the iPod touch to use when you play music; the current equalizer is indicated by the check mark. To turn the equalizer off, select Off.
9. Tap Music.
10. To set a limit to the volume level on iPod touch, tap Volume Limit.
11. Drag the volume slider to the point that you want the maximum volume level to be.
12. To lock this control so that it can't be changed without a passcode, tap Lock Volume Limit.

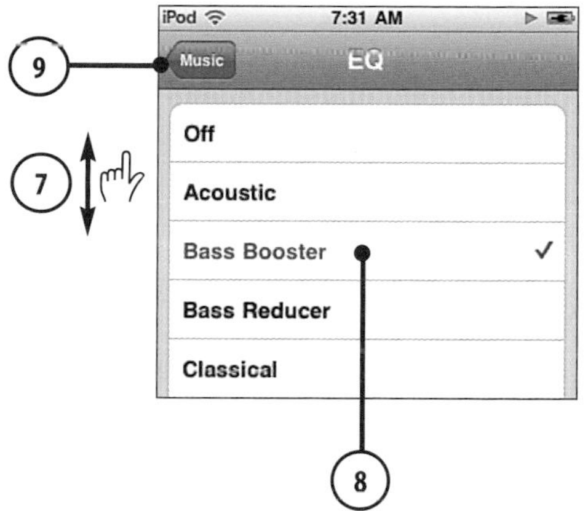

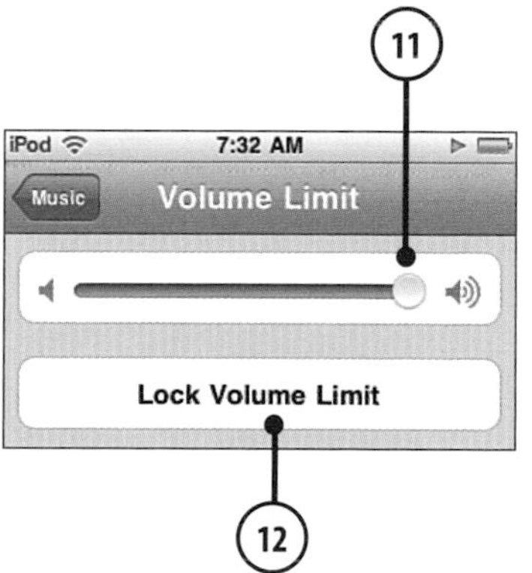

13. Tap a four-digit code.
14. Re-enter the code to confirm it. If the code matches, you return to the Volume Limit screen, and the code is set.
15. To make changes to a locked volume limit, tap Unlock Volume Limit.
16. Enter the code. The volume limit is unlocked, and you can change it again.

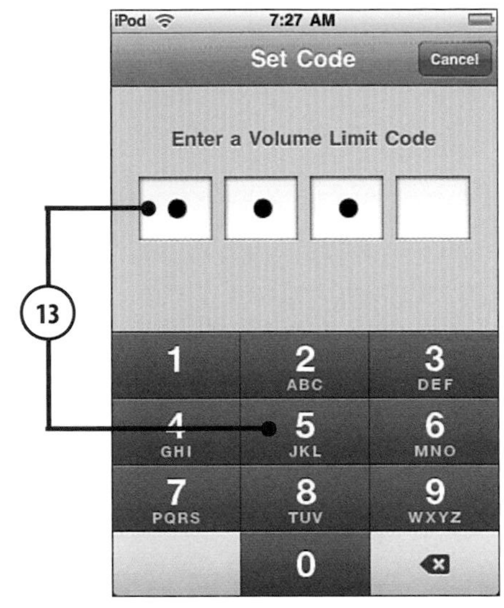

Forgot the Code?

If you forget the passcode, you can reset or restore iPod touch to clear it. See Chapter 15, "Maintaining an iPod Touch and Solving Problems," to learn how.

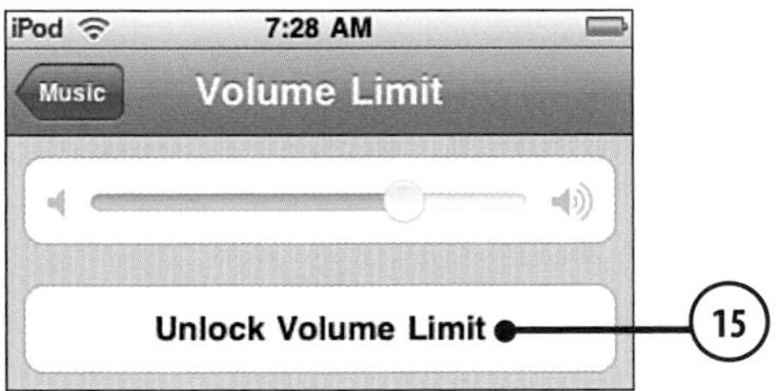

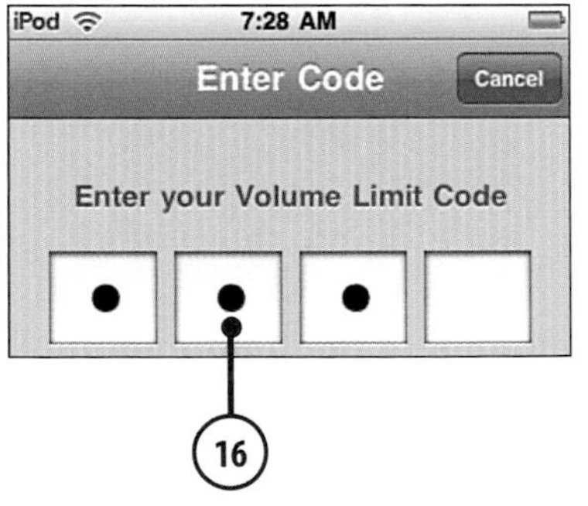

17. Tap Music to move back to the Music Settings screen.

18. To hide lyrics and podcast information on the Now Playing screen, tap Lyrics & Podcast Info ON so its status becomes off. When disabled, you always see the album art for whatever is playing. To show lyrics again, tap OFF so its status becomes ON.

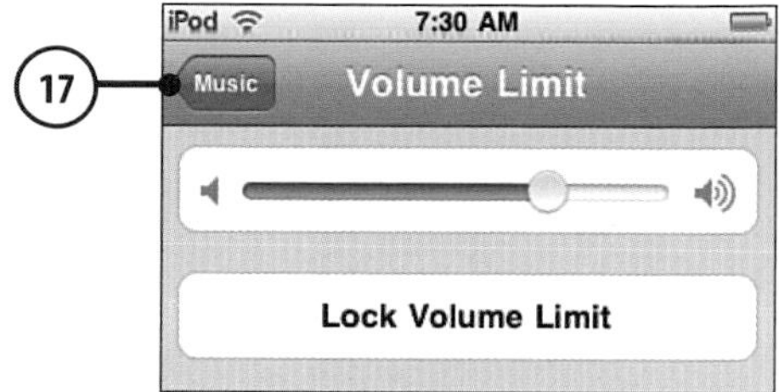

Ping

When it comes to Ping, if you think iTunes meets FaceBook, you'll have the gist of it. Ping enables you to keep information of events and items of interest about people you follow (such as bands or friends) and to keep people informed of things musical of interest to you by allowing people to follow you. You can access Ping using iTunes on a computer and through the iTunes app on your iPod touch.

To get started, enable and configure Ping using iTunes on a computer, as follows:

1. If you aren't signed into your iTunes Store account, sign in.
2. Select Ping on the Source list.
3. Click Turn On Ping.
4. Enter your Apple ID (if necessary), enter your password, and click OK. You move to the Create My Profile page.
5. Complete your profile by creating a nickname, uploading a photo, and entering the other information; then click Continue.
6. On the second page of the Create My Profile form, configure how you want music displayed on your profile, such as Automatically display all music I like, rate, review, or purchase, and click Continue.
7. Configure your privacy settings by choosing to allow people to follow you (and if so, whether you have to grant permission to allow someone to follow you) or not; then click Done. Ping is now set up within iTunes and you see the Welcome to Ping screen.

Once you've set up ping, you can follow people or have people follow you.

To follow artists or other Ping users, perform the following steps:

1. Enter the name of the artist or person you want to follow and press Enter (Windows) or Return (Mac). The artists and other people who can be followed and match your search are shown. (You can also browse for artists to follow by using the links just under the Search tool.)

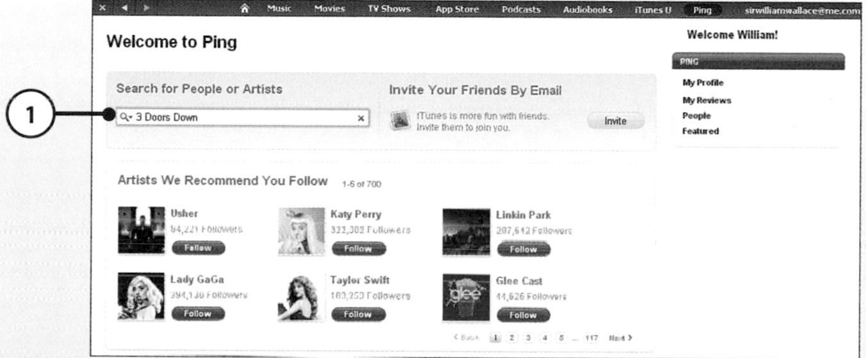

2. Click the Follow button for the artist or person you want to follow. If the artist or person doesn't require authorization for you to follow them, you start following the artist or person immediately. If permission is required, the artist or person has to respond positively to a confirmation email before you will be able to start following them. The status of that person will show Request sent until your request has been approved.

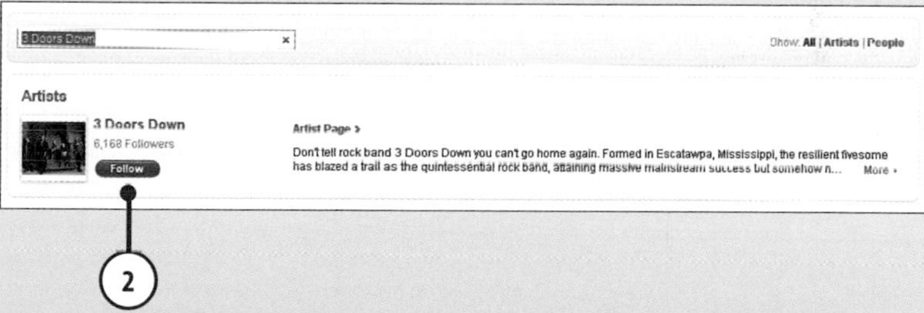

3. Click the Preview Page link. You move back to the Ping Home page and can add more artists and people to follow.

To invite someone to follow you, perform the following steps:

1. Click the Invite button on the Ping Home page.

2. Fill out the Invitation form and click Invite. An email is sent to the person with the message you created. They can then move to Ping and start following you.

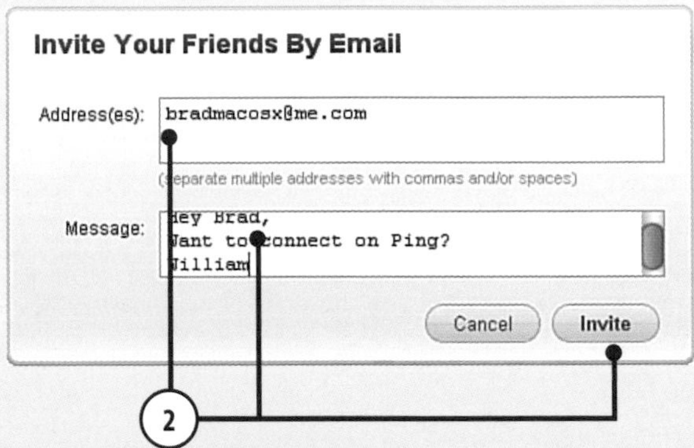

After Ping is set up, here are some pointers for you to start using it:

- When you are following people and people are following you, when you move to the Ping Home page, you see activity related to those people. This can be announcements, new releases of music, and so on. You can also comment on the events, view all comments, and so on.

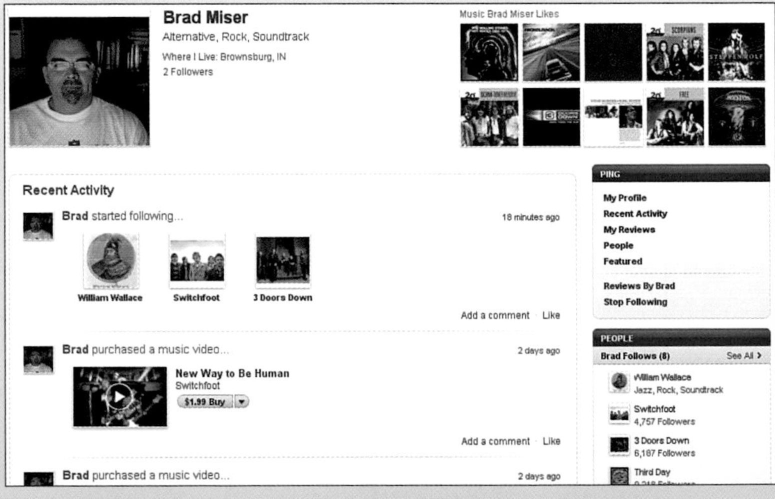

- If you click the People link located in the upper-right corner of the Ping window, you will see two tabs. The People I Follow shows the artists and people you are following. If you click the highlighted name, you move to the artist's or person's profile page where you can see various information about them, recent activity, and so on (depending on the security settings of their account). Click the People Who Follow Me tab to see what is happening with people who are following you. In either case, you can explore activity by browsing the screen or clicking links, such as My Reviews to read reviews the person has posted.

- To change your profile at any time, click the My Profile link in the PING section on the Home page, click the Edit Profile link, and use the resulting screens to make and save your changes.
- At press time, Ping wasn't available in the iTunes app on iPod touches, but it probably will be by the time you read this. To access it, open the iTunes app and tap the Ping tab at the bottom of the screen. The Ping screen has three tabs: Activity shows activity for people you are following. The People tab shows you a list of everyone you follow; you can tap a person to see details. The My Profile tab enables you to change your profile.
- If you want to follow me, search for Brad Miser and click the Follow button.

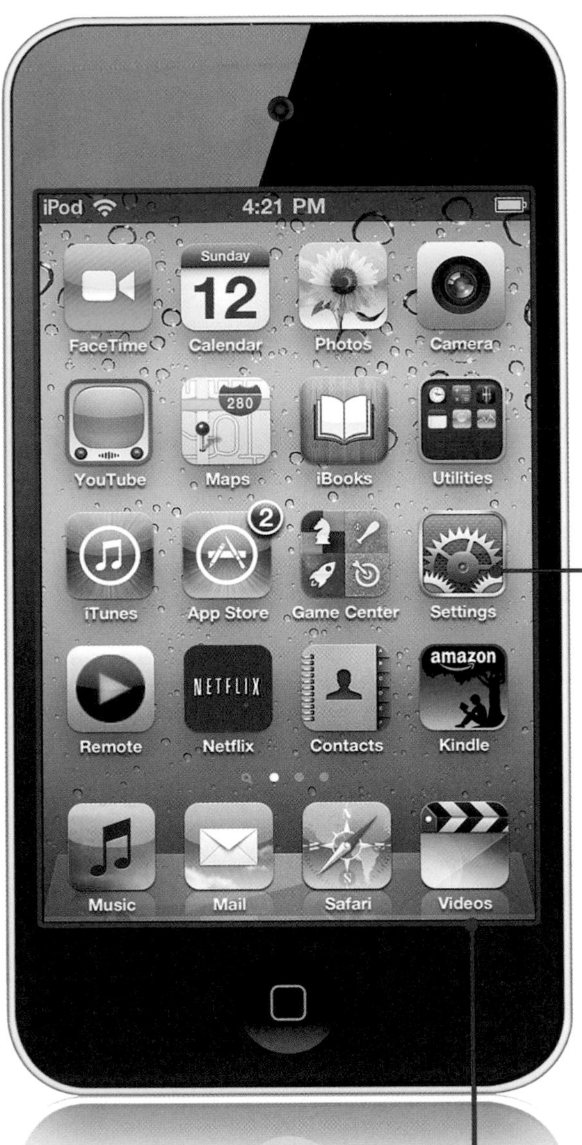

Tap to configure iPod touch for video

Tap to enjoy movies, TV shows, and other video right in the palm of your hand

In this chapter, you explore all the video functionality the iPhoto touch offers. The topics include the following:

- → Finding and watching video content, including movies, TV shows, and video podcasts
- → Configuring iPod touch video settings

6

Watching Movies, TV Shows, and Other Video

Your iPod touch is a great way to enjoy different types of video, including movies, episodes of your favorite TV series, and video podcasts. Be prepared to be amazed; the high quality and portability more than make up for the relatively small screen size (well, relatively small in today's world of 50-inch+ TVs!). Like music and other content, the first step is to find the video you want to watch. Then you use iPod touch's video tools to watch that video. You can also configure some aspects of how your iPod touch plays video content.

Finding and Watching Video

Like listening to audio, watching video is a two-step process. First, find the content you want to watch. Second, select that content and play it.

Finding Video

If you read Chapter 5, "Listening to Music, Podcasts, and Other Audio," you pretty much already know how to find video content on your iPod touch because this is quite similar to finding audio content.

1. On the Home screen, tap the Videos button. The Videos screen appears, showing you the video content on the iPod.
2. Scroll the screen to see all the video content, which is organized by type, such as Movies, TV Shows, Music Videos, and Video Podcasts. Content you haven't watched yet is marked with a blue dot. If you have multiple episodes of a TV series, you see the name of the series and the number of

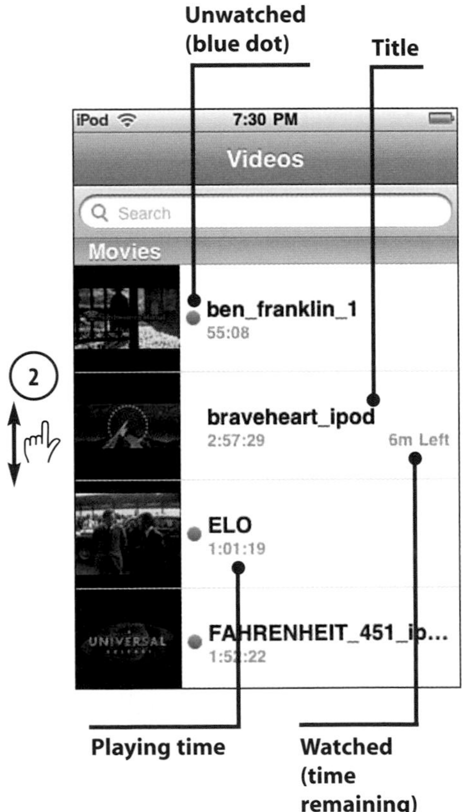

episodes.

3. To watch one of the episodes of a TV series of which more than one is stored on your iPod touch, tap the series. You see the episodes of the series that are available.
4. To watch a movie, an episode of a TV series, or a music video, tap it.
5. Rotate the iPod touch 90 degrees.

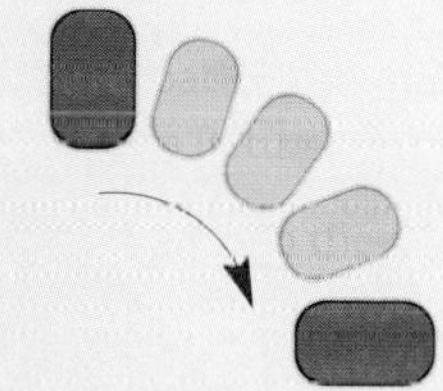

The screen rotates, and the content begins to play.

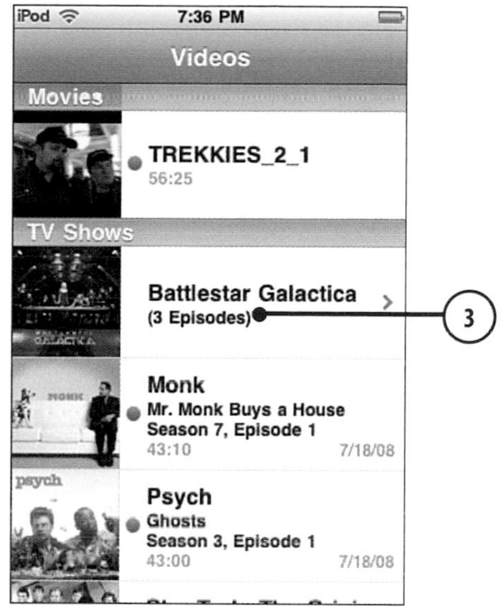

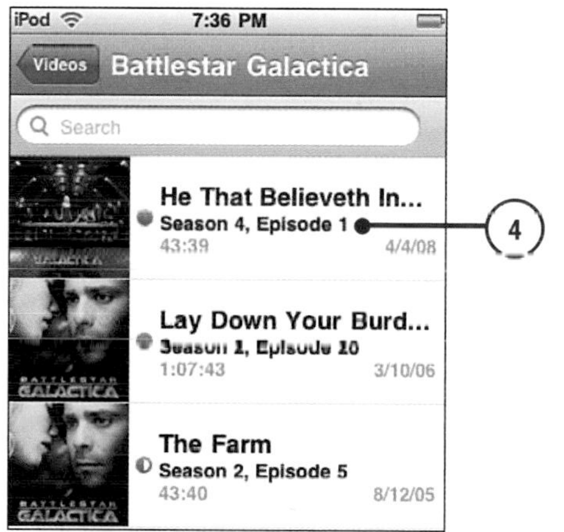

6. Watch and control the video; see the next section for details of controlling video.

Watching Video

When you play video, it is always oriented in landscape mode so that it can fill the screen.

1. Tap the video you are watching. The video controls appear.

Scale This

If native scale of the video is not the same proportion as the iPod touch screen and you play it in its original scale, the video might not fill the screen. When you scale the video, it fills the screen, but some content might be cut off.

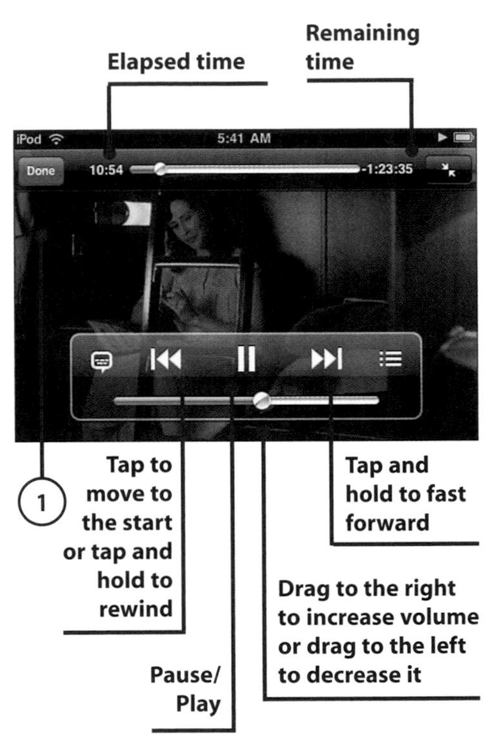

2. Drag the playhead to the right to move ahead or to the left to move backward.
3. Tap the Scale button to scale the video to fit the screen or to show it in its native scale. After a few seconds, the video controls disappear.

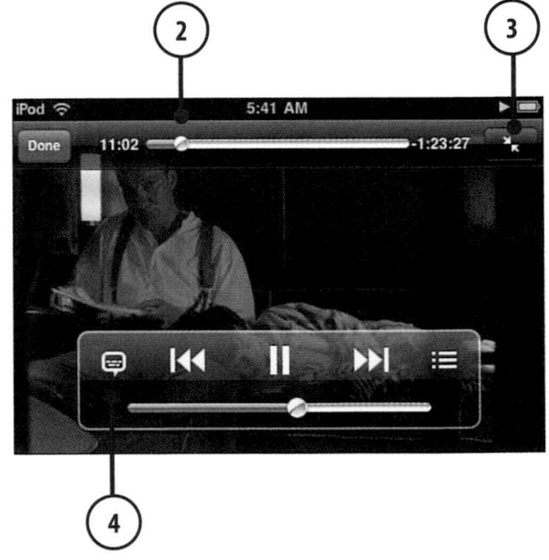

4. To change the language for a movie or TV show, tap the Language button. (Not all movies support this feature.)
5. Tap the language you want to use.
6. Tap Done.

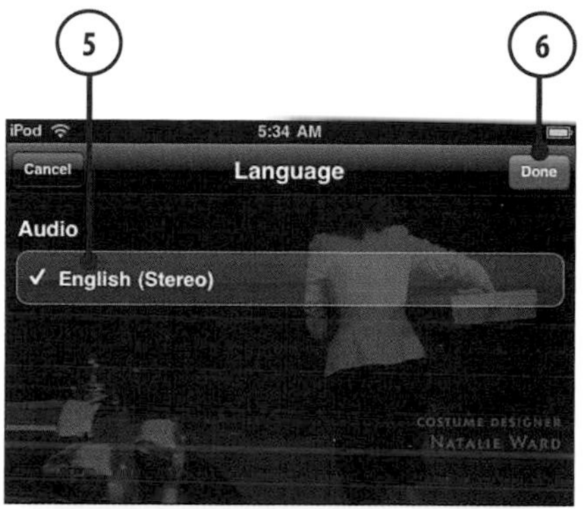

Remember Where You Were

For most kinds of video, the iPod touch remembers where you left off. So if you stop a movie and restart it, the iPod touch picks up where you left off even if you've done a lot of other things since. (You can disable this feature as you learn later in this chapter.)

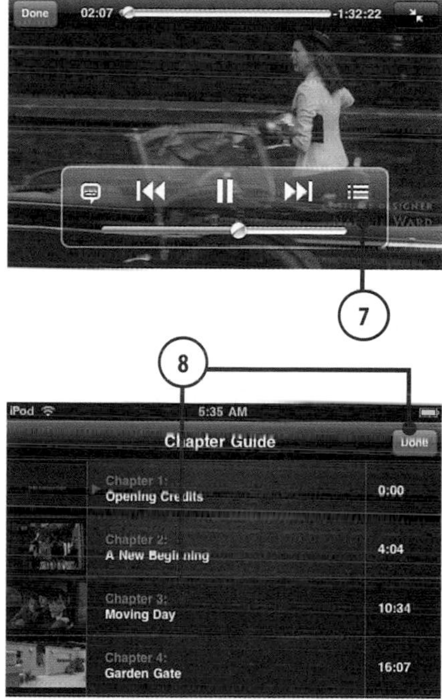

7. To move to a specific chapter in the video, tap the Chapter button. (Not all video content supports this feature.) You move to the movie's Chapter Guide.
8. Tap the chapter you want to watch or tap Done to return to the video at the same location. You move back to the viewing screen, and the video plays.
9. When you finish watching, tap Done. You move back to the Videos screen.

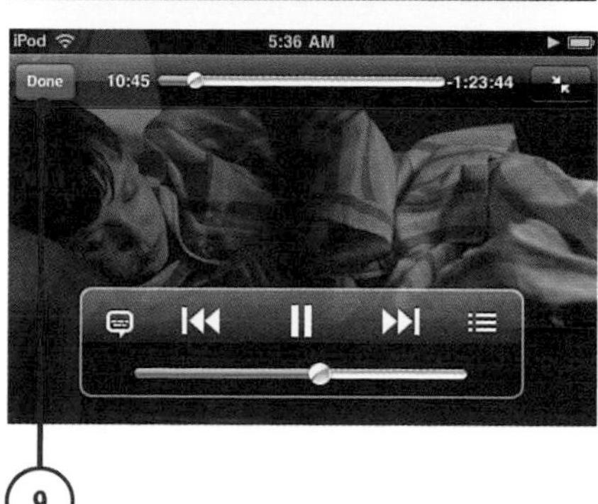

Watching Rented Movies

As you learned in Chapter 3, "Moving Audio, Video, Books, and Photos onto Your iPod touch," you can rent movies from the iTunes Store and move them onto an iPod touch. The steps to watch a rented movie are the same as watching other kinds of video.

When you move to a rented movie, you see important time information about its viewing status and can play it.

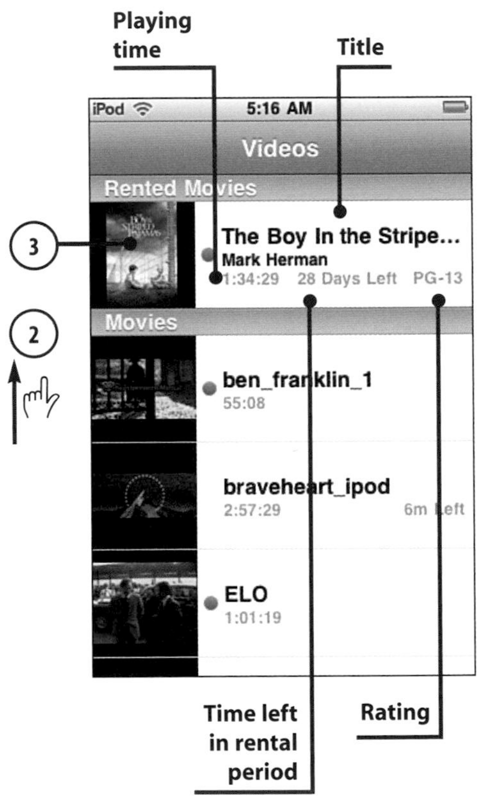

1. On the Home screen, tap the Videos button.
2. Scroll to the top of the screen, where you see the Rented Movies section. Under each rented movie, you see the time remaining in the rental period (days if you haven't watched the movie yet).
3. Tap the rented movie you want to watch. You're prompted with a message to let you know that after you start the movie, you have 24 hours to watch it.
4. Tap OK. The movie starts to play.

5. Use the video controls to play the movie.
6. To stop the movie, tap Done. You move back to the Videos screen.
7. Note how much time you have left to watch the movie, shown in hours. When this period expires, the movie disappears from your iPod touch.

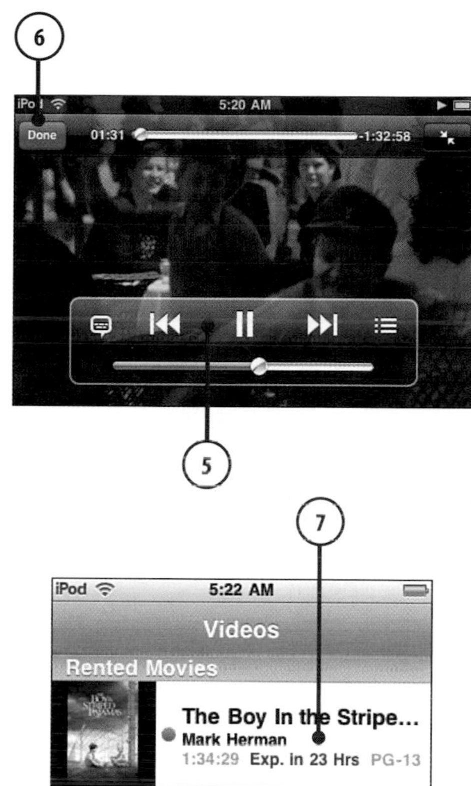

Rental Caveats

You need to be aware that rented movies have two time limitations. One is that you can keep rented movies on your iPod touch for 30 calendar days, starting from the time you downloaded the rented movies to your computer (not from the time when you synced the rented content from your computer to your iPod touch). The second limitation is that when you start playing a rented movie, you have 24 hours to finish watching it. (Though you can watch it as many times as you want within that 24-hour period.) When either of these time periods expires, the rented content disappears from whatever device it is on.

Another difference between rented content and other kinds of content is that rented content can exist on only one device. When you move rented content from your computer to your iPod touch, it disappears from the computer (unlike music or movies you own that remain in your iTunes Library where you listen to or view that content). This also means that rented content can be on only one iPod touch, iPhone, or other kind of iPod at any given time. However, you can move rented movies back and forth among devices as much as you want. So you can start watching a movie on your iPod touch and move it back to your computer to finish watching it (within the 24-hour viewing period, of course).

Watching Video Podcasts

Like the audio podcasts you learned about in the previous chapter, video podcasts are episodic content, though as you can tell by their name, these episodes contain both audio and video content. Another difference is that there are quite a number of podcasts that have only one episode. Watching a video podcast is similar to watching other kinds of video content.

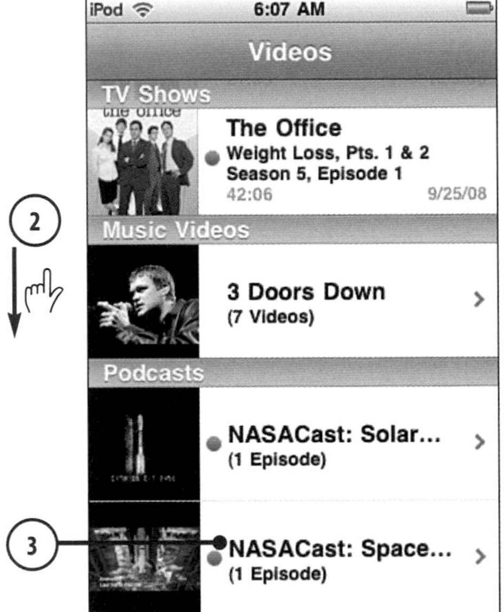

1. On the Home screen, tap the Videos button.
2. Scroll down until you see the Podcasts section.
3. Tap the video podcast you want to watch. You move to the episode list for that podcast.
4. Scroll or search to find the episode you want to view.
5. Tap the episode you want to watch. You move to the viewing screen, and the episode begins to play.

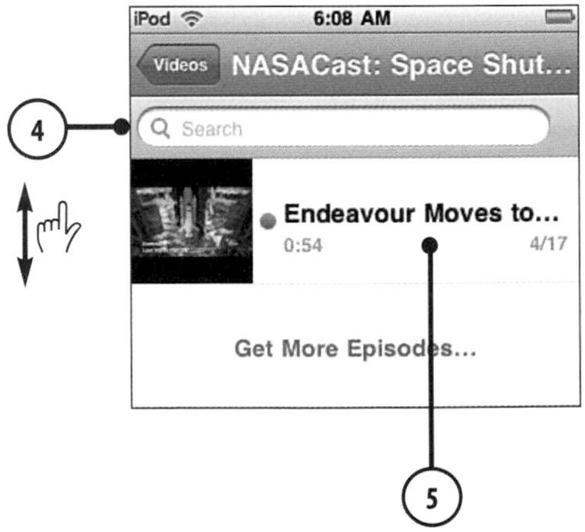

6. Use the video controls to watch the episode.

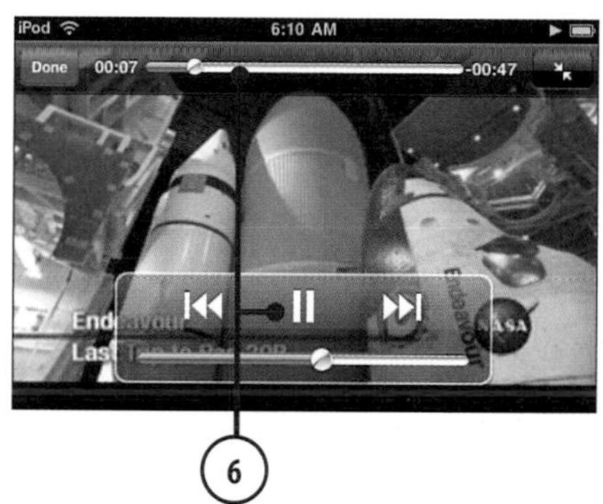

Deleting Video

If you want to free up some of the iPod touch's memory for other things, you can delete video directly from the iPod touch:

1. Move to the Videos screen.
2. Drag left or right on the video you want to delete. The Delete button appears.

Gone but Not Forgotten

When you've added video content to the touch through syncing with your computer, deleting video from the iPod removes it only from the iPod touch. The video content remains in your iTunes Library. You can add video back to your iPod touch again by including it in a future sync. In fact, unless you remove the video content from the sync settings for the iPod touch, it will be moved back onto the touch the next time you sync. If the video content is stored only on your iPod, such as a purchase you've made using the iTunes app since your last sync or a rented movie, it will be permanently deleted. So be careful before tapping that Delete button.

3. Tap Delete. The content is deleted from the iPod touch.

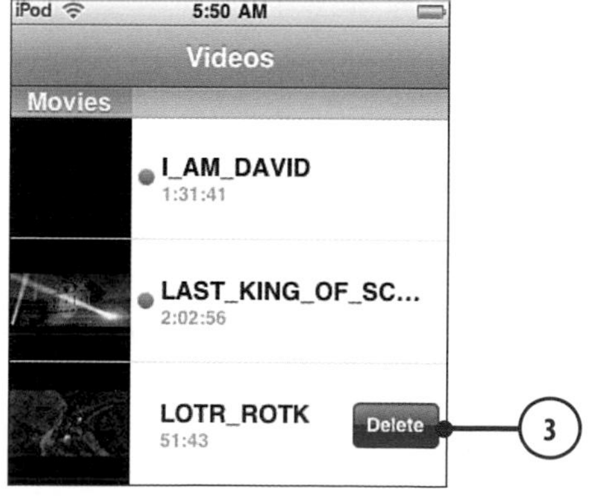

Music Videos

You can access music videos from the Music Videos section of the Videos screen or from the Music screens, such as playlists, artists, and so on. When you play a music video from the Videos screen, it plays in the normal movie player. When you play a music video from Music screens, it plays on the Now Playing screen; instead of seeing album art on the screen, you see the music video.

Configuring iPod touch's Video Settings

There are a few settings you use to configure various aspects of iPod touch's video functionality.

1. Tap the Home button to move to iPod touch's Home screen.
2. Tap Settings.
3. Tap Video.
4. Tap Start Playing.

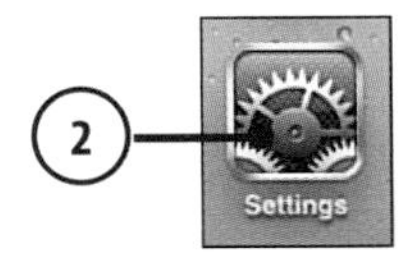

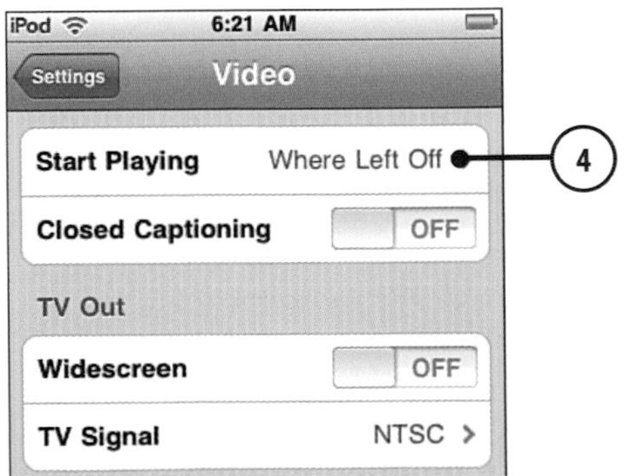

5. Tap Where Left Off to have your iPod touch remember where you last were in a video, so it resumes at the same location when you play it again, or tap From Beginning to have your iPod touch always start video content playback from the beginning.

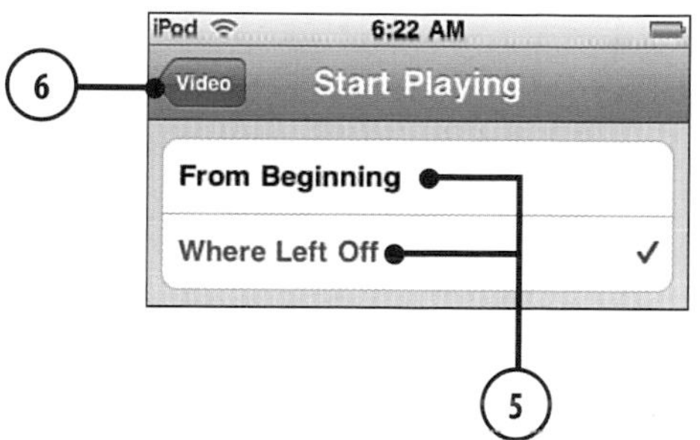

6. Tap Video to move back to the Video screen.
7. To enable or disable Closed Captioning on video, tap the Closed Captioning button. Its status is indicated by ON or OFF. When you tap the button, it toggles between the two states.

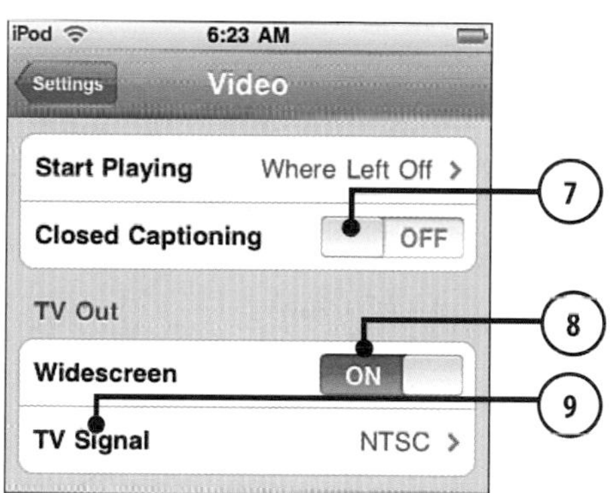

8. To enable or disable widescreen playback, tap the Widescreen button. Its status is indicated by ON or OFF. When you tap the button, it also toggles between the two states.
9. To select a specific output format, tap TV Signal.
10. To choose the NTSC format (for U.S. televisions for example), tap NTSC, or to choose the PAL format (European televisions are some that use this format), tap PAL.
11. Tap Video to return to the Video screen.

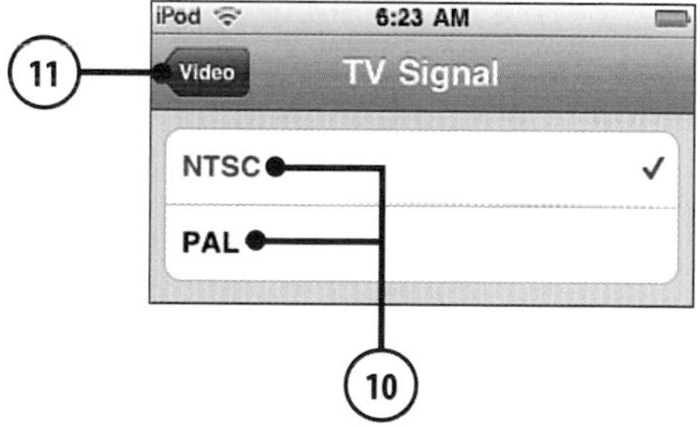

Tap to configure Safari

Tap to have the World Wide Web in the palm of your hand

In this chapter, you explore the amazing web browsing functionality your iPod touch has to offer. The topics include the following:

→ Configuring Safari settings
→ Browsing the Web

Surfing the Web

Wouldn't it be nice to browse the Web wherever you are using a real web browser instead of the modified browsers available on most cell phones or other small, mobile devices? And wouldn't it be nice not to have to be concerned with pages being formatted for proper display on a mobile device? Obviously, considering you have an iPod touch, you know you have all these niceties because iPod touch has a full-featured web browser: Safari. You can browse the Web whenever and wherever you are connected to a Wi-Fi network that offers an Internet connection.

Configuring Safari Settings

Before you surf, take a couple of minutes to configure iPod touch's Safari settings:

1. On the Home screen, tap Settings.
2. Scroll down the page until you see Safari.
3. Tap Safari.
4. To leave Google as the default search engine, skip to step 7. To change the default search engine, tap Search Engine.
5. Tap Yahoo! or Bing. The engine you tapped is now checked to show you that it is the selected search engine.
6. Tap Safari.

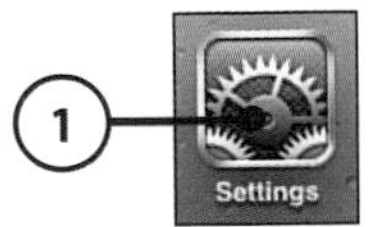

7. Tap AutoFill. This is a great feature that enables you to quickly complete forms on the Web by automatically filling in key information for you.

8. To use contact information stored on your iPod touch to complete forms, tap OFF next to Use Contact Info. Its status becomes ON.

Contact!

To learn how to configure and use contacts, see Chapter 8, "Managing Contacts."

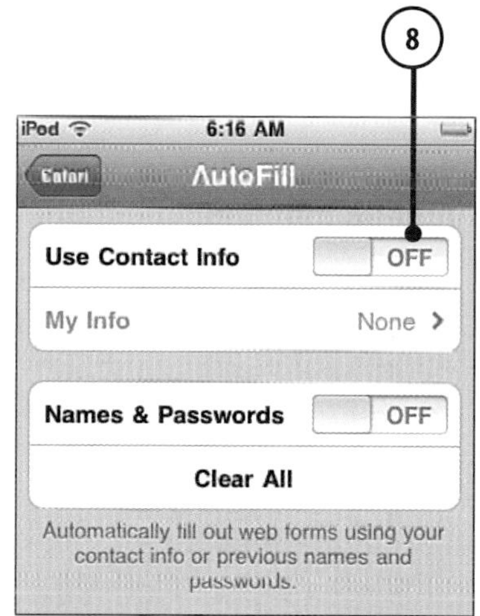

9. Tap My Info. (The first time you configure AutoFill, you can jump immediately to your Contacts and can skip this step.)

Indented Name

If the contact application you use supports this feature (such as the Mac's Address Book), your primary contact information (on the My Card card in Address Book) is indented on the All Contacts list to help you identify it more easily.

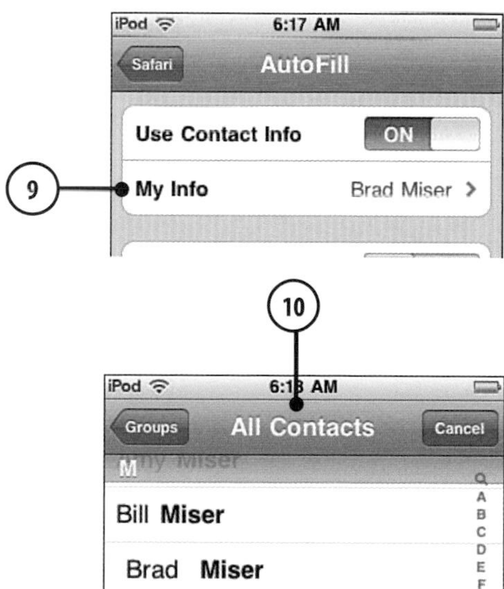

10. Find and tap your contact information. This tells Safari what information to fill in for you on forms, such as your name, address, and so on. You move back to the AutoFill screen and see your name in the My Info section.

11. To enable Safari to remember user names and passwords for websites you log into, tap OFF next to Names & Passwords. Its status becomes ON.

12. Tap Safari.

It's Not All Good

Be careful about allowing Safari to remember usernames and passwords if you access websites with sensitive information, such as a banking website. If Safari remembers this information for you, anyone who uses your iPod touch can log into your account on these sites because Safari automatically fills in the required information to log in. If you lose control of your iPod touch, your sensitive information might be compromised. To remove the usernames and passwords stored on your iPod touch, tap Clear All on the AutoFill screen. When you confirm by tapping Clear AutoFill Data, all the information stored is deleted.

13. Scroll down so you see the Security section.
14. If you don't want Safari to warn you when you visit websites that might be fraudulent, tap ON next to Fraud Warning so its status becomes OFF. Unless you have a good reason to disable this feature, you should leave it turned on.
15. To disable JavaScript functionality, tap JavaScript ON. Its status becomes OFF to show you it is no longer active. Some web pages might not work properly with JavaScript turned off, but it is more secure.
16. To disable pop-up blocking, tap Block Pop-Ups ON. Its status becomes OFF, and pop-ups are no longer blocked. Some websites won't work properly with pop-ups blocked, so you can use this setting to temporarily enable pop-ups while you use a specific website that requires them.
17. To configure how cookies are handled, tap Accept Cookies.

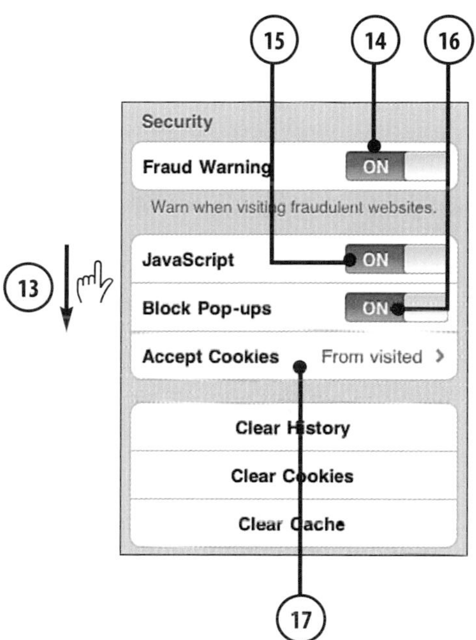

18. Tap the kind of cookies you want to accept. The Never option blocks all cookies. The From visited option accepts cookies only from sites you visit. This is the setting I recommend you choose because it enables websites you visit to store necessary information on your iPod. The Always option accepts all cookies; I don't recommend this option because if you get directed to a site by another site that you didn't intend to visit, its cookies can be stored on your iPod touch.

19. Tap Safari.

20. Scroll to the bottom of the screen.

21. To clear the history of websites you have visited, tap Clear History.

22. Tap Clear History at the prompt. This removes the websites you have visited from your history list. The list starts over, so the next site you visit is added to your history list again.

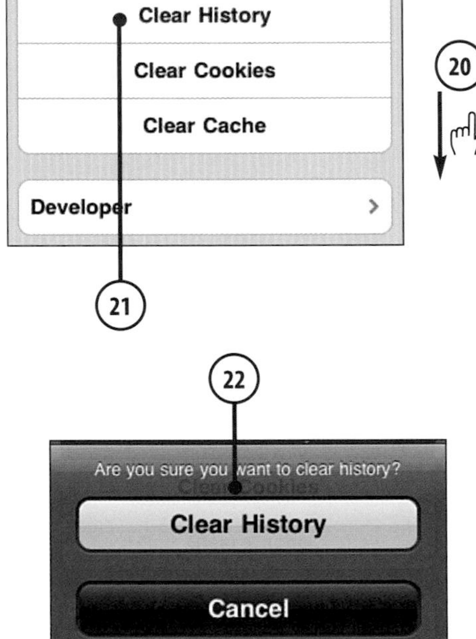

It Never Happened

To remove the information associated with your web browsing, perform steps 22 through 27 and also clear the AutoFill data as described in the previous "It's Not All Good" sidebar.

23. To remove all cookies from iPod touch, tap Clear Cookies.

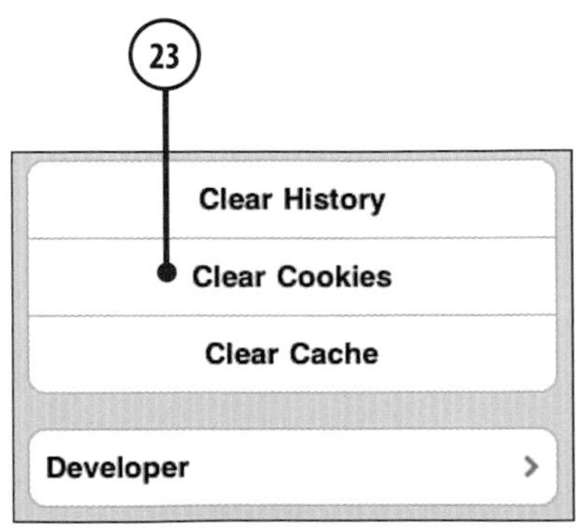

24. Tap Clear Cookies at the prompt. Any sites that require cookies to function re-create the cookies they need the next time you visit them, assuming that you allow cookies.

25. To clear the web browser's cache, tap Clear Cache. The cache stores information from websites so that you can return to that information without downloading it from the Web again.

26. When prompted, tap Clear Cache to confirm the action. The next time you visit a site, its content is downloaded to the iPod touch again.

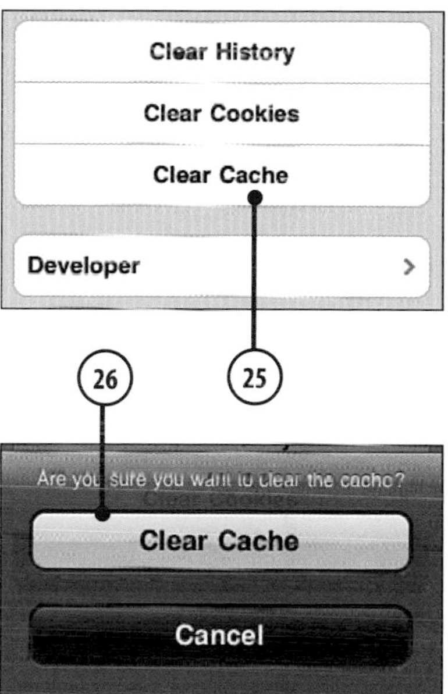

Developer?

The Developer setting enables the Debug Console to be turned ON or OFF. The Debug Console enables website developers to check their websites on an iPod touch for errors so that those sites can be updated to work properly with an iPod touch. If you aren't a website developer, you probably won't need to use this tool. If you are a website developer, enable the tool when you evaluate your website using Safari on an iPod touch.

Got Internet Connection?

An iPod touch gets to the Web via a Wi-Fi network that offers an Internet connection. To learn how to connect an iPod touch to Wi-Fi, see Chapter 2, "Connecting to the Internet, Bluetooth Devices, and iPods/iPhones/iPads."

Browsing the Web on an iPod touch

If you've used a web browser on a computer before, using Safari on an iPod touch will be a familiar experience. If you've not used a web browser before, don't worry because using Safari on an iPod touch is simple and intuitive.

Syncing Bookmarks

You can synchronize your Internet Explorer favorites or Safari bookmarks on a Windows PC or Safari bookmarks on a Mac to your iPod touch so that you have the same set of bookmarks available on your iPod touch that you do on your computer and vice versa. You can do this via the sync process or wirelessly using MobileMe. See Chapter 4, "Configuring and Synchronizing Information on an iPod touch," for details. If you use Internet Explorer or Safari, it's a good idea to synchronize before you start browsing on your iPod touch so that you avoid typing URLs or re-creating bookmarks.

Moving to Websites via Bookmarks

Using bookmarks that you've moved from a computer onto iPod touch makes it easy to get to websites that are of interest to you. You can also create bookmarks on iPod touch (you learn how later in this section) and use them just like bookmarks you've imported from a computer.

1. On the iPod touch Home screen, tap Safari.
2. Tap the Bookmarks button.

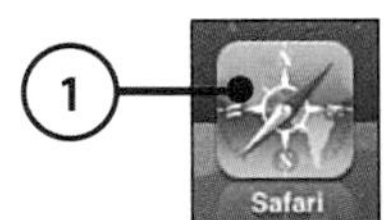

3. Scroll up or down the list of bookmarks.
4. To move to a bookmark, skip to step 9. To open a folder of bookmarks, tap it.

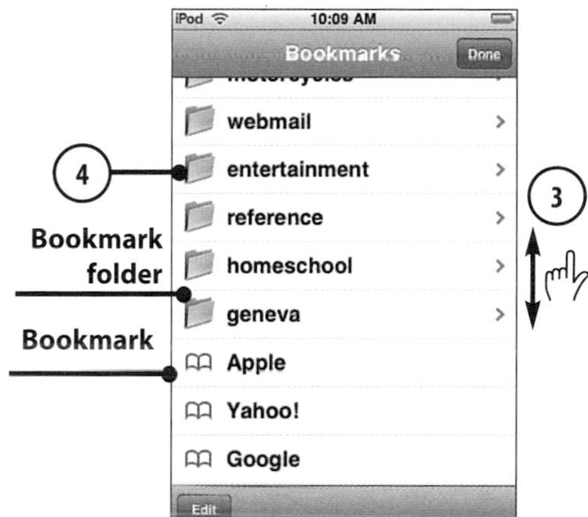

Change Your Mind?

If you decide not to visit a bookmark, tap Done. You return to the page you were previously viewing.

5. Scroll up or down the folder's screen.
6. You can keep drilling down into folders by tapping the folder whose bookmarks you want to see.
7. To return to a previous screen, tap the return button, which is labeled with the name of the current folder you are viewing, the folder you most recently visited, or with Bookmarks if you view a folder on the "top" level of the Bookmarks folder.

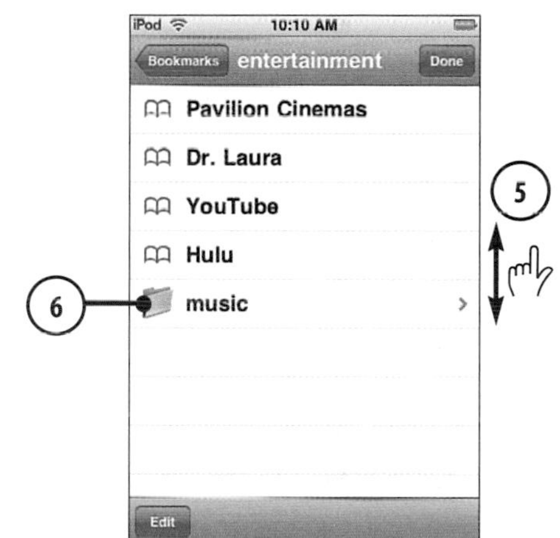

8. Repeat steps 5 through 7 until you see a bookmark you want to visit.
9. Tap the bookmark you want to visit. Safari moves to that website.

10. Use the information in the section "Viewing Websites" later in this chapter to view the web page.

iPod Touch Web Pages

Some websites have been specially formatted for iPhones and iPod touches. These typically have less complex information on each page, so they load faster. When you move to a site like this, you are redirected to the iPod touch version automatically. There is typically a link that takes you to the "regular" version, too. (It's sometimes called the Classic version.) Sometimes the version formatted for handheld devices offers less information or fewer tools than the regular version. Because Safari is a full-featured browser, you can use whichever version you prefer.

Moving to Websites by Typing a URL

Although it might not be fun to type URLs, sometimes that's the only way you have to get to a website.

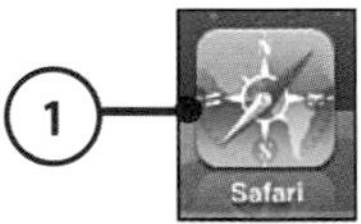

1. On the iPod touch Home screen, tap Safari.

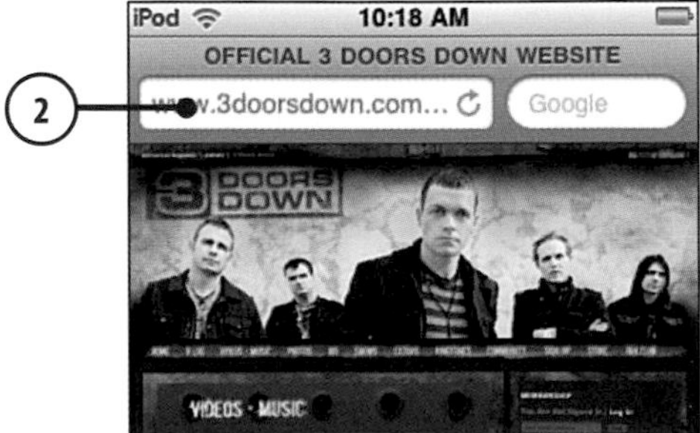

2. Tap in the Address bar. The keyboard appears along with the Search bar. If you've visited a site recently, the URL of the current web page appears in the Address bar, and the page you last visited appears on the screen.

3. If an address appears in the Address bar, tap the Clear (x) button to remove it.

4. Type the URL you want to visit. If it starts with www, you don't have to type "www." As you type, Safari attempts to match what you are typing to a site you have visited previously or to one of your bookmarks and presents a list of those sites to you.

.com for All

Because so many URLs end in .com, there's a handy .com key on the keyboard. You can quickly enter a URL by typing the text before ".com" and then tapping the .com button to complete it.

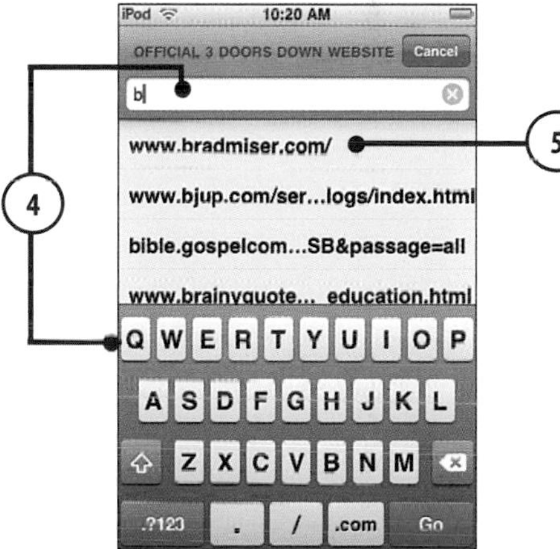

5. If one of the sites shown is the one you want to visit, tap it. You move to that web page; skip to step 8.

6. If Safari doesn't find a match, continue typing until you enter the entire URL.

7. Tap Go. You move to the web page.

8. Use the information in the section that follows to view the web page.

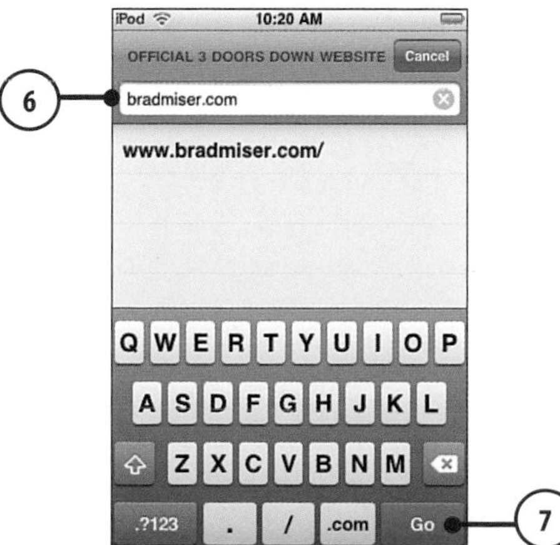

Viewing Websites

Even though your iPod touch is a small device, you'll be amazed at how well it displays web pages designed for larger screens.

1. Use Safari to move to a web page as described in the previous two sections.
2. To scroll a web page, drag your finger right or left, or up or down.
3. To zoom in manually, unpinch your fingers.
4. To zoom in automatically, tap your finger on the screen twice.
5. To zoom out manually, pinch your fingers.
6. To zoom on a column or a figure, tap it twice.

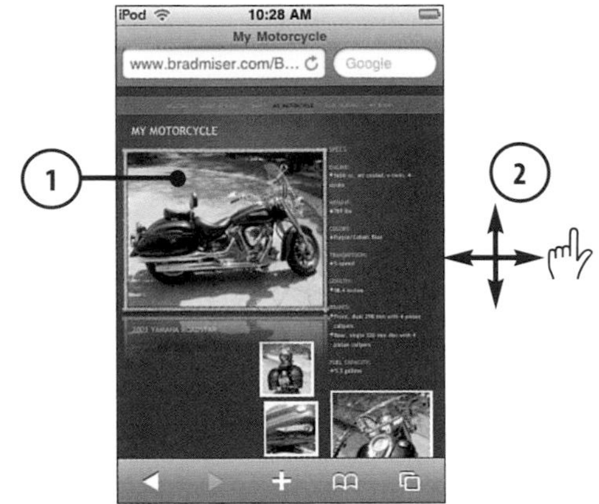

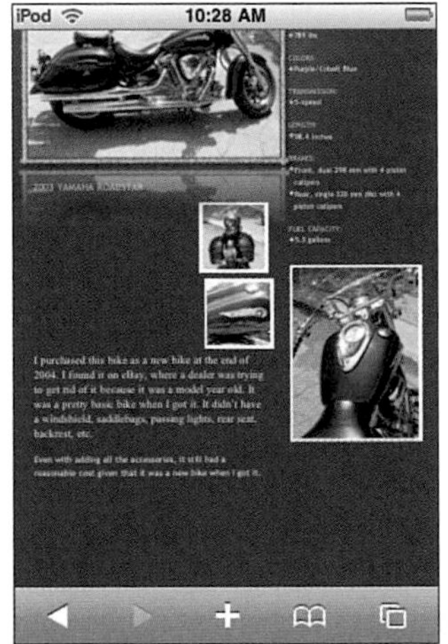

Do More with Links

To see options for a link, tap your finger on it and hold your finger down for a second or so. When you lift your finder, a prompt appears. Tap Open to open the page at which the link points. Tap Open in New Page to open the page in a new Safari window. Tap Copy to copy the link's URL so you can paste it elsewhere, such as in an email message. Tap Cancel to return to the current page and take no action.

7. To move to a link, tap it once. The web page to which the link points opens.

8. Scroll and zoom on the page to read it.

9. To refresh a page, tap Refresh. (Note: while a page is loading, this is the "x" button; tap it to stop the rest of the page from loading.)

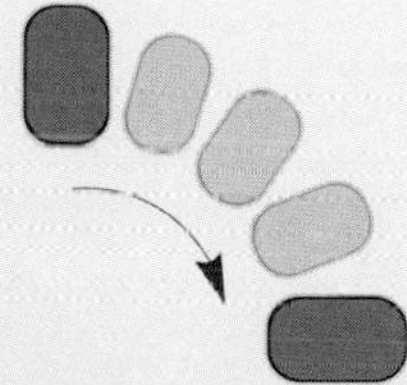

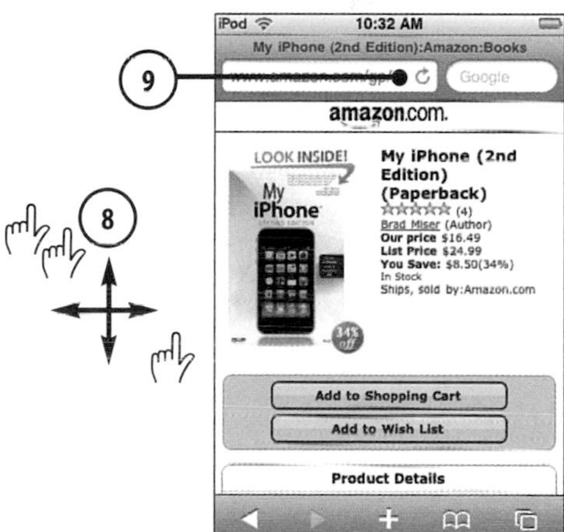

10. To view the web page in landscape mode, rotate the iPod touch 90 degrees.

11. To move to a previous page you've visited, tap Back.

12. To move to a subsequent page, tap Forward.

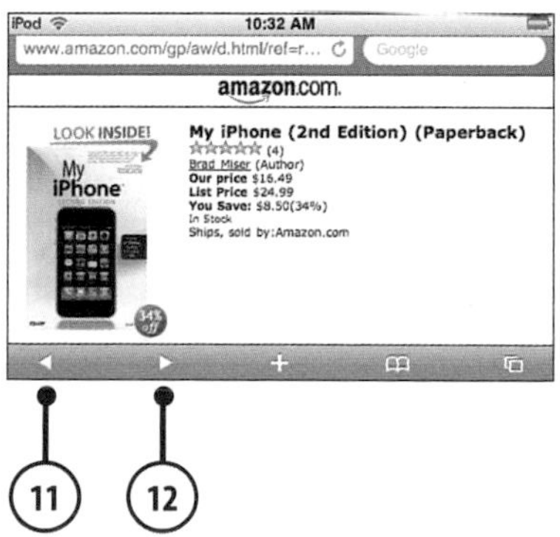

Where Art Thou, Address Bar?

If you lose sight of the Address bar when you scroll pages, tap the status bar, where the time displays, once. You scroll to the top of the screen and can see the Address bar again.

Searching the Web

Earlier you learned that you can set Safari to search the Web using Google, Yahoo!, or Bing by default. Whichever search engine you choose, you search the Web in the same way.

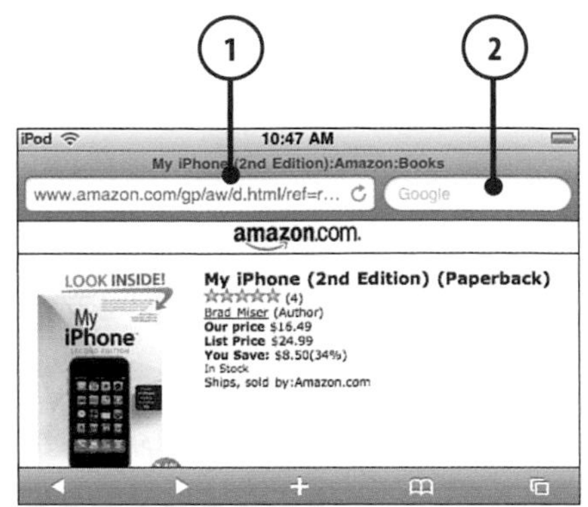

1. Move to a web page.
2. Tap in the Search bar, which has Google, Yahoo! or Bing in the background to show you which engine you are using before you start typing.
3. Type your search word(s). As you type, Safari attempts to find a previous search or suggestion that matches what you type.

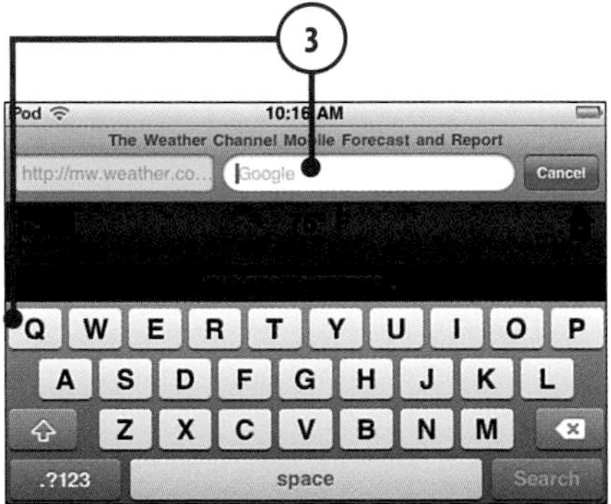

4. To move to a previous search or suggestion, tap it, or when you've entered your search term, tap Search. The search website you use performs the search, and you see the results on the search results page.

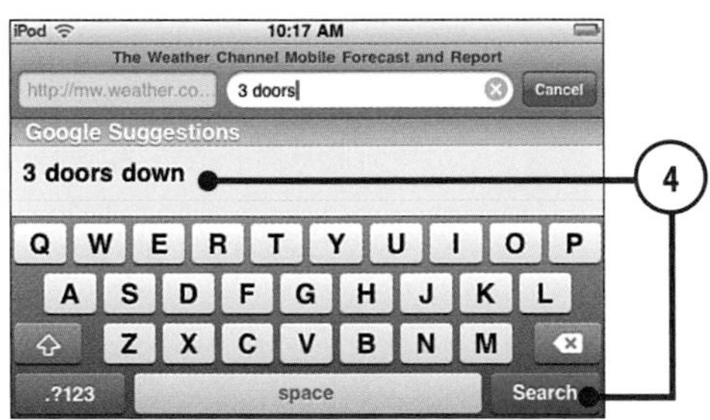

5. Use the search results page to view the results of your search. These pages work just like other web pages. You can zoom, scroll, and click links to explore results.

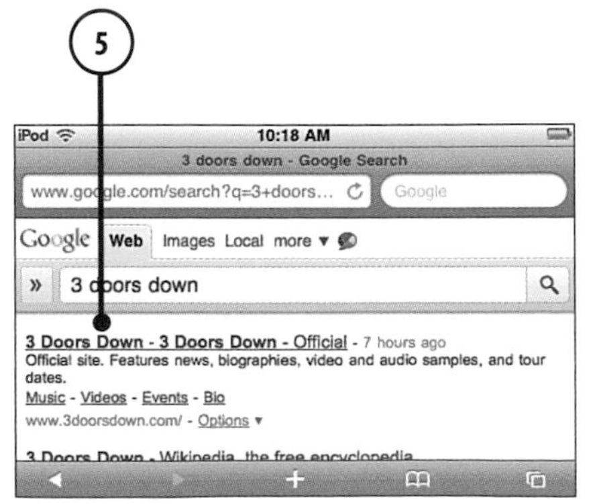

Safari Has a Good Memory

Safari remembers the last search you performed. To clear a search, click the Clear button located at the right end of the Search bar.

Returning to Previous Websites

As you move about the Web, Safari tracks the sites you visit and builds a history list. You can use this list to return to sites you've visited.

1. Open a web page and tap the Bookmarks button.
2. If necessary, tap the Return button until you move to the Bookmarks screen.
3. If necessary, scroll to the top of the page so that you see the History folder.
4. Tap History.

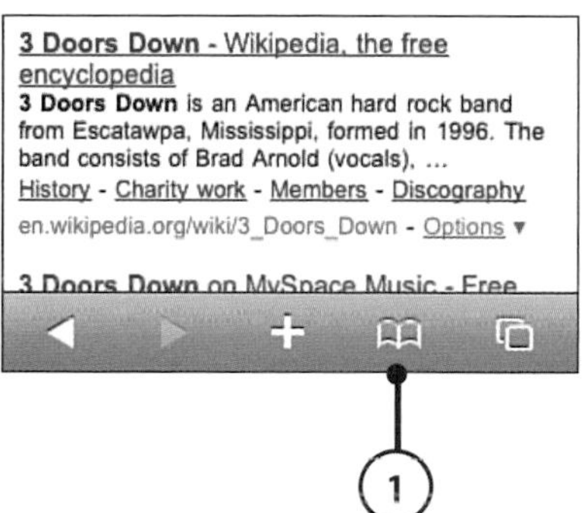

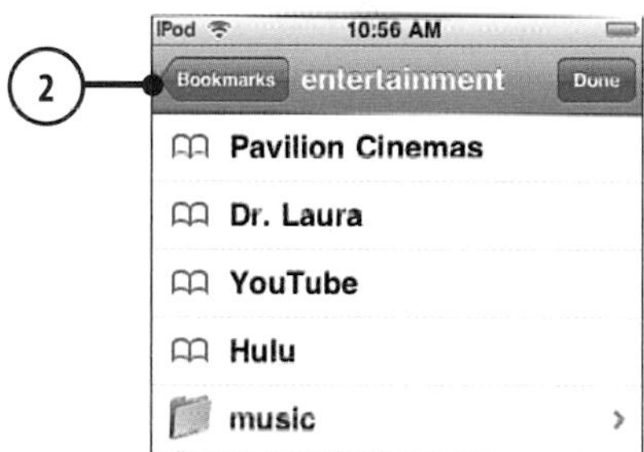

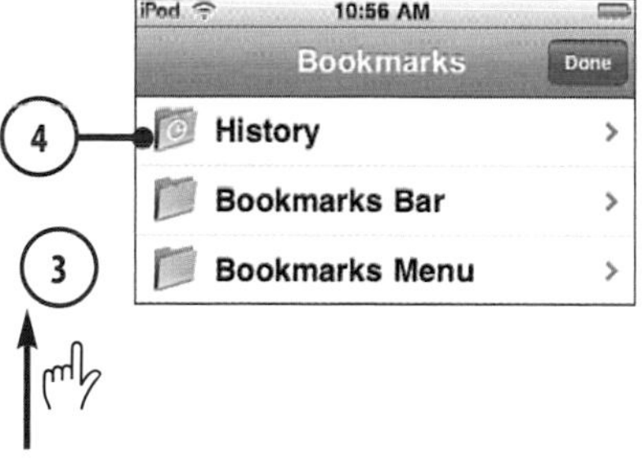

5. Scroll the page to browse all the sites you've visited. The most recent sites appear at the top of the screen. Earlier sites are collected in folders for each day, starting with Earlier Today and moving back one day at a time.
6. If the site to which you want to return is shown on the screen, skip this step; to return to a site that is stored in one of the folders based on the date and time you last visited it, tap the folder containing the site you want to visit. That date's screen appears, and you see the list of sites you visited at that time.
7. Tap the site you want to visit.
8. Use the techniques you previously learned in this chapter to view the content of the page.

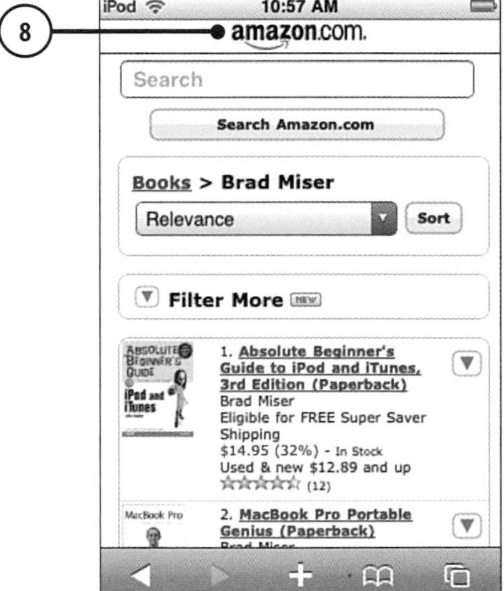

Erasing the Past

To clear your browsing history, tap the Clear button at the bottom of any of the History screens. Tap Clear History at the prompt, and it will be as if you've never been on the Web.

Saving and Organizing Bookmarks

In addition to moving bookmarks from a computer onto your iPod touch, you can add new bookmarks to the iPod touch, and they move onto the computer the next time you sync. You can organize bookmarks on your iPod touch, too.

Saving Bookmarks

1. Move to a web page that you want to save as a bookmark.
2. Tap the Add button.
3. Tap Add Bookmark. The Add Bookmark screen appears. The top field is the name of the bookmark. The middle field shows its URL. The lowest field shows where the bookmark will be stored.
4. Edit the bookmark's name as needed, or to erase the current name (which is the web page's title) and start over, tap the Clear button. Then type the new name of the bookmark.
5. Tap Bookmarks. Starting at the top level, Bookmarks, you see all the folders on the iPod touch in which you can place the bookmark you are saving. The folder that is currently selected is marked with a check mark.

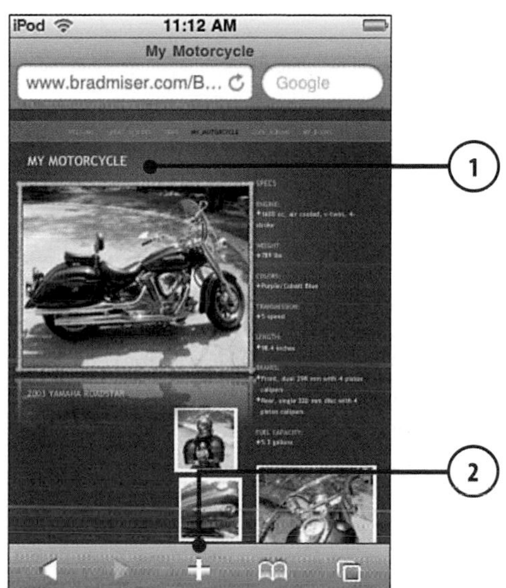

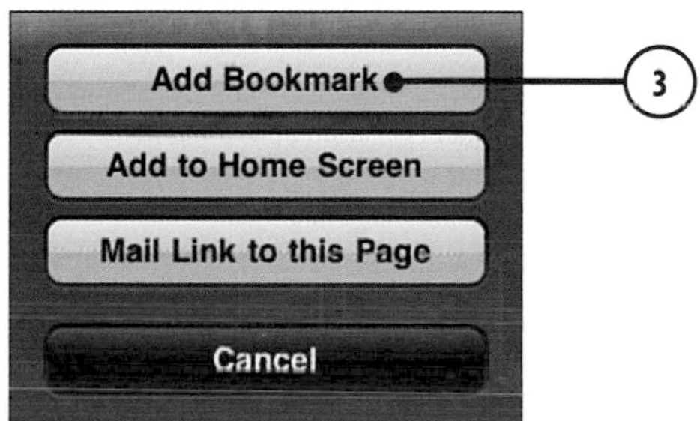

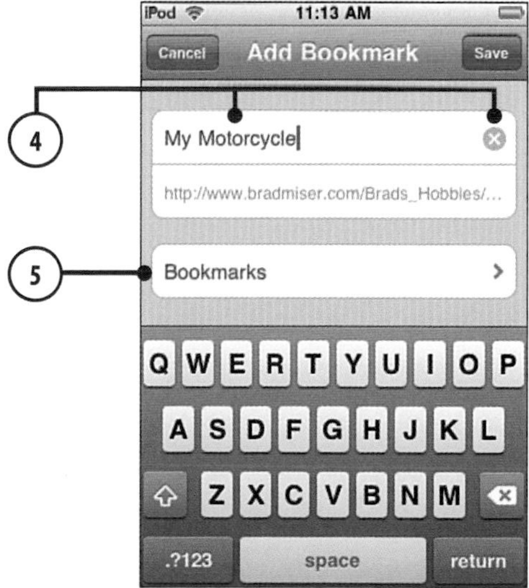

6. Scroll the screen to find the folder in which you want to place the new bookmark. You can choose any folder on the screen.

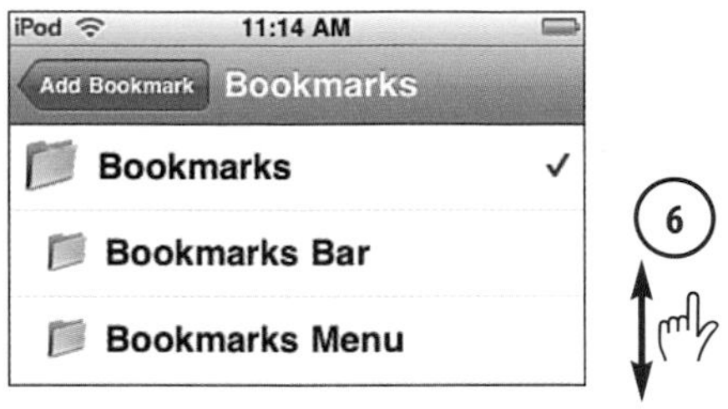

7. To choose a location for the new bookmark, tap it. You return to the Add Bookmark screen, which shows the location you selected.

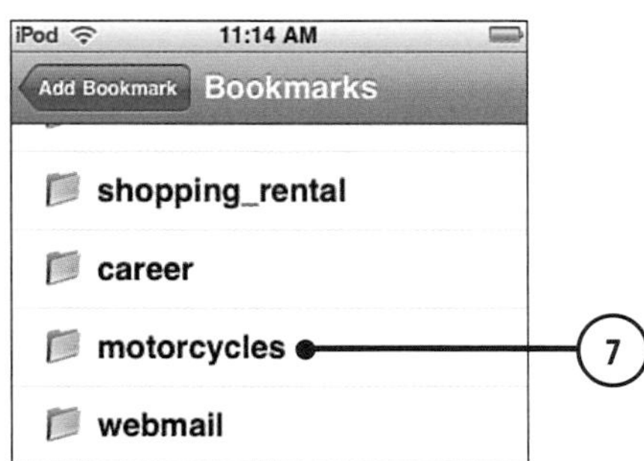

8. Tap Save. The bookmark is created and saved in the location you specified. You can use the Bookmarks tool to return to it at any time.

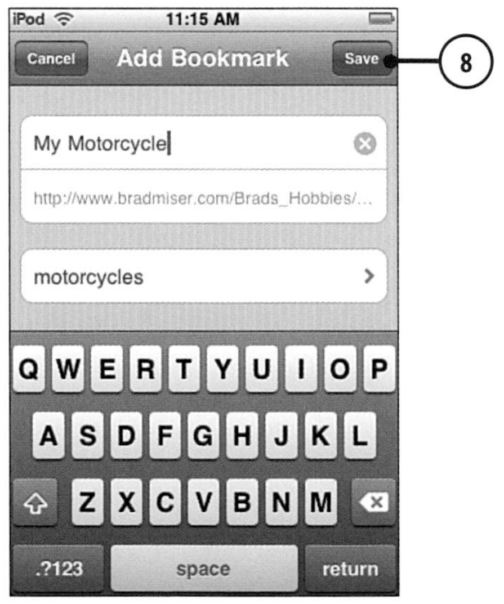

Location, Location

The location shown in the third bar is the last one in which you stored a bookmark. The first time you add a bookmark, this bar is called Bookmarks because that's the default location. After you choose a different location, the bar is relabeled with that location's name, which the iPod touch remembers the next time you add a new bookmark.

It's Not All Good

Unfortunately, bookmarks that you create on the iPod touch are useful on the computer to which they are synced only if you use Internet Explorer or Safari (Windows PCs) or Safari (Mac). If you use Firefox or another web browser, the bookmarks moved onto the computer from the iPod touch are of no value to you because they only appear in one of the supported browsers (Internet Explorer or Safari). You can make them available in other browsers, but that requires going through extra gyrations, which can negate the value of syncing.

Organizing Bookmarks

1. Move to the Bookmarks screen.
2. Tap Edit. The unlock buttons appear next to the folders and bookmarks you can change; some folders, such as the History folder, can't be changed. The List buttons also appear on the right side of the screen, again only for folders or bookmarks you can change.

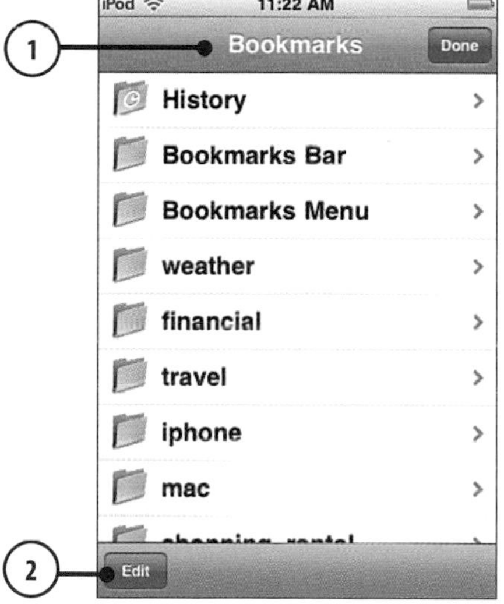

3. Drag the List button next to the bookmark or folder you want to move up or down the list up or down the screen. As you move between existing items, they slide apart to make room for the folder or bookmark you are dragging. The order of the items on the list is the order in which they appear on the Bookmarks screen.
4. To change the name and location of a folder, tap it.
5. Change the name in the name bar.
6. To change the location of the folder, tap the Location bar, which shows the bookmark's current location and is always the lowest bar on the screen.

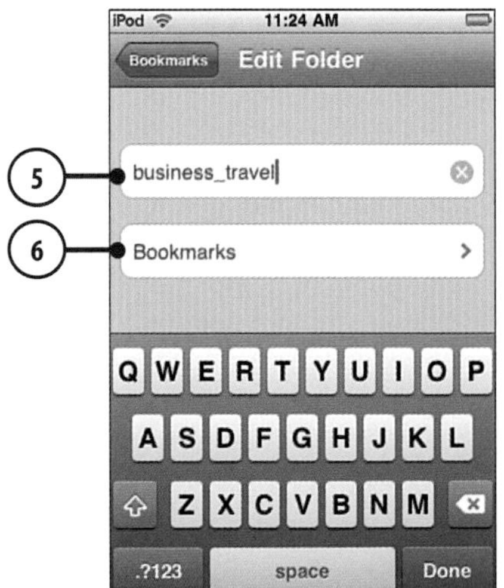

7. Scroll the list of bookmarks until you see the folder in which you want to place the folder.
8. Tap the folder into which you want to move the folder you are editing.
9. Tap Done. You move back to the Bookmarks screen, which reflects any changes you made.
10. Tap a bookmark you want to change. The Edit Bookmark screen appears.

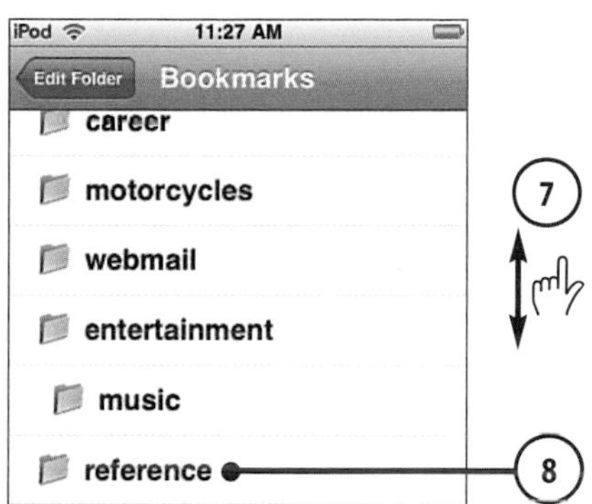

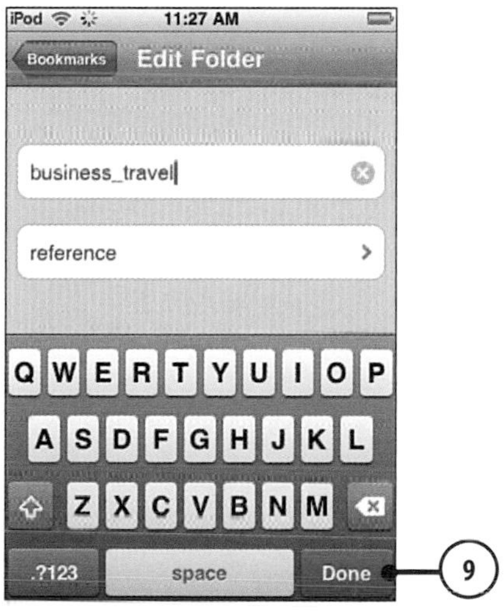

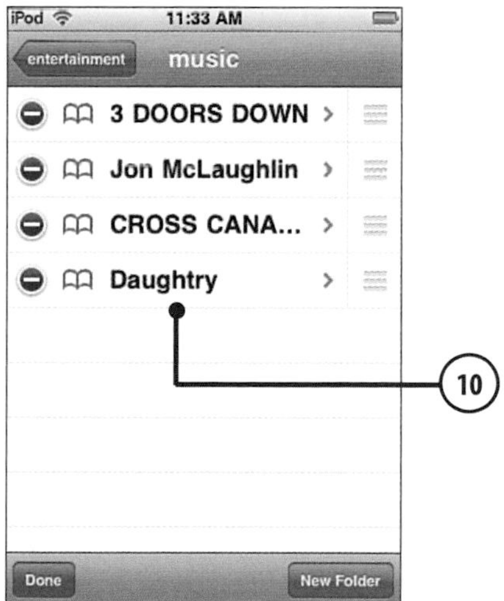

Editing a Bookmark

If the bookmark you want to change isn't on the screen you are editing, tap Done to exit Edit mode. Then open the folder containing the bookmark you want to edit and tap Edit.

11. Change the bookmark's name in the name bar.
12. If you want to change a bookmark's URL, tap the URL bar and make changes to the current URL.
13. To change the location of the folder or bookmark, tap the Location bar and follow steps 7 and 8.
14. Tap Done. You move back to the previous screen, and any changes you made, such as changing the name or location of a bookmark, are reflected.
15. To create a new folder, tap New Folder.
16. Enter the name of the folder.
17. Follow steps 6 though 8 to choose the location in which you want to save the new folder.
18. Tap Done. The new folder is created in the location you selected. You can place folders and bookmarks into it by using the Location bar to navigate to it.

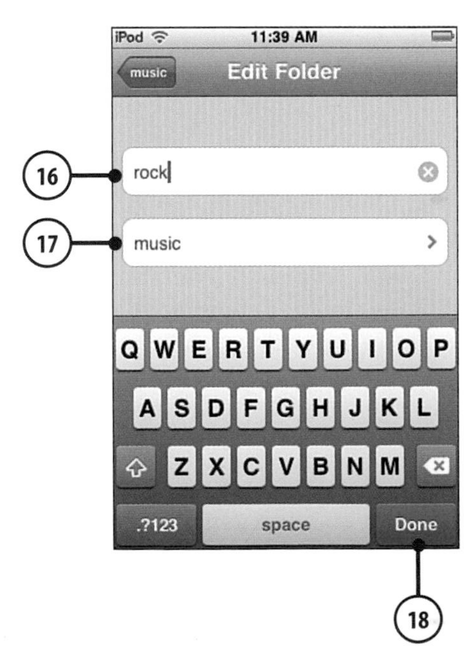

19. Tap Done. Your changes are saved and you exit Edit Bookmarks mode.

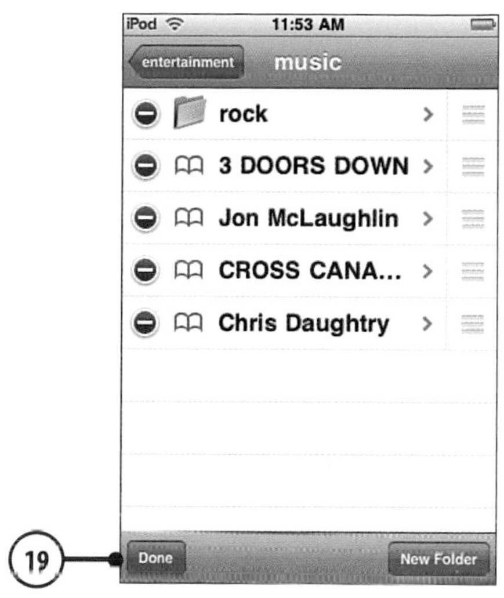

Deleting Bookmarks or Folders

1. Move to the Bookmarks screen containing the folder or bookmark you want to delete.
2. Tap Edit. The Unlock buttons appear next to the folders and bookmarks you can change; some folders, such as the History folder, can't be changed. The List buttons also appear.

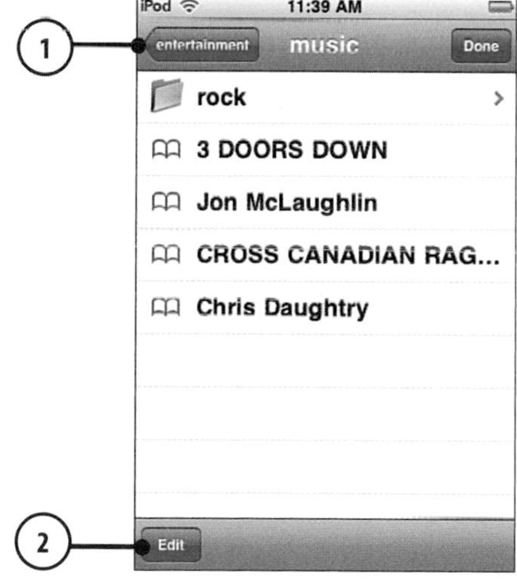

3. Scroll up and down the screen to find the bookmark or folder you want to delete.
4. Tap its Unlock button.
5. Tap Delete. The folder or bookmark is deleted. Deleting a folder also deletes all the bookmarks it contains.
6. Repeat steps 4 and 5 to delete other folders or bookmarks.
7. Tap Done.

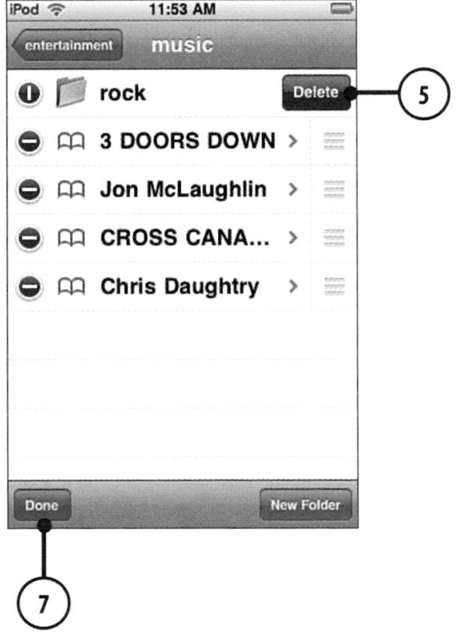

Creating a Bookmark on the Home Screen

You can add a bookmark icon to the Home screen so that you can visit a web page from there; this handy trick saves you several navigation moves that would be required to move into Safari and via typing the URL or using a bookmark to get the page you want to see.

1. Use Safari to move to a web page to which you want to have easy access from the Home screen.
2. Tap the Add button.
3. Tap Add to Home Screen.

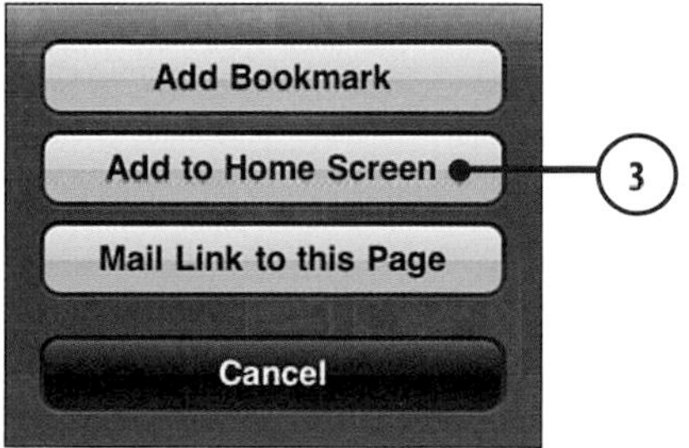

4. If needed, edit the name of the icon on the Home Screen. The default name is the name of the web page, but you will want to keep the name short because it has a small amount of room on its button on the Home Screen.
5. Tap Add. You move to the Home Screen and see the icon you added. You can return to the site at any time by tapping this icon.

Location Is Everything

You can organize the buttons on the pages of the Home Screen so that you can place your web page buttons in convenient locations, and you can create folders on your Home screens to keep your web page icons neat and tidy. See Chapter 14, "Customizing an iPod touch," for details.

Emailing a Link to a Web Page

Sometimes when you visit a web page, you want to share it with others. Using Safari, you can quickly email links to web pages you visit.

1. Use Safari to navigate to a web page whose link you want to email to someone.
2. Tap the Add button.
3. Tap Mail Link to this Page. A new email message is created, and the link to the web page is inserted into the body. The subject of the message is the title of the web page.
4. Complete and send the email message. (See Chapter 9, "Emailing," for all you need to know about using the Mail app.) When the recipient receives your message, he can visit the website by clicking the link included in the email message.

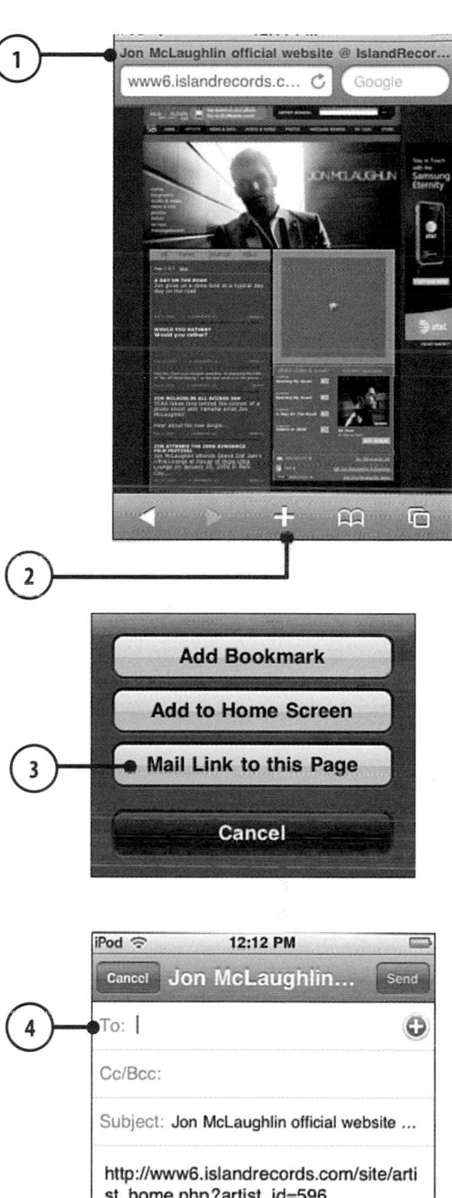

Completing Web Forms

Just like web browsers on a computer, you can provide information through web pages in Safari by completing forms, such as to log in to your account on a website or request information about something. You can manually enter information or use AutoFill to have Safari add the information for you. (AutoFill must be enabled using Safari settings as explained at the beginning of this chapter.)

Completing Forms Manually

1. Open Safari and move to a website containing a form.
2. Zoom in on the fields you need to complete.
3. Tap in a field. If you tapped a text field, the keyboard pops up.
4. Enter the information in the field. (If the site suggests information you want to enter, just tap it to enter it. If the suggestion isn't the information you want to enter, just keep typing.)
5. Tap Next. If there isn't another field on the form, this button is disabled, so skip this step. If it is enabled, you move to the next field on the form.

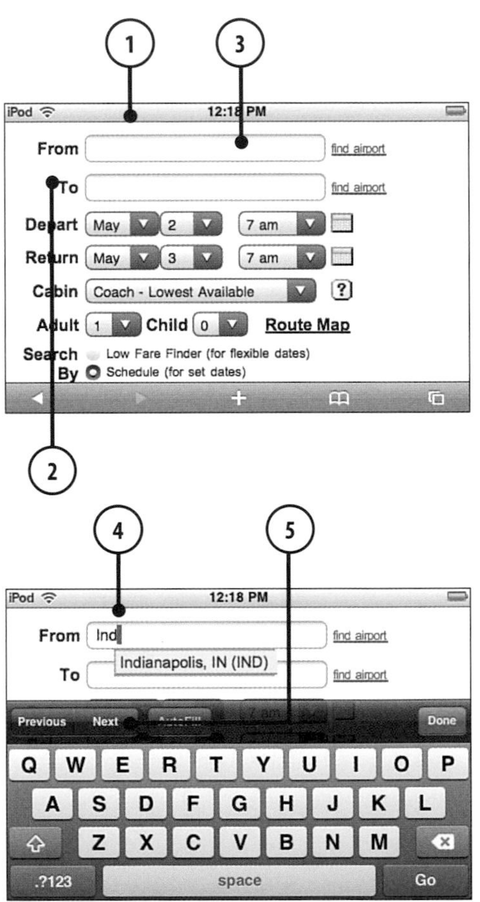

Those Wheels Keep on Spinnin'

When you have to make a selection on a form, such as a date, a selection wheel appears on the iPod touch's screen. You can drag up or down to spin the wheel and then tap on what you want to select to enter that information into a field.

6. Repeat steps 4 and 5 to complete all the fields on the form.
7. Tap Done. The keyboard closes, and you move back to the web page.
8. Tap Search, Submit, Go, Login, or another button to provide the form's information to the website.

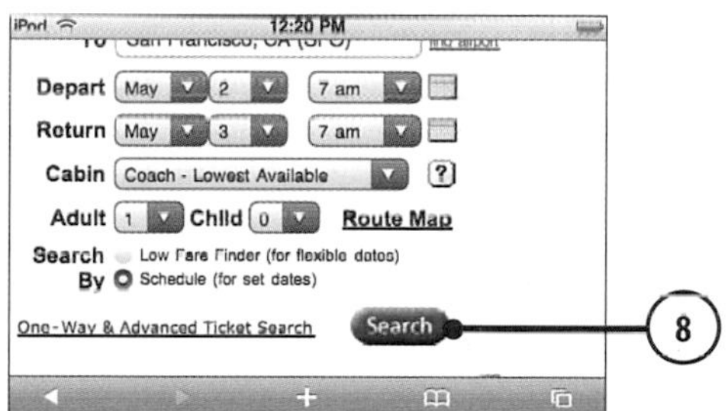

Completing Forms with AutoFill

1. Open Safari and move to a website containing a form. Zoom in on the fields you need to complete and tap in a field. If you tapped a text field, the keyboard pops up.
2. Tap AutoFill. Safari fills any fields it can based on the information in Contacts. Any fields that Safari tries to complete are highlighted in yellow.

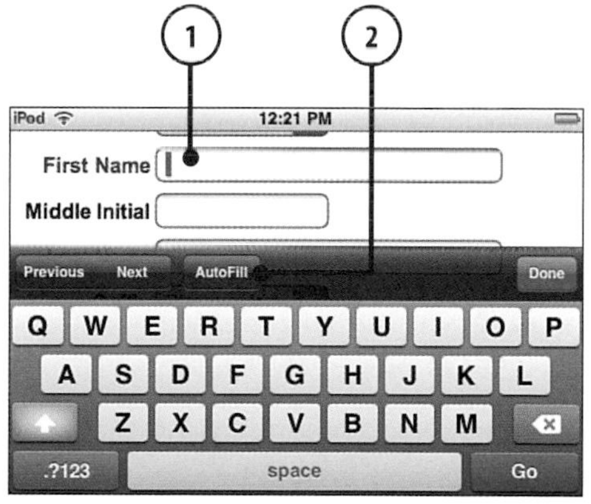

3. Use the steps in the previous section to review all the fields and to edit any that AutoFill wasn't able to complete or that need to be changed.

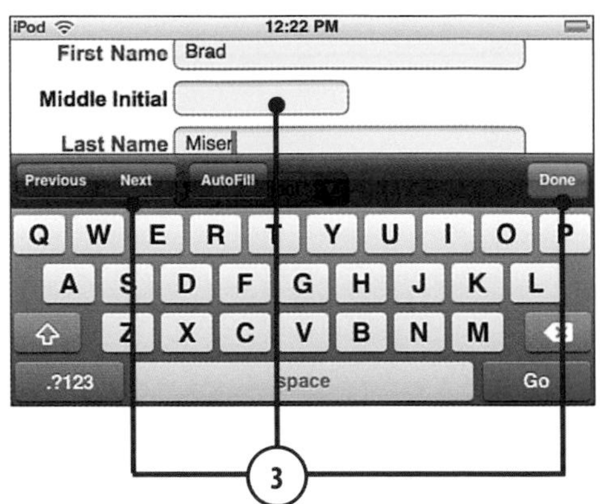

Signing In Automatically

If you enable Safari to remember usernames and passwords, you can log into some websites automatically. When Safari encounters a site for which it recognizes and can save login information, you are prompted to allow Safari to save that information. When saved, this information is entered for you automatically.

1. Move to a web page that requires you to log into an account.
2. Enter your account's username and password.
3. Tap the button to log into your account, such as Continue, Submit, Login, and such. You are prompted to save the login information.
4. To save the information, tap Yes. The next time you move to the login page, your username and password are entered for you automatically. (Tap Never for this Website if you don't want the information to be saved and you don't want to be prompted again. Tap Not Now if you don't want the information saved but do want to be prompted again later to save it.)

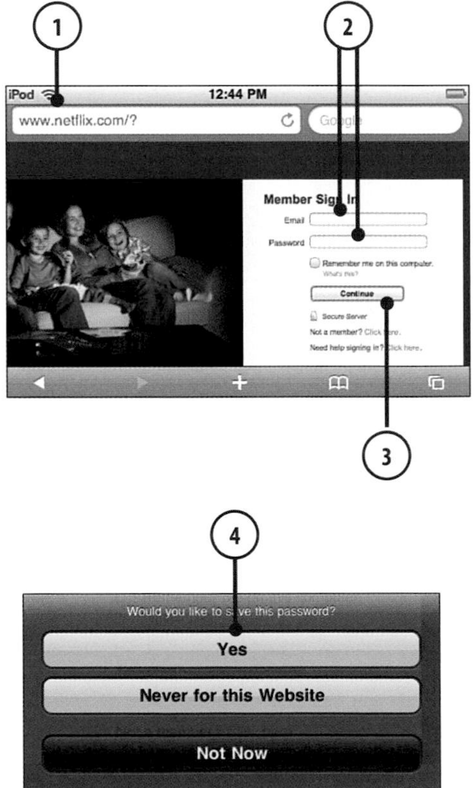

Opening and Managing Multiple Web Pages at the Same Time

Using Safari, you can open and work with multiple web pages at the same time. Some links on web pages open a new page, or you can open a new page manually at any time.

1. Using Safari, open a web page.
2. Tap the Page Manager button.

Safari Keeps Working

As you move to web pages, you can immediately tap the Page Manager button to open more pages. Pages continue to load in the background as you move between the Page Manager and individual pages.

3. Tap New Page. The page you were on moves into the background, and a new web page opens. The counter on the Page Manager button increases by one to show you how many pages are open.

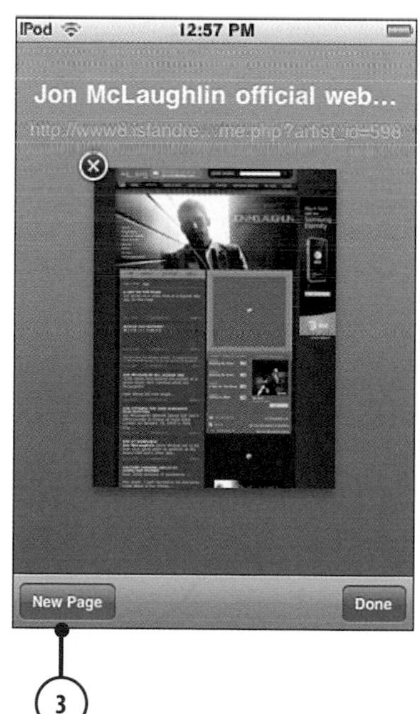

4. Use Safari's tools to move to another web page. You can enter a URL, use a bookmark, perform a search, and so on.
5. View and work with the web page.
6. Repeat steps 2 through 5 to open as many web pages as you want to see.
7. Tap the Page Manager button again. You see a thumbnail representation of each open web page.
8. To move between pages, drag your finger to the left or to the right until the page you want to view is in focus.

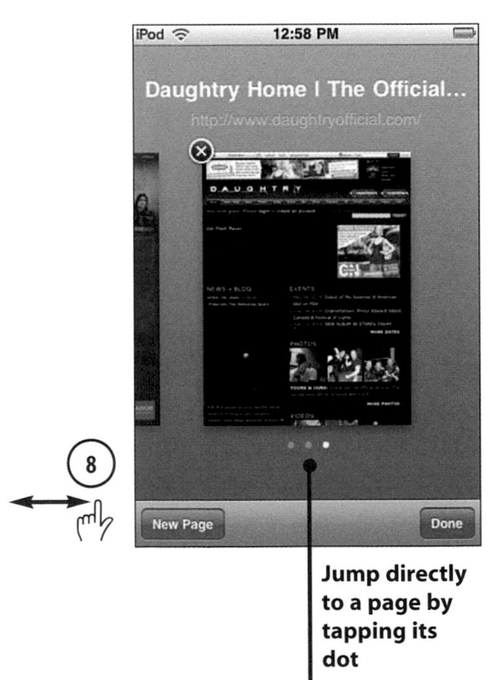

9. To move to the page in focus, tap it or tap Done. You move to the web page and can view it.
10. Tap the Page Manager button. You move back to the Page Manager.
11. To close an open page, tap its Close button. The page closes and disappears from the Page Manager screen, and the counter is reduced by one.

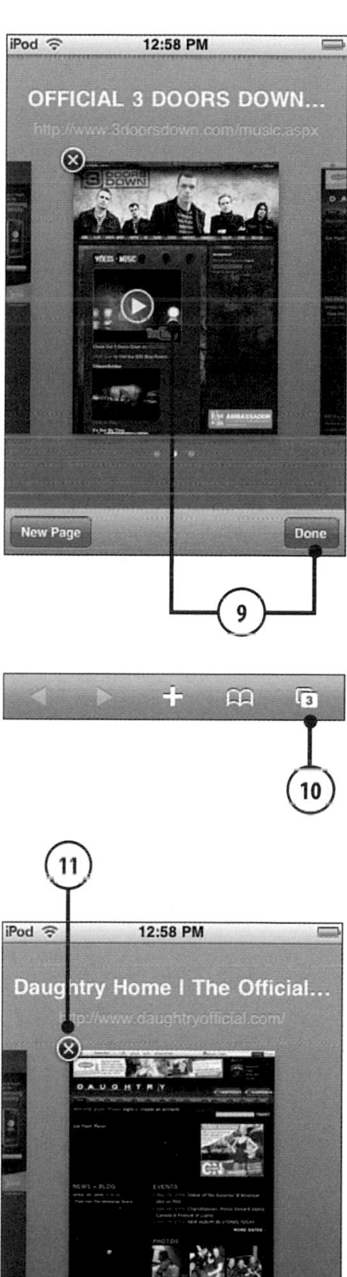

Use Settings to configure how contacts are displayed

Tap here to work with contact information

In this chapter, you learn how to make sure that your iPod touch has the contact information you need when you need it. Topics include the following:

- → Configuring how contacts display
- → Creating contacts on an iPod touch
- → Using contacts on your iPod touch
- → Changing or deleting contacts

Managing Contacts

Contact information, including names, phone numbers, email addresses, and physical addresses, is useful to have on your iPod touch. For example, when you send email, you want to select the appropriate email addresses rather than having to remember them and type them in. Likewise, you might want to pull up addresses on a map in the Maps application.

Configuring How Contacts Display on an iPod touch

Before you start using contacts, make sure that contact information displays according to your preferences. You can determine how contacts sort on lists by first or last name, and you can choose which of those appears first on lists.

1. On the Home screen, tap Settings.
2. Scroll down until you see Mail, Contacts, Calendars.
3. Tap Mail, Contacts, Calendars.
4. Scroll down until you see the Contacts section.
5. Tap Sort Order.
6. To have contacts sorted by first name and then last name, tap First, Last.
7. To have contacts sorted by last name and then first name, tap Last, First.
8. Tap Mail.

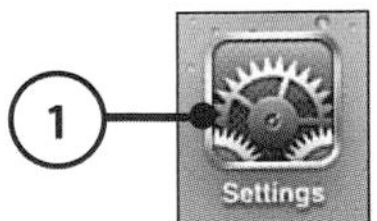

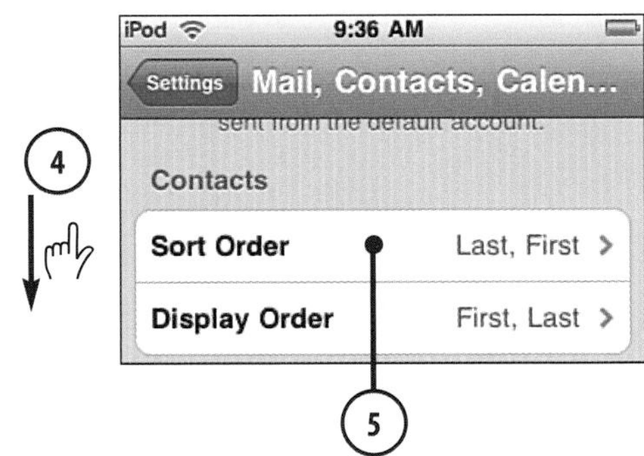

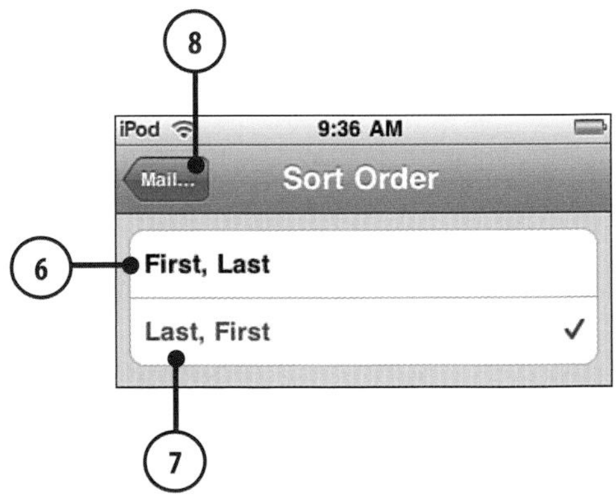

9. Tap Display Order.
10. To show contacts in the format *first name, last name,* tap First, Last.
11. To show contacts in the format *last name, first name,* tap Last, First.
12. Tap Mail.

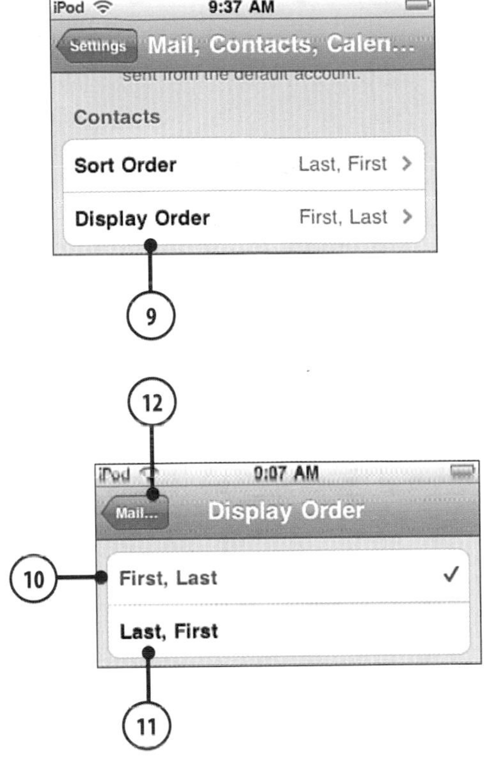

Creating New Contacts While Using an iPod touch

You can create new contacts on an iPod touch in a number of ways. You can start with some information, such as the email address on an email message you receive, and create a contact from it, or you can create a contact manually "from scratch." In this section, you learn how to create a contact from an email message, a location on a map, and manually.

Creating a Contact from a Map

When you view a location on a map, you can create a contact with that location's information.

1. On the Home screen, tap Maps.
2. Use the map to find a location. (Chapter 12, "Using Cool iPod touch Applications," covers the Maps application.)
3. Tap the Info button for the location.
4. Scroll down the screen until you see the Add to Contacts button.
5. Tap Add to Contacts.

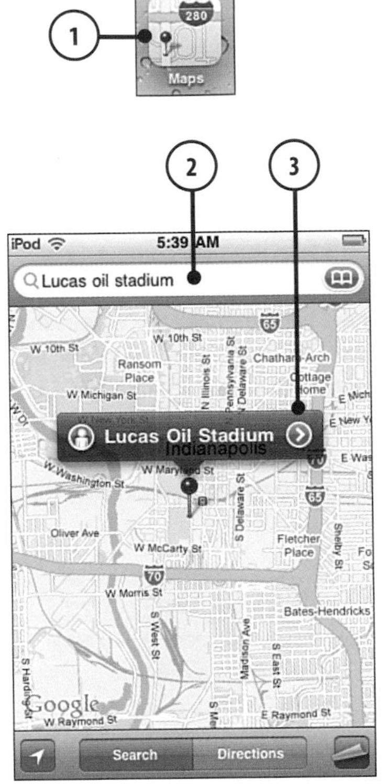

6. Tap Create New Contact. The New Contact screen appears. The iPod touch adds as much information as it can based on the location, such as name, phone number, address, website, and so on.

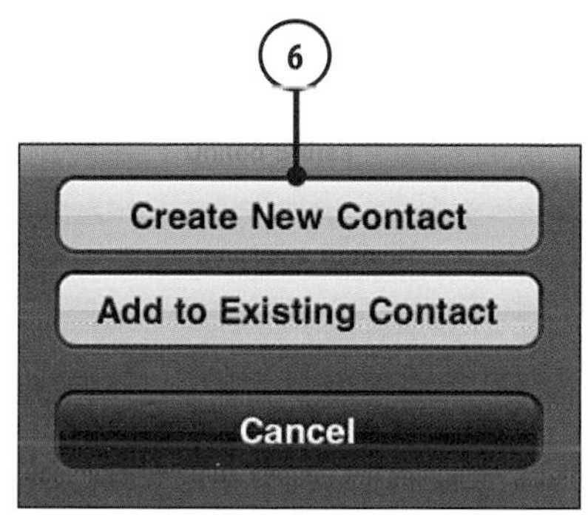

7. Use the New Contact screen to configure the new contact. This works just like when you create a new contact manually, except that you already have information for the new contact, in this case the location name (if it has one), address, and so on. See the next section for details.

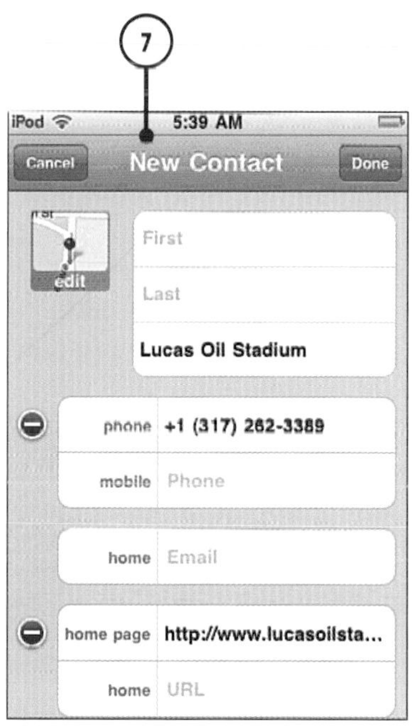

Creating Contacts on an iPod touch Manually

Most of the time, you manage contact information on a computer and move it to your iPod. Or you use information on your iPod touch to create new contacts so that you don't have to start from scratch. When you do have to start from scratch, you can create contacts manually and add all the information you need to them. And you use the same steps to add information to an existing contact, as you learn later in this chapter.

1. On the Home screen, tap Contacts. You see the All Contacts screen.

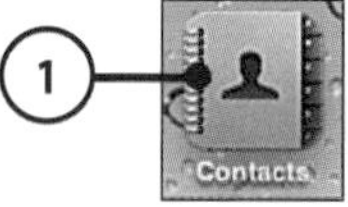

2. Tap the Add button. The New Contact screen appears. You see the information you can include for a contact. You can add more fields as needed using the add field command.

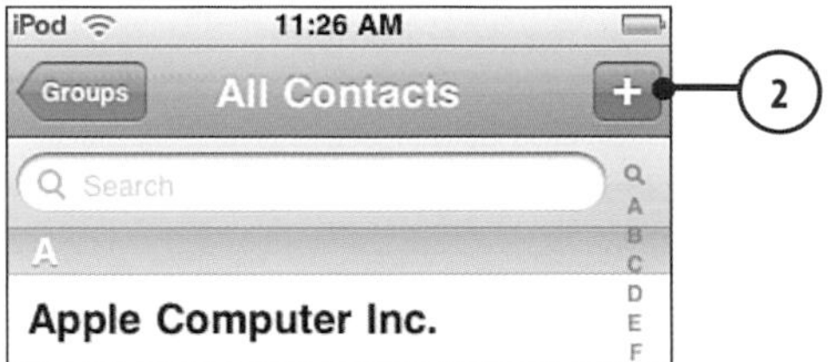

3. To associate a photo with the contact, tap add photo.

4. Tap Choose Photo. The Photo Albums screen appears.

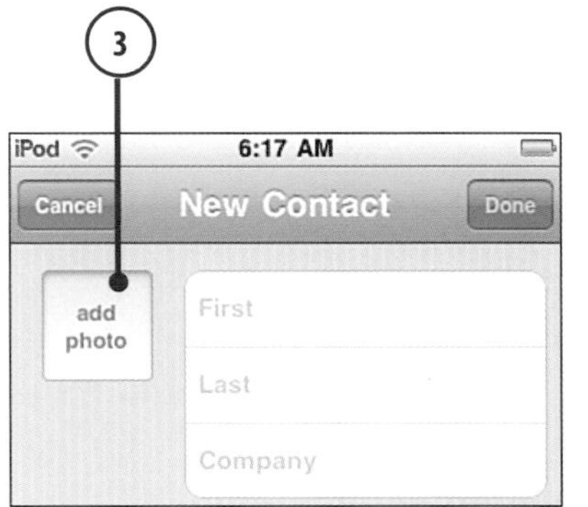

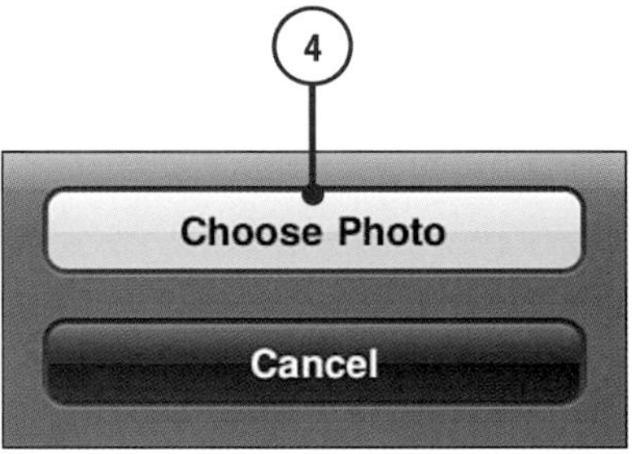

Contact Maps

When you create a contact from an address in the Maps application, the contact "photo" shows the pushpin for the address on the map. You can keep this or replace it with a photo.

5. Use the Photo Album tools to move to, select, and configure the photo you want to associate with the contact (see Chapter 11, "Storing, Viewing, and Sharing Photos").

Contact Photos

To associate a photo with a contact, that photo has to be stored on the iPod touch. You can include photos in the sync process to move them from your computer onto the iPod touch, where you can view them or add them to contacts. See Chapter 11 for the info you need to use the iPod touch's photo tools.

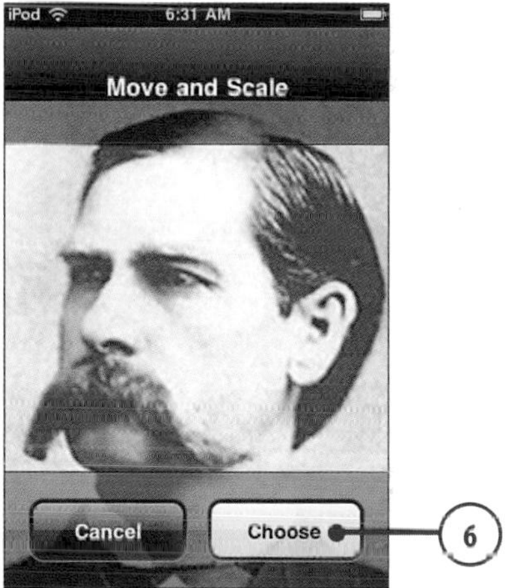

6. After you've configured the photo as you want it to be used, tap Choose. The photo is configured and saved to the contact. You return to the New Contact screen and see the photo you selected.
7. Tap in the First field and enter the contact's first name. (If you are creating a contact for an organization only, leave this field empty.)
8. Tap in the Last field and enter the contact's last name (except if you are creating a contact for an organization, in which case, leave this field empty).

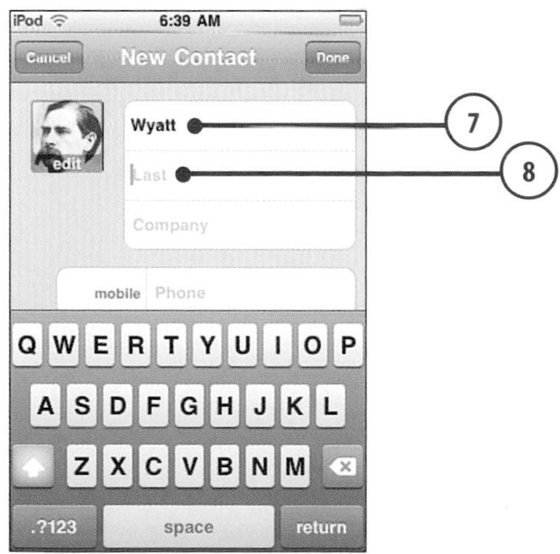

Order, Order

The Display Order preference you set earlier determines whether the First or Last field appears at the top of the screen. It doesn't really matter because the fields are so close that you always see both.

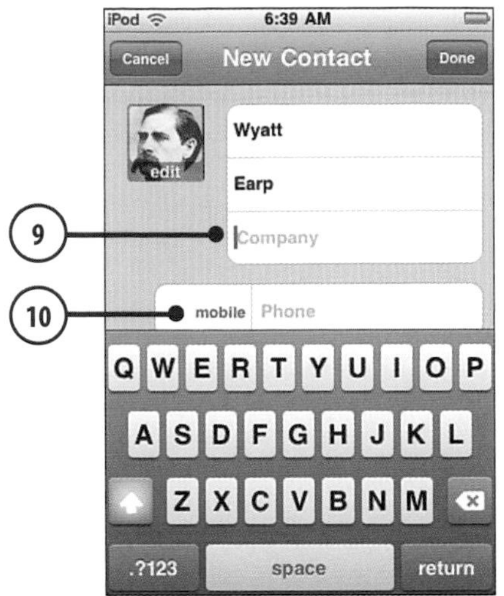

9. Enter the organization, such as a company, with which you want to associate the contact, if any.
10. Tap the label next to the first phone number you want to enter. The resulting Label screen enables you to change the number's label.
11. Tap the label you want to use for the number.
12. Enter the phone number, including area code (and country code if necessary).

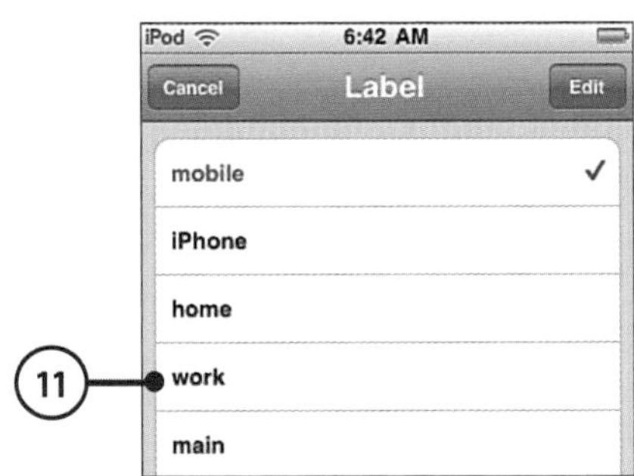

The Fields Grow

As soon as you enter something for one type of contact information, another field of that same type (such as phone number) is added to the contact automatically. When you finish adding information of one type, just ignore the empty fields that the Contacts app created. They won't appear when you view the contact's information.

13. To add another phone number, repeat steps 10 through 12.
14. Scroll down the screen.
15. Tap the label for the first email address field.
16. Tap the label you want to apply to the email address.

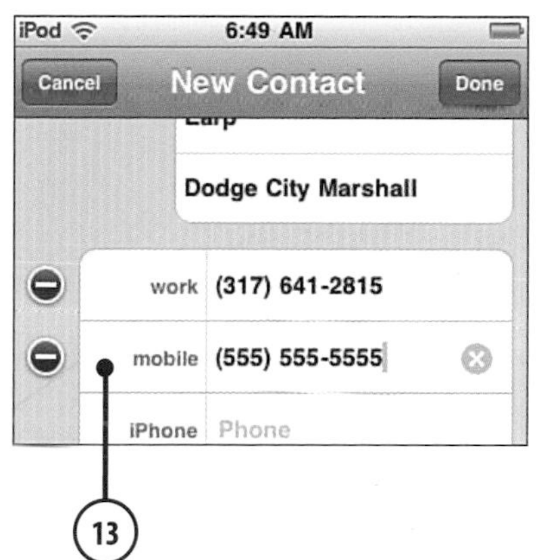

Custom Labels

You can create custom labels for various kinds of contact information. On the Label screen, scroll down the screen and tap Add Custom Label. The Custom Label screen appears. Create the label and tap Save. You can then choose your custom label for the new contact you are creating and for contacts you create or change in the future.

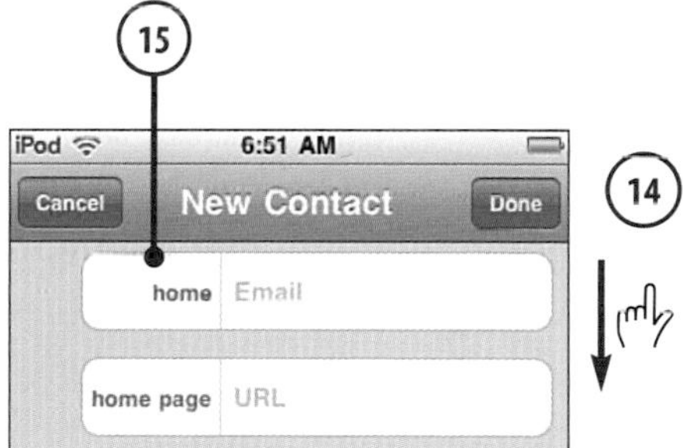

17. Enter the email address.

18. Repeat steps 15 through 17 to add more email addresses.

Edit Labels

If you tap the Edit button on the Label screen, you can delete some labels or add custom labels.

19. If the contact doesn't use FaceTime, or if you want to leave the default ringtone for FaceTime request from the person, skip to step 22. If you want to hear a specific ringtone when you receive a FaceTime request from the person, tap Ringtone.

20. Tap the ringtone you want to use. The ringtone plays.

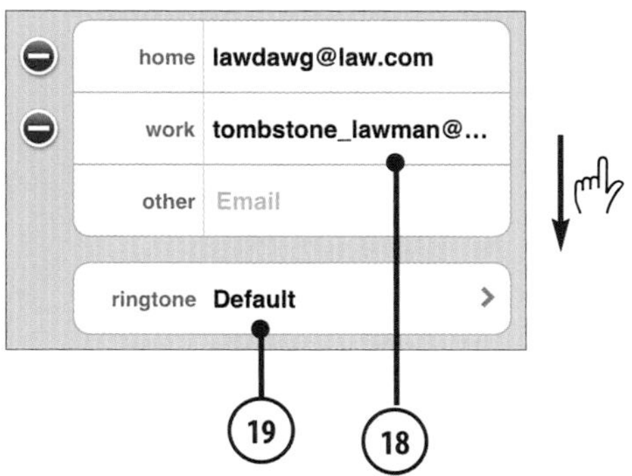

More on FaceTime Ringtones

You can use any of the default ringtones installed on your iPod, or you can add custom ringtones that you purchase from the iTunes Store. You can learn more about FaceTime and ringtones in Chapter 12, "Using Cool iPod touch Applications."

21. Tap Save.

22. Tap the label for the first URL field for the web page you want to associate with the contact.
23. Tap the label you want to apply to the URL.
24. Enter the URL.
25. Repeat steps 20 through 22 to add more URLs.
26. Tap add new address.

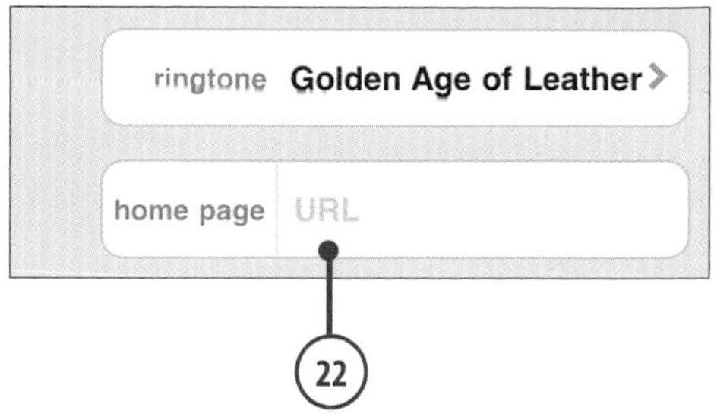

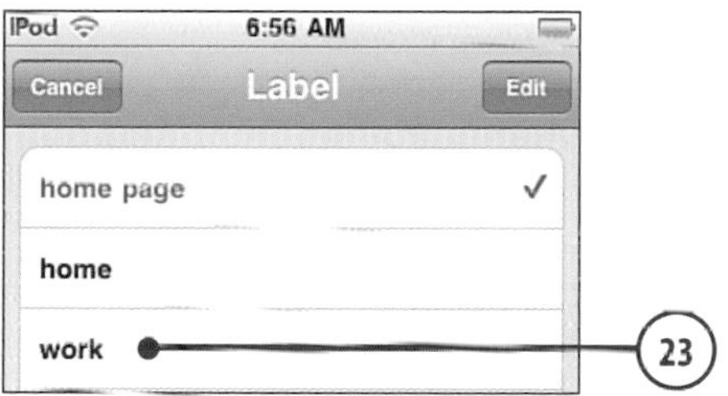

Didn't Mean It?

To remove a field in which you've entered information, tap the red Unlock button next to the field and then tap Delete. If you haven't entered information into a field, just ignore it because empty fields don't appear on the contact screen.

27. Tap the label next to the new address fields.

28. Tap the label you want to apply to the address you are going to enter.
29. Tap the country in which the address is associated; if the default country is correct, skip this and the next step.
30. Tap the country the address is located in.
31. Fill in the address information.

Formats? You Got 'Em

The address formats you see on the contact screens are determined by the country you associate with the address. If the address isn't in the default country, tap that country and use the resulting Country screen to select the appropriate country. When you return to the New Contract screen, you see fields appropriate for that country's addresses.

32. To add another address, repeat steps 24 through 29.
33. To add more fields to the contact, tap add field.
34. Tap the kind of information you want to add.
35. Enter the information for the new field.
36. Repeat steps 31 through 33 to add more fields of various types.
37. When you finish adding information, tap Done.

More on More Fields

When you add more fields to contact information, those fields appear in the appropriate context on the Info screen. For example, if you add a nickname, it is placed at the top of the screen with the other "name" information. If you add an address, it appears with the other address information.

The new contact is created and is ready for you to use, and you see the information you entered on the Info screen. It also is included in the next sync so that it will be added to your contact information on your computer.

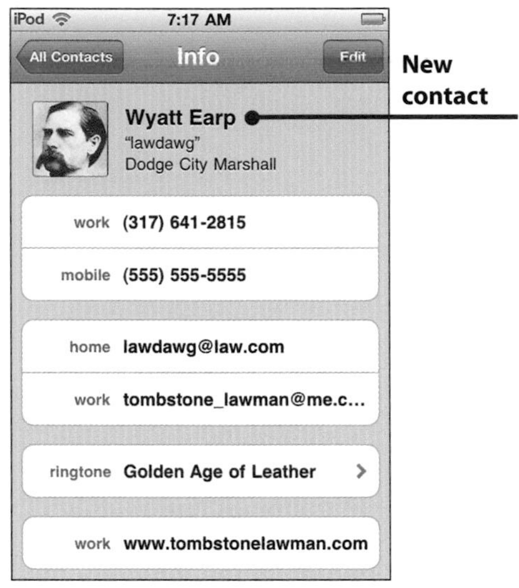

Using Contacts on an iPod touch

There are many ways to use contact information. The first step is always finding the contact information you need. Next is to select the action you want to perform.

Using the Contacts Application

You can access your contact information in the Contacts application. For example, you can search or browse for a contact and then view the detailed information for the contact in which you are interested.

1. On the Home screen, tap Contacts. You see the All Contacts screen with the contacts listed in the view and sort formats you selected, which are last name, first name or first name, last name.

2. Drag your finger up or down to scroll the screen to browse for contact information; flick your finger up or down to scroll rapidly.
3. Tap the index to jump to contact information organized by the first letter of the selected format.
4. Use the Search tool to search for a specific contact.
5. To view a contact's information, tap the contact.

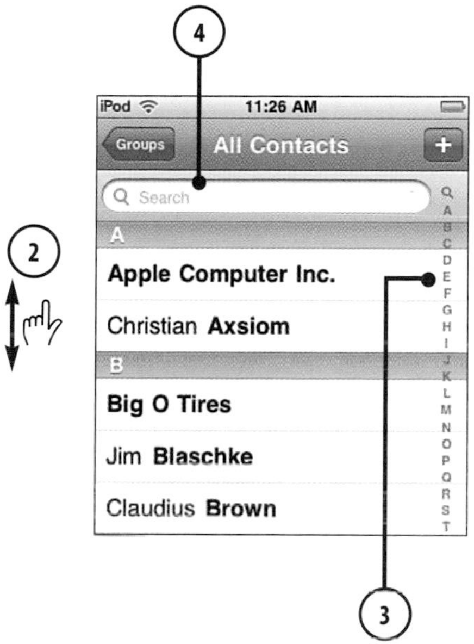

Last Known Contact

The Contacts app remembers where you last were and takes you back there whenever you move into the app. For example, if you view a contact's details and then switch to a different application and back to Contacts, you return to the contact info screen. To move to the All Contacts screen, tap the All Contacts button in the upper-left corner of the screen or tap All Contacts when you are viewing the Groups screen.

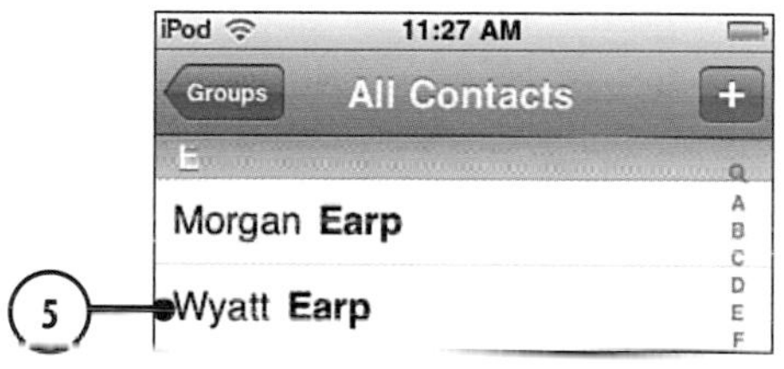

6. Scroll up and down the screen to view all the contact's information.
7. Tap the data and buttons on the screen to perform actions, including the following:
   - **Email addresses**—Tap an email address to create a new email to it.
   - **URLs**—Tap a URL to open Safari and move to the associated website.
   - **Addresses**—Tap an address to show it in the Maps application.
   - **Share Contact**—Tap the Share Contact button. A new email message is created with the contact added as a vCard (virtual address card). Recipients of the message can add the contact information to their own contact applications by importing the vCard.
8. To return to the All Contacts list without performing an action, tap All Contacts.

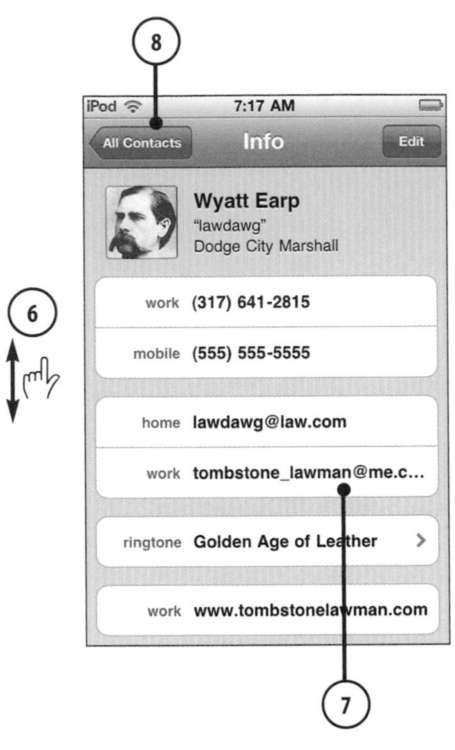

Groupies

In a contact application on a computer, such as Address Book on a Mac, contacts can be organized in groups. When you sync, the groups of contacts move onto the iPod along with the contacts. You can browse or search a group of contacts by moving to the Groups screen by tapping Groups on the All Contacts screen. Then browse your groups and tap the group whose contacts you want to view. Or tap All Contacts to move to the All Contacts screen.

Using Contact Information in Other Applications

You can also access contact information in the context of another application. For example, you can use a contact's email address when you create an email message. When you perform such actions, you use the All Contacts screen to find and select the contact whose information you want to use. The following example shows using contact information to send an email message.

1. Open the application from which you want to access contact information (this example uses Mail).
2. Tap the Add button.
3. To search for a contact, tap in the Search bar. (As you learned earlier, you can also browse the list or use the index to find a contact.)
4. Enter the search text.
5. Tap the contact whose information you want to use. You move back to the application, and the appropriate information is entered.

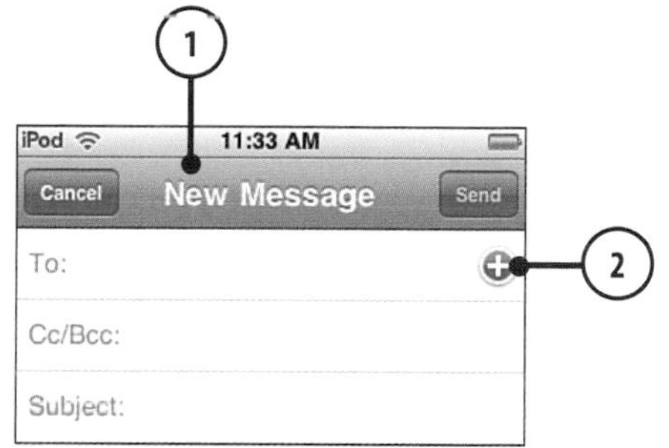

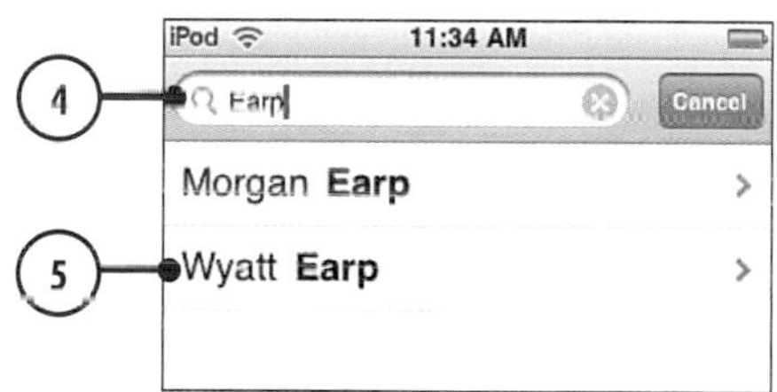

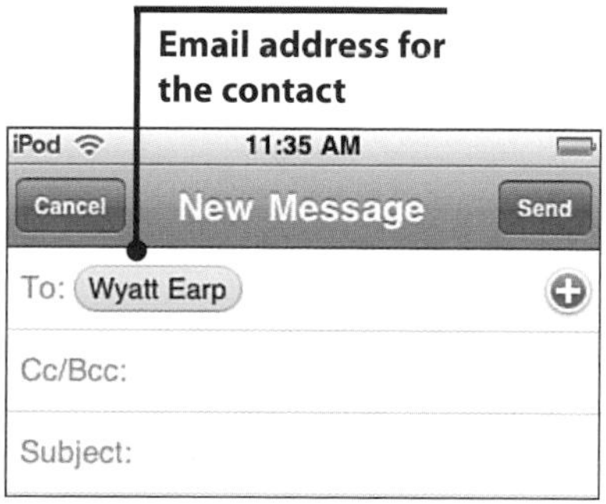

Email address for the contact

Multiple Fields

If you tap a contact who has more than one entry for a type of information, you move to the contact's info screen and then tap on the specific entry you want to use. For example, if a contact has more than one email address, when you tap the contact, you move to the Info screen where you see all the contact's email addresses Tap the one to which you want to address the message.

Changing or Deleting Contacts

When you sync contacts with a computer via iTunes, Exchange, or MobileMe, the changes go both ways. For example, when you change a contact on an iPod touch, the synced contact manager application, such as Outlook, makes the changes for those contacts on your computer. Likewise, when you change contact information in a contact manager on your computer, those changes move to the iPod touch when you sync it. If you add a new contact in a contact manager, it moves to the iPod touch during a sync operation and vice versa.

Changing, Adding, or Removing Information for an Existing Contact Manually

You can change any information for an existing contact on an iPod touch; when you sync, the changes you make move into your contact manager, such as Outlook or Address Book.

1. View the contact's Info screen.
2. Tap Edit. The Info screen moves into Edit mode, and you see Unlock buttons next to each field.

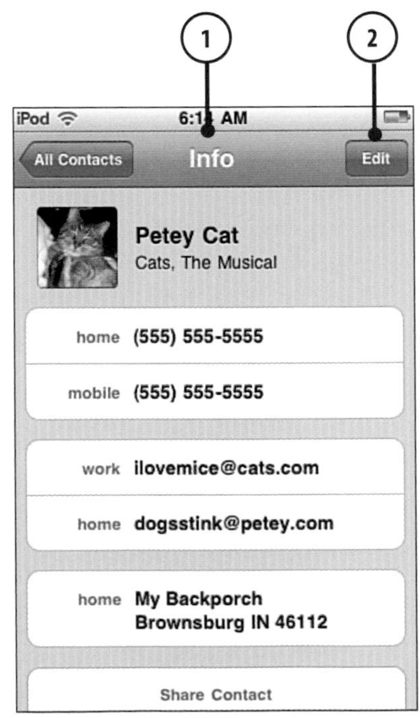

3. Tap a field to change its information; you can change a field's label by tapping it or change the data for the field by tapping that. Use the resulting tools, such as the phone number entry keypad, to make changes to the information. These tools work just like when you create a new contact (see "Creating Contacts on an iPod Touch Manually" earlier in this chapter).
4. To add more fields, tap the bottom label in a section, such as the phone number section, and then select a label for the new field and complete its information. This also works just like when you add a field to a contact you create manually.
5. To remove a field from the contact, tap its Unlock button.
6. Tap Delete. The information is removed from the contact.
7. To change the contact's photo, tap the current photo (which contains the text "edit") and use the resulting tools to select a new photo or change the scale or position of the existing one.
8. When you finish making changes, tap Done. Your changes are saved, and you return to the Info screen.

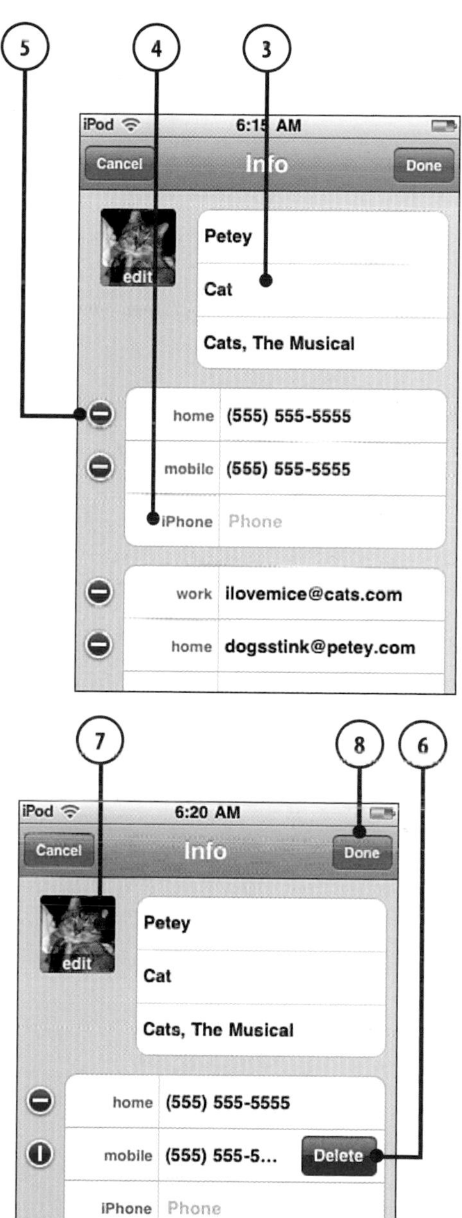

Adding Information to an Existing Contact

As you use your iPod touch, you'll encounter information related to a contact but that isn't part of that contact's information. For example, a contact might send you an email from a different address than you have captured for that contact. When this happens, you can easily add the additional information to an existing contact.

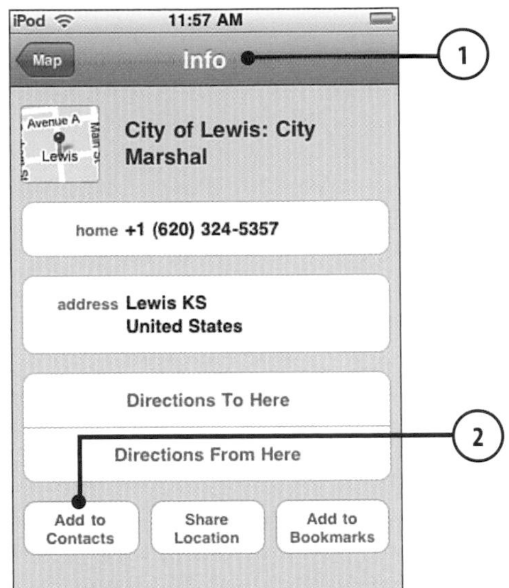

1. Locate the information you want to add to an existing contact, such as a physical address, email address, or website.
2. Tap Add to Contacts or tap Add to Existing Contact (which button you see depends on the type of information you work with).

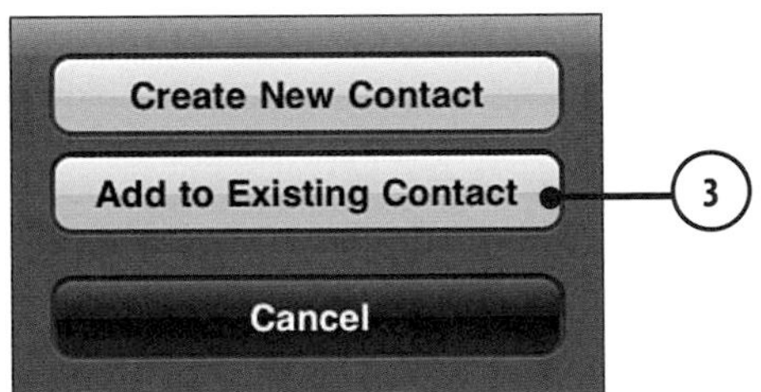

3. Tap Add to Existing Contact. (Skip this step if you tapped Add to Existing Contact in the previous step.)

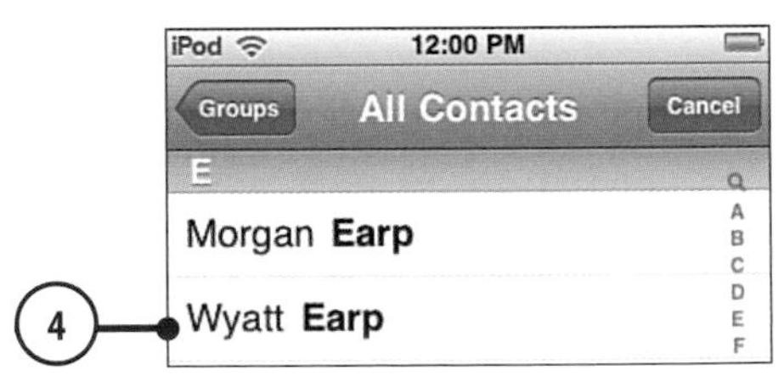

4. Locate and tap the contact to which you want to add the information. The new information is saved to the contact and is highlighted in blue. To change the information, such as its label, tap Edit and follow the steps in the previous section.

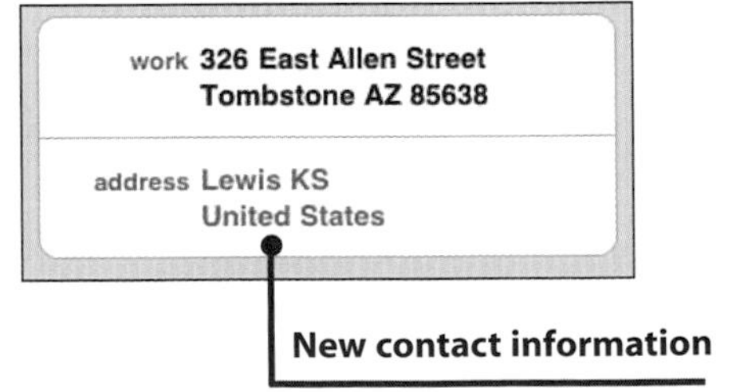

New contact information

Deleting Contacts Manually

To get rid of contacts, you can delete them.

1. Find and view the contact you want to delete.
2. Tap Edit.
3. Scroll to the bottom of the Info screen.
4. Tap Delete Contact.
5. Tap Delete Contact again to confirm the deletion. The iPod touch deletes the contact, and you return to the All Contacts list. The next time you sync, the iPod touch prompts you to approve the deletion on the computer's contact manager, just like other changes you make.

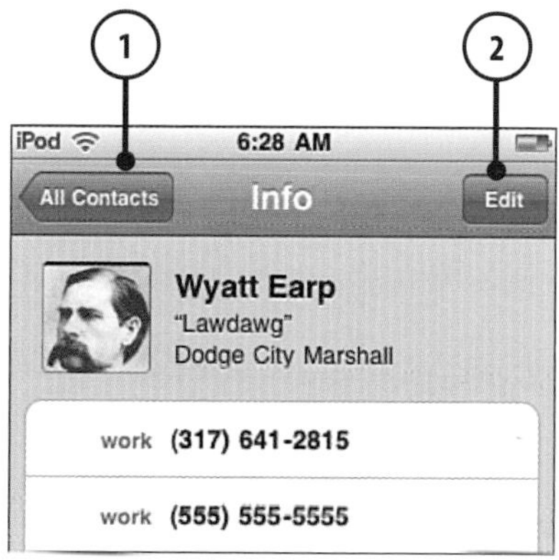

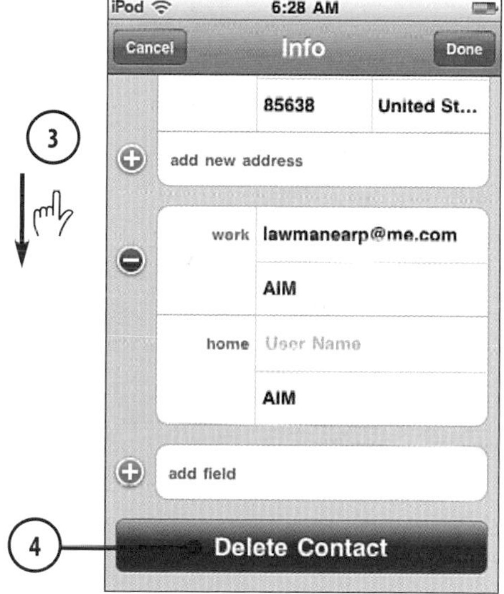

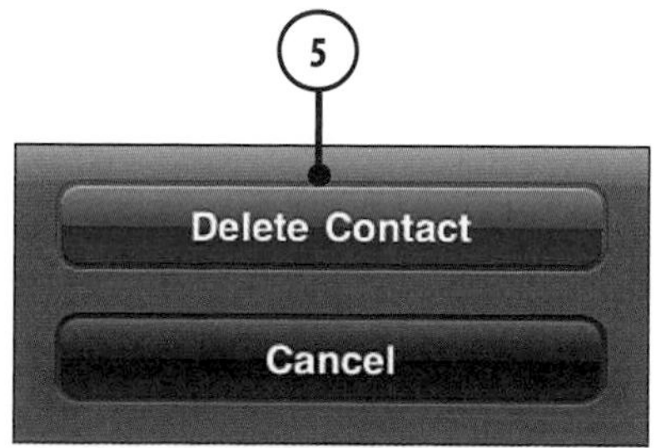

Tap to configure email accounts and settings

Tap to use email

In this chapter, you explore all the email functionality that an iPod touch has to offer. Topics include the following:

- → Configuring email accounts
- → Configuring general email settings
- → Managing email accounts
- → Working with email

Emailing

For most of us, email is an important way we communicate with others, both in our professional and personal lives. Fortunately, your iPod touch has great email tools so that you can work with email no matter where you are. Of course, you need to be connected to the Internet through a Wi-Fi connection to send or receive email—although you can read downloaded messages, reply to messages, and compose messages when you aren't connected.

You can configure multiple email accounts on your iPod so that you can access all of them there. Even better, you can sync an iPod touch's email accounts with your computers so that you access the same email from multiple devices.

Configuring Email Accounts on an iPod touch

Before you can start using an iPod touch for email, you have to configure the email accounts you want to access with it. The iPod touch supports a number of standard email services including MobileMe, Exchange (by far the most widely used email system in business), Gmail, Yahoo!, and AOL. You can also configure any email account that uses POP (Post Office Protocol and no, I'm not making that up) or IMAP (Internet Message Access Protocol); this is good because almost all email accounts provided through ISPs (Internet service providers) use one of these two formats.

You can configure email accounts on an iPod touch in many ways, including the following:

- **Using MobileMe**: You can configure a MobileMe account on an iPod touch with just a few simple steps. When you set up a MobileMe account on an iPod touch, you also configure email access. See Chapter 4, "Configuring and Synchronizing Information on an iPod touch," to learn how to set up a MobileMe account.
- **Syncing email accounts on computers**: You can configure email accounts on an iPod by syncing it with your email accounts on both Windows PCs and Macs. This process is similar to moving other information onto an iPod touch and is also covered in detail in Chapter 4.
- **Configuring Gmail, Yahoo! Mail, or AOL email accounts manually**: Your iPod touch is designed to work with these email accounts and has specific account configuration tools for them. In the next section, you learn how easy it is to set up one of these accounts on your iPod touch.
- **Configuring Exchange email accounts manually**: Microsoft's Exchange email system is the most widely used email in business. Fortunately (or unfortunately, depending on your point of view), you can configure an iPod touch to work with your Exchange email account, so you have access to work-related email. (Hey, an iPod touch can't be all fun and games!)
- **Configuring other email accounts manually**: If you have an account that isn't configured on a computer and isn't one of those listed in the previous bullets, you can add it to an iPod touch manually with just a bit more work.

After you have created email accounts on an iPod touch, you can do some advanced configuration to tweak the way they work.

Configuring Gmail, Yahoo! Mail, or AOL Email Accounts on an iPod touch Manually

An iPod touch is designed to work easily with email accounts from these providers. Although the details vary slightly between these types of accounts, the following steps (which happen to show a Gmail being configured) show you how to configure any of these accounts.

1. On the Home screen, tap Settings.
2. Scroll down the screen.
3. Tap Mail, Contacts, Calendars.
4. Tap Add Account.
5. Tap the kind of account you want to configure. The rest of the steps are for a Gmail account, but configuring Yahoo! Mail or AOL accounts is similar.

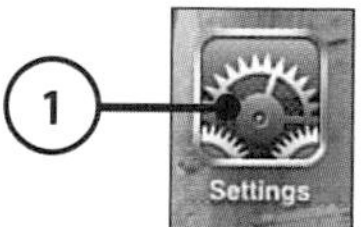

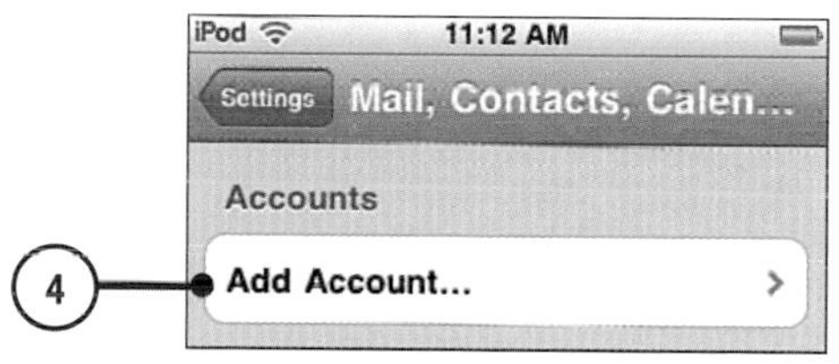

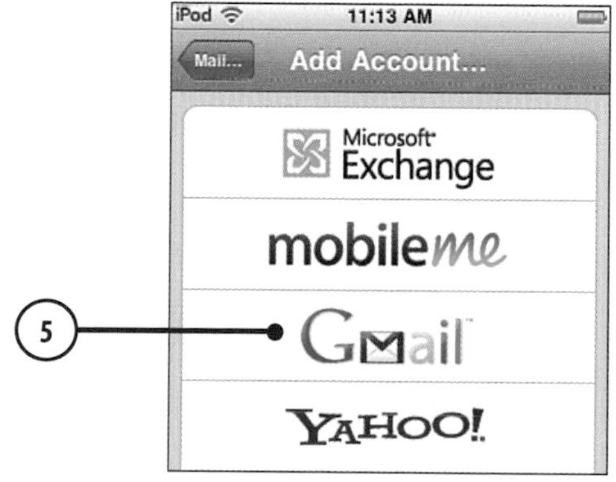

6. Enter your name.
7. Enter your Gmail email address.
8. Enter your Gmail account password.
9. Change the default description, which is your email address, if you want to. This description appears on various lists of accounts.
10. Tap Next. Your account information is verified.
11. Enable the features of the email account you want to access on the iPod, such as Mail, Calendars, Contacts, Notes, and such by tapping the ON status to disable a feature or the OFF status to enable it. (Not all types of email accounts support these features, in which case, skip this step.)
12. Tap Save. The sync settings are saved.
13. To perform advanced configuration of the account, refer to "Performing Advanced Configuration of Email Accounts on an iPod touch," later in this chapter.

Email account configured on this iPod touch

>>> Go Further

WAYS TO EXCHANGE

You can connect an iPod touch to an Exchange account (which can include email, calendar, and contacts) in two ways. One is to go through an Outlook Web Access (OWA) service, which is the service that enables you to access your Exchange account over the Web. The good news is that you don't need any support from your organization's IT department to configure an iPod touch to access your Exchange account via OWA. The other option is for your organization's Exchange system to be configured to support iPod touch email access directly; this does require support from the IT department. Some additional configuration work (and slight expense) is needed by the IT department to enable this.

If you already know you can access your Exchange account through OWA, you're ready to configure your Exchange account on your iPod touch, and you can move ahead with these steps. If you aren't sure, check with your IT department to see if OWA is supported. If it is, use these steps to configure it on an iPod touch. If OWA isn't supported, find out if the Exchange system has been configured to support iPhones and iPod touches. If it has, get the configuration information you need from your IT department and use that to configure your Exchange account on the iPod.

Configuring Exchange Email Accounts on an iPod touch Manually

Microsoft Exchange is the most widely used system for corporate email. iPod touch email is compatible with Exchange, which is good news indeed.

The following steps show you how to configure an Exchange account via Outlook Web Access (OWA):

1. On the Home screen, tap Settings.
2. Scroll down the screen.
3. Tap Mail, Contacts, Calendars.
4. Tap Add Account.
5. Tap Microsoft Exchange.
6. Enter your email address.
7. Enter your domain.
8. Enter your username.

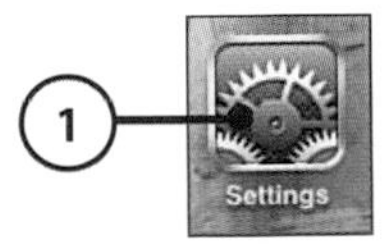

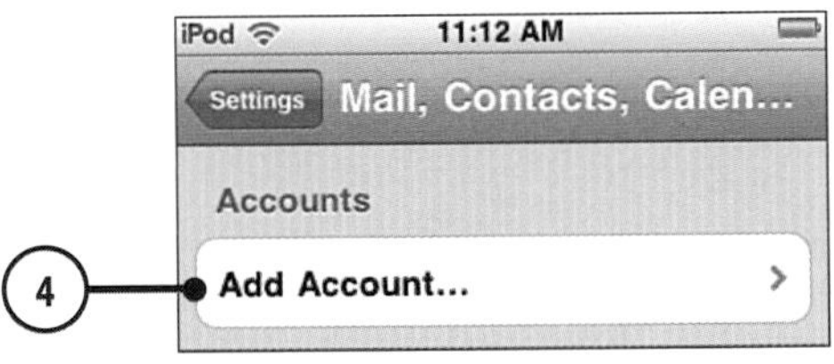

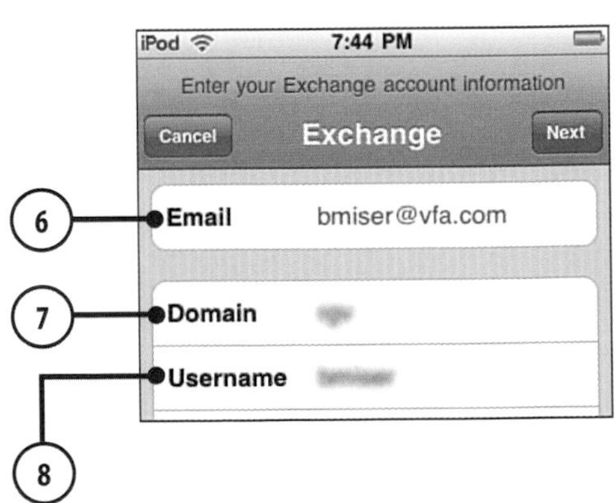

9. Enter your password.
10. Enter a description of the account. (The default is your email address.)
11. Tap Next. The account information is verified, and you see the Exchange screen with your information and some additional fields. (If the information can't be verified, just tap Accept anyway.)

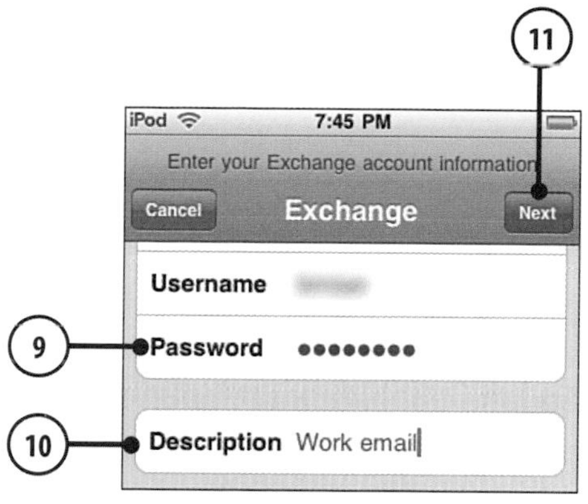

12. Enter the server address. If you use OWA, it might be similar to owa.yourcompany.com. You don't enter the https:// before the address you use to move to the server via a web browser or the /exchange after that address. If you're not using OWA, enter the address provided by your IT department.
13. Tap Next. The account information is verified, and you see the controls that enable you to determine which information is synced on the iPod.

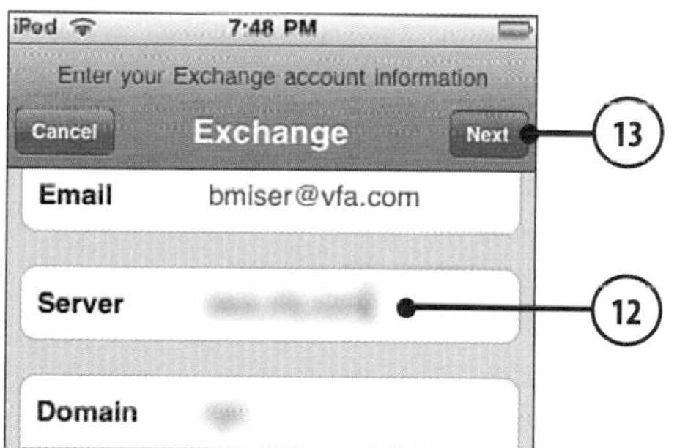

14. Tap ON for any of the information you don't want to be moved onto the iPod; its status becomes OFF to show you it won't be used on the iPod; to include information in the sync, tap OFF so its status becomes ON.
15. Tap Save. The sync is configured, and you move back to the Mail, Contacts, Calendars screen where you see your Exchange account. Under the account description, you see the information that is synced with the account, such as Mail or Calendars.

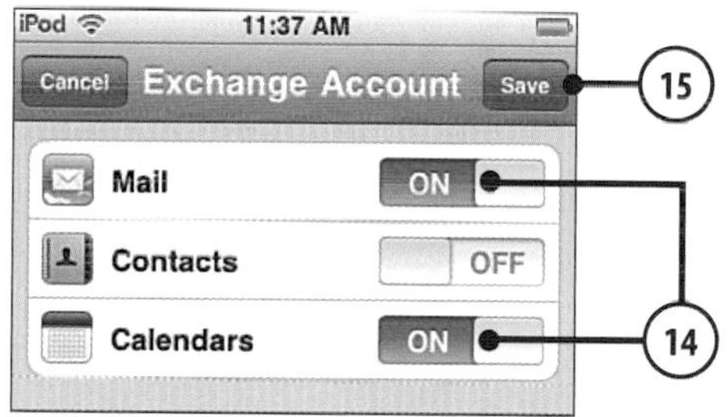

16. Tap your Exchange account.
17. Tap Mail Days to Sync.
18. Tap the amount of time over which Exchange information should be synced. For example, to have one week of Exchange information on your iPod touch, tap 1 Week.
19. Tap the Return button, which is labeled with your email account's description.

Exchange email account

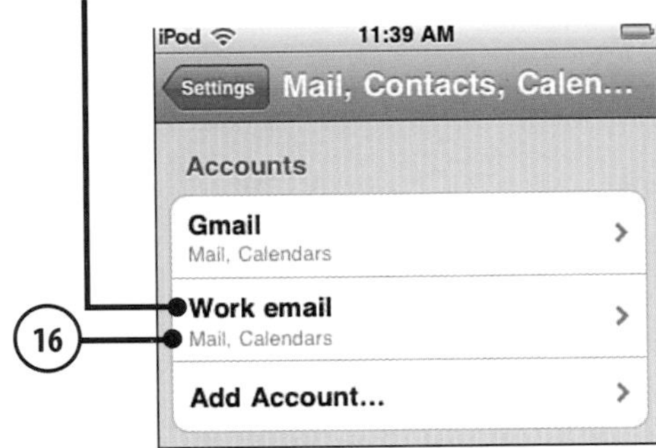

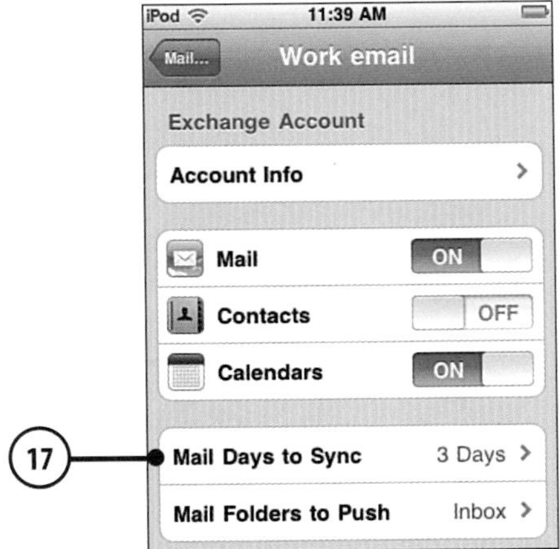

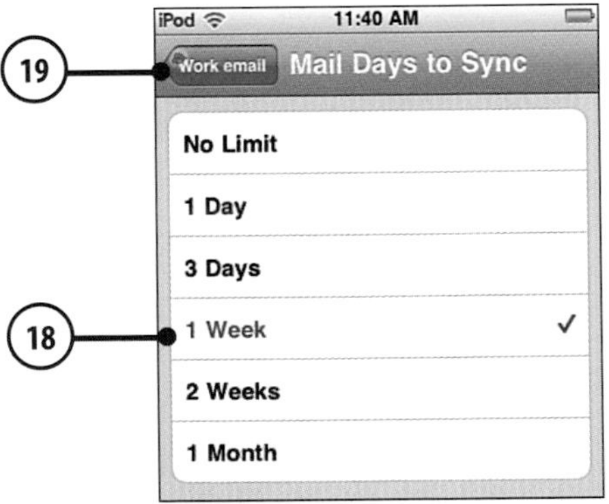

Configuring Other Email Accounts on an iPod touch Manually

If you don't configure an email account via syncing and it isn't one of the "standard" types shown previously, you can still configure it to work on an iPod touch with only slightly more work.

When you obtain an email account, such as accounts that are part of your Internet service from an ISP, you should have received all the information you need to configure that account. If you don't have this information, visit the provider's website and look for information on configuring the email account in an email application. If you already have the account configured on an email client that you aren't syncing for some reason, you can copy the information from the configuration screens in that application. You must have this information to configure the account on the iPod.

With this information in hand, move to the Add Account screen and select Other as the account type. Input the information you received when you obtained the account into the appropriate fields on the resulting screens. This is similar to configuring an Exchange account as described in the previous task, but the details will be a bit different. Just plug the ISP's configuration data into the appropriate fields and you can set up the email account. (In most cases, you have already configured the email account on a computer, so it's easier to move it onto the iPod touch by syncing as explained in Chapter 4.)

Sync 'Em if You've Got 'Em

If you have an email account already configured on a computer, there's no need to configure it manually on an iPod touch. It's much easier just to sync the account onto an iPod touch. See Chapter 4 for the steps to sync email accounts.

>>> Go Further

PROBLEMS SENDING MAIL?

You might have trouble sending email from some kinds of email accounts provided by an ISP when you use a network that isn't provided by that ISP. For example, many email accounts provided by an ISP (such as a cable company) require that any mail sent comes from the IP address associated with that account, which means you can send mail only when you access the Internet from a network with an IP address that the ISP's network recognizes (such as your home network). This won't be the case when you use a Wi-Fi network provided by someone else, such as at a hotel or airport, so you can't send email from these accounts from the iPod touch. You can still receive email for these accounts, but you can't send it.

There are several possible solutions. The easiest one is to select an account from which you can send email when you are outside of your network when you compose or reply to email. (How to do this is explained later in this chapter.) In some cases, you can configure email to be sent by using a specific port. (You usually have to search the ISP's help information to find out what this is.) To do this, you need to use the Advanced configuration settings for the email account with which you are having trouble sending email; these are explained in the following section. The third option is to configure a different email account SMTP server (Simple Mail Transfer Protocol)—the server that sends email—that you can send email from for the account that you can't send mail from; you can use the information in the next section to do this. Finally, you can enable the SMTP server that your iPod touch provider includes if it does provide one; this is also covered in the next section. The simplest solution is to have at least one account through which you can send email from any IP address, such as a MobileMe or Gmail account. (You can obtain a Gmail account for free on google.com). Whenever you aren't using the network associated with the ISP account, simply choose the MobileMe or Gmail account as the from address, and you can send email.

Performing Advanced Configuration of Email Accounts on an iPod touch

Different kinds of email accounts have various sets of advanced configuration options, but you access those options in a similar way. The following steps show the details for a MobileMe account. To do advanced configuration of other accounts, you use similar steps, but the details for the specific accounts depend on the type of account you configure.

1. Move to the Mail, Contacts, Calendars screen.
2. Tap the email account you want to configure.
3. Tap Account Info.
4. Tap Advanced.

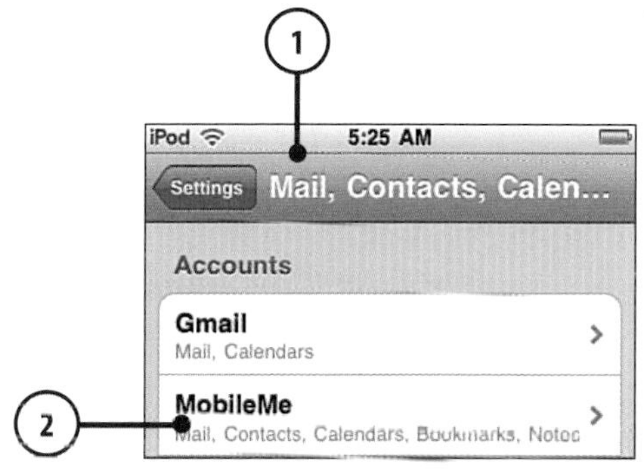

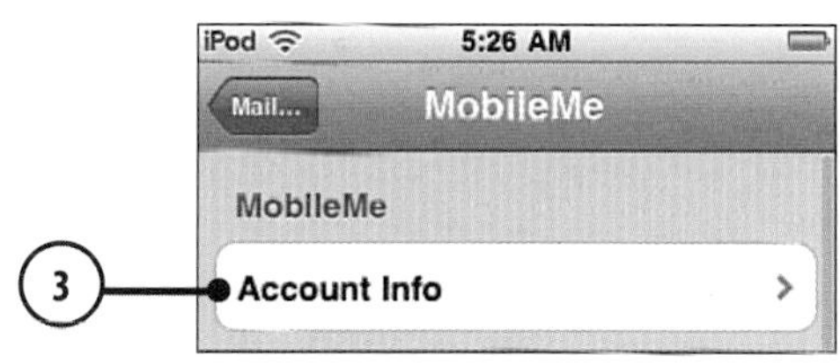

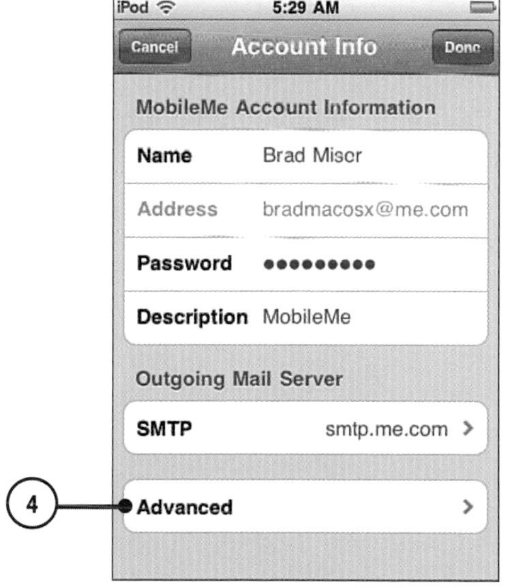

5. Tap Drafts Mailbox.
6. To have drafts of your emails stored on the iPod touch, tap Drafts in the On My iPhone section, or to have them stored on the server, tap Inbox or one of the other folders in the On the Server section. The advantage of storing drafts on the server is that you can work on them from any location that can access your MobileMe account, such as a computer. If you save them on an iPod touch, you can only work on them using the iPod touch.
7. Tap Advanced.
8. Using the information in steps 6 and 7, set the location where your sent mail is stored and where deleted messages are stored. The options are the same as for draft messages.
9. Tap Remove.

10. Choose when you want deleted email to be removed from the server. The longer the timeframe, the more storage space on the server is used for deleted messages, but the longer you can recover those messages.
11. Tap Advanced.
12. Scroll down so you see the Incoming Settings section.
13. If you ever need to change any of the settings that enable you to retrieve email for the account, use the fields in the Incoming Settings section to do so. If you ever change the settings, you need to make sure they match the incoming mail server Information provided for the email account by the provider.
14. Tap Account Info.
15. Tap SMTP. Here, you see all the SMTP servers for the various email accounts configured on your iPod touch. At the top of the screen is the primary server, which is the one that an iPod touch always tries first when you send email from the account you work with. The Other SMTP Servers list shows other configured servers. If a server's status is On, the iPod touch will attempts to send email via that server if the primary fails. It's useful if you have at least two SMTP servers On for each email account.

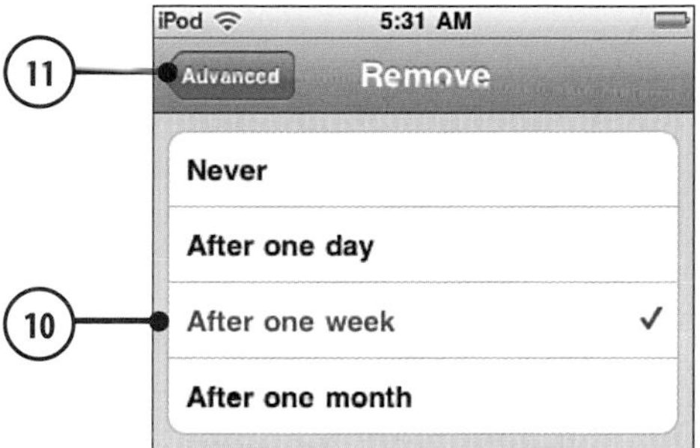

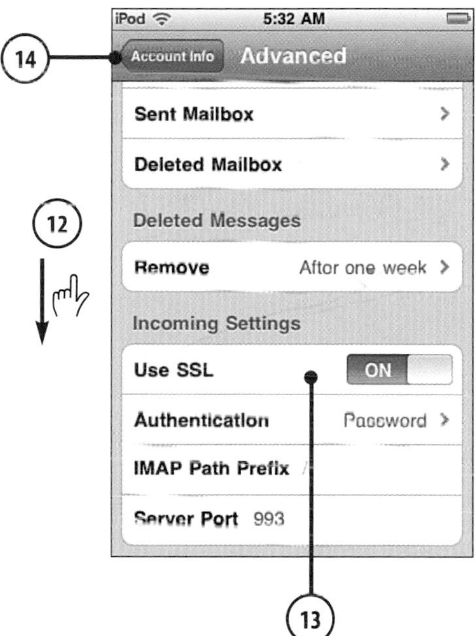

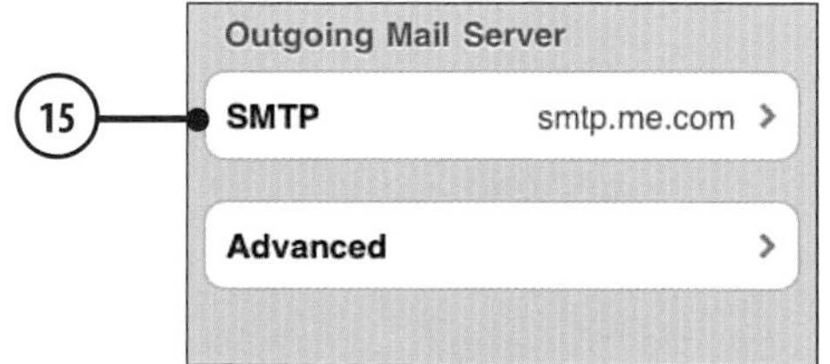

16. If you need to enable or disable the primary server, tap it. You see the configuration screen for that SMTP server.
17. To turn the server off for the account, tap ON; the status becomes OFF, and that server will not be used to send email from the account. (You must have at least one other SMTP server configured to be able to send email from the account.)
18. Tap Done.
19. To configure another SMTP server for the account, tap it on the Other SMTP Servers list.

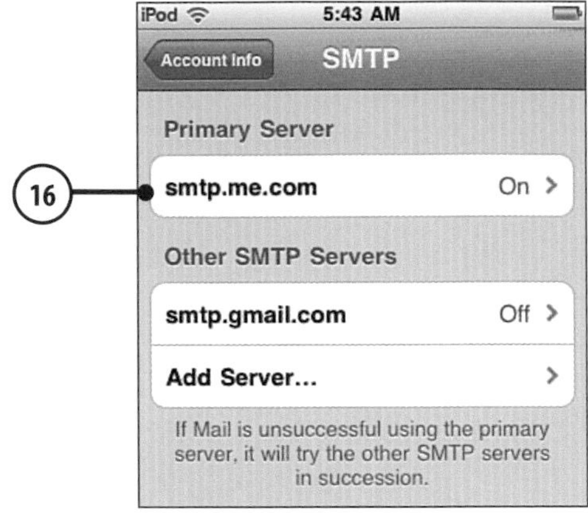

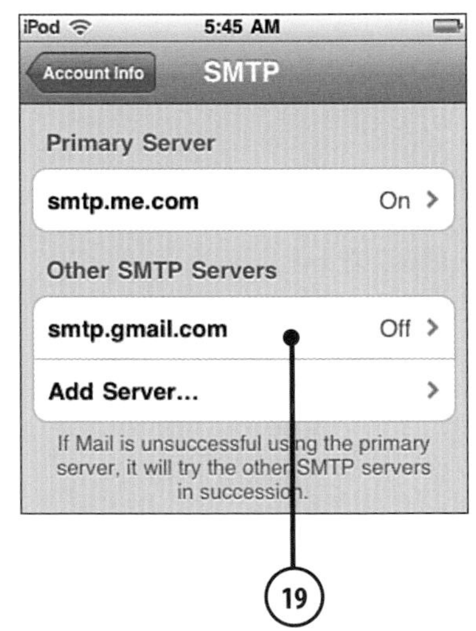

20. To enable the server for the account, tap OFF so the status becomes ON. When sending messages through the primary server fails, the enabled server will be tried.
21. Tap Done.
22. Enable or disable other STMP servers.
23. To add a new SMTP server, tap Add Server.
24. Configure the server with the Add Server screen; you use the same type of settings as when you configure an email account.

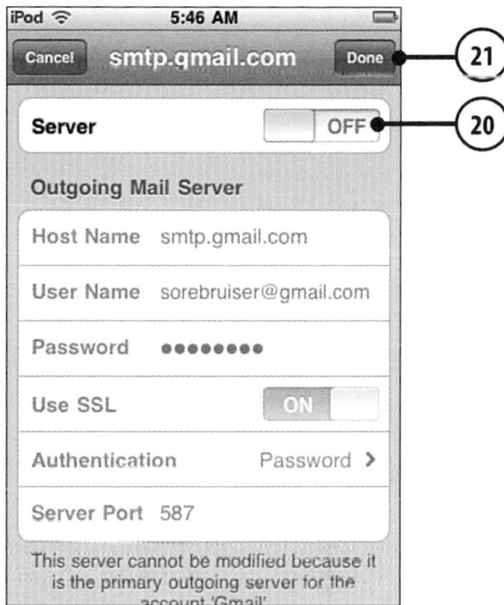

Changing SMTP Server Settings

If the fields for an SMTP server are disabled, it means that the server is the primary for at least one of your email accounts, and so you can't change it from the current one. To make changes to that server, move to the Advanced screen for the email account for which it is the primary SMTP server and use its tools to make the changes to the server settings. Of course, you would only do this if you are having trouble sending email using that server.

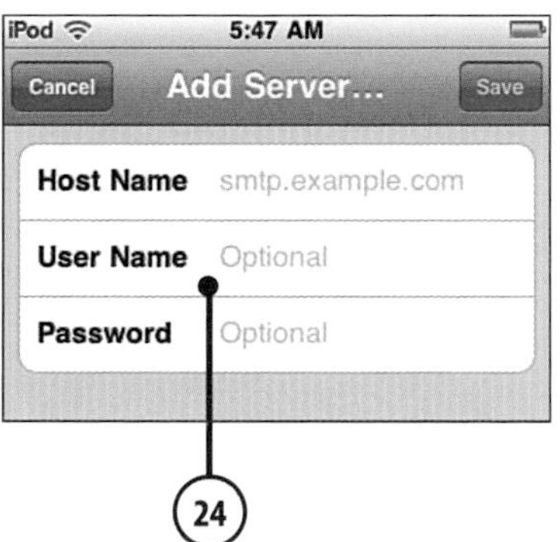

Configuring General Email Settings

You can use several settings to configure how your iPod touch handles your email.

Configuring How Email Is Retrieved

Email is retrieved in several ways on the iPod. Using Push, email is automatically pushed from the email server onto the iPod. Not all email accounts support push (MobileMe and Exchange accounts do), but its benefit is that email on your iPod is in sync with the email server, so you always have your most current email available to you. The downside is that pushing email consumes more battery power because of the constant activity. The touch can also fetch email, which means that it contacts the server at defined intervals to get email. This approach doesn't retrieve email as constantly as pushing, but it does use much less battery power. You can set an iPod touch to fetch email at specific intervals, or you can fetch email manually.

1. Move to the Mail, Contacts, Calendars screen.
2. Tap Fetch New Data.

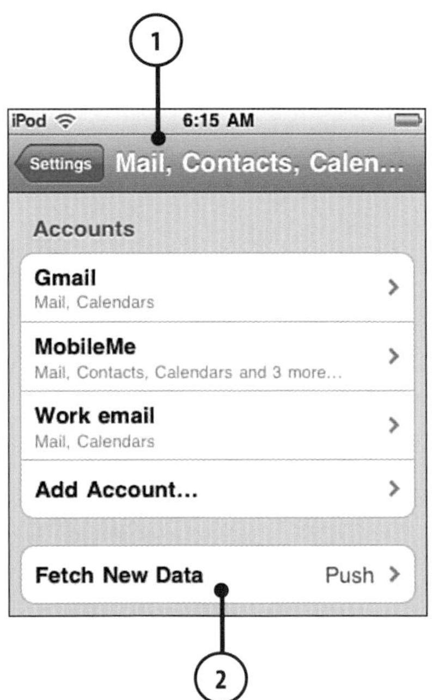

3. To enable email to be pushed, ensure the Push status is ON (if it isn't, tap OFF to turn it on); or to disable push to extend battery life, tap ON so the status becomes OFF.
4. Tap the amount of time when you want an iPod touch to fetch email when Push is OFF and for those accounts that don't support pushing email to your iPod touch; tap Manually if you want to check only for email manually for fetch accounts or when Push is OFF.
5. Scroll down the screen.
6. Tap Advanced. You see a list of all your active email accounts. Next to each account, you see if it is configured to use Push, Fetch, or Manual.
7. To change how an account gets email or other information, tap it. You see the account's screen. The options on this screen depend on the kind of account it is. You always have Fetch and Manual; you see Push only for email accounts that support it.

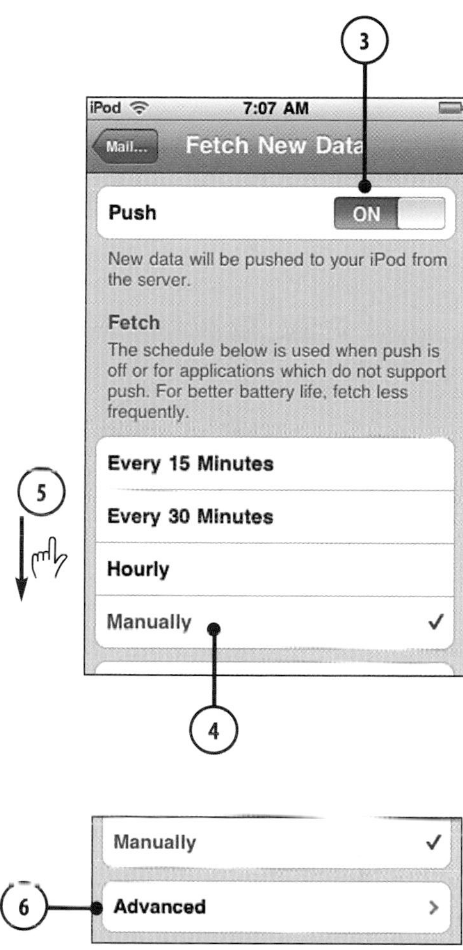

8. Tap the option you want to use for the account; Push, Fetch, or Manual. If you choose Manual, information is retrieved only when you manually start the process, regardless of the general Fetch schedule set on the Fetch New Data screen. If you selected Manually in step 4, you have to manually retrieve email even if you select Fetch on this screen.
9. Tap Advanced.
10. Repeat steps 7 through 9 for each account.
11. Tap Fetch New Data.

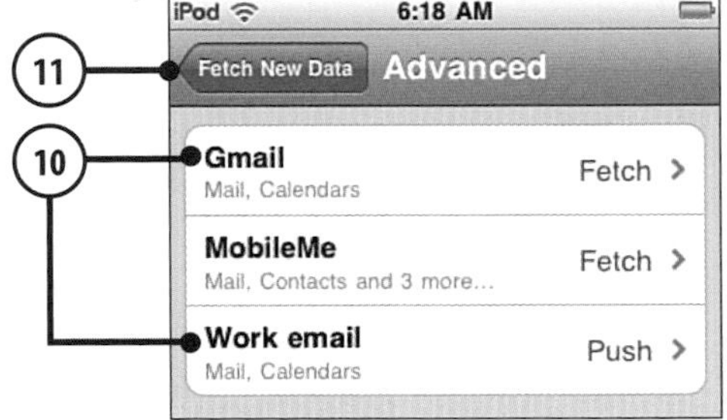

It's Not All Good

WARNING: Editorial comment coming…I find push email distracting and intrusive. One of the benefits of email is that you can use it when you choose to use it. With push enabled for email and your iPod touch configured to notify you each time you receive an email, you might find it distracting as emails come pouring in, and you might be tempted to pay attention to email when you should be paying attention to something else. (If you've ever been in a meeting where people are paying attention to email on their mobile devices instead of paying attention to what's happening around them, you know what I mean.) I find setting most email accounts to Manual is best for me because I control when I deal with email and don't have the distraction of new email coming in automatically. Or set Fetch at a reasonable time, such as every 30 minutes. Email will be retrieved automatically but won't be so distracting. Do we really need a constant stream of email? Additionally, not using Push makes your battery last longer.

Configuring Global Email Settings

Your iPod touch includes a number of settings that affect all your email accounts. You can also set preferences for specific email accounts, as you learn later in this chapter.

1. Move to the Mail, Contacts, Calendars screen.
2. Scroll down until you see the Mail section.
3. Tap Show.
4. Tap the number of recent messages you want an iPod touch to display in the email application.
5. Tap Mail.
6. Tap Preview.

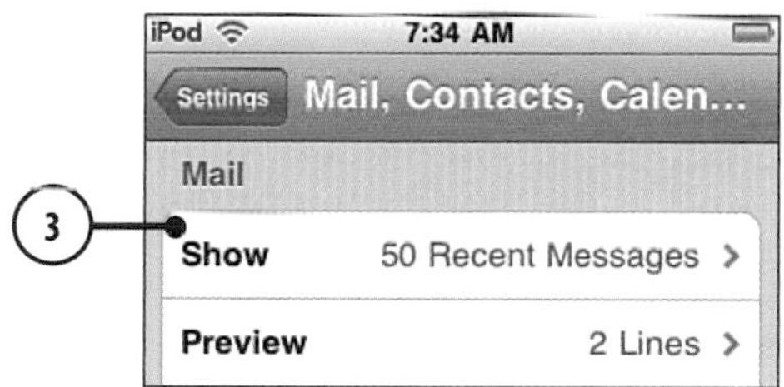

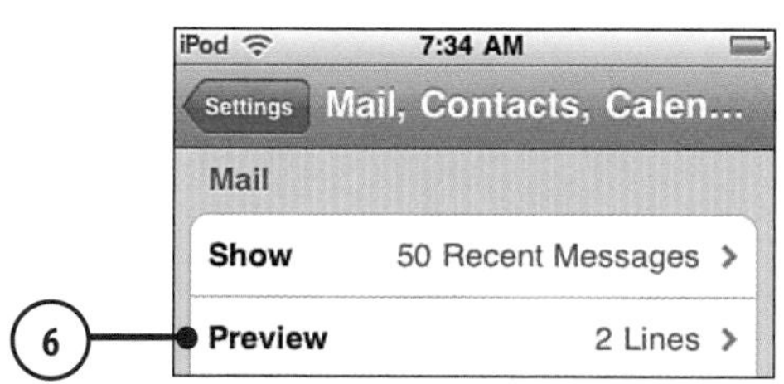

7. Tap the number of lines you want the iPod touch to display for each email when you view the inbox.
8. Tap Mail.
9. Tap Minimum Font Size.
10. Tap the smallest font size you want to use for email. The larger the size, the easier to read, but the less information fits on a single screen.
11. Tap Mail.

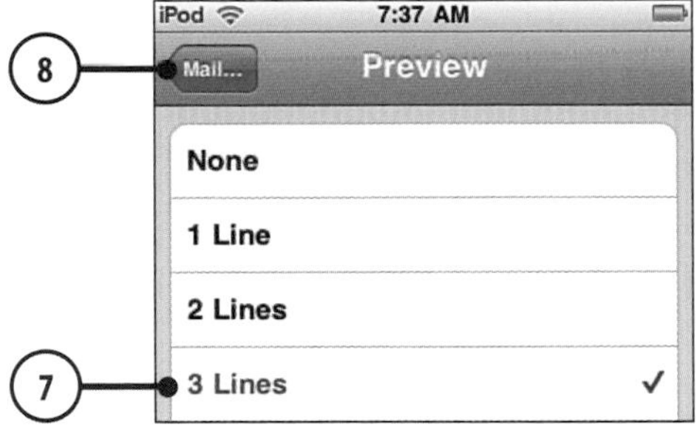

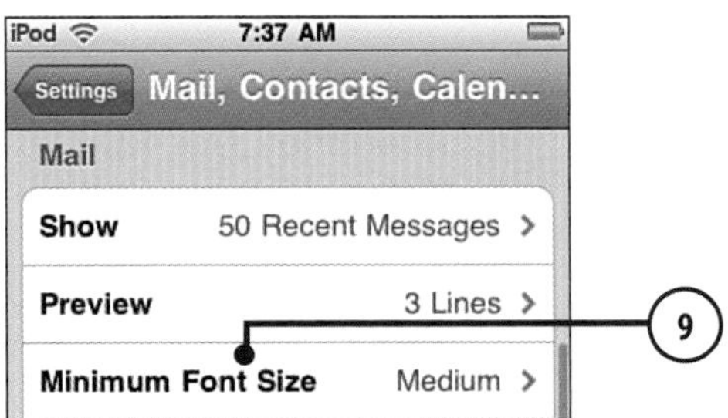

12. Enable the Show To/Cc Label to always see the To and Cc labels in email headers. (With this disabled, you can view this information on a message by tapping Details.)

13. If you don't want to have to confirm your action when you delete messages, ensure that Ask Before Deleting is OFF. When you delete a message, it immediately goes into the trash.

14. If you always want images that are not part of the message to be loaded into a message when you read it, ensure Load Remote Images is ON. If you disable this, you can manually load images in a message. If you receive a lot of spam, you should disable this so that you won't see images in which you might not be interested.

15. If you don't want Mail to organize your messages by thread (which means grouping them based on their subject so that you see all the messages on a single topic on the same screen), disable this feature by tapping Organize by Thread ON so that it's status becomes OFF.

16. If you want to receive a blind copy of each email you send, tap Always Bcc Myself OFF. Its status becomes ON, and each time you send a message, you also receive a copy of it, but your address is not shown to the message's other recipients.

17. Tap Signature.

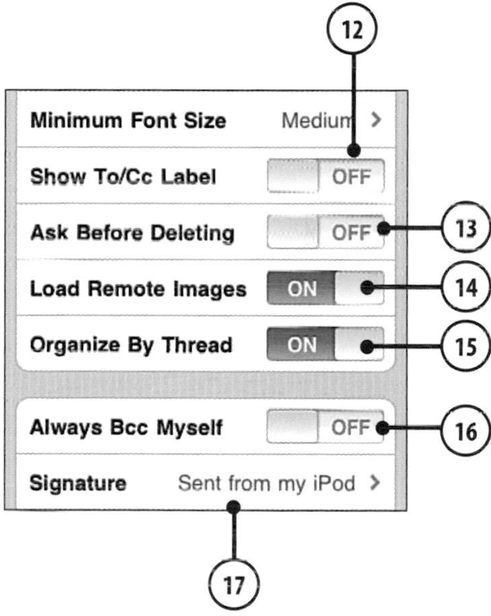

18. Enter the signature you want to append to each message you send. If you don't want an automatic signature, delete all the text on the screen.
19. Tap Mail.
20. Tap Default Account.
21. Tap the account you want to be your default. The default account appears at the top of lists and is used as the From address for emails you send. (Of course, you can change the From address on messages when you create them.) It is also the one used when you send photos, YouTube videos, and so on.
22. Tap Mail. Now enable or disable email sounds.
23. Tap Settings.

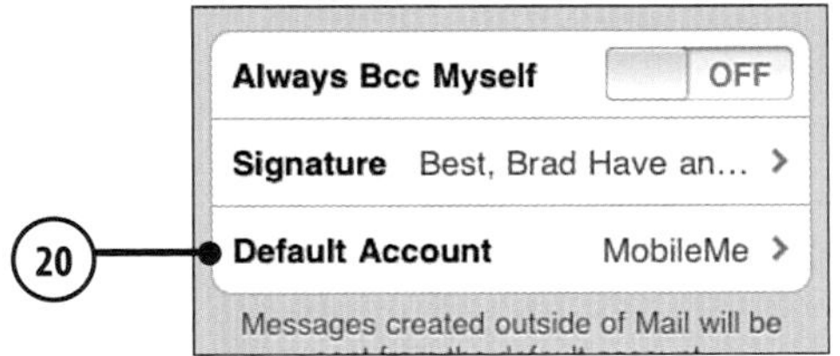

24. Tap Sounds.
25. To hear a sound when you receive new mail, make sure that the ON status for New Mail is shown; tap ON to turn the new mail sound off if you don't want to be notified when you receive messages.
26. To hear a sound when mail is sent, make sure that the ON status for Sent Mail displays; tap ON to turn the sent mail sound off if you don't want to hear this sound.
27. Tap General. Your global email configuration is complete.

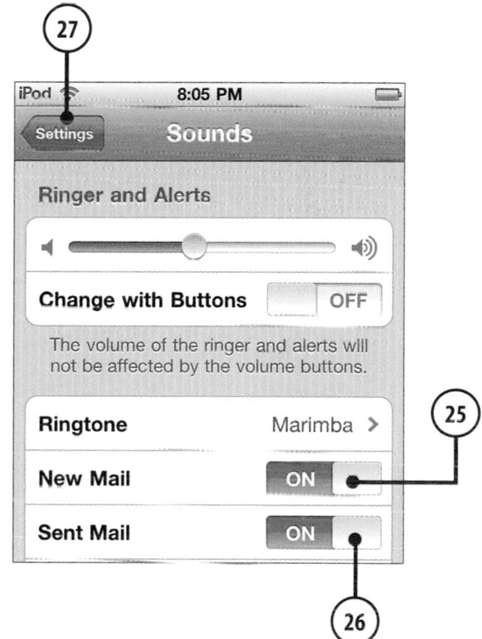

Managing Email Accounts

You can manage your email accounts in a number of ways, including changing their configurations, disabling accounts, or deleting accounts.

Changing Email Account Configurations

As you work with your email accounts, you might need to make changes from time to time. The specific changes you can make depend on the type of account you change. The general steps to change an account follow.

1. Move to the Mail, Contacts, Calendars screen.
2. Tap the account you want to change.
3. Enable the elements of the account you want to use by ensuring they are turned ON. For example, if you don't want to receive email from an account tap Mail ON so its status becomes OFF. That account's inbox is removed from the iPod, and you won't see it in the Mail app. If you disable an element that stores data on the iPod, such as calendars or contacts, you're prompted to delete the existing information when you disable the feature.
4. Configure other options you see. For example, when you configure a Gmail account, you can choose to have your messages archived. For MobileMe, you can enable or disable the Find My iPod touch feature. For an Exchange account, you can set the number of days you want to be included in syncs and the mail folders you want to have pushed to the iPod. Different types of accounts may have other or no options.
5. To reconfigure or update an account's settings, tap Account Info.

6. Use the Account Info screen to change the account's settings. Do this is the same way as when you set up an account.
7. Tap Done.
8. Tap Mail.
9. Repeat steps 2 through 8 to configure the rest of your email accounts.

Avoiding Duplicate Contacts

If you store the same contact information in more than one account, you might want to enable just one of your accounts on the iPod to sync contacts. Otherwise, you may see multiple entries for the same contact from each source (say, one from MobileMe and one from Gmail). If you also have unique contacts in each source, you need to ignore the duplicates.

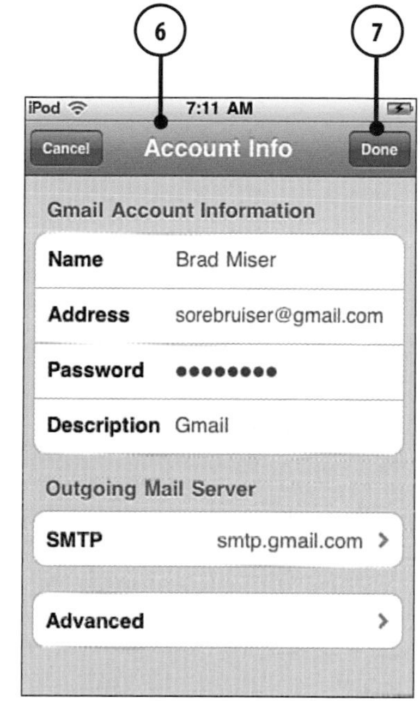

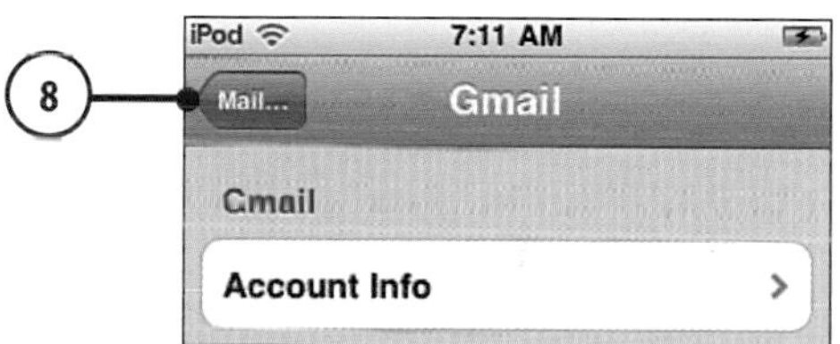

Deleting Email Accounts

If you no longer want to receive email from an account on an iPod touch, you can delete it. Of course, the account still exists; you just won't see it on your iPod. You can still use it with an email application, via the Web, and so on. (You can restore it to an iPod touch by syncing it or by re-creating it manually.) If you just want to temporarily stop using the account instead, disable its sync options as explained in step 3 in the previous task, "Changing Email Account Configurations." About the only situation in which you should delete an email account from the iPod is when you no longer have the account or if the account has become so spammed that you never want to use it again.

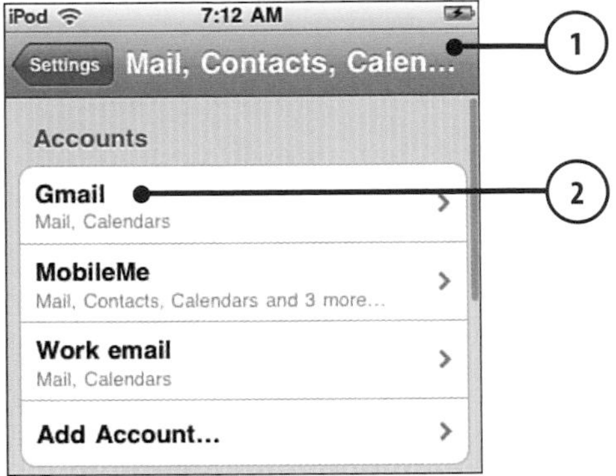

1. Move to the Mail, Contacts, Calendars screen.
2. Tap the account you want to delete.
3. Scroll to the bottom of the screen.
4. Tap Delete Account.
5. Tap Delete Account at the prompt. The account is removed from your iPod touch.

Resurrecting Email Accounts

If the email account you deleted from the iPod touch is part of the synchronization settings for your iPod touch, it will be added to the iPod touch again the next time you sync. To be permanently get rid of it, you also need to remove it from the synchronization settings (see Chapter 4).

Working with Email

With your email accounts and settings configured, you're ready to start using your iPod touch for email. To do this, you use the iPod's Mail app, which offers lots of great features and is ideally suited for working with email on your touch. The Mail app offers a consolidated Inbox, so you can view email from all your accounts at the same time. (In previous versions, you had to move into each account's Inbox separately.) Also, the Mail app organizes your email into threads, which makes following along a conversation convenient.

When you move to the Home screen, you see the number of new email messages you have in the Mail app's icon; tap the icon to move to into the application. Even if you don't have any new email, the Mail icon still leads you to the Mail app.

About Assumptions

The steps in this section assume you have more than one email account configured and actively receiving email on your touch. If you have only one email account active, your Mailboxes screen contains that accounts folders instead of what appears in these figures. Similarly, if you disable the Organize by Thread setting, you won't see messages in threads as these figures show. Instead, you work with each message individually.

Receiving and Reading Email

The iPod touch's Mail app enables you to receive and read email for all the email accounts configured on it and that are active. The Mailboxes screen is the top-level screen in the Mail app and is organized into two sections. The Inboxes section shows the inbox for each account; next to each account, you see the number of new emails received in that account. (A new email is simply one you haven't viewed yet.) At the top of the section, you see the All Inboxes selection that shows the total number of new messages to all accounts. The Accounts screen shows each email account with another counter for new messages; the difference between these sections is that the Inboxes options take you to just the inbox for the selected account, whereas the Accounts options take you to the folders under that account.

1. On the Home screen, tap Mail. The Mail application opens, and you move to the last screen you used. If that isn't the Mailboxes screen, tap the return button in the upper-left corner of the screen until you reach the Mailboxes screen.

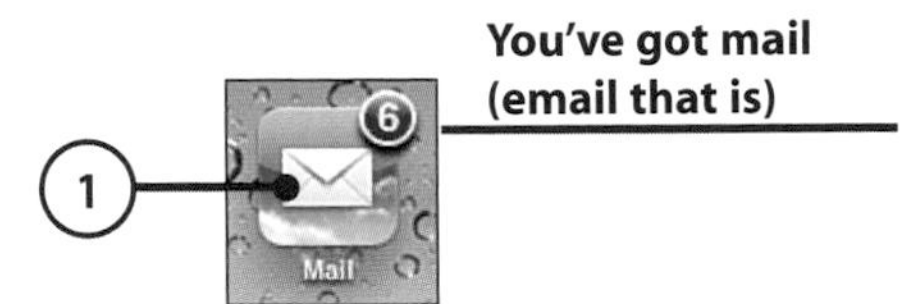

2. To read messages, tap the inbox that contains messages you want to read; tap All Inboxes to see all your messages. You move to the inbox's screen or to the All Inboxes screen, and all the messages in that inbox or in all the inboxes are shown. Various icons indicate the message status, if it is part of a thread, if it has attachments, and so on. At the top of the screen is the Search tool you can use to find specific messages.

Loading More Messages

If more messages are available than are downloaded, tap the Load More Messages link. The additional messages download to the inbox you are viewing.

3. Scroll up or down the screen to browse the messages.

4. If a message you are interested in is in a thread, tap it. (If it isn't part of a thread, skip this step.) The thread's screen appears, and you see all the messages in the thread.

5. To read a message, tap it. As soon as you open a message's screen, it's marked as read, and the new mail counter reduces by one. Just below that is the address information, including who the message is from and who it was sent to. Under that, you see the message's subject along with time and date it was sent. Last, you see the body of the message. If the message has an attachment, you see it at the bottom of the screen.

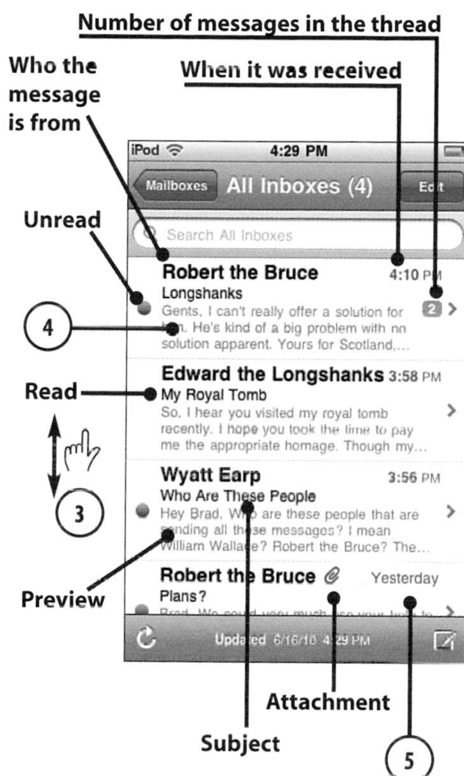

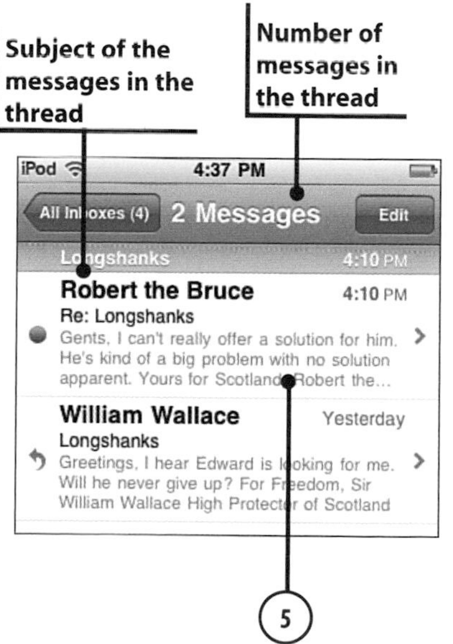

What Doth Make a Thread?

The Mail app identifies a thread by its subject. As replies are made, the messages continue to be categorized by subject because Re: is appended to it. It even remains in the thread if the initial subject continues to be in the message but other words are added.

To/Cc

If you enabled the Show To/Cc Label setting, you see a small "To" or "Cc" next to each message's title where the email address in the message's To or Cc field is associated with one of the email addresses associated with the email accounts configured on your iPod touch. When one of those isn't true, such as when you are part of distribution list, you won't see these labels.

6. Unpinch on the message to zoom in. (If you double-tap text, the selection tools appear.)

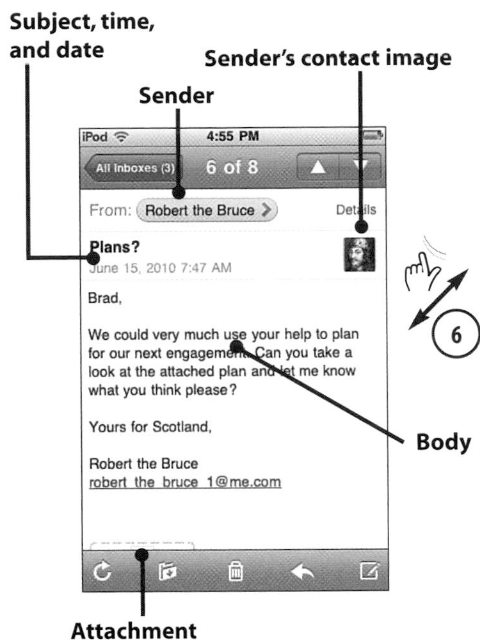

See More Address Info?

Tap the Details link located just under the down arrow at the top of the email screen to show more address information, such as the To and Cc sections. Tap Hide to hide that information again.

7. Rotate the iPod touch 90 degrees to change its orientation.
8. To scroll up or down, left or right, just drag your finger around the screen.
9. Pinch your fingers or double-tap to zoom out.

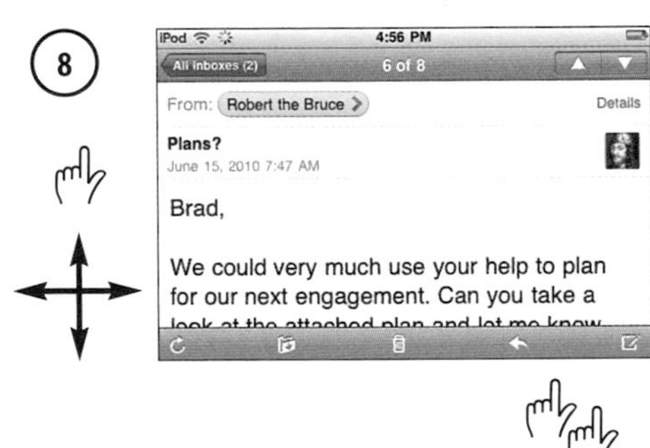

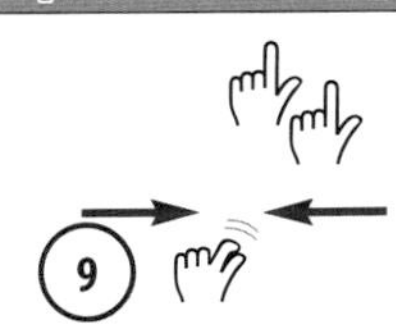

Back in Time

To change the status of a message back to Unread, expand the header by clicking Details and tap Mark as Unread. The message is marked with a blue dot again as if you'd never read it.

Photo Attached

If the message includes a photo, the iPod displays the photo in the body of the email message. You can zoom in or out and scroll to view it just as you can with text.

10. Rotate the iPod touch again to return to the previous orientation.

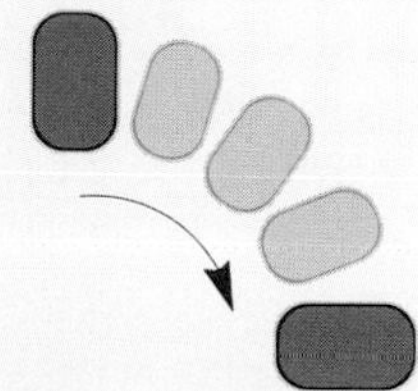

11. To view a message's attachment, tap it. If the attachment hasn't been downloaded yet, it is downloaded into the message and its icon changes to represent the type of file it is; if the attachment has already been downloaded, it opens immediately, and you don't need to tap it again. If the icon remains generic, it might be of a type the iPod can't display.

12. Tap the attachment to view it.

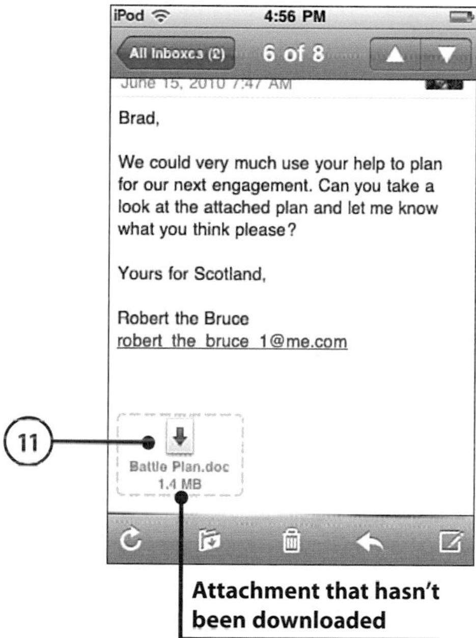

Attachment that hasn't been downloaded

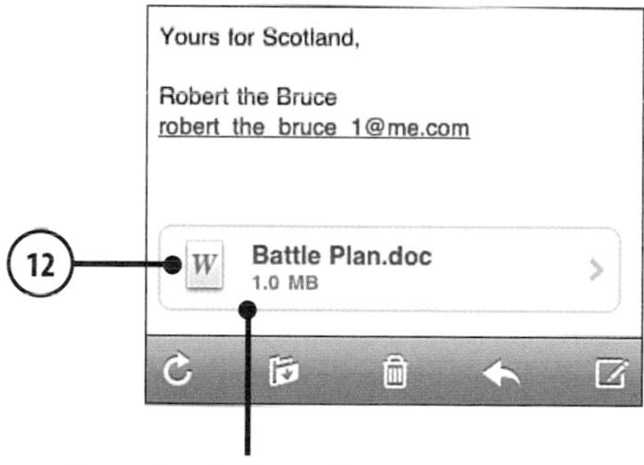

Downloaded attachment

13. Scroll the document by dragging your finger up, down, left, or right on the screen.
14. Unpinch or double-tap to zoom in.
15. Pinch or double-tap to zoom out.
16. Tap Message.
17. To view information for an email address, such as who sent the message, tap it. The Info screen appears; its title tells you how the person relates to the message. For example, if you tapped the email address in the From field, the screen title is From. If the person is on your Contacts list, you see his contact information. If not, you see as much information as an iPod touch can determine based on the email address.
18. Tap Message. You move back to the email.

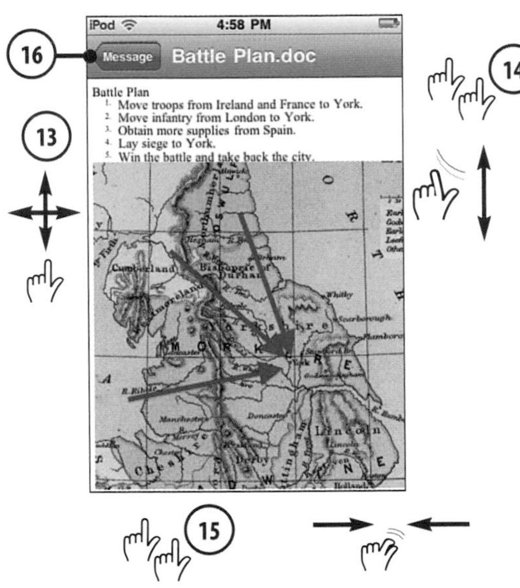

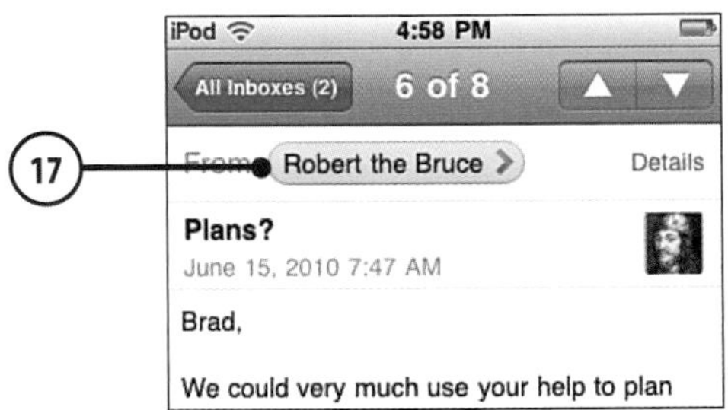

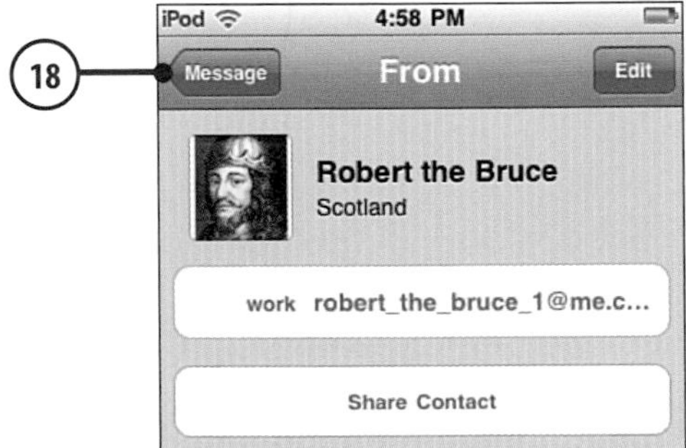

HTML Email

Mail can receive HTML email that behaves like a web page. When you tap a link (usually blue text, but can also be photos and other graphics) in such an email, Safari opens and takes you to the link's source. You then use Safari to view the web page. See Chapter 7, "Surfing the Web," for information about Safari.

19. To read the next message, tap the down arrow.

20. To move to a previous message in the inbox, tap the up arrow.

21. To move back to the inbox, tap the Return button.

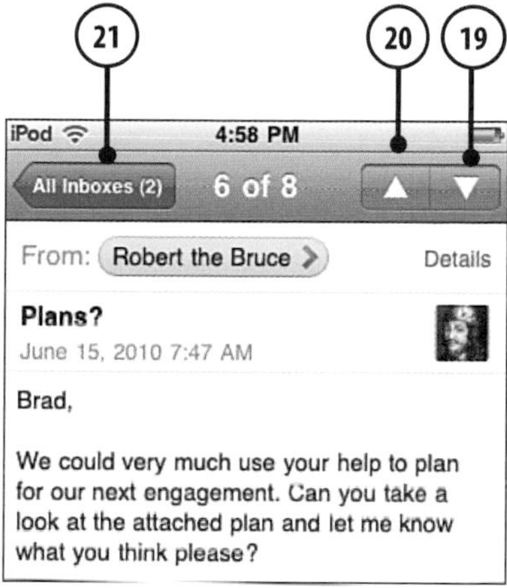

Large Messages

Some emails, especially HTML messages, are large and don't immediately download in their entirety. When you open a large message, you see a message stating that the entire message has not been downloaded. Tap the link to download the rest of the message.

Sending Email

You can send email from any of your accounts.

1. Tap the New Mail button on any Mail screen. A new email message is created. If you tapped the New Mail button while you are on the Mailboxes screen, the From address is the one you set as your default; otherwise, the From address is the email account you work with. Your signature is placed at the bottom of the message's body.

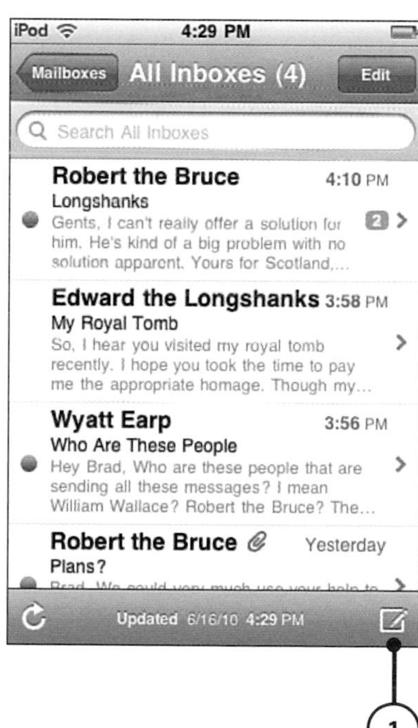

2. To type a recipient's email address, tap the To field and type in the address. As you type, Mail attempts to find matching addresses in your Contacts list or in emails you've sent or received and displays the matches it finds. To select one of those addresses, tap it, and Mail enters the rest of the address for you. Or just keep entering information until the address is complete.

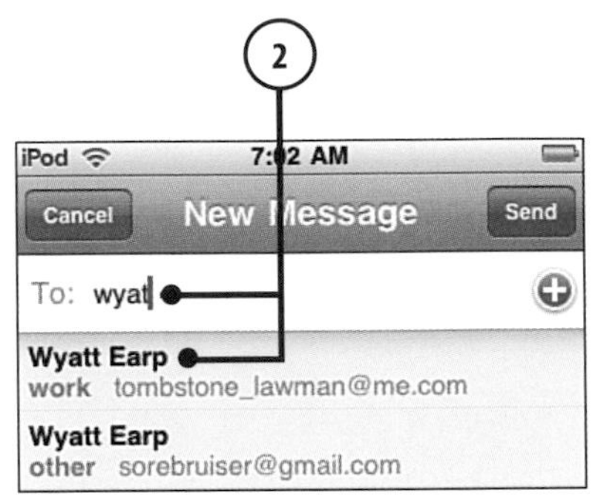

3. To address the email using your contacts, tap the Add button.

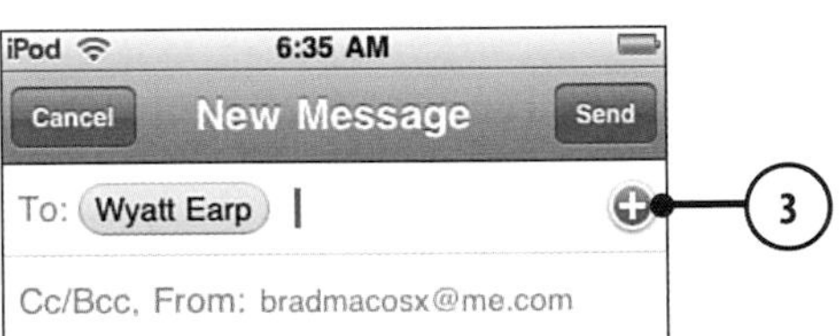

4. Use the All Contacts screen to find and select the contact to which you want to address the message. (See Chapter 8, "Managing Contacts" for the details about working with contacts.) When you tap a contact with one email address, that address is pasted into the To field, and you return to the New Message window. When you tap a contact with more than one email address, you move to the Info screen; tap the address to which you want to send the message.

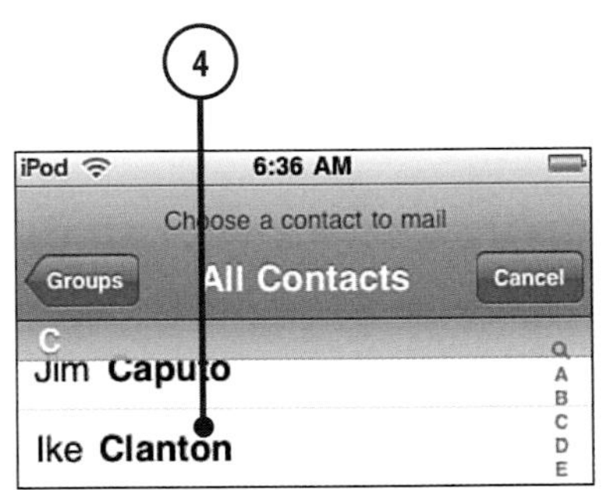

5. Repeat steps 2 through 4 to add all the recipients to the message.

6. Tap the Cc/Bcc, From line. The Cc and Bcc lines expand.

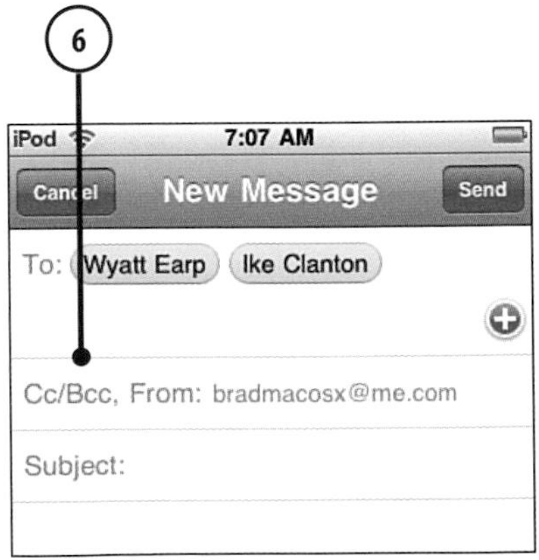

Removing Addresses

To remove an address, tap it so it is highlighted in a darker shade of blue and then tap the Delete button on the iPod touch's keyboard.

7. Use steps 2 though 4 to add recipients to the Cc field.
8. Use steps 2 though 4 to add recipients to the Bcc field.
9. To change the account from which the email is sent, tap the From field. The account wheel appears at the bottom of the screen.
10. Drag up or down the wheel to spin it to see all the addresses available to you.
11. Tap the account from which you want to send the message. It is marked with a check mark, and that address is placed in the From field.
12. Tap in the Subject line. The account wheel closes.

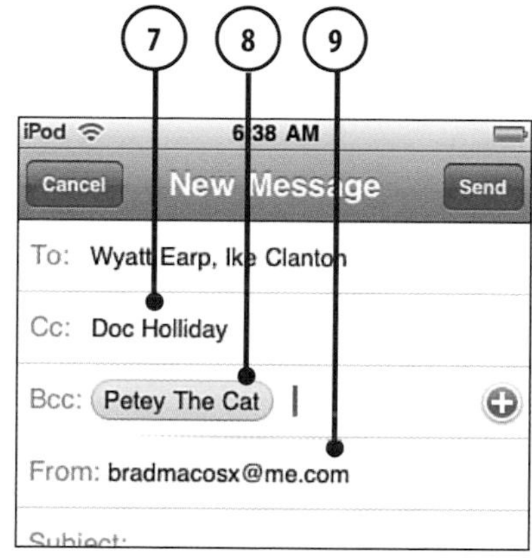

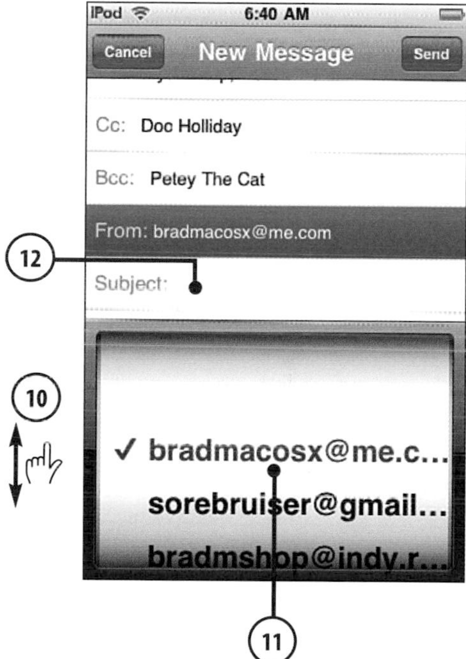

13. Type the subject of the message.
14. Scroll down the screen until you see the body area.
15. Tap in the body, and type the body of the message above your signature. Remember that as you type, Mail attempts to correct spelling and makes suggestions to complete words. To accept a proposed change, tap the space-bar when the suggestion appears on the screen; to ignore a correction, tap the x in the suggestion box. You can also use the copy and paste feature to move text around, and you can edit text using the spell checker and other text tools. (See Chapter 1, "Getting Started with Your iPod touch" for the details of working with text.)
16. To make the keyboard larger, rotate the iPod touch clockwise or counterclockwise.

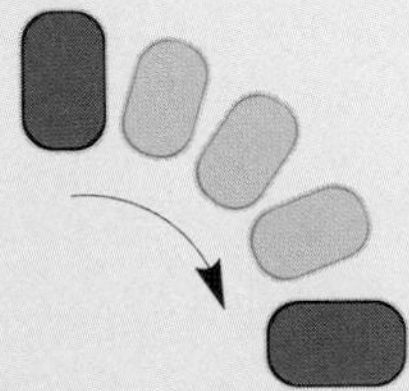

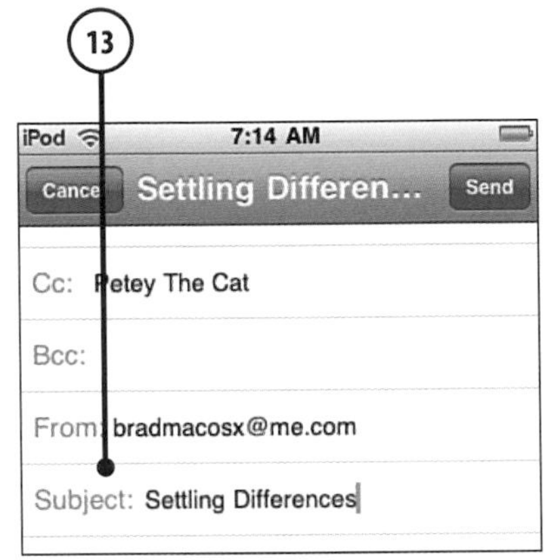

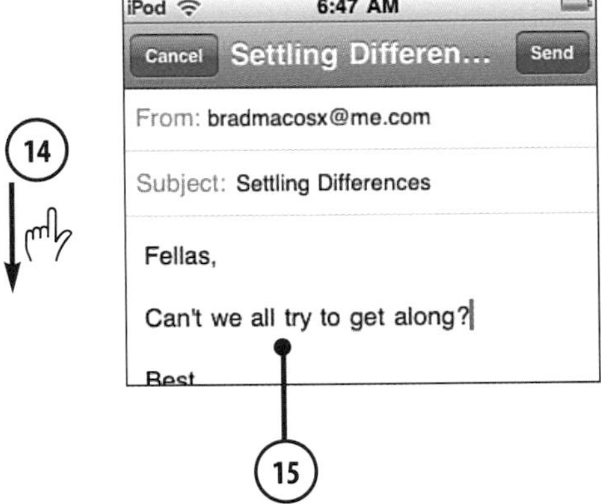

17. When you finish the message, tap Send. You see the progress of the send process at the bottom of the screen.

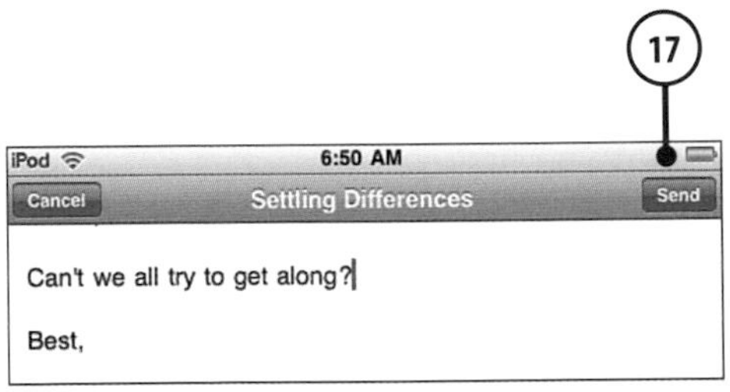

Replying to Email

Email is all about communication, and Mail makes it simple to reply to messages.

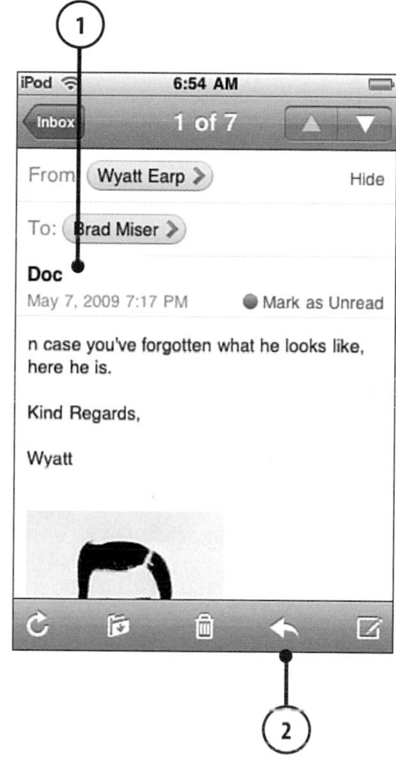

1. Open the message you want to reply to.
2. Tap the Action button.
3. Tap Reply to reply to only the sender or tap Reply All to reply to everyone who received the original message. The Re: screen appears showing a new message. Mail pastes the contents of the original message at the bottom of the body of the new message below your signature. The original content is in blue and is marked with a vertical line along the left side of the screen.

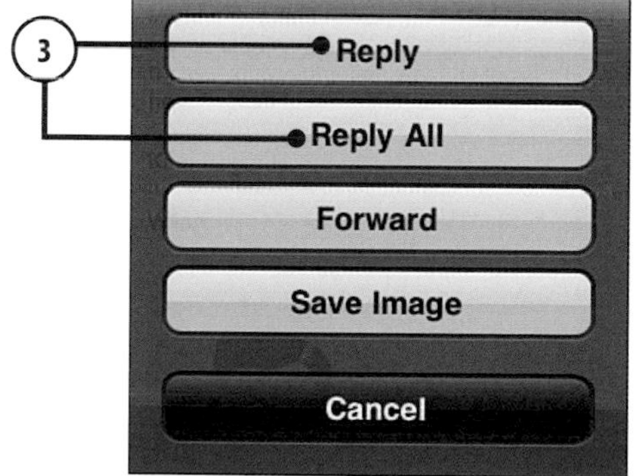

Saving Your Work in Progress

If you want to save a message you are creating without sending it, tap Cancel. A prompt appears; choose Save Draft to save the message; if you don't want the message, tap Delete Draft instead. When you want to work on a draft message again, move to the Drafts folder under the account from which you are sending the message. (You learn how to access folders later in this chapter.) Tap the message, and you move back to the New Message screen as it was when you saved the message. You can make changes to the message and then send it or save it as a draft again.

4. Use the message tools to write your reply, to add more To or Cc recipients, or to make any other changes you want.

5. Tap Send. Mail sends your reply.

Sending Email from All the Right Places

You can send email from a number of different places on your touch. For example, you can share a photo with someone by viewing the photo, tapping the Action button, and then tapping Email Photo. Or you can tap a contact's email address to send an email from your contacts list. For yet another example, you can share a YouTube video. In all cases, the iPod uses Mail to create a new message that includes the appropriate content, such as a photo or link, and you use Mail's tools to complete and send the email.

Forwarding Email

When you receive an email that you think others should see, you can forward it to them.

1. Read the message you want to forward.

2. Tap the Action button.

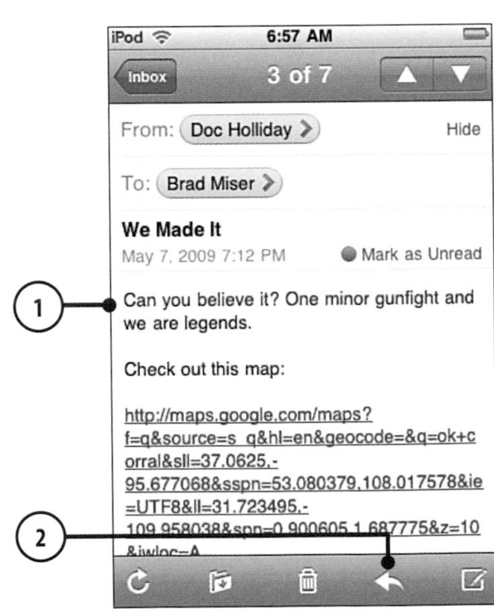

3. Tap Forward; if the message includes attachments, tap Include at the prompt if you also want to forward the attachments or Don't Include if you don't. The Forward screen appears. Mail pastes the contents of the message you are forwarding at the bottom of the message below your signature.

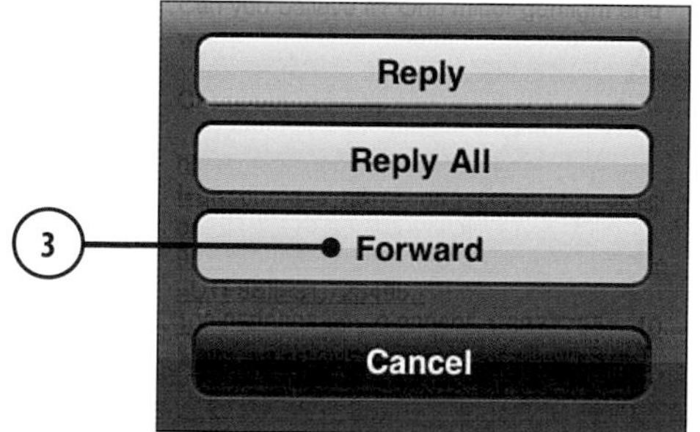

4. Address the forwarded message using the same tools that you use when you create a new message.

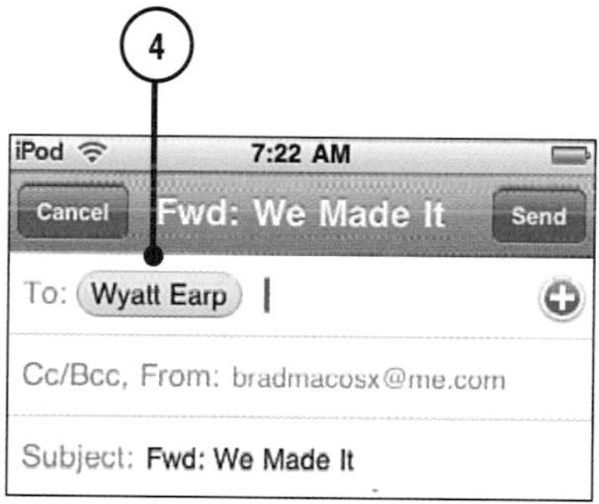

5. Type your commentary about the message above your signature.

Large Messages

Some emails, especially HTML messages, are large so that they don't immediately download in their entirety. When you forward a message whose content or attachments hasn't fully downloaded, Mail prompts you to download the "missing" content before forwarding. If you choose not to download the content or attachments, Mail forwards only the downloaded part of the message.

6. Scroll down to see the forwarded content. Forwarded content is in blue and is marked with a vertical line along the left side of the screen.
7. Edit the forwarded content as needed.
8. Tap Send. Mail forwards the message.

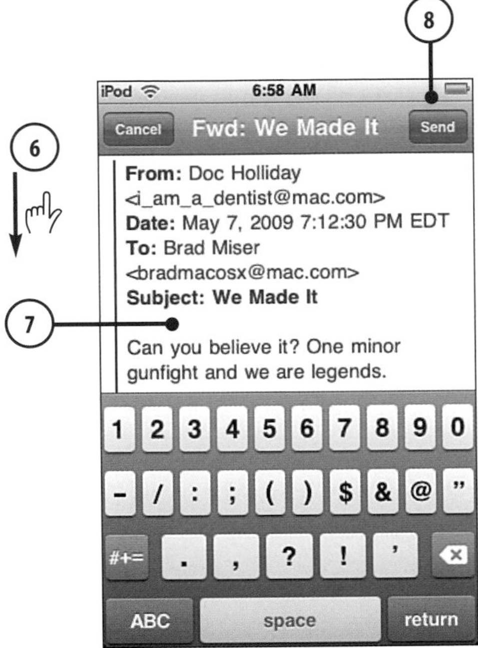

It's Not All Good

You can't create new mail folders on an iPod touch. To create a new folder for an account, use another tool, such as an email application on your computer or the account's website. New folders become available on the iPod touch after you sync the associated email account by retrieving messages.

Managing Email

Following are some ways you can manage your email. You can check for new messages, see the status of messages, and organize messages using the folders associated with your email accounts.

Checking for New Messages

You can check for new mail from any Mail screen by tapping the Get New Mail button. If you get new mail from the Mailboxes screen, messages to all of your accounts are retrieved. If you tap this when you work in a specific account's inbox or folder, only messages to that account are retrieved.

The bottom of the Mail screens always shows the status of the most recent check.

Mail also retrieves messages whenever you move into any inbox or all your inboxes. Of course, it also retrieves messages according to the option you selected. It downloads new messages immediately if Push is enabled or automatically at defined intervals if you've set Fetch to get new email periodically.

Determining the Status of Messages

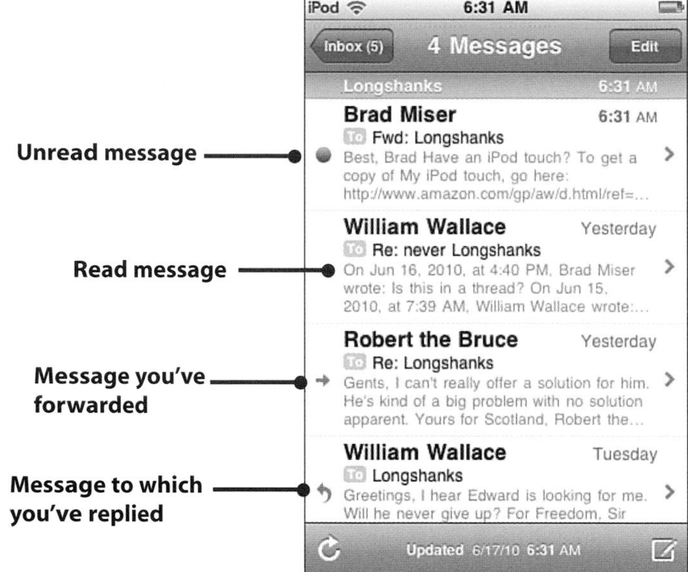

When you view an Inbox, you see icons next to each message to indicate its status (except for messages that you've read but not done anything else with).

Deleting Email from the Message Screen

To delete a message while viewing it, tap the Trash button. If you configure the warning preference, confirm the deletion, and the message is deleted. If you disable the confirmation, the message deletes immediately.

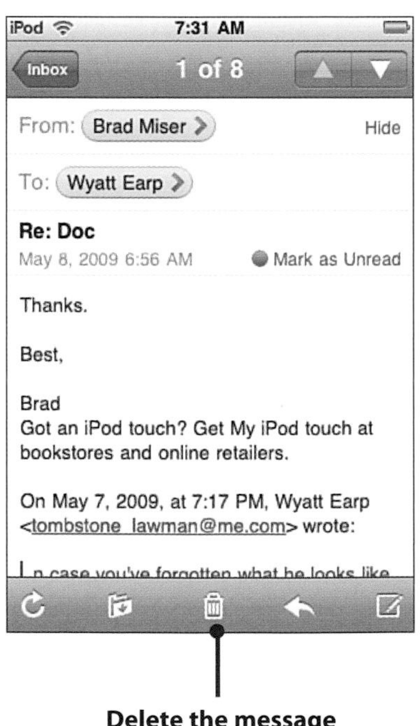

Dumpster Diving

As long as an account's trash hasn't been emptied (you learned how to set when an account's deleted messages are permanently removed earlier in the chapter by configuring the Remove setting for an account), you can work with a message you've deleted by moving to the account's screen and opening its Trash folder.

Deleting Email from the Inbox

1. Move to the screen showing messages you want to delete.
2. Tap Edit. A selection circle appears next to each message, and the Delete and Move buttons appear at the bottom of the screen.
3. Select the messages you want to delete by tapping their selection circles. As you select each message, the counters in the Delete and Move buttons increase by one, and the message's selection circle is marked with a check mark.
4. Tap Delete. Mail deletes the selected messages and exits Edit mode. (If you enabled the warning prompt, you have to confirm the deletion.)

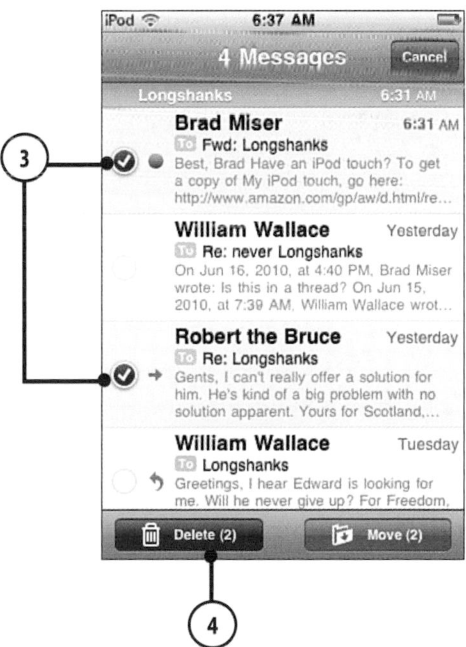

Yet Another Way to Delete

While you are on a screen showing messages, drag your finger to the left or right across a message or a thread. The Delete button appears; if you tapped a thread, the Delete button shows the number of messages in the thread. Tap the Delete button to delete the message or all the messages in the thread.

Organizing Email from the Message Screen

1. Open a message that you want to move to a folder.
2. Tap the Mailboxes button. The Mailboxes screen appears. At the top of this screen, you see the message you are moving. Under that, you see the mailboxes available under the current account.
3. Tap the folder to which you want to move the message. The message moves to that folder, and you move to the next message in the list you were viewing.

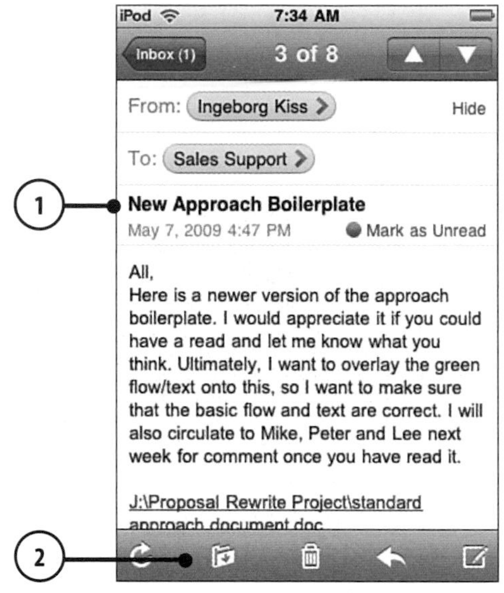

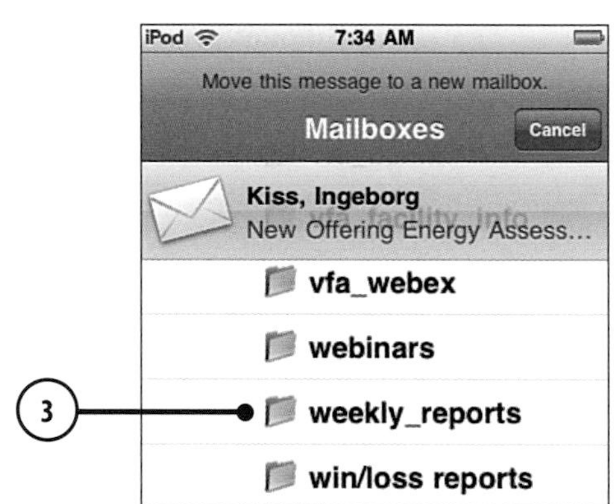

Organizing Email from the Inbox

1. Move to a screen showing email you want to move to a folder.
2. Tap Edit. A selection circle appears next to each message. The Delete and Move buttons appear at the bottom of the screen.

3. Select the messages you want to move by tapping their selection circles. As you select each message, the counter in the Move button increases by one, and the message's selection circle is marked with a check mark.
4. Tap Move.
5. Tap the folder into which you want to place the messages. They are moved into that folder, and you return to the previous screen, which is no longer in Edit mode.

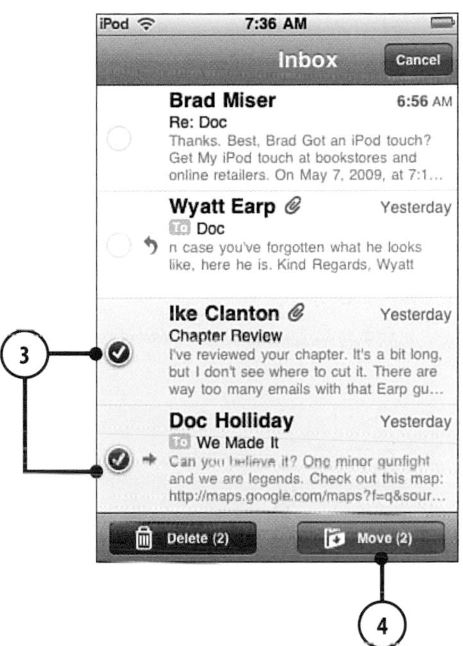

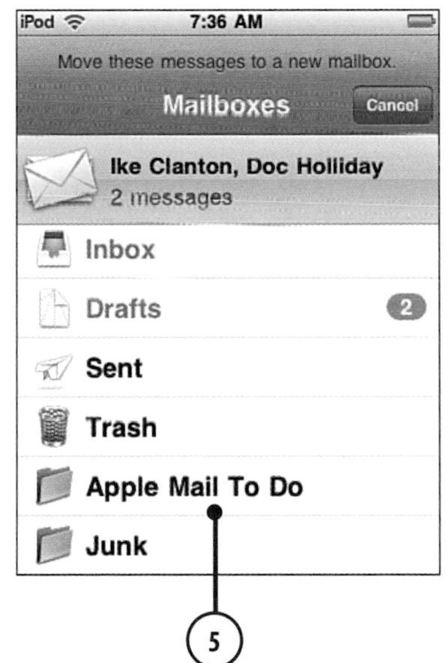

Picking at Threads

If you select a thread, you select all the messages in that thread, and the Delete and Move counters increase by the number of messages in the thread. Whatever action you select is taken on all the thread's messages at the same time.

Viewing Messages in a Folder

1. Move to the Mailboxes screen.
2. Tap the account containing the folders and messages you want to view. You see all the folders for the account.
3. Tap the folder containing the messages you want to view. You see the messages it contains. In some cases, this can take a few moments if that folder's messages haven't been downloaded.
4. Tap a message or thread to view it.

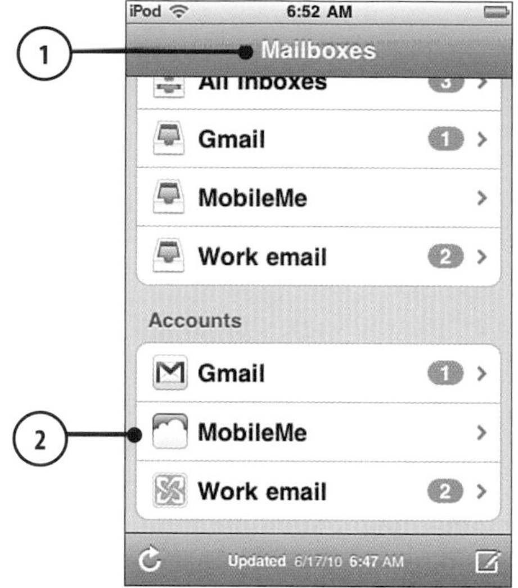

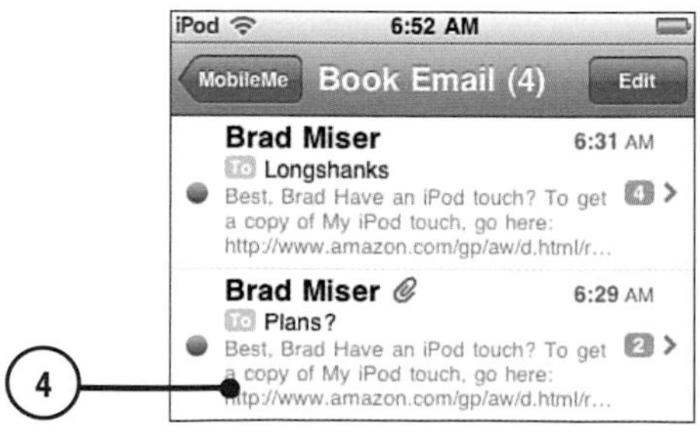

Saving an Image Attached to a Message

1. Move to the message screen of an email that contains one or more photos or images.
2. Tap the Action button.
3. Tap Save X Images, where X is the number of images attached to the message. (If there is only one image, the command is just Save Image.) The images are saved in the Saved Photos album in the Photos application. (See Chapter 11, "Storing, Viewing, and Sharing Photos," for help working with the Photos application.) The next time you sync, the images are moved onto the computer.

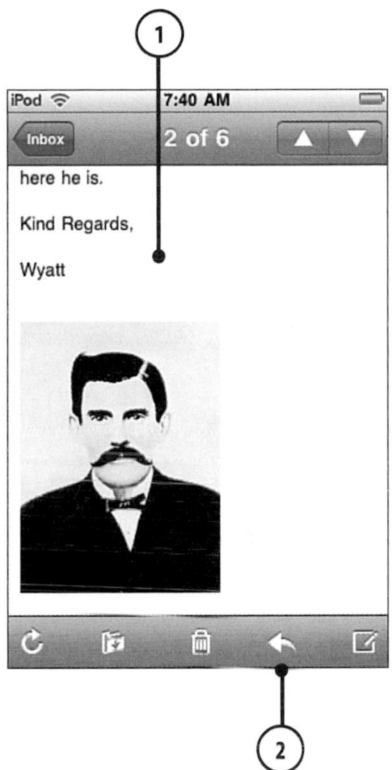

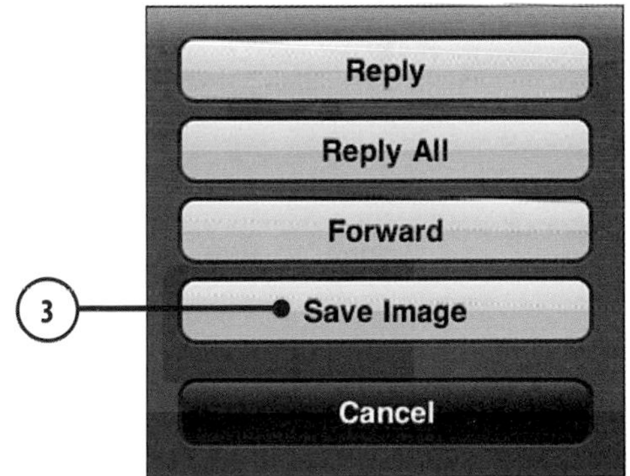

Searching Email

1. Move to the screen you want to search, such as an account's Inbox or a folder's screen.
2. Scroll to the top of the screen.
3. Tap in the Search tool.
4. Tap the message field you want to search: From, To, Subject, or All.
5. Enter the text for which you want to search. As you type, Mail searches the field you selected in step 4 or the entire message if you select All. Messages that meet your search are shown above the keyboard.
6. When you complete your search term, tap Search. The keyboard closes, and you see the messages that met your search.

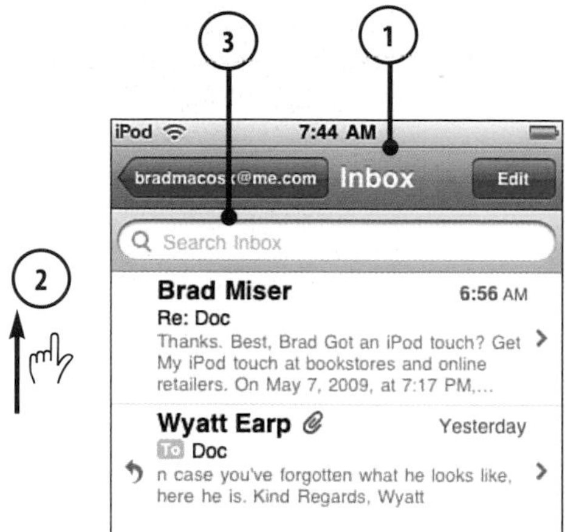

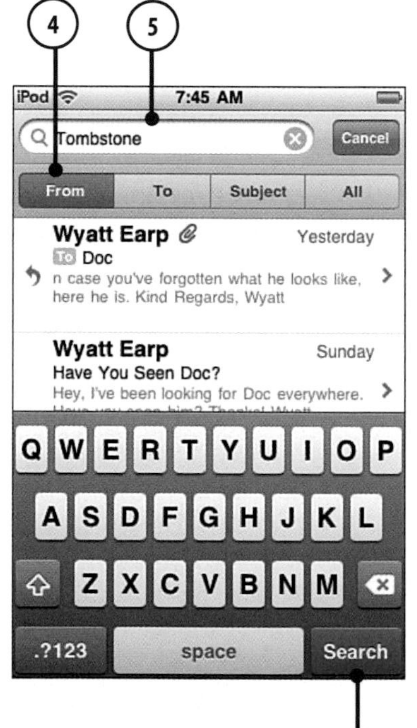

7. Work with the messages you found.
8. To clear a search and exit Search mode, tap Cancel; to clear a search but remain in Search mode, tap the Clear button.

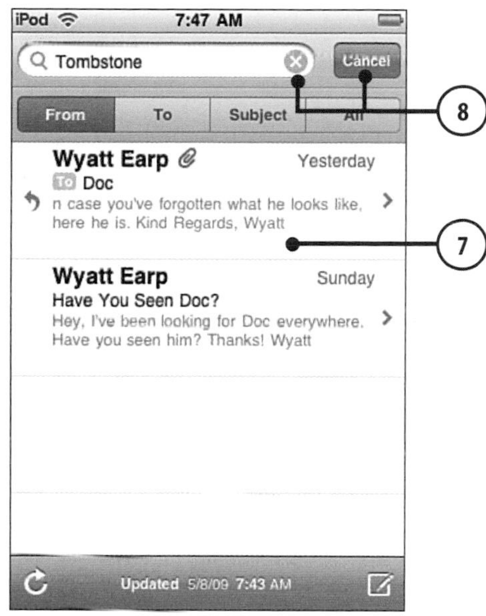

It's Not All Good

The Mail application doesn't include any spam tools. If you configure an already-spammed address on an iPod touch, all the spam is going to come right to your iPod, which can be a nuisance.

The best thing to do is to keep your important addresses from being spammed. Consider using a "sacrificial" email account when you shop and post messages and in the other places where you're likely to get spammed. If you do get spammed, you can stop using the sacrificial account and create another one to take its place. (MobileMe's email aliases are perfect for this.) Or you can delete the sacrificial account from your iPod and continue to use it on your computer where you likely have spam tools in place.

A more complicated way to avoid spam on an iPod touch is by filtering all email through an account that does have spam filtering. For example, you can create a Gmail account and route all your email through it. Use the Gmail account's spam tool to manage the spam and then add only the Gmail account to your iPod touch.

Tap here to see when and where you're supposed to be

Tap here to configure time, date, and calendar settings

Go here to get all the time you need

In this chapter, you explore all the time and calendar functionality that an iPod touch has to offer. Topics include the following:

→ Configuring an iPod touch's calendar, date, and time settings
→ Working with calendars
→ Using an iPod touch as a clock

Managing Calendars and Time

When it comes to time management, an iPod touch is definitely your friend. Using the iPod touch's Calendar application, you can view calendars that have been synchronized with your computer's calendars. Of course, you can also make changes on your iPod touch, and they sync with calendars on your computers so that you have consistent information no matter what device you use. The iPod touch's handy Clock application provides multiple clocks and alarms.

Configuring an iPod touch's Calendar, Date, and Time Settings

You should configure a few time, date, and calendar settings before you start using an iPod touch to manage your calendars and time.

1. On the Home screen, tap Settings.
2. Tap General.
3. Scroll down the screen.
4. Tap Date & Time.
5. To have the iPod touch display time on a 24-hour clock, tap the 24-Hour Time OFF button, which becomes ON to show you that an iPod touch is now showing time on a 24-hour scale. To use a 12-hour clock, tap ON to turn off 24-Hour Time again.
6. Tap Time Zone.

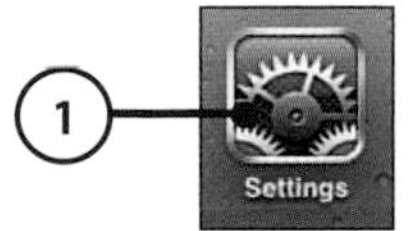

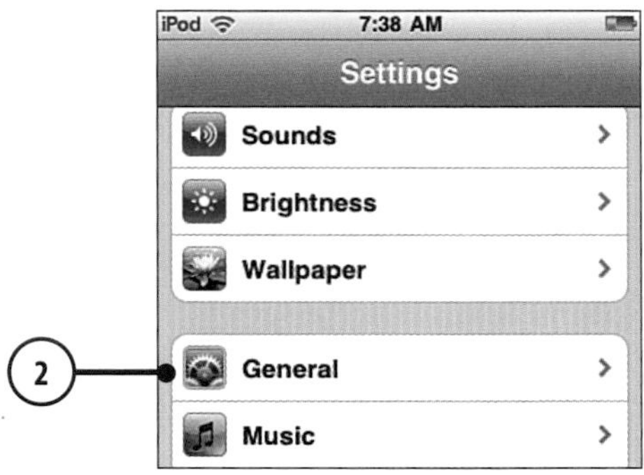

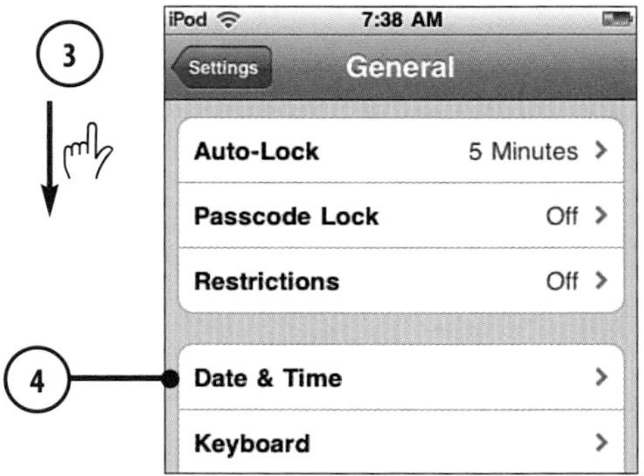

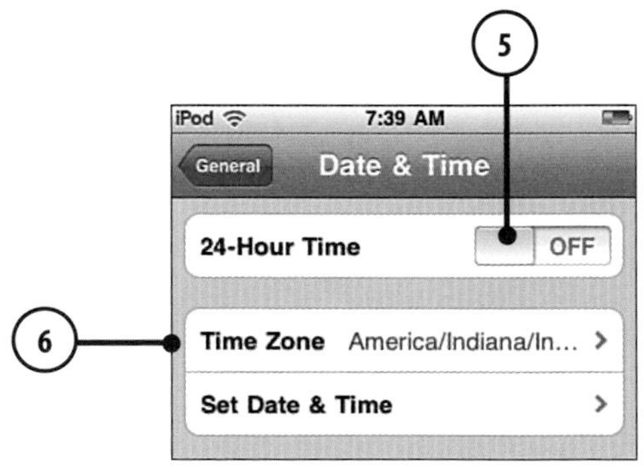

7. Type the name of the city that you want to use to set the time zone. As you type, the iPod lists the cities that match your search.
8. When the city you want to use appears on the list, tap it. (If the city you want isn't on the list, tap one that is in the same time zone.) You move back to the Date & Time screen, which shows the city you selected in the Time Zone field.
9. Tap Set Date & Time.

Have You Got the Time?

The iPod takes the current time and date from your computer when you sync it.

10. Tap the Date button.
11. Drag up and down on the month wheel until the center bar shows the month you want to set.
12. Drag up and down the date wheel until the correct day of the month is shown in the center bar.
13. Scroll and select the year in the same way.

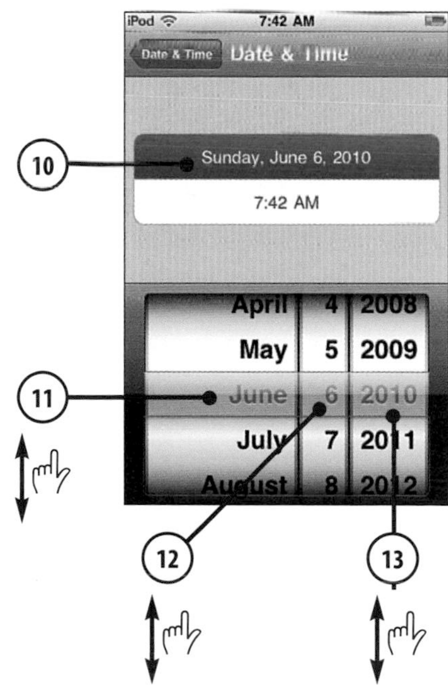

14. Tap the Time button.
15. Scroll the hour wheel until the center bar shows the hour you want to set.
16. Use the minutes wheel to select the minutes you want to set, as shown in the center bar.
17. Tap AM or PM.
18. Tap Date & Time.
19. Tap General.
20. Tap Settings.

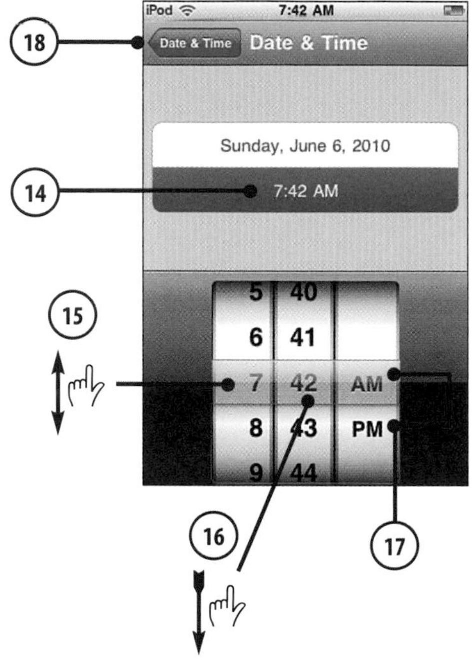

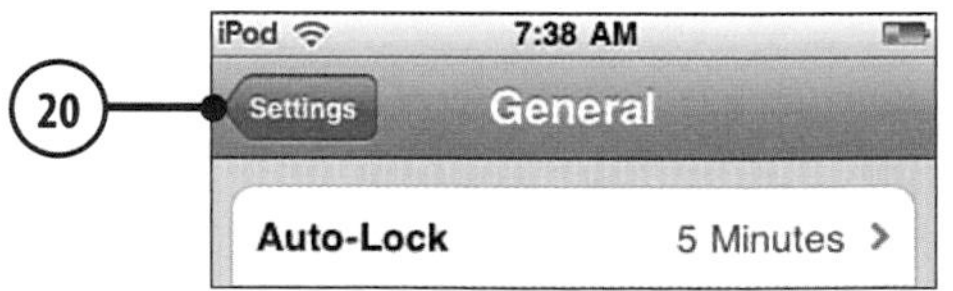

21. Tap Mail, Contacts, Calendars.
22. Scroll down until you see the Calendars section.
23. If you don't want to be alerted when you receive invitations to an event, tap ON next to New Invitation Alerts. Its status becomes OFF to show you that you won't see these alerts. To be alerted again, tap OFF so the status becomes ON.
24. To set the period of time over which past events are synced, tap Sync. (If you haven't set up an account to sync, this option doesn't appear.)
25. Tap the amount of time in the past that you want events to be synced; tap All Events to have all events synced, regardless of their age. When you tap one of the other options, the events within the time frame you select are moved onto your calendar. This can be useful for reference purposes; though the events are in the past, they may be useful to have on your calendar in case you need to refer to them.
26. Tap Mail.

27. Tap Time Zone Support.
28. To have your iPod touch display meeting and event times on its calendars based on the iPod touch's time zone that you set in step 8, tap Time Zone Support ON; it becomes OFF to show you that time zone support is disabled. Skip to step 32.
29. If you leave Time Zone Support ON, tap Time Zone.
30. Type the name of the city that you want to use to set the time zone. As you type, the iPod lists the cities that match your search.
31. When the city you want to use appears on the list, tap it. You move back to the Time Zone Support screen, and the city you selected is shown.
32. Tap Mail.

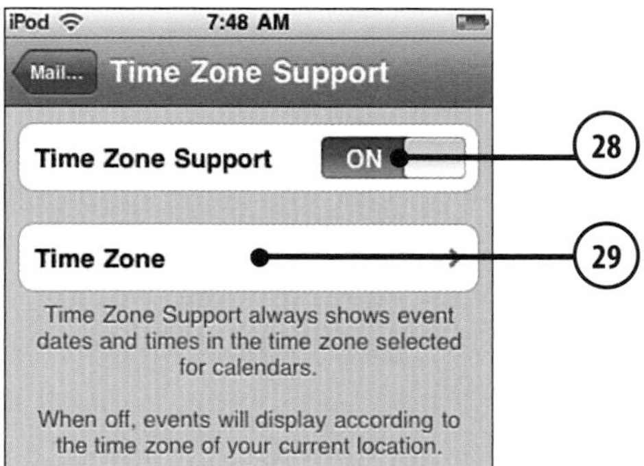

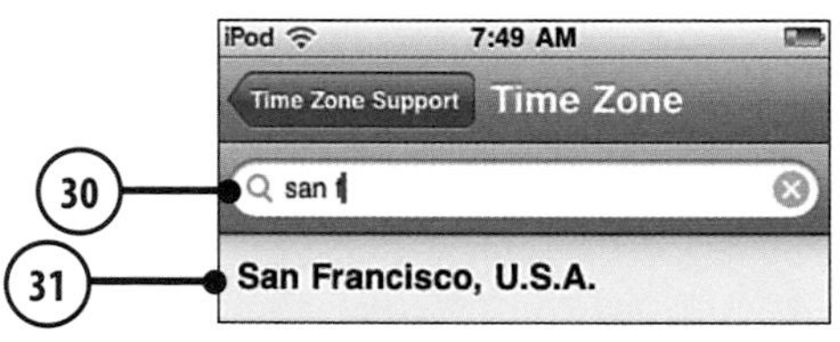

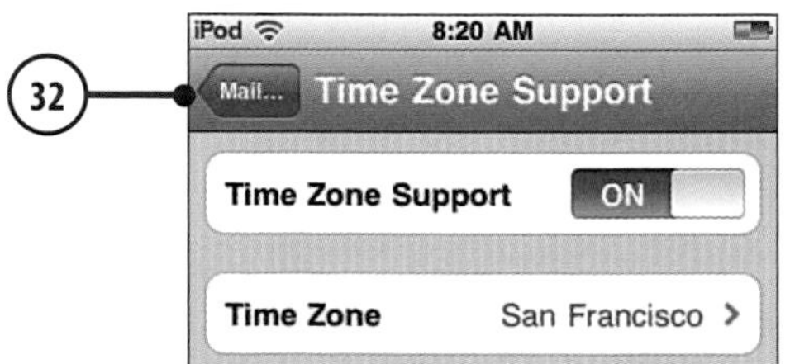

It's Not All Good

The Time Zone Support feature is a bit confusing. If Time Zone Support is ON, the iPod touch displays event times according to the time zone associated with the time zone you select on the Time Zone Support screen. When Time Zone Support is OFF, the time zone used for the calendars is the iPod touch's time zone that you set in step 8.

For example, suppose you set Indianapolis (which is in the Eastern time zone) as the iPod touch's time zone in step 8 and then schedule an event for 10 AM. If you enable Time Zone Support and then set San Francisco as the time zone, the events on your calendars will be shown according to the Pacific time zone because that is San Francisco's time zone rather than Eastern time. The event you set for 10 AM will display as starting at 7 AM because that is the equivalent time in the Pacific time zone. As long as Time Zone Support remains ON, the event remains at this time even if you change the iPod's time zone. If Time Zone Support is OFF and you change the time zone setting for the iPod, the event's time shifts according to the new time zone.

In other words, when Time Zone Support is ON, the dates and times for events become fixed based on the time zone you select for Time Zone support. If you change the iPod touch's time zone, there is no change to the dates and times for events shown on the calendar because they remain set according to the Time Zone support schedule.

In any case, you need to be aware of the time zone you use on your calendars (the one you select if Time Zone Support is on or the time zone of your current location if it is off) and the time zone with which events are associated. With some calendar applications (such as iCal on a Mac), you can associate an event with a specific time zone when you schedule it. This is helpful because the event should be shown at the proper time regardless of the Time Zone Support setting on the iPod touch.

33. Tap Default Calendar. You see the list of all calendars configured on your iPod touch based on its sync settings and any calendars you have created there.
34. Tap the calendar that you want to be the default, meaning the one that is selected unless you specifically choose a different one.
35. Tap Mail.
36. Scroll up the screen. To keep your calendar information current, you can configure information to be pushed from where it is managed, such as an Exchange server or MobileMe, onto your iPod touch whenever changes are made.
37. Tap Fetch New Data.
38. If the status of Push isn't ON, tap OFF so it becomes ON.

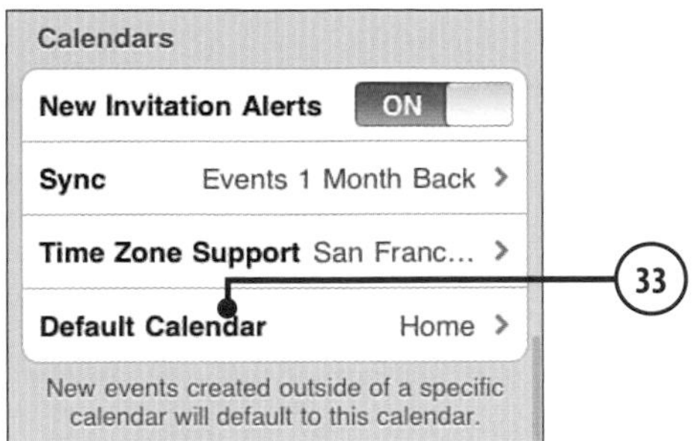

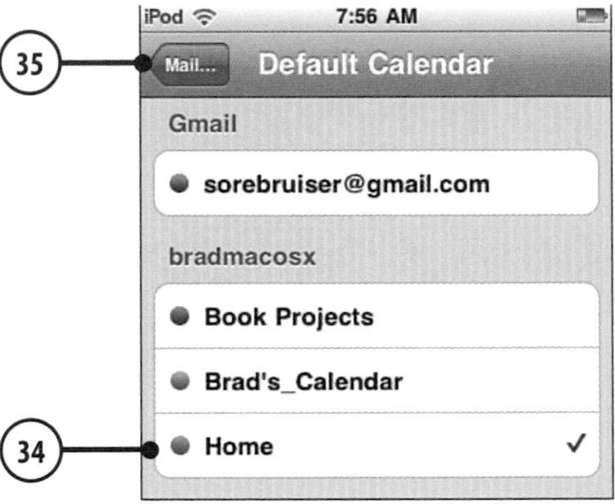

Saving Power

Push syncing causes an iPod touch to use more power, making your battery life shorter. If your calendar or other information doesn't change that fast, use Fetch instead and set a relatively long time between fetches. To do this, move to the Fetch New Data screen and turn Push to OFF. Tap the amount of time between fetches on the list of times, such as Hourly. Your iPod touch fetches the information only at appointed times, saving battery power compared to Push. Choose Manually if you want to fetch information only at your command.

39. Scroll down until you see the Advanced command.
40. Tap Advanced. You see the list of all your accounts. Under each account, you see the information currently being moved to the iPod touch. Along the right edge of the table, you see how the information is moved, either Push, Fetch, or Manual.
41. Tap an account from which you get calendar information.
42. Tap Push to have the account's information pushed onto the iPod touch; tap Fetch to have the information retrieved according to the Fetch schedule; or tap Manual to retrieve new information when you open the Calendar application.
43. Tap Advanced.
44. Repeat steps 41 through 43 for each account providing calendar information.
45. Tap Fetch New Data. Your time, date, and calendar configuration is complete.

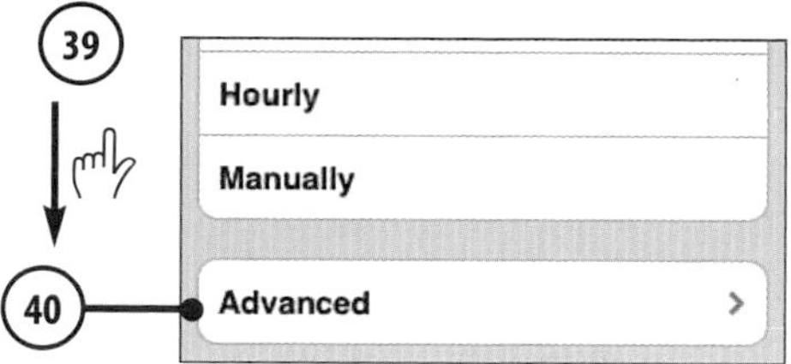

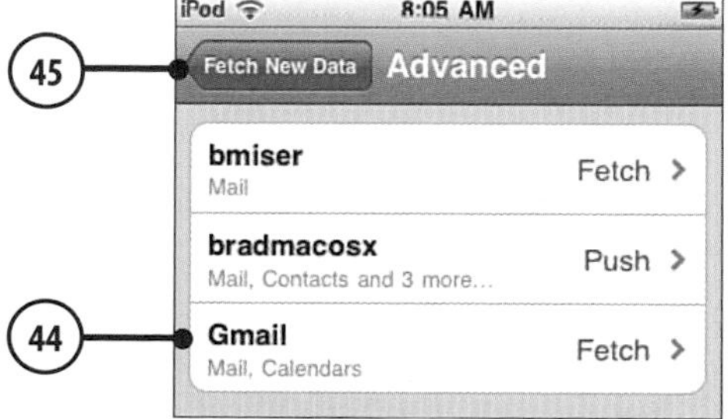

Working with Calendars

Your iPod touch can help you manage your calendars. In most cases, you move calendar information from a computer onto your iPod touch, but you can add events directly to your calendars on the iPod, too. (And when you do, they move to the computer's calendar the next time it syncs.)

You can sync an iPod touch's calendar to calendars on your computers in a number of ways. You can use iTunes, MobileMe, or Exchange (Windows Outlook only) to sync calendar information with Outlook (Window PCs) or iCal (Macs). Syncing calendars is covered along with the other information synching options in Chapter 4, "Configuring and Synchronizing Information on an iPod touch." Before working with your iPod touch's calendars, use Chapter 4 to set up calendar syncing and then come back here.

Viewing Calendars

You use the Calendar application to view your schedule and choose how you view it, such as by month, week, or day.

1. On the Home screen, tap Calendar. You see the most recent calendar screen you were viewing, such as a specific calendar or the Calendars screen. If you see the Calendars button in the upper-left corner of the screen, tap it. (If you have only one calendar on your iPod, the Calendars screen is hidden, and you always move directly to that one calendar; in that case, skip to step 3.) On the Calendars screen, you see a list of all your calendars, grouped by the accounts from which they come, such as Exchange, MobileMe, and so on.

2. Tap the calendars you want to view so that they have a check mark next to their names.
3. Tap a marked calendar to hide it. (It won't have a check mark.)
4. Tap Done. You move to the viewing screen, and the calendars you enabled are shown.

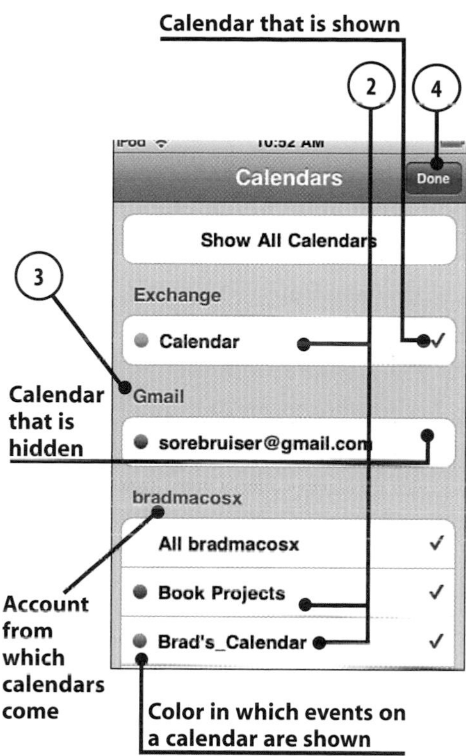

All or Nothing

You can make all your calendars visible by tapping the Show All Calendars button at the top of the Calendars screen; tap Hide All Calendars to do the opposite. After all calendars are enabled or disabled, you can tap individual calendars to show or hide them. You can also hide or show all the calendars from the same account by tapping the All button at the top of the account's calendar list.

5. Tap Month.
6. Tap a date you are interested in. It moves into focus and is highlighted in blue; the event list at the bottom of the screen shows the events associated with that date.
7. Scroll the list of events.
8. To see detailed information for an event, tap it.

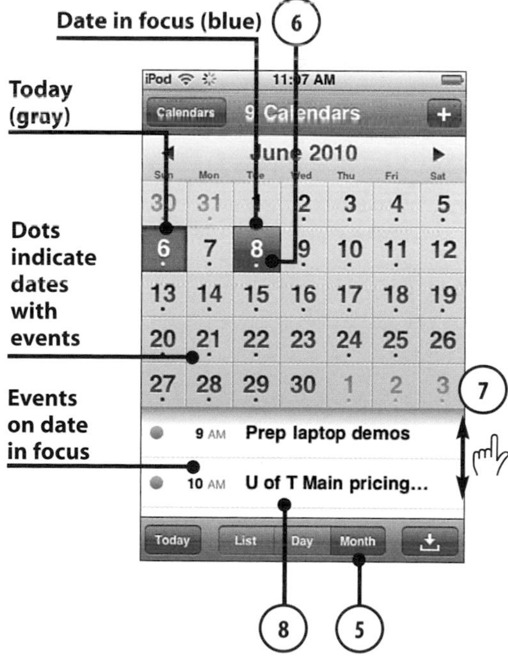

Small Events

The events browser at the bottom of the Month view is small and requires a lot of scrolling. It's usually better to use the Month view to select a date and then switch to the Day view to browse the events on that day.

What's in a Name?

When you view a calendar, its name appears at the top of the screen. When you view multiple calendars, the screen's title shows how many calendars you are viewing. When the screen title is Calendars, you are on the calendar selection screen.

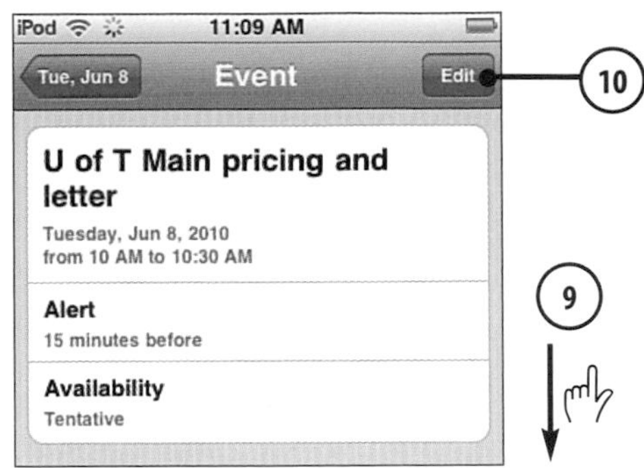

9. Read information about the event; scroll down to see all of it if needed.
10. To change the event, tap Edit.
11. Use the Edit screen to make changes to the event's information. The edit tools work just like when you create a new event; see "Adding Events to the Calendar Manually" later in this chapter for the details.

Where's the Edit Button?

If an event is one to which you have been invited by someone else, you won't see the Edit button; instead you see the Accept, Maybe, or Decline buttons at the bottom of the screen. You can use these to respond to the invitation, as you learn later.

12. When you finish making changes, tap Done.
13. Tap the Return button, now labeled with the event's date.

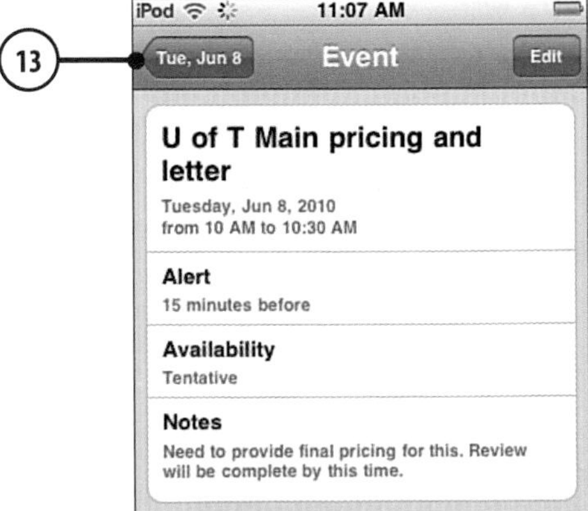

Clear My Calendar!

To delete an event from the calendar, open its Edit screen, scroll to the bottom, and tap Delete Event. Tap Delete Event again, and the event is removed from the calendar.

Searching, Searching

You can search for an event by moving to the List view and entering your search term in the Search tool at the top of the screen. As you type, only events that contain the term for which you are searching appear on the list. The more specific you make your search, the narrower the results will be.

14. To move ahead to the next month, tap Next.
15. To move back to the previous month, tap Back.
16. To move the focus to today, tap Today.
17. Tap List. The view changes to the List view showing the events for each day immediately underneath its heading.
18. Scroll the list of dates.
19. To view or change an event's details, tap it. The Event screen appears; this screen works just as it does when you access it from the Month view.
20. Tap Day.

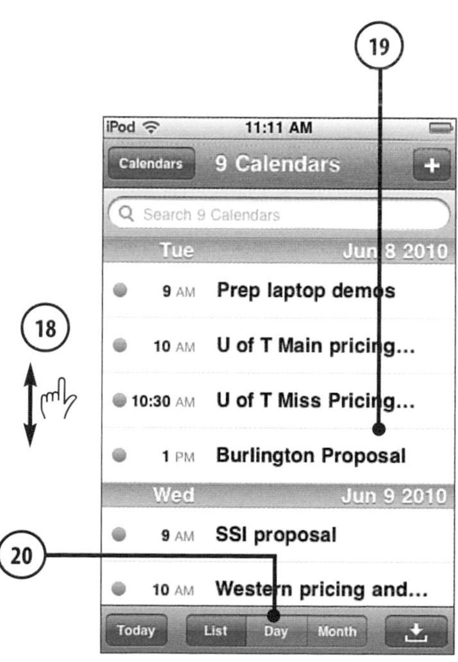

21. Scroll up and down to see the entire day.
22. Tap Back to move to the previous day.
23. Tap Forward to move to the next day.
24. To view or change an event's details, tap it. The Event screen appears; this screen works just as it does when you access it from the Month view.

Adding Events to a Calendar Manually

When you are on the move, you can add events to the calendars on your iPod.

1. View the calendar to which you want to add an event or view multiple calendars; you can add events to any calendar (even if it is not currently enabled) in any view.
2. Tap the Add button.

3. Tap Title Location.
4. With the cursor in the Title bar, type the title of the event.
5. Tap the Location bar and type the location of the event.
6. Tap Done.
7. Tap Starts Ends.

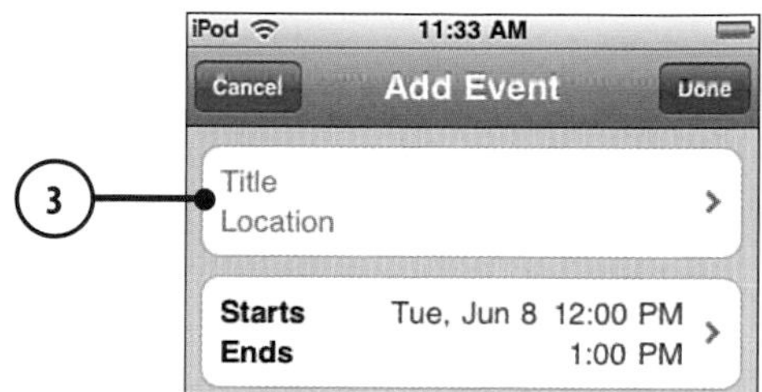

Different Fields for Different Calendars

The information that can be captured in an event is determined by the type of account associated with the calendar on which the event is created. For example, when you create an event on an Exchange calendar, you can indicate your status during the event with the Availability field. When you create an account on a MobileMe calendar, you can add a second alert. This example shows an event on a MobileMe calendar. You create events on other kinds of calendars with similar steps, though you might have different information for those kinds of events.

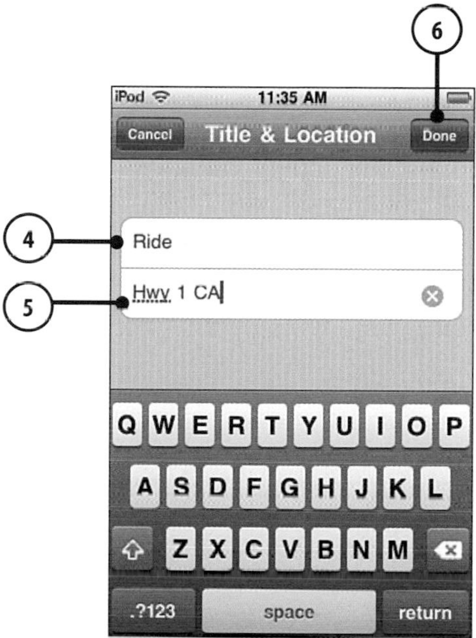

8. Tap Starts.
9. To make the event an all day event, tap All-day OFF; its status becomes ON, and the date selection wheels appear. Follow steps 10 through 16. To set a specific time for the event, leave the All-day status as OFF and complete steps 17 through 23.
10. Drag the month wheel until the event's month is shown in the left bar.
11. Drag the date wheel to set the event's date.
12. Drag the year wheel to set the year in which the event occurs.
13. Tap Ends.
14. Use the month, date, and year wheels to set the end date for the event.
15. Tap Done.

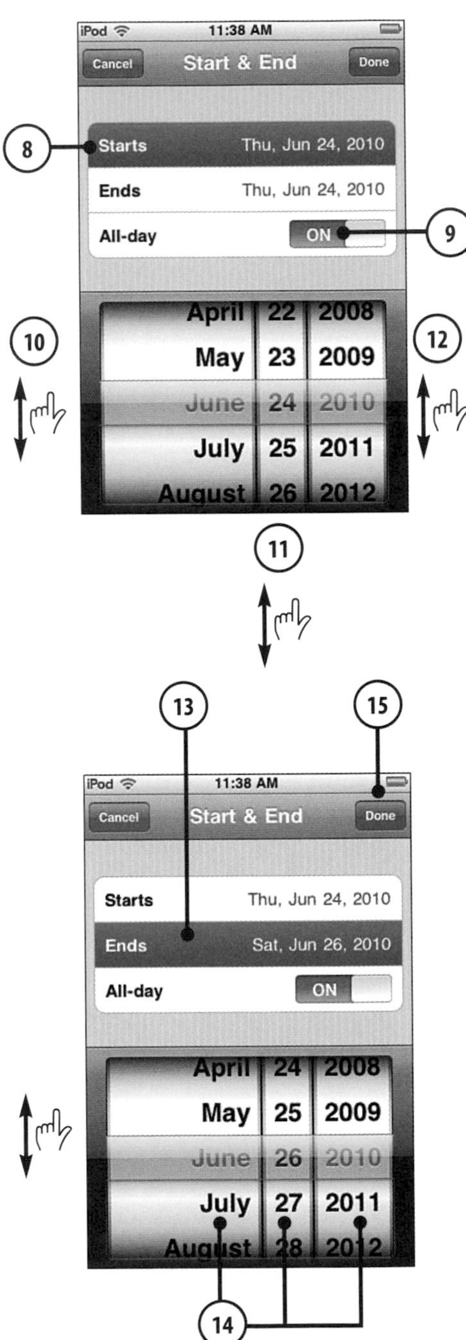

16. Skip to step 24.
17. Scroll the date wheel until the left bar shows the date of the event.
18. Scroll the hour wheel until the center bar shows the hour the event starts.
19. Scroll the minute wheel until the center bar shows the minute the event starts.
20. Tap AM or PM.
21. Tap Ends.
22. Use the date, hour, and minute wheels and tap the AM/PM button to set the end time and date.
23. Tap Done.

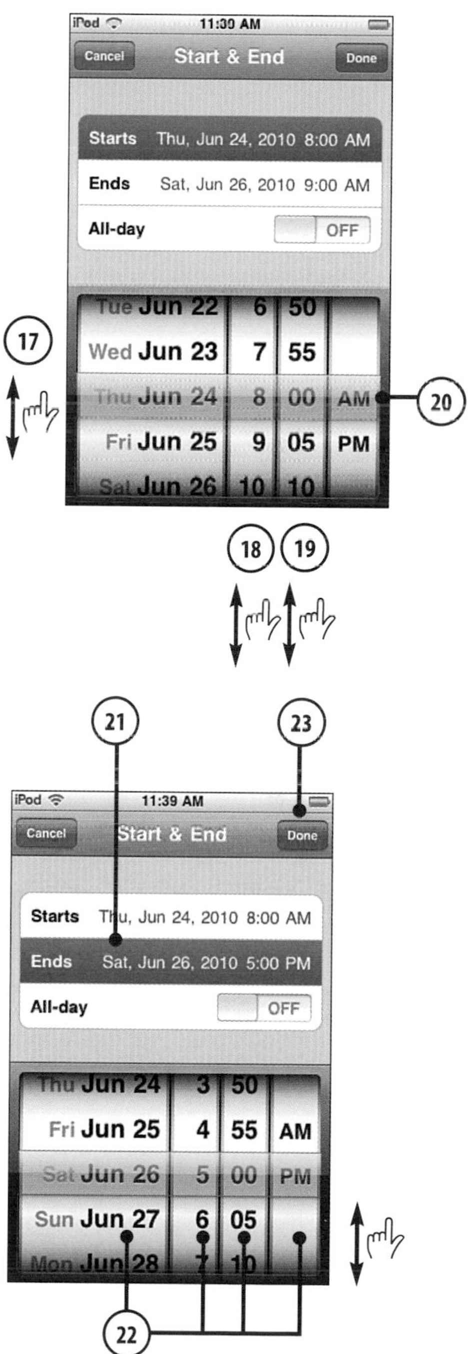

24. To make the event repeat, tap Repeat and follow steps 25 through 30. (For a nonrepeating event, skip to step 31.)
25. Tap the frequency with which you want the event repeated, such as Every Day, Every Week, and so on.
26. Tap Done.
27. Tap End Repeat to set a time at which the event stops repeating, or if you want the event to be repeated forever, skip to step 31.

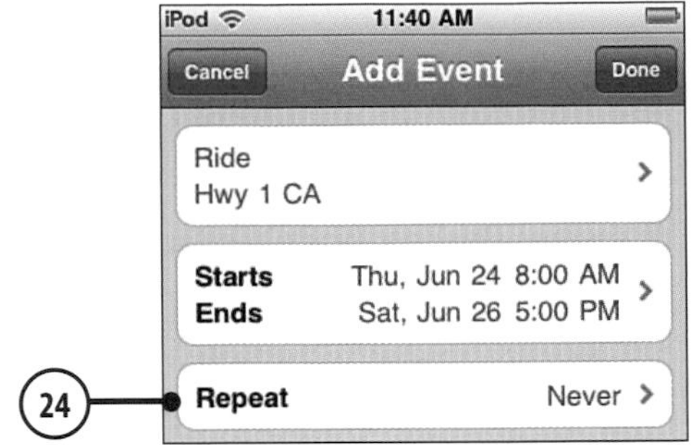

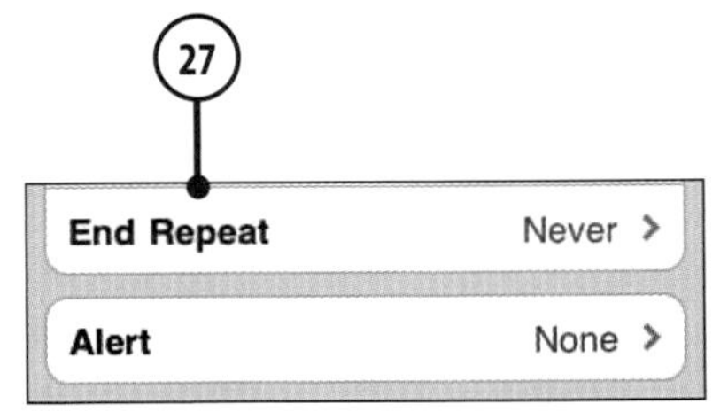

28. To have the event repeat ad infinitum, tap Repeat Forever and skip to step 30.
29. To set an end to the repetition, use the month, date, and year wheels.
30. Tap Done.
31. To set an alert for the event, tap Alert. If you don't want to set an alert, skip to step 37.
32. Select when you want to see an alert for the event.
33. Tap Done.

Alert, Alert!

To hear a sound when an event alert occurs, open the Sounds screen (choose Home, Settings, Sounds), and ensure that ON appears next to Calendar Alerts. If OFF appears, tap it to make event alarms audible and visual. Unfortunately, you can't choose the alert sound for an event. All event alarms use the standard calendar event alarm sound.

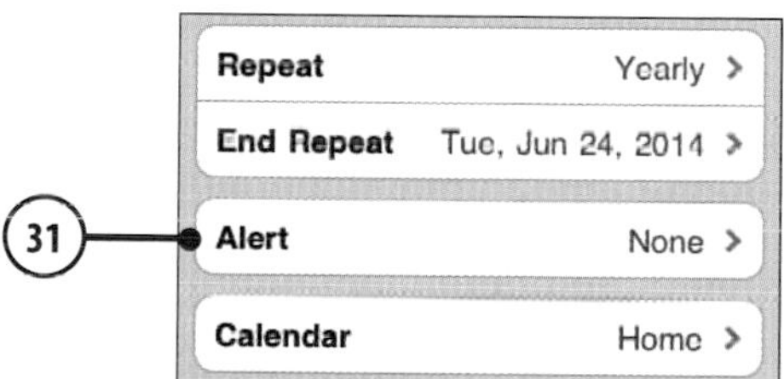

34. To set a second alert, tap Second Alert.

35. Select when you want to see a second alert for the event.

36. Tap Done.

37. To change the calendar with which the event is associated, tap Calendar; to leave the current calendar selected, skip to step 40. (If you change the calendar for the event, it is updated to reflect the information for events associated with the account from which the calendar comes, such as Exchange or MobileMe.

38. Tap the calendar with which the event should be associated.

39. Tap Done.

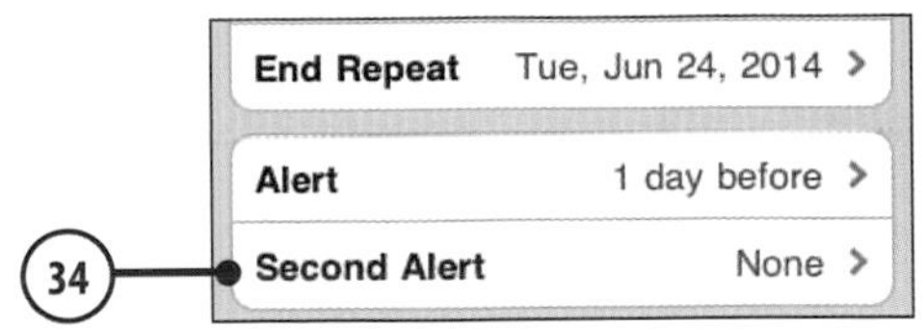

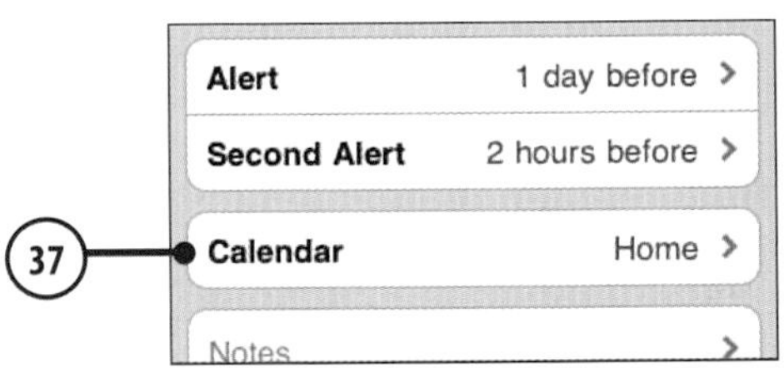

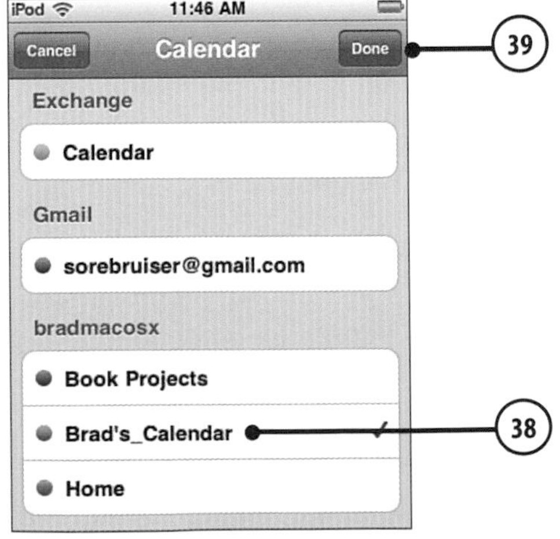

Keeping in Sync

When you sync your iPod touch, information moves both ways. When you add or make a change to a calendar on a synced computer, the changes move to the iPod touch the next time you sync. Likewise, when you add or change events on the iPod touch, those changes move to the calendar on the computer during the next sync.

40. Tap Notes.
41. Type information you want to associate with the event.
42. Tap Done.
43. Tap Done. The event is added to the calendar you selected. Any alarms trigger according to your settings.

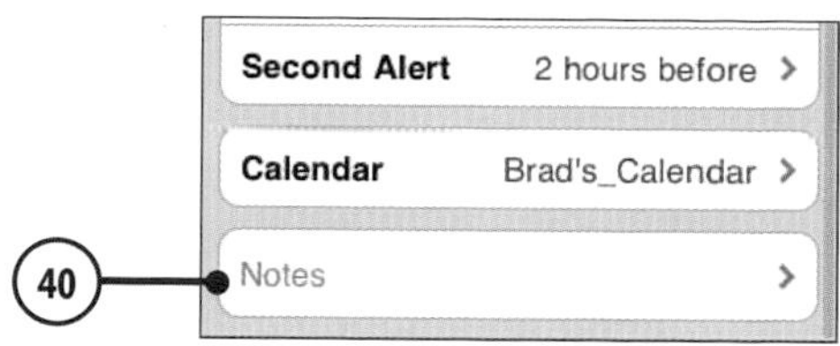

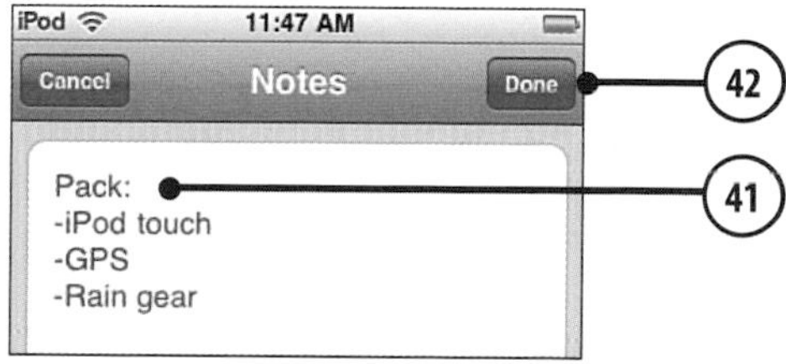

Adding Events to the Calendar by Accepting Invitations

When someone invites you to an event from Outlook via an Exchange account, you receive an invitation notification in the Calendar. You can accept these invitations, at which point the event is added to your calendar, or you can decline the event if you don't want it added to your calendar.

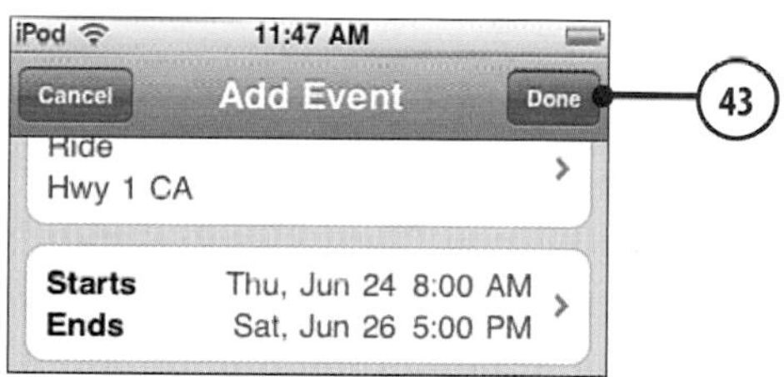

1. When you receive an invitation, you see an alert on the screen; tap View to see the details.
2. Tap the invitation.

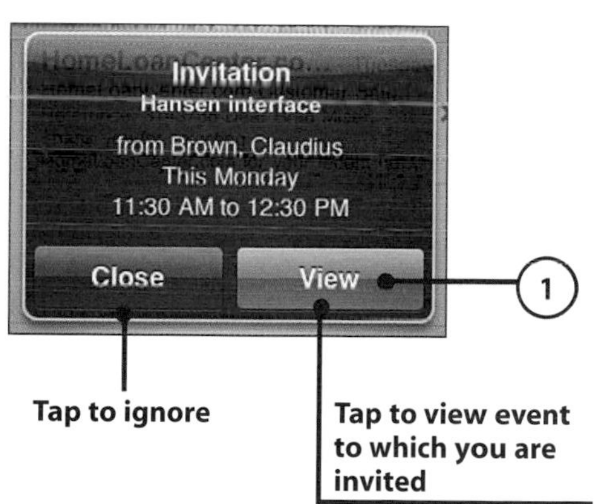

Managing Invitations

If you tap the Close button on an invitation or at any other time, you can always move back to the Invitations screen by tapping the Invitations button in the lower-right corner of the Calendar window. This button also shows the number of invitations you've received but not yet made a decision about.

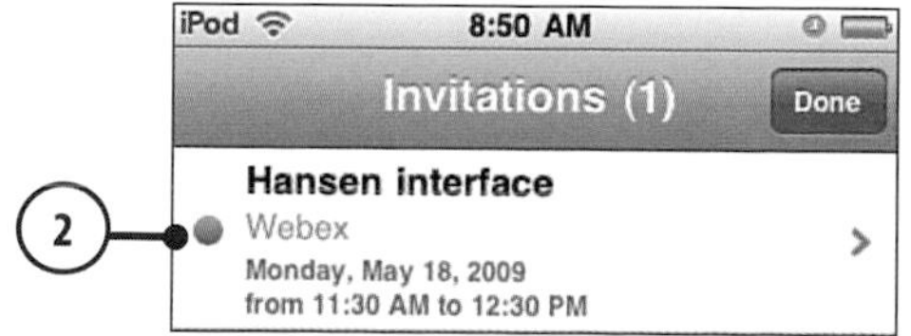

3. Scroll the event to see all its details.
4. View details about whom the invitation is from and attendees by tapping their areas. You move to detail screens for each.
5. To configure an alarm for the event, tap Alert and use the resulting Alert screen to choose an alert.
6. To choose the calendar on which the event should be shown, tap Show in Calendar, and on the resulting screen, tap the appropriate calendar.
7. To add comments to the event, tap Add Comments and use the Comments screen to enter text about the event.
8. Indicate what you want to do with the event by tapping Accept, Maybe, or Decline. If you accept the event or tap Maybe, the event is added to the calendar with the status you indicated. If you decline, the event is not placed on a calendar, and the recipient receives a notice that you have declined.

   After you make a decision, you move to the Invitations screen, where you see the status of all the invitations you've received. Events you've accepted or declined appear briefly and then disappear as the appropriate action is taken (such as adding an event you've accepted to the calendar).

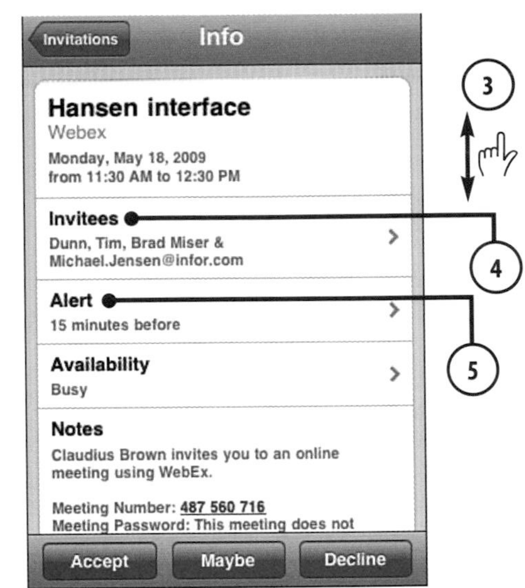

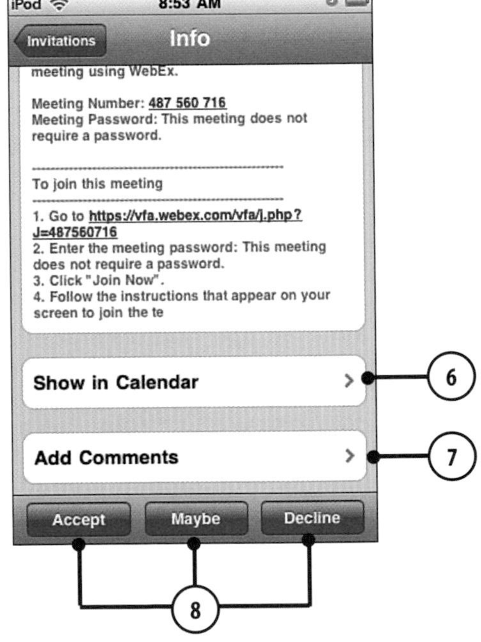

9. Tap Done. You move to the calendar; if you accepted or indicated maybe, the event is added to your calendar.

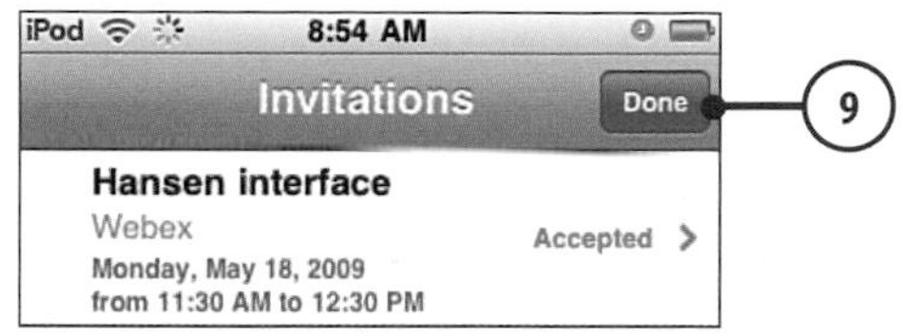

It's Not All Good

The current version of the Mail application can't do what it should with attachments that are event invitations (.ics files). That means when you receive an email invitation to an event, you can't add it to a calendar on your iPod touch by opening the attachment (which is what should happen and what does happen when you use an email application on a computer). If you can see the event's information in the subject line of the email message, you can create an event on your calendar manually, but invitations from some email applications don't have this information, so they are useless to you on your iPod touch. You need to work with iCal or other calendar applications to accept or reject these invitations. You can view details about an invitation if it comes from Outlook via Exchange, but even so, you can't make a decision about the invitation from Mail.

The only kind of events that come as invitations are meeting requests from Outlook that come in through an Exchange account. To make a decision about these events, you have to use the Invitations screen within the Calendar application.

Also you can't invite other people to events that you set up on an iPod touch for many kinds of calendars (you can invite people to events when you create them on Exchange calendars); you have to use a calendar application on a computer to do that.

Hopefully, these issues will be resolved with a future iPod touch software update, and all invitations will work like those sent via Exchange. In the current version, working with invitations and with meetings that involve other people is limited unless everyone involved uses Exchange, so you have to rely on your calendar application on a computer to manage them properly. This has been a longstanding issue, which is unfortunate because it really limits the usefulness of the iPod touch for managing meetings with others, unless everyone uses Exchange accounts.

Working with Event Alarms

When an event's alarm goes off, you see an onscreen alert and hear the calendar event sound (if it is enabled). Tap View Event to view details on the Event screen or tap Close to dismiss the alarm.

If the event has a second alarm, it also goes off according to the schedule you set. Handle it the same way as you did the first alarm.

Using an iPod touch as a Clock

An iPod touch is also useful as an alarm clock, timer, and stop watch. In addition to the primary time you learned to set earlier in the chapter, you can set clocks for a variety of locations.

Telling Time with an iPod touch

Your iPod touch displays the current time at the top of most of its screens for easy viewing.

When your iPod touch is locked/asleep and you press the Sleep/Wake button or the Home button, it shows the current time and date. If you don't unlock the iPod, it goes to sleep again in a few seconds, making this an easy way to check the current time and date without using much battery power.

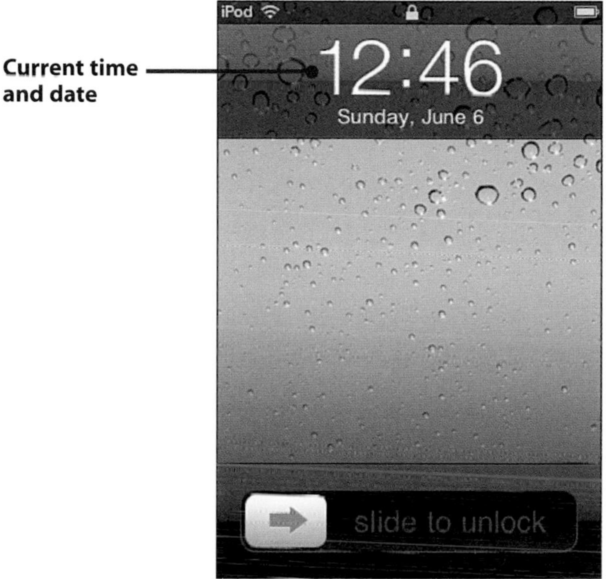

Using the Clock Application

You can use the Clock app to display a number of clocks with each clock having a specific time zone associated with it. This makes it possible to know the time in several locations at once. Even better, you can configure multiple alarms to remind you of important events, such as getting out of bed. The Clock app also provides a basic but serviceable stopwatch and timer.

Creating, Configuring, and Using Clocks

You can create multiple clocks, with each showing the time in a different time zone. If you travel a lot or if you know people in different time zones, this is an easy way to see the time in multiple locations.

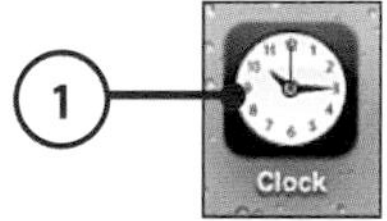

1. On the Home screen, tap Clock.

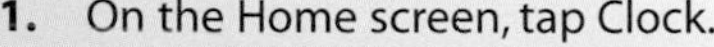

Like Night and Day

Based on the associated time zone, a clock's face is black if the current time is between sunset and sunrise (in other words, it's dark there) or white if the time there is in daylight hours.

2. Tap World Clock. You see a clock for each location you have configured.
3. To add a clock, tap the Add button.
4. Type the name of the city with which the clock is associated; this determines the clock's time zone. As you type, the iPod touch tries to match cities to what you type and presents a list of matching cities to you.
5. Tap the city you want to associate with the clock. You return to the World Clock screen, and the clock is created, showing the current time in that city.

Missing City

If the iPod can't find the specific city you want, just choose a city in the same time zone. The city you select determines the time zone of the clock. However, there is an issue with the clock's name, which is addressed in the "It's Not All Good" section in this task.

6. To remove a clock or to change the order in which they appear on the screen, tap Edit.
7. Tap the Unlock button next to the clock you want to delete.
8. Tap Delete. The clock is deleted.
9. Repeat steps 7 and 8 until you've deleted all the clocks you no longer want to see.
10. Drag clocks up and down the screen by their list icons to reorganize them.
11. Tap Done.

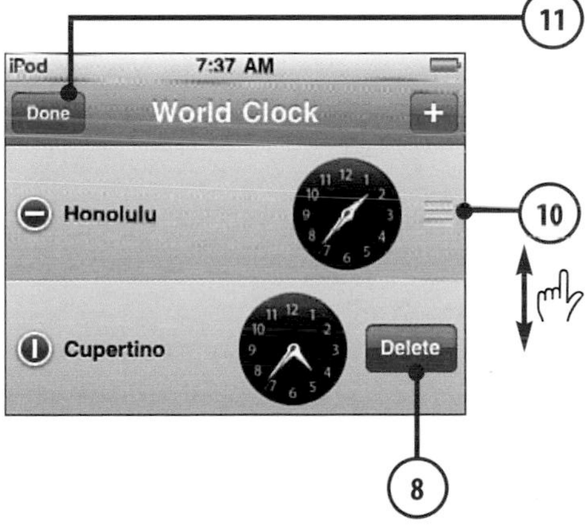

It's Not All Good

Unfortunately, you can't rename clocks to reflect the actual city in which you are interested. So if you can't find the specific city you want when you set the time zone, make sure that you select one that you easily recognize as being in the same time zone as the city where you really want to know the time.

Setting and Using Alarms

Your iPod touch is a handy alarm clock on which you can set and manage multiple alarms.

1. On the Home screen, tap Clock.
2. Tap Alarm. You see the currently set alarms, listed by their times, with the earlier alarms toward the top of the screen.
3. To add an alarm, tap Add.

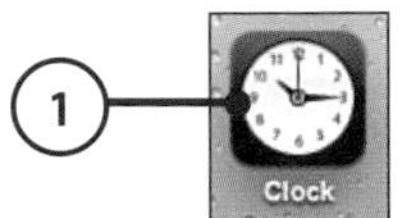

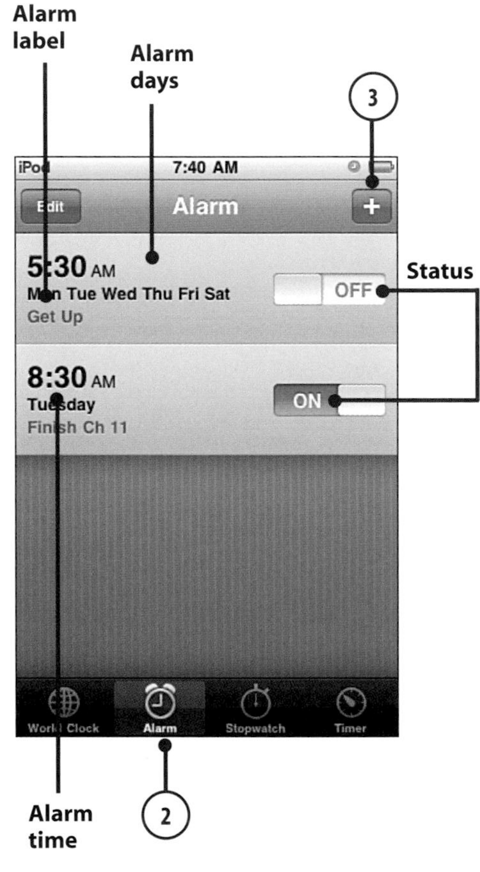

4. To configure the alarm to repeat, tap Repeat; to set a one-time alarm, skip to step 8.
5. Tap the day of the week on which you want the alarm to repeat. It is marked with a check mark.
6. Repeat step 5 as many times as you need; however, the most frequently an alarm can repeat is once per day. Of course, you can create multiple alarms for the same day.
7. Tap Back. The Repeat option shows you the days you selected for the alarm to repeat.
8. To choose the alarm sound, tap Sound.

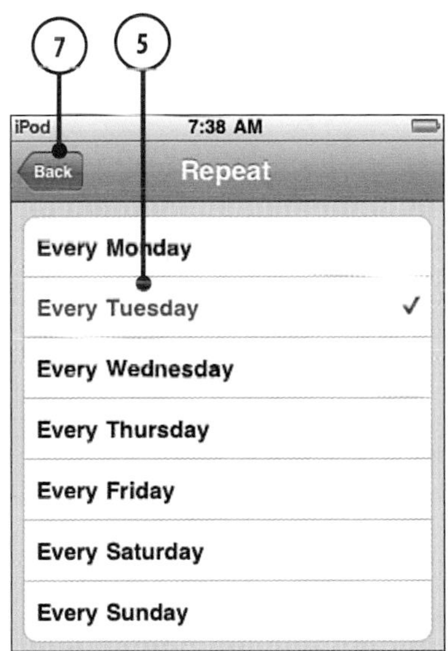

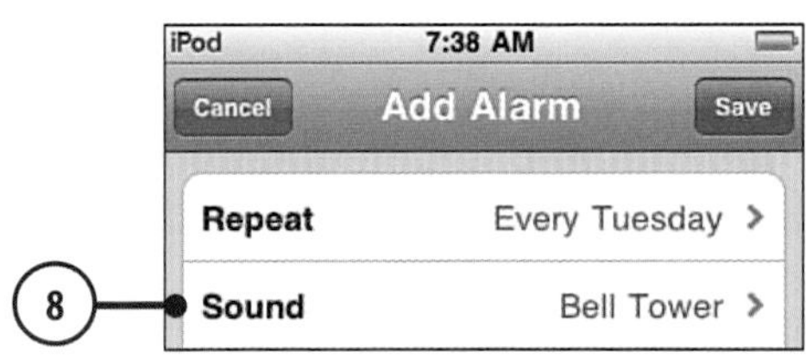

Silent Alarm

If you select the None sound, you won't hear anything when the alarm goes off, but a visual alarm displays.

More Sounds

If you've added ringtones to your iPod (see Chapter 12, "Using Cool iPod touch Applications"), you can choose any of them as the alarm sound for an event. On the Sound screen, you see the following categories: Purchased shows the ringtones you bought from the iTunes Store, Custom shows sounds you've created, and Standard shows the iPod's default sounds.

9. Browse the list of available sounds.
10. Tap the sound you want to use for the alarm. You hear the sound, and it is marked with a check mark.
11. After you select the sound you want to use, tap Back. You move back to the Add Alarm screen, which now shows the sound that will play when the alarm goes off.
12. To disable the Snooze function, tap ON. Its status becomes OFF. When an alarm sounds and you dismiss it, it won't appear again. With Snooze set to ON, you can tap Snooze to dismiss the alarm, and it returns at 10-minute increments until you dismiss it.
13. To name the alarm, tap Label. The label is what appears on the screen when the alarm activates, so you might want to give it a meaningful title. (To leave the default label, which is "Alarm," skip to step 17.)
14. To remove the current label, tap the Clear button.
15. Type a label for the alarm.
16. Tap Back. You return to the Add Alarm screen, which shows the label you created.

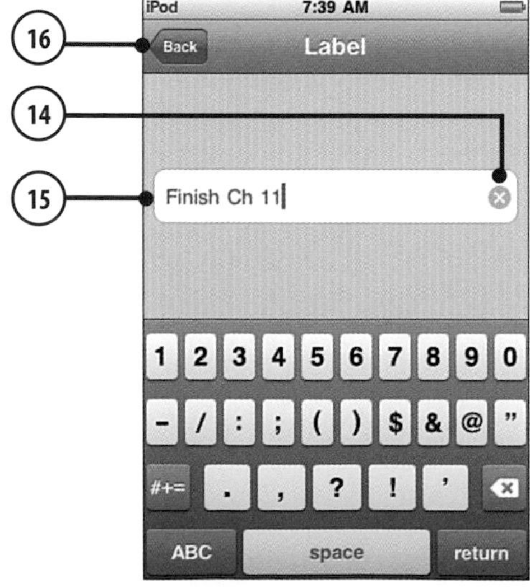

17. Scroll the hour wheel until you see the hour you want to set in the left bar.
18. Scroll the minute wheel until you see the minute you want to set in the center bar.

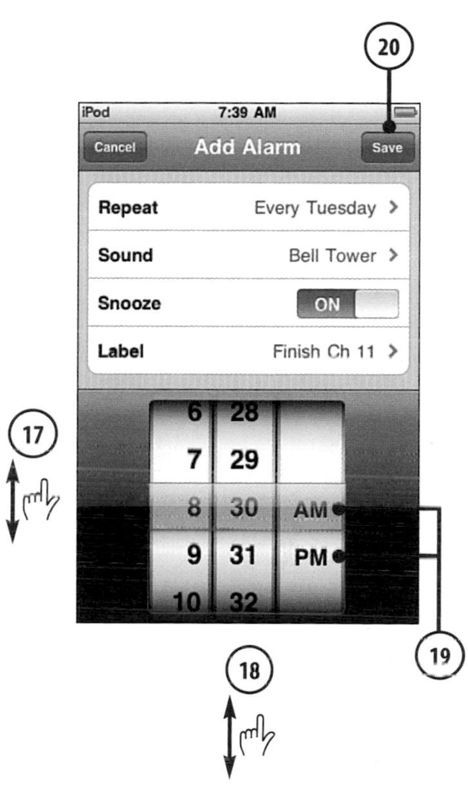

How iPod touch Alarms Are Like Those on Bedside Clocks

You can't set an alarm for a specific date; they are set only by day of the week, just like a bedside alarm clock. To set an alarm for a specific date, configure an event on the calendar and associate an alarm with that event.

19. Tap AM or PM.
20. Tap Save. You return to the Alarm screen, which now shows the new alarm you set. When the appointed time arrives, the alarm sounds and displays on the screen (or just displays on the screen if it is a silent alarm).

Changing Alarms

You can change existing alarms in several ways.

1. Move to the Alarm screen.
2. Tap Edit. Unlock buttons appear next to each alarm.

3. To delete an alarm, tap its Unlock button.
4. Tap Delete. The alarm is deleted.
5. To change an alarm, tap it.
6. Use the controls on the Edit Alarm screen to make changes to the alarm. These work just as they do when you create an alarm. (See the preceding task, "Setting and Using Alarms," for details.)
7. Tap Save. The alarm is changed, and you return to the Alarms screen.

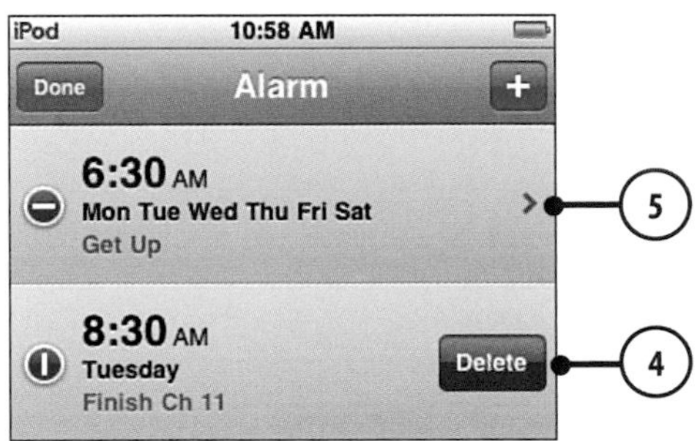

8. To disable an alarm, tap ON. Its status becomes OFF, and it is no longer active.
9. To enable an alarm, tap OFF. Its status becomes ON, and it sounds and appears at the appropriate times.

Managing Alarms

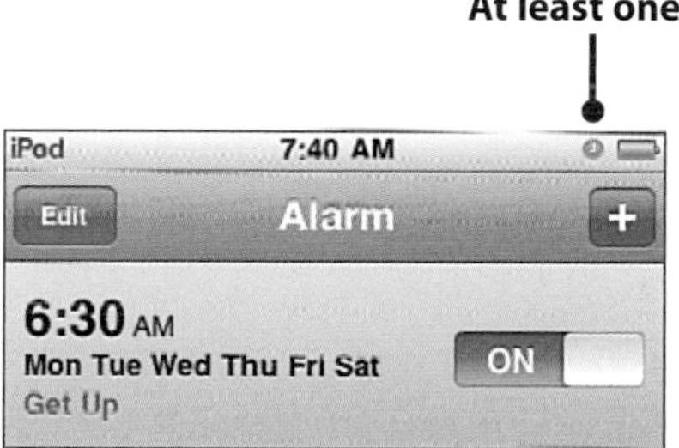

When at least one alarm is active, you see the Alarm Clock icon in the upper-right corner of the screen next to the Battery icon.

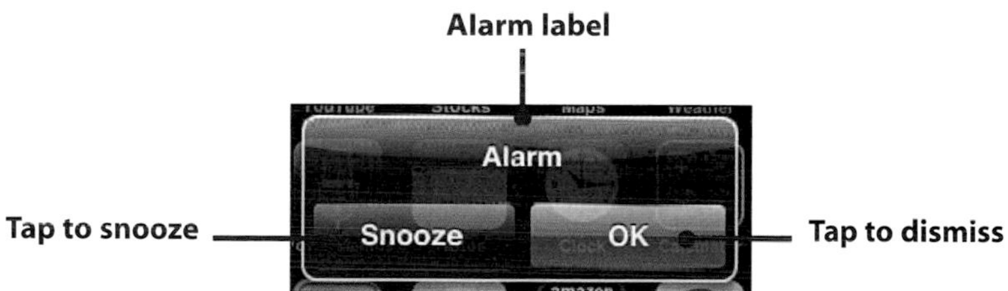

When an alarm triggers, you see an onscreen message and hear the sound associated with it. If the alarm is snooze-enabled, tap Snooze to dismiss it; it returns in 10 minutes. To dismiss the alarm completely, tap OK. You can also dismiss an alarm by pressing the Sleep/Wake button.

Not Dismissed So Easily

When you dismiss an alarm, it isn't deleted, but its status is set to OFF. To re-enable the alarm, move to the Alarm screen and tap its OFF button. The status becomes ON, and the alarm activates at the next appropriate time.

>>> Go Further

MORE TIME

The Clock app also has a full-function stopwatch; tap the Stopwatch button to access it. Tap the Start button to start the count; tap the Lap button to set lap times or the Stop button to stop the stopwatch. As you set lap times, they are recorded on a list on the app's screen along with the lap number. At the top, you see the time of the current lap, whereas the larger readout shows you the total time. To start over, tap Reset.

If you want to count down a certain amount of time, tap the Timer button. Use the hour and minute wheels to set the amount of time you want for the countdown. Then tap the When Time Ends button to select the end sound for the timer. Tap Start; when the time you selected passes, you hear the end sound and see an onscreen message.

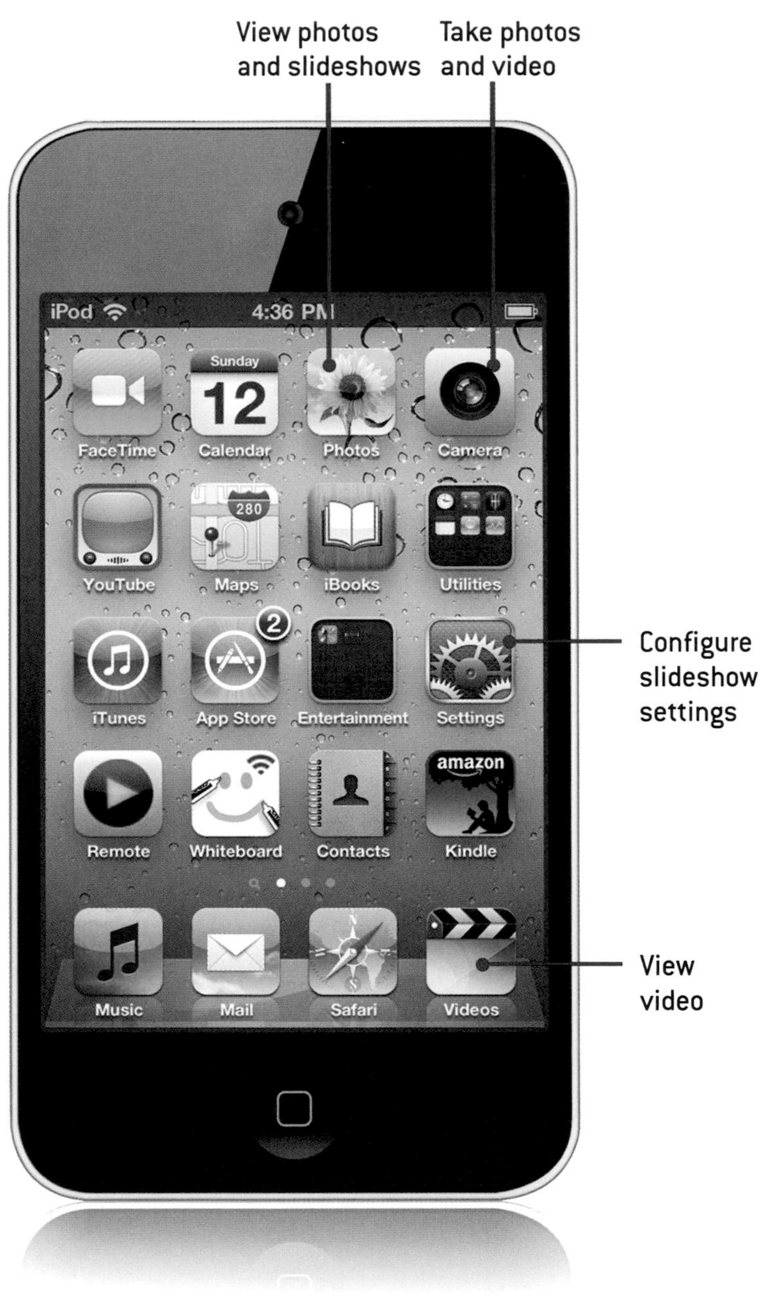
View photos and slideshows
Take photos and video
Configure slideshow settings
View video
iPod
4:36 PM
Sunday
12
FaceTime
Calendar
Photos
Camera
280
YouTube
Maps
iBooks
Utilities
2
iTunes
App Store
Entertainment
Settings
amazon
Remote
Whiteboard
Contacts
Kindle
Music
Mail
Safari
Videos

In this chapter, you'll explore all the photo and video functionality that the iPod touch has to offer. Topics include the following:

- → Taking photos with your iPod touch
- → Taking video on an iPod touch, 4th generation
- → Viewing and working with photos on an iPod touch
- → Viewing, editing, and working with video on an iPod touch, 4th generation
- → Moving photos and video from an iPod touch onto a computer

Working with Photos and Video

If you have a 4th-generation IPod touch, you can use it to take photos and video. Because you're likely to have your iPod with you all the time, it is very handy to be able to capture snapshots and video clips wherever you happen to be.

If you have an earlier generation iPod touch, you aren't completely out of the game. You can move photos from a computer onto the touch, and you can capture them from email attachments or screenshots.

Whether you've captured them on your iPod touch or moved them from a computer onto your iPod touch, you can view your photos individually and as slideshows. If you decide some of the photos you've taken on your iPod touch are worthy of adding to your photo collection, you can move them from your iPod touch onto your computer. If you have an iPhoto 3GS or iPod touch 4th generation, you can view and edit video and move it to your computer just like you move photos.

Taking Photos with Your iPod touch

With an iPod touch, 4th generation, you can take photos using either the back-side or front-side camera. When you use the back-side camera, you can zoom in or out. You can choose an area to focus on with both cameras. (If you have an earlier model, see the Going Further sidebar at the end of this task to learn other ways to capture photos on your iPod.)

1. On the Home screen, tap Camera. The Camera screen appears; initially it has a shutter, but after a few moments the window opens, and you start seeing through the iPod touch's camera.

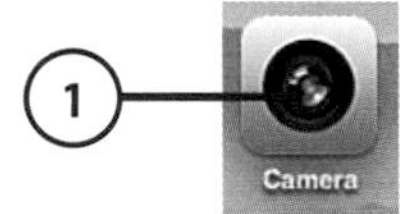

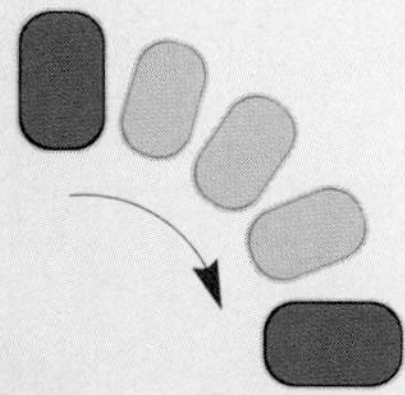

2. To capture a photo in landscape mode, rotate the iPod touch so that it's horizontal; of course, you can use either orientation to take photos just as you can with any other camera.

Sensitive, Isn't It!

The iPod touch's camera is sensitive to movement, so if your hand moves while you are taking a photo, it's likely to be blurry. Sometimes, part of the image will be in focus while part of it isn't, so be sure to check the view before you capture a photo. This is especially true when you zoom in. If you are getting blurry photos, the problem is probably your hand moving while you are taking them.

3. Ensure the Photo/Video switch is set to Photo.
4. Tap the Lens Change button to switch the camera being used for the photo. When you change the lens, the image briefly freezes and then you start seeing through the other lens.
5. Tap the screen where you want the image to be focused. The focus box appears where you tapped. If you are using the back-side lens, the Zoom slider appears. If you are using the front-side lens, you can't zoom, so skip to step 8.
6. Drag the Zoom slider toward the + to zoom in or toward the – to zoom out.
7. If you changed the zoom setting, tap the primary subject of the photo again to refocus. The blue focus box shows you where the iPod touch's camera is focusing.
8. Continue using the zoom and focus controls along with moving the camera until the photo is properly framed.
9. Tap the Camera button. The iPod touch captures the photo, and the shutter closes briefly while the photo is re-corded. When the shutter opens again, you're ready to take the next photo.
10. To take more photos, repeat steps 4 through 9. To see the photo you most recently captured, tap the Thumbnail button. The photo appears on the screen with iPod touch's photo-viewing controls.

11. Use the photo-viewing tools to view the photo (see "Viewing and Working with Photos on an iPod touch" later in this chapter for the details).
12. To delete a photo, tap the Trashcan and then tap Delete Photo. The iPod touch deletes the photo, and you see the next photo in the Photo Roll album.
13. Tap Done. You move back into the Camera app, and you can take more photos.

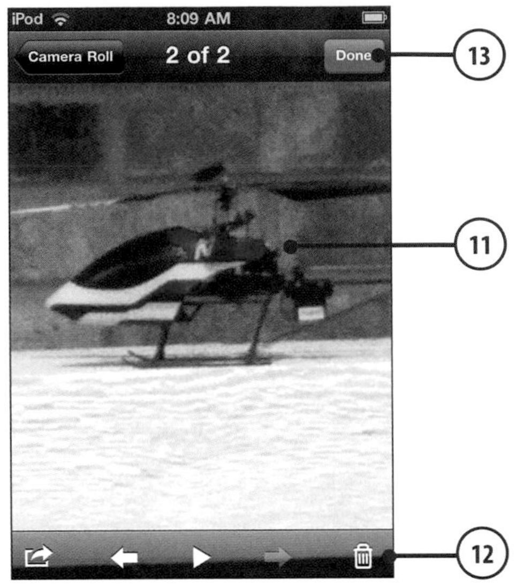

Shutter Sounds

When you capture a photo, you hear the iPod touch's shutter sound, unless you have muted it.

>>> Go Further

MOVING PHOTOS

You can move photos onto all models of the iPod touch in several ways:

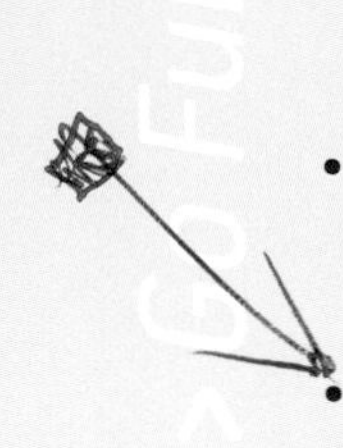

- **Syncing**: You can move photos from a computer onto your iPod touch through the sync process. This is explained in Chapter 3, "Moving Audio, Video, Books, and Photos onto Your iPod touch."
- **Saving attachments**: When you receive email messages that have photos attached, you can save those photos onto your iPod touch. This is covered in Chapter 9, "Emailing."
- **Taking screenshots**: There are times when it is useful to capture screen images of your iPod touch's screen (such as when you are writing a book about the iPod touch). The iPod touch screen capture function enables you to take a picture of whatever is on your iPod touch's screen at any point in time.

When the screen you want to capture appears, hold down the Home button and press the Wake/Sleep button. The screen flashes white, and you hear the shutter sound to indicate that the capture has been taken. The resulting image is stored in the Saved Photos album. You can view the screenshots you capture, email them, or move them onto a computer, as you can with other kinds of photos.

Taking Video with an iPod touch

With an iPod touch 4th generation, you can capture video. Here's how.

1. On the Home screen, tap Camera.
2. To capture video in landscape mode, rotate the iPod touch so that it's horizontal; of course, you can use either orientation to take video just as you can with any other videocamera.

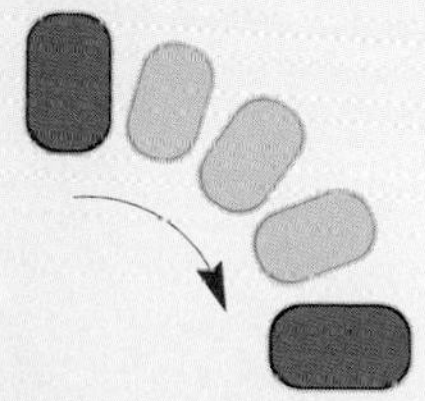

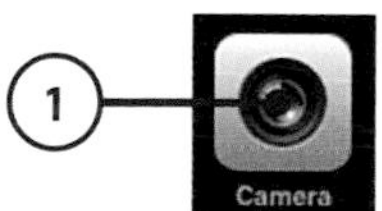

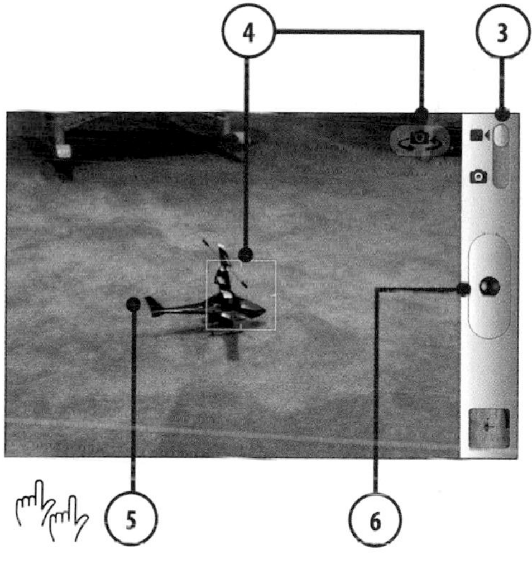

3. Set the Photo/Video switch to Video.
4. Choose the lens and use focus controls to frame the starting image for the video, just like setting up a still image (see steps 4 through 9 of the previous task). (You can't zoom when taking video.)
5. To change the proportion of the video image to widescreen, double-tap the screen. Black bars appear at the top and bottom of the screen.
6. To start recording, tap the Record button. The iPod touch starts capturing video; you see a counter on the screen showing how long you've been recording.

You Are Recording

When you tap the Record button, you hear the start/stop recording tone. When you stop recording, you hear the same tone.

7. To stop recording, tap the Record button again.
8. To preview the video clip, tap the Thumbnail button.
9. Use the video tools to view or edit the clip (see "Viewing, Editing, and Working with Video on an iPod touch" later in this chapter for the details).

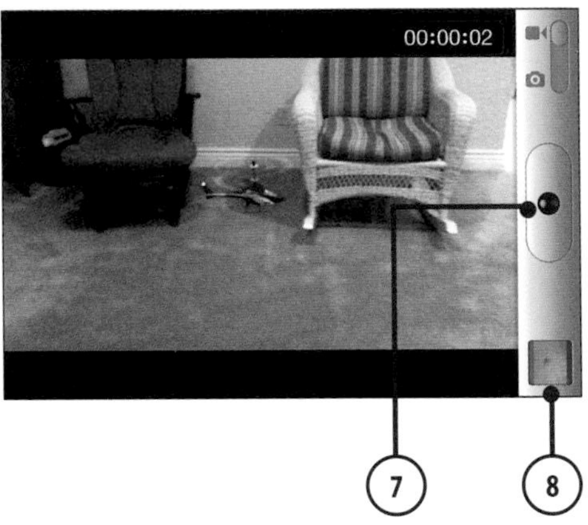

Viewing and Working with Photos on an iPod touch

After you've loaded your iPod touch with photos, you can use the Photos app to view them individually and as slideshows. You can also use the photos on iPod touch for a number of tasks, such as setting iPod touch's wallpaper or emailing them.

Viewing Photos Individually

The Photos app enables you to view your photos individually.

1. On the Home screen, tap Photos. The Photo Albums screen appears. Along the bottom of the screen are buttons for up to four ways you can find photos to view:

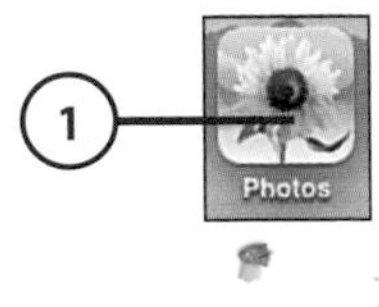

- **Albums**—This screen organizes photos by album. The Camera Roll album contains photos and videos you've taken, images you've saved from emails, or screenshots you've captured. The Photo Library contains all the images (except for those in the Camera Roll album) on your iPod touch. The rest of the items are photo albums or other collections that you've moved from a computer onto your iPod touch.
- **Events**—Events are collections of photos based on time (such as all the photos taken on the same day) or some other criteria, such a vacation.
- **Faces**—iPhoto enables you to tag people in photos with names. You can use the Faces option in the Photos app to find photos to view based on the people in those photos.
- **Places**—When photos have been tagged with location information (either automatically through a camera with a GPS locator, such as when they were taken on an iPod touch, or manually by tagging in a photo application), you can find photos to view by selecting a location on the map.

No Events, Faces, or Places?

The Photos app gets information about albums, events, faces, and places from the photo application from which the photos were synced. If the application you use doesn't support one of these concepts or you don't tag photos with this information, such as places (which tags photos with the location at which they were taken), then that option will be hidden, and you have to use one of the others to find the photos you want to view. iPhoto on the Mac supports all these features; photo applications on Windows might or might not, so you just have to explore the specific application you use to find out. If you don't have any photos with places or faces, you won't even see the respective tabs.

2. To view photos by album, tap Albums and continue to step 3; to view photos by events, skip to step 6; or to view photos by place, skip to step 10.
3. Browse the screen until you see an album containing photos you want to view.
4. Tap the album you want to view. You see the preview screen for that album with a thumbnail for each photo it contains.

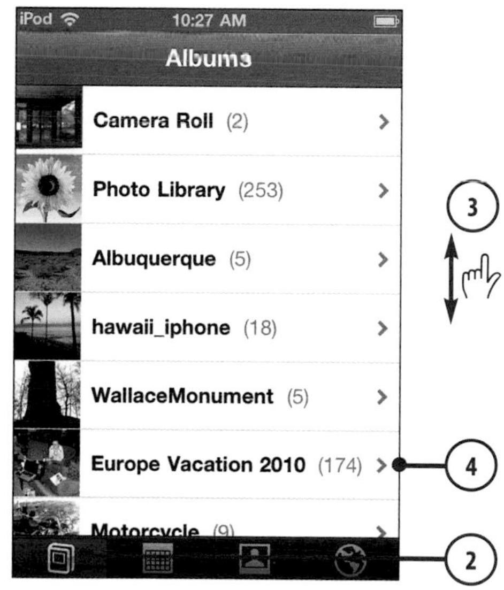

5. Browse the album to see all the photos it contains; to view photos in the album, skip to step 16.

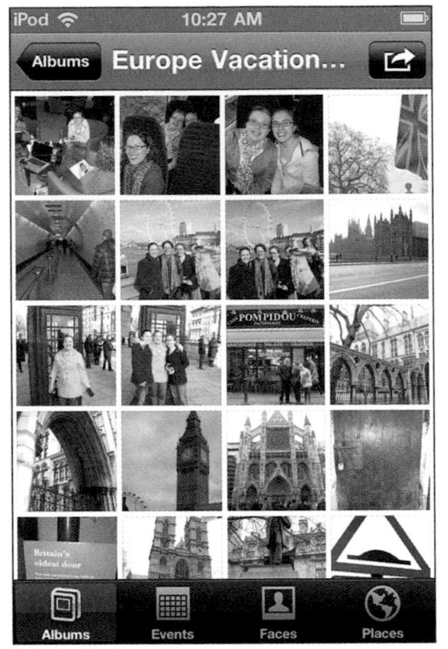

How Many Photos?

When you browse the Albums, Events, or Faces list, you see the number of photos each item contains in the gray parentheses to the right of the item's name. When you tap a location on the map, you see the number of photos associated with that place. When you view photos, you see the number of the photo you view instead of the number in the source containing that photo at the top of the screen (such as 57 of 174).

6. Tap Events. You see the events that have been synced on the iPod touch.
7. Browse the list of events.
8. Tap the event containing the photos you want to view.

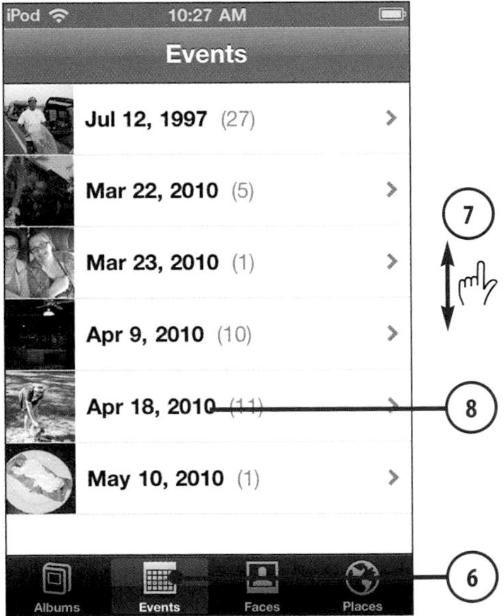

9. Browse the photos in the event; to view photos in the event, skip to step 16.
10. Tap Places. You see a map of the globe; each location with which photos are associated is marked with a pushpin.
11. Double-tap or unpinch on an area on the map to zoom in.
12. Drag on the map to move around the globe.

Viewing with Faces

Viewing photos by Faces is similar to the other options. Tap the Faces tab and then tap the person whose photos you want to view. You see the photos on the iPod touch that have been tagged with that person's name. You can browse and view these just like photos in events or albums.

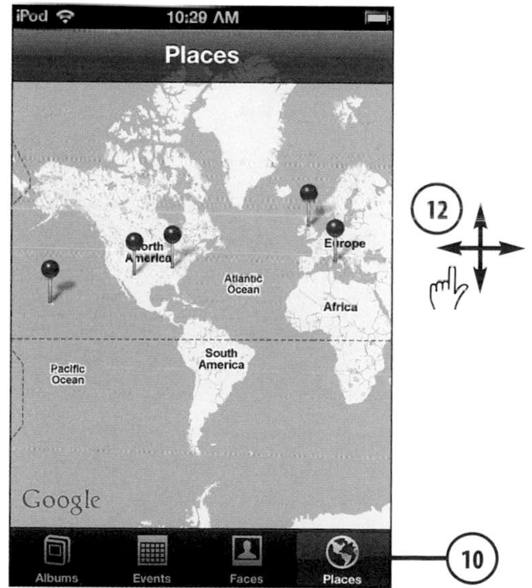

13. Tap a pushpin at a location. You see the number of photos associated with that location.

14. To browse the photos for a location, tap its Info button.

15. Browse the photos for the location.

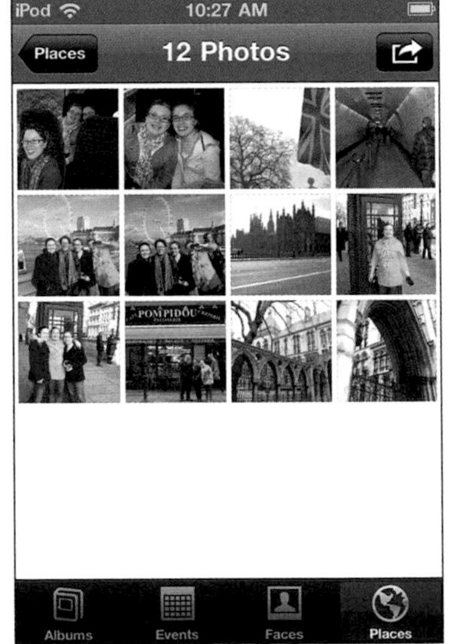

16. To view a photo, tap it. The photo display screen appears. When the photo first appears, the photo viewing controls appear on the screen. After a moment, they disappear.
17. Tap Forward or drag to the left to view the next photo in the group (album, event, face, or place).

Orientation Doesn't Matter

Zooming, unzooming, and browsing a photo works in the same way in both orientations.

18. Tap the Back button or drag to the right to view the previous photo in the album.

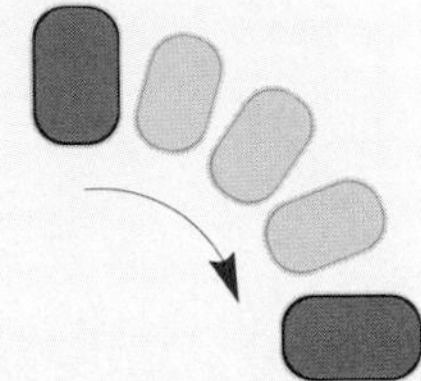

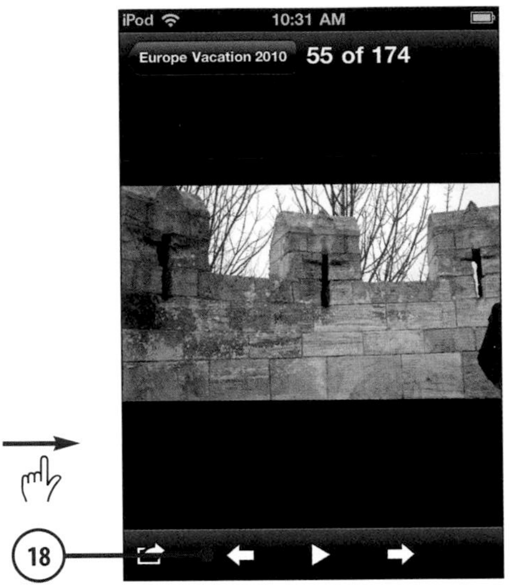

19. To view the photo in landscape orientation, rotate your iPod touch 90 degrees.
20. Unpinch or double-tap on the photo to zoom in.
21. When you are zoomed in, drag on the photo to scroll in it.

22. Pinch or double-tap on the photo to zoom out.
23. Tap anywhere on the photo to show the toolbar.
24. Tap the return button, which is labeled with the source's name. You move back to the source's browse screen.

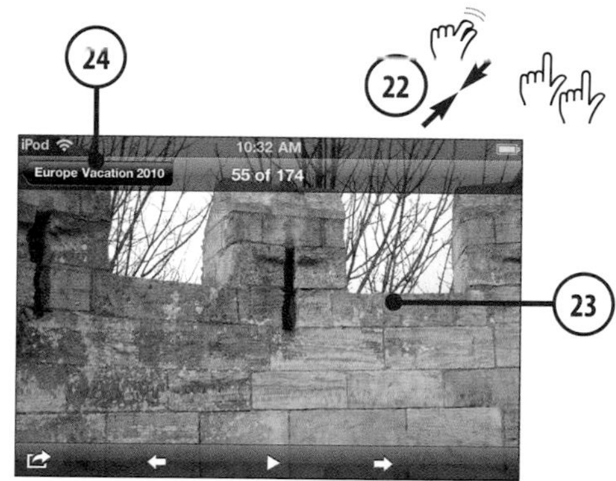

Viewing Photos as a Slideshow

You can view photos in slideshows. Before you start watching your own slideshows, take a few moments to configure iPod touch's slideshow settings to set your slideshow preferences.

Configure Slideshow Settings

1. On the Home screen, tap Settings.
2. Scroll down until you see Photos.
3. Tap Photos.

4. Tap Play Each Slide For.
5. Tap the amount of time you want each slide in a slideshow to appear on the screen.
6. Tap Photos.
7. Tap Transition.
8. Tap the transition you want to use when slides change.
9. Tap Photos.
10. To make slideshows repeat until you stop them, tap Repeat OFF. Its status becomes ON to indicate you have to stop slideshows manually. When the status is OFF, slideshows play through once and then stop.
11. To view photos in a random order in a slideshow, tap Shuffle OFF. Its status becomes ON so you know photos will appear in random order during slideshows. To have photos appear in the order they are in the selected album, tap ON so the status becomes OFF.

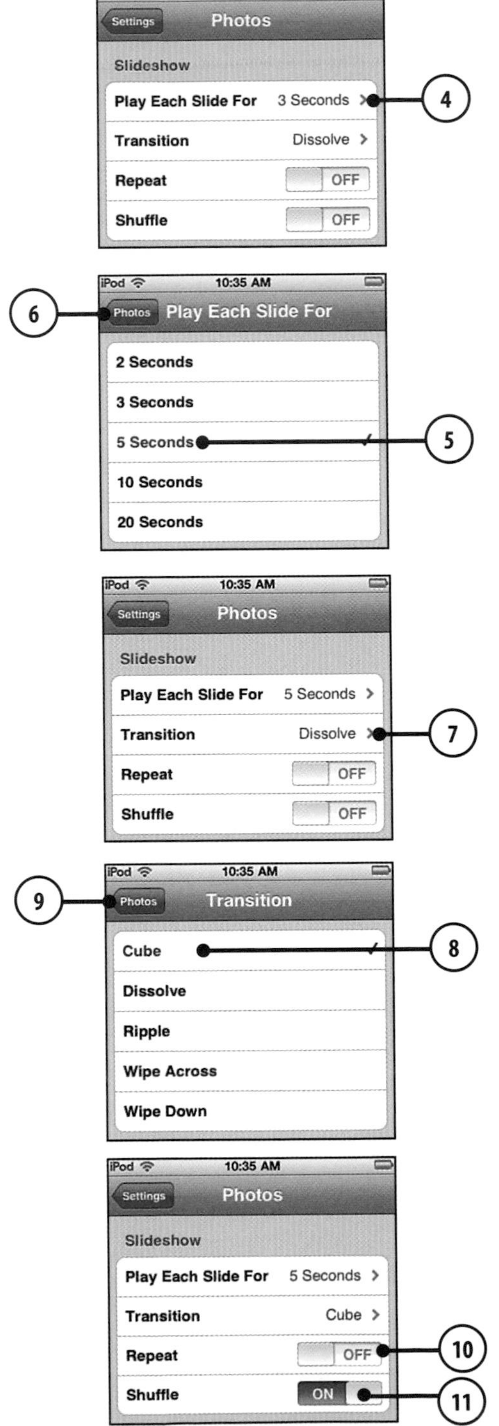

Watching Slideshows

1. On the Home screen, tap Photos.
2. Choose the source of photos you want to view in a slideshow and browse it. You can start a slideshow from photos in any of the categories you see (Albums, Events, Faces, or Places).
3. Tap the source of photos you want to view in a slideshow.
4. Tap the first photo in the selected source. (If you don't care about the order of photos in the slideshow, you can tap any photo to start.)
5. Tap Play. The slideshow begins to play.

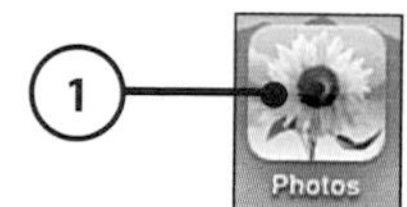

It's Not All Good

Unfortunately, you can't associate music with a slideshow so that the music plays automatically when you watch the slideshow. If you want to hear music while a slideshow plays, use the iPod app to start the music and then move to and start the slideshow.

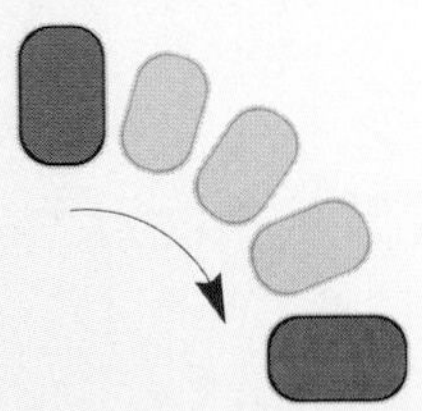

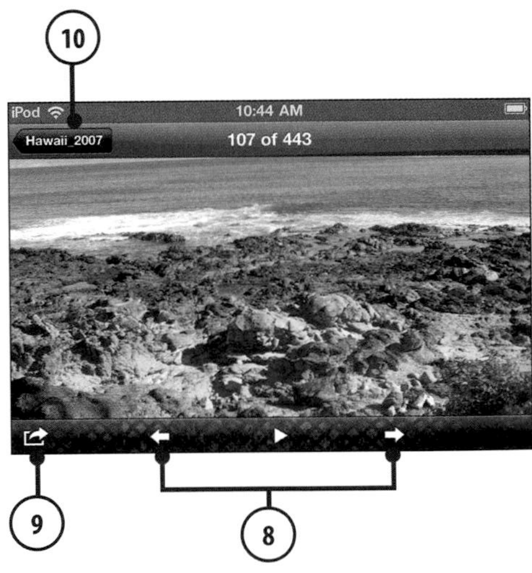

6. To view the slideshow in landscape mode, rotate the iPod touch. The slideshow plays, each slide appearing on the screen for the length of time you set. The transition you selected is used to move between photos. If you set slideshows to repeat, the slideshow plays until you stop it; if not, it stops after each photo has been shown once.
7. To stop the slideshow before it finishes, tap the screen. The photo controls appear, and the slideshow stops at the current photo.
8. To move to the next or previous photo, tap the Forward button or tap the Back button.
9. To perform various actions on a photo, such as using it as wallpaper, tap the Action button. This is covered later in this chapter.
10. When you're done with the slideshow, tap the return button, which is labeled with the album's name.

Deleting Photos or Video from an iPod touch

You can only delete photos and videos in the Camera Roll album from your iPod touch. (To remove photos that are loaded onto iPod touch via syncing with a computer, you must change the sync settings so those photos are excluded and then resync.) To delete a photo or video you've taken with iPod touch's camera, captured as a screenshot, or downloaded from email, take the following steps.

1. Move to the Photos application and open the Camera Roll source.
2. Tap the photo you want to delete.
3. Tap the Trash icon.
4. Tap Delete Photo. The Trash icon opens and "swallows" the photo, at which point it is deleted. You see the next photo in the Camera Roll source.

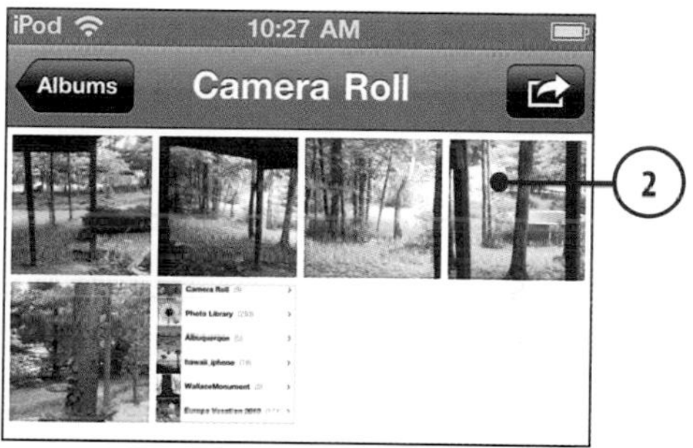

Emailing a Photo

You can email photos via iPod touch's Mail application starting from the Photos app.

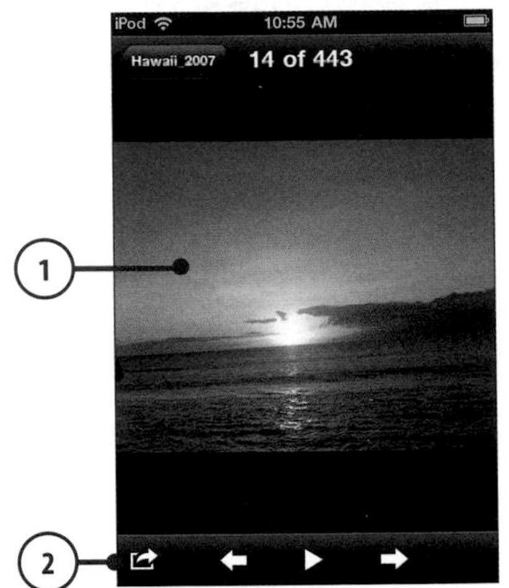

1. View the photo you want to send in an email.
2. Tap the Action button.
3. Tap Email Photo. A new email message is created, and the photo is added as an attachment. (In some cases, you are prompted to select the size of the photo to send. If this happens, tap the size you want the user to receive. Higher resolution photos are better, but are also larger files. If the recipient has a low bandwidth connection, choose a low resolution version of the photo.)

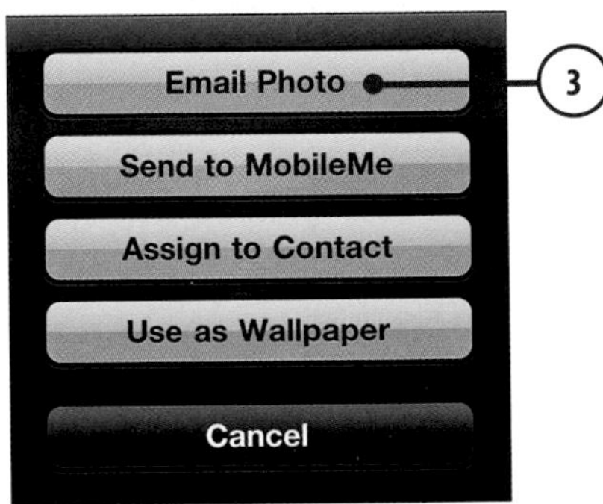

4. Use the email tools to address the email, add a subject, type the body, and send it. (See Chapter 9, "Emailing," for detailed information about using your iPod touch's email tools.) After you send the email, you move back to the photo.

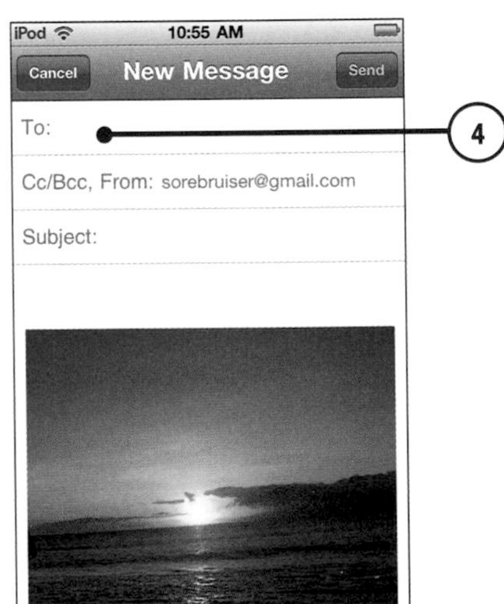

Images from Email

As you learned in Chapter 9, when you save images attached to email that you receive, they are stored in the Camera Roll photo album just like photos you take with the iPod touch.

Sending a Photo to MobileMe

If you have a MobileMe membership, you can post photos from the iPod touch directly to your MobileMe galleries on the Web, where they can viewed or downloaded.

1. View the photo you want to move to the Web.
2. Tap the Action button.
3. Tap Send to MobileMe.
4. Add a title and description for the photo. (The description is optional.)
5. Scroll down the screen until you see the albums on your MobileMe website.

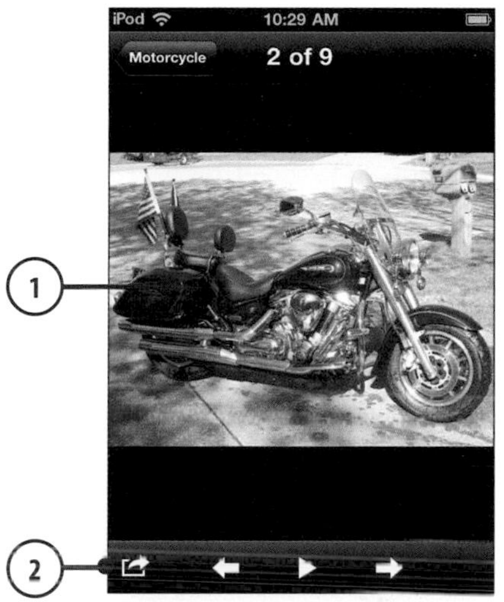

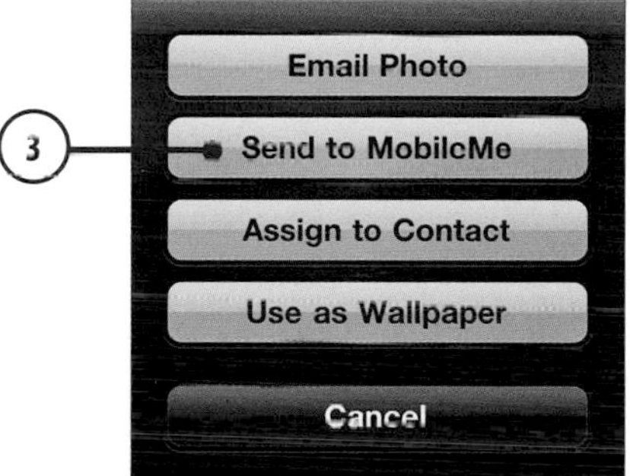

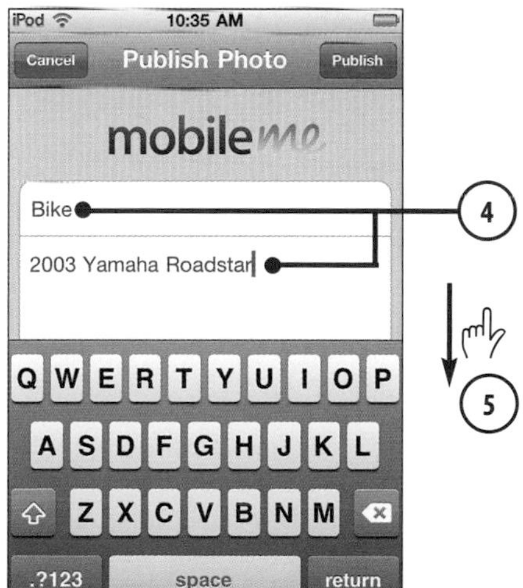

6. Tap the album to which you want the photo posted.
7. Tap Publish. The photo is posted to the album you selected.
8. Tap the action you want to perform, such as Tell a Friend, which sends a message inviting someone to visit your published photo, or View on MobileMe to view the published photo.

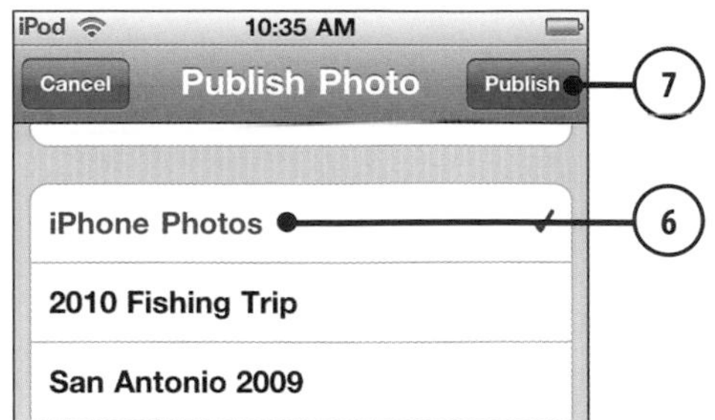

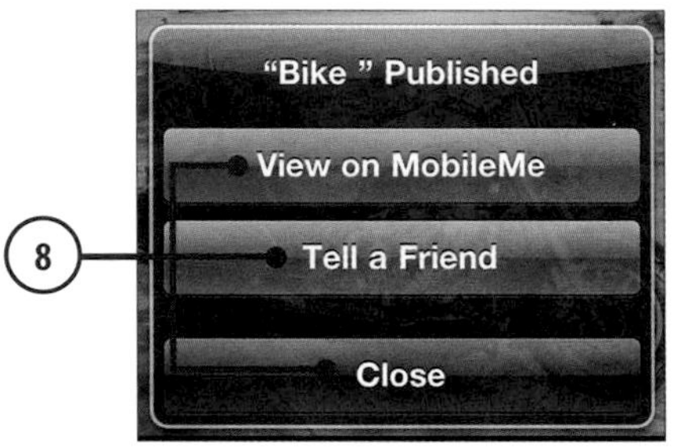

iPod touch photo posted on the web

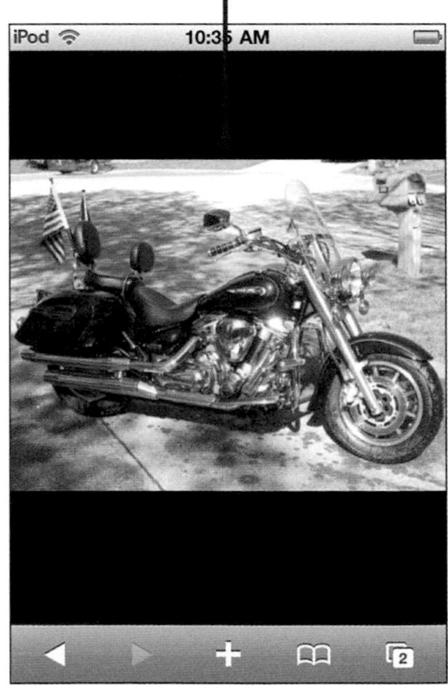

Assigning a Photo to a Contact

You can assign photos on your iPod touch to your contacts. When you assign a photo to a contact, you see that photo when the contact calls you, when you receive email from the contact, and so on. You can assign any photo to a contact, but you get the best results when you use a photo that you've taken with iPod touch because it will scale to full screen when the person calls you; other kinds of photos appear as thumbnails instead.

1. Take the photo you want to assign to a contact. If the photo you want to use already exists on iPod touch, skip this step.
2. View the photo you want to associate with a contact.
3. Tap the Action button.
4. Tap Assign to Contact. (For more information on working with contacts, see Chapter 8, "Managing Contacts.")

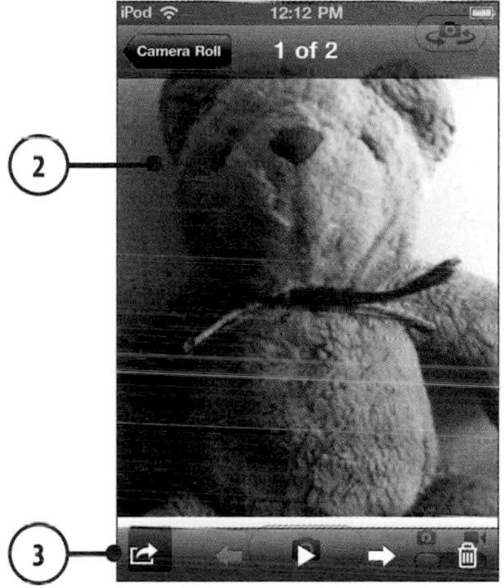

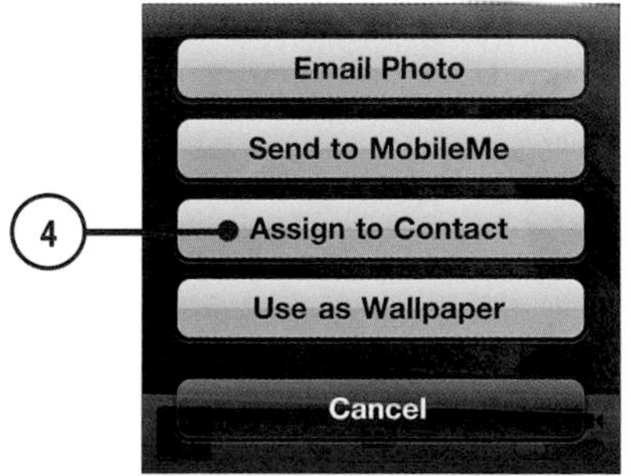

5. Find and tap the contact with which you want to associate the photo.
6. Drag and pinch or unpinch the image until the part you want to add to the contact shows on the screen the way you want to see it.
7. Tap Set Photo. The photo is saved to the contact; when iPod touch interacts with that contact, such as when you receive a request for a FaceTime session, the photo is displayed on iPod touch's screen. You return to the photo.

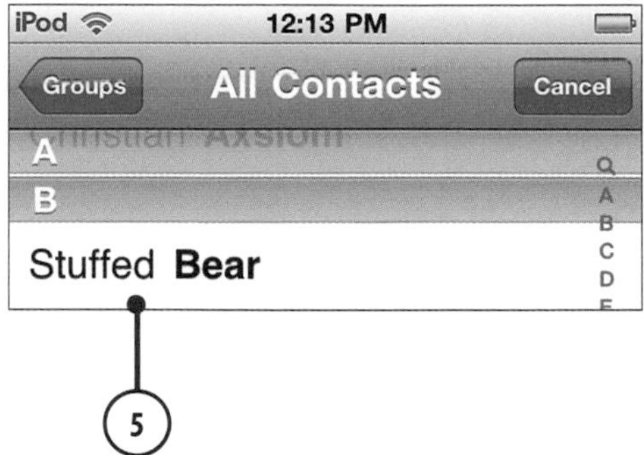

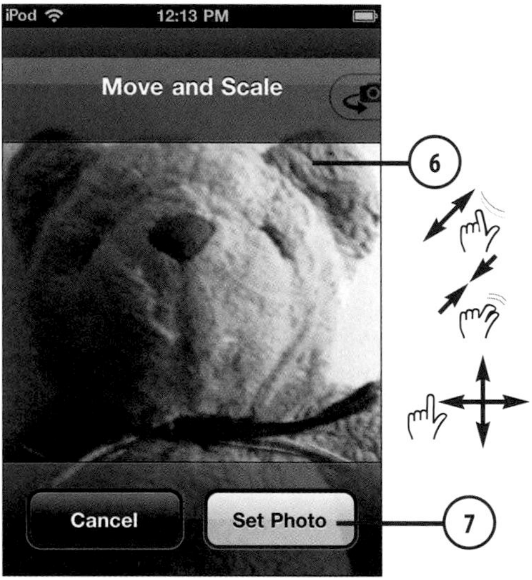

Deleting Contact Photos

When a photo is associated with a contact, even if you delete the original photo taken with the the iPod touch, the photo remains with the contact. (You can only delete photos taken with the touch; photos that are transferred from a computer must be removed from the sync to be removed from the touch.) Contact photos are quite small, so don't worry about them using lots of your iPod touch's memory. To delete a photo from a contact, edit the contact information and tap the photo. Then tap Delete Photo. See Chapter 8 for more information about editing contacts.

Using a Photo as Wallpaper

Your iPod touch's wallpaper appears when you wake it up but before you unlock it and as the background for your Home screens. You can use any photo stored on your iPod touch to customize your wallpaper in either location.

1. View the photo you want to use as wallpaper.
2. Tap the Action button.
3. Tap Use as Wallpaper.
4. Drag and pinch or unpinch the image until the part you want to use as wallpaper shows on the screen the way you want to see it.
5. Tap Set.
6. Tap the location to which you want to apply the custom wallpaper.

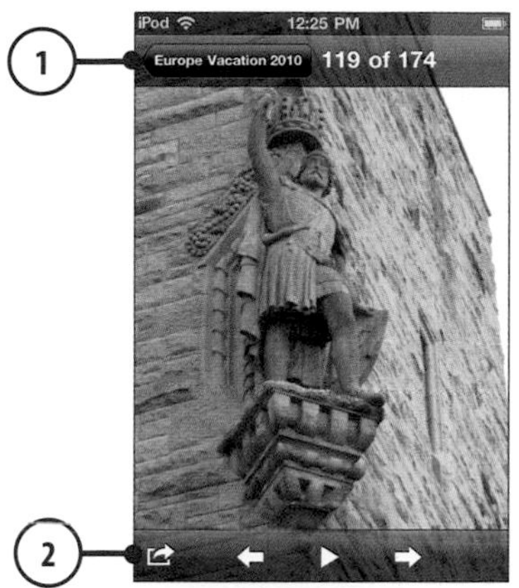

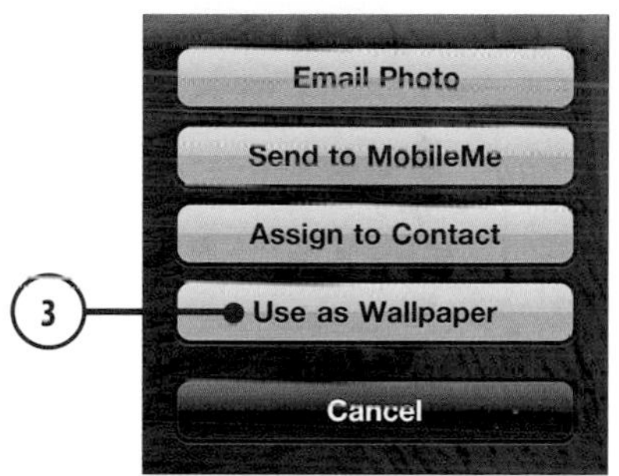

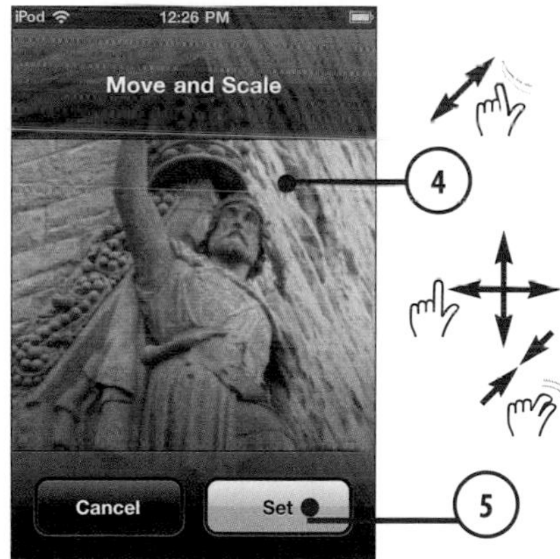

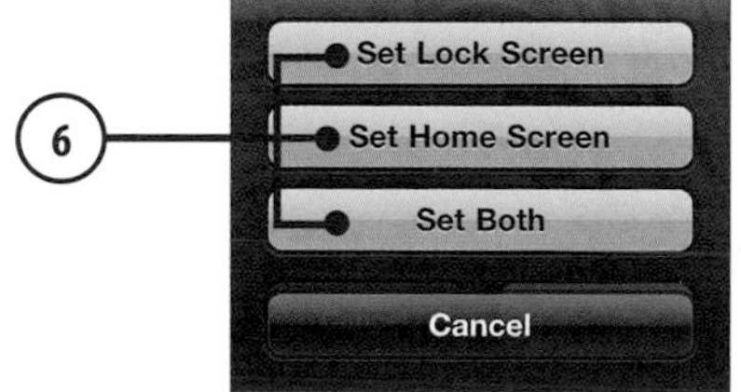

Sharing Photos

You can share a group of photos with others as easily as you can email an individual photo. Check this out.

1. Open the source containing the photos you want to share.
2. Tap the Action button.
3. Tap the photos you want to share.
4. Tap Share.
5. Tap Email to attach the selected photos.
6. Complete and send the email.

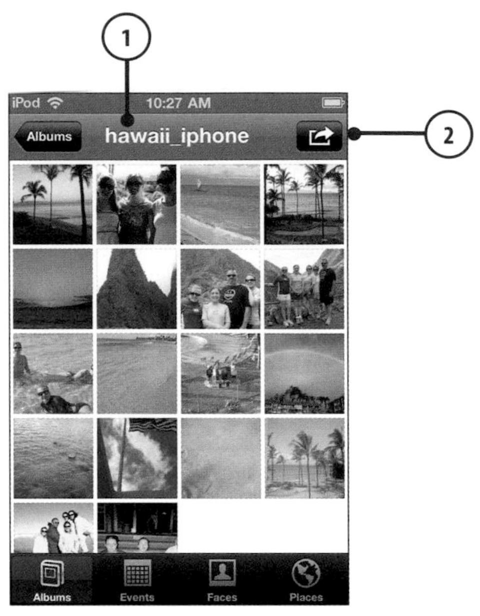

Copy (or Delete) 'Em

If you tap the Copy button, the images you selected are copied to the iPod touch's clipboard. You can then move into another application and paste them in. When you are working with the Camera Roll source, you can delete selected photos by tapping the Delete button.

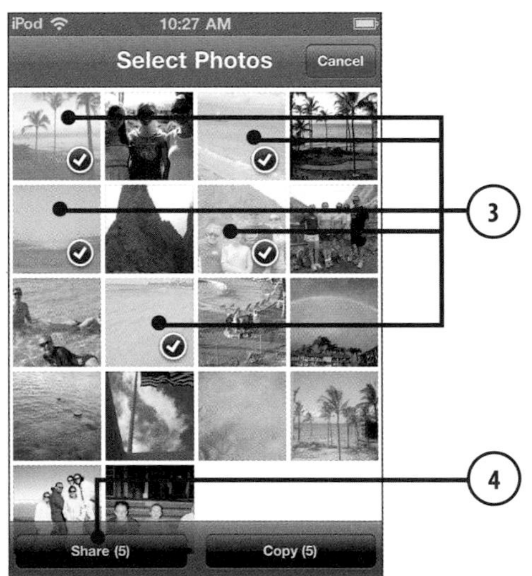

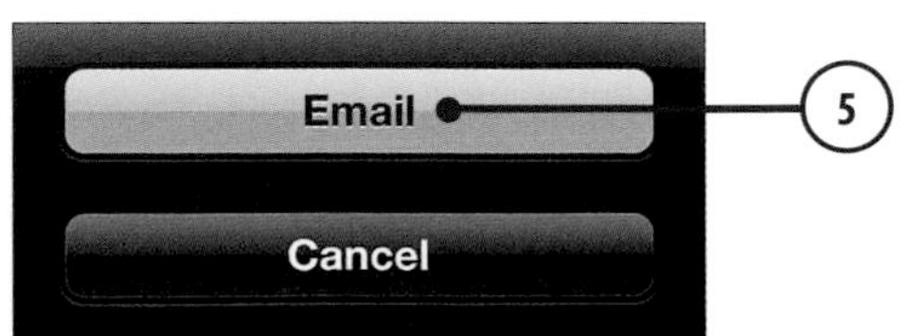

Viewing, Editing, and Working with Video

As you learned earlier, if you have an iPod touch 4th generation, you can capture video clips. Once captured, you can view clips stored there, edit them, and share them.

Watching Video

Watching videos you've captured with your iPod touch is simple.

1. Move to the Photos application and open the Camera Roll source. Video clips have a camera icon and running time at the bottom of their icons.
2. Tap the clip you want to watch.
3. Tap either Play button. The video plays. After a few moments, the toolbars disappears.

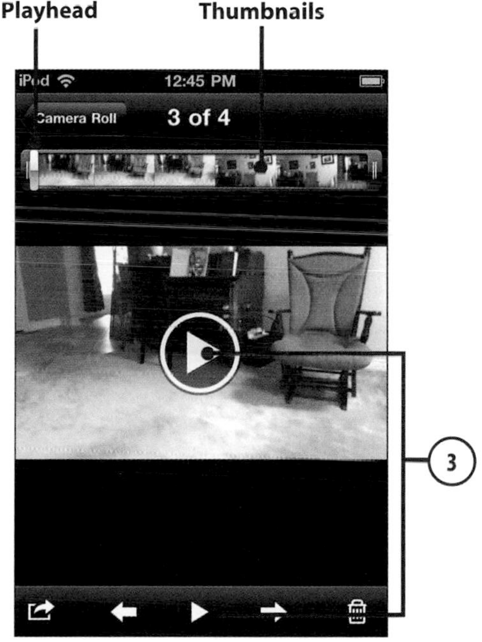

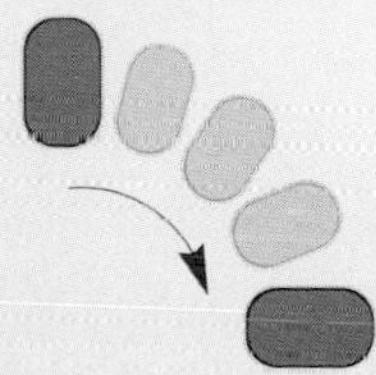

4. Rotate the video to change its orientation.

5. Tap the video. The toolbars reappear.
6. To pause the video, tap Pause.
7. To view the next video clip (or photo if that's what's next in the source you are working with), tap the Next button.
8. To view the previous clip (or photo if that's what's next in the source you are working with), tap the Previous button.
9. To jump to a specific point in a clip, drag the playhead to where you want to start playing it; if you hold your finger in one place for a period of time, the thumbnails expand so your placement of the playhead can be more precise. When you lift your thumb, the playhead remains at its current location; if the clip is playing, it resumes playing from that point.

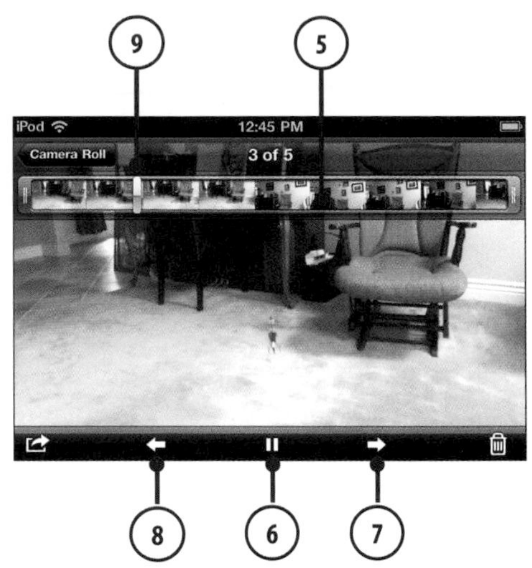

Editing Video

You can trim a video clip to remove unwanted parts. Here's how you do it.

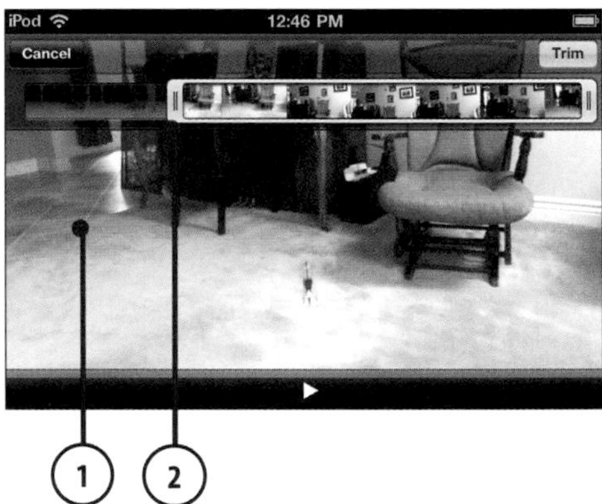

1. View the video you want to edit.
2. Drag the left crop marker to where you want the edited clip to start. As soon as you move the crop marker, the part of the clip that is inside the selection is highlighted in the yellow box; the Trim button also appears.
3. Drag the right crop marker to where you want the edited clip to end.
4. Tap Trim.

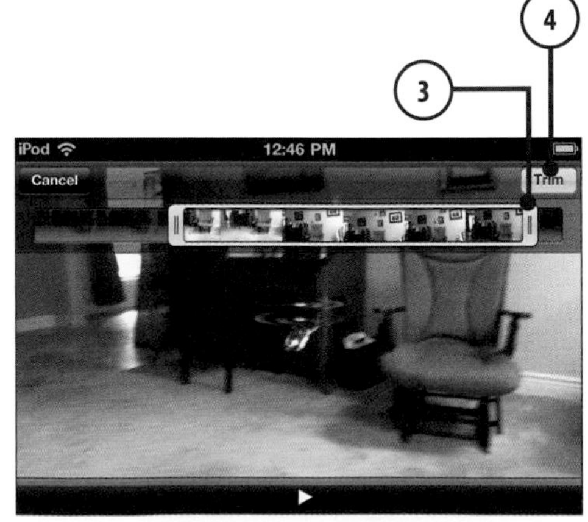

5. Tap Trim Original to edit the clip and replace the original version with the edited version or Save as New Clip to create a new clip containing only the frames between the crop markers. The frames outside the crop markers are removed from the clip. The clip is trimmed and replaces the original clip or a new clip is created depending on the option you selected.

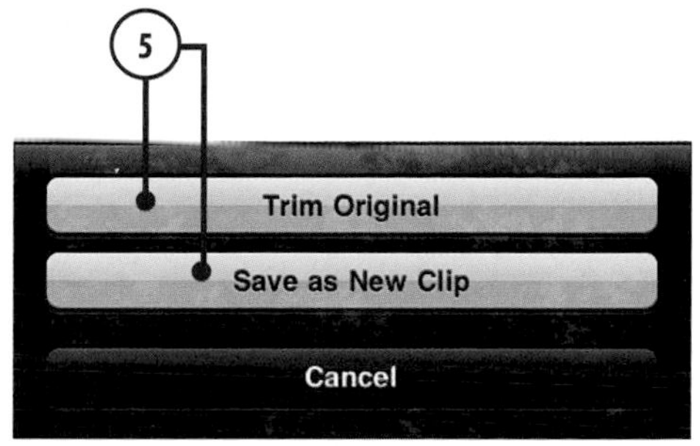

Go Further

THERE'S AN APP FOR THAT

For more powerful video editing on your iPod touch, download the iMovie app. This app provides a much more powerful video editor. You can use themes to design a video, add music, include titles and photos, and much more. For more information on downloading and installing apps, see Chapter 13, "Installing and Maintaining iPod touch Applications."

Deleting Video

To remove a video clip from your iPod touch, tap the Trashcan icon and then tap the Delete Video button at the prompt.

Sharing Video

You can share videos you've taken on your iPod touch by email, text message, MobileMe, or YouTube. (You must have a MobileMe or YouTube account to share videos over those services.) Sharing videos via email, text message, or MobileMe is just like sharing photos. Move to the clip, tap the Action button, and tap Email, Video, MMS, or Send to MobileMe (see the steps to perform these tasks with photos earlier in this chapter for details).

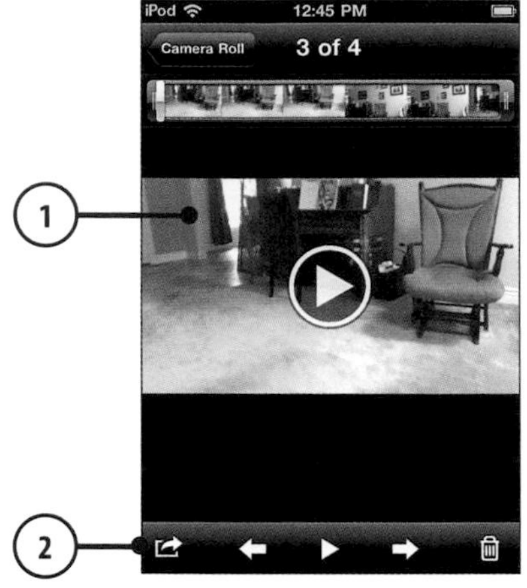

You can share your videos on YouTube by performing the following steps.

1. View the video you want to share.
2. Tap the Action button.
3. Tap Send to YouTube. The video is compressed for YouTube.
4. Enter your YouTube username and password, and tap Sign In. You don't have to do this every time; it depends if you've signed out of your account. If you aren't prompted to log in, you already are.

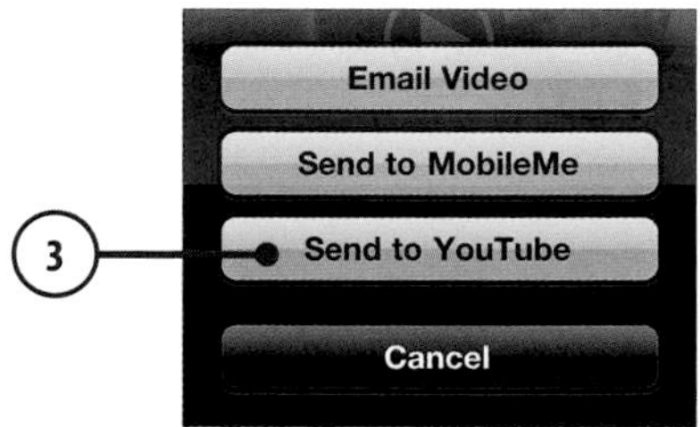

5. Enter a title and description of the video clip.
6. Enter one or more tags.
7. Associate the clip with a category.
8. Tap Publish. The clip is posted to YouTube.

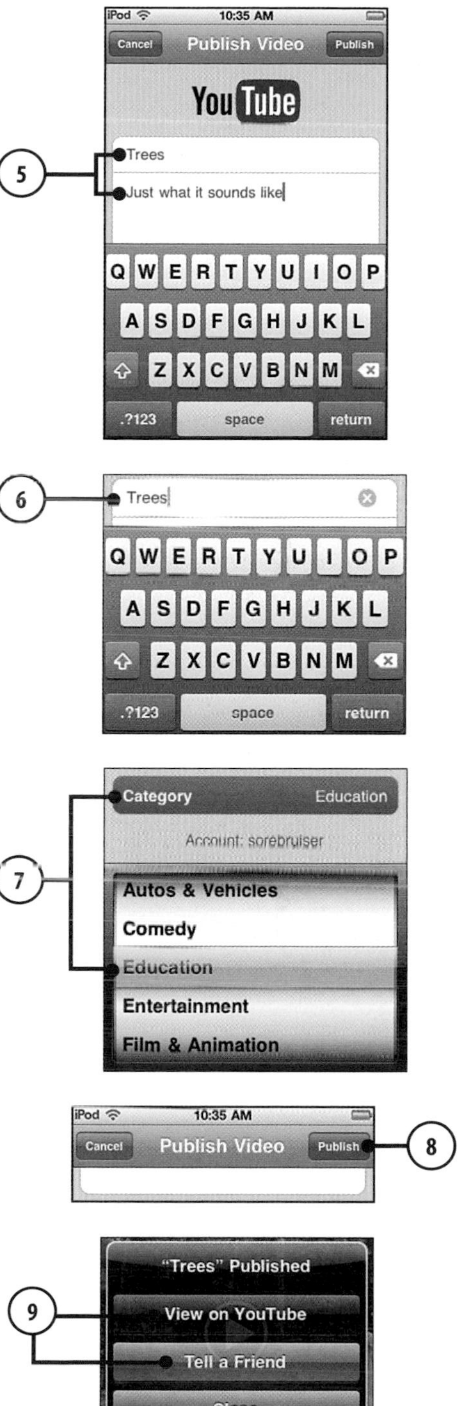

Time Equals Battery

If you publish large video files over a slow connection, the process can take a while. And, during this process, your iPod touch is chugging battery power. Be aware of your battery's charge status and how long it will be before you can recharge your iPod touch before you publish videos. Otherwise, you might end up with a partially published video and a powerless iPod touch.

9. Tap the action you want, which can be View on YouTube to immediately view your posted clip or Tell a Friend to send a message that contains a link to your video.

Moving Photos from Your iPod touch to a Computer

As you use your iPod touch to take photos or video, you're going to want to move some of the content you capture to your computer. How you do this depends on the kind of computer and application you use.

Moving Photos from Your iPod touch to a Windows PC

How you move photos from your iPod touch to a Windows PC depends on the specific application you use to manage your digital photos. Most applications designed to import photos from a digital camera should also work with your iPod touch. For example, you can import photos from an iPod touch into Adobe Photoshop Elements. Or, you can just use Windows default tools to move photos and video from the iPod onto your computer, at which point you can use them in any application you have that can work with photos and video.

The following steps show you how to import photos and video using Windows XP's Microsoft Scanner and Camera Wizard. Importing them using other applications will follow a similar process, although the specific steps you follow and options you have will be different:

1. Connect the iPod to your computer. The Apple iPod dialog appears.
2. Select the action you want to take; in this case, select Microsoft Scanner and Camera Wizard.
3. If you want this action to be performed each time you connect your iPod (when it has photos and video to import), check the Always use this program for this action check box.
4. Click OK.

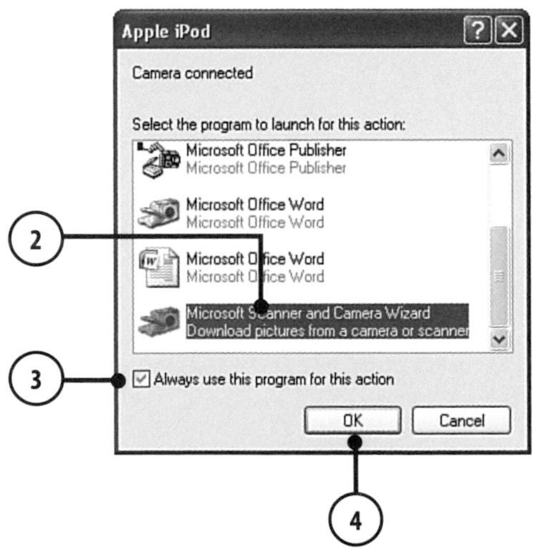

5. Click Next.
6. Check the check boxes for each photo and video you want to import onto the computer.
7. Click Next.
8. Enter a name for the photos and videos you are importing or select and existing folder; this will be the name for the folder in which the imported content will be stored.
9. Choose a location in which to store the folder you created or selected in step 8.
10. If you want to delete the photos and video from the iPod after they have been imported, check the Delete pictures from my device after copying them check box.
11. Click Next. The photos and video are downloaded from the iPod onto the computer; you see a progress window on the screen.

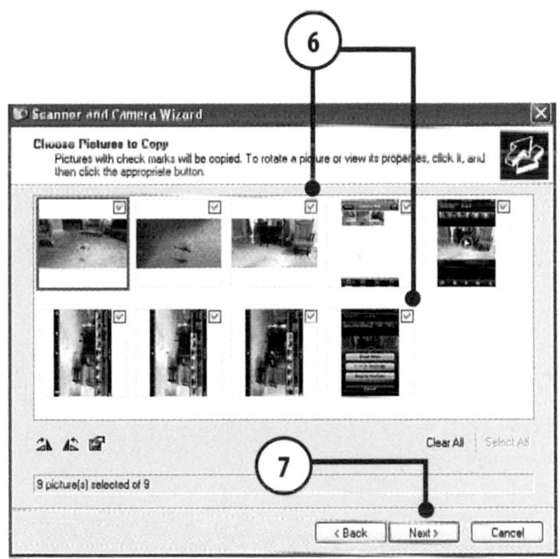

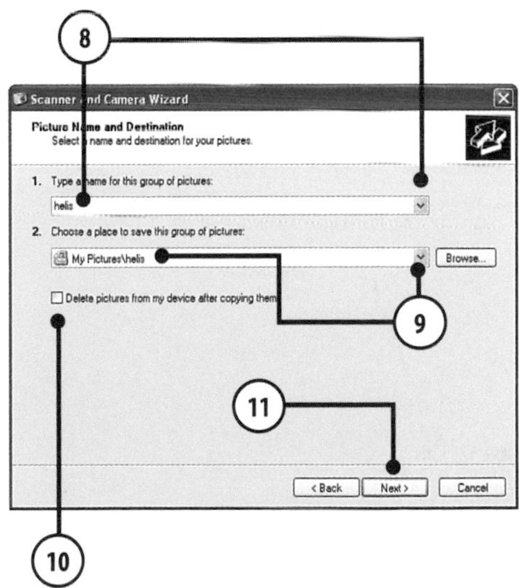

12. Select the action you want to take on the imported content, such as publishing them to the Web; or click Nothing if you don't want to take any action.
13. Click Next.
14. Follow the on-screen prompts to complete the action you selected in step 13. For example, if you selected Nothing in step 12, when you click Finish, the folder into which you imported the photos and video will open.

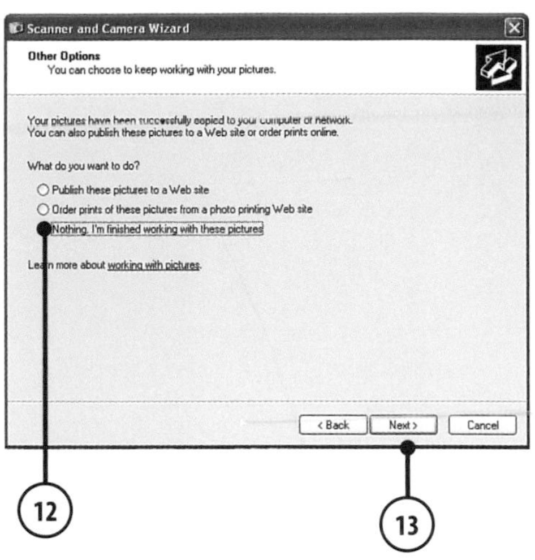

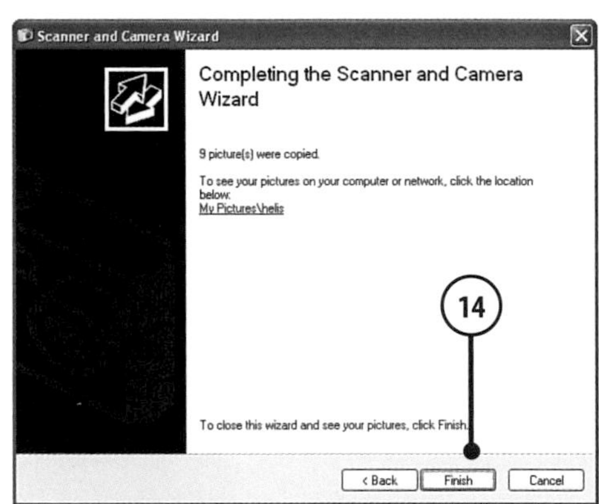

Moving Photos from an iPod touch to a Mac

The iPod touch is designed to move its photos into your iPhoto Library easily.

1. Connect your iPod touch to a Mac. If there are photos or videos on your iPod touch, iPhoto opens automatically and moves into Import mode. The iPod touch is selected as the import source.
2. Enter an event name for the photos you want to import in the Event Name field.
3. Enter a description of the photos you want to import in the Description field.

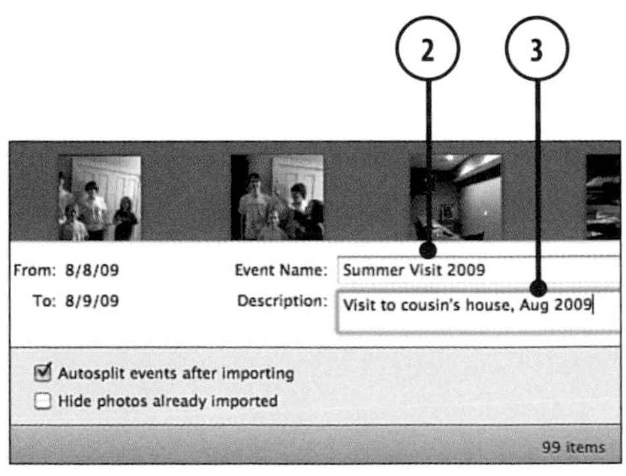

4. Click Import All. Photos and videos are copied from the iPod touch into iPhoto.
5. Click Delete Photos if you want to delete the photos and videos from the iPod touch or Keep Photos if you want them to remain on the iPod touch.
6. Use iPhoto to work with the photos and videos you imported from iPod touch.

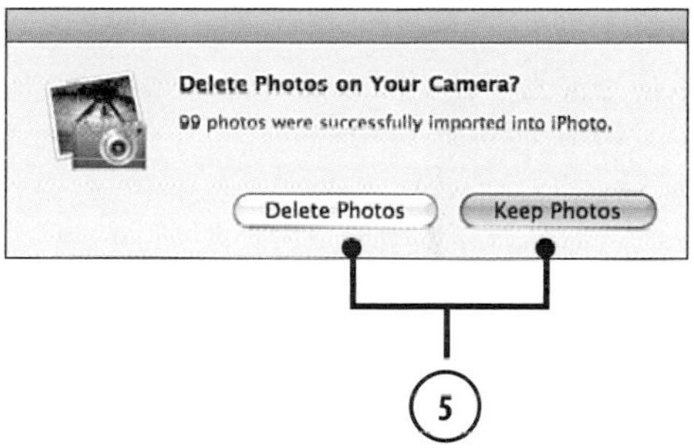

Moving Video from iPhoto (on Macs) to iTunes

When you transfer video from your iPod touch to iPhoto, the iPhoto application can't play the video clips. When you double-click a clip, it opens in the QuickTime Player application where you can watch it. If you want to add your clips to iTunes, click the Action button on the QuickTime Player toolbar and choose iTunes. Select the format for the clip, and it is added to your iTunes Library. Select the Movies source and you can watch your videos in iTunes. You can also include them in the sync settings to move them back to the iPod touch.

Apps make the iPod touch one of the most amazing devices ever

In this chapter, you explore functionality provided by some of the great applications available for your iPod touch. The topics include the following:

- → Video conferencing
- → Reading books
- → Tracking stocks
- → Finding your way with maps
- → Watching the weather

Using Cool iPod touch Applications

You've seen that your iPod touch is packed with amazing functionality. However, so far we've scratched only the surface of what the iPod touch can do. In this chapter, you discover functionality provided by some of the useful applications available for your iPod touch. Some applications installed by default, but you have to download the iBooks application. (Downloading applications requires that you connect to the Internet; see Chapter 2, "Connecting to the Internet, Bluetooth Devices, and iPods/iPhones/iPads," for help with that task.

Getting Some FaceTime (4th Generation or Later)

FaceTime enables you to see and hear people you want to communicate with. This feature exemplifies what's great about the iPod touch; it takes very complex technology and makes it simple. FaceTime works great, but there are two conditions that have to be true for you and the people you want some FaceTime with. Both people have to use an iPod touch (4th generation or later) or and iPhone (4 or later) that has FaceTime enabled. And each device has to be connected to a Wi-Fi network with Internet access. When these conditions are true, communicating with FaceTime is easy.

More Details

To be able to use FaceTime, you also need an Apple ID and email address. I've assumed this is the case since you need both of these to get the most out of your iPod.

Setting Up FaceTime

Before you can start getting your FaceTime, you need to configure it with the following steps:

1. Tap Settings on the Home screen.
2. Tap FaceTime. If you've already entered your Apple ID elsewhere, such as in the iTunes app, your Apple ID is entered for you and you can skip to step 4.

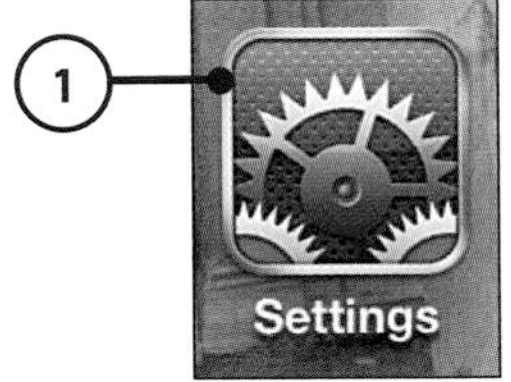

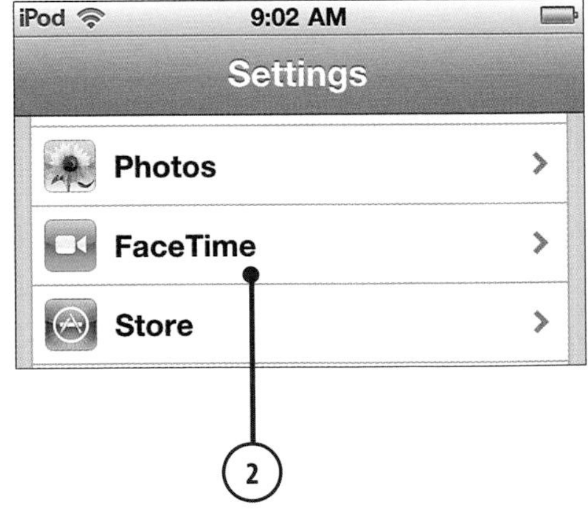

3. Enter your Apple ID.
4. Enter your password.
5. Tap Sign In.

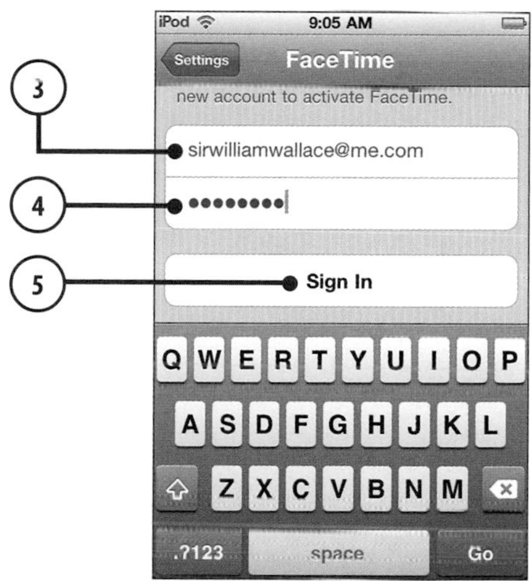

No ID?

If you don't have an Apple ID, tap Create New Account to get one.

6. Verify the email address you want people to use to request a FaceTime session is correct; if it isn't, update it.
7. Tap Next.
8. Check the email account you entered in step 6. You should have received a verification email from Apple. Follow its instructions to verify that the email address you entered is correct. Once that happens, the information you entered will be verified on the iPod.

9. If you want to use multiple email addresses for FaceTime, tap Add Another Email and follow the screens to configure.
10. If you want to disable FaceTime at any point, tap ON next to FaceTime so its status becomes OFF. You won't be able to use FaceTime until you enable it again.
11. Tap Settings.

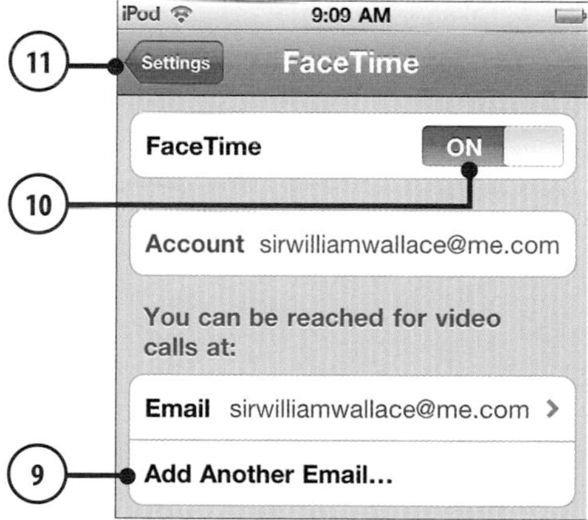

Dump the Address

If you want to stop using an email address for FaceTime, tap it, and on the resulting screen, tap Remove This Email.

12. Tap Sounds. Configure the ringtone, which is one of the sounds you hear when someone requests a FaceTime session with you.
13. Tap Ringtone.
14. Browse the sounds available to you. If you added ringtones by purchasing them using the iTunes app on an iPhone and synching with your iTunes Library (at press time, the iTunes app on an iPod doesn't support ringtones), you see them in the Purchased section. If you've created your own ringtones, you see them in the Custom section. In the Standard section, you see the default ringtones.
15 Tap a sound to play it. It is marked with a check mark to show it is the selected sound.
16 After you select the ringtone you want, tap Sounds.

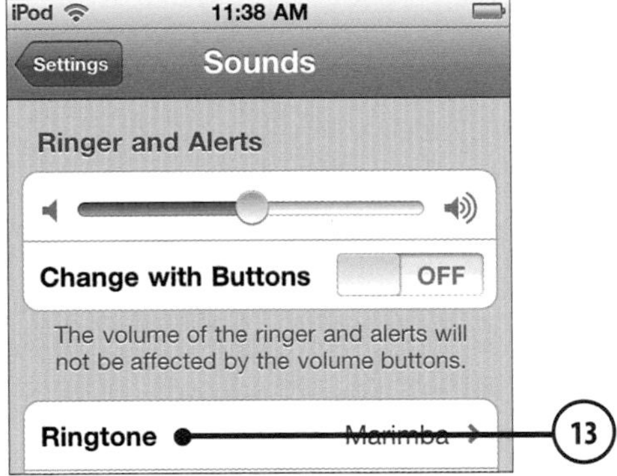

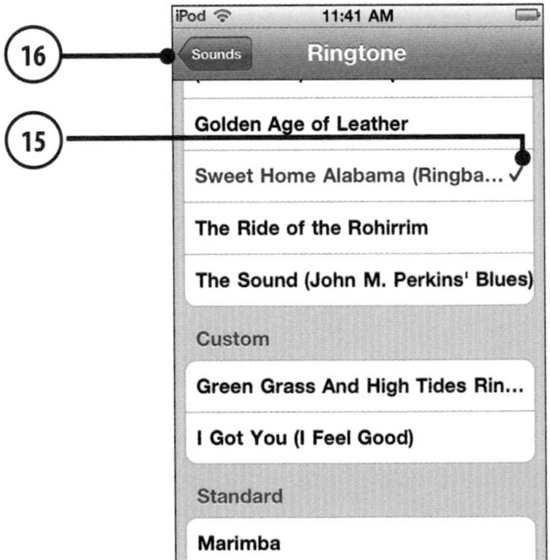

17. Use the slider to set the volume level for the ringtone you selected. You're now FaceTime ready.

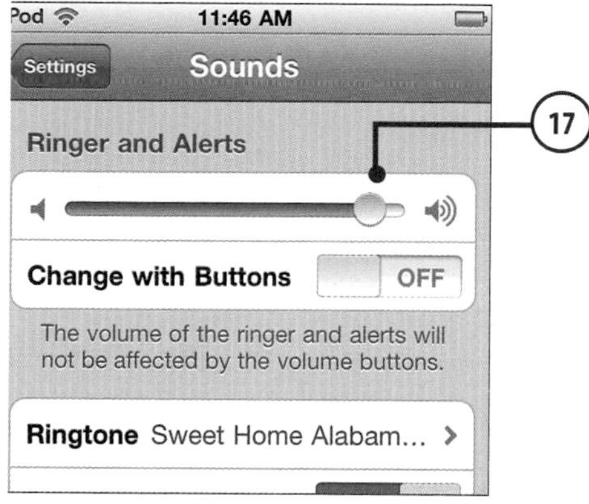

Making a FaceTime Call

FaceTime is a great way to communicate with someone because you can hear and see them. Because the iPod touch has cameras facing each way, it's also easy to show something to the person you are talking with. You can start a session with someone who has either an iPhone 4 (or later) or an iPod touch (4th generation or later). If you want to FaceTime with an iPhone owner, you must have the phone number associated with the iPhone stored with the person's contact information. If you want to FaceTime with an iPod touch user, you use the email address associated with that person's FaceTime configuration (also stored in the Contacts app).

We Have Contact

For information about configuring and working with your contacts, see Chapter 8, "Managing Contacts."

1. Tap the FaceTime icon.
2. Find and tap the contact with whom you want to FaceTime.

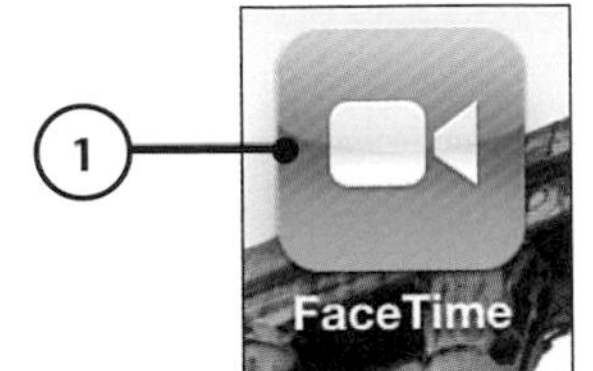

No Contact?

If you don't move directly into your contacts, tap the Contacts tab at the bottom of the FaceTime window.

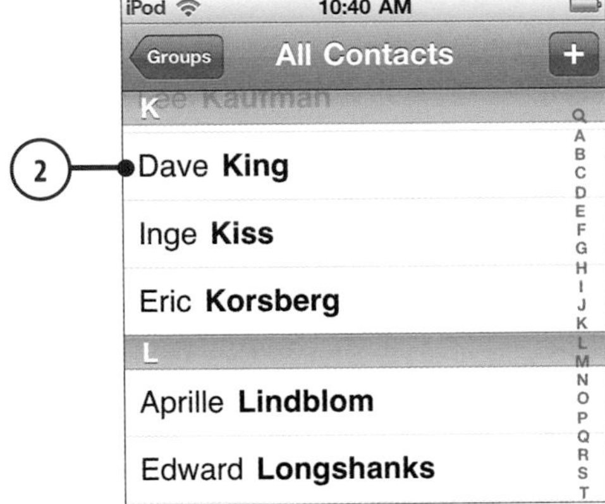

3. Scroll down until you see the FaceTime button.
4. Tap FaceTime.
5. Tap the information you want to use for the FaceTime call. This needs to be the FaceTime email address for an iPod touch user or the phone number for an iPhone user.

   The iPod touch attempts to make a FaceTime connection.

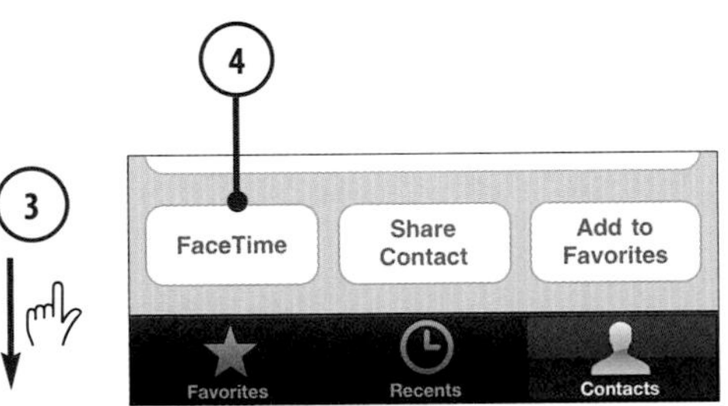

No FaceTime for You!

If the person you are trying to FaceTime with isn't able to connect via FaceTime (for example, FaceTime is disabled or the device is not connected to the Internet), you see a warning message and the process terminates.

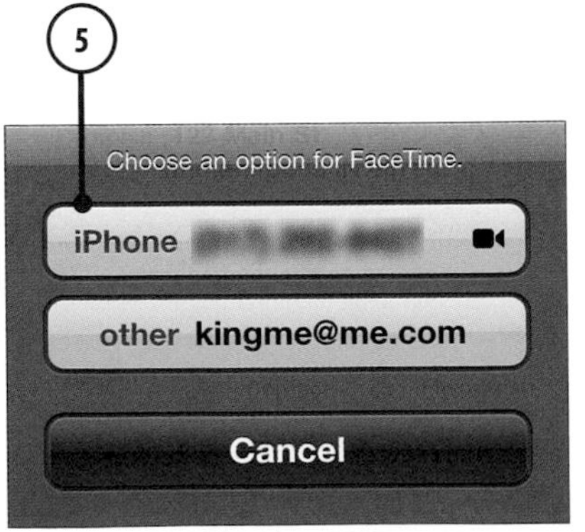

When the connection is complete, you see the other person in the large window and a preview of what he is seeing in the small window.

6. During the FaceTime session, you can do the following:
   - Drag the preview window around the screen to change its location.
   - Mute your side of the conversation.
   - End the FaceTime session.
7. To use the camera on the backside of the iPhone, tap the switch button. The other person will now see whatever you have that camera pointed at.

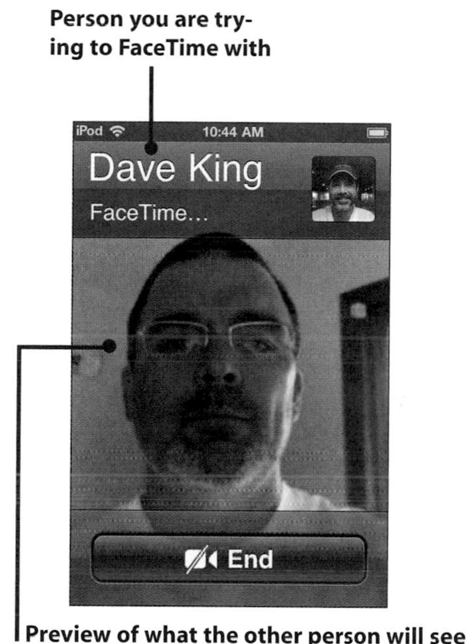

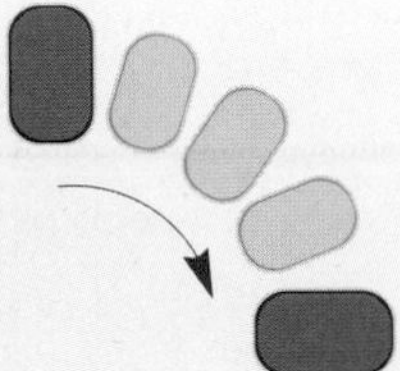

8. Rotate your iPod touch to change the orientation to landscape. This impacts what the other person sees (as reflected in your preview), but you continue to see the other person in his iPhone's current orientation.

   If the other person changes his camera, you see what his backside camera is pointing at.

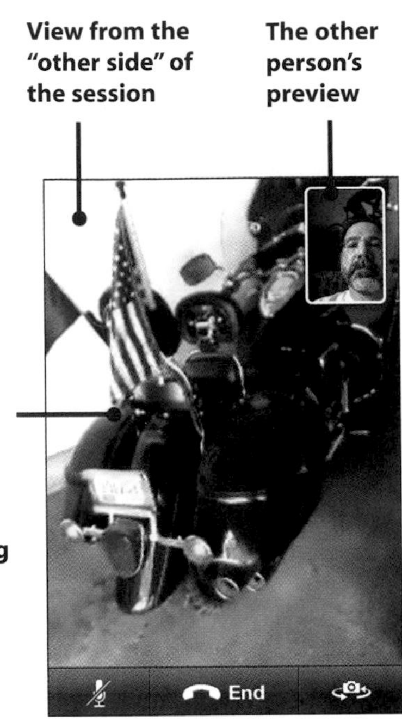

Updated FaceTime Icon

After you've successfully FaceTimed with someone, a camera icon is added to the FaceTime button on the Info page so you know the person can FaceTime.

Just Missed You

Anytime a FaceTime session is requested (either by you or to you), it is considered a missed call. You see the number of missed calls in a red circle on the FaceTime icon for new missed calls. When you view the Recents tab in the FaceTime app, this counter is set to 0 again.

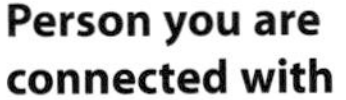

8. To end the session, tap End.

Accepting a FaceTime Call

When someone tries to FaceTime with you, you hear a chiming noise followed by the ringtone you've select, and you see the FaceTime message showing who is trying to connect with you. You can either decline by tapping Decline or start the session by tapping Accept. If you accept, the session starts and you have the same options as when you start a FaceTime session.

More on FaceTime

The FaceTime app has three tabs at the bottom of its window. Tap the Contacts tab to request a FaceTime session by using contacts. If you tap the Recents tab, you see a list of all the FaceTime sessions you've had (in black) or missed (in red). You can tap a recent session to start another one with the same person. To see more information about a session, tap the Info button along the right side of the screen. The third tab, Favorites ,is where you can store shortcuts to FaceTime info you want to be able to access quickly. Tap the Add button (+) and tap the contact you want to add as a favorite. Then tap the specific information (such as the FaceTime email address) that you want on the favorites list. To request a FaceTime session, move to your Favorites list and tap the favorite you want to connect with.

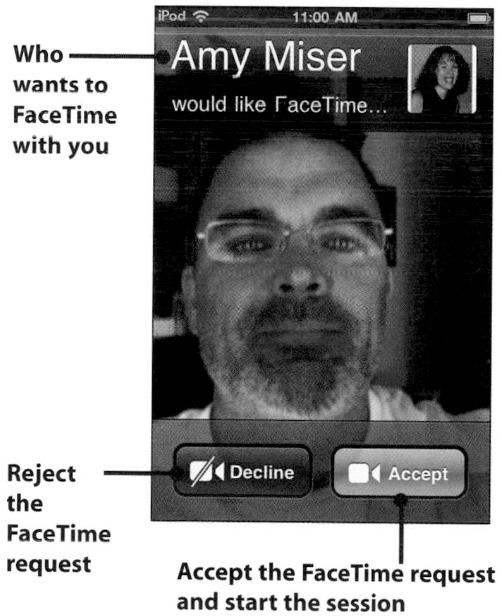

Reading Books with iBooks

The iBooks application enables you to download and read thousands of books on your iPod touch. You can carry a library of books with you and enjoy the benefits of e-reading wherever you are. To start with iBooks, download and install it from the App Store (see Chapter 13, "Installing and Maintaining iPod touch Applications," for the details of downloading applications on your iPod touch). You can read portions of books (samples) and then, if you decide that you want to read the rest of the story, you can easily upgrade to the full book.

Moving Books onto Your iPod touch

In Chapter 3, "Moving Audio, Video, Books, and Photos onto Your iPod touch," you learn how to use iTunes to stock iBooks' Bookshelf with great reading material.

Finding Books to Read

When you launch iBooks, you see the Bookshelf where your books are stored. You can browse and search your bookshelf and, when you find a title of interest, you can take it off the digital shelf and start reading. You can browse books by their covers (steps 2 and 3) or use a configurable list (steps 4 through 6). You can also search for specific books (step 7). After you've found a book, reading it is a simple tap.

1. Move to the Home screen and tap iBooks.

iBooks and PDFs

iBooks is also a reader for PDF documents. You can change the view of your Library by tapping Books to see books or PDFs to see PDF files. You can view PDFs in the same way that you read books in the iBooks app. When you view a PDF attached to an email message, you're prompted to view it in iBooks or Mail.

2. Scroll up the screen to reveal the View buttons and search bar.
3. Tap the Cover button.
4. Browse your books by their covers.
5. Tap the List button to browse books by various groupings.
6. Tap the criterion by which you want to see the books, such as Titles or Authors. The books are reorganized by the criterion you selected.
7. Browse your books.

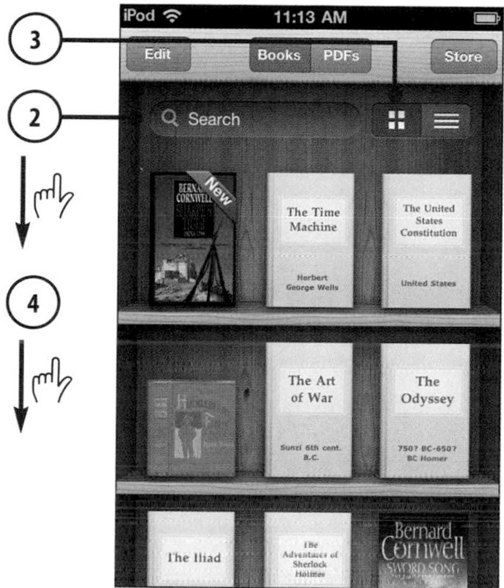

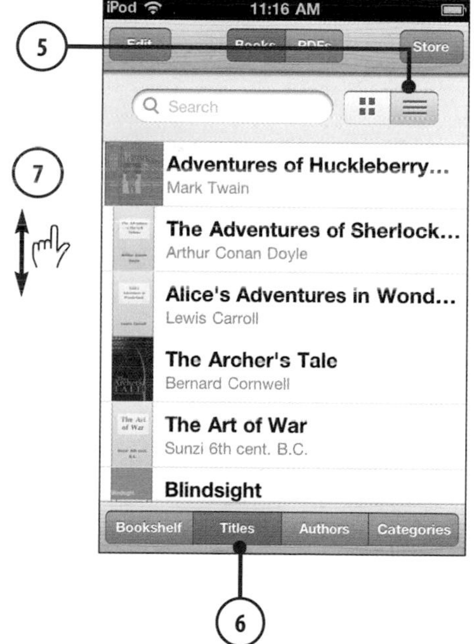

8. To search for a book, type text in the Search tool; the text can be in the book's title, author name, and so on. Books that meet your search criterion are shown on the shelf.

9. To read a book you've found (by browsing or searching), tap its cover. It opens and you see the most recent page you viewed or the first page if you've never opened the book before.

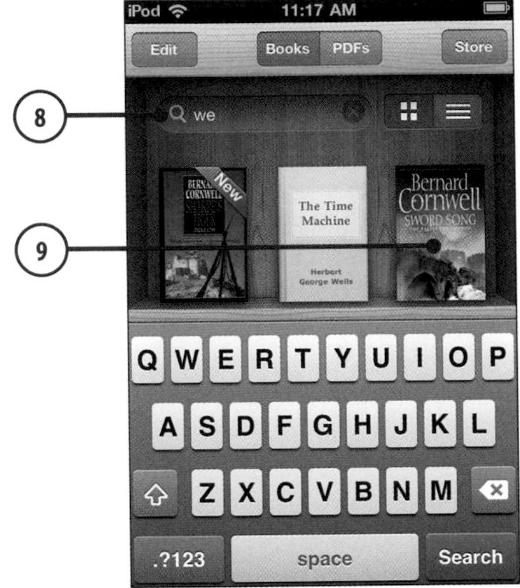

Reading Books

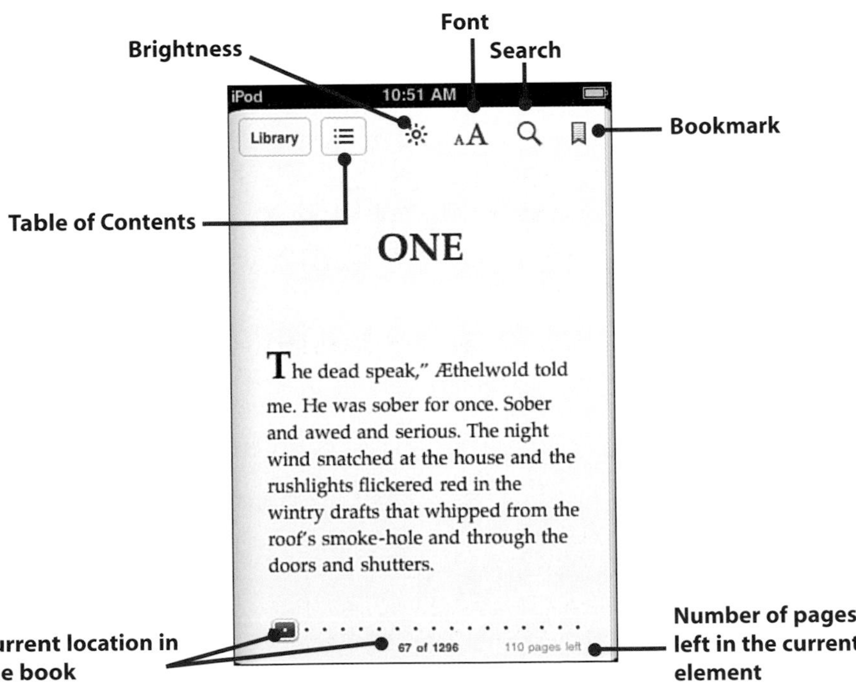

iBooks offers many features that make reading digital books even better than reading the paper version. The reading screen provides lots of information about and controls for your books.

Following are some of the great ways you can use iBooks to read:

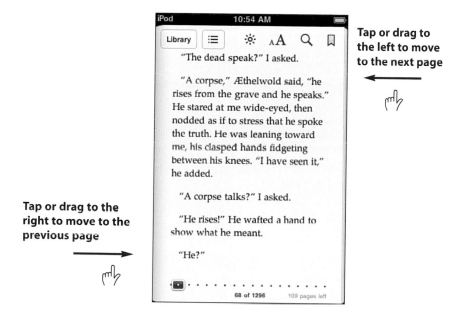

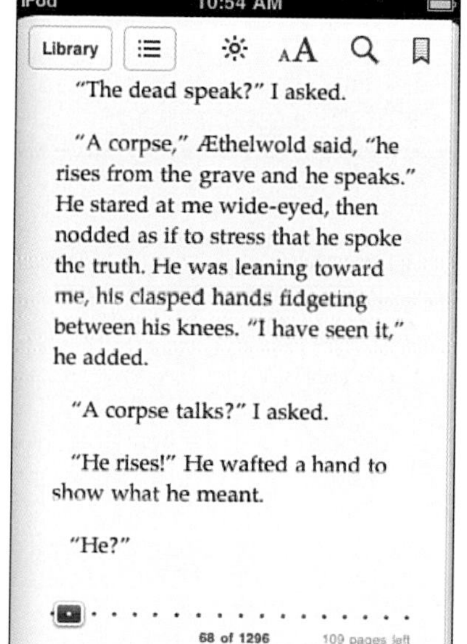

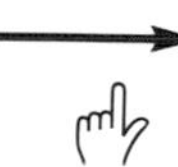

- **Turn the page**: To move to the next page, tap on the right side of the screen or drag your finger to the left to flip the page. To move to a previous page, tap on the left side of the screen or drag your finger to the right.
- **Hide/Show controls**: Tap the center of the screen to show or hide the controls; the book title replaces the top buttons when the controls are hidden.

It's All Relative

The page numbers you see in iBooks are actually screen numbers. When you change the iPod's orientation, font, or another factor that causes iBooks to change the layout of a book's screens, the page location and total page count also change to reflect the current number of screens in the book and element (such as chapter).

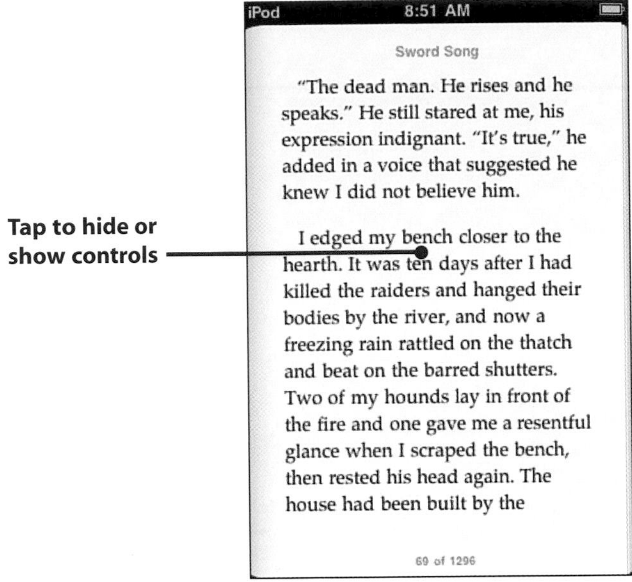

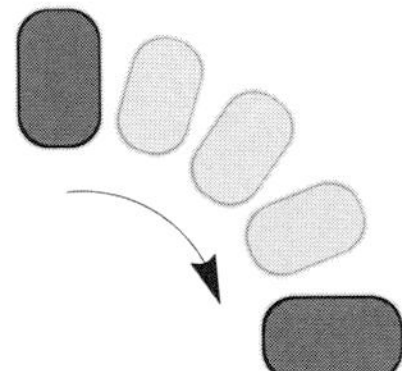

- **Rotate to read in landscape**: Rotate the iPod to change the book's orientation. iBooks will repaginate the book.

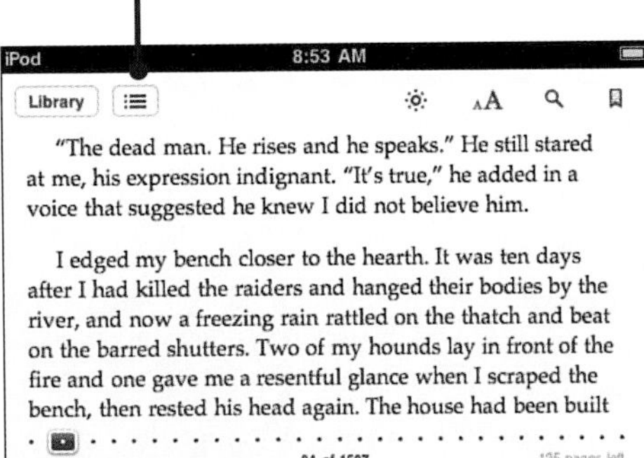

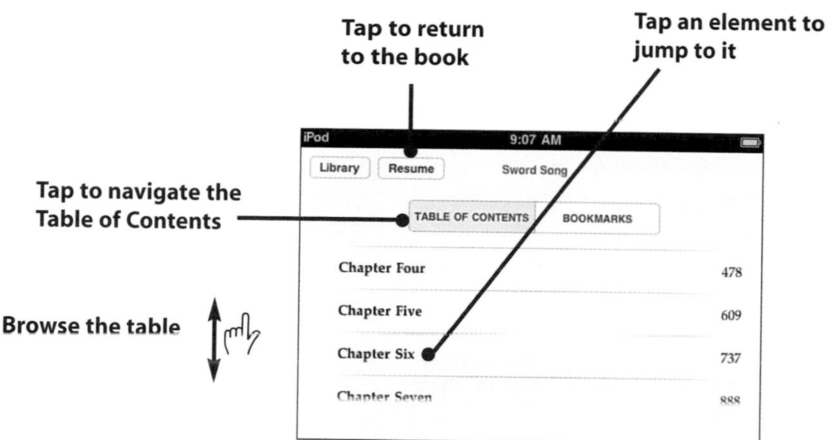

- **Navigate with the Table of Contents:** Tap the Table of Contents button; then tap the Table of Contents tab. Browse the book's table of contents and tap the location to which you want to jump. To return to your previous location, tap Resume.

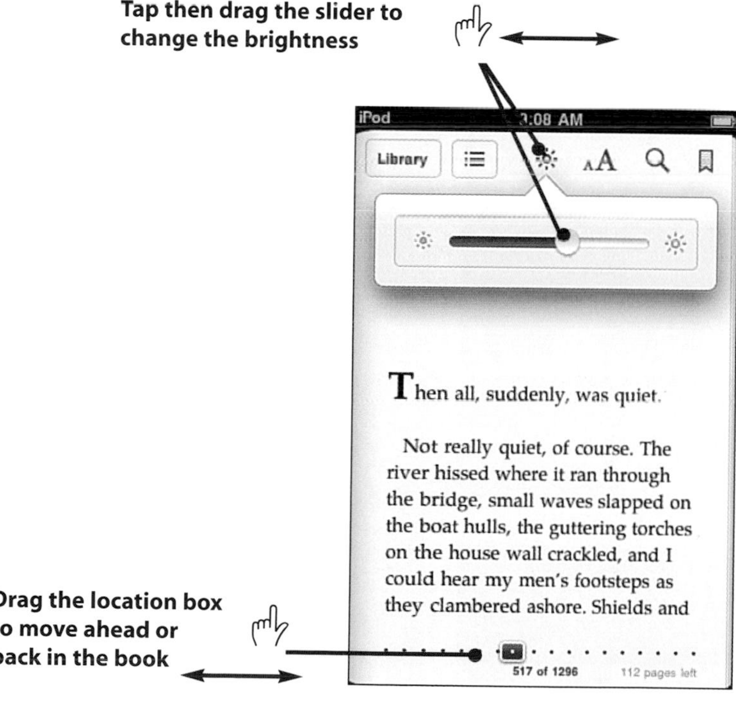

- **Brightness**: Tap the Brightness button and then drag the slider to the left or right to change the screen brightness.
- **Change pages quickly**: Drag the location box to quickly scroll ahead or back in the book. As you drag, the chapter and page number of the box's current location appears in a pop-up box. When you release the box, you jump to its current location.

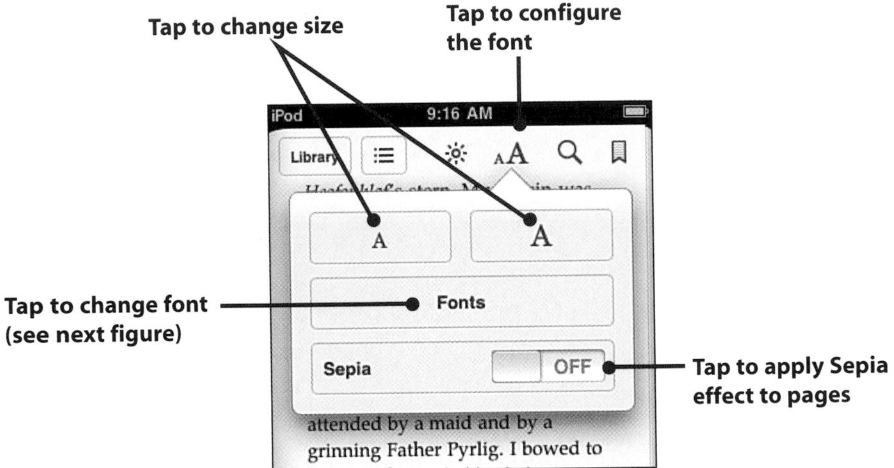

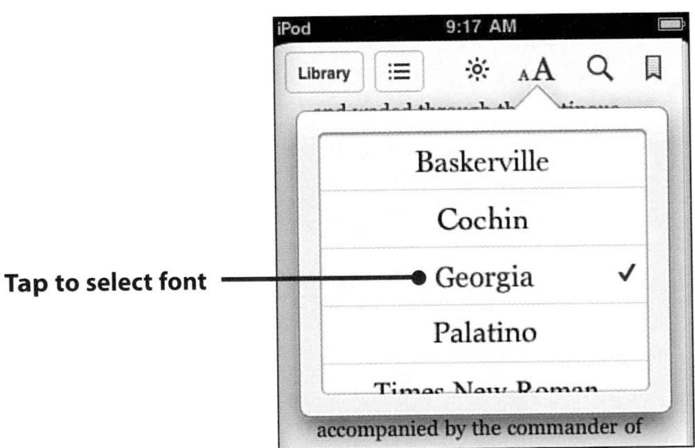

- **Change font**: When you tap the Font button, the Font palette appears. Use the size buttons to change the size of the font displayed; as you change the size, iBooks resizes the book's font in the background. Tap the Fonts button; the list of available font types appears. Tap the font type you want to use; iBooks reformats the book with that style in the background. Tap the Sepia OFF button to enable iBooks to apply Sepia tones to the book's pages. Tap the Font button on the menu bar or tap outside of the Font palette to close it.

It's Not All Good

When you tap the Fonts button, the list of font types replaces the other controls on the Font palette. Unfortunately, you can't return to the other controls without first closing the palette and reopening it. Not a big deal because it only requires a couple of quick taps, but this makes adjusting both font type and size more difficult than it needs to be.

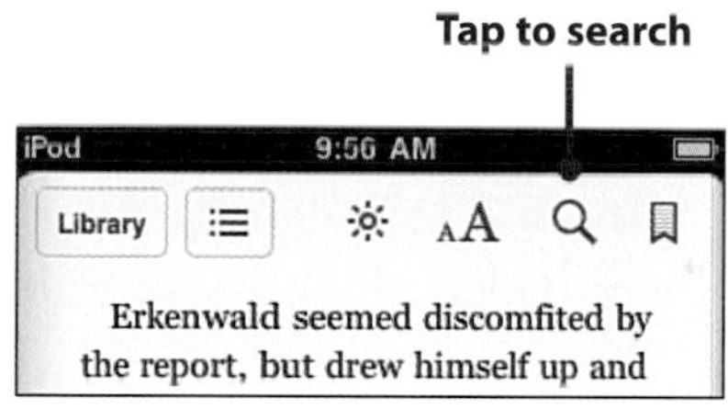

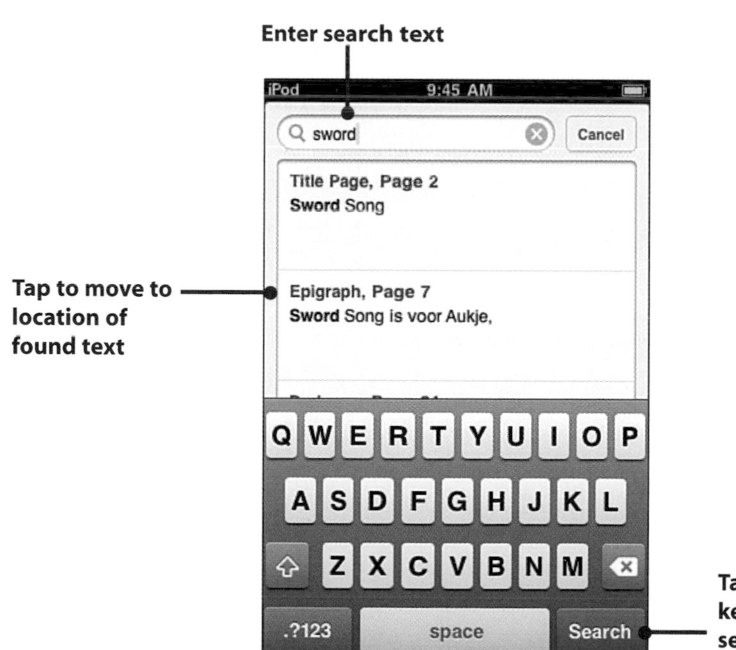

- **Search**: Tap the Search button to search for specific text in the book. Type the text for which you want to search. iBooks searches the book and presents matches to you; the more specific you make your search, the narrower the list of results will be. When you finish entering your search text, tap Search to close the keyboard to see the full list of results. Tap a result to move to it in the book; the search term is highlighted on the page. To return to the search results page, tap the Search button again. When the keyboard is hidden, you can tap the Search Google button to perform a web search or the Search Wikipedia to search the Wikipedia website.

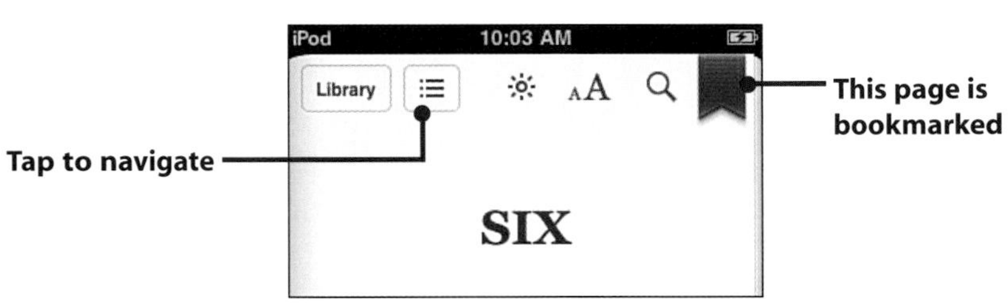

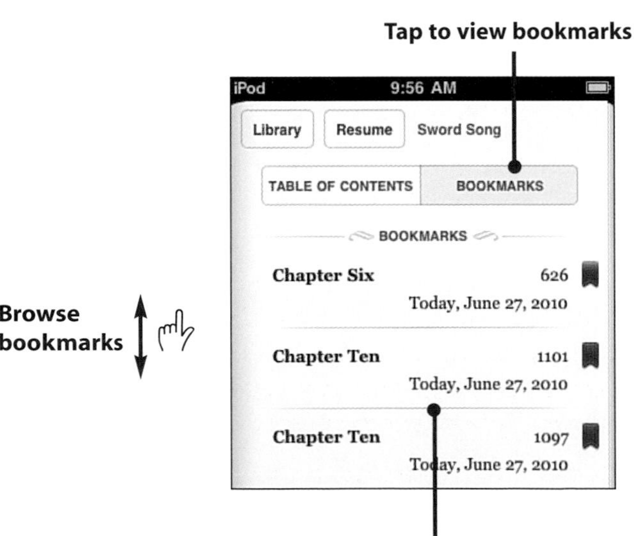

- **Navigate with bookmarks:** When you want to be able to return to a location in the book, tap the Bookmark button. The page is marked and a red bookmark appears on it. To return to a bookmark, tap the Table of Contents button and then tap the Bookmarks tab. You see a list of all the bookmarks in the book; the chapter, page number, and time when the bookmark was created are shown. Tap a bookmark to return to its location. To remove a bookmark, move to is location and tap it; the bookmark will be deleted.

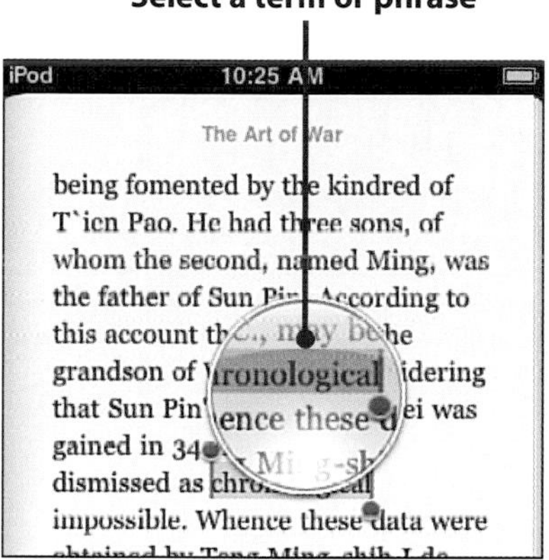

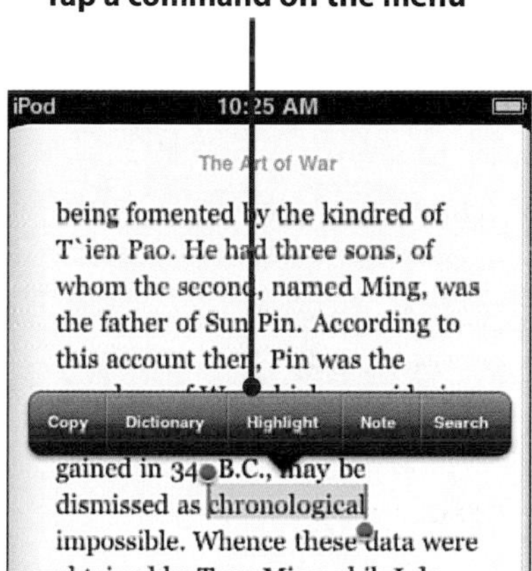

- **Use other great features:** Select some text on a page; when you are done, a menu with the following commands appears:
    - Tap Copy (shown only for non-protected works) to copy the selected text.
    - Tap Dictionary to look up the selected text in a dictionary.
    - Tap Highlight to highlight the selection; when you select a highlighted term, a menu appears that enables you to change the highlight color, add a note, or remove the highlight.
    - Tap Note to create a note attached to the selected text; after you've created a note and tapped Done; the text is highlighted and you see the note icon on the right side of the screen (tap this icon to read or edit the note). Tap text with a note associated with it and you can change the highlight color or remove the note.
    - Tap Search to perform a search for the selected text.

Watching Stocks

The iPod touch's Stocks application can help you monitor stocks or market indices in which you are interested. First, set up the stocks or indices you want to track. Second, track those stocks or indices.

Configuring the Stocks Application

You can add any stock or market index to the Stocks application; all you need to know is the stock's ticker symbol, which you can easily find on the web.

1. Move to the Home screen and tap Stocks.
2. Tap the Info button. The Stocks screen appears; on this screen, you configure the stocks you want to track and the information you want to see.

3. To remove a stock or index from the list, tap its Unlock button.
4. Tap Delete. The stock or index is removed from the application.
5. To change the order in which stocks or indices appear, drag them up or down the list by their list buttons.
6. To add a stock or index, tap the Add button.

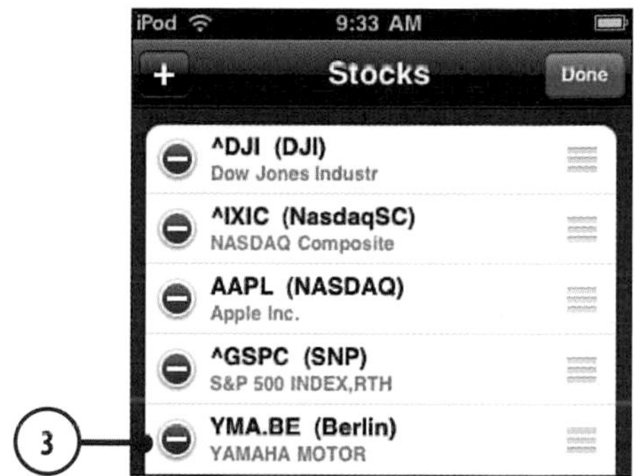

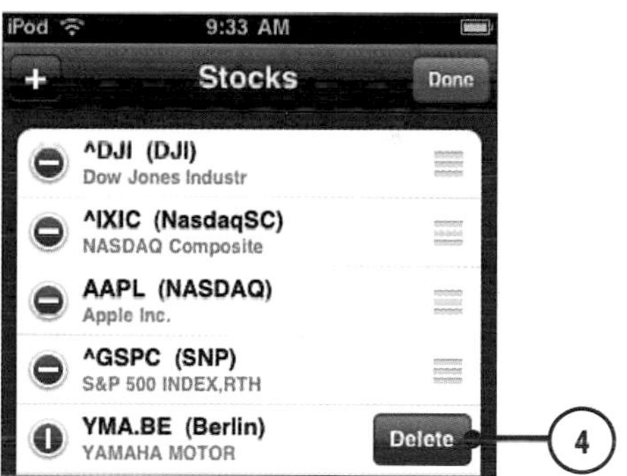

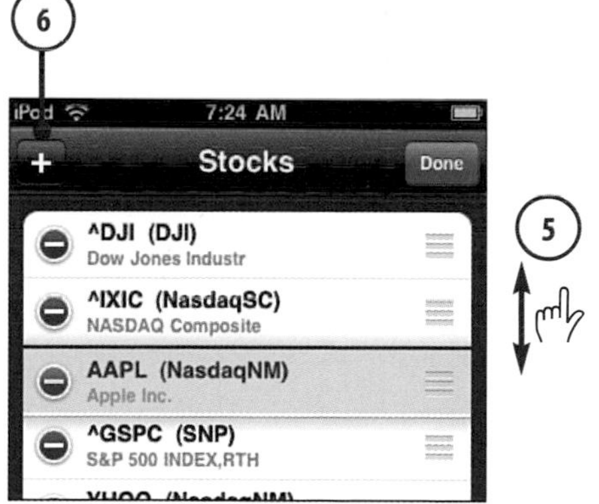

7. Enter the company name or stock's or index's symbol or as much as you know of any of this information. As you type, the application attempts to find items that match your search.
8. Scroll the list of results.

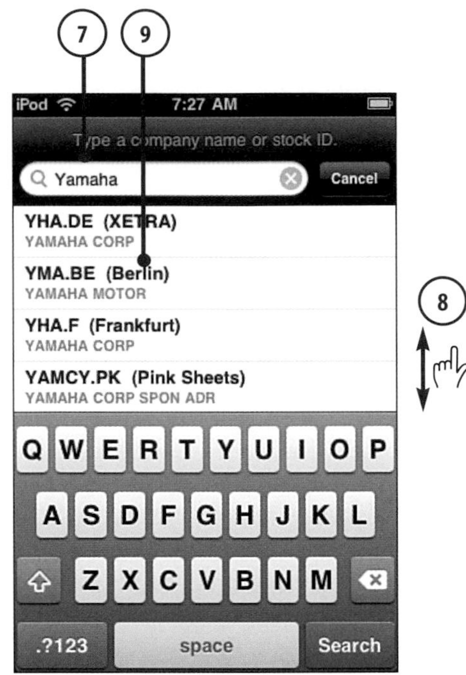

The Full List

To close the keyboard so that you see more results on the screen, tap Search.

9. Tap a stock or index you want to add to the application. You return to the Stocks screen, and the stock you tapped is added to the list.
10. Repeat steps 3 through 9 to remove or add stocks and organize the list until the Stocks screen shows the stocks and indices you want to track in the order in which you want them to appear.
11. Tap % if you want changes to stock values to display as a percentage; tap Price if you want changes to stock values to display as a dollar amount; or tap Mkt Cap if you want to see values by their market capitalization.
12. Tap Done. You return to the Stocks application and see the stocks and indices you have configured in the upper part of the screen.

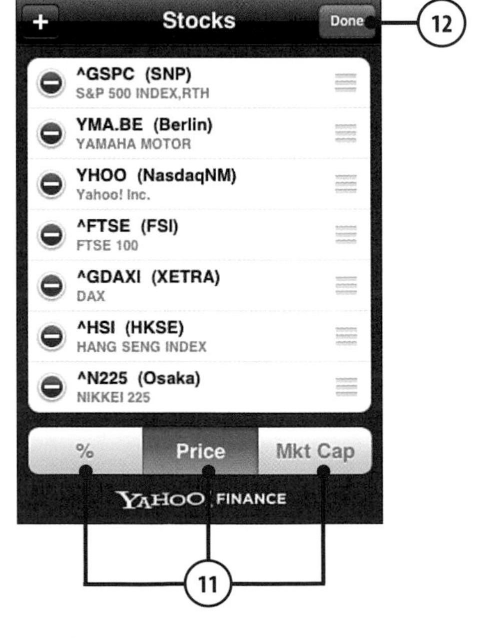

Tracking Stocks

With the Stocks application customized to your stock and index interests, you can quickly see how your favorites are performing.

1. Open the Stocks application.
2. Browse the screen to see the entire list of stocks and indices.
3. Tap the stock or index in which you are interested. The performance graph at the bottom of the screen is updated to show the performance of what you selected.
4. Tap the time frame in which you're interested, from 1 day to 2 years. The graph refreshes to cover the period you selected.
5. Tap the change indicators to move from percentage to price to market capitalization.
6. Drag across the graph to the right. You see details about the selected item.

7. Drag across the graph to the right again. You see news articles and videos.

8. Drag to browse the articles and videos.

9. To read an article or watch a video, tap it. You move to the web via Safari.

10. Read the article or watch the video.

Red Is Bad, Green Is Good

Values shown in red are bad, meaning they've decreased, whereas values in green are good, meaning they've increased.

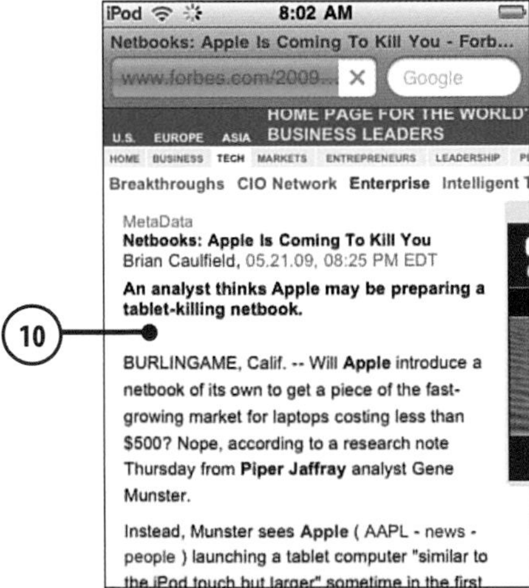

11. Press the Home button twice and then tap the Stocks button on the App toolbar to return to the Stocks application.
12. Tap the Yahoo! button. Safari opens and moves to a Yahoo! page for the selected item.
13. Use the web page to read about the item.
14. Press the Home button twice and then tap the Stocks butto on the App toolbar to return to the Stocks application.

Going Further with Stocks

If you rotate the iPod 90 degrees, you see a large graph showing the performance of each index and stock you are tracking. Drag quickly across the screen to the left or right to move to the previous or next stock or index. Tap and hold your finger down while you drag across a graph to see the exact value on a specific date.

Finding Your Way with Maps

The Maps application just might be one of the most useful iPod touch applications, especially if you are directionally challenged like I am. Using the Maps application, you can find the location of addresses using Google Maps. You can also get directions from one address to another, and maps are linked to your contacts, so you can quickly show the location of any address in your contacts on a map and then get directions.

A number of ways exist to find locations on the map, such as by searching or by using a contact's address. After you find a location, you can use that location for different purposes, such as to create directions.

Tap Maps to find your way.

To open the Maps application, tap the Maps button on the Home screen. The application appears, and you can start finding your way.

Where Am I?

The arrow button in the lower-left corner of the Maps screen is to show your current location. Tap the button and allow Maps to use Location Services to find your location. When the app can find you, it places a blue dot on your current location. Tap the button again to center your location on the map. You must be connected to the Internet for this to work, and whether Location Services can find your location depends on how you are connected. Unlike the iPhone, which can use GPS or cellular data to locate you, the iPod's location service is somewhat limited because it usually isn't possible to stay connected to a Wi-Fi network as you travel around.

Finding a Location by Searching

You can search for locations in many ways. Your search can be specific, such as an address, or your search can be more general, such as a search for gas stations or restaurants.

1. Tap Search.
2. Tap in the Search bar.

Easy Searching

As you enter a search, an iPod touch attempts to match what you type with recent searches. As it finds matches, it presents the list of matches to you. Tap a search on the list to perform it. The Maps app also remembers the context of your last search, so if you want to change the general area of the search item, you should include a state or ZIP code in the search term. For example, if you search for an address in one state and then perform a general search (such as for libraries), Maps searches in the area of the address for which you previously searched. To change that context, enter the state or ZIP code where you want to search (such as libraries Indiana to find libraries in Indiana).

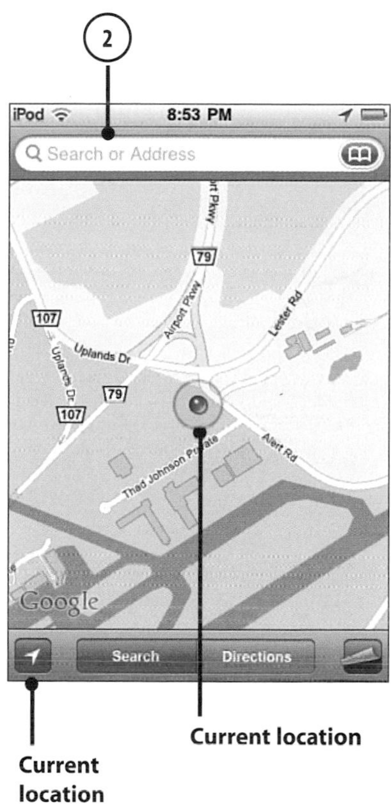

3. Type your search. You can enter an address, city, category, or just about anything else. The more specific your search term, the more likely it is that you can find the location. But general searches can be helpful, such as a search for gas stations.

4. If you see a location on the list you want to see, tap it, otherwise, tap Search. The map appears, and the locations that meet your search criteria are marked with push pins; the location that an iPod touch thinks is most likely to be the one you are looking for has the Info bar above it.

Clear a Search

To clear a search, tap the Clear button, which is the gray circle containing an "x," located at the right end of the Search bar.

5. To see information about a location, tap the arrow in its Info bar.

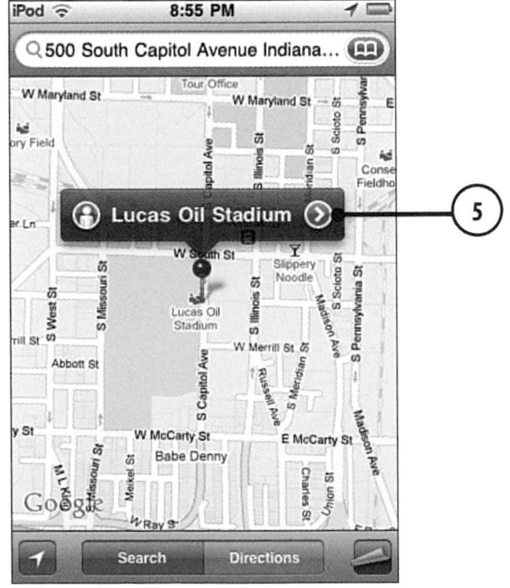

Using Bookmarks, Recents, or Contacts to Find a Location

Bookmarks enable you to save locations and return to them easily. (See the "Working with Maps" task later in this chapter to learn how to set bookmarks.) Recents is a list of locations that you've worked with recently. You can also use a contact's address from your Contacts list to move to a specific location on the map.

1. Open the Search screen and tap the Lists button in the Search bar.
2. Tap Bookmarks, Recents, or Contacts. The screen related to what you tapped appears. The rest of these steps show the Recents screen. When you tap Bookmarks, you see a list of your bookmarks; tap one to show it on the map. When you tap Contacts, use the All Contacts screen to find and select the address you want to show.
3. Browse up or down the list to see all the recent locations available to you. Locations are identified by type, such as contacts, search, and so on.
4. Tap the location you want to see on the map. You move back to the map, and the recent location is shown.
5. Use the information in the next task to find out more information about the location and to change the map's view.

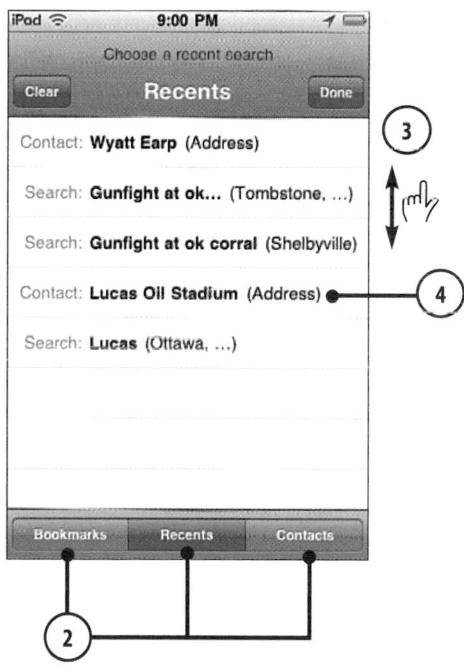

Working with Maps

After you find locations on a map, you can work with them for a variety of purposes.

1. Using the techniques (such as searching for a location) explained in the previous sections, find locations in which you are interested.
2. To zoom in on a location, double-tap the map near the location or unpinch the map.
3. To scroll the map, drag your finger up or down and left or right.
4. Zoom out by pinching your fingers together on the screen.
5. Tap a location's pushpin. You see the name of the location.
6. Tap the More Info arrow. The Info screen appears.

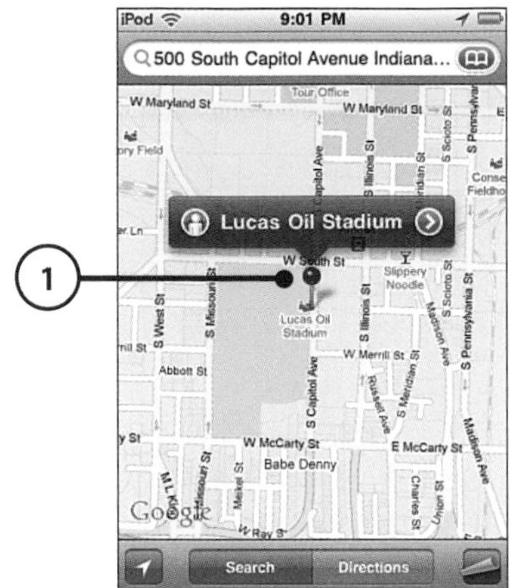

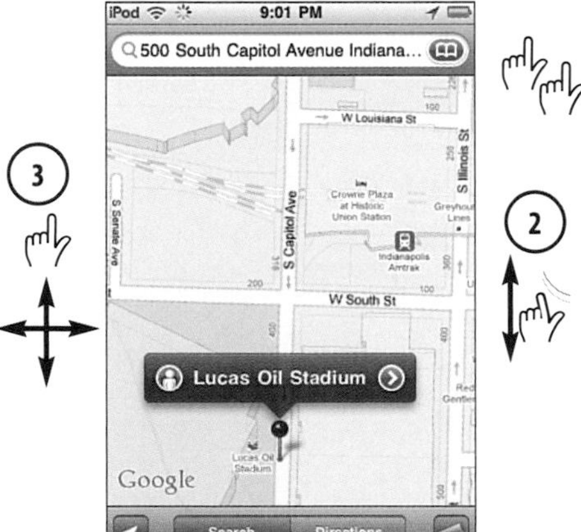

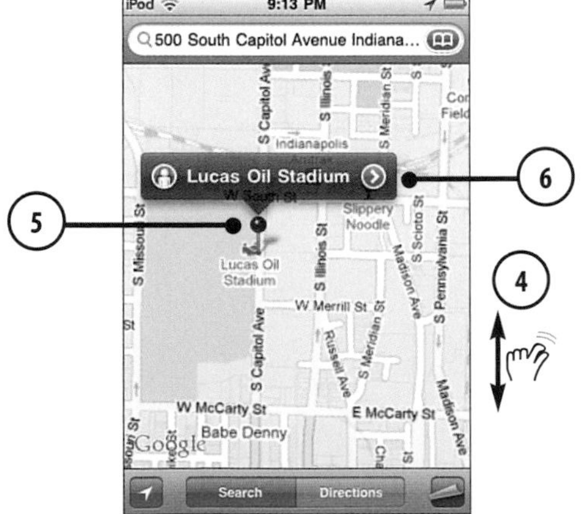

7. If the location has a URL, tap it to move to the location's webpage.
8. Scroll down the screen.
9. To set a bookmark for the location, tap Add to Bookmarks.
10. Use the keyboard to make changes to the bookmark's name.
11. Tap Save. The location is added to your bookmarks, and you return to the Info screen.

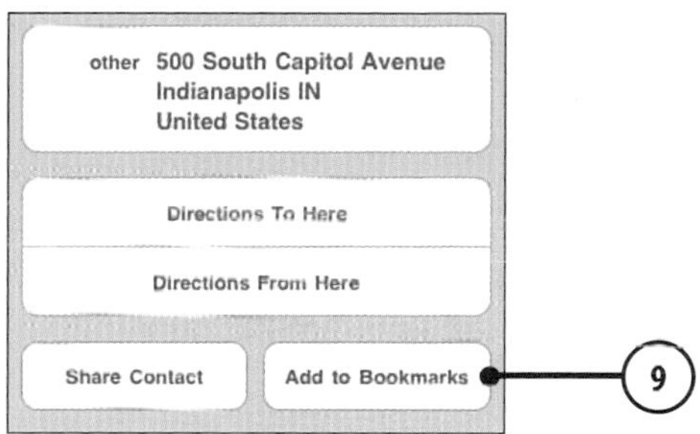

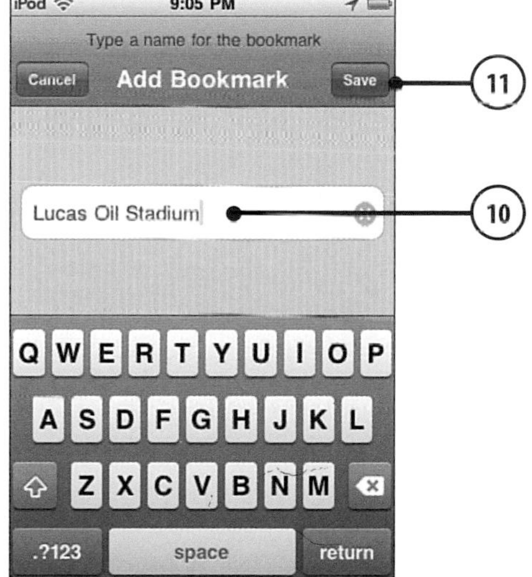

12. To add the address on the map to an existing contact or to create a new contact with the address, tap Add to Contacts. Use the resulting tools to configure contact information (see Chapter 8, "Managing Contacts").

13 To send a link to the location to someone else, tap Share Location and complete and send an email.

Buttons Come and Go

The buttons you see on a location's Info screen depend on the status of that location. For example, if you've already added the location as a bookmark, the Add to Bookmarks button doesn't appear.

Getting Directions

The Maps application can generate driving directions between two locations along with an estimate of how long the trip will take.

1. Tap the Directions button. The Start and End boxes appear.

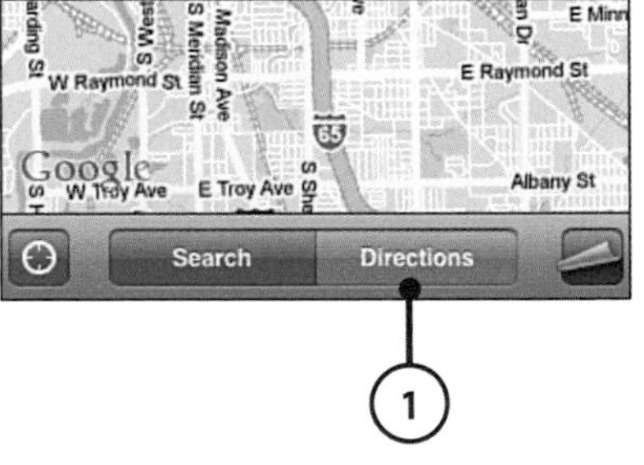

2. Find the start location by searching for it or by using the Lists button to select it from a list. For example, you can use a bookmark, recent item, or contact information to set a location along with searching for a location.

3. Find the end location by searching for it or by using the Lists button to select it from a list.

4. Tap Route. A path from the start location to the end location is generated and appears on the map in a purple line. The start point is shown as a green pushpin, whereas the end point is a red pushpin. The default route is for driving a car.

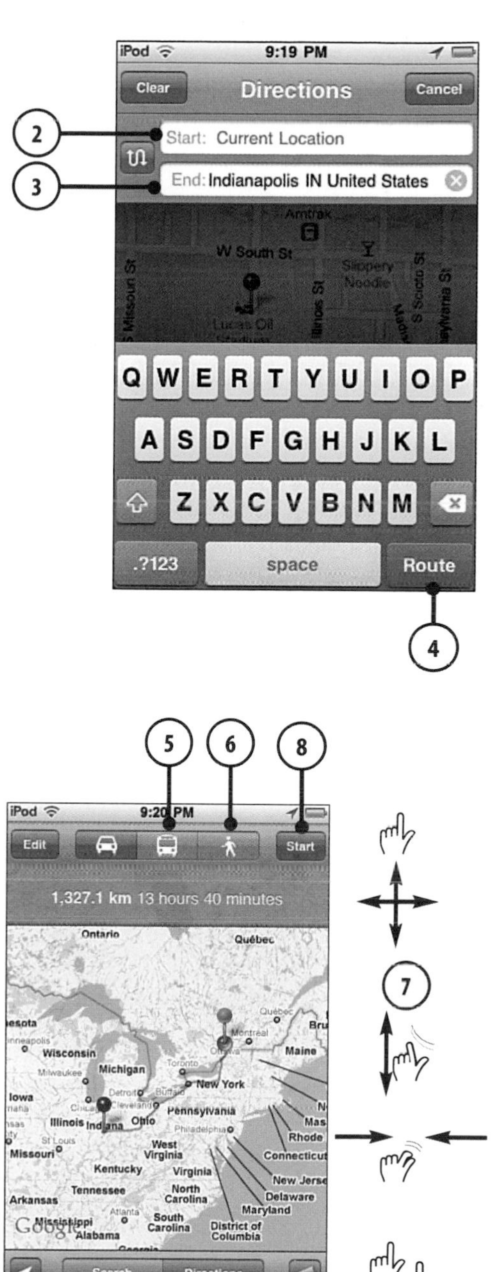

Can't Tell if You're Coming or Going?

You can start the direction process from a location's Info screen by tapping the Directions to Here or Directions from Here button to set that location as the starting point or endpoint.

5. Tap the Transit button to see a route using public transportation.

6. Tap the Walking button to see walking directions.

7. Zoom or scroll the map as needed to view the entire route.

8. When you're ready to start moving along the route, tap Start. You see the first leg of the route. Instructions and information about the leg appear at the top of the screen.

Going Back Again

To quickly reverse the current route, tap Edit. Then tap the Reverse button, which is located to the left of the Start and End fields.

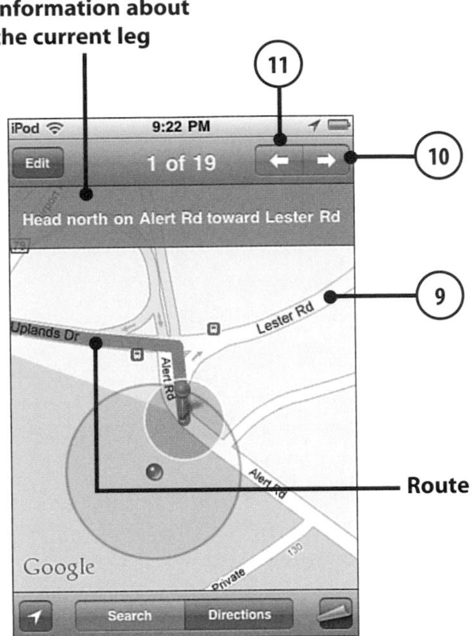

9. Follow your location along the first leg of the route. As you approach the next segment of the route, you see a circle on the route.
10. After you've made the change to get onto the next segment of the route, tap the Forward button to move to the next segment on the map.
11. To move to a previous segment, tap the Back button.

>>> Go Further

MORE ON MAPS

Maps does more than I have room in this chapter to show. When you view a map, tap the Options button, which is the sheet with a folded corner located in the lower-right corner of the screen. On the resulting menu, you see various tools. You can use the Drop Pin command to place your own pushpins on the map (very useful for creating directions when you don't know the exact address of where you want to go). You can use the Show Traffic to see traffic conditions. You can show a satellite view by tapping Satellite or show the map and a satellite view by tapping Hybrid. Tapping List shows you a route in list form; click a segment to see it on the map.

Watching the Weather

The Weather app is a handy way to get information about weather in specific locations quickly and easily.

Choosing Weather Locations

Configure the Weather application with the areas you are interested in.

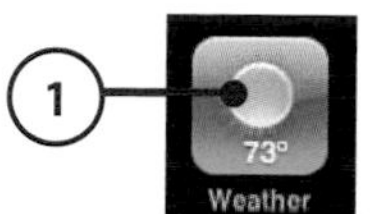

1. Move to the Home screen and tap Weather.
2. Tap the Info button. The Weather screen appears. On this list, you see all the locations that the application currently shows.
3. To add a location, tap the Add button.

4. Enter a city's name or ZIP code using the keyboard. Cities that match your search are shown.
5. To add a city to the application, tap it. You move back to the Weather screen, and the city you added is listed.
6. To delete a city, tap the Unlock button. The Delete button appears.
7. Tap Delete.
8. Perform steps 3 through 8 until the list contains all the cities about which you want weather information.
9. Drag cities up or down the list by their List buttons to change the order in which their screens appear.
10. To have temperatures displayed in degrees Fahrenheit , tap °F.
11. To have temperatures displayed in degrees Celsius, tap °C.
12. Tap Done.

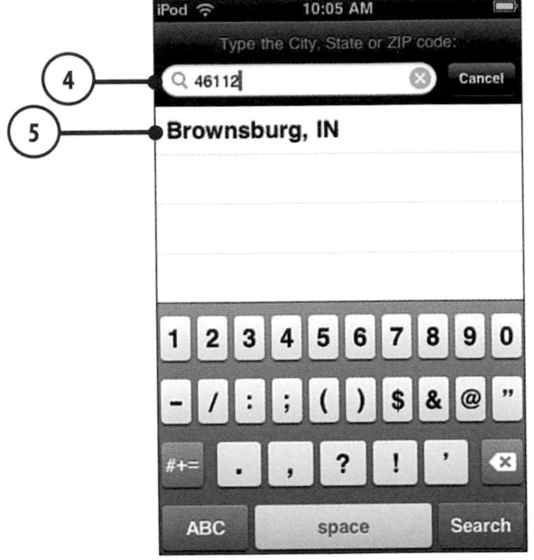

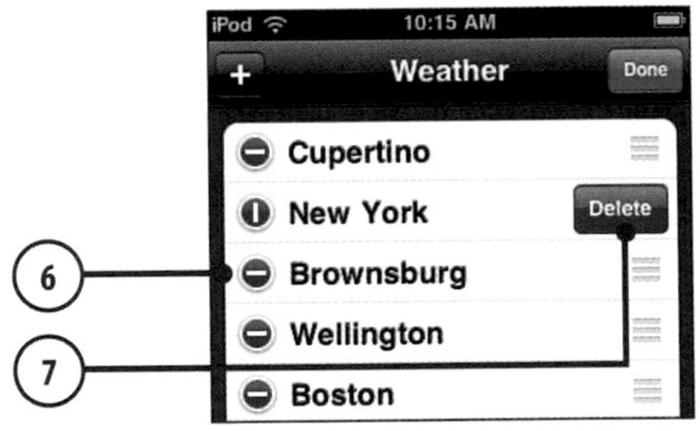

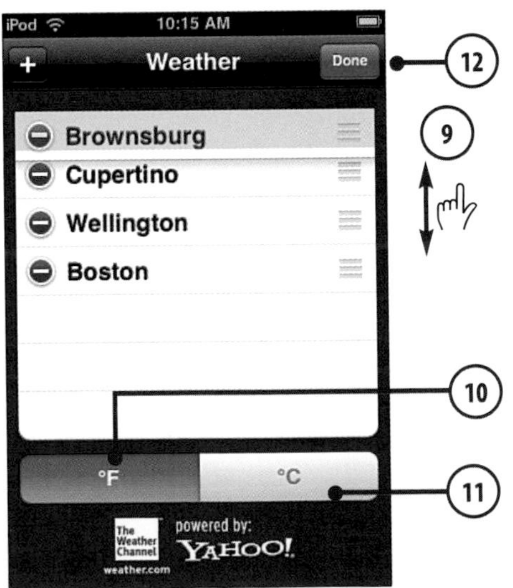

Viewing Weather Information

With the Weather app, getting weather information is simple.

1. Move to the Home screen and tap Weather. You see weather for the last city you viewed.
2. To see weather for the next location, drag to the left or right.
3. To jump to a specific location, tap its button. You have to know where the location is on the list; for example, if a city is third on the list, tap the third button.

   To move to a website about a location, view its weather and tap the Yahoo! button. The web browser opens, and you move to the Yahoo! page for that city that provides more detailed weather information, event information, and so on.

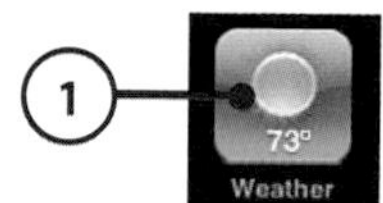

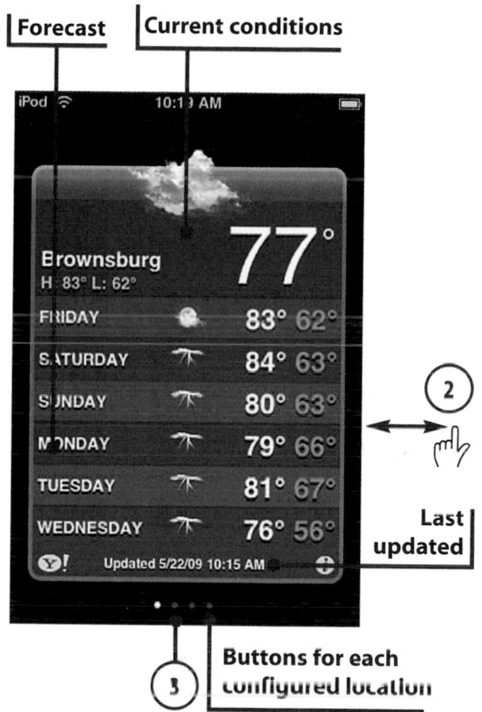

>>> Go Further

OTHER USEFUL DEFAULT APPS

Voice Memos enables you to record sounds through a microphone connected through the headphone port or dock connector. You can play back memos you record and send them to others via email. The Notes app enables you to create and save text notes. You can view or email them; although it won't replace a word processor, it can be a useful way to capture snippets of text. The Calculator enables your iPod touch to do everything that a $0.99 calculator does; it's simple and handy. If you rotate the iPod touch so that it is in landscape mode, it becomes a more sophisticated scientific calculator. The YouTube application enables you to watch YouTube videos.

voice memos in utilities
CALCULATOR " "

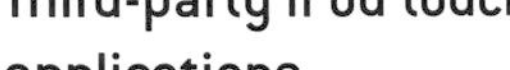

Third-party iPod touch applications

In this chapter, you explore how to install, maintain, and manage third-party applications on your iPod touch. The topics include the following:

- Using iTunes to find and install iPod touch applications
- Using the App Store application to find and install iPod touch applications
- Using iPod touch applications you install
- Maintaining iPod touch applications
- Removing applications from iPod touch

13

Installing and Maintaining iPod touch Applications

Your iPod touch is quite a powerful device and supports a full suite of programming tools. That's a good thing because this capability has unleashed the creativity of developers around the world, and thousands of applications are available to you. Apple's marketing campaign for the iPhone (which almost equally applies to the iPod touch) implies that if you want to do something, you can find an app for it. That is quite a claim, but it also happens to be pretty accurate.

With all these applications available to you, there's a potential for complexity in finding and installing applications that interest you. Fortunately, with iTunes and the App Store application, you can quickly find and install applications. The tools you need to maintain your applications are also built-in, so you don't have to spend much time or effort making sure you use the latest versions of your favorite apps. And using applications you install is similar to using the default applications you learned about in the previous chapter. Managing the applications on your iPod touch isn't hard either, but you need to know a few things.

Using iTunes to Find and Install iPod touch Applications

The iTunes Store has many applications that you can download and install on your iPod touch. Many of these are free, whereas others have a license fee (which you pay through your iTunes Store account). Downloading applications from the iTunes Store is similar to downloading audio and video content. (That topic is covered in detail in Chapter 3, "Moving Audio, Video, Books, and Photos onto Your iPod touch.")

Like moving other kinds of content onto iPod touch from the iTunes Store, this process has two steps. The first is to download applications to your iTunes Library. The second is to move those applications onto iPod touch by syncing it with iTunes.

Downloading Applications from the iTunes Store

You can use the iTunes Store to browse for and download applications.

1. Open iTunes and select iTunes Store on the Source list.
2. Click App Store. You move to the App Store Home page.
3. Click the iPhone button. (The iPod touch uses the same application set as the iPhone.) You can click the various links you see to find applications, or you can search for applications. The rest of these steps demonstrate searching for an application.
4. Enter the term for which you want to search, such as the application name, in the Search tool and press Enter (Windows) or Return (Mac). The apps that meet your search criterion are shown.

See All, Know All

Apps on the various screens in the store are organized in many ways, such as New and Noteworthy, Staff favorites, and so on. All these groupings have the See All link that you can click to view all the apps in that grouping.

5. Browse the results; when you find an application in which you are interested, click its icon. You move to the application's description screen, where you can read about the application (including user reviews) and look at screenshots.

Just Download It

You don't have to view an application's details to download it. Just click the button next to the application's icon while you browse to start the download process. This button is labeled FREE for no-fee applications, or it contains the license cost of the application and BUY.

6. Check the requirements to make sure the application is compatible with your iPod touch. Some applications support only iPhones, and you need to make sure you use a supported version of the iPhone OS. (See Chapter 15, "Maintaining an iPod touch and Solving Problems," to learn how to update your iPod touch's software.)
7. Review the description, view screenshots, and read the user reviews on the application's page.
8. When you're ready to download the application, click the Free App button if it is a free application or the Buy App button, which also shows the cost if it has a license fee.

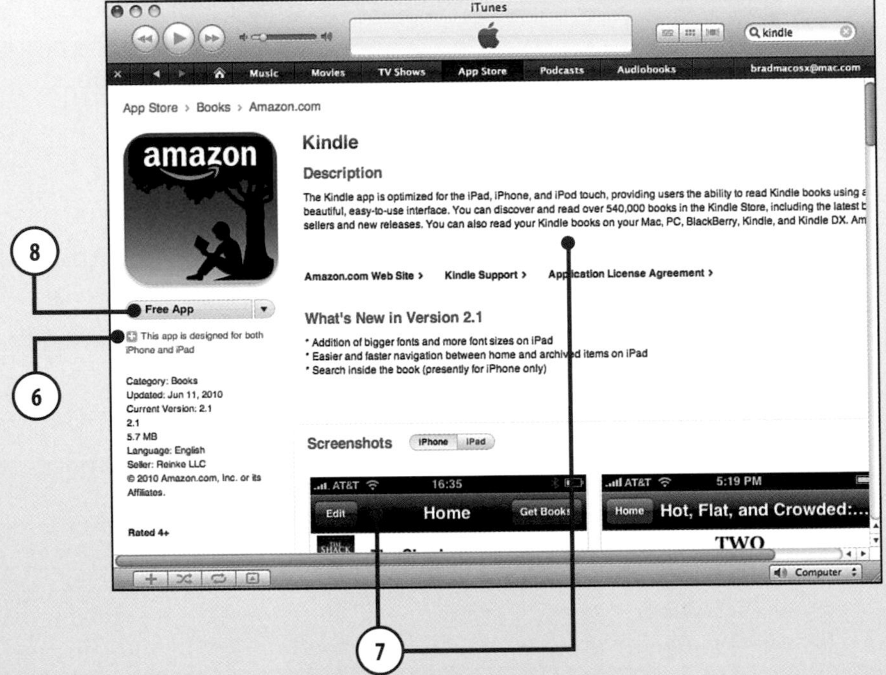

9. If you aren't signed into your iTunes Store account, do so at the prompt by entering your Apple ID and password (or AOL screen name and password) and then clicking Buy or Get (depending on if the app is free or not). The application is downloaded to your iTunes Library. (You can view the applications you have downloaded by clicking Applications on the Source list.)

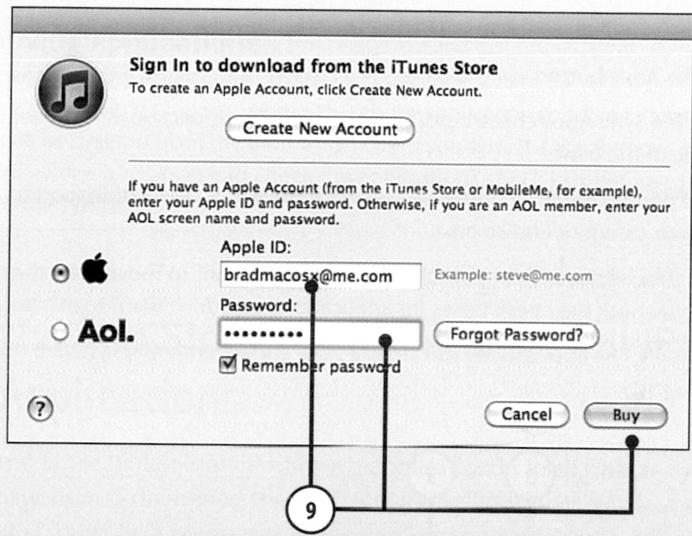
Sign In to download from the iTunes Store
To create an Apple Account, click Create New Account.
Create New Account
If you have an Apple Account (from the iTunes Store or MobileMe, for example), enter your Apple ID and password. Otherwise, if you are an AOL member, enter your AOL screen name and password.
Apple ID:
bradmacosx@me.com
Example: steve@me.com
Password:
Aol.
Forgot Password?
Remember password
Cancel
Buy
9

Searching for Apps in All the Right Places

You can also search for iPod touch applications using the Power Search tool. Click the Power Search link located in the Quick Links section in the top-right side of the iTunes Store Home page. Choose Apps on the Power Search drop-down list and then enter a title or description, developer name, or category. On the Device Compatibility drop-down list, choose iPod touch. If you want to limit the results to include only free applications, check the Search only for free applications check box. Click Search. Any applications that meet your criteria are shown. You can also click the Power Search link on the screen showing the results of a search to perform another search.

These steps show you how to find applications by category; the other options are similar:

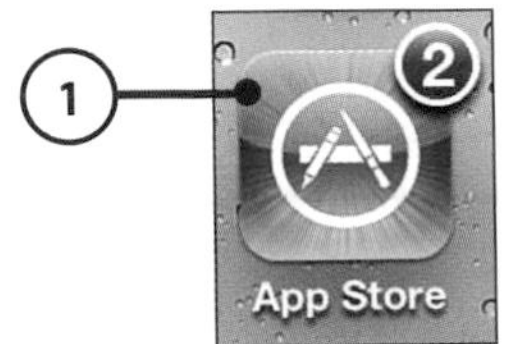

1. Move to the Home screen and tap App Store. At the bottom of the App Store screen, you see the buttons you can use to choose a method to find applications.
2. Tap Categories.
3. Browse the list until you see a category of interest.
4. Tap a category in which you are interested.
5. If the application has subcategories, browse the subcategories; if you move directly to applications, skip to step 9.
6. Tap a subcategory in which you are interested.

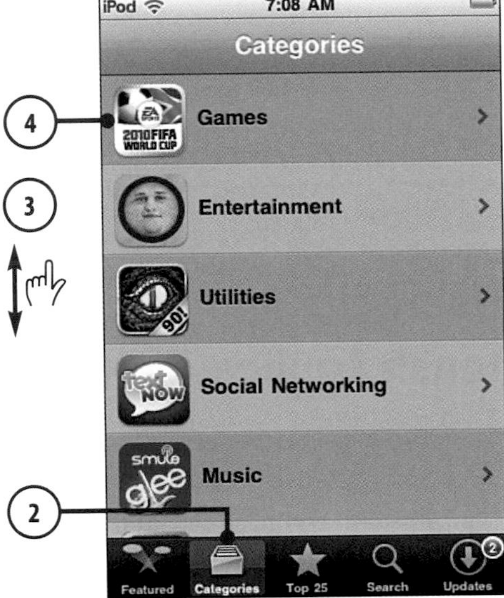

7. Tap the Top Paid button to see the most frequently downloaded applications that require a license fee; tap Top Free to see the most popular free applications; or tap Release Date to see the applications most recently added to the store.
8. Browse the applications. For each application, you see its icon, developer, name, user ranking, number of user reviews, and its cost (a price or Free).
9. Tap an application in which you are interested. You move to the application's Info screen.

Wait, There's More

Only a certain number of items are downloaded to the screens you browse; when you reach the bottom of the current list, you see the *number* More text, where *number* is the number of items you can add to the list. Tap that text to add those items to the list you are browsing. You can continue this process until you've seen all there is to see.

10. Read the application's description.
11. To read reviews and see screenshots, scroll down the screen.

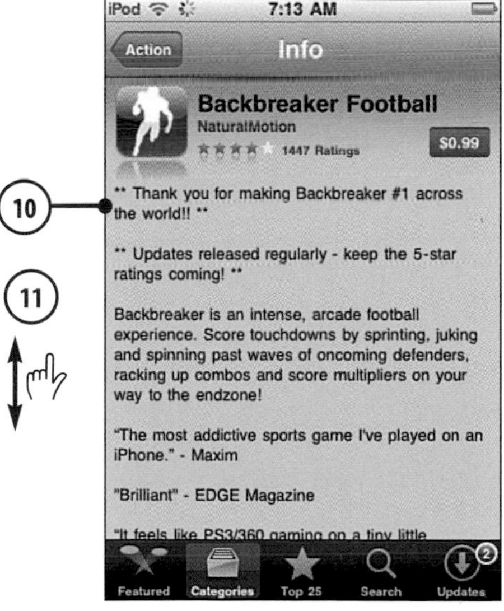

12. Browse screenshots by dragging. If the app is landscape-oriented, rotate the iPod so the screenshots make sense. (Note that the screen you view doesn't reorient like most screens do, but at least the screenshots themselves look better.)

13. Scroll down. (If you've rotated the iPod, you'll want to move it back to the Portrait orientation.)

Feeling Generous?

To give the application to someone else, tap Gift This App and follow the onscreen instructions to send the application to another iPod touch or iPhone user.

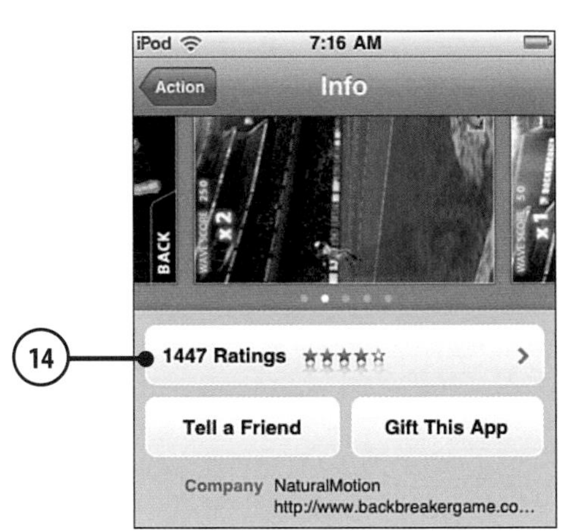

14. Tap the Ratings link, which is labeled with the average user rating and the number of ratings received. You move to the application's Reviews screen where you see user reviews for the application.
15. Scroll the screen to read reviews.
16. Tap Info.

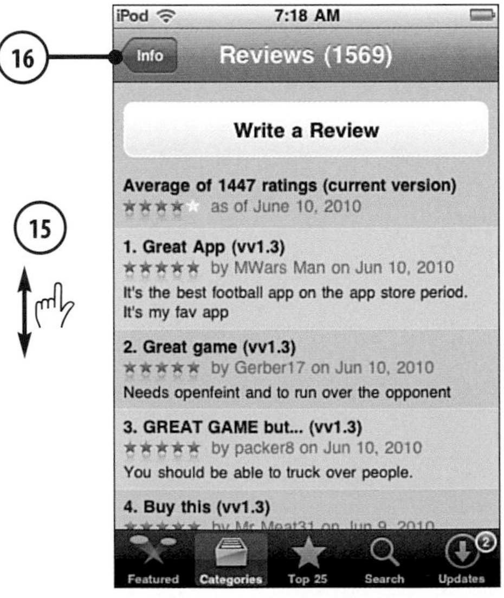

Make Your Voice Known

After you have used an application, you can add your own review by moving back to its Reviews screen and tapping Write a Review. You move to the Submit Review screen where you have to enter your iTunes Store account information before you can write and submit a review.

17. Scroll to the top of the screen.

18. To download the application, tap FREE if it is a free application, or tap the price to download the application if it has a license fee. The button becomes INSTALL if it is a free application or BUY NOW if it has a license fee.

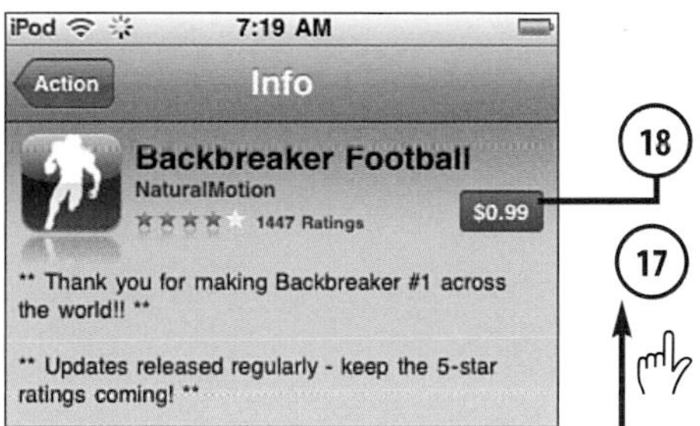

Gotta Share?

If you decide an application is one someone you know should know about, move to the application's Info screen and tap Tell a Friend. An email message is created with a link to the application. Complete and send the email.

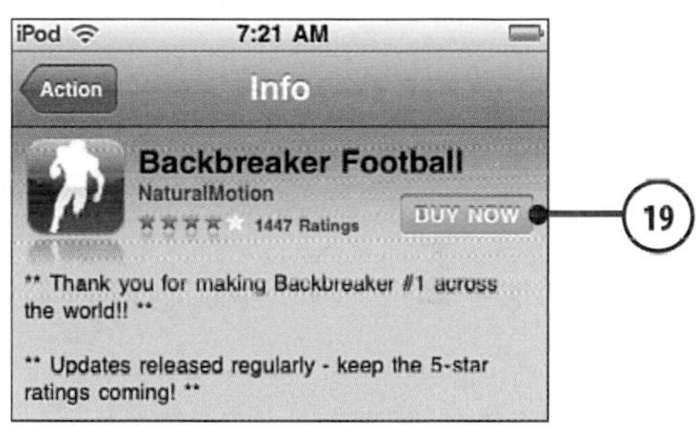

19. Tap INSTALL or BUY NOW.

20. If prompted to do so, enter your iTunes Store password and tap OK.

    The application is downloaded to the iPod touch. You move to the Home screen where you see the application's icon with the word "Loading" under it.

    After the application is downloaded, it installs, and you see the progress bar and "Installing" under the application's icon.

    When the installation is complete, you see the application's icon, and it is ready for you to use. (The next time you sync your iPod touch, the application is also added to your iTunes Library.)

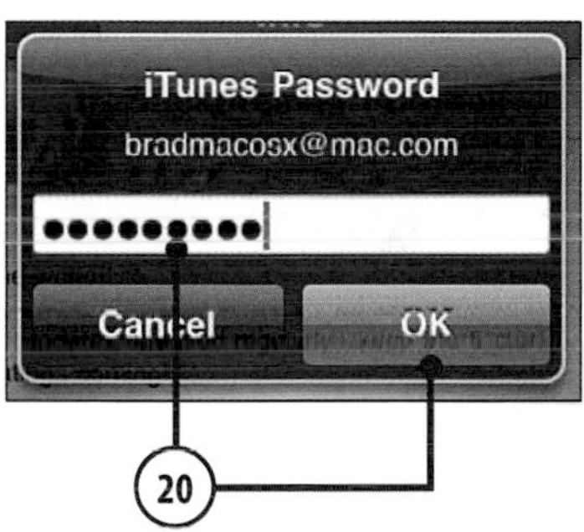

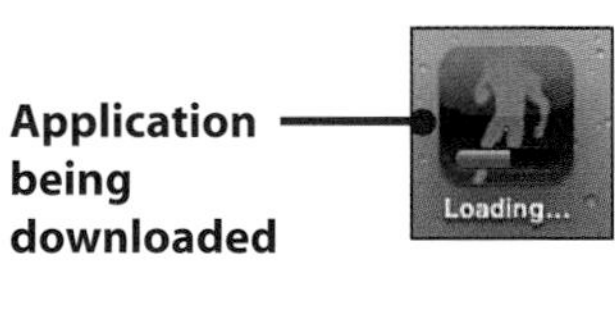

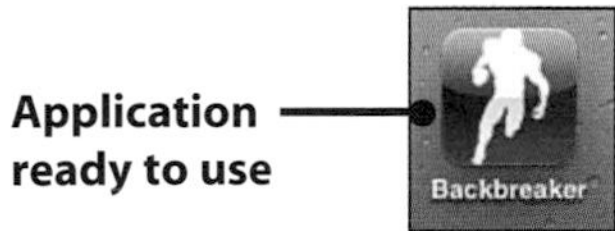

Keep the Home Screen Organized

As you add application icons to the Home screen, you can place icons on the various pages of the Home screens and use folders to organize your screens to make them as efficient for you as possible. To learn how, see Chapter 14, "Customizing an iPod touch."

Syncing Apps

The next time you sync your iPod, the apps you've added using the App Store app will be copied into your iTunes Library. From there you can install them on other devices, such as an iPhone or iPad. This also gives you a good way to back up your apps should something happen to your iPod. Though, unlike audio and video content you purchase from the iTunes Store, you can download apps you purchase multiple times; you only have to pay for apps the first time you download the current version. (Most updates are free, but some have a cost associated with them.) Still, if you keep all your apps and other downloads in your iTunes Library backed up, it is much easier to recover from a major issue if you have everything included in your backup.

Using iPod touch Applications You Install

Running application

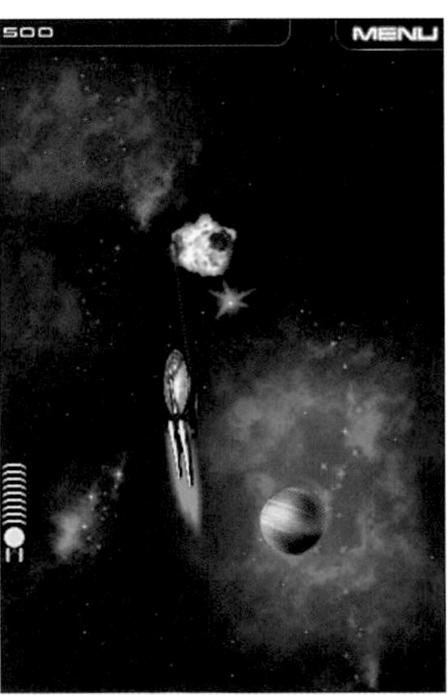

After you install applications, you use them just like iPod touch's default applications. Tap the application's icon on the Home screen, and it opens. At that point, how you use the application depends on the specific one you use.

Tap to configure an installed application's settings

Some applications enable you to configure preferences using the Settings app. To see which of your applications provide settings, open the Settings screen and scroll to the bottom. If you see an application, tap its name to access its settings.

Maintaining iPod touch Applications

Like applications you use on a computer, iPod touch applications are regularly updated. When updates are available for applications installed on your iPod, you see a counter on the App Store icon that indicates updates for some or all your installed applications are available.

To update your applications, perform the following steps.

1. Move to the Home screen and tap App Store.
2. Tap Updates. The number of applications for which updates are available is shown in the red circle on the Updates button. On the Updates screen, you see all the installed applications for which an update is available. For each application, you see its developer, name, the version number of the update, and the release date.
3. Scroll the screen to see all the updates available.

All at Once

To download and install all available updates, tap Update All in the upper-right corner of the Updates screen.

4. Tap the application that you want to update.
5. Read about the update.
6. If the update is free (most are), tap FREE; if it isn't, tap the button showing the cost of the update. The button becomes the INSTALL button for a free update or BUY NOW for an update that has a fee.

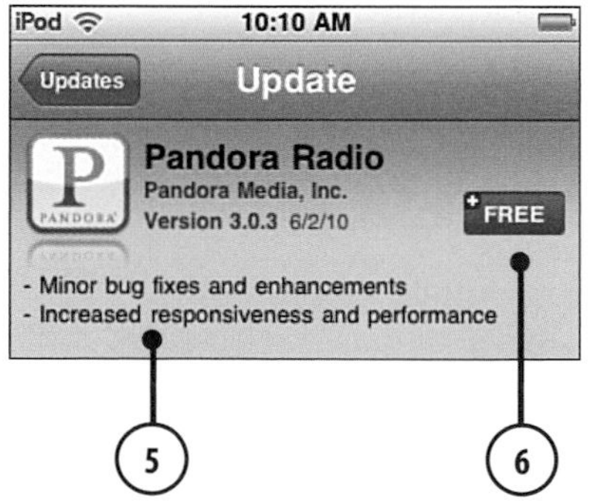

7. Tap INSTALL or BUY NOW.
8. If prompted to do so, enter your iTunes Store password and tap OK.

   The update begins to download to iPod touch. You move back to the Home screen, where you see the updated application's icon with the word "Loading" under it.

   When the download process is complete, you see the progress of the installation process under the icon.

   When installation is complete, the status information disappears. The next time you run the application, you use the updated version.

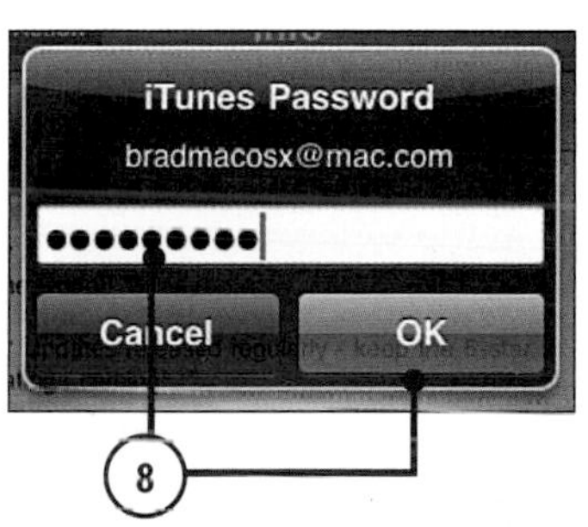

Using iTunes to Check for Updates

You can also update applications via iTunes. Next to the Apps source, you see the number of applications in the Library for which updates are available. Click the Apps source on the Source list, and click the *X* Updates Available link (where *X* is the number of updates available) at the bottom of the iTunes window. Click the Download All Free Updates button in the upper-right corner of the iTunes window to click an application's GET UPDATE button to update just that application. The updates are downloaded into your iTunes Library. The next time you sync your iPod touch, the updates are moved from your iTunes Library onto the iPod touch.

Update is downloading

Update is installing

Updated application

Removing Applications from an iPod touch

Not all that glitters is gold, and not all iPod touch applications are worth keeping. You can get rid of iPod touch applications you don't use.

If you delete an application that you installed from the iTunes Library or if you synced the iPod touch since you installed the application (at which time, that application was moved from iPod touch to your iTunes Library), it will be added to iPod touch again the next time you sync if that application is still included in the sync settings.

To permanently remove an application from an iPod touch, you can remove it from the sync settings or delete the application from the Applications source in iTunes if you're sure you won't want to reinstall it at some point.

To permanently remove an application from both locations, remove it from the Apps source on the iTunes Source list and also remove it from the iPod touch. Before you do that though, you need to carefully consider if you really want to permanently remove the application, depending which of two situations you are in.

One situation is if you've purchased the application, in which case, you should keep a copy in your iTunes Library but remove it from the sync settings and then delete it from the iPod touch; this will allow you to reinstall the application at some point in the future without paying for it again.

The other situation is if the application manages data for you that isn't available elsewhere; when you delete an application from your iPod touch, all the data it manages goes away, too. Make sure you have that data backed up or available elsewhere before you delete an application.

Except for these caveats, the steps to delete an application from iPod touch are simple.

1. Move to the page of the Home screen showing the icon for the application you want to delete.
2. Tap and hold the icon of the application you want to delete until the icons on the screen start shaking and the Delete buttons appear.

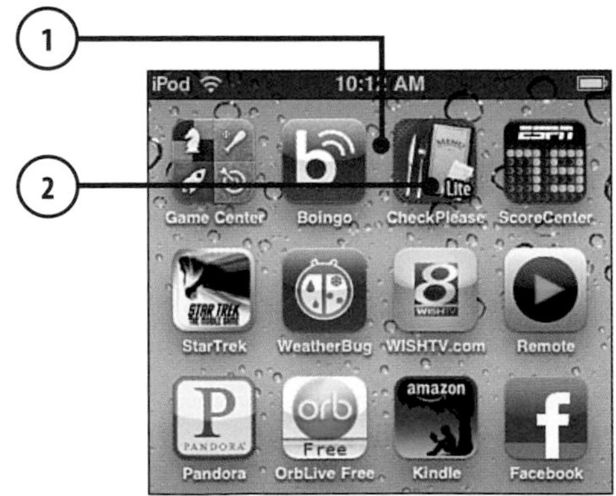

3. Tap the Delete button for the application you want to delete.
4. Tap Delete at the prompt. The application and all its data are deleted from the iPod.

Set custom wallpaper
Customize the icons that appear on your Home screens
Use folders to organize your apps
Use Settings to customize how your iPod touch looks and works
iPod
6:11 AM
Saturday
18
FaceTime
Calendar
Photos
Camera
280
YouTube
Maps
iBooks
Utilities
iTunes
App Store
Entertainment
Settings
Apple - iPod
Remote
Clock
Contacts
Music
Mail
Safari
Videos

In this chapter, you explore ways you can make your iPod touch more your own. The topics include the following:

14

- → Customizing your Home screens
- → Accessing iPod touch settings
- → Configuring general sound settings
- → Setting screen brightness
- → Setting wallpaper
- → Configuring other general settings

Customizing an iPod touch

If you've read previous chapters on various iPod touch functions, such as listening to music or emailing, you've customized your iPod by using its Settings tools. Many of those settings relate directly to functionality discussed in other chapters, which is why they are covered there. However, a number of an iPod touch's settings are more general in nature, which is where this chapter comes into play.

Some examples include sound settings, screen brightness, and so on. Although you might not use these functions every day, they do enable you to make your iPod work more the way you want it to.

One of the most useful customizations is to configure your iPod touch's Home screens so they are the most convenient for you (which doesn't actually involve using the Settings application, but this chapter seemed like the best place to tell you about it).

Customizing Your Home Screens

The iPod touch's Home screens are the starting point for anything you do because these screens contain the icons that you tap to access the functions you want to use. The Home screens come configured with default icons in default locations. You can change the location of these icons to be more convenient for you, and as you add applications and create your own web page icons, it becomes even more important that you organize your Home screens so that you can quickly get to the items you use most frequently. You can move icons around the same screen, you can move icons between the pages of the Home screen, and you can organize icons within folders. You can perform these actions using the iPod or you can use iTunes.

Using the iPod to Customize Your Home Screens

You can organize your Home screens using the iPod's tools. This is convenient because you don't need a computer, and it's easy to set up your screens anyway you want.

1. Press the Home button to move to a Home screen.
2. Drag across the Home screen until the page containing an icon you want to move appears. (If you drag all the way to the left, the iPod touch Search screen appears.)

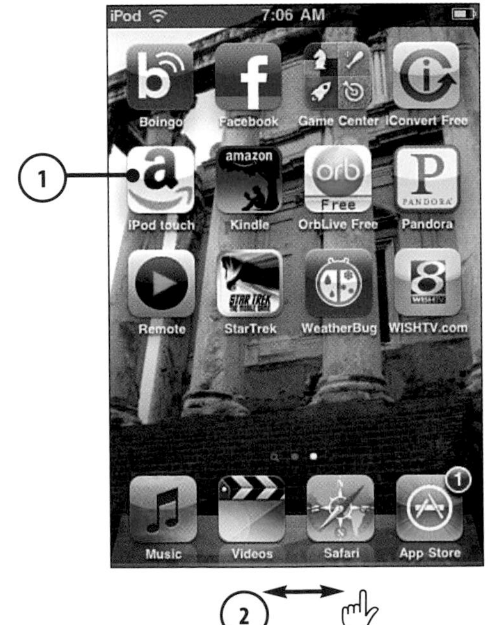

3. Tap and hold any icon. After a moment, the icons begin jiggling, and you also see Delete buttons (x) next to certain icons. The jiggling indicates that you can move icons on the Home screens. The Delete button indicates you can remove the icon; which deletes the item (app or web page link).

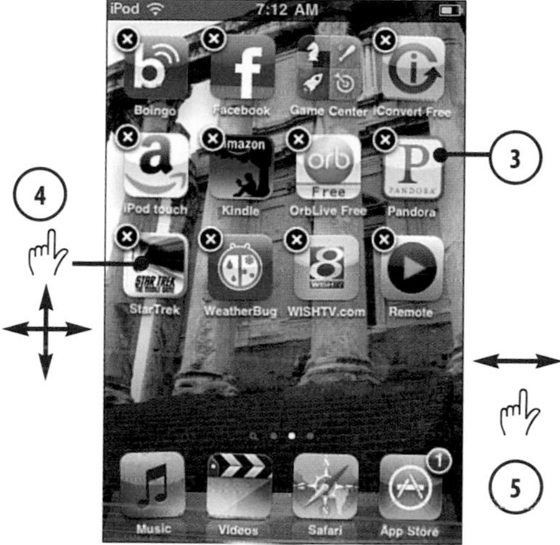

4. Tap and hold down on an icon you want to move and drag it to a new location on the current screen; as you move the icon around the page, other icons separate and are reorganized to enable you to place the icon in its new location.

5. To move the icon onto a different page, drag it to the right or left side of the screen until you see the page on which you want to place the icon and drop it on its new location. As you drag an icon between others on the page, they also spread apart to make room for the newcomer.

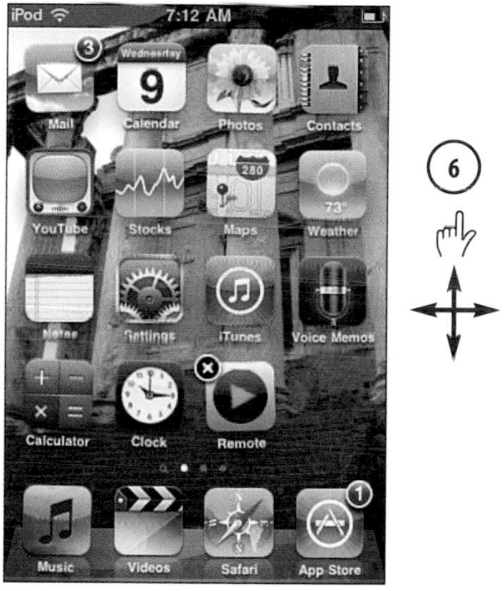

6. When the icon is in the position you want, lift your finger up. The icon is placed in that location.

7. To organize icons into folders, drag one icon on top of another one that you want to be in the same folder; when the first icon enlarges, lift your finger up. The two icons are placed into a new folder, which is named based on the type of icons you place within it. The folder opens and you see its default name.

8. To edit the name, tap in the name field and make changes to it. (To clear the current name, tap the x.)

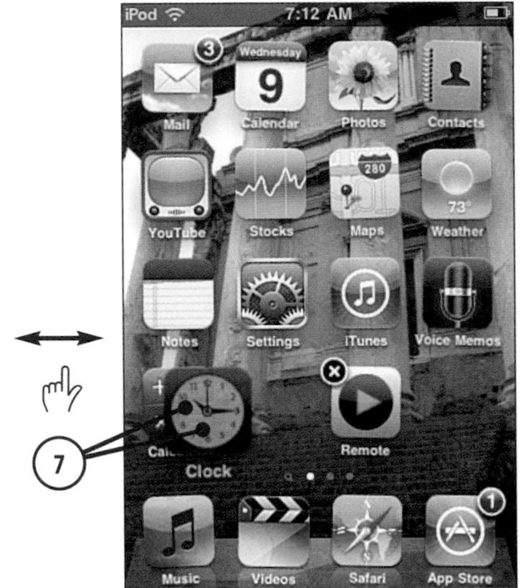

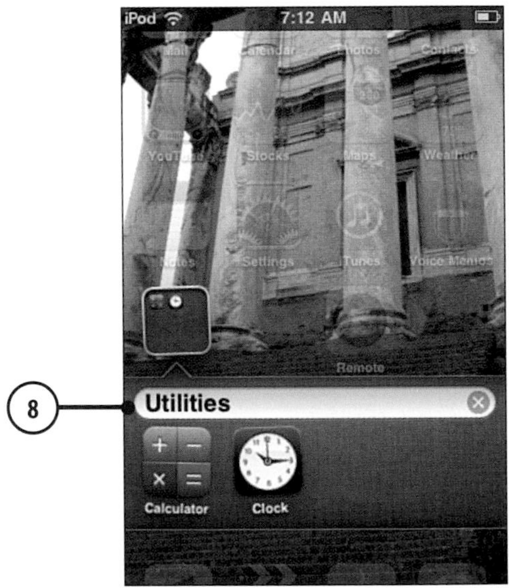

9. Tap Done.
10. Continue dragging icons onto the folder to add more to it; you can drag icons from different pages and drop them onto the folder. Each time you add a new icon, you see its mini-icon with the folder's icon. You can add up to 12 icons to a single folder.
11. To change the icons within a folder, double-tap its icon. The folder opens; the icons remain in the jiggle mode to indicate you can change the folder's contents.

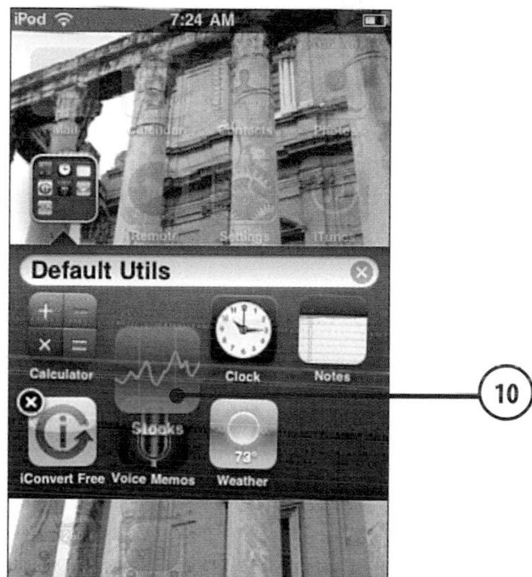

12. Drag icons around within the folder to change their locations.
13. To remove an icon from a folder, drag it out of the folder and onto the Home screen in the background. The folder closes, and you can place the icon anywhere on the Home screens.
14. When you finish configuring a folder, tap outside it on the Home screen background. The folder closes, and you can continue customizing the Home screens.
15. Place the folder in the location you want it just as you do with other icons.

Deleting Folders

To delete a folder, remove all the icons from it. The folder is deleted.

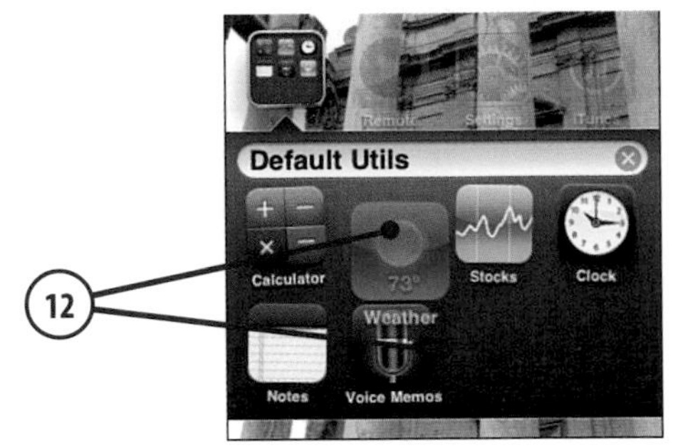

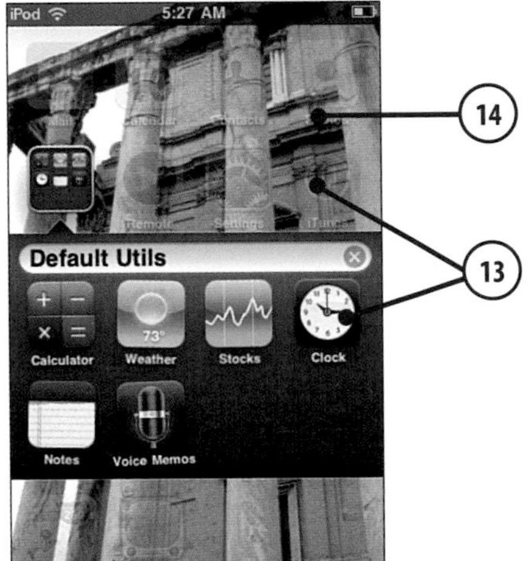

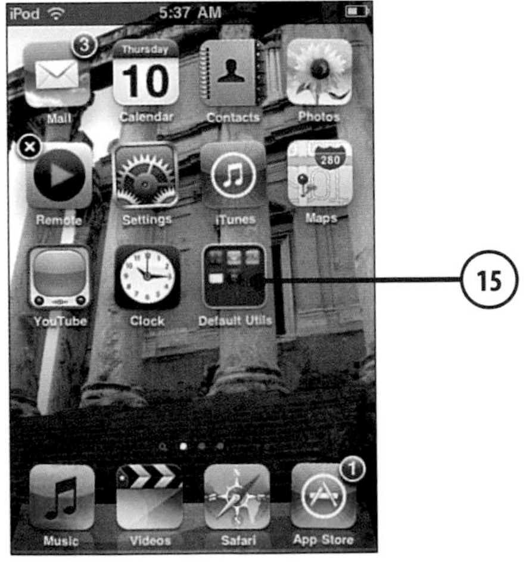

16. To remove an icon, tap its Delete button.

17. Tap Delete. The icon is deleted from the iPod.

18. Continue organizing the pages of your Home screen until they are what you want them to be.

19. When you are happy with your Home screens, press the Home button. The icons are locked in their current positions, they stop jiggling, and the Delete buttons disappear.

Icons You Can Delete and Those You Can't

You can delete only icons for things you've added to your iPod touch, which are either applications you've installed or bookmarks to web pages you've added; when you delete an icon, you also delete the application or bookmark, and it is no longer on your iPod touch. You can't delete any of the default applications, which is why their icons don't have Delete buttons. If you don't use some of these icons, move them to pages of your Home screen that you don't use very much so that they don't get in your way, or create a folder for unused icons and store all of them there, out of your way.

Changing Icons on the Main Toolbar

The icons on the main toolbar at the bottom of the screen are fair game for reorganization, too. You can move them around within the toolbar, or you can drag them up onto the pages of the Home screen and replace them with icons from there. You can also place folders on this toolbar, which makes accessing any of the apps with a folder possible from any Home page screen. The only difference between the icons on the main toolbar and those on the pages of the Home screen is that the main toolbar is always visible when you view a Home screen, so you want to keep the four icons you use most often there.

Using iTunes to Customize Your Home Screens

You learned in Chapter 13, "Installing and Maintaining iPod touch Applications," how to use iTunes to install applications. You can also use iTunes to customize your Home screens.

1. Connect the touch to your computer.
2. Select the iPod on the Source list.
3. Click the Apps button.
4. Click the Home screen you want to organize. It is shown in the window.

Home Screens

The Home screens that have content (and so appear on the iPod) are the ones with the black background and on which you see mini-icons. The bottom Home screen is gray, indicating it is empty. When you add an icon to that screen, it becomes active and you can add and organize just like the other screens. You can have up to 11 Home screens on your iPod.

To remove a Home screen, remove all the icons from it. It disappears from iTunes and from the iPod (when you sync it).

5. Drag icons around the Home screen to change its organization. As you move an icon around, the other icons slide apart to make room for it.

6. Drag an icon from the current screen onto one of the thumbnails to change the screen on which the icon is located. As the icon moves over the thumbnail, the large Home screen becomes the one you are dragging the icon onto.

7. To create a folder, drag one icon onto an icon that you want to be in the same folder.

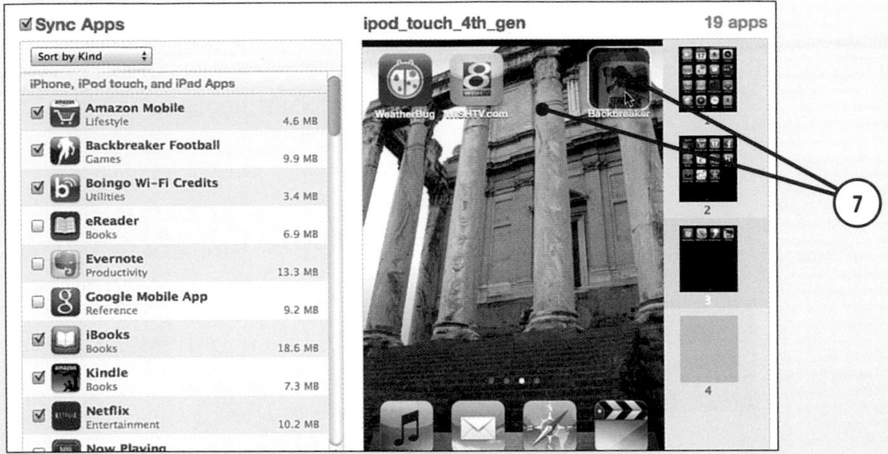

8. If you want to change the default name of the folder (which is based on the type of icons you've added to it), type the new name of the folder in the name box.

9. To close the folder, click on the Home screen outside the folder.

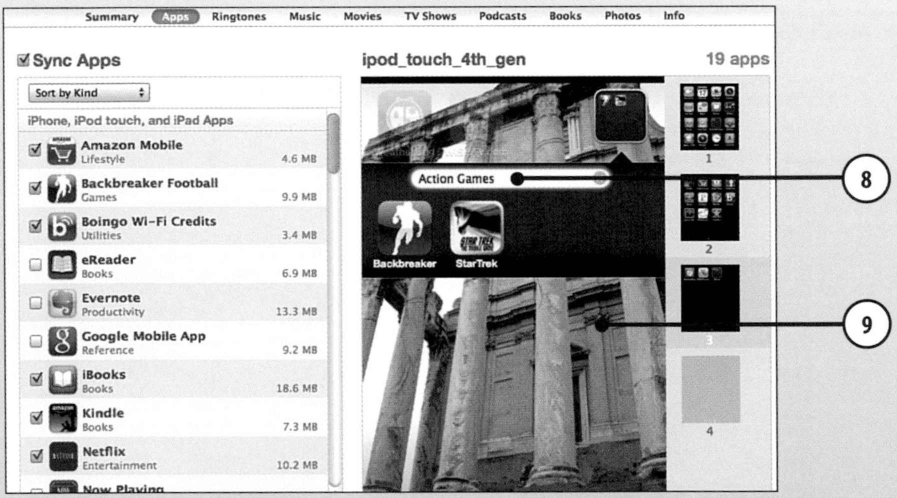

10. To add icons to the current Home screen, check the check boxes for the apps you want to add.

11. To remove apps from the Home screens (and the iPod of course), uncheck their check boxes or click the "x" button that appears when you hover over an icon.

12. To add an icon to an existing folder, drag the icon on top of the folder.

13. To organize icons within a folder, double-click it to open it.

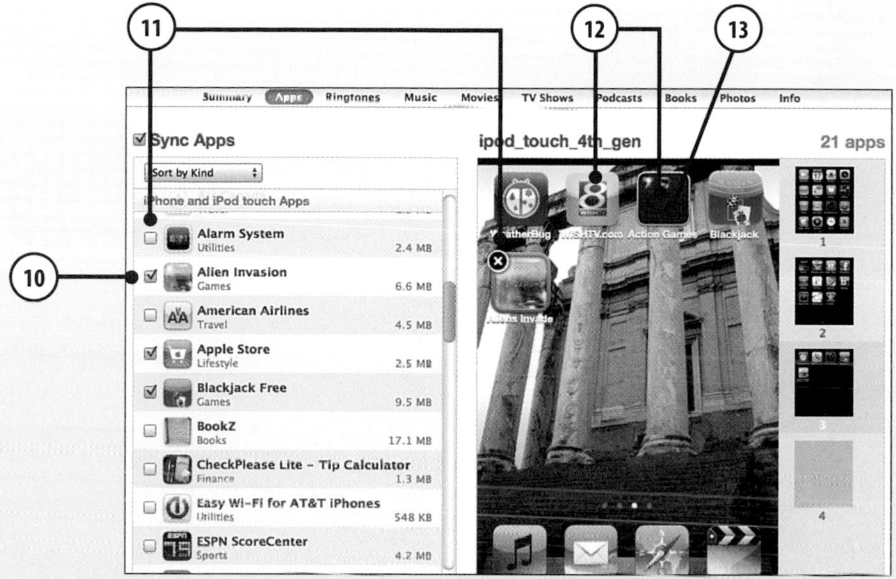

14. Drag the icons around within the folder to set their locations.
15. To remove an icon from a folder, but not from the iPod, drag it out of the folder and drop it onto the current Home screen or onto the thumbnail of a different one.
16. When your Home screens are the way you want them to be, click Apply. A sync is performed and the Home screens on the iPod are configured the way you designed them to be.

Dumping Folders

To remove a folder, remove all the icons from within it, either by dragging them outside of the folder or removing them from the iPod. When the last icon is removed, the folder will be deleted.

Accessing iPod touch Settings

To configure the rest of the options explained in this chapter, first move to the Home screen and tap the Settings button. The Settings screen appears; scroll to see and use all the settings available. The following sections describe various setting options and show you how to configure them. In all cases, start by moving to the Settings screen and then performing step 1.

Use the Settings screen to access and configure the rest of the options explained in this chapter

(If a setting isn't explained in this chapter, it is covered in the chapter about the related topic. For example, the Network setting is explained in Chapter 2, "Connecting to the Internet, Bluetooth Devices, and iPods/iPhones/iPads.")

App Settings

Many apps include settings you can use to configure how the applications work or look. These are grouped together at the bottom of the Settings screen. They work similarly to the default settings; tap the app whose settings you want to configure and use the resulting screens to configure it.

Configuring General Sound Settings

You learned about most of an iPod touch's sound settings in earlier chapters. Some sound settings are more general to an iPod touch, and the following steps describe how to access and change them.

1. Tap Sounds.
2. To change the iPod's volume level for the ringer and alert sounds, drag the slider to the left or right.
3. To be able to change the volume of the ringer and alerts with the Volume buttons, tap OFF next to Change with Buttons. Its status becomes ON and you can change the volume of these types of sounds with the button. If this is OFF, you can only change this volume with the slider. (The Volume buttons always change the level of audio.)
4. If you don't want your iPod touch to make a sound when you lock it, tap Lock Sounds ON. Its status becomes OFF to show you that the sound when you lock an iPod touch is disabled, and the iPod touch no longer makes this sound when you press the Wake/Lock button to put it to sleep and lock it. Tap OFF to re-enable this sound.
5. If you don't like the audible feedback when you tap keys on the iPod touch's virtual keyboard, tap Keyboard Clicks ON to disable that sound. Its status becomes OFF, and an iPod touch's keyboard is silent as you type on it. Tap OFF, and the audible feedback returns.

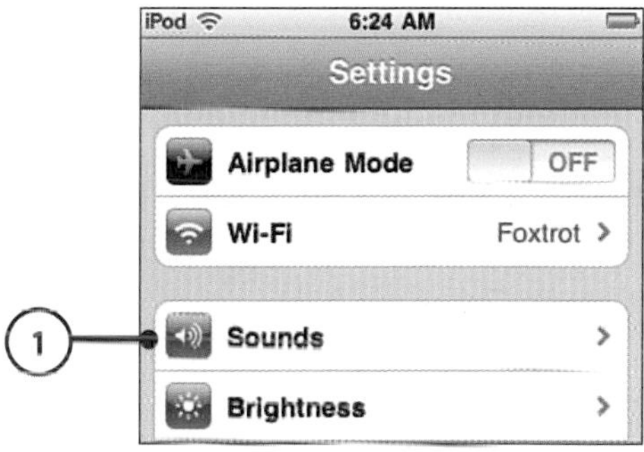

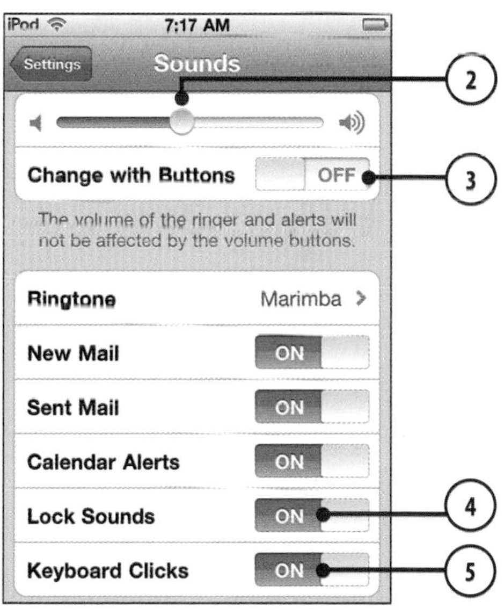

Hearing Things?

When you tap any of the settings on the Sounds screen, you hear the associated sound.

Setting Screen Brightness

Because you continually look at an iPod touch's screen, it should be the right brightness level for your eyes. However, the screen is also a large user of battery power, so the less bright an iPod touch's screen is, the longer its battery lasts. You have to find a good balance between viewing comfort and battery life. Fortunately, your iPod touch has a brightness feature that adjusts for current lighting conditions automatically.

1. Tap Brightness.
2. Tap the ON button to disable the Auto-Brightness feature; its status becomes OFF. Tap OFF to enable this feature again; when enabled, an iPod touch's screen dims when you are in low-level lighting conditions.
3. Drag the slider to the right to raise the base brightness or to the left to lower it. A brighter screen uses more power but is easier to see.

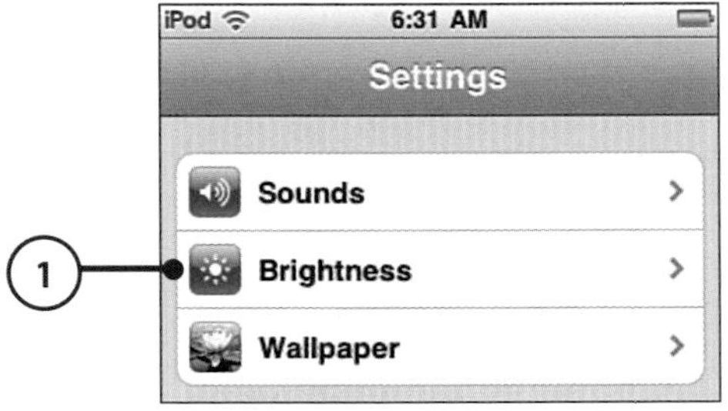

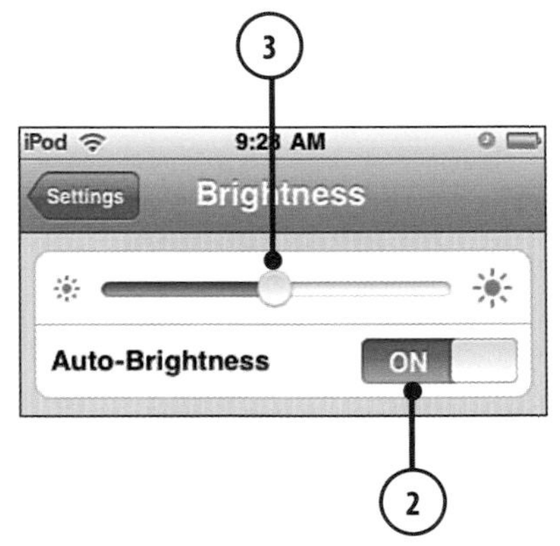

A Bright Idea

The Auto-Brightness feature adjusts the screen brightness based on the lighting conditions in which you are using the iPod touch. You'll get more battery life with Auto-Brightness on, but you might not be comfortable with the screen when you use the iPod where there isn't a lot of ambient light. Try using your iPod touch with this feature enabled to see if the automatic adjustment bothers you. You can always set the brightness level manually if it does.

Setting Wallpaper

When an iPod touch is awake but locked, you see its wallpaper. You also see wallpaper behind the icons on Home screens. If you have a third- or later-generation iPod touch, you can set the wallpaper in both of these places using either the default wallpaper collection or by choosing a photo you've moved onto your iPod touch. To use one of an iPod touch's default images as your wallpaper, perform the following steps:

1. Tap Wallpaper.
2. Tap the Lock screen icon to set its wallpaper, or tap the Home screen icon to set wallpaper there (if you are not using a third-generation or later version, you have only one option). If you don't have any photos stored on the iPod touch, you move directly to the default wallpaper images and can skip to step 4. If you have added images to the iPod touch, the Wallpaper screen appears, and you see the sources of wallpaper available to you.

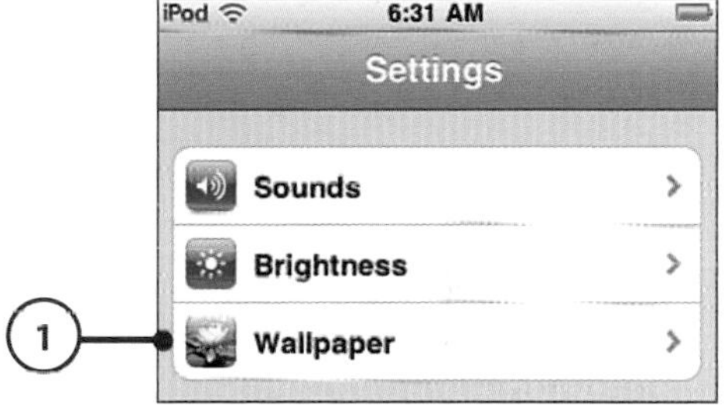

3. Tap Wallpaper. The default wallpaper images appear.
4. Tap the image you want to use as wallpaper. You see a preview of the image you selected.
5. Tap Set. The next time you move to the screen you selected in step 2, you see the wallpaper you selected.
6. Repeat steps 2 through 5 to set the wallpaper for the other screen.

Using Your Photos as an iPod touch Wallpaper

To learn how to add photos to an iPod touch so that they are available as wallpaper, see Chapter 11, "Working with Photos and Video." You can select any of the sources of your photos on the Wallpaper screen to use the photos they contain as wallpaper by tapping the source you want to use instead of Wallpaper in step 3. You then scale and move your own images to customize how they appear as wallpaper; unlike the default wallpaper images, which you have to use as they are.

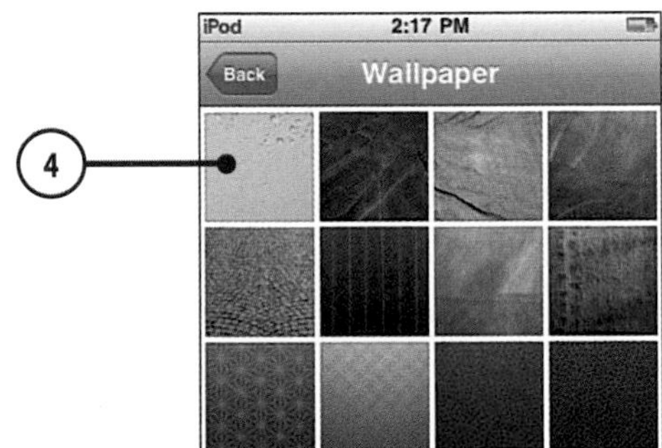

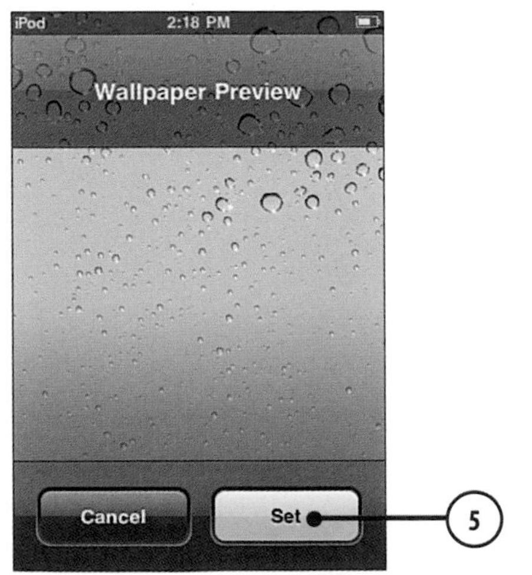

Configuring Other General Settings

An iPod touch has a large number of other general setting tweak how it works. For all these, move to the Settings scre General to start.

Customizing Through Applications

The most powerful way to customize how your iPod touch works is by installing applications. See Chapter 13 for information about installing applications.

Getting Information about an iPod touch

The About function provides lots of information about your iPod touch. Some of this can be useful for troubleshooting or other purposes.

1. Tap About.
2. Scroll up and down the screen to view its information, such as the number of songs, videos, photos, and applications stored on it; its memory; software version number; serial number; and so on.

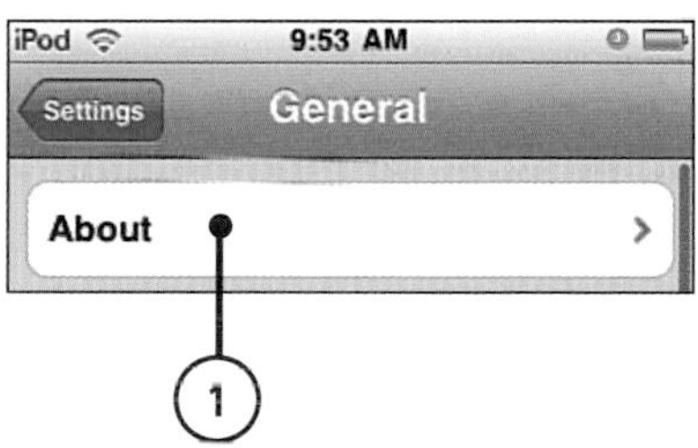

Legalese

If you want to kill some time, move to the bottom of the About screen and tap Legal. Enjoy!

Location Icon

When you are working with an app that is currently using Location Services, you see the Location Services icon in the upper-right corner of the screen (next to the battery icon).

Configuring Location Services

If you don't want applications, such as Maps, to access your iPod touch's current location, you can disable this feature. Of course, if you do, applications that rely on this won't work properly.

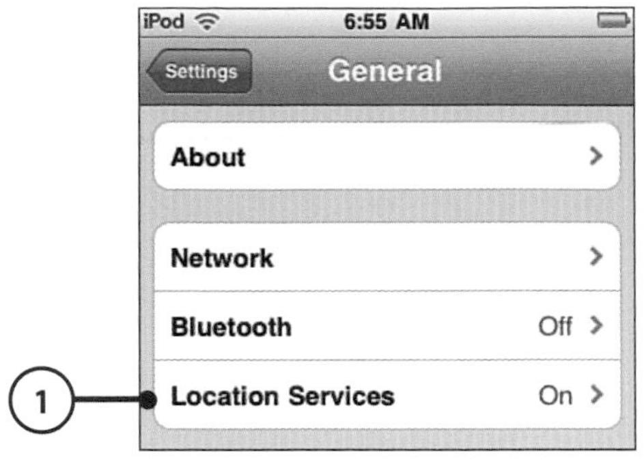

1. Tap Location Services. Under the Location Services control, you see a list of all the applications that have identified your location at least once; those that have done so within the past 24 hours are marked with the Location Services icon.

2. Tap the Location Services ON button. The status becomes OFF to indicate that the iPod can't access the services it uses to identify where it is.

Apps that have used Location Services to locate your iPod

3. Tap Turn Off at the prompt. (To reenable Location services, tap OFF so that the status becomes ON.)

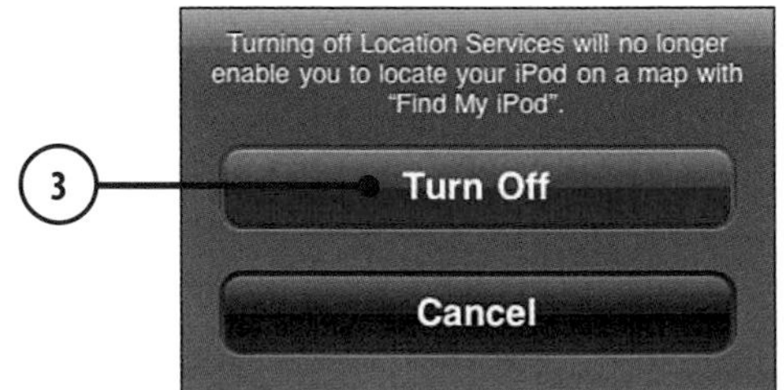

Don't Find Me!

To disable a specific application's access to Location Services so it can't use those services to locate the iPod, tap its ON button. The status becomes OFF and that specific application can't identify your location; if location is required for the application to function, it won't work properly until you re-enable its access to Location Services.

Where Oh Where Has My iPod Gone?

If you have MobileMe and have your account configured on your iPod, you can use the Find My iPod feature to try to show its location. For this to have a chance of working, the Location Services feature must be enabled. When it is, you can log into your MobileMe website and use the Find My iPod option, which attempts to show the iPod's location on a map.

Securing Your iPod touch

Your iPod touch has a number of ways to protect it, which is important considering the information that can be stored there. You can also limit the functions and type of content available on it. To secure your iPod touch, perform the following steps:

1. Tap Auto-Lock.
2. Tap the amount of idle time you want to pass before the iPod automatically locks and goes to sleep. You can choose from 1 to 5 minutes; choose Never if you want to manually lock your iPod touch. I recommend that you keep Auto-Lock set to a relatively small value to conserve your iPod touch's battery and to make it more secure. Of course, the shorter you set this time to be, the more frequently you have to unlock it.
3. Tap General.

4. If you want to secure the content on your iPod touch with a passcode, tap Passcode Lock.
5. Tap Turn Passcode On.
6. Enter a four-digit passcode.

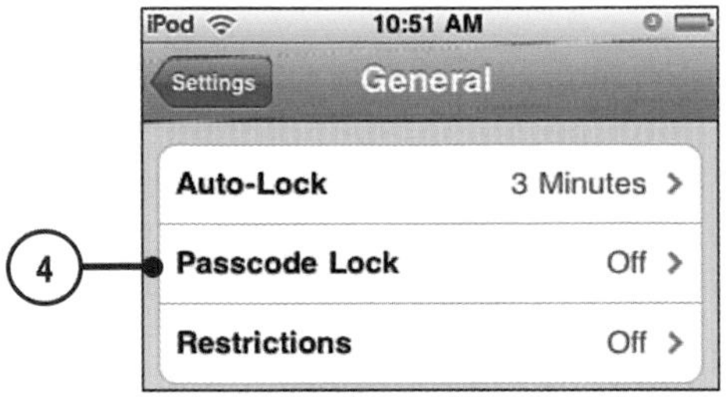

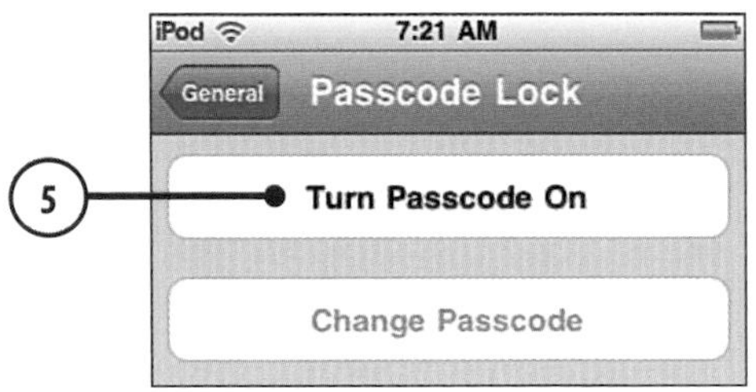

Are You Complex?

By default, your passcode is a simple four-digit number. If you want to have a more complex (and more secure) passcode, tap ON next to Simple Passcode. Its status becomes OFF, the passcode field becomes more flexible, and you can enter text and numbers. This is more secure, especially if you use a code eight characters or longer that includes both letters and numbers. The steps to set a complex password are similar; the difference is that you use the keyboard to configure the passcode instead of the numeric keypad.

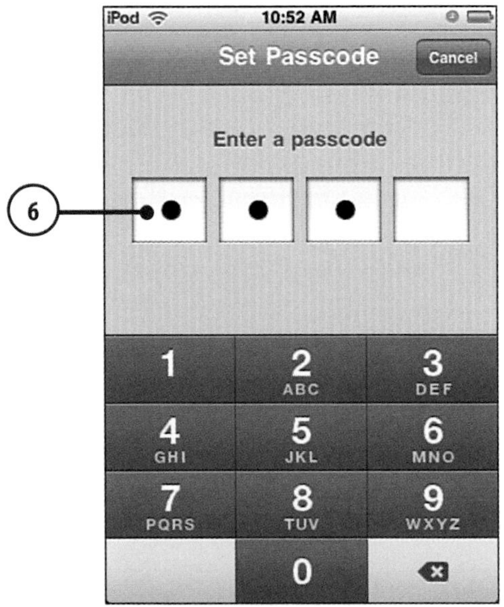

7. Re-enter the passcode. If the two passcodes match, you see the Passcode Lock screen.
8. To disable the passcode, tap Turn Passcode Off and enter the passcode. To set it again, repeat steps 5 through 7.
9. To change your passcode, tap Change Passcode. You then enter your current passcode and enter your new passcode twice. You return to the Passcode Lock screen, and the new passcode takes effect.
10. To set the amount of time the iPod is locked before a passcode is required to unlock it, tap Require Passcode.
11. Tap the amount of time the iPod touch is locked before the passcode takes effect. (This assumes you've set a passcode of course.) The shorter this time is, the more secure an iPod touch is, but also the more times you'll have to enter the passcode if your iPod touch goes to sleep frequently.
12. Tap Passcode Lock.

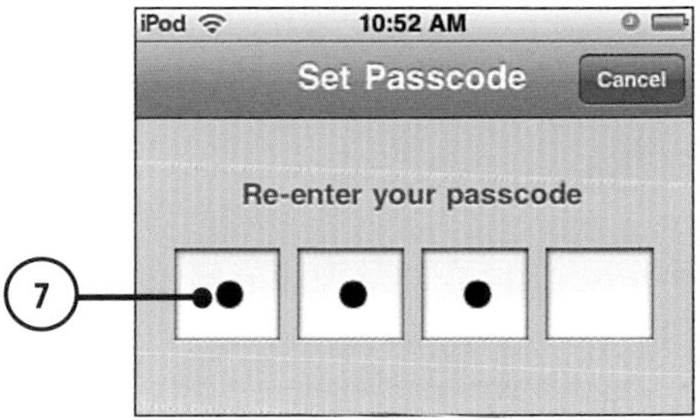

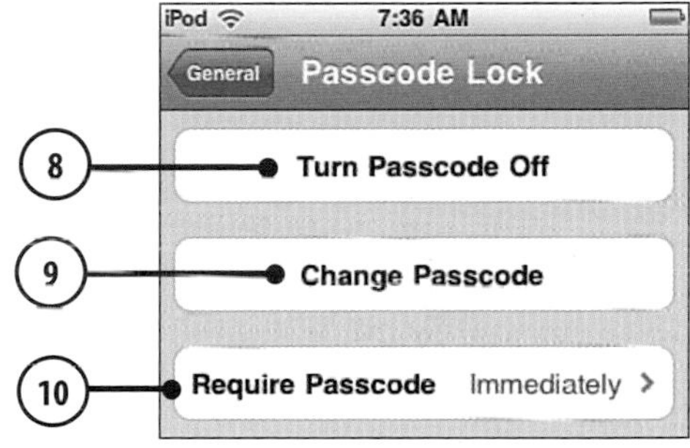

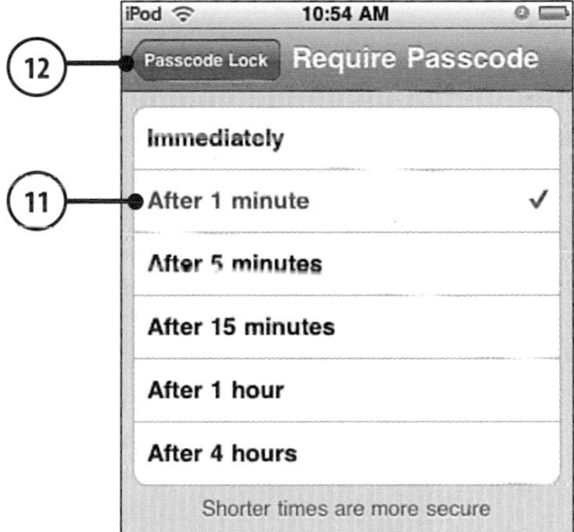

13. If you want the iPod touch to automatically erase all your data after an incorrect passcode has been entered 10 times, tap Erase Data OFF.

14. Tap Enable. The status of Erase Data becomes ON. Should you or anyone else be unable to enter the correct passcode on the eleventh try, your data (basically any changes you've made to the contents of the iPod touch) will be erased from the iPod touch.

15. Tap General.

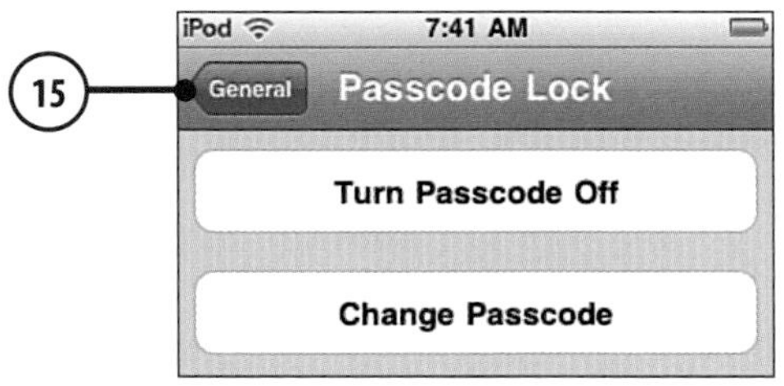

16. To limit the kind of content or functions that can be used on your iPod touch, tap Restrictions.

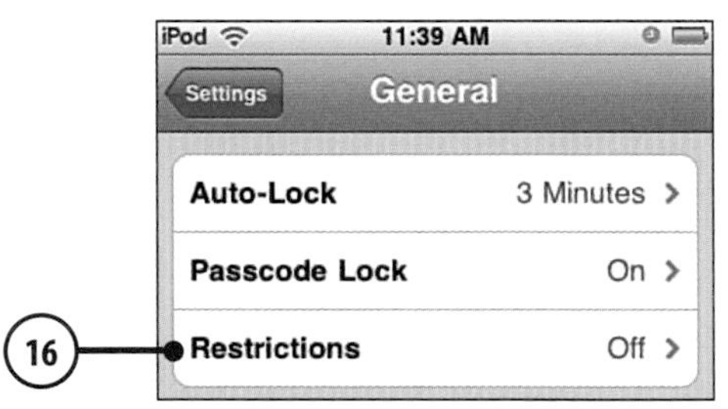

17. Tap Enable Restrictions.

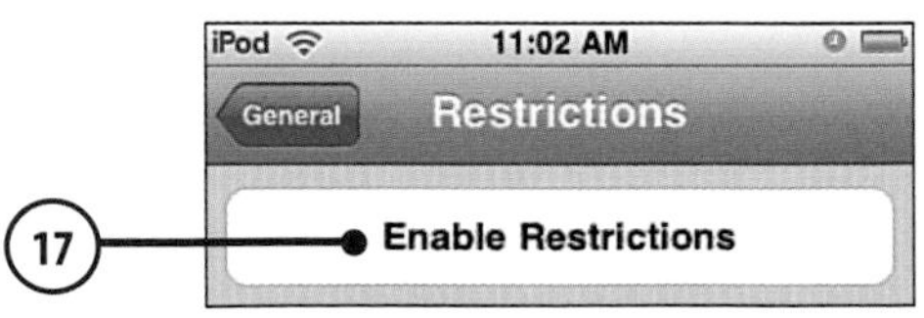

18. Create a restrictions passcode. You have to enter this passcode to change the content restrictions.

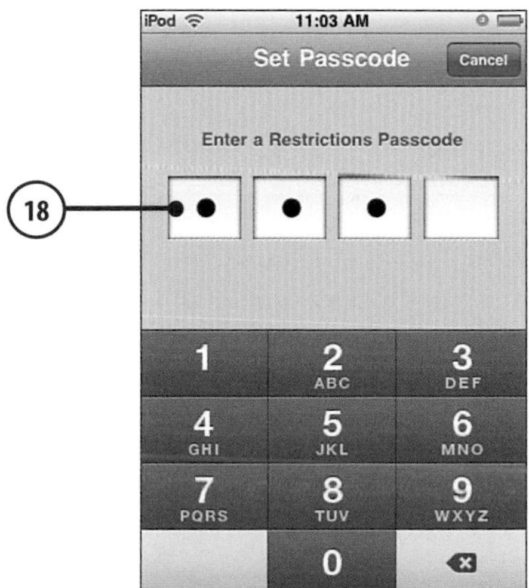

19. Re-enter your restrictions passcode. You return to the Restrictions screen, and the Allow buttons and Allowed Content functions are enabled.

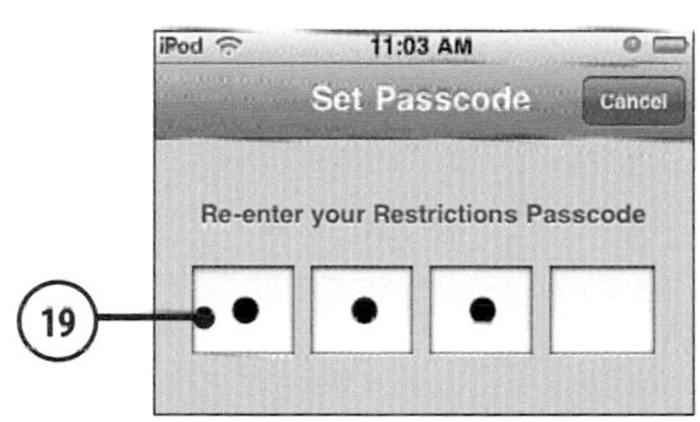

20. Tap the ON button next to each function you want to disable. Its status becomes OFF to show you that content or function can't be accessed. For example, to prevent web browsing, tap ON next to Safari; its status becomes OFF, and the Safari icon is removed from the Home screen and can't be used. With the other controls, you can prevent access to YouTube videos, the iTunes Store application, the App Store application, and Location Services.

21. To prevent purchases from being made within applications, tap ON next to In-App Purchases. Its status becomes OFF, and purchases can't be made from within applications. This is a good way to prevent unintended purchases, particularly when someone else is using your iPod touch.

22. Scroll down to see all the Allowed Content controls.

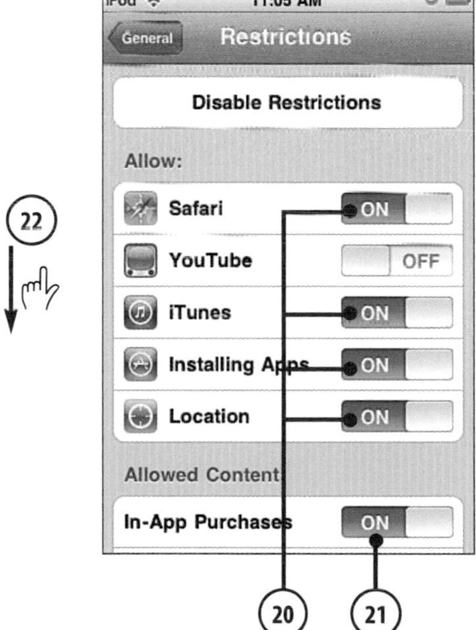

Dueling Passcodes

There are two passcodes: the Auto-Lock passcode and the Restrictions passcode. Each controls access to their respective functions. You can use different passcodes for each or use the same passcode so that you only have to remember one.

23. Tap Ratings For.
24. Tap the country whose rating system you want to use for content on your iPod.
25. Tap Restrictions.

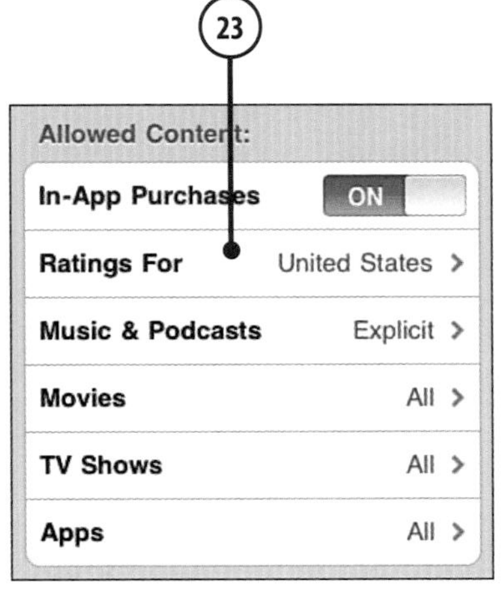

Whose Ratings?

The country you select in step 24 determines the options you see in steps 30, 33, and 36. The steps show the United States rating systems; if you select a different country, you see rating options for that country instead.

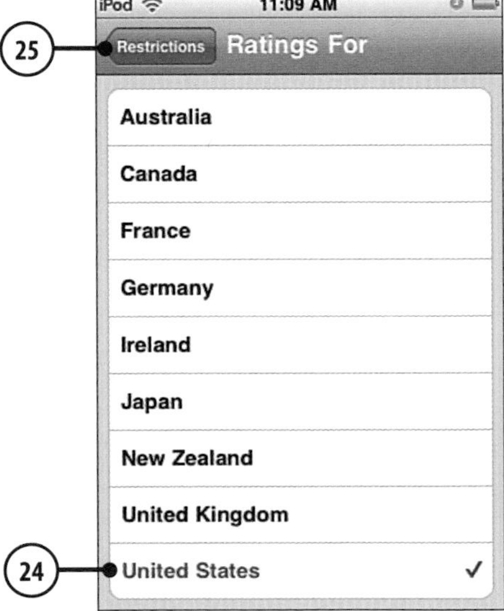

26. Tap Music & Podcasts.
27. To prevent content tagged as explicit In the iTunes Store from being played, tap ON so its status becomes OFF. Any explicit content will not be played.
28. Tap Restrictions.
29. Tap Movies.
30. Tap the highest rating of movies that you want to be playable (for example, tap PG to prevent R and NC-17 movies from playing); tap Allow All Movies to allow any movie to be played; or tap Don't Allow Movies to prevent any movie content from playing. Prevented movie ratings display highlighted in red.
31. Tap Restrictions.

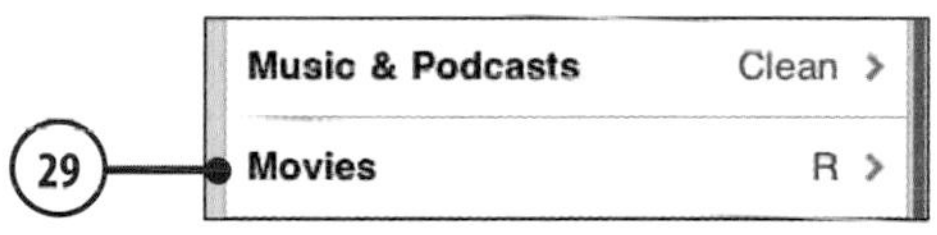

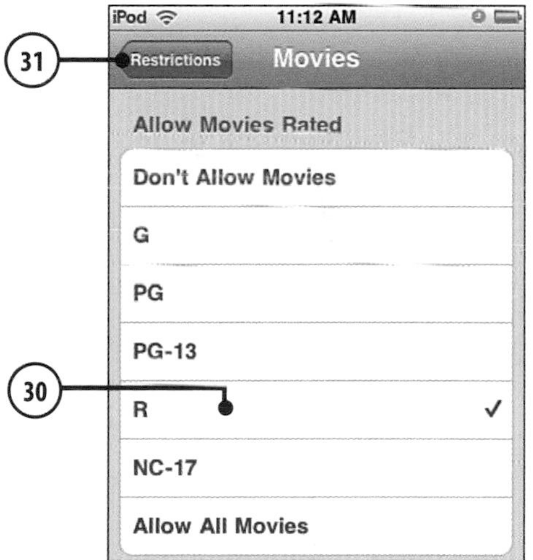

32. Tap TV Shows.
33. Tap the highest rating of TV shows that you want to be playable (for example, tap TV-14 to prevent TV-MA shows from playing); tap Allow All TV Shows to allow any show to be played; or tap Don't Allow TV Shows to prevent any TV content from playing. Prevented ratings display in red.
34. Tap Restrictions.
35. Tap Apps.
36. Tap the highest rating of application that you want to be available (for example, tap 12+ to prevent 17+ applications from working), tap Allow All Apps to allow any application to be used, or tap Don't Allow Apps to prevent all applications.
37. Tap Restrictions.

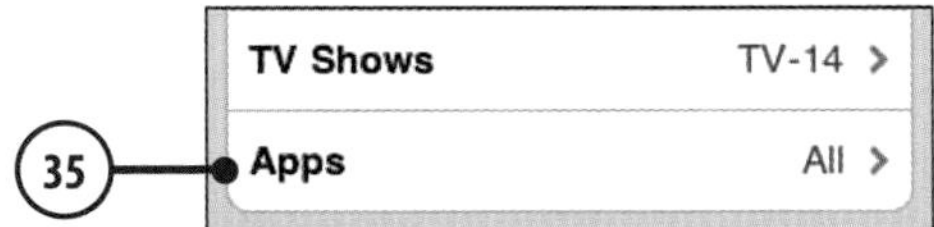

Where's My Good Stuff?

When you change content restriction settings, such as allowing explicit content after it was prevented, you might have to re-sync your iPod touch for those changes to take effect. For example, if you prevent R-rated movies from playing and then allow them to play again, you might need to re-sync your movie content for those movies to appear on the iPod.

When you try to perform an action that requires a passcode, you are prompted to enter the required passcode. When you do so successfully, you can perform the action, such as unlocking your iPod touch or changing its restrictions. (If you set the passcodes to be different, make sure you enter the appropriate one.)

Automatic Erase

When you have enabled the Erase Data function and you enter an incorrect passcode when unlocking your iPod touch, you see a counter showing the number of unsuccessful attempts. When this reaches 10, all the data on your iPod touch will be erased on the next unsuccessful attempt.

Configuring Search Options

You can search the contents of your iPod with its Search tool, which you access by browsing to the Home page or by tapping the magnifying icon just above the toolbar on the Home screens. You can configure how you search your iPod with the following steps:

1. Tap Spotlight Search.

2. Tap any category of content that you don't want to be included in searches. When a category has a check mark, it will be included; when a category doesn't have a check mark, it is ignored when you search.

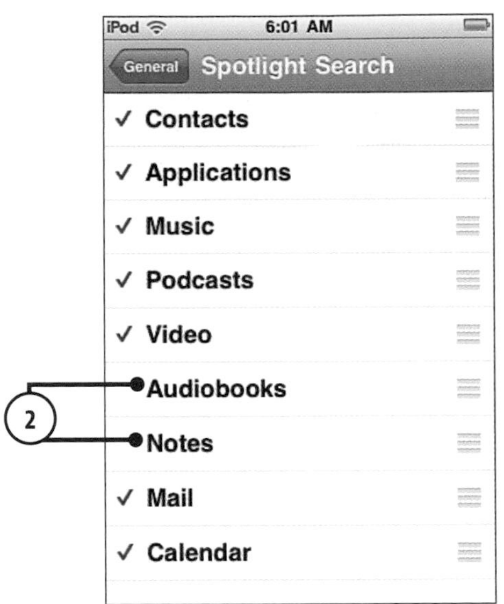

3. Drag the list button next to a category up or down the screen to move it up or down on the list. Categories that are higher on the Spotlight Search screen display toward the top of the results. For example, if Mail is the top item on the list, emails appear at the top of the results screen when you search.

4. Repeat steps 2 and 3 until you've configured searches so that only categories you want to search are included and the results appear in the order you prefer.

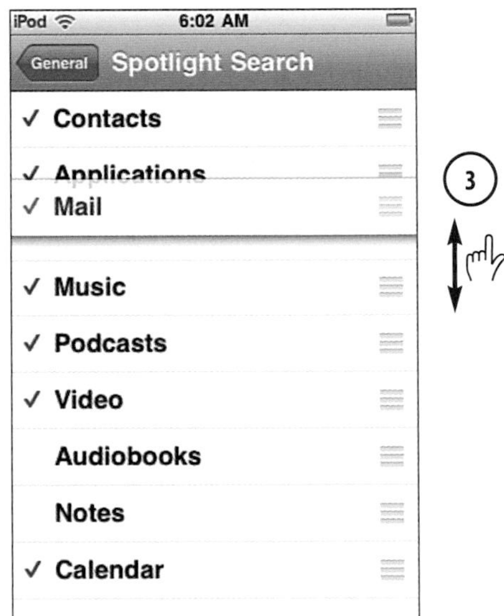

Configuring the Keyboard

As you've seen, you use the iPod touch's keyboard for lots of things, such as emailing, surfing the Web, and so on. There are a number of settings that determine how the keyboard works.

1. Tap Keyboard.

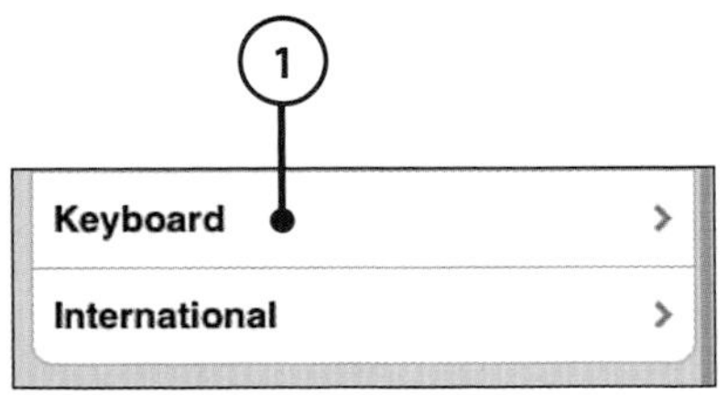

2. To disable the automatic spell checking/correction, tap Auto-Correction ON so its status becomes OFF. Your iPod touch no longer suggests spelling as you type.
3. To prevent your iPod touch from automatically capitalizing as you type, tap Auto-Capitalization ON. Its status becomes OFF, and the iPod touch no longer changes the case of letters as you type them.
4. If you don't want the iPod to use the Spell Check feature as you type, tap ON next to Check Spelling to disable it. When you want to have your spelling checked again, tap OFF so its status becomes ON.
5. To enable the Caps Lock key, tap Enable Caps Lock OFF. The status becomes ON, and when the keyboard appears, you can use the Caps Lock key.
6. To disable the shortcut that types a period followed by a space when you tap the space bar twice, tap "." Shortcut ON. Its status becomes OFF, and you must tap a period and the space bar to type these characters.
7. To change the keyboard's configuration, tap International Keyboards (covered in the next section).

Setting International Options

You can configure various aspects of how the iPod touch to reflect the countries and standards you want to reflect.

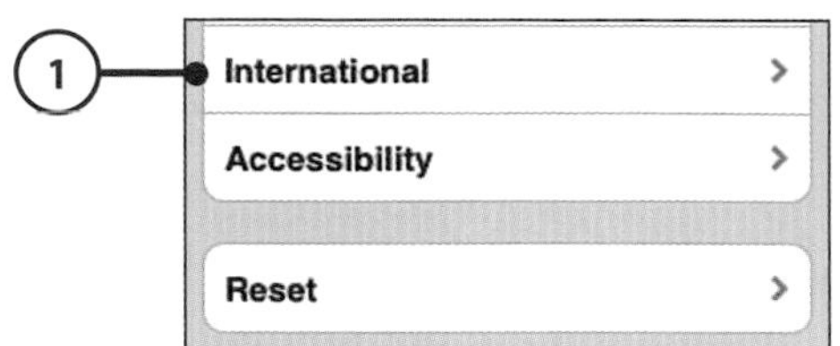

1. Tap International.
2. Tap Language.
3. Tap the language you want to use. The selected language is marked with a check mark.
4. Tap Done. Your iPod touch starts using the language you selected.
5. Tap Voice Control.

6. Tap the language you want to speak to enter voice commands.
7. Tap International.
8. Tap Keyboards.
9. Tap the language for which you want to configure a keyboard.

Multilingual?

To add keyboards in other languages, tap the Add New Keyboard command and select the language for the new keyboard. Then follow steps 9 through 12 to configure its layout.

10. Tap the layout option for the iPod's virtual keyboard.
11. Tap the layout option for external keyboards you use, such as a Bluetooth keyboard.
12. Tap Keyboards.

Removing and Reordering Keyboards

To remove a keyboard, tap Edit. Then tap the Unlock button next to the keyboard you want to remove. Tap Delete. To change the order in which keyboards are listed and used, drag the keyboards up and down the list.

13. Tap International. The number of keyboards you have enabled is shown on the right side of the screen in the Keyboards option.
14. Tap Region Format.

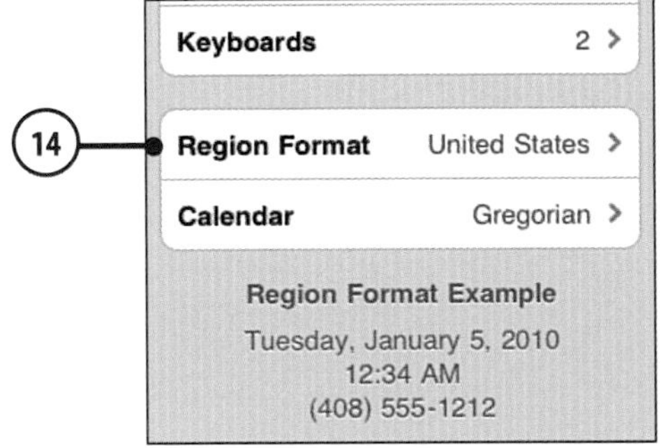

15. Tap the region whose formats you want to use. Some regions have alternative format choices; you can choose from among the format options used in those regions.
16. Tap International. At the bottom of the International screen, you see examples of the format you selected.
17. Tap Calendar.
18. Tap the type of calendar you want to use.
19. Tap International.

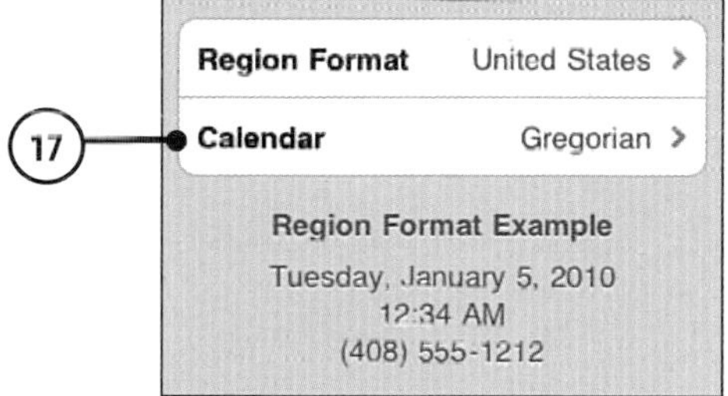

When you have more than one language enabled, a Globe button appears on an iPod touch's keyboard to the left of the space bar. Tapping this button cycles through each of the enabled keyboards; each keyboard's name appears briefly as you tap its button. When you reach the language you want to use, you can type using the characters for that language.

Tap to change keyboards.

>>> Go Further

THE ACCESSIBLE IPOD

If you tap the Accessibility option, you see a large number of options you can configure to make your iPod more accessible. You can enable Voice Over to have the iPod guide you through screens by speaking their contents. Zoom magnifies the entire screen. Large Text enables you to increase the size of the text displayed for easier reading. White on Black changes the screen from dark characters on a light background to light characters on a dark background. Mono Audio makes all audio come out in one channel. Speak Auto-text has the iPod speak corrections it suggests to you, such as auto-capitalizations. Triple-click Home configures the action when you press the Home button three times.

Resetting an iPod touch

Although time machines are a staple in science fiction, it isn't often you get the chance to go back in time in real life. You can use the reset tools to return your iPod touch to a previous state of configuration. This can be useful for troubleshooting or if you simply determine that a previous configuration was better than the one resulting from your changes. For example, it's much easier to return the Home screens to their default conditions using the reset function than it is manually moving icons back to their original positions.

1. Tap Reset.
2. To reset all settings to the defaults, tap Reset All Settings and then tap Reset All Settings again to confirm. All the iPod touch's settings return to the default states.
3. To reset all settings and delete all content (such as music), tap Erase All Content and Settings; tap Erase iPod at the prompt. All the iPod's settings return to defaults, and all content you've added is erased.
4. To return only the network settings to defaults, tap Reset Network Settings and then Reset Network Settings again at the prompt. You need to reconfigure the iPod touch to connect to a network or other iPods/iPhones/iPads.
5. To return an iPod touch to its default dictionary, tap Reset Keyboard Dictionary followed by Reset Dictionary at the prompt. Any words you've added to an iPod touch's dictionary are removed, and it returns to its default state.
6. To return the Home screen to the default layout, tap Reset Home Screen Layout and Reset Home Screen again at the prompt. Icons on the Home screen are returned to their default locations.
7. To reset the warnings your iPod touch has sent you when you use Location Services, tap Reset Location Warnings and then Reset Warnings. The next time the iPod touch needs to warn you about a location service, you see the appropriate warning.

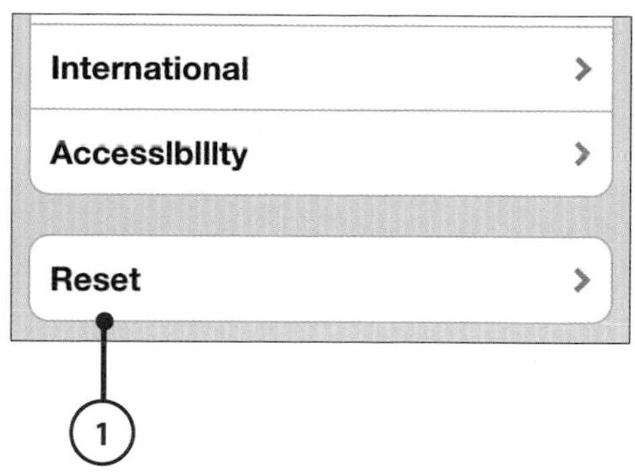

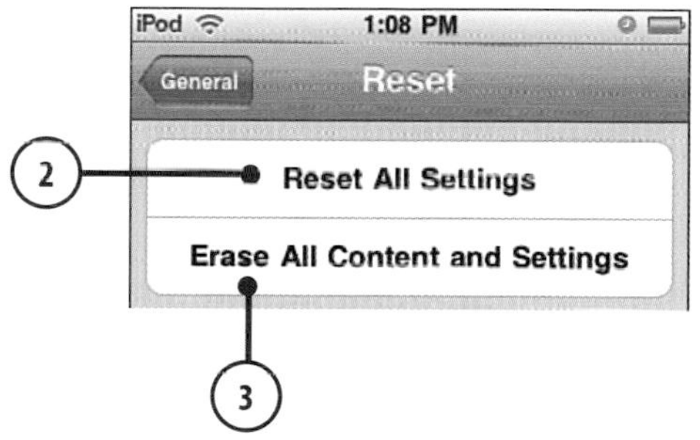

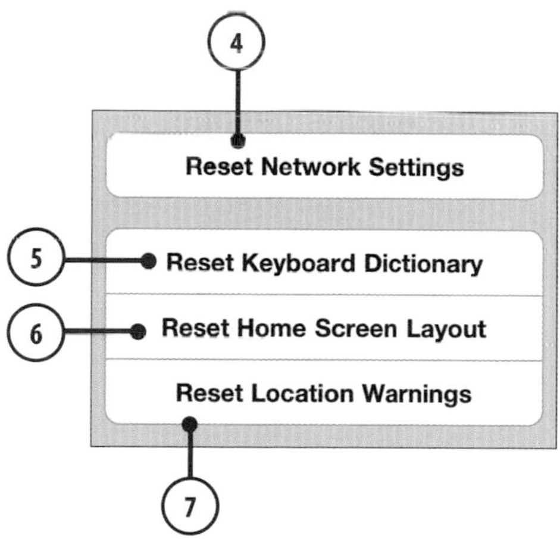

An iPod touch is easy to maintain
and isn't likely to give you much trouble
iPod
4:36 PM
Sunday
12
FaceTime
Calendar
Photos
Camera
280
YouTube
Maps
iBooks
Utilities
2
iTunes
App Store
Entertainment
Settings
amazon
Remote
Whiteboard
Contacts
Kindle
Music
Mail
Safari
Videos

In this chapter, you learn how to keep an iPod touch in top shape and what to do should problems happen. Topics include the following:

15

- → Maintaining an iPod touch
- → Solving iPod touch problems

Maintaining an iPod touch and Solving Problems

You probably noticed that this is a short chapter, and there is a good reason for that: An iPod touch works very well, and you are unlikely to have problems with it, especially if you keep iTunes and the iPod touch's software current. When problems do occur, you can usually solve them with a few simple steps. If that fails, there's lots of help available for you on the Internet.

Maintaining an iPod touch

Some basic maintenance tasks keep an iPod touch in top working condition. Even better, you can do most of these tasks with just a couple of mouse clicks because you can configure iTunes to do most of the work for you.

Maintaining iTunes

As you've learned in this book, iTunes is a vital partner for your iPod touch. You should keep iTunes current to ensure that you have the latest bug fixes, new features, and so on. Fortunately, you can configure iTunes to maintain itself.

Maintaining iTunes on Windows PCs

You can easily update iTunes on a Windows PC, but it's even better to have iTunes update itself automatically.

1. In iTunes, choose Edit, Preferences.
2. Click the General tab.
3. Check the Check for new software updates automatically check box.
4. Click OK. The dialog closes. iTunes checks for updates automatically. When it finds an update, it prompts you to download and install it.

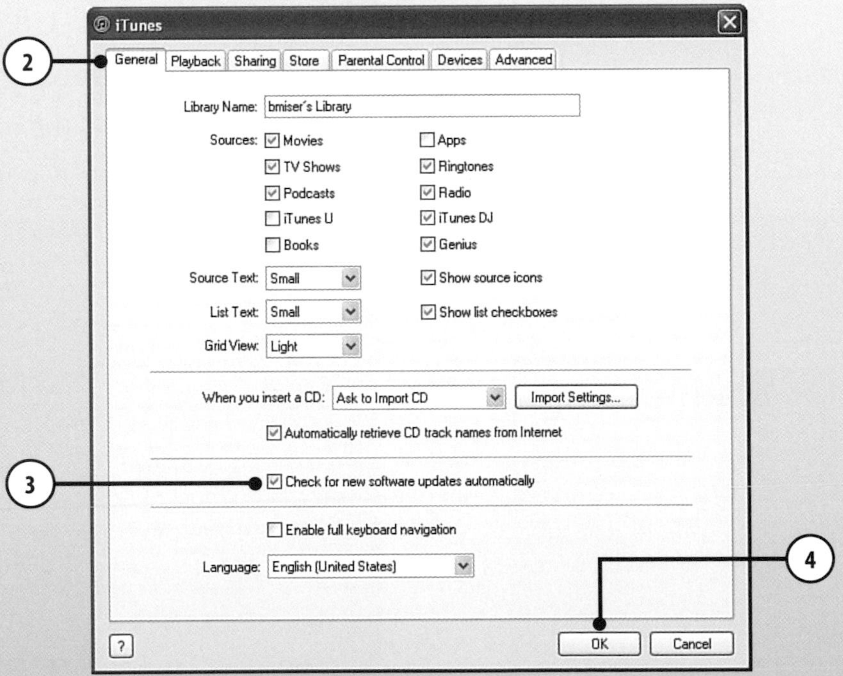

Check for Updates Now Windows

To check for updates at any time, choose Help, Check for U…ates. iTunes checks for … see a message telling … oad and install it.

… ave iTunes update itself

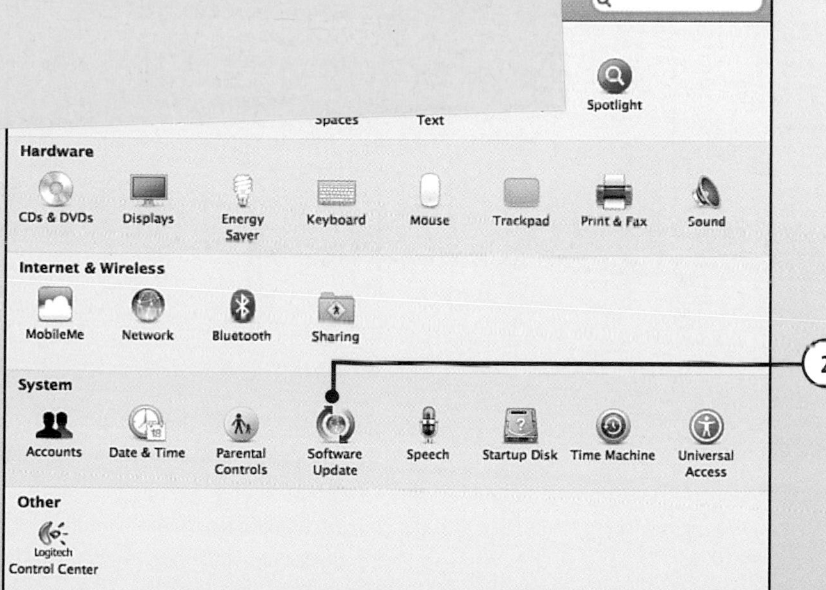

Check for Updates Now Mac

To check for updates at any time, open the Apple menu and choose Software Update. The Software Update application runs. If it finds an update to iTunes or to any other Apple software, you are prompted to download and install them.

3. Check the Check for updates check box.
4. Choose the frequency that Mac OS X checks for updates on the pop-up menu, such as Weekly.
5. Check the Download updates automatically check box. The Mac checks for updates for iTunes, along with all the other Apple software on your Mac according to the time frame you selected. When it identifies an update, it downloads the update automatically and prompts you to install it or prompts you to download and install it, depending on the kind of update it is.

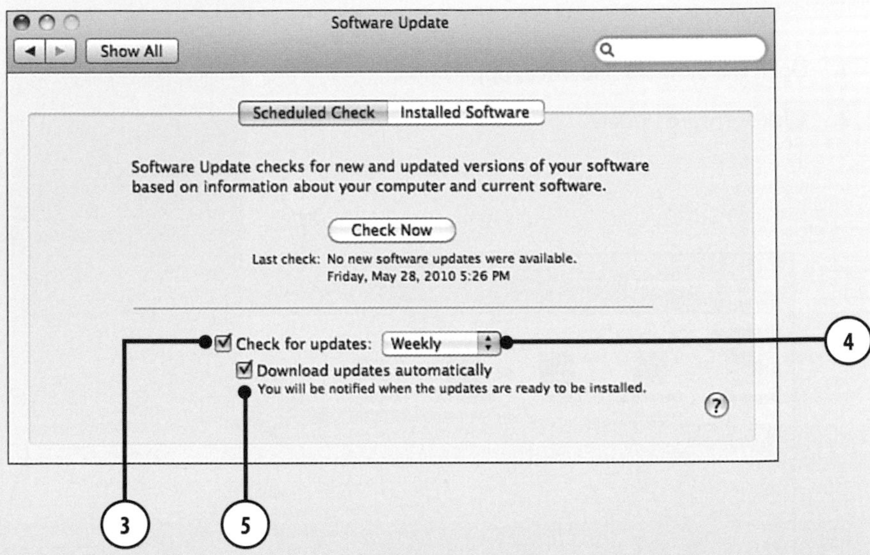

Maintaining an iPod touch's Software

One of iTunes' functions is to maintain an iPod touch's software. Periodically, iTunes checks for updates to the iPod touch operating system software iOS. When iTunes finds an update, it installs it for you; the next time you connect your iPod touch to your computer, you are prompted to install the update. You can allow the update when you are prompted about it and follow the onscreen instructions to install it, or you can update your iPod's software manually by performing the following steps.

1. Connect your iPod touch to your computer.
2. Select your iPod touch on the Source list.
3. Click the Summary button. You see the current version of the iPod touch's software at the top of the pane.
4. If a newer version of the iPod touch software has already been downloaded to your computer and you want to install it, click Update; to see if a newer version is available and download it, click Check for Update. If you manually check for an update and you're using the current version of the iPod touch's software, you see a dialog telling you so, and you can skip the rest of these steps. If you aren't using the current version, the update is downloaded to your computer and the button becomes Update.

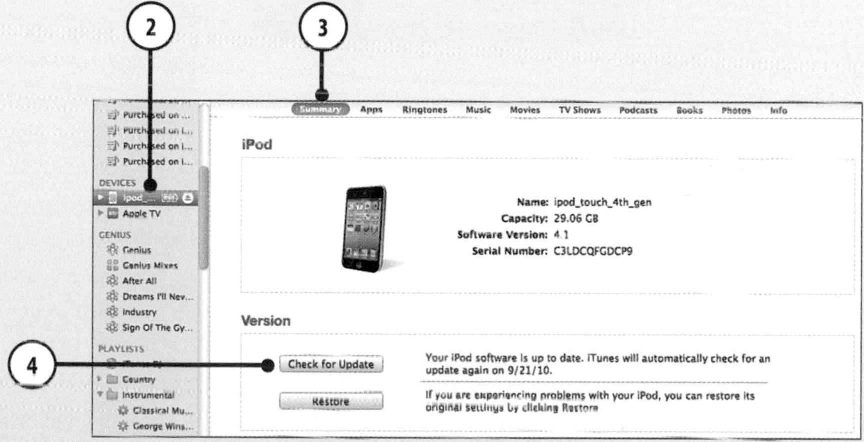

5. Click the Update button and follow the onscreen instructions to download and install the updated software onto your iPod touch.

   When the software has been downloaded and installed, the iPod touch is automatically restarted. As the process proceeds, you see various status messages in iTunes. Eventually, the iPod touch disappears from iTunes, is restarted, and becomes available in iTunes again, and you see that your software is now the current version.

Maintaining an iPod touch's Power

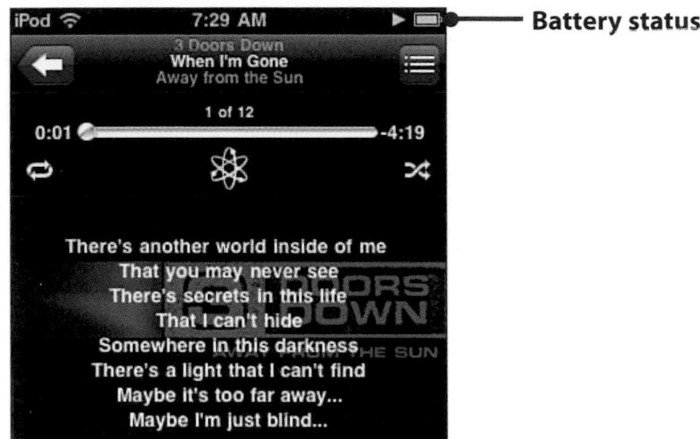

Obviously, an iPod touch with a dead battery isn't good for much. As you use your touch, you should keep an eye on its battery status. As long as the battery status is green or is at least partially filled, you're okay. As the iPod gets low on power, the battery status icon becomes empty and eventually turns red (on some screens, the status is always in black and white, in which case you should pay attention to how much it is filled rather than color). Two separate warnings alert you when the battery lowers to 20% and then again at 10%. If you keep going from there, the iPod touch runs out of power and shuts down. Of course, it gives you plenty of warning through onscreen messages before this happens.

Sync Regularly and Often

You should sync your iPod touch frequently. Syncing your iPod does several things for you. One is to charge its battery for as long as it's connected to your computer. Another is to update the content on your touch. Last, but by no means least, you should sync to keep your iPod's information backed up on your computer. If you run into a major problem that requires restoring or erasing your iPod touch, you can recover its data from the backup. If you wait a long time between syncs/backups and encounter a problem, you could run out of battery power, or if something worse happens, lose data.

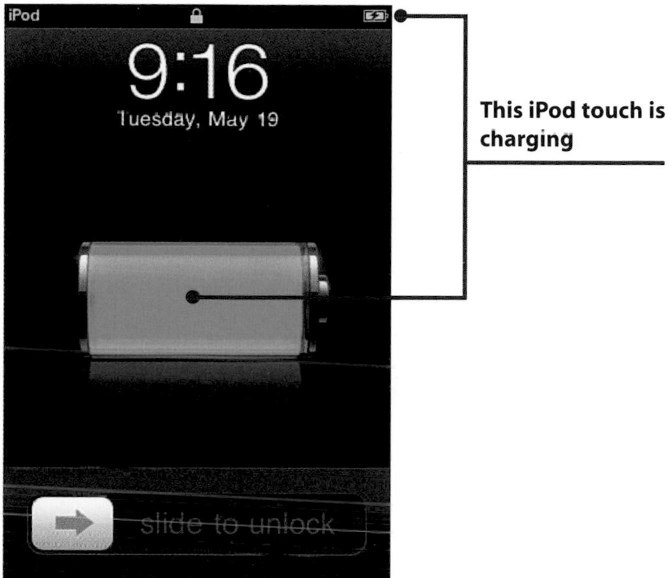

Fortunately, it's easy to avoid running out of power by keeping your iPod touch charged. The good news is that all you have to do is to connect the iPod touch to your computer, and its battery charges. While this is occurring, you see the charging icon in the upper-right corner of the screen, and if you wake the iPod, a large battery icon showing the relative state of the battery appears on its screen. When charging is complete, the battery status icon replaces the charging icon in the upper-right corner of the screen, the large battery icon disappears, and you see your iPod touch's wallpaper if it's locked, or you see whatever screen you happen to be using if it isn't locked.

You can also connect an iPod touch to an external charger if your computer isn't handy. This charges the battery, but of course, doesn't sync or back up your iPod's contents.

Topping Off

It's a good idea to keep your an iPod touch's battery topped off; this type of battery actually does better if you keep it charged rather than letting it run down all the way before recharging. Periodically, say every month or two, you might want to let your iPod run completely out of power and then recharge it to maximize its life. The key point is, as Apple puts it, to "keep the electrons moving." So, don't let your iPod sit with no activity for long periods of time.

In addition to keeping your touch's battery charged, consider the following recommendations to maximize the amount of time you can use the iPod between charges:

- Put your iPod touch to sleep when you aren't using it by pressing the Sleep/Wake button.

- Set Auto-Lock to a small interval, such as 1 Minute. When an iPod touch locks, it goes to sleep immediately, which puts it in low-power mode (Settings, General, Auto-Lock).

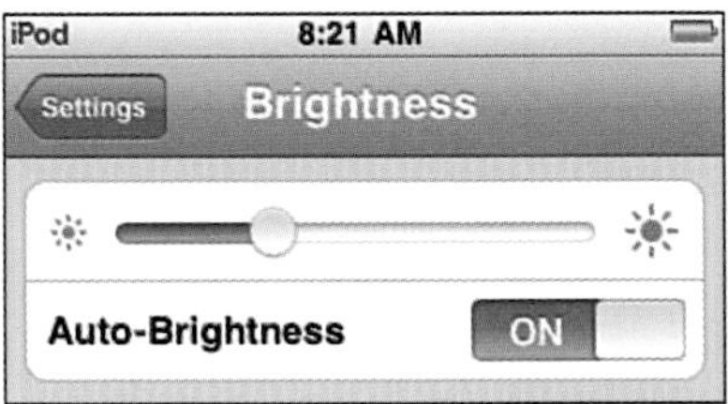

- Set the brightness of the screen to a low but comfortable level and leave Auto-Brightness turned on (Settings, Brightness).

- Disable features you don't use, especially those that communicate with other devices. Specific suggestions follow:

- If you don't use Bluetooth devices, make sure Bluetooth is turned off (Settings, General, Bluetooth OFF).

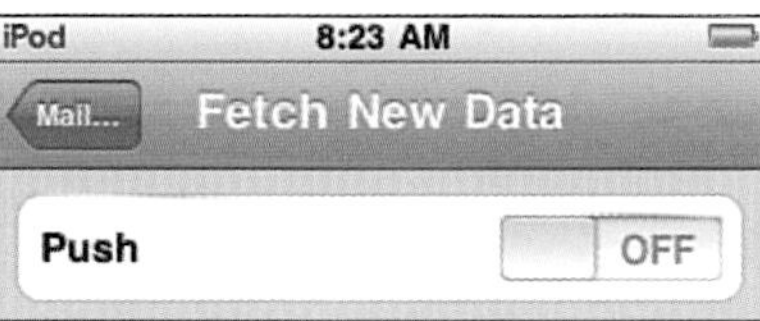

- If you don't need email to be pushed to any email accounts, disable email Push (Settings; Mail, Contacts, Calendars; Fetch New Data; Push OFF).

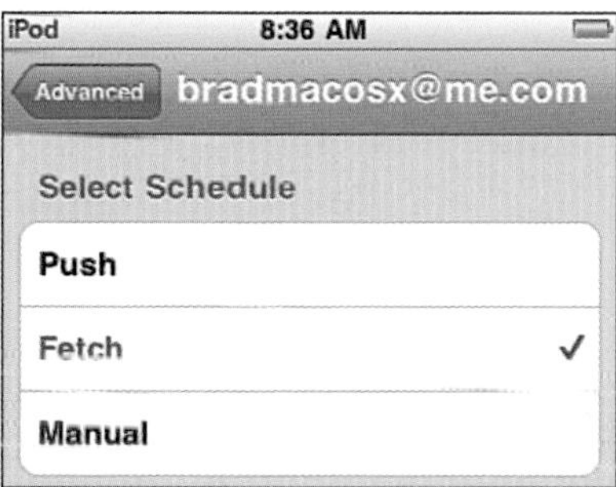

- If you do need email pushed to some accounts, disable Push for the accounts you don't need email pushed to by setting them to Fetch (Settings; Mail, Contacts, Calendars; Fetch New Data; Advanced; email account; Fetch).

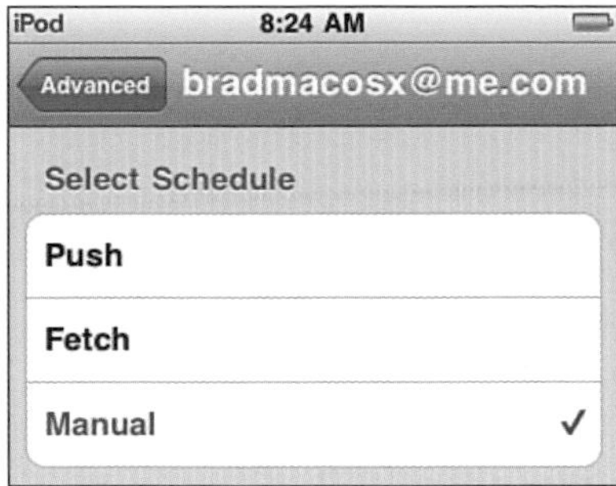

- Set email to be manually fetched instead of automatically fetched (Settings; Mail, Contacts, Calendars; Fetch New Data; Advanced; email account; Manual).

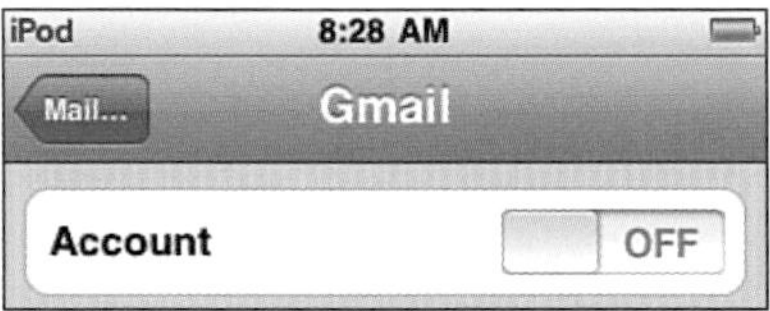

- Inactivate email accounts you don't need to use at all (Settings; Mail, Contacts, Calendars; email account; Account OFF). (You can turn only some kinds of email accounts off; for others, such as MobileMe accounts, you can disable specific information for the account, such as mail, calendars, contacts, and so on by turning that type of information off. This also saves power because whenever information is moved onto or from the iPod, power is used. So, disabling types of information you don't need to use saves a small amount of power, but if you don't need the information anyway, it doesn't hurt anything to turn it off.)

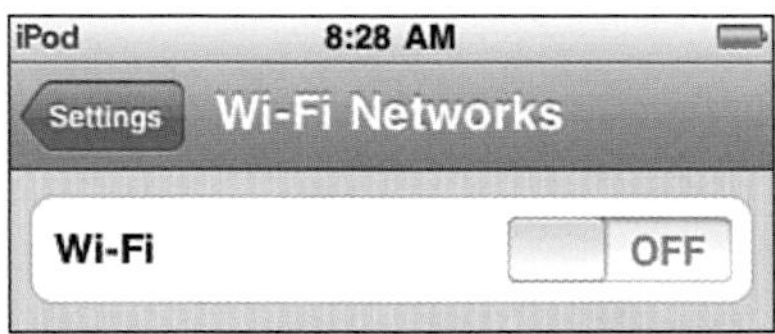

- When you don't need to connect to the Internet or other iPod touches/iPhones, turn Wi-Fi off (Settings, Wi-Fi, Wi-Fi OFF).

- When you want to disable all transmitting and receiving functions (Wi-Fi and Bluetooth), enable the Airplane mode (Settings, Airplane Mode ON).

The airplane icon appears when the iPod is in Airplane mode

Cleaning an iPod touch's Screen

The iPod touch's onscreen controls are amazing. But because you use them by tapping and dragging your fingers on the screen, the screen gets smudged over time and with use. You can clean the screen using a very soft cloth, ideally one intended for this purpose, by rubbing it carefully. You should never spray any cleaners directly onto an iPod touch's screen. However, you can apply a slight amount of glass cleaner to a soft cloth and gently wipe the iPod touch's screen to clean it.

Keeping a Clean Screen

If the smudges on the screen bother you, consider adding a clear plastic protector to the screen. There are many kinds of these available (some cases come with one), but they all work in the same way in that they have a side that clings to the screen. You touch the other side, which is more resistant to smudges than is an iPod touch's glass screen. Using a protector sheet does change the feel of using and the look of an iPod touch so you might or might not like using one. However, even if the look and feel of a protector sheet isn't ideal, it can also help guard against scratches. Although an iPod touch's screen is quite tough, it can be scratched, so you might want to trade off the slight degradation resulting from using a protector sheet against the possibility of a permanent scratch on the screen.

Solving iPod touch Problems

Even a device as reliable as your iPod touch can sometimes run into problems. Fortunately, the solutions to most problems you encounter are simple. If a simple solution doesn't work, a great deal of detailed help is available from Apple, and even more is available from the community of iPod touch users.

The problems that you can address with the simple steps described in this section vary and range from such issues as the iPod touch hanging (won't respond to commands) to not being visible in iTunes when connected to your computer (can't be synced). No matter which problem you experience, try the following steps to solve them.

Restarting an iPod touch

If an iPod touch starts acting up, restart it.

1. Press and hold the Sleep/Wake button until the red slider appears on the screen.
2. Drag the red slider to the right. The iPod touch powers down.
3. Press and hold the Sleep/Wake button until you see the Apple logo on the screen. The iPod touch restarts. When the Home screen appears, try using the iPod touch again. If the problem is solved, you're done.

Restarting the Computer and iTunes

If iTunes can no longer see your iPod, restart the computer and open iTunes again.

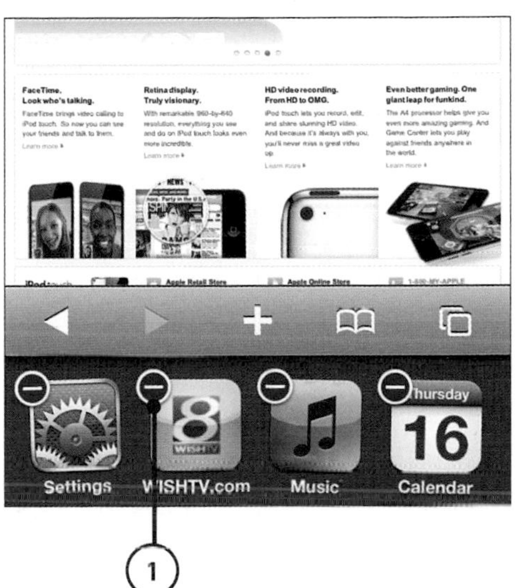

1. Disconnect the iPod touch from the computer.
2. Restart the computer.
3. After the computer restarts, connect your iPod touch to it. iTunes should open, and the iPod touch should be selected on the Source list. If so, all should be well. If not, you need to try something else.

All USB Ports Are Not Created Equal

If your computer can't see your iPod touch when it's connected, try a different USB port. You should use a USB port on the computer itself rather than one on a keyboard or USB hub.

Resetting an iPod touch

If restarting an iPod touch or the computer doesn't help, try resetting an iPod touch using the following escalation of steps.

1. If an application freezes or starts acting oddly while you are using it, press the Home button twice; on the App bar, press and hold the application's icon until it starts jiggling and the minus button

appears. Press the minus button. (This feature is available only on iPod touches that are third generation or later.) The application quits. Complete any running processes and then proceed to the next step.

2. Restart the iPod touch using the previous steps. If the problem goes away, you're done. If not, continue to the next step.
3. If you can't restart the iPod touch normally, press and hold down both the Home button and the Sleep/Lock buttons for at least 10 seconds. You should see the Power Off slider; if you do, shut down and then restart the iPod touch. If you don't see the slider, the iPod touch should turn itself off and then restart; you can release the buttons when you see the Apple logo on the screen. If the problem goes away, you're done. If not, continue.
4. If you can use the iPod touch's controls, proceed with the following steps. If you can't use any of its controls, you need to restore the iPod touch, which is explained in the next section.
5. On the Home screen, tap Settings.
6. Tap General.
7. Scroll down until you see the Reset command.
8. Tap Reset.
9. Tap Reset All Settings.

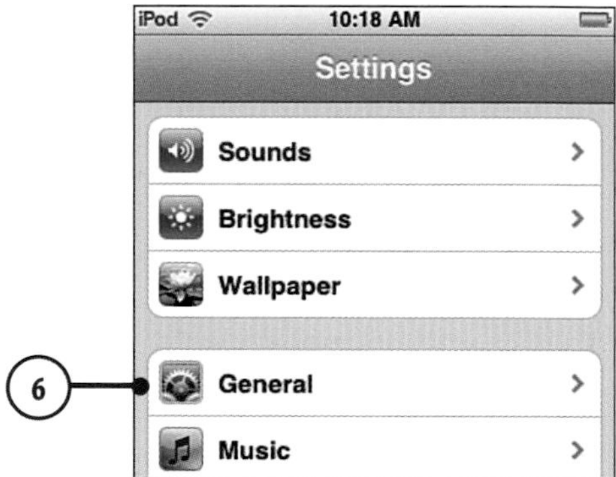

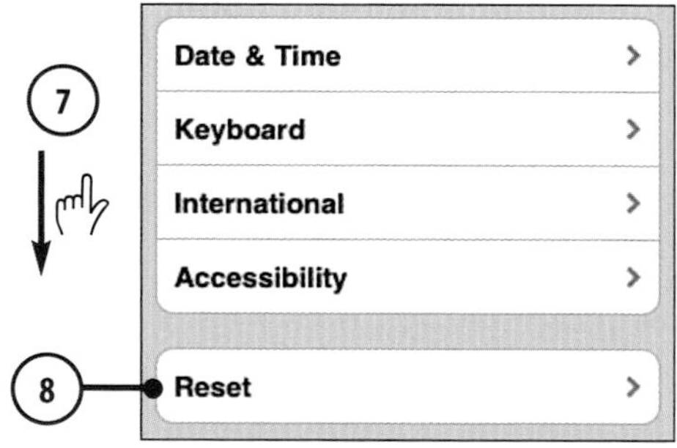

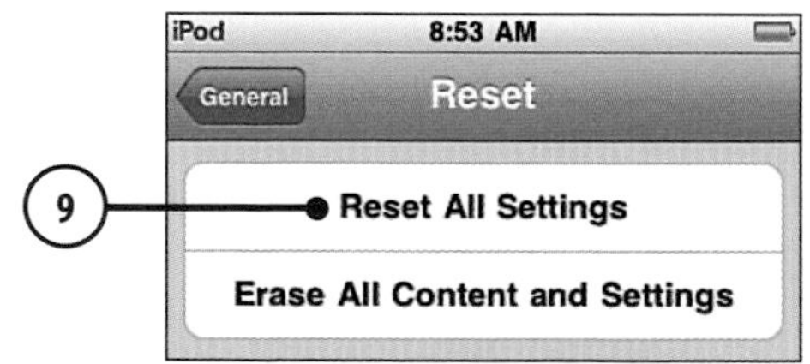

10. Tap Reset All Settings at the prompt. All settings on the iPod touch reset to their defaults, and the iPod touch restarts. If the problem goes away, you're done—except for reconfiguring your settings, of course. If not, continue.

11. Repeat steps 5 through 8 to move back to the Reset screen.

Reset Specific Areas

If you experience problems in a specific area, such as connecting to a network, try resetting just that area (for example, Reset Network Settings) before you pull out the big gun by erasing the iPod touch.

12. Tap Erase All Content and Settings. When you do this, you lose all the content on your iPod touch. Make sure that you have that content elsewhere before you erase your iPod. If the content is in your iTunes Library, you're fine. But if you've added information that you have not synced to iTunes, such as contacts, directly onto the iPod touch, you lose that information when you erase it, and you shouldn't perform this step unless you've tried all the other solutions.

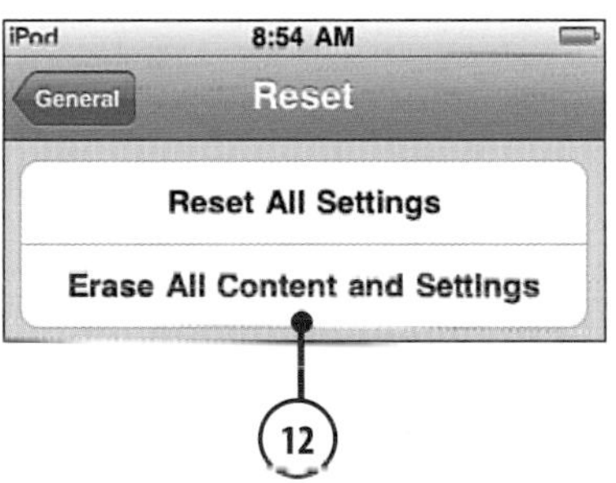

13. Tap Erase iPod at the prompt. The iPod touch is erased, and it should return to like-new condition. You have to sync it again, reconfigure its settings, and so on. If the problem recurs, you must restore the iPod touch.

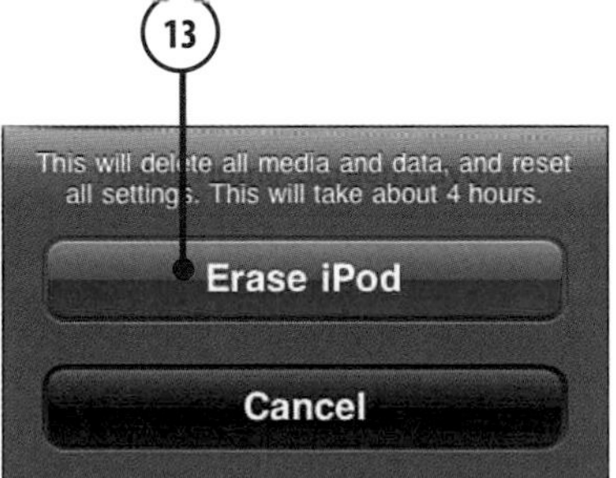

Restoring an iPod touch

The most severe action you can take on your iPod touch is to restore it. When this happens, the iPod touch is erased, so you lose all its contents, and its current software is overwritten with the latest version. If you have added information to your iPod touch since it was last backed up (when you last connected it to the computer), that information is lost when you restore your iPod touch—so be careful before doing this. If none of the other steps corrected the problem, restoring the iPod touch should.

1. Connect the iPod touch to your computer.
2. Select the iPod touch on the Source list.
3. Click the Summary button.
4. Click Restore. Remember that you lose everything on your iPod touch when you restore it, so make sure that you have all its data stored elsewhere, such as in your iTunes Library, before you do this.

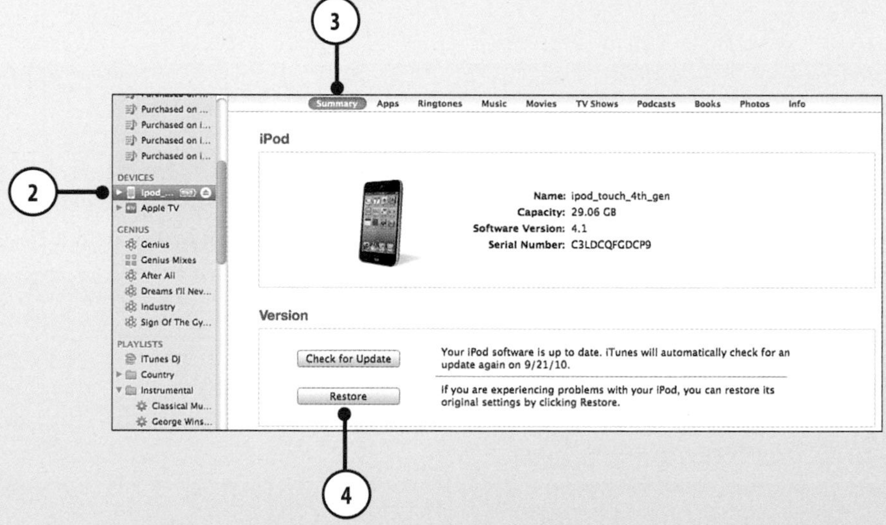

5. Click Restore in the dialog.

6. Read the information about the current version of the iPod touch's software and click Next.
7. Click Agree. The current version of the iPod touch's software is downloaded to your computer, and iTunes reinstalls it on your iPod touch. This process takes a while because iTunes downloads the current version of the iOS to your computer. You see several progress indicators along the way. The iPod touch restarts and iTunes begins reinstalling its software. When the process is complete, you see a message explaining what has happened.

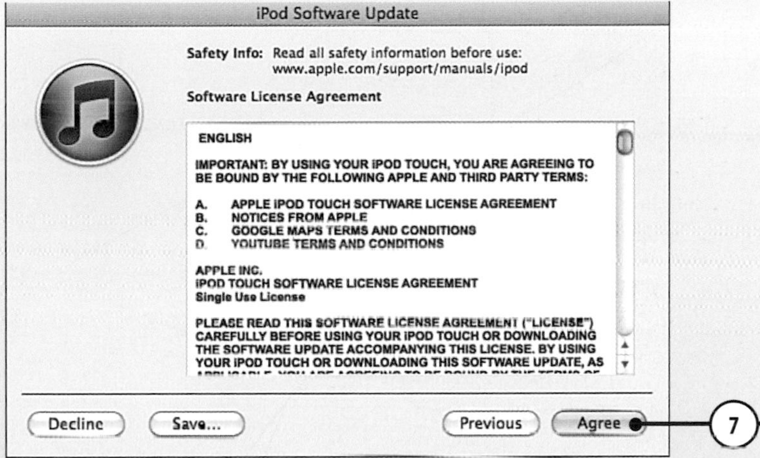

8. Click OK. The iPod touch is restarted, and you see the Set Up Your iPod screen.

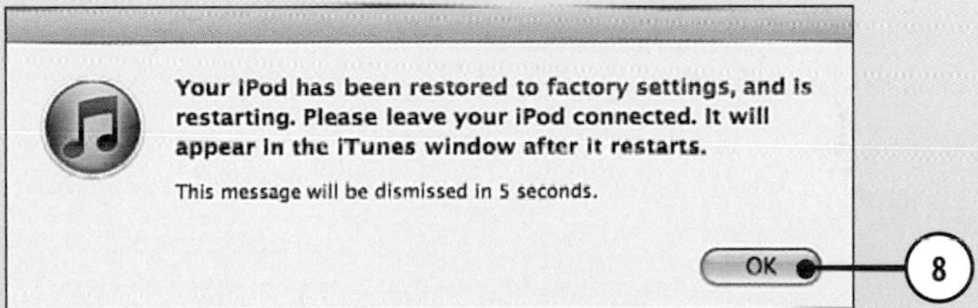

Starting Over

If you want to start at the beginning, select the Set Up as a New iPod radio button in step 9 instead. Follow the onscreen prompts. When that process is complete, you're prompted to name and reconfigure the iPod touch as you did when you first started using it.

9. Click the Restore from the backup of radio button.
10. On the pop-up menu, choose your iPod touch's name.
11. Click Continue. iTunes restores the iPod touch from the backup.

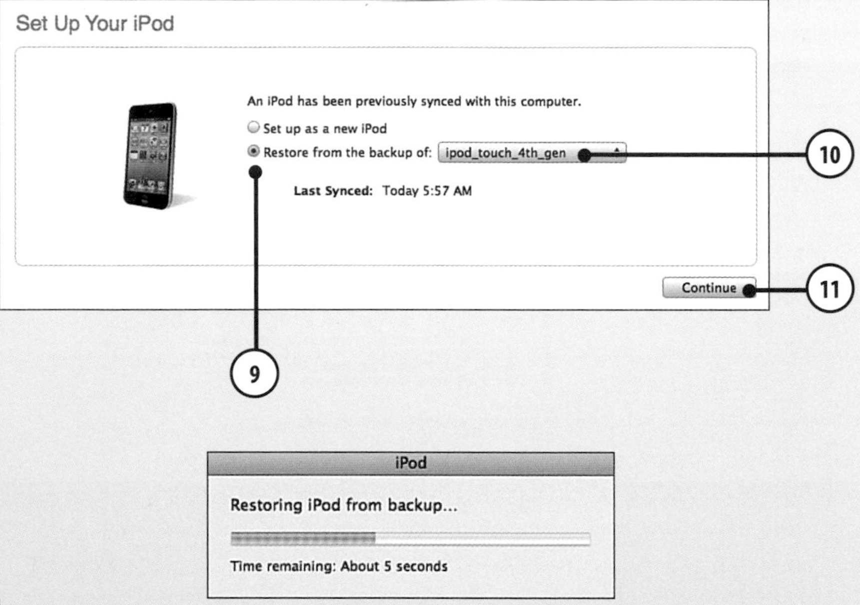

12. Click OK in the completion dialog. The iPod touch is synced according to the settings stored in the backup. When the sync process is complete, the iPod touch should be back in working condition with all your content restored to it. If you have a lot of content, this process can take a while because the sync is done starting with the iPod touch's memory being "empty."

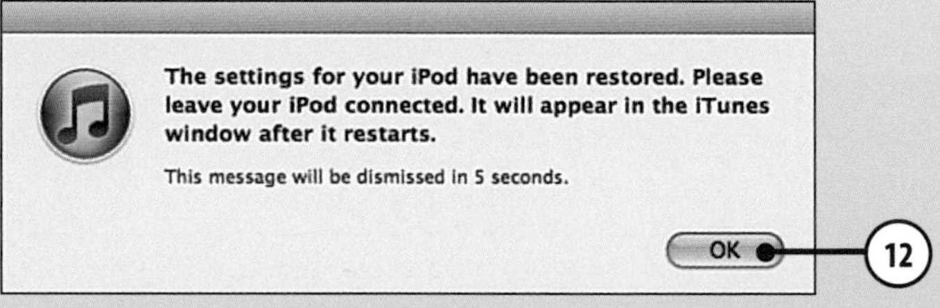

How Does It Remember?

You might wonder how an iPod touch can be restored. It's because iTunes backs up critical iPod touch data and settings on your computer. Each time you sync, this information is backed up on the computer so that it is available again when it is needed, such as when you restore your iPod touch. You should connect your iPod touch to your computer regularly even if the content you sync hasn't changed much. This ensures the iPod touch's backup is current.

Reinstalling iTunes

If iTunes continues to be unable to see your iPod touch and the touch appears to be working normally, reinstall iTunes on your computer. (This is much more likely on a Windows PC than on a Mac.) See Chapter 1, "Getting Started with Your iPod touch," for instructions on downloading and installing iTunes on your computer.

No iTunes Content Worries as Long as You Back Up

iTunes stores content, such as music and video, in a different location than the application. You can reinstall iTunes without disturbing your iTunes content. Of course, you should always have your iTunes content backed up, such as storing it on DVD or an external hard drive, in case something happens to your computer. If a problem with your computer causes you to lose audio or video you've purchased from the iTunes Store, you have to pay for it again. So be sure you back up your iTunes content regularly.

Trouble Sending Email from an iPod touch?

If you are sure you've configured an email account correctly and you can receive email to that address but you can't send any from that address, the provider of the account probably doesn't allow sending email from any IP address except those it provides. This is most common when the email account is provided through an Internet service provider, such as a cable company. You have a couple of solutions. One is to access your email through the provider's web email interface. The other is to add a second email account (such as a Gmail account) to your iPod and use that account when you want to send email. See Chapter 9, "Emailing," for information about choosing the account through which you are sending email.

Getting Help with iPod touch Problems

If none of the previous steps solve the problem, you can get help in a number of ways:

- **Apple's website**—Go to www.apple.com/support/. On this page, you can access all kinds of information about iPod touches, iTunes, and other Apple products. You can browse for help, and you can search for answers to specific problems. Many of the resulting articles have detailed, step-by-step instructions to help you solve problems and link to more information.
- **Web searches**—One of the most useful ways to get help is to do a web search for the specific problem you're having. Just open your favorite search tool, such as Google, and search for the problem. You are likely to find many resources to help you, including websites, forums, and such. If you encounter a problem, it's likely someone else has, too, and has probably put the solution on the Web.
- **Me**—You're welcome to send email to me for problems you're having with your iPod touch. My address is bradmiser@me.com. I'll do my best to help you as quickly as I can.

Index

A

B

C

D

N

O

P

T

U

V

W

X-Y-Z